The Lisbon Treaty

Law, Politics, and Treaty Reform

PAUL CRAIG

OXFORD
UNIVERSITY PRESS

OXFORD
UNIVERSITY PRESS

Great Clarendon Street, Oxford, OX2 6DP,
United Kingdom

Oxford University Press is a department of the University of Oxford.
It furthers the University's objective of excellence in research, scholarship,
and education by publishing worldwide. Oxford is a registered trade mark of
Oxford University Press in the UK and in certain other countries

First published 2010
First published in paperback 2013

British Library Cataloguing in Publication Data

Data available

ISBN 978–0–19–959501–3 (Hbk)
ISBN 978–0–19–966495–5 (Pbk)

Printed in Great Britain by
CPI Group (UK) Ltd, Croydon, CR0 4YY

This book is for Anita and Ciaran

Preface to the paperback edition

For the avoidance of any doubt, this is a not a second edition of this book, and thus Chapters 1–11 have remained unchanged. Chapter 12 is however new. It is a detailed analysis of the financial crisis that has dominated the EU over the past two years. The chapter begins by charting the economic and constitutional assumptions that under-pinned the Maastricht settlement concerning EMU, followed by a brief explanation of the crisis itself. The discussion then turns to the responses to the crisis. These were complex and varied, but nonetheless two kinds of measure are discernible, those designed to assist Member States in economic difficulty, and those to increase supervision over national budgetary policy. These measures are analyzed, including the legal difficulties attendant upon them. This is followed by consideration of further measures that will be enacted in the light of high-level deliberations as to what is required for a 'genuine economic and monetary union'. The chapter concludes with analysis of the broader political, economic, and legal consequences of the crisis for the EU and its relationship with the Member States.

Contents

List of Abbreviations

ACP	African, Caribbean, and Pacific
ADR	alternative dispute resolution
AFSJ	Area of Freedom, Security and Justice
CAP	Common Agricultural Policy
CATS	Article 36 Committee (*Comité de l'Article Trente Six*)
CCP	Common Commercial Policy
CEN	European Committee for Standardization
CENELEC	European Committee for Electrotechnical Standardization
CFI	Court of First Instance
CFSP	Common Foreign and Security Policy
CLWP	Commission's Legislative and Work Programme
CSDP	Common Security and Defence Policy
DCFR	Draft Common Frame of Reference
EC	European Community
ECB	European Central Bank
ECHR	European Convention on Human Rights
ECJ	European Court of Justice
ECSC	European Coal and Steel Community
EDA	European Defence Agency
EDP	Excessive Deficit Procedure
EEAS	European External Action Service
EFSF	European Financial Stability Facility
EFSM	European Financial Stabilisation Mechanism
EIP	Excessive Imbalance Procedure
EMU	economic and monetary union
ENP	European Neighbourhood Policy
EPC	European Political Community
ESCB	European System of Central Banks
ESM	European Stability Mechanism
EU	European Union
Europol	European Police Office
FAC	Foreign Affairs Council
FFA	financial assistance facility agreement
FRA	Fundamental Rights Agency
GAC	General Affairs Council
GAERC	General Affairs and External Relations Council
GDP	gross domestic product
IGC	intergovernmental conference
IMF	International Monetary Fund
IPM	Interactive Policy Making
JHA	Justice and Home Affairs

EUROPEAN TREATIES, CONVENTIONS,
AND OTHER LEGAL INSTRUMENTS

1

Reform, Process, and Architecture

It was a long road from Nice to Lisbon. The ratification of the Lisbon Treaty was the culmination of attempts at Treaty reform in the EU, which began after the Nice Treaty and lasted for nearly a decade.[1] An understanding of the reform process is therefore essential in order to understand the Lisbon Treaty, more especially because there is much commonality between it and the Constitutional Treaty.

The discussion begins in 2001, the period between the Nice Treaty and the Laeken Declaration. Political developments in this period were crucial for the emergence of the Convention on the Future of Europe. The focus then shifts to the Convention, and identifies in temporal perspective five factors that shaped the Convention process, and enabled Giscard d'Estaing to present a Constitutional Treaty to the intergovernmental conference (IGC).

The story continues with the IGC that led to agreement on the Constitutional Treaty in June 2004, the subsequent demise of this Treaty after the negative referenda in France and the Netherlands, and the re-starting of the Treaty negotiations in 2007, culminating in signature of the Lisbon Treaty in December 2007 and its subsequent ratification.

The penultimate section of the chapter outlines the architecture of the Lisbon Treaty, an understanding of which is essential for subsequent discussion. The chapter concludes with reflections on the process of Treaty reform, and the lessons that can be learned from the 'long walk to Lisbon'.

1. From Nice to Laeken: The Shaping of the Reform Agenda

We should never forget that the 'beginning started at the end'. The road to Laeken began with the Declaration on the Future of the Union appended to the Nice Treaty.[2] It is important to remember at the outset what the Declaration 'declared'.

---

[1] P Craig, 'Constitutional Process and Reform in the EU: Nice, Laeken, the Convention and the IGC' (2004) 10 EPL 653.
[2] Treaty of Nice, Declaration 23 [2001] OJ C80/1.

It began with an air of congratulation at what had been achieved in the Nice Treaty.[3] The Declaration then called for a 'deeper and wider debate' about the future of the EU, which would 'encourage wide-ranging discussion with all interested parties'.[4] It set a timetable for this process to be continued through initiatives to be set out in a Declaration made at the Laeken European Council in December 2001. The Laeken Declaration should address, *inter alia*, the delimitation of competences, the status of the Charter of Fundamental Rights, simplification of the Treaties, and the role of national Parliaments in the European architecture.[5] It would then be for the IGC in 2004 to make the necessary Treaty changes 'after these preparatory steps'.[6]

It would nonetheless be mistaken to believe that the content of the Laeken Declaration, and the establishment of the Convention on the Future of Europe, were somehow pre-ordained after Nice. The calendar year 2001 between Nice and Laeken saw the emergence of consensus among the major institutional players about two crucial issues.

The first concerned the content of the reform agenda. It came to be accepted that the four issues left over from the Nice Treaty were not discrete. It came to be recognized that competences, and the status of the Charter, resonated with other issues concerning the institutional balance of power within the EU, and also with the vertical distribution of authority between the EU and the Member States. It became clear that the ideal of simplification of the Treaties could not realistically be accomplished without considering substantive modification in the existing Treaty provisions. The very fact that the Nice Declaration stated that future reform should address *inter alia* the four issues adumbrated above lent further weight to the expansion of the topics for discussion that resulted in the Laeken Declaration.

There was also growing consensus on the second issue, the reform process. If a broad range of issues was to be discussed, if the next round of Treaty reform was not simply to be a further episode in tinkering with the Treaties, then the idea that the result, whatsoever it might be, should be legitimated by input from a broader 'constituency' than hitherto assumed greater force. There was an element of 'traditional reform fatigue', leading to the desire for new institutional mechanisms that could consider matters central to the future of the EU.

(a) The Council and the European Council

The debate on the 'Future of Europe' was formally opened on 7 March 2001, by the Prime Ministers of Sweden and Belgium, who held the Council Presidency for the first and second half of 2001, and by the President of the Commission

---

[3] ibid paras 1–2.   [4] ibid para 3.   [5] ibid para 5.   [6] ibid para 7.

and the President of the European Parliament. The 'futurum' website was inaugurated.[7]

The Goteborg European Council in June 2001 was an important step on the road to Laeken, and its approach was influenced by a paper prepared by the Secretary-General.[8] The paper contributed to the growing realization that the four issues identified in the Nice Declaration could not be considered in isolation and that debate about the future of Europe would necessarily address fundamental issues of institutional competence. This was acknowledged by the Goteborg European Council, which made reference to the Secretary-General's Report, and recognized that modernization of Community institutions would be central to future reforms.[9]

The deliberations of the Goteborg European Council concerning the reform process were shaped by a paper prepared by the Swedish Presidency of the Council.[10] It canvassed a number of options as to how the debate about the future of Europe should be taken forward, such as classic IGC mode, and the establishment of a small group of 'wise men'. It also raised the possibility of 'creating a broad and open preparatory forum',[11] drawing on the process used for the Charter of Fundamental Rights. The Goteborg European Council was relatively brief about the specifics of the reform process, but the Presidency paper put the Convention model firmly on the agenda and the European Council noted that the debate about the future of Europe 'involving all parts of society' should be actively pursued.[12]

The themes apparent in the first half of 2001 concerning both the content of the reform agenda and the reform process were developed by Belgium, which occupied the Presidency in the second half of 2001. This is readily apparent from the Press Release issued by the Belgian Presidency on 9 September 2001, at the conclusion of an informal meeting of foreign ministers. The reform agenda was conceptualized in terms of a broad analysis of the strengths and weaknesses of the European model, and this was coupled with specific attachment to the Convention model for the reform process, which was regarded as a democratic, transparent, and credible mechanism for future reform.

This growing consensus about the approach to content and process was affirmed by later meetings of the General Affairs Council (GAC).[13] Thus the GAC 'favoured an approach consisting of enlarging on the themes and objectives listed in the Nice Declaration, in the form of questions, with the

---

[7] <http://europa.eu/institutional_reform/index_en.htm>.
[8] Preparing the Council for Enlargement, POLGEN 12, 9518/01, Brussels 7 June 2001.
[9] Goteborg European Council, 15–16 June 2001, [16]–[18].
[10] Report on the Debate on the Future of the European Union, POLGEN 14, 9520/01, Brussels 8 June 2001.
[11] ibid [56].
[12] Goteborg European Council (n 9) [15].
[13] 2372nd Council Meeting, General Affairs, 12330/01, Brussels 8–9 October 2001.

dual aim of making the Union meet its citizens' expectations more successfully while functioning more effectively'.[14] The GAC also confirmed the broad convergence of views in favour of the Convention model, detailing matters such as the number and type of participants, the establishment of a Praesidium, and support from a Secretariat.[15]

The GAC meetings paved the way for the Laeken European Council.[16] In terms of the reform agenda, the Laeken Declaration gave the formal imprimatur of the European Council for the broadening of the issues left open post-Nice. These issues may always have been the tip of the iceberg. The Laeken Declaration nonetheless made this explicit. The four issues post-Nice became the 'headings' within which a plethora of other questions were posed, which raised virtually every issue of importance for the future of Europe. In terms of the reform process, the Laeken Declaration formally embraced the Convention model with a composition designed to enhance the legitimacy of the results that it produced, whatsoever those might be.

(b) The Commission

The willingness of the European Council and the Council to expand the reform agenda and to adopt the Convention model for the reform process was clearly crucial. It should, however, also be recognized that the other main institutional actors were pressing in the same direction.

This is apparent from one of the Commission's early contributions, six weeks after the inauguration of the future of Europe debate. The Commission made clear its belief that the four questions identified in the Nice Declaration were not the only ones to be considered when reflecting on the future of the Union. The debate should address

the transparency and democratic legitimacy of the Union and its institutions and cover ... all the questions that arise concerning the process of European integration, whether they relate to its final objectives, its institutional structures or its policies.[17]

While the Commission was more circumspect about the precise format for the reform process, it indicated its interest 'in a formula based on the agreement which led to the drafting of the Charter of Fundamental Rights'.[18]

The same themes are evident in Commission speeches between April and December 2001. Romano Prodi called for the Laeken Declaration to establish

---

[14] ibid 18.
[15] ibid 18. See also, 2386th Council Meeting, General Affairs, Brussels 19–20 November 2001, 11.
[16] Laeken European Council, 14–15 December 2001.
[17] Commission Communication, On Certain Arrangements for the Debate about the Future of the European Union, 25 April 2001, 4.
[18] ibid 3.

'an ambitious and comprehensive agenda'.[19] This would be discussed in the only way acceptable to citizens, in a Convention,[20] more especially so given that the Nice European Council had shown that the common European interest could not emerge from the regular IGC process.[21] Traditional State diplomacy could not, said Prodi, 'launch a full European constitutional process in a way which will seem credible in the eyes of the people'.[22] Individual Commissioners pressed in the same direction. Antonio Vitorino argued that the subject matter of the reform debate must be wide-ranging and that the Convention model should be employed.[23] These sentiments were echoed by Michel Barnier. He argued that the four topics identified in the Nice Declaration could not be considered in isolation since they necessarily resonated with broader issues concerning the purpose and legitimacy of the EU as a whole, which should be addressed via the Convention model.[24]

The Commission reiterated these views on the eve of the Laeken Summit. The Laeken Declaration should broaden the scope of the questions posed in the Nice Declaration since it was, for example, not possible to discuss competences without considering what the Member States of the Union wished to do together,[25] albeit without thereby calling into question 50 years of European integration.[26] The broadened agenda should be legitimated through the broadest possible consensus, which meant that the reforms should be deliberated using the Convention model.[27]

(c) The European Parliament

The European Parliament pressed strenuously in the same direction as the other major institutional actors. This is apparent in its Resolution concerning the Future of the European Union in May 2001.[28] It expressed regret at the narrow compass of the Nice Treaty, and noted that a Union of 27 Member States required more thoroughgoing reform in order to guarantee democracy,

---

[19] On the Road to Laeken, Speech by Romano Prodi to the European Parliament, Speech/01/326, 4 July 2001, 4.
[20] ibid 3.
[21] Speech to the European Parliament's Committee on Constitutional Affairs, Romano Prodi, Speech/01/343, 10 July 2001, 3.
[22] Building the Community and the New Challenges Facing the Union, Romano Prodi, University of Pisa, Speech/01/458, 12 October 2001, 4.
[23] The Convention as a Model for European Constitutionalisation, Humboldt University, Berlin, 14 June 2001.
[24] Why Europe Matters, 17 October 2001; Speech to the European Parliament's Committee on Constitutional Affairs, 19 November 2001.
[25] Communication from the Commission on the Future of European Union, Renewing the Community Method, COM(2001) 727 final, 4.
[26] ibid 5.
[27] ibid 3–4, 8.
[28] The Treaty of Nice and the Future of the European Union, A5–0168/2001.

effectiveness, transparency, and governability.[29] The medium through which such reform should be pursued should be radically different from the IGC model, which the European Parliament argued had outlived its usefulness as a method for Treaty reform. The Convention model should be employed, thereby enabling a wider participation of affected interests.[30] Consensus between the European Parliament and national Parliaments in favour of the Convention model was secured by July 2001.[31]

The European Parliament's aspirations were reiterated forcefully in the Report of the Committee on Constitutional Affairs for the Laeken European Council.[32] The Report reaffirmed the need to proceed beyond the strict confines of the issues identified in the Nice Declaration, and elaborated the particular topics that should be discussed in the reform process,[33] most of which found their way into the Laeken Declaration. The Report also pressed for adoption of the Convention model and set out in detail how it might operate.[34]

2. The Convention on the Future of Europe: From Talking Shop to Draft Constitutional Treaty

The content of the Lisbon Treaty is, as will be seen, very similar to that of the Constitutional Treaty. It is therefore important to understand the way in which the Constitutional Treaty emerged, and the forces that shaped its content. It is only by doing so that one can understand the Lisbon Treaty itself.

The Laeken European Council duly instituted the Convention on the Future of Europe, which began work in March 2002.[35] It was chaired by Valery Giscard d'Estaing, with two Vice-Chairmen, Giuliano Amato and Jean-Luc Dehaene. There was one representative from each of the 15 Member States, 30 members of national Parliaments, two from each Member State, 16 Members of the European Parliament (MEPs) and two Commission representatives. There were also representatives from the accession candidate countries, who could take part in the proceedings without, however, being able to prevent any consensus that might emerge among the Member States. The members of the Convention could be replaced by alternate members if they were not present. Observer status was accorded to the European Ombudsman and to members of

---

[29] ibid [1]–[2].
[30] ibid [5]–[7].
[31] Second Meeting with National Parliaments on Future of Europe Secures Consensus in favour of a Convention to Prepare for Treaty Reform, 16 July 2001.
[32] Report on the Laeken European Council and the Future of the European Union, A5-0368/2001.
[33] ibid [2]–[4].
[34] ibid [6]–[21].
[35] Laeken European Council, 14–15 December 2001, Annex 1, 24. The seminal work on the Convention on the Future of Europe is, P Norman, *The Accidental Constitution, The Making of Europe's Constitutional Treaty* (EuroComment, 2nd edn, 2005).

the Economic and Social Committee, the European social partners, and the Committee of Regions. The Presidents of the Court of Justice and of the Court of Auditors could be invited by the Praesidium to address the Convention.

The Praesidium of the Convention was composed of the Convention Chairman and Vice-Chairmen and nine members drawn from the Convention, these being the representatives of all the governments holding the Council Presidency during the Convention, two national parliament representatives, two European Parliament representatives, and two Commission representatives.

It is important to recognize at the outset that the Convention was given a relatively short period to complete its work. It was instructed to finish its deliberations within a year, and to present its conclusions to the European Council meeting in the summer of 2003. It is equally important to understand that the Convention decided at an early stage to proceed via consensus, rather than formal voting, which thereby gave the Praesidium considerable power to determine whether the requisite consensus had been reached.[36]

The Convention used a three-stage methodology. There was the listening stage from March till June 2002, when the main emphasis was on general statements concerning the missions of the Union. This was followed by the examination stage, in which Working Groups considered particular topics. This exercise occupied the latter half of 2002. There was then the proposal stage, in which the Convention discussed draft articles of the Constitution, normally on the basis of proposals from the Working Groups.

This was the formal architecture of the Convention deliberations. It tells us little about the real issues that shaped the framing of the Constitutional Treaty. The analysis that follows identifies the key factors that enabled the Convention to produce the Constitutional Treaty.

(a) Spring 2002: a viable way forward through Working Groups

The organization of working groups was central to the attainment of the Convention goals.[37] The time limit within which the Convention had to consider the issues assigned to it by the Laeken Declaration was very tight. This was even more so once it became clear that the Convention wished to produce a 'complete Treaty'. Working groups were therefore a necessary step if the tasks were to be completed within the designated time. The possibility of establishing such groups was expressly envisaged in Article 15 of the Convention's Working Methods, and the decision to establish such groups was made in May 2002.[38] This made good sense. The groups facilitated detailed discussion of the kind that could not take place in plenary, and they enabled more Convention members to be engaged than would otherwise have been possible.[39]

---

[36] Norman (n 35) 37–38.   [37] ibid ch 5.
[38] CONV 52/02, Working Groups, Brussels 17 May 2002.   [39] ibid [1].

Six groups were initially established. It was clear that there would have to be groups concerned with rights and competences, and these were duly established as groups two and five respectively. The establishment of separate groups dealing with subsidiarity and the role of national Parliaments was somewhat less obvious, but these became groups one and four. The remaining two groups dealt with classic legal and economic issues respectively, the legal personality of the Union being assigned to group three, and the implications of a single currency for closer economic cooperation being assigned to group six. Each working group was set a deadline to fit in with the schedule of plenary meetings in autumn 2002. Four further working groups on external action, defence, simplification of instruments, and the area of freedom, security, and justice were established in early autumn 2002. A working group on social Europe was created towards the end of 2002, making 11 in all.

However, working groups were consciously not used for certain issues, the most important example being the inter-institutional distribution of power. This was left for discussion in plenary sessions, in large part because of its centrality and the controversial nature of the relevant issues.

(b) Autumn 2002: the defining 'convention moment'—the decision to press for a Constitutional Treaty

The decision to press for a Constitutional Treaty was perhaps *the* defining Convention moment. It is tempting to think that the Convention on the Future of Europe was created in order to produce a draft Constitutional Treaty. This is to read a sense of historical inevitability into events with the benefit of hindsight. The reality was far less pre-ordained.

Talk of a constitutional text featured only at the very end of the Laeken Declaration in the context of Treaty simplification. The language of the Declaration was cautious to say the least: 'the question ultimately arises as to whether this simplification and reorganization might not lead in the long run to the adoption of a constitutional text in the Union'.[40] It is true that in the opening ceremony Giscard mentioned the possibility of a Constitutional Treaty emerging from the Convention,[41] and it can be accepted that some Convention members might always have hoped that this would be attained.[42] Many Member States, however, felt that the Convention might be nothing more than a high-level talking shop, which produced recommendations.[43] There was therefore nothing inevitable about the Convention producing a coherent constitutional document. This was not a foregone conclusion.

[40] Laeken European Council, 14–15 December 2001.
[41] Norman (n 35) 39.   [42] ibid 44.
[43] Norman (n 35) 34–35; P Norman, 'From the Convention to the IGC (Institutions)' (Federal Trust, September 2003) 2.

The reality was that the Convention developed its own institutional momentum and vision. The idea took hold that the Convention should produce a coherent document, and that this should take the form of a Constitutional Treaty.[44] Thus the Praesidium rejected a proposal in July 2002 that the Convention should ask the Commission to prepare a draft Constitutional Treaty, since this would imply that the Convention had shirked its own responsibilities.[45] The defining 'Convention moment' when the idea that a Constitutional Treaty should be drafted by the Convention took hold was September 2002.[46]

A paper from the Secretariat, entitled *Simplification of the Treaty and Drawing up of a Constitutional Treaty*, was central to this process.[47] The Secretariat discussed options for making the Treaties more accessible, such as Treaty simplification, codification, and merger, and pointed to difficulties or limitations with such options. It then raised the possibility of drawing up a Basic Treaty, which addressed matters such as the values of the Union, citizenship, institutions, decision-making procedures, competences and the like. It thus laid the initial foundations for what was to become Part I of the Constitutional Treaty.[48]

Matters then moved rapidly. There was a plenary session on 12–13 September 2002, two days after the Report from the Secretariat.[49] The Chairman of the Convention, Giscard d'Estaing, drew together the impending reports from the working groups, with the Secretariat paper, which was to provide the foundation for the new Treaty architecture. This made it possible for the Convention to 'reflect on the form of the end product, ie the draft Constitutional Treaty for Europe'. The plenary session at the beginning of October 2002 carried forward these initiatives.[50] The debate revealed broad consensus for the idea that there should be a single legal personality, which would supplant the legal personalities of existing bodies. This would then 'pave the way for merger of the treaties into a single text', which would consist of two parts, 'the first, fundamental part, containing provisions of a constitutional nature, and the second mainly policies'.[51]

It was not fortuitous that the membership of the Convention altered in the late autumn of 2002, shortly after the Convention's aspirations to produce a concrete document became apparent.[52] The foreign ministers of Germany and France joined the Convention. The Member States began to realize that this

---

[44] There was considerable uncertainty as to whether the Convention should seek to produce a Constitution or a Constitutional Treaty, Norman (n 35) 63–64.

[45] Norman (n 35) 54.

[46] ibid 54–55.

[47] CONV 250/02, Simplification of the Treaties and Drawing up of a Constitutional Treaty, Brussels 10 September 2002.

[48] ibid 11–15.

[49] CONV 284/02, Summary Report on the Plenary Session—Brussels 12 and 13 September 2002, Brussels 17 September 2002.

[50] CONV 331/02, Summary Report on the Plenary Session—Brussels 3 and 4 October 2002, Brussels 11 October 2002.

[51] ibid 2, 4.   [52] Norman (n 35) 129–133.

Convention might produce a constitutional document for the EU. It was better then to be on the inside, shaping whatever might emerge, rather than merely making comments from the sidelines.

(c) Autumn 2002: sketching the constitutional architecture through the Preliminary Draft Constitutional Treaty

Giscard d'Estaing was true to his word, and the Preliminary Draft Constitutional Treaty was presented to the second plenary session in October 2002.[53] Its publication[54] was an astute political move, notwithstanding the fact that there was much that was unclear or ambiguous.

The Draft represented an exercise in 'outline constitutional architecture'. It was premised on the idea of a single Treaty with three parts, the first containing the constitutional principles, the second dealing with Union policies, and the third with general provisions concerning ratification and the like. It identified the different 'rooms' within each part. The extent to which these 'rooms' had content varied considerably. The 'room' dealing with the EU institutional balance of power was largely empty, simply listing Articles that would deal with the powers of the principal EU institutions, while saying nothing as to what those powers actually were. The 'rooms' that dealt with topics such as competence and rights had some 'furniture'.

The publication of the Preliminary Draft Constitutional Treaty was astute nonetheless. It was important 'internally', sending a message to Convention members that progress was being made towards something concrete and providing a framework for the conclusions of the working groups. It was equally important 'externally' for the relationship between the Convention and key State players. The document lent credence to the idea that a Constitutional Treaty would emerge from the Convention, a matter which was not pre-ordained ahead of time. Its publication served to acclimatize State players to the fact that something real might emerge from the Convention, while allowing time for their comments to be considered. As Norman states, 'publication of the skeleton gave a palpable boost to the Convention's proceedings and structured the subsequent discussions'.[55]

(d) Winter and spring 2003: internal and external discourse about institutions

The year 2002 ended relatively smoothly. The working groups continued their deliberations with varying degrees of success and consensus, presenting their

---

[53] CONV 378/02, Summary Report of the Plenary Session—Brussels 28 and 29 October 2002, Brussels 31 October 2002.
[54] CONV 369/02, Preliminary Draft Constitutional Treaty, Brussels 28 October 2002.
[55] Norman (n 35) 59.

conclusions for discussion within plenary sessions from autumn 2002 onwards. When sufficient consensus emerged from plenary sessions the Secretariat began work in earnest on drafting articles concerning the topic, such as competence or rights, thereby fleshing out the relevant Article identified in the Draft Constitutional Treaty. The Convention then discussed these draft articles and amendments were tabled.

The beginning of 2003 arrived and there had as yet been no formal discussion about institutions. The contentious nature of the issues surrounding the inter-institutional division of power was evident in the process employed at the Convention. The Convention's general three-stage methodology, the listening phase, the examination stage through working groups, followed by the proposal stage, did not apply to institutions. There was no working group. It was felt that the issues were too contentious to be dealt with other than in plenary session. This is reflected in the fact that the title on Institutions was empty in the Preliminary Draft Constitution. It was a 'room' without content.

The key to understanding the deliberations about institutions is to recognize that they were shaped by discourse within and outside the Convention, and that the Praesidium exercised greater power over these proposals than any other matter on the reform agenda.

The formal, internal Convention discussions began in earnest in January 2003.[56] The Praesidium presented a reflection paper on the Functioning of the Institutions,[57] which served as the basis for discussion in the plenary session at the end of January 2003. It is important to appreciate the range of difficult institutional issues that were on the table. These included, *inter alia*, the method of choosing the Commission President, the composition of the Commission, the Council formations, the functions of the European Council, whether there should be a longer-term President of the European Council as opposed to the rotation system, the composition of the European Parliament, and its role within the legislative process. The diversity of views on these matters was readily apparent from discussions within the plenary session at the end of January 2003.[58] There was a reasonable degree of consensus on some matters, such as the co-equal status of the European Parliament within the legislative process. It was equally clear that there were serious divisions of opinion concerning the locus of executive power, more especially the respective roles of the Commission and the European Council.[59] The division of opinion was between the larger and the smaller States, with the Commission lining up with the latter group.

---

[56] CONV 473/02, Summary Report on the Plenary Session—Brussels 20 December 2002, Brussels 23 December 2002.

[57] CONV 477/03, The Functioning of the Institutions, Brussels 10 January 2003.

[58] CONV 508/03, Summary Report on the Plenary Session—Brussels 20 and 21 January 2003, Brussels 27 January 2003.

[59] P Craig, 'The Constitutional Treaty: Legislative and Executive Power in the Emerging Constitutional Order' (EUI Working Paper No 7, 2004).

The external discourse on these issues had a marked impact on the internal Convention deliberations. As Grevi notes, the key phrase in shaping the formal Convention agenda for 2002 may have been 'everything but institutions', but the key phrase for the debate in other circles was 'nothing but power'.[60] The institutional division of power was like Banquo's ghost, ever present, lurking in the background. The very fact that the institutional issues so clearly concerned the locus of power within the EU meant that Heads of State, national Parliaments, and interest groups all contributed to this debate. This was especially so in relation to the location of executive power within the EU, as exemplified by the debate about the future shape of the European Council. The larger Member States, in the form of Spain, the UK, and France, made it clear that they supported the idea of a longer-term, strengthened Presidency of the European Council. This became known as the 'ABC' view, expressed by Aznar, Blair, and Chirac.[61] In January of 2003, just when the Convention was beginning to deliberate about institutions, Germany was brought on board. This was made clear in a Franco-German paper, in which Germany accepted the idea of a long-term Presidency of the European Council, with the *quid pro quo* being that France accepted that the Commission President should be elected.[62] The importance attached to the future shape of executive power was also apparent in what Grevi has termed a non-paper leaked by the UK Government in January 2003 concerning the European Council.[63] The UK paper favoured very extensive powers for the President of the European Council, with fundamental implications for the way in which the EU would operate.[64] The vision for the EU contained in the 'ABC view' and the Franco-German paper provoked a fierce reaction from small Member States and accession States.[65]

We can now return to the internal Convention deliberations and the power wielded by the Praesidium. The views of the larger Member States necessarily impacted on the internal Convention discourse. This was all the more so given the change in the membership of the Convention in the late autumn of 2002. The most significant change in this respect was what Norman has termed the

---

[60] G Grevi, 'The Europe We Need: An Integrated Presidency for a United Europe' (European Policy Centre, December 2002) 5.

[61] Norman (n 35) 110–112.

[62] ibid 143–148.

[63] G Grevi, 'Options for Government of the Union' (Federal Trust, March 2003) 6; Norman (n 35) 112.

[64] This paper envisioned the President of the European Council preparing and controlling its agenda; developing jointly with the Commission President the multi-annual strategic agenda; being head of the Council Secretariat that would become 'his administration'; chairing the General Affairs and External Relations Council; chairing teams of chairs of sectoral Council formations; approving agendas for sectoral Councils; chairing trialogue meetings with the Commission and the EP; and attendance at Commission meetings as an observer when the President of the European Council so decides; 'ownership' of major summits with great powers; coordination and supervision on aspects of crisis management and defence.

[65] Norman (n 35) 148–150.

invasion of the foreign ministers:[66] Joschka Fischer and Dominique de Villepin both joined the Convention, as did foreign ministers from some other Member States. They were powerful figures and made numerous contributions to the institutional deliberations. The Franco-German paper, set against the background of the 'ABC' view, shaped developments inside the Convention concerning the disposition of executive power. It set the tone of subsequent debate about the Presidency of the Union. It had a marked impact on Giscard d'Estaing's thinking. He may well have inclined to this view in any event. The Franco-German paper, when combined with the opinions of the UK and Spain, nonetheless shaped his thinking. He was not about to produce a Draft Constitution for the IGC that contained key provisions about the institutional disposition of power that were opposed by the larger Member States, and therefore doomed to failure.

The manner of announcement of the constitutional provisions on the Presidency of the European Council was nonetheless dramatic. The proposals were leaked to the press on 22 April 2003, just as he was unveiling them to the Praesidium, with the consequence that Praesidium members were 'flabbergasted and furious'.[67] The proposals 'provoked shock and awe in about equal measure, particularly among the integrationist Convention members from the European Parliament and some of the smaller Member States'.[68] It is safe to say that they were not welcomed by the Commission either. The 'shock and awe' provoked by the Giscard proposals was explicable because they not only provided for an extended Presidency of the European Council, which was to be the highest authority of the Union, but also accorded the European Council a range of other powers, and its own bureaucratic support mechanism. It is true that the most developed form of these proposals did not survive long within the Convention. Substantial parts hit the 'cutting room floor', but the result as expressed in the Draft Constitution nonetheless embodied the central idea of an extended Presidency for the European Council and enhancement of its power.

The Praesidium submitted its proposals to the Convention in April 2003.[69] Full discussion of the draft articles concerning institutions only occurred in the plenary session on 15–16 May 2003,[70] and this revealed serious differences of view on central issues. The Praesidium realized that it needed more time for reflection and therefore did not make any amendments to these articles in its initial global draft of 28 May 2003.[71] There was no second reading in plenary

---

[66] Norman (n 43) 2; Norman (n 35) 129–133.

[67] Norman (n 35) 189.

[68] Norman (n 43) 3.

[69] CONV 691/03, Institutions, Brussels 23 April 2003; CONV, Summary Report of the Plenary Session—Brussels 24 and 25 April 2003, Brussels 30 April 2003.

[70] CONV 748/03, Summary Report of the Plenary Session—Brussels 15 and 16 May 2003, Brussels 27 May 2003. See also, CONV 709/03, Summary Sheet of Proposals for Amendments relating to the Union's Institutions, Brussels 9 May 2003.

[71] CONV 783/03, Summary Report on the Plenary Session—Brussels 30 and 31 May 2003, Brussels 16 June 2003.

about these articles. The Praesidium opted instead for consultations with the four constituent groups, governments, MEPs, national MPs, and the Commission, which took place on 4 June 2003.[72] Formal text of the revised articles on the institutions only became available on 10 June,[73] a mere three days before the concluding session on 13 June.[74] It is clear moreover, as will be seen below, that the Praesidium, and the Secretariat, exercised considerable power in deciding on the ultimate content of these provisions of the Constitution and which amendments should be adopted.

The Convention process in relation to institutions can obviously be criticized. It should, however, be placed in perspective. This may not serve to justify the process in this respect, but it does help us to understand what occurred. It was not self-evident that the Convention would seek to draft a Constitution. Many of the Member States felt that it might be nothing more than a high-level talking shop, which produced recommendations.[75] It nonetheless quickly became evident that the Convention had more far-reaching aspirations to produce a formal constitutional document. The decision to postpone discussion of institutions is readily explicable. It was clear that this topic would be divisive. If it had been placed on the agenda in the latter part of 2002, then it would have overshadowed the work on other issues. It might have undermined the entire constitution-making process.

The contrast with what occurred is instructive. The Convention, via working groups, concentrated on important issues, such as the Charter of Rights, competences, legal personality and the like. There were differences of opinion on these matters, but they were less marked than those on institutions. Progress on these matters allowed the Praesidium to publish the Preliminary Draft Constitution in the autumn of 2002. This may well have been a skeletal document. It did, however, reinforce the sense that the Convention really was going to produce a constitutional document, and allowed key national players to absorb the idea.

(e) Spring and summer 2003: centralization of initiative to the Praesidium and the Secretariat in the closing stages

The closing stages of the Convention[76] saw the increasing centralization of initiative to the Praesidium and the Secretariat.

The European Council refused to extend the time for the Convention deliberations. The President of the Convention informed the members in April

[72] CONV 770/03, Part I, Title IV (Institutions)—Revised Text, Brussels 2 June 2003; CONV 771/03, Consultations with the Component Groups, Brussels 2 June 2003.
[73] CONV 797/03, Revised Text of Part One, Brussels 10 June 2003.
[74] CONV 814/03, Summary Report of the Plenary Session—Brussels 11 and 13 June 2003, Brussels 19 June 2003.
[75] Norman (n 43) 2.   [76] Norman (n 35) chs 15–17.

that the European Council required the Convention to present its conclusions to the European Council meeting in Greece on 20 June. Giscard d'Estaing recognized that this was a firm deadline to which the Convention had to work.[77] He acknowledged also that the tight time frame required flexibility in the Convention's working methods.[78]

The tight time scale increased the centralization of initiative to the Praesidium and the Secretariat. They already had the principal responsibility for drafting the detailed articles of the Constitutional Treaty. Their power in this respect was strengthened because the working groups were largely disbanded once they had presented their final reports, although it was possible to reconvene such groups if this was required. The centralization of initiative was enhanced by the very limited time scale within which amendments to the draft Articles could be made. This was normally a week, a short time by any standards given the complexity and controversial nature of some of the Articles. It fell, moreover, to the Praesidium to decide which amendments should be taken seriously. A plethora of amendments were tabled to all draft Articles, and it was not uncommon for there to be 50 or more. It was the Praesidium, and in some instances a small number within the Praesidium, that 'grouped' the amendments, decided which 'groups' had most support, and which should be taken up.

The tightness of the timetable, with the consequential centralization of power and scant time for deliberation about amendments, was of course less than satisfactory. It certainly did not conform to some 'ideal-type' vision of the final stages of drafting a Constitution or Constitutional Treaty. The Convention, however, did not exist within an ideal-type world. It conducted its task against the real world conditions laid down by the European Council. Once the deadline was set the Praesidium had little choice but to take a more pro-active role. If it had not done so the Constitutional Treaty would not have been presented to the European Council in June 2003, and might not even have been ready by autumn 2003.

We should be similarly realistic about the Praesidium's role in relation to the prioritization of amendments. The absence of the strict deadline would, to be sure, have allowed greater time for deliberation about the amendments. It would still have been necessary for someone to be pro-active in deciding which of the amendments should be pursued. This could not have been readily accomplished by any simple voting method, even assuming that voting had been chosen as the method for resolving such matters. The number and range of amendments precluded this solution. Whether a member might vote for or against amendment X concerning topic A would depend on the alternatives, and there would

[77] CONV 696/03, Summary Report of the Plenary Session 24 and 25 April, Brussels 30 April 2003.
[78] CONV 721/03, Letter from the Chairman to Members of the Convention Concerning the Convention's Working Methods During its Final Stages, Brussels 8 May 2003.

often be many placed on the table. Moreover, preferences for or against amendment X on topic A might commonly be affected by the outcome in relation to amendment Y on topic B, which was related to, but distinct from, topic A.

3. The Inter-Governmental Conference: Deliberation, Discord, and Decision

(a) The IGC deliberations: an Italian autumn

Giscard d'Estaing duly delivered the Draft Constitutional Treaty to the European Council in June 2003.[79] However, the IGC deliberations did not begin in earnest until the autumn under the Italian Presidency. The outcome is well known. The Member States failed to agree on the Constitutional Treaty in the December meeting of the European Council.

The early view, embodied in the Laeken Declaration, was that the Convention deliberations would be no more than the 'starting point for the discussions in the Intergovernmental Conference, which will take the ultimate decisions'.[80] This was in line with the view that the Member States hold the reins of power in grand constitutional moments. It was nonetheless unclear when the IGC initially convened whether it would seek to reopen the Convention's text. There were some Member States who favoured acceptance of the text as it stood, mindful of the dangers of opening Pandora's Box. However, they made it clear that if the text were reopened then there were issues that they would place on the table for reconsideration. Other Member States were less reticent, and pressed for reconsideration of certain provisions. The latter view won the day, and the IGC proceeded to 'pick its way' through the Constitution, albeit not in any very systematic manner.

The IGC discussed a plethora of particular issues during this period, including detailed aspects of areas such as economic policy, criminal law, defence, and the Common Foreign and Security Policy (CFSP).[81] It was not surprising, however, that the IGC deliberations were dominated by institutional issues. No attempt will be made to evaluate the complex issues surrounding the desirability or otherwise of the changes proposed by the IGC to the institutional provisions. These issues will be considered in subsequent chapters.[82] The objective is rather to give a brief flavour of the institutional issues that occupied the IGC in this

---

[79] CONV 820/03, Draft Treaty Establishing a Constitution for Europe, Brussels 20 June 2003; CONV 850/03, Draft Treaty Establishing a Constitution for Europe, Brussels 18 July 2003; this is the final version of the Convention's work, submitted in July 2003, in which some changes were made from the version submitted in June 2003.

[80] Laeken European Council, 14–15 December 2001, 5.

[81] CIG 52/1/03, PRESID 10, IGC 2003-Naples Ministerial Conclave: Presidency Proposal, Brussels 25 November 2003.

[82] Chs 2, 3.

autumnal period. The changes were important because many were retained in the final version of the Constitutional Treaty and in the Lisbon Treaty.

The IGC considered the internal organization of the Commission. The Draft Constitution embodied a two-tier system for Commissioners, 15 of whom could vote, while the remainder could not.[83] This was a compromise between those who favoured a smaller, tighter Commission, and those who advocated the continued presence of one Commissioner from each Member State. This compromise was however deeply problematic. The Commission expressed opposition in the strongest possible terms, describing the relevant provisions of the Draft Constitution as 'complicated, muddled and inoperable'.[84] The Italian Presidency addressed the issue,[85] although it seemed that the IGC would persist with the divide between voting and non-voting Commissioners, while attempting to clarify the responsibilities of the latter group.[86]

The organization of the Council received considerable attention. The Draft Constitution proposed a combined Legislative and General Affairs Council (LGAC). When the LGAC acted in its legislative capacity each Member State's representation was to be composed of one or two representatives at ministerial level with relevant expertise, which would reflect the business on the Council's agenda.[87] This did not prove acceptable to the IGC.[88] The majority of the Member States favoured according legislative power to each of the Council formations, rather than having one dedicated Legislative Council, and this view was incorporated in a revised version placed before the IGC by the Italian Presidency.[89]

The IGC also proposed more general changes to the regime of Council formations.[90] The combined LGAC was discarded. There was to be a General Affairs Council, GAC, with the task of ensuring consistency in the work of the different Council formations. The GAC would, as in the Draft Constitution, prepare and ensure the follow-up to meetings of the European Council in liaison with both the President of the European Council as well as the Commission.[91] The provisions concerning the Foreign Affairs Council, FAC, remained the same.[92] The European Council would still make the decision concerning the

---

[83] CONV 850/03 (n 79) Art I-25(3).

[84] A Constitution for the Union, Opinion of the Commission, pursuant to Art 48 of the Treaty on European Union, on the Conference of representatives of the Member States' governments convened to revise the Treaties, COM(2003) 548 final, [2].

[85] CIG 6/03, Preparation of the IGC Ministerial Meeting on 14 October 2003: Questionnaires, Brussels 7 October 2003.

[86] IGC 2003-Naples Ministerial Conclave (n 81) 4–5.

[87] CONV 850/03 (n 79) Art I-23(1).

[88] CIG 9/03, PRESID 1, Questionnaire on the Legislative Function, the Formations of the Council and the Presidency of the Council of Ministers, Brussels 15 October 2003.

[89] CIG 39/03, PRESID 5, Council Presidency and Council Formations, Brussels 24 October 2003.

[90] ibid.   [91] IGC revised Art I-23(2).   [92] IGC revised Art I-23(3).

list of other Council formations.[93] A consequence of discarding the LGAC was that each of the Council formations would deliberate and vote on legislation within its respective area. The method of choosing the Presidency of the Council formations was altered.[94] They were to be held by Member State representatives in the Council on the basis of equal rotation, in accordance with a Protocol devised by the IGC. The Protocol embodied in essence a 'team system' for the Presidency of Council formations, other than the GAC and FAC. This meant that the Presidency of those other Council formations would be held collectively by pre-established groups of three or four States, for a period that was still being negotiated, but which would be somewhere between one and two years.

There was also discussion about voting within the Council, the definition of qualified majority voting (QMV), and the areas to which QMV, as opposed to unanimity, should apply.[95] Some States were happy with the Convention draft, others wished to be more adventurous, yet others wished to be more cautious, at least with respect to the retention of unanimity for voting in certain areas. The Italian Presidency was reluctant to reopen the Convention definition of QMV, which can be readily understood given the Byzantine nature of previous discussions on the matter. It did, however, accept that further reflection on the matter was necessary and that it might have to be placed on the table of the European Council meeting.[96]

(b) The Brussels European Council December 2003: the 'winter of our discontent'

As autumn turned to winter the Italian Presidency sought to prepare the ground for the Brussels European Council meeting in December 2003. It pursued a double-edged strategy, as is clear from documentation submitted to the European Council. It submitted one document in the form of revised texts on issues that the Presidency felt were sufficiently resolved by the IGC deliberations to be able to be put forward as concrete proposals.[97] It also submitted a much shorter document concerning sensitive issues that were intended to be the focus of the discussion at the December meeting.[98] These were the existence or not of some reference to Europe's Christian roots in the Preamble; the composition of the Commission; the rules on QMV; and the minimum threshold of seats in the European Parliament.

---

[93] IGC revised Art I-23(4).
[94] IGC revised Art I-23(6).
[95] CIG 38/03, PRESID 4, IGC—Qualified Majority Voting, Brussels 24 October 2003.
[96] CIG 52/1/03, PRESID 10, IGC 2003—Naples Ministerial Conclave (n 81) 4.
[97] CIG 60/03, ADD 1, PRESID 14, IGC 2003—Intergovernmental Conference (12–13 December): Addendum 1 to the Presidency Proposal, Brussels 9 December 2003.
[98] CIG 60/03, ADD 1, PRESID 14, IGC 2003—Intergovernmental Conference (12–13 December): Addendum 2, Brussels 11 December 2003.

Commentators and participants initially expected the Brussels European Council to be a 'three shirter'. There is an amusing article waiting to be written about 'sartorial metaphors within European discourse', more especially so given the talk of 'hats' within the Convention in the context of the Presidency of the EU. Suffice it to say that the 'three shirter' signified an expectation that the European Council would extend beyond the normal two-day period, thereby necessitating the extra supply of fresh clothing. It was thought that there would be lengthy discussions, quite possibly extending throughout the nights, as the *dramatis personae* hammered out some form of consensus on the issues that still divided them. That had been the case in the past, most recently with the IGC that produced the Nice Treaty.

Matters turned out very differently. As the date for the meeting approached, concerns were expressed that a deal might not be brokered. MEPs who were former Convention members drew up a list of ten critical points that they expected to see in the final Constitution. It was the issue of vote-weighting in the Council, with its implications for QMV, which proved most difficult. This saw France and Germany pitted against Spain and Poland, with the former pair insisting that the number of votes wielded by the latter two States should be reduced. Agreement could not be reached on this topic, the European Council broke up early, and the participants went home with some clean clothes.

The 'assignment of blame' for failure to agree on the Constitution began quickly. Fingers were pointed at Spain and Poland for being intransigent; similar accusations were levelled at France and Germany, and Berlusconi was criticized for not doing enough to resolve the problem. The 'payback' for failure to agree on the voting issue was equally rapid. On 16 December the leaders of France, Germany, UK, Sweden, Austria, and the Netherlands signed an open letter calling for EU spending to be capped from 2007 onwards. This would have significant consequences for Spain and Poland who would be principal beneficiaries of EU funding and hence suffer from any cap on spending. It is difficult to regard the timing of this letter as unrelated to the failure at Brussels.

(c) The Brussels European Council June 2004: the Irish secure agreement

The Presidency passed to Ireland for the first six months of 2004, with the Dutch set to follow for the second half of 2004. The Irish conducted bilateral negotiations with the relevant players. However, it was the tragedy of the bombing in Madrid which proved to be the turning point. This led to a change of government in Spain. The incoming government quickly made it clear that it wished to see the IGC process revived and that it was willing to re-enter discussion about voting rights within the Council.

It should not be thought, however, that agreement on the Constitutional Treaty was inevitable thereafter. It remained unclear until the last moment whether the voting rights issue could be resolved and whether other matters, such as Blair's red lines, could be accommodated. However, the Brussels European Council in June 2004 managed to secure agreement on the Constitutional Treaty.[99]

4. From Constitutional Treaty to Lisbon Treaty: Crisis, Reflection, and Ratification

(a) 2005: 'Ratification' and 'Reflection'

The final version of the Constitutional Treaty[100] had to be ratified in accordance with the constitutional requirements or choices of each Member State. Fifteen Member States ratified the Treaty. It was generally thought that problems with ratification would be most pronounced in the UK, but this was never tested because progress with ratification came to an abrupt halt when France and the Netherlands rejected the Constitutional Treaty in their referenda in 2005.[101] A number of Member States therefore postponed the ratification process. The European Council in 2005 decided that discretion was the better part of valour and that it was best for there to be a time for 'reflection', during which Member States were encouraged to engage in debate about the EU with their own citizens.

The negative referenda in France and the Netherlands, coupled with the period of reflection, not surprisingly generated discourse as to whether it was wise for the EU ever to have embarked on this ambitious constitutional project. This was reflected in the jibe 'if it ain't broke, why fix it?' On this view grand constitutional schemes of the kind embodied in the Constitutional Treaty were unnecessary, because the EU could function perfectly well on the basis of the Nice Treaty, and dangerous, because the very construction of such a constitutional document would bring to the fore contentious issues concerning matters such as the range of EU competences, the supremacy of EU law over national law, and the inter-institutional division of power, which were best resolved through less formal mechanisms, as opposed to hard-edged constitutional provisions that invited high-profile constitutional controversy.

There is force in this view. It should nonetheless be recognized that the four issues left over from the Nice Treaty were not discrete. They raised, both directly

---

[99] Council of the European Union, Brussels European Council, Presidency Conclusions 10679/04, ADD 1, CONCL 2, Brussels 18 June 2004.

[100] Treaty Establishing a Constitution for Europe [2004] OJ C316/1; J Ziller, *La nouvelle Constitution europeéne* (La decouverte, 2005); J-C Piris, *The Constitution for Europe: A Legal Analysis* (Cambridge University Press, 2006); O de Schutter and P Nihoul, *Une Constitution pour l'Europe: réflexions sur les transformations du droit de l'Union europeéne* (Larcier, 2004).

[101] R Dehousse, 'The Unmaking of a Constitution: Lessons from the European Referenda' (2006) 13 *Constellations* 151.

and indirectly, broader issues concerning the nature of the EU, its powers, mode of decision-making, and relationship with the Member States and their parliaments. The dissatisfaction with piecemeal IGC Treaty reform, monopolized by the Member States, should moreover not be forgotten. If this traditional process had been adhered to in relation to the broadened reform agenda there would have been a raft of criticism about the 'legitimacy and representativeness deficit' inherent in the classic IGC model.

A related, but distinct, set of issues concerned the way in which the Convention operated. Thus some cast doubt on the participatory credentials of the Convention, pointing to the increasing centralization of initiative in the Praesidium, especially in the latter stages of the Convention, which left scant time for deliberation of amendments. This was problematic and did not conform to some 'ideal-type' vision of drafting a Constitution. However, the Convention did not exist within an ideal-type world. It conducted its task against the real world conditions laid down by the European Council. Once the European Council reaffirmed the deadline the Praesidium had little choice but to take a more pro-active role, since otherwise the Constitutional Treaty would not have been presented to the European Council in June 2003. The absence of the strict deadline would, moreover, still have required 'someone' to have been pro-active in deciding which amendments should be pursued.

There was also a vibrant discourse as to what should happen in the light of the negative referenda in France and the Netherlands.[102] Some argued that while the rejection of the Constitutional Treaty by the French and Dutch voters had little to do with its content, grand constitution making was neither necessary, nor desirable, since there was already a relatively stable constitutional settlement in place. The EU should rather get on with its normal business.[103] Others broadly agreed with this diagnosis of the French and Dutch referenda, but maintained that the EU needed some constituent document as it moved forward in the new millennium.[104] Yet others saw the rejection of the Treaty as evidence of a deeper malaise within the EU, which should not be ignored.[105]

(b) January to June 2007: from reflection to action

In 2006 the European Council commissioned Germany, which held the Presidency of the European Council in the first half of 2007, to assess and report

---

[102] G de Búrca, 'The European Constitution Project after the Referenda' (2006) 13 *Constellations* 205.

[103] A Moravcsik, 'Europe without Illusions: A Category Error' (2005) 112 Prospect, available at <http://www.prospectmagazine.co.uk/landing_page.php>.

[104] A Duff, 'Plan B: How to Rescue the European Constitution', Notre Europe, Studies and Research No 52, 2006.

[105] L Siedentop, 'A Crisis of Legitimacy' (2005) 112 Prospect, available at <http://www.prospectmagazine.co.uk/landing_page.php>.

on the current state of discussion concerning the Constitutional Treaty. This would then serve as the basis for measures to be taken by the French Presidency in the second half of 2008 at the latest. It was nonetheless unclear at the time how much progress Germany would be able to make in gaining acceptance of the Treaty, or some revised version thereof.

The German Presidency, however, was keen to move matters forward in 2007. The objective was to see whether an agreement could be brokered between the Member States that would pave the way for acceptance of some revised Treaty reform. To this end, the German Government engaged in well-organized and astute diplomacy, inquiring of each Member State which issues in the Constitutional Treaty it would require to be changed in order for that State to ratify any amended document. This enabled Germany to bring to the table in the June 2007 European Council a detailed mandate of the changes that should be made to the Constitutional Treaty, in order that a revised Treaty could successfully be concluded.

The German Presidency sought agreement in the European Council in June 2007[106] on the outlines for a revised version of the Constitutional Treaty, which led to the birth of the Reform Treaty. The European Council concluded that 'after two years of uncertainty over the Union's treaty reform process, the time has come to resolve the issue and for the Union to move on'.[107] It was agreed to convene an IGC,[108] which was to carry out its work in accord with the detailed mandate provided in Annex I of the conclusions of the European Council, and finish its deliberations by the end of 2007.[109] The IGC was to be conducted under the overall responsibility of the Heads of State or Government, assisted by members of the General Affairs and External Relations Council. A representative of the Commission was to participate in the Conference, and the European Parliament was to be closely 'associated with and involved in the work of the Conference with three representatives'.[110]

The amount of work done prior to the June 2007 meeting was readily apparent from the detailed mandate in Annex I drawn up for the IGC that was to take place in the second half of 2007. Annex I began with 'general observations' about the next stage of Treaty reform. The IGC was asked to draw up a Treaty to be called the Reform Treaty, which would amend the existing Treaties with a 'view to enhancing the efficiency and democratic legitimacy of the enlarged Union, as well as the coherence of its external action'.[111] The Reform Treaty was to contain two principal substantive clauses, which amended respectively the Treaty on the European Union TEU, and the EC Treaty, the latter of which would be renamed the Treaty on the Functioning of the European Union, TFEU. The Union should have a single legal personality and the word 'Community' throughout would be replaced by the word 'Union'.[112]

---

[106] Brussels European Council, 21–22 June 2007.   [107] ibid [8].
[108] ibid [10].   [109] ibid [11].   [110] ibid [12].
[111] ibid Annex I, [1].   [112] ibid Annex I, [2].

The 'general observations' within the Annex were also structured to excise the 'C' word, constitution, from the Reform Treaty. Thus the Reform Treaty would operate as an amendment to the existing treaties, rather than by way of repealing all existing treaties as envisaged by the Constitutional Treaty.[113] The TEU and TFEU that were to make up the Reform Treaty were not to have a constitutional character. This was said to be so for a number of reasons:[114] the term 'constitution' was not to be used; the 'Union Minister for Foreign Affairs' was to be called High Representative of the Union for Foreign Affairs and Security Policy; the terms 'law' and 'framework law' were to be abandoned, and the existing terminology of regulations, directives, and decisions was to be retained; there was to be no flag, anthem, or motto; and the clause in the Constitutional Treaty concerning the primacy of EU law was to be replaced by a declaration.

The European Council's reasoning was readily explicable in political terms: the imperative was to conclude this stage of Treaty reform, and insofar as the constitutional terminology of the Constitutional Treaty was felt to be a political obstacle then it was to be ditched. This can be acknowledged, but it should nonetheless be recognized that the arguments set out above as to why the Reform Treaty was not to have a constitutional character were weak to say the very least. Insofar as the Constitutional Treaty partook of the nature of a constitution, none of the changes identified by the European Council were significant. A constitutional document does not cease to be so because the words law or lawmaking are not used, nor because of the change in nomenclature of the Union Minister for Foreign Affairs, nor for any of the other reasons listed. There is, of course, room for genuine debate as to whether the Constitutional Treaty was truly a constitutional document,[115] but insofar as it was the reasons for differentiation provided by the European Council were unconvincing.

The remainder of the European Council's mandate for the 2007 IGC consisted of 16 pages of detailed provisions concerning modifications that were to be made to the TEU and the TFEU. They related to matters such as competences, the Common Foreign and Security Policy, the enhanced role of national parliaments, the Charter of Fundamental Rights and the area of freedom, security, and justice. This did not, however, mask the fact that the great majority of the changes introduced by the Constitutional Treaty looked set to remain within the Reform Treaty.

(c) July to December 2007: the IGC and the Lisbon Treaty

Matters then moved rapidly. An IGC was convened in order to take forward the formulation of the Reform Treaty. Portugal held the Presidency of the Council

---

[113] ibid Annex I, [1].   [114] ibid Annex I, [3].

[115] S Griller, 'Is this a Constitution? Remarks on a Contested Concept' in S Griller and J Ziller (eds), *The Lisbon Treaty, EU Constitutionalism without a Constitutional Treaty?* (Springer, 2008) 21–56.

in the second half of 2007 and was keen that the matter should be concluded during its Presidency, in part because the President of the Commission was from Portugal, and in part because Portugal could then attach its name to the amending Treaty.

The 2007 IGC was power politics with a vengeance. We had grown accustomed to the fact that even traditional IGCs would be relatively open, with discussion papers available on the internet and time for the 'people' to form some view as to the planned reforms. This sense was fuelled by the more inclusive process used in relation to the Charter of Fundamental Rights and the Constitutional Treaty. The Lisbon Treaty was, by way of contrast, forged by the Member States and Community institutions, and there was scant time afforded for further deliberation. Thus the detailed version of the Reform Treaty of October 2007 allowed only two weeks before the Member States were required to signal their consent, and scant time for any one else to digest its detailed provisions.

The justification for this accelerated process was apparent when one perused the content of the Lisbon Treaty, but it was, for obvious reasons, a justification that those engaged in the IGC could not too openly avow, this being that the Lisbon Treaty was indeed the same in most important respects as the Constitutional Treaty. The issues had been debated in detail in the Convention on the Future of Europe after a relatively open discourse, and were considered once again in the IGC in 2004. There was therefore little incentive or appetite for those engaged in the 2007 IGC to reopen Pandora's Box.[116] This argument could not, however, be pressed too explicitly by those taking part in the 2007 IGC, since they would be open to the criticism that they were largely re-packaging provisions that had been rejected by voters in two prominent Member States,[117] more especially given that key Member States sought to press forward with ratification of the Lisbon Treaty without recourse to any (further) referendum.

The 2007 IGC produced a document that was signed by the Member States on 13 December 2007,[118] although the appellation was changed to the Lisbon Treaty in recognition of the place of signature. It required ratification by each Member State. The hope that this stage of Treaty reform could be hastily concluded was dashed, however, when Ireland rejected the Lisbon Treaty in a referendum. This obstacle was overcome by a second Irish referendum in October 2009, after concessions were made to overcome Irish objections expressed in the earlier referendum. The final hurdle proved to be the reluctance

---

[116] G Tsebelis, 'Thinking about the Recent Past and Future of the EU' (2008) 46 JCMS 265.

[117] This was so regardless of the fact that the reasons for the 'no' vote in France and the Netherlands may have had relatively little to do with the new provisions contained in the Constitutional Treaty.

[118] Conference of the Representatives of the Governments of the Member States, Treaty of Lisbon Amending the Treaty on European Union and the Treaty Establishing the European Community, CIG 14/07, Brussels 3 December 2007, [2007] OJ C306/1.

of the Czech President to ratify the Lisbon Treaty, but he did so reluctantly after a constitutional challenge to the Treaty had been rejected by the Czech Constitutional Court.

5. Lisbon Treaty: Architecture and Structure

(a) Formal architecture

It is axiomatic that every Treaty has its own architecture, which serves to shape the ordering and placing of particular Treaty provisions, more especially when the amending Treaty makes significant institutional changes to the status quo ante. It would indeed be natural to denominate this in terms of 'constitutional architecture', but for the fact that the word 'Constitution' has been consciously excised from the Lisbon Treaty. It is nonetheless necessary to understand and evaluate the '(constitutional) architecture' of the Lisbon Treaty, since this is important in and of itself, and because it facilitates understanding of the more particular amendments that will be considered in later chapters.

So, let us be clear about the basics. The Lisbon Treaty amends the Treaty on European Union and the Treaty Establishing the European Community. The Lisbon Treaty itself has seven Articles, of which Articles 1 and 2 are the most important, plus numerous Protocols and Declarations. Article 1 contains the amendments to the Treaty on European Union, TEU, and contains some of the principles that govern the EU, as well as revised provisions concerning the Common Foreign and Security Policy and enhanced cooperation. Article 2 amends the EC Treaty, which is renamed the Treaty on the Functioning of the European Union. The EU is henceforth to be founded on the TEU and the TFEU, and the two Treaties have the same legal value.[119] The Union is to replace and succeed the EC.[120] The Lisbon Treaty contains an Annex with a Table of Equivalences for the revised Treaty as a whole. This provides the reader with the new numbering of Articles for the entire Treaty. A consolidated version of the Lisbon Treaty now contains the new numbering and references to the old provisions where appropriate.[121] These renumbered Treaty Articles will be used throughout the discussion of the Lisbon Treaty.

(b) Substantive architecture: general

The Constitutional Treaty had a pretty clear 'constitutional architecture', and this was so irrespective of what one felt about particular provisions thereof.

---

[119] Art 1 para 3 TEU.
[120] ibid.
[121] Consolidated Versions of the Treaty on European Union and the Treaty on the Functioning of the European Union [2008] OJ C115/1, [2010] OJ C83/1.

Part I contained the important principles concerning the nature and operation of the EU legal order, even if reference to the substantive provisions of Part III of the Constitutional Treaty was necessary in order to understand the more detailed meaning of particular principles.

The Lisbon Treaty fares less well in this respect. The revised TEU functions to some extent as the repository of the constitutional principles for the EU. This is especially true in relation to Title I-Common Provisions, Title II-Democratic Principles, and Title III-Provisions on the Institutions. The Articles included within these Titles undoubtedly address matters of a constitutional nature, concerning, for example, the locus of legislative power within the EU and the establishment of the newly-expanded role of President of the European Council. There are nonetheless matters not included within the revised TEU, which had properly been in Part I of the Constitutional Treaty. Thus, for example, the rules concerning competence, aside from a brief mention in the TEU,[122] are to be found in the TFEU,[123] as are the provisions concerning the hierarchy of norms,[124] and the important principles relating to budgetary planning.[125]

This was perhaps inevitable, given the fate of the Constitutional Treaty and the political need to take forward the reforms in a manner that would be more in accord with the status quo. This explains the continued use of the basic divide between the TEU and the EC, albeit with the latter renamed as the TFEU. The framers of the Lisbon Treaty nonetheless also had to ensure that there was some difference to the 'naked eye' between what was contained in the revised TEU, and what had been included within Part I of the Constitutional Treaty. The drafters of the Lisbon Treaty were therefore caught in a dilemma: the natural desire to frame the revised TEU so as to embrace the EU's important constitutional principles had to be tempered by the political need to produce a document that did not simply replicate Part I of the Constitutional Treaty.

The Lisbon Treaty has, however, made improvements in the architecture of what will henceforth be the TFEU. It is divided into seven Parts. Part One, entitled Principles, contains two Titles, the first of which deals with Categories of Competence, the second of which covers Provisions having General Application. Part Two deals with Discrimination and Citizenship of the Union. Part Three, which covers Policies and Internal Actions of the Union, is the largest Part of the TFEU with 24 Titles.[126] The most noteworthy change in this respect is that the provisions on Police and Judicial Cooperation in Criminal Matters, the Third Pillar of the old TEU, have been moved into the new TFEU. They have been integrated with what was Title IV EC, dealing with Visas, Asylum etc, and is now

---

[122] Arts 4, 5 TEU.   [123] Arts 2–6 TFEU.
[124] Arts 288–292 TFEU.
[125] Art 312 TFEU.
[126] The Titles are as follows: I-Internal Market; II-Free Movement of Goods; III-Agriculture and Fisheries; IV-Free Movement of Persons, Services and Capital; Title V-Area of Freedom, Security and Justice; VI-Transport; VII-Common Rules on Competition, Taxation and Approximation of Laws;

Title V of the TFEU, renamed the Area of Freedom, Security and Justice. Part Four of the TFEU covers, as before, Association of Overseas Countries and Territories. Part Five, by way of contrast, is new and deals with External Action by the Union, bringing together a range of subject matter with an external dimension.[127] Part Six of the TFEU is concerned with Institutional and Budgetary Provisions, while Part Seven covers General and Final Provisions.

(c) Substantive architecture: the pillar structure and the Common Foreign and Security Policy

The impact of the Lisbon Treaty on the Second and Third Pillar[128] will be considered in subsequent chapters.[129] The present focus is on the general approach in the Lisbon Treaty to matters that had hitherto been dealt with in the Second and Third Pillars.

The approach to the Common Foreign and Security Policy (CFSP) in the Lisbon Treaty largely replicates that in the Constitutional Treaty, subject to the change of nomenclature, discussed below, from Union Minister for Foreign Affairs to High Representative of the Union for Foreign Affairs and Security Policy. The distinctive nature of the rules relating to the CFSP means that in reality there is still a separate 'Pillar' for such matters. The rules relating to the CFSP remain distinct and executive authority continues to reside with the European Council and the Council. It is the European Council, acting unanimously on a proposal from the Council, which identifies the strategic interests and objectives of the CFSP.[130]

This is further emphasized by Article 24 TEU, which provides that: the CFSP is subject to specific rules and procedures; it is defined and implemented by the European Council and the Council acting unanimously, except where the Treaties provide otherwise; that the adoption of legislative acts is excluded;[131] and the CFSP is to be put into effect by the High Representative of the Union for Foreign Affairs and Security Policy and by Member States, in accordance with the Treaties.

VIII-Economic and Monetary Policy; IX-Employment; X-Social Policy; XI-The European Social Fund; XII-Education, Vocational Training, Youth and Sport; XIII-Culture; XIV-Public Health; XV-Consumer Protection; XVI-Trans-European Networks; XVII-Industry; XVIII-Economic, Social and Territorial Cohesion; XIX-Research and Technological Development and Space; XX-Environment; XXI-Energy; XXII-Tourism; XXIII-Civil Protection; XXIV-Administrative Cooperation.

[127] The principal issues covered by Part Five are: the common commercial policy, cooperation with third countries and humanitarian aid, restrictive measures, the making of international agreements, and the EU's relations with third countries and international organizations.

[128] A valuable detailed analysis can be found in S Peers, *Statewatch Analysis of the EU Reform Treaty*, available at <http://www.statewatch.org/>.

[129] Chs 9 and 10.

[130] Art 22 TEU.

[131] Art 352(4) TFEU, which is the amended Art 308 EC, specifically precludes the use of this provision in relation to the CFSP.

Article 24 TEU also emphasizes the 'specific role' of the European Parliament and the Commission in this area as defined by the Treaties. The European Court of Justice (ECJ) continues to be largely excluded from the CFSP.[132] It does, however, have jurisdiction in relation to Article 40 TEU, which is designed to ensure that exercise of CFSP powers do not impinge on the general competences of the EU, and vice versa; the ECJ also has jurisdiction under Article 275 TFEU to review the legality of decisions imposing restrictive measures on natural or legal persons adopted by the Council under Chapter 2 of Title V TEU.

(d) Substantive architecture: the pillar structure and Police and Judicial Cooperation in Criminal Matters

The approach in the Lisbon Treaty to the CFSP can be contrasted with that in relation to the Third Pillar, which is moved from the TEU and merged with the provisions of what was Title IV EC, dealing with immigration, asylum and civil law. This forms a new Title V TFEU, the Area of Freedom, Security and Justice, which has five chapters dealing with: general provisions; policies on border checks, asylum, and immigration; judicial cooperation in civil matters; judicial cooperation in criminal matters; and police cooperation. The detailed provisions largely reflect those in the Constitutional Treaty, subject to some amendments mandated by the European Council in June 2007. The Lisbon Treaty has therefore largely followed the Constitutional Treaty in 'de-pillarizing' this aspect of EU law.

This development is to be welcomed, as is the fact that, subject to transitional provisions, the normal jurisdiction of the ECJ is generally applicable within this area. Thus the old Article 35 EU, which limited the ECJ's jurisdiction under the Third Pillar, is repealed by the Lisbon Treaty. The exception is Article 276 TFEU, which continues to preclude the ECJ from reviewing the validity or proportionality of operations carried out by the police or other law-enforcement services of a Member State or the exercise of the responsibilities incumbent upon Member States with regard to the maintenance of law and order and the safeguarding of internal security. Article 267 TFEU, the preliminary ruling procedure, is modified such that if the question raised by the national court relates to a person in custody, the ECJ must act with the minimum of delay.

Less welcome is the preservation of the various opt-outs and reservations to Justice and Home Affairs, which have been extended to cover the new Title V TFEU, and therefore embrace policing and criminal law.[133] This was part of the 'deal' negotiated by the UK in the 2007 negotiations concerning the Lisbon Treaty.

---

[132] Art 24 TEU, Art 275 TFEU.
[133] S Peers, *Statewatch Analysis, EU Reform Treaty Analysis No 4: British and Irish Opt-Outs from EU Justice and Home Affairs (JHA) Law*, 26 October 2007, available at <http://www.statewatch.org/news/2007/aug/eu-reform-treaty-uk-ireland-opt-outs.pdf>.

6. Reflections on Constitutional Reform

Norman has rightly emphasized that the negotiations that resulted in the Constitutional Treaty were in many ways 'a tale of the unexpected'.[134] He notes that the Constitutional Treaty handed to the Italian Presidency in July 2003 was 'in many ways an accidental Constitution',[135] in the sense that the Laeken Declaration envisaged a less ambitious final document. Norman is equally firm in his conclusion that there was nothing inevitable about other key stages within the Convention, such as the timing of the early draft Constitution in autumn 2002, the invasion of the foreign ministers, or the Franco-German paper on institutional reform that did so much to shape later discussion.[136] With this by way of background, we can consider some of the issues concerning content and process in this latest and most protracted round of Treaty reform.

(a) Content

In terms of content, some might argue that the reform agenda was too ambitious and that the focus should have been on the four 'discrete' issues set out in the Nice Declaration. We should be careful in this respect. The issues left open after Nice were not discrete, and if reform had concentrated solely on them there would have been a raft of criticism that it had failed to address deeper problems about the functioning of the EU. The negative referenda in France, the Netherlands, and Ireland spoke volumes about the need for the EU to engage with the people, and there were undoubtedly real concerns about aspects of the EU. The disenchantment and lack of engagement with the European project among certain sections of society is a serious concern and must be addressed. The reality is nonetheless that the rationales for the negative votes in these referenda, especially those in France and the Netherlands, had relatively little to do with the principal changes made by the Constitutional or Lisbon Treaties.

There is of course room for disagreement as to the resulting content of the Lisbon Treaty. Thus some have been critical about the further federalization which they believed to result from, for example, the further shift from unanimity to qualified majority in the Council. Others, by way of contrast, have been equally critical about what they saw as the increased intergovernmentalism in the Treaty, focusing on, for example, enhanced Member State influence in the provisions concerning the inter-institutional distribution of power, the creation of the long-term Presidency of the European Council and the like. There are also significant differences of view concerning particular provisions of the Lisbon Treaty. Thus some have applauded the distribution of competences, while others

---

[134] Norman (n 35) 313.   [135] ibid 313.   [136] ibid 313–315.

have been critical, arguing that the provisions were unclear and uncertain. There is a similar spectrum of views on matters such as the balance between the social and economic dimensions of the EU as reflected in the new Treaty. Such differences of view on these and other matters are inevitable and will be considered in detail in the subsequent chapters.

(b) Process

In terms of process, it might be tempting to think that the Convention process was defective, or that it had been oversold by way of comparison with traditional IGC techniques. We should be careful before subscribing to these conclusions.

The sentiments expressed by the key players between Nice and Laeken were genuine. There was disenchantment with the traditional IGC approach to EU reform, more especially after the experience with the discussions leading to the Nice Treaty. If this traditional process had been adhered to in relation to the broadened reform agenda there would have been criticism about the 'legitimacy and representativeness deficit' inherent in the classic IGC model. It has moreover been argued by Risse and Kleine that the Convention method fares better than the traditional IGC model in terms of input, throughput, and output legitimacy.[137]

It is true that the realization that the Convention might well produce a formal Constitutional Treaty led to some intergovernmentalization of the Convention process. This is exemplified by the way that certain Member States changed their representatives to the Convention, installing high profile players such as foreign ministers in place of their original members. It is apparent also in the way in which State actors intervened in a deliberate manner from outside the Convention in order to influence the proceedings therein.

These developments did not, however, make the Convention just another IGC in disguise. State actors were always part of the Convention. The fact that State players recognized that the Convention deliberations were more important than they initially believed, and therefore wished to have greater input, did not mean that they had a monopoly in the discursive process.

It is true also that the Convention process was overlaid by the traditional IGC model. This was however to be expected. It would have been possible in theory for the outcome of the Convention deliberations to be dispositive with no amending role for the IGC. The reality is that the Member States would not accept this, nor are they likely to do so in the foreseeable future. The process of EU reform is therefore likely to be a blend of the Convention model and the IGC.

---

[137] T Risse and M Kleine, 'Assessing the Legitimacy of the EU's Treaty Revision Methods' (2007) 45 JCMS 69.

There will doubtless also be continuing debate concerning the process that led to the Lisbon Treaty. For some, the decision to press ahead with the Treaty which replicated 90 per cent of what had been in the Constitutional Treaty was either illegitimate, or at the very least dangerous in ignoring the negative votes in referenda from two prominent Member States, more especially because there was scant opportunity to consider the Lisbon Treaty before signature or ratification. For others, the decision to press ahead with this Treaty was justified. They point to the fact that the changes introduced by the Lisbon Treaty played little part in the negative votes in France and the Netherlands, and that insofar as those votes were reflective of a deeper malaise with the EU, it was all the more important to put in place a decision-making structure that would better enable the EU to meet the challenges of the new millennium.

We shall return to these issues in the concluding chapter after considering the principal changes brought about by the Lisbon Treaty. The discussion begins by considering the impact of the Treaty on the inter-institutional distribution of power in the EU.

2

Legislation, Regulation, and Participation

The inter-institutional balance of power within the EU is central to the new constitutional order, when viewed from the perspectives of legitimacy, democracy, and efficacy. It is therefore not surprising that this topic has been contentious. This chapter assesses the changes made by the Lisbon Treaty, which relate to legislative power broadly conceived. It draws together three areas that are central to any such assessment.

The first part of the chapter examines the way in which the Lisbon Treaty has altered the process for the making of primary legislative acts. There are, as will be seen, numerous amendments that are relevant to this issue. These will be analysed legally and politically, in order to estimate their likely impact on EU decision making.

The focus in the second part shifts to the new regime for the passage of delegated acts. These are formally classified in the Lisbon Treaty as non-legislative acts, but this merely signifies that they were not made in accordance with a procedure for the making of legislative acts. The reality is nonetheless that many such provisions are in substantive terms rules of a legislative nature, which bear close analogy to rule-making or delegated legislation in national systems. There have in the past been considerable tensions as to power over the making of such provisions. This was the world of Comitology, but the fate of this committee system is uncertain under the Lisbon Treaty and the implications for the inter-institutional division of power could be far-reaching.

The third part of the chapter is concerned with participatory democracy. The EU has been vocal in its support for greater involvement of the citizenry in the EU, but it has nonetheless been equivocal, politically and legally, as to how far it wishes to go in this respect. It has in reality been reticent to recognize any legally enforceable participation rights. The Lisbon Treaty now contains a provision on participatory democracy which will be analysed in order to see whether EU policy might alter in the future.

The chapter concludes with detailed analysis of the overall impact of the changes made by the Lisbon Treaty on democracy in the EU.

1. Legislative Power and Democracy

The Lisbon Treaty made a number of changes to the making of legislative acts, which are relevant to the overall assessment of democracy in the EU.

(a) Legislative acts: initiation and agenda setting

(i) Legislative initiation: continuity and change

The Lisbon Treaty preserves previous orthodoxy in relation to legislative initiation. It formalized the pre-existing legal position, whereby the Commission has the right of legislative initiative. This had hitherto been the case because Treaty articles generally stipulated that Community legislation could only be made in this manner. The Commission retained its 'gold standard', the right of legislative initiative, which was formalized in the Lisbon Treaty: Union legislative acts may only be adopted on the basis of a Commission proposal, except where the Treaties provide otherwise.[1]

The reality prior to the Lisbon Treaty was nonetheless that many legislative initiatives originated in the Council itself, or in the European Council. The legislative process in relation to such measures was formally initiated by the Commission, but the impetus for their introduction often lay with the Council. The Council thus made liberal use of the power to request the Commission to undertake studies the Council considered 'desirable for the attainment of the common objectives, and to submit to it any appropriate proposals', and this power has been retained in the Lisbon Treaty.[2]

The position of the European Parliament in relation to legislative initiation has in formal terms remained the same. It can still request the Commission to submit any appropriate proposal on matters on which it considers that a Union act is required for the purpose of implementing the Treaties. If the Commission does not submit a proposal, it must inform the European Parliament of the reasons.[3] The Commission hitherto has not accepted that it must automatically pursue a matter referred to it in this manner, but the Framework Agreement on relations between the Parliament and Commission signed in 2000 included a provision under which the Commission committed itself to undertake 'a prompt and sufficiently detailed response' to such requests.[4] The European Parliament, however, also accepted that it should be cautious in its use of this power.[5] Thus any request to the Commission would emanate from an own-initiative report of

---

[1] Art 17(2) TEU.   [2] Art 241 TFEU.   [3] Art 225 TFEU.

[4] Framework Agreement on relations between the European Parliament and the Commission, C5–349/2000, [2001] OJ C121/122, para 4. The Agreement was revised in 2005, [2006] OJ C117/123.

[5] Rules of Procedure of the European Parliament (16th edn, 2006) rules 39, 45.

the responsible European Parliament committee, and authorization from the Conference of Presidents was required before such a report could be drawn up. The relevant committee also had to establish that no such proposal was included in the annual legislative programme, that the preparations of such a proposal had not started or were unduly delayed, or that the Commission had not responded positively to earlier requests from the committee responsible or contained in resolutions adopted by the European Parliament.[6]

It remains to be seen whether other changes made by the Lisbon Treaty have an impact, directly or indirectly, on the European Parliament's role in the initiation of particular legislative acts. The new rules for the appointment of the Commission President may prove relevant in this respect. Thus the Lisbon Treaty provides that the European Council, acting by qualified majority, taking into account the elections to the European Parliament and after having held the appropriate consultations, proposes to the European Parliament a candidate for President of the Commission. It is then for the European Parliament to elect this candidate by a majority of its component members. If the candidate does not obtain the required majority, the European Council, acting by a qualified majority, must propose a new candidate within one month, who is then elected by the European Parliament following the same procedure.[7]

The basic idea is thus that, subject to the control by the European Council, the Commission President will be a person who is acceptable to the dominant grouping in the European Parliament. It remains to be seen how this works in practice. The candidate for President of the Commission will have to win support from the majority within the European Parliament. This may well entail discussion not only of the candidate's overall vision for the EU, but more detailed specification of the legislative programme for the forthcoming years. The candidate will be mindful of the need for this programme to appeal to the majority within the European Parliament, which may therefore be able to exercise leverage at this stage on the legislative proposals that should be initiated in the forthcoming session.

(ii) Legislative agenda setting: continuity and change

The impact of the Lisbon Treaty on the setting of the overall legislative agenda is less certain. The pre-existing position was that the Commission produced its annual work programme in the autumn of the year before it was to take effect.[8] While this programme was designed, *inter alia*, to influence the EU's policy

[6] The EP's resolution also had to indicate the appropriate legal basis and be accompanied by detailed recommendations and must respect the principle of subsidiarity and the fundamental rights of citizens.

[7] Art 17(7) TEU.

[8] <http://ec.europa.eu/atwork/synthesis/index_en.htm>; Annual Policy Strategy for 2010, COM(2009) 73 final; Strategic Objectives 2005–2009, COM(2005) 12 final; <http://ec.europa.eu/atwork/programmes/index_en.htm>.

agenda, the Commission's freedom for manoeuvre was constrained by pre-existing commitments, and by Council Presidencies that had their own work programme/priorities that influenced the Commission agenda. The role of the European Council and Council in this respect was modified in the new millennium. In 2002 the Seville European Council reformed the way in which the European Council and Council operated. It provided that the six Presidencies concerned, in consultation with the Commission, should draw up a joint proposal, which was submitted to the General Affairs and External Relations Council (GAERC) for adoption by the European Council in the form of a multi-annual strategic programme lasting three years. The first such programme was produced in 2003.[9] This three-year programme in turn led to annual operational programmes submitted by the two Presidencies to the GAERC, which would then finalize the programme.[10] This programme was influenced by the Commission programme, and by external events.[11]

This general pattern is likely to continue for the future. There are nonetheless provisions of the Lisbon Treaty that impact directly on the setting of the legislative agenda. Article 15(1) TEU states that the European Council must provide the EU with the necessary impetus for its development and define the EU's general political directions and priorities. This modifies the previous Treaty formulation by mandating that the European Council should define the EU's priorities, as well as its general political direction. This language is mandatory, and the additional task of defining the EU's priorities is not expressly qualified by the adjective 'general'. It might be argued that the word 'general' should be read onto priorities, but nothing requires this conclusion. The existing formulation makes sense as it stands. If the Treaty framers had wished to limit the European Council they could have said 'and shall define... its general priorities'.

This has implications for the role of the new Presidency of the European Council. This novel institutional development will be considered in the next chapter. Suffice it to say for the present that there is an obvious connection between the extended tasks of the European Council and the President's role, since the President must, *inter alia*, chair the European Council and drive forward its work.[12] The work of the European Council now includes setting priorities for the EU, and hence the President will have the obligation to drive this forward. These legal provisions could with justification be regarded as a classic example of law catching up with political reality, given that the European Council has in effect been playing an important role in relation to setting priorities for some considerable time. The formal recognition of this within the Lisbon Treaty is nonetheless significant, more especially so because the very

---

[9] POLGEN 76, 15047/03, Multi-annual Strategic Programme, Brussels 20 November 2003.
[10] Seville European Council, Annex II, Brussels 24 October 2002, 23–24.
[11] F Hayes-Renshaw and H Wallace, *The Council of Ministers* (MacMillan, 2nd edn, 2006) ch 6.
[12] Art 15(6) TEU.

existence of a President of the European Council with tenure of up to five years means that the incumbent is more likely to develop a vision of the EU's priorities over that time.

The Lisbon Treaty is also supportive of the Commission in this respect. Thus Article 17(1) TEU provides, *inter alia*, that the Commission shall initiate the EU's annual and multi-annual programming with a view to achieving inter-institutional agreements. Thus while the Commission is accorded a general right to initiate particular pieces of Union legislation,[13] it also has the right and duty to initiate the Union's more general programming strategy. The language of Article 17(1) TEU serves to reinforce the sense of shared executive power: the Commission initiates the Union's annual and multi-annual programming with a view to achieving inter-institutional agreement.

It is unclear how far, if at all, these provisions of the Lisbon Treaty will alter the previous legal and political landscape. It might be argued that Article 17(1) TEU places the Commission in the driving seat in setting the overall legislative agenda, and that the pre-existing Seville strategy, whereby the European Council developed its own multi-annual programme, would be inconsistent with this. It is nonetheless doubtful whether the new regime will differ markedly from that which preceded it. The Commission is empowered under Article 17(1) TEU to initiate the annual and multi-annual programming with a view to reaching inter-institutional agreement, and hence it expressly envisages input from the other institutional players. It could moreover be argued that this Article should not be regarded as the exclusive method whereby such strategic visions are developed, more especially given that the European Council is charged with responsibility for defining the general political direction and priorities of the EU. Thus even if the Lisbon Treaty were to be interpreted in formalistic terms such that the Commission was to have the formal right to initiate annual and multi-annual programming, parity of reasoning would dictate that the Commission would be obliged to factor in, and accord weight to, the priorities for the EU as defined by the President of the European Council. These provisions, viewed overall, therefore embody and exemplify the sharing of executive power that is a characteristic of the Lisbon Treaty.[14] This view is reinforced by Declaration 9 of the Lisbon Treaty. It embodies a draft Decision on Council formations, but also provides that the General Affairs Council shall ensure consistency in the work of the Council formations in the framework of multi-annual programmes in cooperation with the Commission.

(b) The European Parliament: voting and empowerment

There is a real sense in which the European Parliament emerged as a winner in the Lisbon Treaty. The principal reason for this is to be found in the provisions

---

[13] Art 17(2) TEU.   [14] See ch 3 below.

concerning the legislative process, and more specifically those concerning the ordinary legislative procedure. These provisions of the Lisbon Treaty follow directly those in the Constitutional Treaty.[15]

In relation to 'primary legislation', inter-institutional balance, as opposed to separation of powers, has characterized the relationship, *de jure* and *de facto* between the major players. The European Parliament and the Council both partake in the consideration of legislation and do so now on an increasingly equal footing. The European Parliament and the Council are said to exercise legislative and budgetary functions jointly.[16] This is embodied in Article 14(1) TEU, which provides that the European Parliament shall, jointly with the Council, exercise legislative and budgetary functions, and this provision is replicated in relation to the Council in Article 16(1) TEU.

The co-decision procedure is now deemed to be the ordinary legislative procedure,[17] and this procedure consists in the joint adoption by the European Parliament and the Council of a regulation, directive, or decision on a proposal from the Commission.[18] The reach of the ordinary legislative procedure has been extended to cover more areas than hitherto, including, for example, agriculture,[19] services,[20] asylum and immigration,[21] the structural and cohesion funds,[22] and the creation of specialized courts.[23] The European Parliament and the Council must meet in public when considering and voting on a draft legislative act.[24]

This is to be welcomed and represents a natural development of the reforms in the legislative process that began in 1986. The Single European Act 1986 (SEA) constituted a watershed in Community inter-institutional relations. The Member States rejected far-reaching proposals for Treaty reform advanced by the European Parliament prior to the SEA, but they were nonetheless persuaded to accept some institutional reform, whereby the European Parliament was given real power in the legislative process for the first time, through the creation of the cooperation procedure. The advent of this procedure was all the more important given that it applied to harmonization measures enacted under the new Article 95 EC, which was the provision used for the enactment of much single market legislation post-1986.

The cooperation procedure began the transformation of the legislative process. The previous reality encapsulated in the maxim that the 'Commission proposes, the Council disposes' changed. There were now three players in the game, which had wide-ranging ramifications. The Commission recognized the need for increased inter-institutional cooperation. It had to draft proposals with an eye as to what would 'play' with Parliament as well as the Council.[25]

---

[15] Arts I-20(1), I-23(1), I-34(1), and III-396 CT.   [16] Art 14(1) and Art 16(1) TEU.
[17] Arts 289 and 294 TFEU.   [18] Art 289 TFEU.   [19] Art 43(2) TFEU.
[20] Art 56 TFEU.   [21] Arts 77–80 TFEU.
[22] Art 177 TFEU.   [23] Art 257 TFEU.   [24] Art 15(2) TFEU.
[25] M Westlake, *The Commission and the Parliament: Partners and Rivals in the European Policy-Making Process* (Butterworths, 1994) 37–39.

Coreper, the gatekeeper for the Council, now had to consider the views of the European Parliament, as well as the Council and Commission.[26] The European Parliament's powers in the legislative process were 'transformed from the weak and essentially unconstructive power of delay to a stronger and potentially constructive role in the drafting of legislation'.[27]

It was but a few years later that the Treaty on European Union, TEU, introduced the co-decision procedure, Article 251 EC. It was revised by the Treaty of Amsterdam, which strengthened further the role of the European Parliament.[28] It became the method for making much important Community legislation, and areas previously governed by the cooperation procedure were upgraded to co-decision.[29] The European Parliament used its veto power under Article 251 sparingly, although decision-making still took place under its shadow. It is more difficult to generalize about the amendments secured by the European Parliament. There is research indicating that European Parliament amendments modified the Commission proposal, but did not significantly alter it.[30] This is to some extent unsurprising, since draft legislative proposals were discussed with the European Parliament and Council/Coreper before co-decision was initiated, thereby accommodating diverse opinion. Where this dialogic process still left major differences of view the European Parliament and Council might well propose amendments, which forced the Commission to modify the measure significantly, as with the Services Directive.[31]

The co-decision procedure generally worked well, allowing input from the European Parliament, representing the electorate directly, and from the Council, representing State interests. It provided a framework for a deliberative dialogue on the content of legislation between the European Parliament, Council, and Commission. The extension of the ordinary legislative procedure to new areas is a natural development, building on what occurred in earlier Treaty reform. It enhances the legitimacy of EU legislation and its democratic credentials by enabling the European Parliament to have input into the making of legislation in these areas.

We should nonetheless be mindful of the way in which co-decision has operated more recently, which has reduced the 'space' for meaningful dialogue

---

[26] J Lewis, 'National Interests, Coreper' in J Peterson and M Shackleton (eds), *The Institutions of the European Union* (Oxford University Press, 2nd edn, 2006) ch 14.
[27] Westlake (n 25) 39.
[28] Joint Declaration on Practical Arrangements for the New Co-Decision Procedure [1999] OJ C148/1.
[29] <http://ec.europa.eu/codecision/index_en.htm>.
[30] A Kreppel, 'Moving beyond Procedure: An Empirical Analysis of European Parliament Legislative Influence' (2002) 35 Comparative Political Studies 784; R Thomson and M Hosli, 'Who has Power in the EU? Council, Commission and Parliament in Legislative Decision-making' (2006) 44 JCMS 391.
[31] Proposal for a Directive of the European Parliament and of the Council, on services in the internal market, COM/2004/2 final/3; EP Committee on the Internal Market and Consumer Protection, A6–0409/2005, Rapporteur Evelyne Gebhardt; Amended Proposal for a Directive of the European Parliament and of the Council, on services in the internal market, COM(2006) 160 final.

within the co-decision procedure. The institutionalization of trilogues has been of particular importance in this respect.[32] The trilogue contains represen-tatives from the Council, European Parliament, and Commission, normally no more than ten, from each institution. These informal meetings have been common since the mid-1990s and were originally devised so as to precede and exist alongside formal meetings of the Conciliation Committee with the object of facilitating compromise. There is, however, now evidence that they have moved 'earlier up' in the co-decision process, such that trilogues are increasingly com-monly used to broker inter-institutional compromise at first reading and prior to second reading, thereby limiting the potential for meaningful dialogue by a broader range of members of the European Parliament and Council.[33] The scale of this change is brought home from the Report of the Vice-Presidents respon-sible for Conciliation, who noted that in the period 2004–2009 72 per cent of legislative acts were concluded at first reading, with another 10.8 per cent at early second reading, largely as a result of increased use of such informal negoti-ations.[34] This is, as Bunyan states, regrettable because 'deals' are done in secret, with no readily available documents, and because 'the process removes mean-ingful debate, disagreements, options, votes from both the Committee meetings and the plenary session'.[35]

(c) The Council: formations and voting

We have already seen that under the Lisbon Treaty the Council, jointly with the European Parliament, exercises legislative and budgetary functions; and that it carries out policy-making and coordinating functions as laid down in the Treaties.[36] This replicates the approach taken in the Constitutional Treaty.[37]

The Treaty negotiations concerning the Council focused on two other issues: its internal organization, and the voting rules. The resolution of both issues in the Lisbon Treaty largely echoes that in the Constitutional Treaty.

(i) Council formations: legislative functions

There was significant debate in the Convention on the Future of Europe as to the internal organization of the Council. The Draft Constitution provided for a

---

[32] European Parliament, *Conciliations and Co-decision, A Guide to How Parliament Co-legislates* (DV/547830EN.doc, 2004) 13–15; M Shackleton and T Raunio, 'Codecision since Amsterdam: A Laboratory for Institutional Innovation and Change' (2003) 10 JEPP 171, 177–179.

[33] D Curtin, 'The Council of Ministers: The Missing Link?' in L Verhey, P Kiiver and S Loeffen (eds), *Political Accountability and European Integration* (Europa Law Publishing, 2009) ch 12.

[34] Activity Report 1 May–13 July 2009 of the Delegations to the Conciliation Committee, CM\787539EN.doc.

[35] T Bunyan, 'Abolish 1st and 2nd Reading Secret Deals—Bring Back Democracy "Warts and All" ', 6, available at <http://www.statewatch.org/analyses/no-84-ep-first-reading-deals.pdf>.

[36] Art 16(1) TEU.   [37] Art I-23(1) CT.

Legislative and General Affairs Council (LGAC).[38] When the LGAC acted in its legislative capacity each Member State's representation was to be composed of one or two representatives at ministerial level with relevant expertise, which would reflect the business on the Council's agenda. The rationale for this structure was that the Council would have a specific legislative formation, and that one of the two Member State representatives might become a quasi-permanent fixture who would develop more general expertise in European matters. It would then enable this Council formation to develop a broader view of EU legislation taken as a whole.

The solution embodied in the Draft Constitution was, however, rejected by the IGC. The Italian Presidency of the IGC distributed a questionnaire to the Member States, asking, *inter alia*, whether the Council's legislative function should be exercised by a single Council formation, or whether a legislative function should be exercised by each of the Council formations.[39] The majority of the Member States favoured according legislative power to each of the Council formations, rather than having one dedicated Legislative Council. The IGC therefore rejected the idea of the combined LGAC,[40] and this was reflected in the final version of the Constitutional Treaty.[41]

The Lisbon Treaty adopted the same view, rejecting the idea of a combined LGAC. Thus Article 16(6) TEU provides for a General Affairs Council (GAC) with the task of ensuring consistency in the work of the different Council formations. The GAC prepares and ensures the follow-up to meetings of the European Council, in liaison with the President of the European Council as well as the Commission. Article 16(6) also provides for the Foreign Affairs Council (FAC). A consequence of discarding the idea of the combined LGAC is that each Council formation votes on legislation within its area. Meetings of Council formations are therefore divided into two parts dealing with legislative and non-legislative functions, and the meeting must be in public when the Council formation acts in a legislative capacity.[42] Specific provision is made for the Committee of Permanent Representatives, which is charged with preparing the work of the Council and carrying out tasks assigned to it by the Council.[43]

There is much to be said for the IGC view that the General Affairs and Legislative functions should be separated. The two are distinct. It would almost certainly create an excessive burden on one body for it to have responsibility for

[38] CONV 850/03, Draft Treaty Establishing a Constitution for Europe, Brussels 18 July 2003, Art I-23.
[39] Conference of the Representatives of the Governments of the Member States, Questionnaire on the Legislative Function, the Formations of the Council and the Presidency of the Council of Ministers CIG 9/03, PRESID 1, Brussels 15 October 2003.
[40] Conference of the Representatives of the Governments of the Member States, Council Presidency and Council Formations, CIG 39/03, PRESID 5, Brussels 24 October 2003.
[41] Art I-24 CT.
[42] Art 16(8) TEU; M de Leeuw, 'Openness in the Legislative Process in the European Union' (2007) 32 ELRev 295.
[43] Art 16(7) TEU, Art 240 TFEU.

both issues. This is especially so given that the General Affairs Council will have its hands full in ensuring the overall co-ordination of the Council's work.[44]

There is more room for debate about the desirability or not of a separate Legislative Council. The principal arguments in favour are that it would have engendered greater legislative coherence,[45] and emphasized the two-chamber character of the EU legislative process. The argument against was that it could lead to loss of expertise by way of comparison with exercise of legislative power by the sectoral Councils. It could also be disadvantageous by leading to differential treatment for legislative acts and delegated acts. Thus there could be problems of overall coherence if a dedicated legislative Council dealt with legislative acts and other sectoral Councils were responsible for oversight of delegated acts within their assigned area.

(ii) Chairing Council formations: the contested terrain

Resolution of the issue as to whether there should be a separate Legislative Affairs Council did not lead to inter-institutional tensions. There were, however, considerable power struggles in the debates on the Constitutional Treaty concerning who should preside over the Council formations.

The role of the new President of the European Council within the Council was especially important in this respect. Certain proposals from the UK in January 2003,[46] and the original plan for the European Council announced by Giscard D'Estaing, accorded the President of the European Council considerable power within the Council. This is exemplified by the battles over the GAC. The centrality of this Council formation explains why some Member States sought to have the President of the European Council be the President of the GAC.[47] The Commission argued by way of contrast that the consistency task of the GAC should be performed in conjunction with the Commission.[48] It sought more generally to confine the President's duties to chairing the European Council, and representing the Union in the Common Foreign and Security Policy (CFSP), while excluding the President from organizing the work of the Council.[49] The European Parliament expressed similar concerns.[50]

---

[44] Conference of the Representatives of the Governments of the Member States, Reply from the Commission to the Questionnaire on the Legislative Function, the Formations of the Council and the Presidency of the Council of Ministers, CIG 35/03, DELEG 26, Brussels 15 October 2003, 2.

[45] ibid 2.

[46] G Grevi, 'Options for Government of the Union' (Federal Trust, March 2003) 6.

[47] Conference of the Representatives of the Governments of the Member States, Reply from the UK to the Questionnaire on the Legislative Function, the Formations of the Council and the Presidency of the Council of Ministers, CIG 34/03, DELEG 25, Brussels 15 October 2003.

[48] A Constitution for the Union, Opinion of the Commission, pursuant to Art 48 of the Treaty on European Union, on the Conference of Representatives of the Member States' governments convened to revise the Treaties, COM(2003) 548 final, para 17.

[49] ibid para 14.

[50] European Parliament, Report on the Draft Treaty establishing a Constitution for Europe and the European Parliament's Opinion on the Convening of the Intergovernmental Conference, A5–0299/2003/Final, para 20.

Neither side won out in the Constitutional Treaty. The compromise embodied in that Treaty[51] has been taken over into the Lisbon Treaty, which now provides as follows. The High Representative of the Union for Foreign Affairs and Security Policy presides over the FAC.[52] The European Council decides by qualified majority on the list of the other Council formations, and the Presidency of these formations.[53] The Presidency of Council formations other than the FAC must be in accord with the principle of equal rotation.[54]

A Draft Decision was included in the Lisbon Treaty, which embodies in essence a 'team system' for the Presidency of Council formations, other than the FAC.[55] The essence of this schema is that the Presidency of the Council, other than the FAC, is held by pre-established groups of three Member States for a period of 18 months. The groups are made up on a basis of equal rotation among the Member States, taking into account their diversity and geographical balance within the Union. Each member of the group in turn chairs for a six-month period all configurations of the Council, with the exception of the FAC. The other members of the group assist the Chair in its responsibilities on the basis of a common programme. It is open to members of the team to decide on alternative arrangements among themselves.

The draft Decision also makes provision for the chairing of important preparatory bodies that serve the Council. Coreper is to be chaired by a representative of the Member State that chairs the GAC. The Chair of the Political and Security Committee is held by a representative of the High Representative of the Union for Foreign Affairs and Security Policy. The chair of the preparatory bodies of the various Council configurations, with the exception of the FAC, is held by the member of the group chairing the relevant configuration, unless decided otherwise.

The provisions in the Lisbon Treaty concerning the Council may have resolved some of the inter-institutional tensions in the preceding debates, but there are nonetheless issues concerning power and influence within Council formations to which we shall return later.[56]

---

[51] Art I-24 CT.

[52] Art 18(3) TEU.

[53] Art 16(6) TEU, Art 236 TFEU.

[54] Art 16(9) TEU.

[55] Declaration 9, which adopts the same schema as worked out for the Constitutional Treaty; Council 16517/09, Council Decision laying down measures for the implementation of the European Council Decision on the exercise of the Presidency of the Council, and on the chairmanship of preparatory bodies of the Council, Brussels 30 November 2009; Council 16520/09, Decision of the Council (General Affairs) establishing the list of Council configurations in addition to those referred to in the second and third subparagraphs of Article 16(6) of the Treaty on European Union, Brussels 26 November 2009.

[56] Ch 3.

(iii) Council voting rules: the shift from unanimity to qualified voting

The Lisbon Treaty increased the areas to which qualified majority voting applies, although unanimity is still the rule in over 70 areas. It will come as no surprise that there was considerable disagreement about the requirements for a qualified majority in the Council, and the shift from unanimity to qualified majority.[57] The requirements for a qualified majority have always been a battleground between the Member States, and more especially between small, medium-sized, and large Member States. Intra-institutional tensions have therefore characterized debates on this issue.

Article 16(3) TEU stipulates that the Council shall act by qualified majority, except where the Treaty provides otherwise. The provisions in the Lisbon Treaty on the definition of a qualified majority are complex, and are the same as those in the Constitutional Treaty.[58] The basic rule that will operate from 1 November 2014 is set out in Article 16(4) TEU. A qualified majority is defined as at least 55 per cent of the members of the Council, comprising at least 15 of them and representing Member States comprising at least 65 per cent of the population of the Union. A blocking minority must include at least four Council members, failing which the qualified majority shall be deemed attained. There are therefore three criteria to be taken into account for a qualified majority: a certain percentage of Member States in the Council; a certain number of Member States; and a certain percentage of the EU's population.

The default rule defining a qualified majority is, however, subject to exceptions. Thus, where the Council does not act on a proposal from the Commission or the High Representative for Foreign Affairs the qualified majority must be 72 per cent of the members of the Council, comprising 65 per cent of the population of the EU.[59] It is therefore more difficult for the Council to adopt a measure in the relatively rare instances where it does not act on a proposal from the Commission or from the High Representative.

There are also separate rules specifying the requirements for a qualified majority where not all Member States vote in the Council.[60] In these circumstances a qualified majority is at least 55 per cent of the members of the Council representing the participating Member States, comprising at least 65 per cent of the population of these States. A blocking minority must include at least the minimum number of Council members representing more than 35 per cent of the population of the participating Member States, plus one member, failing which the qualified majority shall be deemed attained. These rules are subject to qualification where the Council does not act on a proposal from the Commission or from the High Representative of the Union for Foreign Affairs and Security

---

[57] J Rideau, 'Conflits et compromise constitutionnels sur la composition de la Commission et la vote a la majorité qualifiée au Conseil' in C Kaddous and A Auer (eds), *Les Principes Fondamentaux de la Constitution Européenne* (Helbing & Lichtman, Bruylant, LGDF, 2006) 165–179.
[58] Art I-25(1) CT.   [59] Art 238(2) TFEU.   [60] Art 238(3) TFEU.

Policy: the qualified majority must then be at least 72 per cent of the members of the Council representing the participating Member States, comprising at least 65 per cent of the population of these States.

The rules that operate until 31 October 2014, and the transitional rules applicable between 1 November 2014 and 31 March 2017, are set out in a Protocol attached to the Lisbon Treaty.[61] Between 1 November 2014 and 31 March 2017, when an act is to be adopted by qualified majority, a member of the Council can request that it be adopted in accordance with the qualified majority as defined under the rules in the Nice Treaty.[62]

It has been estimated that the voting rules in the Lisbon Treaty rules will increase the probability of securing the passage of legislation through the Council as compared with those under the Nice Treaty.[63] The demographic component of the new rules also increases the relative power of the larger Member States in the Council.[64] The significance of this depends, however, on voting behaviour post-Lisbon. Thus academic study has shown that voting in the Council has been relatively rare, even in areas where qualified majority voting operates, and that decision making by consensus has been the norm. The authors accept that voting rules remain significant, in part because they provide the 'shadow' against which consensus operates in the Council and preliminary bodies such as Coreper. This does not alter the fact that explicit voting has been rare and that when it occurs the dissentient is often a single State.[65]

The shift towards qualified majority voting in more areas raised, not surprisingly, critiques of loss of sovereignty through surrender of the national veto that accompanies unanimity. The most obvious response is that unanimity renders decision making excessively difficult in a Union of 27 Member States.

There is in addition a less obvious but equally important response. The assumption that unanimity is the best protection of national sovereignty is based implicitly on the argument that sovereignty is best safeguarded by maximizing veto points and inaction. This may be true, but it may not. It is axiomatic that if a veto power exists it resides with every Member State. Whether unanimity is the best protector of national sovereignty depends therefore on whether a State believes that maximizing the possibility of inaction through multiple veto points is better for the national interest than a qualified majority voting rule which increases the possibility of action, with some attendant risk that the particular

---

[61] Protocol (No 36) On Transitional Provisions, Title II. See also Declaration 7, which contains a Draft Council Decision concerning transitional arrangements.

[62] Protocol (No 36), Art 3.

[63] R Baldwin and M Widgrén, 'Council Voting in the Constitutional Treaty. Devil in the Details' CEPS Policy Brief 6–7 (No 53, July 2004).

[64] Baldwin and Widgrén (n 63); Y Devuyst, 'The European Union's Institutional Balance after the Treaty of Lisbon: "Community Method" and "Democratic Deficit" Reassessed' (2008) 39 Georgetown Jnl Int Law 247, 302–303.

[65] F Hayes-Renshaw, W van Aken, H Wallace, 'When and Why the EU Council of Ministers Votes Explicitly' (2006) 44 JCMS 161.

State will be forced to accept a measure that it dislikes. This in turn depends on whether a State believes that if there is a unanimity rule it is more likely to be 'vetoed against', thereby preventing action which it believes to be desirable, than it is to be an 'exerciser of the veto' itself.

A State may well decide on this calculus that sovereignty and the national interest are indeed better protected via qualified majority than unanimity. This was in effect part of the rationale for the UK Conservative Party acceptance of the most important shift from unanimity to qualified majority in the EU's history, through acceptance in the Single European Act 1986 of Article 95 EC, which became the principal vehicle for enactment of single market legislation. The unanimity rule in Article 94 was felt to be impeding the market liberalization desired by the Conservative Party and Prime Minister Thatcher, hence the willingness to sacrifice the veto for the enhanced possibility of Community action.

(iv) Council voting rules: the general passerelle clause

The Lisbon Treaty also embodies a general 'passerelle' clause enabling modification to the voting rules in the Council. This is contained in Article 48(7) TEU. It provides that where the TFEU or Title V of the TEU provides for the Council to act by unanimity in a given area or case, the European Council may adopt a decision authorizing the Council to act by a qualified majority in that area or in that case, subject to the caveat that this cannot apply to decisions with military implications or those in the area of defence. It stipulates further that where the TFEU provides for legislative acts to be adopted by the Council in accordance with a special legislative procedure, the European Council may adopt a decision allowing for the adoption of such acts in accordance with the ordinary legislative procedure. The European Council when making such decisions acts by unanimity after obtaining the consent of the European Parliament, which shall be given by a majority of its component members.

Any such initiative taken by the European Council must be notified to the national Parliaments. If a national Parliament makes known its opposition within six months of the date of such notification, the decision referred to above shall not be adopted. In the absence of opposition, the European Council may adopt the decision. The implications of this clause and other related provisions will be considered in a later chapter.[66]

(d) National Parliaments: input and subsidiarity

Evaluation of the changes made by the Lisbon Treaty to the legislative process would be incomplete without consideration of the role accorded to national

---

[66] Ch 11.

Parliaments. This takes us into the terrain of subsidiarity and the exercise, as opposed to the existence, of EU competence.[67] The competence dimension of subsidiarity will be considered below.[68] The present discussion focuses directly on the role of national Parliaments in the EU legislative process.

Article 12 TEU complements the previous provisions on representative and participatory democracy in the EU, and deals with the role of national Parliaments in EU decision making. The Article draws together the different ways in which national Parliaments play a role in the EU, including through scrutiny of draft EU legislative acts; by ensuring respect for subsidiarity; by taking part, within the framework of the area of freedom, security, and justice, in the evaluation mechanisms for the implementation of the Union policies in that area, and through being involved in the political monitoring of Europol and Eurojust's activities; by taking part in the revision procedures of the Treaties; by being notified of applications for accession to the Union; and by taking part in the inter-parliamentary cooperation between national Parliaments and the European Parliament. The real substance of the national Parliaments' role in the legislative process is, however, found in two Protocols attached to the Treaty.

The Protocol on the Role of National Parliaments in the EU[69] mandates that Commission consultation documents, the annual legislative programme, and draft legislative acts must be sent to national Parliaments at the same time as they are forwarded to the Council and the European Parliament.[70] There must, save in cases of urgency, be an eight-week period after receipt of draft legislative acts by national Parliaments before such acts are placed on the provisional agenda of the Council for adoption. There must also, subject to a caveat for cases of urgency, be a ten-day period between the placing of a draft legislative act on the provisional agenda for the Council and the adoption of a position by the Council.[71] National Parliaments in addition receive the agendas and outcomes of Council meetings at the same time as they are sent to national governments.[72] The Protocol also makes provision for inter-parliamentary cooperation.

The Protocol on the Role of National Parliaments should be read in tandem with the Protocol on the Application of the Principles of Subsidiarity and Proportionality.[73] It imposes an obligation to consult widely before proposing legislative acts.[74] The Commission must provide a detailed statement concerning proposed legislation so that compliance with subsidiarity can be appraised. The statement must contain some assessment of the financial impact of the proposals, and there should be qualitative and, wherever possible, quantitative indicators to substantiate the conclusion that the objective can be better attained at Union level.[75] The Commission must submit an annual report on the application of

---

[67] Arts 5(3)–(4) TEU.   [68] Ch 5.
[69] Protocol (No 1), On the Role of National Parliaments in the European Union.
[70] ibid Arts 1–2.   [71] ibid Art 4.   [72] ibid Art 5.
[73] Protocol (No 2), On the Application of the Principles of Subsidiarity and Proportionality.
[74] ibid Art 2.   [75] ibid Art 5.

subsidiarity to the European Council, the European Parliament, the Council, and to national Parliaments.[76] The European Court of Justice (ECJ) has jurisdiction to consider infringement of subsidiarity under Article 263 TFEU, brought by the Member State, or 'notified by them in accordance with their legal order on behalf of their national Parliament or a chamber of it'.[77] These aspects of subsidiarity will be considered below.[78]

The most important innovation in the Protocol on Subsidiarity is the enhanced role accorded to national Parliaments.[79] The Commission must send all legislative proposals to the national Parliaments at the same time as to the Union institutions.[80] A national Parliament or Chamber thereof, may, within eight weeks, send the Presidents of the Commission, European Parliament, and Council a reasoned opinion as to why it considers that the proposal does not comply with subsidiarity.[81] The European Parliament, Council, and Commission must take this opinion into account.[82] Each national Parliament has two votes,[83] and where non-compliance with subsidiarity is expressed by national Parliaments that represent one third of all the votes allocated to them, the Commission must review its proposal.[84] The Commission, after such review, may decide to maintain, amend, or withdraw the proposal, giving reasons for the decision.[85] Where a measure is made in accordance with the ordinary legislative procedure, and at least a simple majority of votes given to national Parliaments signal non-compliance with subsidiarity, then the proposal must once again be reviewed, and although the Commission can decide not to amend it, the Commission must provide a reasoned opinion on the matter and this can, in effect, be overridden by the European Parliament or the Council.[86]

It remains to be seen how subsidiarity operates in practice. It is clear that there will continue to be many areas in which the comparative efficiency calculus in Article 5(3) TFEU favours Union action, more especially in an enlarged Union. It is equally clear that subsidiarity has had an impact on the existence and form of EU action. If Union action is required, the Commission will often proceed through directives rather than regulations, and there has been a greater use of guidelines and codes of conduct.

---

[76] ibid Art 9.   [77] ibid Art 8.
[78] Chs 4–5.
[79] J-V Louis, 'National Parliaments and the Principle of Subsidiarity—Legal Options and Practical Limits' in I Pernice and E Tanchev (eds), *Ceci n'est pas une Constitution—Constitutionalization without a Constitution?* (Nomos, 2009) 131–154; G Bermann, 'National Parliaments and Subsidiarity: An Outsider's View' ibid 155–161; J Peters, 'National Parliaments and Subsidiarity: Think Twice' (2005) European Constitutional L Rev 68.
[80] Subsidiarity and Proportionality (n 73) Art 4. The national Parliaments must also be provided with legislative resolutions of the EP, and common positions adopted by the Council.
[81] ibid Art 6.   [82] ibid Art 7(1).
[83] ibid Art 7(1).
[84] ibid Art 7(2). This threshold is lowered to one-quarter in certain cases concerning the area of freedom, justice, and security.
[85] ibid Art 7(2).   [86] ibid Art 7(3).

Time will tell how far the new provisions in the Protocol according greater power to national Parliaments affect the incidence and nature of EU legislation. Much will depend on the willingness of national Parliaments to devote the requisite time and energy to the matter. The national Parliament has to submit a reasoned opinion as to why it believes that the measure infringes subsidiarity. It will have to present reasoned argument as to why the Commission's comparative efficiency calculus is defective. This may not be easy. It will be even more difficult for the requisite number of national Parliaments to present reasoned opinions in relation to the same Union measure so as to compel the Commission to review the proposal. The Commission is nonetheless likely to take seriously any such reasoned opinion, particularly if it emanates from the Parliament of a larger Member State.

2. Delegated Acts and Power

The discussion thus far has focused on the impact of the Lisbon Treaty on legislative acts, and the consequences for the inter-institutional division of power and democracy within the EU. This discussion would be incomplete, however, if it did not take account of the new regime for delegated acts introduced by the Lisbon Treaty. There will be detailed analysis of the Lisbon Treaty concerning the hierarchy of norms in a subsequent chapter.[87] The present discussion will focus on their effect on the pre-existing balance of power.[88] Historical understanding is especially important in this context.

(a) Political history: contestation and power

In the 1960s the Luxembourg Accords enabled the Member States to block measures that injuriously affected their vital interests, while Coreper acted as gatekeeper and allowed Council input into the making of primary legislation. However, it quickly became apparent that Member States sought influence over secondary norms and created an institutional mechanism to facilitate this.

It is common in democratic statal systems for primary legislation to be complemented by secondary norms which flesh out the principles contained in the enabling statute. This is so for a number of reasons. The legislature may not be able to foresee all ramifications of primary legislation; it may have neither time, nor expertise, to address all issues in the original legislation; and measures

---

[87] Ch 7.
[88] P Craig, 'The Hierarchy of Norms' in T Tridimas and P Nebbia (eds), *European Law for the Twenty-First Century, Rethinking the New Legal Order, Volume 1* (Hart, 2004) ch 5; P Craig, *EU Administrative Law* (Oxford University Press, 2006) ch 4.

consequential to the original statute may have to be passed expeditiously. The secondary norms may be individualized decisions. They will, however, commonly be legislative in nature: general rules applicable to all those falling within a certain factual situation. The method by which such measures are made varies in the Member States. The premise in some systems is that norms of a legislative nature should be legitimated through some degree of legislative oversight. This legitimation from the 'top' via the legislature may be complemented by legitimation from the 'bottom' through participation in rulemaking by affected parties. The premise in other regimes is that the executive should have some autonomous power to make secondary norms, the principal check being judicial review.

It is important to dispel any illusion that the primary legislation captures all issues of principle, while secondary norms address insignificant points of detail. This does not represent reality. Secondary norms may address issues of principle or political choice that are just as controversial as those dealt with in the primary legislation. It is equally the case that for those to whom the law applies it makes little difference whether it takes the form of a legislative or a delegated act, since both are equally the law of the land.[89]

This is especially so in the EU, which has been characterized as a regulatory State,[90] where secondary regulations will often deal with matters of principle or political contestation. This serves to explain the birth of the committee system known as Comitology.[91] The Commission has articulated a picture of the 'Community method' in which it sees itself as the Community executive with principal responsibility for the making of such secondary norms. The original Treaty was, however, ambiguous in this respect.

The disposition of primary legislative power in the Rome Treaty was relatively clear; the maxim the 'Commission proposes, the Council disposes' held true for most areas. The disposition of power over secondary norms rules was less clear. The Commission's claim for authority over such norms was based on Article 155 EEC, which provided that in order to ensure the proper functioning and

---

[89] *Making the Law, The Report of the Hansard Society Commission on the Legislative Process* (1993) 42.

[90] G Majone, 'The Rise of the Regulatory State in Europe' (1994) 17 West European Politics 77; G Majone, *Regulating Europe* (Routledge, 1996); G Majone, 'Europe's "Democratic Deficit": The Question of Standards' (1998) 4 ELJ 5.

[91] R Pedler and GF Schaefer (eds), *Shaping European Law and Policy: The Role of Committees and Comitology in the Political Process* (European Institute of Public Administration, 1996); C Joerges, K-H Ladeur and E Vos (eds), *Integrating Scientific Expertise into Regulatory Decision-Making: National Traditions and European Innovations* (Nomos, 1997); C Joerges and E Vos (eds), *EU Committees: Social Regulation, Law and Politics* (Hart, 1999); E Vos, *Institutional Frameworks of Community Health and Safety Legislation: Committees, Agencies and Private Bodies* (Hart, 1999); M Andenas and A Turk (eds), *Delegated Legislation and the Role of Committees in the EC* (Kluwer Law International, 2000); C Bergstrom, *Comitology, Delegation of Powers in the European Union and the Committee System* (Oxford University Press, 2005); T Christiansen, 'Administrative Fusion in the European Union: Reviewing a Decade of Comitology Reform' in U Diedrichs, A Faber, F Tekin, and G Umbach (eds), *Europe Reloaded: Differentiation or Fusion?* (Baden-Baden: NOMOS Verlag, 2010).

development of the common market the Commission should, *inter alia*, 'exercise the powers conferred on it by the Council for the implementation of the rules laid down by the latter'. This was, however, an uncertain foundation for the assertion of Commission authority. This was in part because, as the ECJ acknowledged,[92] Article 155 was optional and became operative when the Council conferred power on the Commission. It was in part because of ambiguity as to the meaning of 'implementation'. The word could refer to the 'making' of secondary rules, or alternatively to the 'execution' of the primary regulation or directive, connoting the need for measures to ensure that the primary regulation or directive was properly applied.[93] The reality was that the Rome Treaty provided little by way of definitive guidance on the making of secondary norms, or the conditions that could be attached to this process.

Political reality is nonetheless often the catalyst for legal development. Comitology was born in the context of the Common Agricultural Policy (CAP).[94] It rapidly became clear that administration of the CAP required detailed rules in ever-changing market circumstances. Recourse to primary legislation was impracticable. The Member States were, however, wary of according the Commission a blank cheque over implementing rules, since power once delegated without encumbrance generated legally binding rules without the option for further Council oversight. This wariness was heightened by tensions between Council and Commission in the mid-1960s leading to the Luxembourg Accords. The creation of the committee system also facilitated interaction between national administrators and resolution of disagreement between the Member States, who might agree on the regulatory principles for an area, but disagree on the more detailed ramifications thereof.

The net result was the birth of the management committee procedure, embodied in early agricultural regulations. The committee, composed of national representatives with expertise in the relevant area, was involved with the Commission in the deliberations leading to the secondary regulations, which were immediately applicable, subject to the caveat that they could be returned to the Council if they were not in accord with the committee's opinion. The Council could then take a different decision by qualified majority within one month. The committee methodology rapidly became a standard feature of delegation of power to the Commission. It was not long before the more restrictive version, the regulatory committee procedure, was created: if the committee failed to deliver an opinion, or if it gave an opinion contrary to

---

[92] Case 25/70 *Einfuhr- und Vorrasstelle fur Getreide und Futermittel v Koster, Berodt & Co* [1970] 2 ECR 1161, [9].

[93] Case 16/88 *Commission v Council* [1989] ECR 3457, [11]–[13].

[94] C Bertram, 'Decision-Making in the EEC: The Management Committee Procedure' (1967–68) 5 CMLRev 246; P Schindler, 'The Problems of Decision-Making by Way of the Management Committee Procedure in the EEC' (1971) 8 CMLRev 184; C Bergstrom, *Comitology, Delegation of Powers in the European Union and the Committee System* (Oxford University Press, 2005) ch 2.

the recommended measure, the Commission would have to submit the proposal to the Council, which could then act by qualified majority. There was a safety net, or *filet*, such that if the Council did not act within three months of the measure being submitted to it, then the proposed provisions could be adopted by the Commission. The desire for greater political control reached its apotheosis in the *contre-filet* version of the regulatory committee procedure: the normal regulatory committee procedure applied, subject to the caveat that the Council could, by simple majority, prevent the Commission from acting even after the expiry of the prescribed period.

The legitimacy of the management committee procedure was considered by the ECJ in *Koster*.[95] The German court asked whether the procedure was consistent with the institutional balance in the Treaty. If the ECJ had found against the legitimacy of the procedure it would have created serious problems, given the importance attached by the Council to input into the making of secondary norms. The ECJ avoided any such conflict by upholding the legitimacy of the management committee procedure. It reasoned that Article 155 EC accorded the Council discretion to confer implementing powers on the Commission, and that therefore the Council could determine the rules to which the Commission was subject when exercising such powers. Moreover, because the committee could not take any decision, but merely served to send the matter back to the Council, the ECJ held that it did not distort the institutional balance within the EEC. Judicial support for the political status quo was evident once again in *Tedeschi*,[96] where the ECJ upheld the legality of the regulatory committee procedure.

The process for the passage of Community primary legislation was transformed post the Single European Act 1986. It came to be increasingly accepted that the three major institutional players all had a role to play. This premise was not shared in relation to the passage of secondary norms, and the period from the SEA to the Nice Treaty and beyond saw continuing contestation as to power over the making of such provisions.

Prior to the SEA, Comitology had been based on an admixture of legislative choice, backed by judicial approval. The SEA legitimated Comitology via the new third indent of Article 202 EC, which stipulated that the Council should confer on the Commission, in the acts adopted by the Council, powers for the implementation of the rules which the Council laid down, and that it could impose certain requirements in respect of the exercise of these powers. These procedures had to be consonant with principles and rules laid down in advance. The Council could also reserve the right, in specific cases, to exercise directly implementing powers itself.

---

[95] *Koster* (n 92).
[96] Case 5/77 *Carlo Tedeschi v Denkavit Commerciale Srl* [1977] ECR 1555.

Article 202 EC demanded that the committee procedures should take place in accordance with rules laid down in advance, and this was the catalyst for the first Comitology Decision in 1987.[97] It was an improvement on the status quo ante, reducing the basic committee procedures to three, advisory, management, and regulatory, with two variants of both the management and regulatory committee procedures, plus safeguard committee procedures. The beneficial impact of the Decision was qualified, however, by the Council's insistence that it should not be taken to affect the plethora of procedures applicable to existing committees.

The Commission and the European Parliament were, however, dissatisfied with the Comitology regime, albeit for different reasons. For the Commission the Treaty amendment to Article 202 was a 'plus', insofar as it embodied the general principle that the Council should confer implementing power on the Commission, unless the Council provided reasons why it should reserve implementing power to itself, although judicial review of this issue has not generally been searching.[98] It was nonetheless a defeat for more far-reaching Commission ambitions, since it entered the SEA negotiations hoping to secure amendment to Article 211 EC, whereby it would have implementing power without prior authorization from the Council, coupled with a strictly limited number of committee procedures, and a clear preference against regulatory committees.[99]

This aspiration was itself reflective of deeper Commission concerns about Comitology. The Commission's long-standing view was that the passage of 'implementing' provisions was part of the executive function, the authority for which should properly reside with the Commission. Thus, while it was content to accept advisory committees it was unhappy with management and regulatory committees that cramped what it regarded as its proper sphere of executive autonomy. The political and normative foundation for this assumption is contestable to say the least. It is premised on the argument that everything that occurs after the passage of the primary legislation should be regarded as part of the executive function. The reality is that while some secondary norms made pursuant to Comitology may simply be concerned with issues of technical detail, in many other instances the primary legislation may provide guidance but still leave issues of principle and political choice to be resolved through secondary norms that are legislative in nature. Given that this is so, the Commission's claim that such measures fall naturally within its sphere of 'executive' autonomy conceals more than it reveals.

The 1990s also saw increased opposition to Comitology by the European Parliament. It expressed disquiet over Comitology from the very outset, but the

---

[97] Council Decision 87/373/EEC of 13 July 1987 laying down the procedures for the exercise of implementing powers conferred on the Commission [1987] OJ L197/33.
[98] Case C-257/01 *Commission v Council* [2005] ECR I-345, [53]; Case C-378/00 *Commission v European Parliament and Council* [2003] ECR I-937.
[99] C-D Ehlermann, 'The Internal Market Following the Single European Act' (1987) 24 CMLRev 361.

European Parliament's opposition grew commensurately with its increased status in the making of primary regulations and directives. The reason for this is not hard to divine. It had been on the sidelines of the legislative process for the first three decades of the Community's existence. This changed with the introduction of the cooperation and co-decision procedures. The significance of these gains was undermined, however, by the European Parliament's exclusion from the making of secondary norms, which would often entail important issues of principle, practical detail, or political choice.

The European Parliament fought the battle against Comitology on the legal and political front.[100] It argued that Article 202 could not be regarded as the basis for Comitology where the primary acts were adopted pursuant to co-decision, but only for such acts adopted by the Council alone. The Council rejected this view,[101] and drew comfort from the ECJ which held, albeit without detailed consideration, that acts of the Council covered those undertaken jointly with the European Parliament pursuant to co-decision, as well as acts made by the Council alone.[102] The ECJ's jurisprudence, moreover, served to empower the Council and Commission at the expense of the European Parliament by adopting a broad concept of implementation. Thus, while the ECJ insisted that the primary regulation or directive must embody its 'essential elements', it interpreted this loosely, thereby allowing a broad range of implementing measures to be adopted through secondary regulations according to Comitology procedures from which the European Parliament was largely excluded.[103] The European Parliament also contested the committee procedures through the political process.[104] The process of legislative attrition was wearing for all involved and hostilities were temporarily lessened through the *Modus Vivendi* in 1994:[105] the relevant committee of the European Parliament would be sent general draft implementing acts at the same time as the Comitology committee set up by the basic act.

The position of the European Parliament was improved by the revised Comitology Decision, made pursuant to Declaration 31 of the Treaty of

---

[100] K Bradley, 'Maintaining the Balance: The Role of the Court of Justice in Defining the Institutional Position of the European Parliament' (1987) 24 CMLRev 41; K Bradley, 'Comitology and the Law: Through a Glass Darkly' (1992) 29 CMLRev 693; K Bradley, 'The European Parliament and Comitology: On the Road to Nowhere?' (1997) 3 ELJ 230.

[101] J-P Jacque, 'Implementing Powers and Comitology' in Joerges and Vos (n 91) ch 4.

[102] Case C-259/95 *European Parliament v Council* [1997] ECR I-5303, [26]; Case C-378/00 (n 98) [40].

[103] Case C-156/93 *European Parliament v Commission* [1995] ECR I-2019, [18]–[22]; Case C-417/93 *European Parliament v Council* [1995] ECR I-1185, [30].

[104] R Corbett, *The European Parliament's Role in Closer EU Integration* (MacMillan, 1998) 347–348.

[105] *Modus Vivendi* of 20 December 1994 between the European Parliament, the Council and the Commission concerning the implementing measures for acts adopted in accordance with the procedure laid down in Article 189b of the EC Treaty [1996] OJ C102/1.

Amsterdam. Its passage was difficult,[106] and it was finally adopted in 1999.[107] The management and regulatory committee procedures were simplified to some degree. There were efforts to make the system more accessible to the public. The European Parliament was accorded a greater role than hitherto. It was given power concerning rules made pursuant to the regulatory procedure, and the European Parliament could now indicate by resolution that draft implementing measures, submitted to a committee pursuant to a primary act adopted by co-decision, would exceed the implementing powers in that act. The European Parliament was also given a right to be informed by the Commission of committee proceedings, receive committee agendas, voting records, and draft measures submitted to the committees for implementation of primary law made under the co-decision procedure. In a subsequent agreement between the European Parliament and the Commission,[108] the latter stated that it would also forward to the European Parliament, at its request, specific draft measures for implementing basic instruments even if not adopted under co-decision, where they were of particular importance to the European Parliament. The European Parliament can, moreover, request access to minutes of committee meetings.[109]

The European Parliament's position was further improved by the 2006 amendment to the 1999 Decision,[110] the catalyst for this being belated acceptance of the European Parliament's objection to the 1999 Comitology Decision where co-decision applied.[111] It introduced a new 'regulatory procedure with scrutiny', which gives the European Parliament greater rights than hitherto. The legal and political significance of this reform will be considered more fully below, when discussing the fate of Comitology under the Lisbon Treaty.

Comitology has been much discussed by political scientists as well as lawyers. Rational choice institutionalists regard it as an exemplification of their principal/agent thesis. Member State principals delegate four functions to supranational agents: monitoring compliance; the resolution of incomplete contracts among principals; the adoption of regulations in areas where the principals would be biased or uninformed; and setting the legislative agenda so as to avoid the 'endless cycling' that would otherwise result if this power were exercised by the

---

[106] Bergstrom (n 91) 249–264.

[107] Council Decision 99/468/EC of 28 June 1999 laying down the procedures for the exercise of implementing powers conferred on the Commission [1999] OJ L184/23; K Lenaerts and A Verhoeven, 'Towards a Legal Framework for Executive Rule-Making in the EU? The Contribution of the New Comitology Decision' (2000) 37 CMLRev 645.

[108] Agreement between the European Parliament and the Commission on procedures for implementing Council Decision 99/468/EC of 28 June 1999 [2000] OJ L256/19, [2].

[109] Case T-188/97 *Rothmans v Commission* [1999] ECR II-2463.

[110] Council Decision 2006/512/EC of 17 July 2006 amending Decision 1999/468/EC laying down the procedures for the exercise of implementing powers by the Commission [2006] OJ L200/11.

[111] Proposal for a Council Decision Amending Decision 1999/468/EC laying down the procedures for the exercise of implementing powers conferred on the Commission, COM(2002) 719 final, 2.

principals themselves.[112] The principals must, however, ensure as far as possible that the agents do not stray from the preferences of the principals themselves. Thus, on this view Comitology constitutes a control mechanism whereby the Member State principals exert control over supranational agents. The Member State principals recognized the need for delegation of power over secondary norms to the supranational agent, the Commission, but did not wish to give it a blank cheque, hence the creation of committees through which Member State preferences could be expressed, with the threat of recourse to the Council if agreement could not be reached with the Commission. It is assumed that the representatives on Comitology echo their Member State exogenous preferences and bargain within the committees.[113] The variants of committee procedure reflect the Member States' ability to impose the degree of control that best suit their interests.

This view has been challenged by sociological institutionalists and constructivists. They contend that decision making within Comitology is best viewed as a form of deliberative supranationalism.[114] Governments might be unaware of their preferences on the particular issue. The national delegates on the committees will often regard themselves as a team dealing with a transnational problem, and become representatives of an inter-administrative discourse characterized by mutual learning. Comitology is portrayed as a network of European and national actors, with the Commission acting as coordinator. The national representatives in the deliberative process are willing to call their own preferences into question in searching for a Community solution.[115]

There have not surprisingly been empirical studies designed to test these rival hypotheses.[116] There may well be something to both hypotheses. Thus, even if the creation of Comitology committees conforms to the rational choice hypothesis, this does not mean that the national representatives will necessarily always function in interstate bargaining mode. They might operate in a manner more akin to deliberative supranationalism. However whether they do so may depend on the subject matter, and conclusions reached in the context of, for example, food safety committees, may not be applicable in other areas.

---

[112] M Pollack, *The Engines of Integration, Delegation, Agency and Agenda Setting in the EU* (Oxford University Press, 2003) 6.

[113] ibid ch 2.

[114] C Joerges and J Neyer, 'From Intergovernmental Bargaining to Deliberative Political Processes: The Constitutionalization of Comitology' (1997) 3 ELJ 273; J Neyer, 'The Comitology Challenge to Analytical Integration Theory' in Joerges and Vos (n 91) ch 12; C Joerges, 'Good Governance through Comitology?' in Joerges and Vos (n 91) ch 17.

[115] Joerges and Neyer (n 114) 315.

[116] Pollack (n 112); F Franchino, 'Control of the Commission's Executive Functions: Uncertainty, Conflict and Decision Rules' (2000) 1 European Union Politics 63; M Pollack, 'Control Mechanism or Deliberative Democracy: Two Images of Comitology' (2003) 36 Comparative Political Studies 125.

(b) Treaty reform: Commission objectives

The Commission's primary goal has been to dismantle the established Comitology regime, at least insofar as it entails management and regulatory committees, and to persuade the Member States to accept a regime of *ex ante* and *ex post* constraints on non-legislative acts of the kind that are now contained in the Lisbon Treaty, with the hope that the Member States might be persuaded to modify the existing Comitology oversight mechanisms for delegated regulations. This is apparent from a series of high-profile Commission communications.[117]

The Commission's desire to have greater autonomy in this area has been apparent for some time,[118] and was an explicit feature of the White Paper on *European Governance*.[119] The key to the White Paper was the Commission's conception of the 'Community method',[120] with the Commission representing the general interest and the Council and the European Parliament as the joint legislature, representing the Member States and national citizens respectively. This is in itself unexceptionable. It is the implications that the Commission drew from it that are interesting in the light of subsequent developments.

It was, said the Commission, necessary to revitalize the Community method.[121] The Council and the European Parliament should limit their involvement in primary Community legislation to defining the essential elements.[122] This legislation would define the conditions and limits within which the Commission performed its executive role. It would, in the Commission's view, make it possible to do away with the Comitology committees, at least so far as they had the powers presently exercised by management and regulatory committees. There would instead be a simple legal mechanism allowing the Council and European Parliament to control the actions of the Commission against the principles adopted in the legislation. The possibility of enhancing the Commission's control over delegated regulations by abolishing or amending the Comitology procedure was raised again by the Working Group on Simplification.[123]

It is generally accepted that the Commission 'punched below its weight' in the process of Treaty reform, especially in the deliberations that led to the

---

[117] European Governance, COM(2001) 428 final, [20]–[29]; Institutional Architecture, COM (2002) 728 final, [1.2], [1.3.4]; Proposal for a Council Decision Amending Decision 1999/468/EC Laying Down the Procedures for the Exercise of Implementing Powers Conferred on the Commission, COM(2002) 719 final, 2; Final Report of Working Group IX on Simplification, CONV 424/ 02, Brussels 29 November 2002, 12.

[118] Bergstrom (n 91).

[119] COM(2001) 428 final. The White Paper provoked a variety of critical comment, see Mountain or Molehill? A Critical Appraisal of the Commission White Paper on Governance (Jean Monnet Working Paper 6/01) <http://centers.law.nyu.edu/jeanmonnet/papers/papers01. html>.

[120] COM(2001) 428 final, 8.   [121] ibid 29.

[122] ibid 20.   [123] Working Group IX (n 117) 12.

Constitutional Treaty.[124] If, however, it transpires that the Commission has successfully undermined Comitology in the new Treaty regime then this could be of real significance for the inter-institutional balance of power in the EU. It is to the new provisions that we now turn.

(c) The Lisbon Treaty: delegated and implementing acts

The Constitutional Treaty introduced a hierarchy of norms, which distinguished between different categories of legal act, and used terms such as 'law', 'framework law' and the like.[125] The European Council of June 2007, which initiated the process leading to the Lisbon Treaty, decided that the terms 'law', and 'framework law' should be dropped. The rationale given was that the Lisbon Treaty was not to have a 'constitutional character',[126] although it is not readily apparent why the terminology of 'law' or 'framework law' should be assumed to have such a character. It was nonetheless decided to retain the existing terminology of regulations, directives, and decisions. A version of the hierarchy of norms is nonetheless preserved in the Lisbon Treaty, which distinguishes between legislative acts, non-legislative acts of general application, and implementing acts. The legal difficulties flowing from the new regime of legal acts will be considered in detail below.[127] The primary focus of the present discussion is on the implications for the inter-institutional balance of power between the Commission, Council, and European Parliament.

Article 289 TFEU defines a legislative act as one adopted in accordance with a legislative procedure, either the ordinary legislative procedure, which is the successor to co-decision, or a special legislative procedure.

Article 290 TFEU deals with what are now termed non-legislative acts of general application, whereby power to adopt such acts is delegated to the Commission by a legislative act. Such non-legislative acts can supplement or amend certain non-essential elements of the legislative act, but the legislative act must define the objectives, content, scope, and duration of the delegation of power. The essential elements of an area cannot be delegated. The legislative act must specify the conditions to which the delegation is subject. Such conditions may allow the European Parliament or the Council to revoke the delegation; and/or enable the European Parliament or the Council to veto the delegated act within a specified period of time. Acts made pursuant to Article 290 TFEU are to be known as delegated acts.[128]

The third category in the hierarchy of norms, implementing acts, is dealt with in Article 291 TFEU. Member States must adopt all measures of national law

---

[124] P Norman, *The Accidental Constitution, The Making of Europe's Constitutional Treaty* (Euro-Comment, 2nd edn, 2005).
[125] Arts I-33–39 CT.
[126] Brussels European Council, 21–22 June 2007, Annex 1, [3].
[127] Ch 7.   [128] Art 290(3) TFEU.

necessary to implement legally binding Union acts. Where uniform conditions
for implementing legally binding Union acts are needed, those acts shall confer
implementing powers on the Commission, or, in certain cases on the Council.
It is for the European Parliament and Council to lay down in advance the rules
and general principles concerning mechanisms for control by Member States of
the Commission's exercise of implementing powers.

It should be recognized that the distinction between legislative and non-
legislative acts is formal in the following sense. Legislative acts are defined
as those enacted via a legislative procedure, either ordinary or special; non-
legislative acts are those that are not enacted in this manner. This should not,
however, mask the fact that the latter category of delegated acts will often be
legislative in nature, in the sense that they will lay down binding provisions of
general application to govern a certain situation. This is implicitly recognized in
the nomenclature used in the Lisbon Treaty, which speaks of delegated acts
having 'general application'. This moreover accords with the use made of
'secondary regulations' under the regime prior to the Lisbon Treaty. Such
regulations were commonly used to flesh out the meaning, scope, or interpretation of provisions in the 'parent regulation' in a manner analogous to the use
made of delegated legislation, secondary legislation, or rulemaking in national
legal systems. It is interesting to contrast the label attached to delegated acts in
the Lisbon Treaty with the Convention on the Future of Europe Working
Group's more honest depiction of these acts as a new category of legislation.[129]

(d) Delegated acts: survival of Comitology

There are undoubtedly 'positives' to be drawn from the new regime in the Lisbon
Treaty. The controls contained in Article 290 TFEU are important, more
especially so since they accord the European Parliament the simple power to
reject a non-legislative act. Viewed from this perspective, the European Parliament emerges as a winner from the Lisbon Treaty in relation to delegated acts as
well as legislative acts, because it is given an important power that it did not
have hitherto.[130] The legal status of Comitology in relation to delegated acts will
ultimately be decided by the ECJ. It is therefore important to consider Article
290 TFEU on alternative scenarios in which Comitology continues to exist, and
in which it does not. The Commission may well hope that Article 290 TFEU
signals the demise of Comitology, at least for management and regulatory
committees. This is the likely legal conclusion, but the contrary arguments
should at least be examined.

[129] Final Report of Working Group IX (n 117) 8.
[130] P Craig, 'The Role of the European Parliament under the Lisbon Treaty' in S Griller and
J Ziller (eds), *The Lisbon Treaty, EU Constitutionalism without a Constitutional Treaty* (Springer,
2008) 109–134.

The ECJ could conclude that Comitology can continue to exist because it would operate within Article 290(2)(b) TFEU. This enables the Council and European Parliament to veto a delegated act. The argument would then be that Comitology is simply an informational device used by the Council in deciding whether to exercise its veto power, and that it does not constitute an independent or separate constraint. There are indeed echoes of this type of reasoning in the ECJ's earlier jurisprudence on Comitology. Thus in *Koster*[131] the ECJ conceptualized Comitology committees as not distorting the institutional balance within the Community, because they did not take decisions themselves, but merely served to send the matter back to the Council. This argument could moreover be reinforced by suitably framed wording in future Union legislation. Thus the legislative act delegating power to the Commission could explicitly state that in deciding whether to exercise the veto power over particular delegated acts the Council and European Parliament will draw on opinions provided by management and regulatory committees.

The alternative legal route to validate the continued existence of Comitology committees would be for the ECJ to interpret Article 290(2) TFEU as a non-exhaustive list of conditions. The legislative act could therefore specify conditions other than those listed, including Comitology.

(e) Delegated acts: demise of Comitology

The more likely interpretation, however, is that Article 290 TFEU will be read as spelling the demise of Comitology in relation to delegated acts, at least insofar as management and regulatory committees are concerned. This is because Article 290 TFEU makes no mention of such committees and because even the 2006 version of the Comitology procedures would create an imbalance between the Council and the European Parliament within Article 290, which is formally built on institutional parity between the two bodies in relation to control over delegated acts. This is reflected in the Report of the European Parliament's Committee of Legal Affairs, which expressed its unequivocal opposition to any continuation of Comitology committees in the post-Lisbon world.[132]

The Commission's Communication to the Council concerning Articles 290 and 291 In December 2009 was implicitly premised on the demise of management and regulatory committees,[133] and this was made explicit in its later Communication on Article 291.[134] The Commission in the former document emphasized

---

[131] Case 25/70 *Koster* (n 92) [9].

[132] Committee on Legal Affairs, On the Power of Legislative Delegation, A-7 0110/2010, Rapporteur J Sjazcr, 11–12.

[133] Implementation of Art 290 of the Treaty on the Functioning of the European Union, COM (2009) 673 final.

[134] Proposal for a Regulation of the European Parliament and of the Council laying down the rules and general principles concerning mechanisms for control by Member States of the Commission's exercise of implementing powers, COM(2010) 83 final, 2.

that Article 290 TFEU prescribed no procedures for the passage of delegated acts. It acknowledged that such measures would have to comply with the limits and criteria in the legislative act, but stressed nonetheless that the Commission had a large measure of autonomy in the making of delegated acts.[135] Comitology was like Banquo's ghost, hovering in the background, but never directly acknowledged. In a 14-page document there was but one brief section devoted to consultation with national experts and the change from the status quo ante was marked indeed. Thus the Commission, without mentioning the previous committee regime, accepted that it would systematically consult with national experts in the making of delegated acts, but stressed that the experts would have a 'consultative rather institutional role in the decision-making procedure'.[136] When the consultations were concluded the experts would merely be informed of the Commission's conclusions and how it intended to proceed.[137]

The Council's response to the Commission document was interesting. While the Commission devoted but one small section to consultation with national experts, the Council dealt almost entirely with this issue, having suddenly realized the implications of the new regime.[138] The very fact that this response came but two days after the Commission Communication was indicative of the issue's significance. Thus while the Council formally welcomed the Commission's paper it then stressed the importance it attached to consultation with national experts. Such consultation should, said the Council, be undertaken in time to allow for meaningful input by national experts, and delegated acts should be accompanied by 'explanatory memoranda setting out in a detailed manner the grounds for the act and providing information about the preparatory work undertaken by the Commission'.[139] Such commitments were in the Council's view essential to 'create confidence in the new procedure foreseen under Article 290 of the TFEU and to ensure a smooth and fruitful operation of the delegation of powers'.[140]

We must also be mindful of the European Parliament's response to the Commission's paper. It makes for interesting reading, more especially the contribution of the Legal Affairs Committee,[141] which formed the basis for the resolution of the European Parliament.[142] The resolution began by noting the 'delicacy' of delegation, whereby the Commission is instructed to exercise a power that is intrinsic to the legislator's own role.[143] This is more especially so because delegated acts can have 'important implications in many areas',[144] the

---

[135] COM(2009) 673 (n 133) [4.1].   [136] ibid [4.2].   [137] ibid [4.2].
[138] Council 17477/09, Implementation of the Treaty of Lisbon, Article 290, Article 291, Brussels, 11 December 2009.
[139] ibid Annex I.
[140] ibid Annex I.
[141] Committee on Legal Affairs A-7 0110/2010 (n 132).
[142] European Parliament resolution of 5 May 2010 on the power of legislative delegation (2010/2021(INI)).
[143] ibid Preamble C.   [144] ibid Preamble E.

corollary being that the co-legislators must be able to control democratically the exercise of power delegated to the Commission. The European Parliament took the view that the controls listed in Article 290, revocation of the delegation and veto of a delegated act, were not exhaustive, and that other mechanisms, such as a requirement of express approval by the European Parliament and Council of each delegated act, or repeal of a delegated act already in force, could also be envisaged.[145] It was moreover essential that the legislator should be able to monitor the use of delegated power properly. This required *inter alia*: consultation in the preparation of delegated acts; arrangements for the transmission of documents to the relevant Parliamentary committee, including successive drafts of delegated acts and comments received thereon; and minimum periods for objection by Parliament and the Council.[146]

(f) Delegated acts: the inter-institutional balance of power

It seems likely that an Inter-Institutional Agreement or Common Understanding will be framed between the Commission, Council, and European Parliament as to the *modus operandi* of Article 290 TFEU, and this is expressly envisaged in the resolution of the European Parliament.[147] The implications of the new regime for the inter-institutional balance of power will perforce depend on the details of any such agreement. There are nonetheless certain points that can be made at this juncture, which will continue to have salience for the balance of power in the post-Lisbon world.

First, the Council gains little if anything from the new regime. It already had a veto power through the mechanisms of the management and regulatory committee procedures. It might be argued that even if Comitology in the form of management and regulatory committees disappears from the terrain of delegated acts, the Commission will, as we have seen, nonetheless still engage with national representatives through advisory committees, and that it has an interest in doing so.[148] This may be so. The remainder of this discussion nonetheless proceeds on the not unreasonable assumption that if the Council insisted on certain controls over the last 40 years then those controls mattered. Institutional players do not commonly fight battles that are irrelevant or unimportant for the disposition of power. Likewise, if the Commission has gone to considerable lengths to devise a scheme for delegated acts with the express intent that it might lead to the demise of a regime that it has resisted for many years, then the assumption once again is that this matters, and that it will not necessarily be business as usual under the new regime.

---

[145] ibid [2].   [146] ibid [10].   [147] ibid [9]–[10].
[148] P Ponzano, 'Executive and Delegated Acts: The Situation after the Lisbon Treaty' in Griller and Ziller (n 130) 135–143.

Second, we should be mindful of the trade-off that is inherent in this scheme for non-legislative acts. In essence the pre-existing regime was based on generalized ex ante input into the making of the delegated norms, with the possibility of formal recourse to the Council in accordance with the Comitology procedures. It allowed for regularized, general, and detailed input into the content of such norms by Member State representatives, with increasing control exercised by the European Parliament, more especially since the 2006 reforms. If Article 290 TFEU is read so as to preclude Comitology then the constraints therein are premised on a system of ex ante specification of standards in the primary law, combined with the possibility of some control ex post should the measure not be to the liking of the European Parliament or Council.

Third, the controls contained in Article 290(2) TFEU are not mandatory. The conditions of application to which the delegation is subject 'shall' be determined in the legislative act. These 'may' entail the possibility of revocation of the delegation by the European Parliament or the Council, or a condition whereby the delegated regulation enters into force only if there is no objection expressed by the European Parliament or the Council within a specified period of time. These controls will therefore only operate where they are written into the legislative act.[149] The wording of the analogous provision in the Constitutional Treaty was consciously altered to make it clear that 'these conditions do not constitute a mandatory element of such a law or framework law'.[150]

Fourth, the methods of control in Article 290(1) TFEU will be difficult to monitor and enforce. Non-legislative acts can only amend or supplement 'certain non-essential elements of the legislative act', and cannot cover the 'essential elements of an area'. These must be reserved for the legislative act, which must also define the 'objectives, content, scope and duration of the delegation of power'. It will often be difficult, however, for the Council and the European Parliament to specify with exactitude the criteria that should guide the exercise of delegated power by the Commission. They may have neither the knowledge nor the time to delineate in the legislative act precise parameters for the exercise of regulatory choices. The real issues about the assignment of regulatory risks will often only be apparent when the matter is examined in detail. It was for these very reasons that the Comitology process was first created. It will therefore not be easy for the legislative act to define with precision the 'objectives, content, scope and duration' of the delegation. If these requirements are to be taken seriously then there will have to be oversight by the Union courts. They will have to enforce a non-delegation doctrine, striking down delegations where the legislative act is insufficiently precise about the 'objectives, content, scope and duration' of the delegation. Whether the ECJ would be willing to do this with vigour remains to be seen, and history does not indicate vigorous judicial enforcement

---

[149] COM(2009) 673 (n 133) 7–8.   [150] CONV 724/03, Annex 2, 93.

of such criteria.[151] Even if compliance with these criteria is taken seriously by the ECJ, important regulatory choices will still be dealt with through delegated acts for the reasons given above: the parameters for the exercise of regulatory choices will frequently only become apparent when the provisions of the legislative act are worked through in greater detail in the delegated acts. The very depiction of delegated acts as non-legislative serves, whether intentionally or not, to dispel fears that the Commission is making legislative choices of its own volition. The reality is that secondary regulations often deal with complex regulatory choices or policy issues, which are not rendered less so by the fact that they are concerned with matters of detail or technicality. To the contrary, the devil is often in the detail, which is of course the very reason why the Comitology committees were created in the first place, so as to allow Member State oversight of these complex regulatory choices. The fact that the matters are often complex and detailed does not alter this important fact. The committees were created precisely because the Member States sought greater regulatory input into the detail of secondary regulations than allowed for in the then existing Treaty provisions, and this occurred as soon as the need to delegate extensive powers to the Commission became a reality. They have been part of the institutional landscape for over 40 years. They were established to accord Member States an institutionalized method for input into the content of delegated legislation. These regulatory choices will not disappear. They will continue to be made through the new style non-legislative acts.

Fifth, we should be equally mindful of the limits to the (non-mandatory) controls in Article 290(2) TFEU. Revocation of the delegation might be useful as an ultimate weapon, but is ill-suited to fine-tuned control over the content of a particular non-legislative act. This can only be achieved by recourse to the other control specified, the veto power given to the European Parliament and Council. This, too, is a blunt tool, in the sense that neither the Council nor the European Parliament is accorded any formal right to propose amendments to a delegated act, but only the power to prevent its entry into force. The threat of the veto might be *de facto* leverage to secure amendment to a delegated act, but this does not alter the fact that Article 290(2) contains no formal power to amend. The exercise of the veto power is, moreover, crucially dependent on understanding of the relevant measure. Neither the Council nor the European Parliament will be in a position to decide whether to object to the measure unless they understand its content. The Member State representatives on the Council clearly have neither the time nor expertise to perform this task unaided. The European

---

[151] Case 156/93 *European Parliament v Commission* [1995] ECR I-2019; Case 417/93 *European Parliament v Council* [1995] ECR I-1185. Experience from other legal systems is mixed. The non-delegation doctrine in the USA has, eg, provided little by way of control of broad regulatory choices accorded to agencies, AC Aman and WT Mayton, *Administrative Law* (West Group, 2001) ch 1; JM Rogers, MP Healy, and RJ Krotoszynski, *Administrative Law* (Aspen Publishers, 2003) 312–345.

Parliament committees might develop such expertise. They have hitherto been able to draw on informational resources from Comitology committees, but if such committees cease to operate in relation to delegated acts, then the relevant European Parliament committee will have less material to help it to comprehend the relevant measure and decide whether to object to it. Even if advisory committees of Member State representatives are retained under the new regime, there is no certainty that the European Parliament would be able to access any information about the content of the delegated act in the manner that it has done hitherto. It is for this very reason that the Committee on Legal Affairs placed such emphasis on the flow of information from Commission to the relevant committees of the European Parliament, including information about successive drafts of delegated acts.[152]

Finally, the preceding difficulties will be more pronounced given that the European Parliament and Council have to raise any such objection within a period specified by the legislative act. The period will vary depending on the area, but it will probably be relatively short, with the norm being two months. The Council and European Parliament will therefore have to 'get their act together' pretty quickly if either institution seeks to prevent the non-legislative act becoming law. The reality is therefore that the Council will only be able to make a reasoned choice concerning a draft delegated act within the limited time available if it re-invents the very type of national expert oversight that the Commission hoped to dismantle through the Lisbon Treaty provisions, or what amounts to the same thing, *de facto* to invest advisory committees with power of the kind hitherto exercised by its more powerful siblings, management and regulatory committees. This is equally true of the European Parliament's committees. They will have to function in a world where they can no longer rely on informational resources coming from Comitology committees.

(g) Implementing acts: Comitology and the inter-institutional balance of power

The law in this area has become more complex because the Lisbon Treaty, following the Constitutional Treaty, recognizes a third category of legal act, the implementing act, Article 291 TFEU. There are, as will be seen in a subsequent chapter, very real difficulties in deciding when such provisions can or should be made.[153] Reference should be made to that discussion when considering the present analysis, which focuses directly on the role of Comitology. There are four points to note in this regard.

First, the continuance of Comitology is envisaged by Article 291 TFEU. Article 291(2) provides that where uniform conditions for implementation

---

[152] Committee on Legal Affairs A-7 0110/2010 (n 132) 10.   [153] Ch 7.

are needed the requisite implementing powers must be conferred on the Commission, or in limited instances the Council. The acts thereby adopted are termed implementing acts. Article 291(3) then stipulates that the European Parliament and the Council shall lay down in advance by means of a legislative regulation enacted by the ordinary legislative procedure the rules and principles concerning mechanisms for control by the Member States of the Commission's implementing powers.

Second, there is nothing in Article 291(3) which stipulates the form or nature of the controls over the Commission's implementing powers. Article 291(3) is framed in terms of 'control by Member States'. It is not even framed in terms of the Council, and says nothing of control by the European Parliament. This has been emphasized by the Commission in its proposed regulation on Article 291, where it stated that the Council has no role in controlling the exercise of implementing powers when they are conferred on the Commission, and that it was for the Member States 'and they alone' to exercise the controls devised pursuant to Article 291.[154] The draft regulation on Article 291 will be examined in detail in a later chapter.[155] Suffice it to say for the present that the Commission has proposed a new Comitology system to apply to implementing acts, where there are two types of committee regime termed the advisory and examination procedure.

Third, the divide between delegated acts and implementing acts is not clear,[156] and it has important implications since the institutional controls over the two kinds of act differ. This is likely to generate inter-institutional litigation, more especially so since the Council and European Parliament are given no role in relation to implementation acts, although they will have access to relevant Comitology documentation. Thus there could well be instances where the Commission seeks to have recourse to implementation acts, and this is challenged by the European Parliament or the Council on the ground that the relevant measures either supplement or amend the legislative act, and hence should have been made pursuant to Article 290 as a delegated act, thereby enabling the European Parliament and Council to exercise the controls specified in that Article. The European Parliament has already sounded a warning bell in this respect, stating that special attention should be given to the relative use of Articles 290 and 291 'in order to fully preserve the legislator's prerogatives'.[157]

Finally, it is important to appreciate the way in which the Lisbon Treaty has altered the pre-existing position. The preceding discussion has been premised on the assumption that some version of Comitology applies only in relation to implementing acts, and not in relation to delegated acts. The assumption is based on the fact that there is no mention of Comitology procedures in Article 290, which deals with delegated acts. This will represent a marked change from the

---

[154] COM(2010) 83 (n 134) 2.   [155] Ch 7.
[156] Ch 7.   [157] European Parliament resolution (n 142) [20].

previous regime. The 'cause' of this shift resides ultimately in ambiguity as to the meaning of the word implementation. It can bear the meaning that it had in the previous Treaty, Article 202 EC: delegated rule making or decision making subject to Comitology conditions. Implementation can also mean the execution of other norms without any supplementation or amendment. The Comitology procedure hitherto applied to implementation in the first sense of this term: it was the condition attached to delegated rule making or decision making by the Commission.

The discussion in the Convention on the Future of Europe revealed an important shift in thought. The Comitology procedures were not mentioned in relation to the making of delegated regulations, even though this was the true analogy with the status quo ante, the implication being that they would be replaced by the controls on delegated acts now found in Article 290(2) TFEU. The Convention documentation considered the legitimacy of Comitology primarily in the context of implementing acts, where the emphasis was on implementation in its second sense, as execution or application. This was apparent in the literature from the Working Group.[158] It was apparent again in other Convention documentation.[159] Thus the Praesidium stated that several amendments were opposed to the then current committee mechanisms, and wished to delete any reference to Comitology-type controls, while other comments proposed confining the control mechanisms to advisory committees alone. The Praesidium considered that this was a matter for secondary legislation and therefore did not amend the Article. The assumption was therefore that in the future Comitology would be relevant only in the context of implementing acts, and not in relation to delegated regulations, even though this was in stark contrast to the circumstances where Comitology is currently used.

3. Participatory Democracy and Inclusion

The Lisbon Treaty includes Article 11 TEU, which was borrowed directly from the Constitutional Treaty,[160] save for the fact that the Lisbon Treaty omits the actual heading 'participatory democracy'. Article 11 TEU provides that:

1. The institutions shall, by appropriate means, give citizens and representative associations the opportunity to make known and publicly exchange their views in all areas of Union action.

2. The institutions shall maintain an open, transparent and regular dialogue with representative associations and civil society.

---

[158] Final Report of Working Group IX on Simplification (n 117) 9.
[159] CONV 724/03, Annex 2, 94.   [160] Art I-47 CT.

3. The European Commission shall carry out broad consultations with parties concerned in order to ensure that the Union's actions are coherent and transparent.

4. Not less than one million citizens who are nationals of a significant number of Member States may take the initiative of inviting the European Commission, within the framework of its powers, to submit any appropriate proposal on matters where citizens consider that a legal act of the Union is required for the purpose of implementing the Treaties.

The provisions concerning representative and participatory democracy were regarded as important in the Convention on the Future of Europe,[161] and there was some academic commentary.[162] We should therefore resist the temptation to regard these provisions of the Constitutional Treaty[163] as rhetorical flourishes, with little if any substance, or to ignore the analogous provisions of the Lisbon Treaty when evaluating the overall picture of democracy within the EU. This is more especially so because they are expressed in mandatory language and might well have more bite to them than is captured by the imagery of rhetorical flourish. Before embarking on this exercise, it is, however, important to step back and consider in general terms the legal and political protection afforded to participation before the Lisbon Treaty.

(a) The EC Treaty: promise and performance

Prior to the Lisbon Treaty there was a good deal of rhetoric concerning participation and inclusion, much of which was directed towards enhancing the overall legitimacy of the EU. The reality was nonetheless that the extent to which the judicial or political organs were willing to commit to legally binding participation rights was decidedly limited. This is a complex story, which cannot be told fully here, but the essence of the approach can nonetheless be conveyed.[164]

The Community courts provided little assistance in this respect. They were active in promoting due process rights in adjudication, regarding this as a fundamental right and being willing to apply it irrespective of whether the legislature had made any provision for such hearing rights.[165] Their stance was markedly different when the applicant claimed participation rights in the making of norms of a legislative nature. The Community courts consistently resisted such claims, denying consultation rights unless they were expressly provided by the

---

[161] Norman (n 124) 176–178, 218.

[162] C Kaddous, 'L'initiative citoyenne: un instrument de démocratie directe a l'échelle de l'Union européenne' in Kaddous and Auer (n 57) 317–328.

[163] Arts I-46–47 CT.

[164] Craig, *EU Administrative Law* (n 88) ch 10; J Mendes, *Participation in EU Rulemaking, A Rights-Based Approach* (Oxford University Press, 2011).

[165] Case C-49/88 *Al-Jubail Fertilizer v Council* [1991] ECR I-3187, [15]; Cases T-33–34/98 *Petrotub and Republica SA v Council* [1999] ECR II-3837; Case C-458/98 P *Industrie des Poudres Spheriques v Council and Commission* [2000] ECR I-8147, [99].

relevant Treaty article, or by a regulation, directive, or decision. The *Atlanta* case is the leading authority.[166] The applicant sought compensation for damage caused by a Community regulation concerning the bananas market. It argued, *inter alia*, that the Court of First Instance (CFI) had erred in finding that the right to be heard in an administrative procedure affecting a specific person could not be transposed to the process leading to a regulation, more especially because it was irrelevant to the individual concerned whether his legal situation was affected as a result of an administrative or a legislative procedure. The applicant sought to rely on *Al-Jubail* to show that the absence of a Treaty provision requiring consultation in relation to a legislative procedure did not allow a hearing to be dispensed with.[167] The ECJ rejected the argument. It held that the case law according a right to be heard related only to acts of direct and individual concern to the applicant. It could not be extended to the procedure culminating in legislation involving a choice of economic policy and applying to the generality of traders concerned. The only obligations of consultation incumbent on the Community legislature were those laid down by the Treaty article in question.[168] This approach was reaffirmed by later authority.[169] The Community courts were similarly unwilling to draw any legal consequences from the fact of participation in the making of the legislative measure, concluding that this did not give the applicant any preferential position when it came to challenging such a measure.[170]

Individuals have drawn some succour from the political process, but the results have nonetheless been mixed. Regulations or directives have granted participation rights in a number of important areas, but the most prominent instances have entailed the grant of such rights in relation to national regulatory bodies, rather than the Commission.[171] The Commission has been reluctant to accord

---

[166] Case C-104/97 P *Atlanta AG v Commission* [1999] ECR I-6983.

[167] ibid [31]–[32].

[168] ibid [35]–[39].

[169] Case C-258/02 P *Bactria Industriehygiene-Service Verwaltungs GMbH v Commission* [2003] ECR I-15105, [43]; Case C-263/02 P *Commission v Jego-Quere & Cie SA* [2004] ECR I-3425, [47]; Case T-13/99 *Pfizer Animal Health SA v Council* [2002] ECR II-3305, [487]; Case T-70/99 *Alpharma Inc v Council* [2002] ECR II-3495, [388]; Case T-135/96 *UEAPME v Council* [1998] ECR II-2335, [69]–[80].

[170] Case C-10/95 P *Asociacion Espanola de Empresas de la Carne (Asocarne) v Council* [1995] ECR I-4149, [39]; Case C-263/02 P *Jego-Quere* (n 169) [48]; Case T-583/93 *Stichting Greenpeace Council (Greenpeace International) v Commission* [1995] ECR II-2205, [56]. The Community courts were willing to accord standing where the applicant was given rights to complain in the making of the initial decision, Case 26/76 *Metro-SB-Großmärkte GmbH & Co KG v Commission* [1977] ECR 1875; Case 169/84 *Compagnie Francaise de l'Azote (COFAZ) SA v Commission* [1986] ECR 391; Case T-435/93 *ASPEC v Commission* [1995] ECR II-1281; Case T-380/94 *AIUFFASS v Commission* [1996] ECR II-2169.

[171] See, eg, Directive of the European Parliament and of the Council 2002/21/EC of 7 March 2002 on a common regulatory framework for electronic communications networks and services (Framework Directive) [2002] OJ L108/33, Art 6; Directive 2003/35/EC of the European Parliament and of the Council of 26 May 2003 providing for public participation in respect of the

legally enforceable participation rights in relation to its own legislative or policy proposals. It has proceeded mainly through measures that are not legally binding, but which nonetheless became more effective over time. It made increasing use of Green and White Papers when important areas of EC policy were being developed, inviting comments on an ad hoc basis to particular legislative initiatives. The Commission generalized this approach in its 2002 Communication on Consultation,[172] and gave it more practical force through Interactive Policy Making (IPM),[173] which is a principal component of 'Your Voice in Europe'.[174] The 2002 Communication was an important step in fostering consultation within the EU, but its limitations should also be noted. Consultations were used only for the more major policy initiatives,[175] and areas such as the Open Method of Coordination and rule making subject to Comitology were excluded from the ambit of the Communication.[176]

The asymmetry between treatment of the Member States and the Commission was marked. It is exemplified by changes to the participatory requirements imposed on Member States in the context of pollution prevention and control. This regime was strengthened in 2003 by a provision entitled 'access to justice', which required Member States to provide access to a review procedure before a court of law or other independent and impartial body to enable challenge to the substantive or procedural legality of decisions that were subject to the public participation provisions of the Directive.[177] This reinforcement of participation rights against the Member States may well be laudable. The Commission, however, showed no inclination to apply analogous precepts of 'access to justice' to itself. This is readily apparent from its response to comments received on the draft of its Communication about consultation, which had suggested that the consultation standards should be included in a legally binding document. The Commission's response was peremptory. The principles and minimum standards in the Communication were specifically stated not to be legally binding,[178] and the Commission offered this terse justification.[179]

[A] situation must be avoided in which a Commission proposal could be challenged in the Court on the grounds of alleged lack of consultation of interested parties. Such an overly-legalistic approach would be incompatible with the need for timely delivery of policy, and with the expectations of the citizens that the European Institutions should deliver on substance rather than concentrating on procedures.

drawing up of certain plans and programmes relating to the environment and amending with regard to public participation and access to justice Council Directives 85/337/EEC and 96/61/EC, [2003] OJ L156/17, Art 4.

[172] Towards a Reinforced Culture of Consultation and Dialogue – General Principles and Minimum Standards for Consultation of Interested Parties by the Commission, COM(2002) 704 final.
[173] ibid 6–7. [174] <http://ec.europa.eu/yourvoice/index_en.htm>
[175] COM (2002) 704 (n 172) 15–16. [176] ibid 16.
[177] Dir 2003/35 (n 171) Art 4(4).
[178] COM(2002) 704 final (n 172) 10, 15. [179] ibid 10.

(b) Lisbon Treaty: promise and expectation

Article 11 TEU should not be ignored when evaluating the overall picture of democracy within the EU, more especially given the concerns voiced over time as to the connection between the EU and its citizens. Article 11 is expressed in mandatory language and might well have more bite than imagined. The EU has already begun work on the power of citizens' initiative contained in Article 11(4) TEU.[180] The salient issue is therefore whether the inclusion of this Article will signal any change in legal and political terms from the previous position. Article 11 will almost inevitably be relied on by claimants in litigation, and the ECJ will necessarily be compelled to face difficult interpretative issues as to the concrete implications that are drawn from these principles.

The ECJ might choose to interpret the Article narrowly, thereby effectively leaving the matter to the political institutions. It might, for example, fasten on the phrase 'by appropriate means' within Article 11(1) to conclude that the obligation on the EU institutions that citizens should have the opportunity to make their views known and publicly exchange their views in all areas of Union action could be satisfied by techniques such as 'Your Voice in Europe'. The ECJ might likewise interpret the mandatory obligation in Article 11(3) that 'the European Commission shall carry out broad consultations with parties concerned in order to ensure that the Union's actions are coherent and transparent' as providing no foundation for participation rights in the context of delegated acts.

The reality is nonetheless that such narrow interpretation is problematic. Thus although the 'Your Voice in Europe' initiative has been valuable it will not normally touch the more detailed provisions that citizens will often wish to comment on where they affect their lives in some direct manner, and it is precisely the detailed secondary regulations that are of direct concern for those who come within their remit. A narrow interpretation does not moreover sit well with the injunction in Article 11 TEU that citizens and representative associations shall have the opportunity to make known their views in all areas of EU action, that there should be open, transparent, and regular dialogue between EU institutions and civil society, and that the Commission shall carry out broad consultations with parties concerned in order to ensure that the Union's actions are coherent and transparent. A restrictive interpretation of Article 11 would therefore send a very negative message about the nature of participatory democracy in the EU, and risk turning a provision that was meant to convey a positive feeling about the inclusive nature of the EU and its willingness to engage with its citizenry, into one that carried the opposite connotation.

---

[180] Council 8796/10, Proposal for a Regulation of the Council and of the European Parliament on the Citizens' Initiative, Brussels 21 April 2010; Proposal for a Regulation of the Council and of the European Parliament on the Citizens' Initiative, COM(2010) 119 final.

4. Conclusion

(a) Legislative acts: democracy, improvement, and deficit

It is clear that hitherto the EU has rested on the twin-fold legitimacy of the Member States, as represented in the Council, and their peoples, as represented in the European Parliament. This precept is now formally embodied in Article 10 TEU, which copies the relevant provision from the Constitutional Treaty.[181] It stipulates that the functioning of the Union is founded on representative democracy; that citizens are directly represented at EU level by the European Parliament; that Member States are represented in the European Council by Heads of State or Government and in the Council by their governments, which are themselves democratically accountable either to their national Parliaments, or to their citizens; that citizens shall have the right to participate in the democratic life of the Union and that decisions shall be taken as openly and as closely as possible to them; and that political parties at European level contribute to forming European political awareness and to expressing the will of citizens of the Union.

There is a rich literature on EU democracy.[182] A prominent focal point in the debate is as to whether EU democracy should be judged primarily in terms of

---

[181] Art I-46 CT.

[182] S Garcia (ed), *European Identity and the Search for Legitimacy* (Pinter, 1993); J Hayward (ed), *The Crisis of Representation in Europe* (Frank Cass, 1995); A Rosas and E Antola (eds), *A Citizens' Europe, In Search of a New Order* (Sage, 1995); J Weiler, U Haltern and F Mayer, 'European Democracy and its Critique' in J Hayward (ed), *The Crisis of Representation in Europe* (Frank Cass, 1995); R Bellamy, V Bufacchi, and D Castiglione (eds), *Democracy and Constitutional Culture in the Union of Europe* (Lothian Foundation Press, 1995); S Andersen and K Eliassen (eds), *The European Union: How Democratic Is It?* (Sage, 1996); R Bellamy and D Castiglione (eds), *Constitutionalism in Transformation: European and Theoretical Perspectives* (Blackwell, 1996); R Bellamy (ed), *Constitutionalism, Democracy and Sovereignty: American and European Perspectives* (Avebury, 1996); F Snyder (ed), *Constitutional Dimensions of European Economic Integration* (Kluwer, 1996); R Dehousse (ed), *Europe: The Impossible Status Quo* (Macmillan, 1997); D Curtin, *Postnational Democracy, The European Union in Search of a Political Philosophy* (Kluwer, 1997); R Corbett, *The European Parliament's Role in Closer EU Integration* (Palgrave, 1998); J Weiler, *The Constitution of Europe* (Cambridge University Press, 1999); C Hoskyns and M Newman (eds), *Democratizing the European Union* (Manchester University Press, 2000); B Laffan, R O'Donnell, and M Smith, *Europe's Experimental Union: Rethinking Integration* (Routledge, 2000); F Mancini, *Democracy and Constitutionalism in the European Union* (Hart, 2000); K Neunreither and A Wiener (eds), *European Integration after Amsterdam, Institutional Dynamics and Prospects for Democracy* (Oxford University Press, 2000); R Prodi, *Europe As I See It* (Polity, 2000); K Nicolaidis and R Howse (eds), *The Federal Vision, Legitimacy and Levels of Governance in the United States and the European Union* (Oxford University Press, 2001); A Moravcsik, 'In Defence of the "Democratic Deficit": Reassessing Legitimacy in the European Union' (2002) 40 JCMS 603; Y Mény, 'De la démocratie en Europe: Old Concepts and New Challenges' (2003) 41 JCMS 1; W van Gerven, *The European Union, A Polity of States and Peoples* (Hart, 2005); A Follesdal and S Hix, 'Why there is a Democratic Deficit in the EU: A Response to Majone and Moravcsik' (2006) 44 JCMS 533; R Bellamy, 'Still in Deficit: Rights, Regulation and Democracy in the EU' (2006) 12 ELJ 725; A Menon and S Weatherill, 'Democratic Politics in a Globalising World: Supranationalism and Legitimacy in

input or output.[183] Thus a significant feature of the democracy deficit argument is the 'disjunction between power and electoral accountability'. It is axiomatic within national systems that the voters can express their dislike of the incumbent party through periodic elections. There may be limits to electoral accountability, but the bottom line is that governments can be changed if they incur electoral displeasure. In the EU, legislative power has been divided between the Council, European Parliament, and Commission, with the European Council playing a significant role in shaping the overall legislative agenda. The voters therefore have no direct way of signifying their desire for change in the legislative agenda. European elections can alter the complexion of the European Parliament, but it is only one part of the legislative process. The Commission, Council, and European Council have input into the legislative agenda, but they cannot be voted out by the people. My own view is that democratic input is indeed central when thinking about EU decision making, but that there are nonetheless structural reasons why, although there can be improvements in this respect, it cannot be perfectly realized.[184] It is therefore important to consider the implications of the Lisbon Treaty for EU democracy, more especially from the input perspective.

There is no doubt that the Lisbon Treaty has improved democratic input by rendering the system more truly 'parliamentary' than hitherto. The European Parliament has been empowered through the extension of the ordinary legislative procedure to new areas, and has greater control over the appointment of the Commission President than hitherto. Thus, while the European Council retains ultimate power over choice of Commission President, it is unlikely to attempt to force a candidate that is of a different persuasion from the dominant party or coalition in the European Parliament. The Lisbon Treaty thus generally coheres with recent practice, and goes some way to improving the linkage between policy and politics in the EU. Insofar as the EU has been depicted as a polity in which policy is divorced from party politics, a formal linkage between the dominant party/coalition in the European Parliament and the appointment of the Commission President serves to strengthen the connection between policy and party politics, the assumption being that the designated President of the Commission will share broadly similar political views on policy to that of the dominant party in the European Parliament. This will thereby alleviate the disjunction of power and responsibility that has underpinned previous critiques of the EU.

the European Union' LSE, Law, Society and Economy Working Papers 13/2007; R Bellamy, 'Democracy without Democracy? Can the EU's Democratic "Outputs" be Separated from the Democratic "Inputs" Provided by Competitive Parties and Majority Rule?' (2010) 17 JEPP 2; G Majone, 'Transaction-Cost Efficiency and the Democratic Deficit' (2010) 17 JEPP 150.

[183] See, eg, Moravcsik, Majone, Follesdal and Hix, Bellamy, Menon and Weatherill (n 182).

[184] P Craig, 'Integration, Democracy and Legitimacy' in P Craig and G de Búrca (eds), *The Evolution of EU Law* (Oxford University Press, 2010) ch 1.

We should nonetheless be mindful of the obstacles that subsist to a closer link between policy and politics in the EU, even after the Lisbon Treaty reforms. Four such factors deserve mention.

First, a general precept of democracy is that the voters can remove the party in power and replace it with another, whose policies are preferred. This basic precept is not fully met in the EU. The EU policy agenda is not exclusively in the hands of the European Parliament and/or Commission. The Council and the European Council have input both *de jure* and *de facto*. The extended Presidency of the European Council is likely to increase this tendency further, since the incumbent will have the time and opportunity to develop a set of ideas for the EU in the way that the pre-existing regime of six-monthly rotating presidencies rendered difficult. It should moreover be noted that the Lisbon Treaty, like the Constitutional Treaty, accords the Commission the power to initiate the Union's annual and multiannual programming with a view to achieving inter-institutional agreements.[185] This is explicitly premised on the assumption that other institutional players will and should have an impact on the development of politics and policy. Thus even if the European Parliament and Commission President were very closely allied in terms of the EU's substantive political vision, the policy that emerges will necessarily also bear the imprint of the political vision of the Council and European Council.

Second, the absence of a developed party system at the EU level is also important in this respect. A coherent political agenda normally emerges at national level because it is developed by rival parties, which formulate the contending political packages offered to voters. The absence of a developed party system at the EU level means that elections to the European Parliament are fought by national political parties in which national political issues often predominate, with the result that there is little by way of a clear political agenda on EU issues that is proffered to the voters to choose from. The MEPs sit within cross-national political groupings of left, centre, right wing and the like, but they will not come to the European Parliament with a coherent overall agenda that is readily discernible to voters.

Third, the President of the Commission may well be *primus inter pares*, but he or she is still only one member of the Commission team. The other Commissioners will not necessarily be of the same political persuasion as the President or the dominant party in the European Parliament and it has been common for Commissioners to have varying political backgrounds. Thus even if there is some commonality of view between Commission President and European Parliament in terms of policy, this will not necessarily be shared by all Commissioners. Nor, insofar as this is perceived to be a problem, can it be resolved through European Parliament hearings of individual Commissioners.

---

[185] Art 17 TEU.

A fourth factor that has reduced the linkage between policy and party politics concerns the very nature of the issues that the EU regulates. It is true that the scope of the EU's competence has been expanded by successive Treaty amendments. It is true also that certain issues which have more recently fallen within the EU's competence are highly political, such as those covered by the area of freedom, security, and justice. It nonetheless remains the case that many of the most 'political' issues at national level, or matters that cause the most pronounced tensions between the left and right wing, are issues over which the EU either has no competence, or only limited competence. These include direct taxation, the reach and nature of the welfare state, education, crime, health and the like.

There are, moreover, structural political limits to the realization of input democracy in the EU. The present disposition of power is premised on the twin conceptions of legitimacy identified earlier, now embodied in Article 10 TEU: the people are represented through the European Parliament and the Member States in the Council and the European Council. This very division of power means that it is not possible under existing arrangements for the people directly to vote out those in power and substitute a different party with different policies, since Member State representatives in the Council and European Council are not chosen in this manner. There is no doubt that a system could in principle be designed that would come closer to this. It would in theory be possible to have a regime in which the people voted directly in European elections for two constituent parts of the legislature, the European Parliament and Council, and also for the President of the European Council. However, even this would not ensure that the people could exercise electoral control over the direction of EU policy, since the European Council would still be populated by Heads of State who would continue to have a marked influence over the policy agenda.

Insofar as the 'cure' for the democratic deficit is felt to lie in granting the 'people' more power over policy choice than hitherto through the ability to vote out those whom they dislike and replace them with another party, and insofar as this would require changes of the kind mentioned in the previous paragraph, it could then lead to the critique that the EU was becoming a super-State. The inter-institutional disposition of power that would be required to meet this version of the democratic deficit would entail diminution of State power in the Council and European Council, and there would be questions as to Member State willingness to partake in a supranational polity in which their own influence over the policy agenda would be severely curtailed. There could moreover be considerable constitutional difficulties for those that predicate membership of such a polity on Member States being 'Masters of the Treaty'.

Insofar as the 'cure' for the democratic deficit is said to entail limiting the power of the EU, it is premised on the assumption that such power would simply be repatriated to the Nation State, with a net 'gain' in terms of democracy. This will not occur, at least not in the simple terms depicted here. The reality is that cross-border flows of goods create international policy externalities, which in turn create incentives for policy co-ordination.[186] The key issue then becomes not whether States interact, but how. They can do so by ad hoc international agreements. Some more permanent form of international cooperation may be preferred to reduce the transaction costs of ad hoc coordination and lend credibility to Member State bargains. The salient point here is that diminution of EU power does not equate with simple repatriation of power to the nation state. The reality is that ad hoc international agreements would fill the gap where policy coordination was required between states. These are made and administered by national executives, with relatively little control by the legislature. It is by no means self-evident that this constitutes a net gain for democracy.

(b) Delegated acts: power, value choices, and control

The implications of the new provisions for delegated and implementing acts will only become apparent over time. Assuming that Article 290 TFEU is interpreted so as to preclude Comitology in relation to delegated acts this would represent perhaps the most significant shift in institutional power in the Lisbon Treaty. It will increase Commission regulatory autonomy, and is likely to decrease control by the other institutional players. It is true that the Council and European Parliament have the veto power, but this is not a net gain for the Council and the efficacy of such control is crucially dependent upon the informational resource previously provided to the Council by the Comitology committees. Thus the Council could not possibly exercise meaningful review of legislative acts without the gatekeeping and informational functions performed by Coreper and the working parties that feed into it. The need for such functions to be undertaken by some institutional player is *a fortiori* the case in relation to delegated acts, which outstrip legislative acts by at least four to one. Those functions were hitherto provided by Comitology committees.

The choice is therefore stark. Advisory committees might *de facto* be transformed into more powerful bodies, furnishing the detailed advice on which the Council will decide to exercise its veto, in which case we would in effect have déjà vu all over again, and the reinvention of the old order. The alternative could be demise of management and regulatory committees in relation to delegated acts,

[186] A Moravcsik, 'Preferences and Power in the European Community: A Liberal Intergovernmentalist Approach' (1993) 31 JCMS 473; W Wessels, 'The Modern West-European State and the European Union: Democratic Erosion or a New Kind of Polity?' in S Andersen and K Eliassen (eds), *The European Union: How Democratic Is It?* (Sage, 1996) ch 4; G Majone, 'The European Community Between Social Policy and Social Regulation' (1993) 31 JCMS 153 and 'The Rise of the Regulatory State in Europe' (1994) West European Politics 1; P Craig 'Integration, Democracy and Legitimacy' in P Craig, and G de Burca (eds), *The Evolution of EU Law* (Oxford University Press, 2nd edn, 2010) ch 1.

and advisory committees not taking up 'the slack', with the consequential increase in Commission regulatory autonomy. Commentators may well differ as to the desirability of these outcomes. Those who believe that enactment of regulatory provisions pursuant to legislative acts falls naturally within the sphere of the 'executive function', which should reside with the Commission, will welcome the developments in the Lisbon Treaty. Those like the present author, who believe that it is often fortuitous whether things end up in primary legislation or in a delegated act, and who believe also that the latter may entail complex regulatory choices that are just as 'political' as the former, will disagree.

Triangular relationships often produce tensions and paradoxes, and the dynamic between Commission, Council, and European Parliament in this area is no exception. The Committee on Legal Affairs expressed its regret that the Commission Communication on Article 290 appeared to 'understand neither the extent nor the significance of the changes in the Union's constitutional and legal framework ushered in by the Treaty of Lisbon'.[187] The reality is surely to the contrary. The Commission understood full well the implications of the new order, for which it had pressed for nearly two decades. The truth is that each corner of the institutional triangle had different goals which it sought to maximize.

For the Commission this was the embodiment in the Treaty of a regime like Article 290, which would enable it to press for the demise of management and regulatory committees. The fact that it did not then shout this from the rooftops in its Communication on Article 290 was simply sound political sense. For the European Parliament the demise of Comitology and formal equality of status with the Council was the major prize, in some quarters at least, as reflected in the views of the Legal Affairs Committee. The paradox here is that this may yet prove to be a Pyrrhic victory unless its committees really can perform the scrutiny functions demanded under the new regime without any direct connection to the informational resource hitherto provided by Comitology committees. For the Council the dominant theme was dropping the ball. There is no evidence that the Member States understood the full implications of the changes made by Article 290, which is not so surprising given that attention was concentrated on other institutional issues in the hectic first half of 2003. There was scant time for consideration of the hierarchy of norms in plenary sessions, and relatively few understood the arcane divide between delegated and implementing acts.

The paradox here may yet prove to be Council resilience in the face of formal Treaty norms. The Council has resisted attempts to prise away its power over secondary norms for 40 years. Its attitude is unlikely to change overnight or the next decade. If the Council cannot have management and regulatory committees it might well try to preserve the substance of the status quo ante by *de facto* investing the committees composed of their national representatives with powers

---

[187] Committee on Legal Affairs A-7 0110/2010 (n 132) 11.

analogous to those that existed hitherto. The sensible thing in practical terms would indeed be for the Council and European Parliament to join forces and pool resources in relation to new advisory committees that oversee delegated acts.

There is, in any event, an institutional paradox lurking in the new regime. The provisions on the hierarchy of norms were designed to simplify matters. The consequence of the changes will, however, be increased institutional complexity in relation to the committees that inhabit the EU world. A modified version of Comitology will operate in relation to implementing acts, but these committees will be different from those that will be used by the Council to inform itself about the content and desirability of delegated acts. It is doubtful whether the framers of the Lisbon Treaty intended this, but then history is replete with instances of change producing unintended consequences.

(c) Participatory democracy: expectation, hope, and fulfilment

The future of the provisions concerning participatory democracy within the Lisbon Treaty remains to be seen. The EU institutions are mindful of the need to put some flesh on the bare bones of these provisions, as attested to by the speed with which proposals in relation to the Citizen's Initiative have been brought forward. Whether real life is breathed into the other principles contained in Article 11 TEU is more uncertain. The desire to enhance EU legitimacy by doing so has in the past been tempered, often severely, by the desire to get things done without participatory input, or at the very least without any binding obligation to engage in such process. Article 11 has nonetheless 'upped the stakes'. To be sure, the political and legal players can construe this provision narrowly, but the political cost of so doing has been raised by the very embodiment of these participatory ideals within the Treaty.

3

Executive Power, Contestation,
and Resolution

The most divisive issues in the debates that led to the Constitutional Treaty concerned executive power, and the 'solutions' embodied in that Treaty were largely carried over into the Lisbon Treaty. This chapter examines the tensions concerning executive power and the way in which they were 'resolved' in the Lisbon Treaty, the focus being on the legal provisions and the political implications of the new regime.[1]

It is important to note at the outset that there is no precise definition of executive power in the EU.[2] We know, in formal terms at least, that legislative power under the Lisbon Treaty captures the making of legislative acts.[3] The very nature of executive power is more difficult to define in substantive terms. It varies as between nation states and national constitutions often provide scant assistance in defining the locus and scope of executive power.[4] We can nonetheless identify a core set of tasks that are commonly undertaken by the executive branch of government. The executive will commonly play a major role in planning the overall priorities and agenda for legislation. It will normally have principal responsibility for foreign affairs and defence. The executive will have an important say in the structure and allocation of the budget. It will also have responsibility for the effective implementation of agreed policy initiatives and legislation.

While there may be some measure of agreement that these issues constitute 'executive' functions, we should nonetheless note a duality latent in use of the word 'executive', which connotes both 'follow' and 'lead'. The former captures the idea of execution, in the sense that the executive has responsibility for implementing legislation and policy enacted elsewhere, commonly by the

---

[1] P Craig, 'European Governance: Executive and Administrative Powers under the New Constitutional Settlement' (2005) 3 I-CON 407; Y Devuyst, 'The European Union's Institutional Balance after the Treaty of Lisbon: "Community Method" and "Democratic Deficit" Reassessed' (2008) 39 Georgetown Jnl Int Law 247.

[2] D Curtin, *Executive Power in the European Union, Law, Practices and the Living Constitution* (Oxford University Press, 2009).

[3] Art 289 TFEU.

[4] P Craig and A Tomkins (eds), *The Executive and Public Law, Power and Accountability in Comparative Perspective* (Oxford University Press, 2006).

legislature. The functions commonly ascribed to the executive cannot however all be conceptualized in this manner. Agenda setting and decisions about priorities connote leading rather than following, and this is equally true of power over foreign policy and defence.[5] The fact that we identify these as executive functions can be traced back to the monarch as repository of executive authority, and this identification has largely survived the transfer of executive authority from monarch to government.

This duality in the meaning of the word executive is just as prevalent in the EU as it is in Nation States, as will be apparent in the ensuing discussion. The issues raised by the disposition of executive power in the EU are complex. The initial sections focus on particular topics, including the locus of executive power as epitomized by the struggles that led to the creation of the new long-term President of the European Council; power over Council formations; the creation of an EU High Representative for Foreign Affairs and Security Policy; the election of the Commission President; the internal organization of the Commission; and the role of agencies in the new Lisbon regime. The political tensions surrounding each topic will be analysed, as will the 'resolution' captured by the relevant provisions of the Lisbon Treaty.

The Lisbon Treaty is premised on shared executive power and the focus in the latter parts of the chapter shifts to the way in which the overall regime of executive power is likely to function in the post-Lisbon world. There will be discussion of the relative merits of unitary and shared executive power; examination as to how the institutional players are likely to interact in different executive spheres; and consideration of shared executive power from the perspective of legal and political accountability.

1. Process

The provisions of the Lisbon Treaty concerning executive power largely follow those in the Constitutional Treaty. The process that led to the Constitutional Treaty was considered in detail in Chapter 1. We should nonetheless briefly recall the relevant parts of that analysis for the purposes of the present discussion because it affects the substance of the provisions that emerged from the Convention on the Future of Europe, which were then embodied in the Constitutional Treaty.

The contentious nature of the discussions about institutions was evident in the process used at the Convention. The Convention generally employed a three-stage methodology. There was the listening stage from March till June 2002. This was followed by the examination stage, in which Working Groups

---

[5] D Curtin and M Egeberg, 'Tradition and Innovation: Europe's Accumulated Executive Order' (2008) 31 West European Politics 369.

considered particular topics. This exercise occupied the latter half of 2002. There was then the proposal stage, in which the Convention discussed draft articles of the Constitution.

The process was very different in relation to institutions. There was no Working Group. It was felt that the issues were too contentious to be dealt with other than in plenary session. This is reflected in the fact that the title on Institutions was empty in the original preliminary Draft Constitution. The Convention discussions about institutions only began in earnest in January 2003. It rapidly became apparent that there were serious divisions of opinion between the larger and the smaller States, with the Commission lining up with the latter group. The absence of a Working Group on institutions did not, however, lead to more detailed deliberation in the plenary sessions of the Convention.

The Praesidium submitted its proposals to the Convention in April 2003.[6] Full discussion of the draft articles only occurred in the plenary session on 15–16 May 2003,[7] and this revealed serious differences of view. The Praesidium realized that it needed more time for reflection and therefore did not make any amendments to these articles in its initial global draft of 28 May 2003.[8] There was no second reading in plenary of these articles. The Praesidium opted instead for consultations with the four constituent groups, governments, MEPs, national MPs, and the Commission, which took place on 4 June 2003.[9] Formal text of the revised articles on the institutions only became available on 10 June,[10] a mere three days before the concluding session on 13 June.[11] It is clear, moreover, that the Praesidium, and the Secretariat, exercised considerable power in deciding on the ultimate content of these provisions and in deciding which amendments should be adopted.[12]

The Convention process in relation to institutions has been considered above.[13] While it was far from perfect, the decision to postpone discussion of institutions was nonetheless readily explicable. It was clear that this topic would be divisive. If it had been placed on the agenda in the latter part of 2002, then it would have overshadowed the other work. The contrast with what occurred is instructive. The Convention, via Working Groups, concentrated on important issues. There were differences of opinion on these matters, but they were less

[6] CONV 691/03, Institutions, Brussels 23 April 2003; CONV, Summary Report of the Plenary Session—Brussels 24 and 25 April 2003, Brussels 30 April 2003.
[7] CONV 748/03, Summary Report of the Plenary Session—Brussels 15 and 16 May 2003, Brussels 27 May 2003. See also, CONV 709/03, Summary Sheet of Proposals for Amendments relating to the Union's Institutions, Brussels 9 May 2003.
[8] CONV 783/03, Summary Report on the Plenary Session—Brussels 30 and 31 May 2003, Brussels 16 June 2003.
[9] CONV 770/03, Part I, Title IV (Institutions)—Revised Text, Brussels 2 June 2003; CONV 771/03, Consultations with the Component Groups, Brussels 2 June 2003.
[10] CONV 797/03, Revised Text of Part One, Brussels 10 June 2003.
[11] CONV 814/03, Summary Report of the Plenary Session—Brussels 11 and 13 June 2003, Brussels 19 June 2003.
[12] pp 14–16.   [13] pp 14–16, pp 30–31.

marked than those on institutions. Progress on issues assigned to Working Groups allowed the Praesidium to publish the preliminary Draft Constitution in the autumn of 2002. This strategy also enabled discussion about institutions to take place 'offline' in 2002.

The issue of the institutional division of power, especially executive power, was, however, like Banquo's ghost, ever present, lurking in the background. As Grevi notes, the key phrase in shaping the formal Convention agenda for 2002 may have been 'everything but institutions', but the key phrase for the debate in other circles was 'nothing but power'.[14]

2. The President(s) of the Union

(a) One President or two: hats and labels

It is fitting to begin the discussion with the most divisive issue, which was the debate about the Presidency of the EU. This at times bordered on the arcane, and much of the discussion was redolent of a 'milliner's' tale: the talk was of one hat, two hats, shared hats and the like. This should not mask the issues of real power that were at stake. Two main positions were staked out.

A prominent version of the 'single hat' view was that there should be one President for the Union as a whole; the office of President should be connected formally and substantively with the locus of executive power within the Union; and the President of the Commission should hold this office. The Presidency of the European Council should continue to rotate on a six-monthly basis. The real 'head' of the Union would be the President of the Commission, whose legitimacy it was hoped would be increased by election.

A prominent version of the 'separate hats' view was that there should be a President of the Commission and a President of the European Council, and that executive power would be exercised by both. It was central to this view that the Presidency of the European Council would be strengthened. It would no longer rotate between States on a six-monthly basis. It was felt that this would not work within an enlarged Union, and that greater continuity of policy would be required. This view was advocated by a number of the larger States, but was opposed by some of the smaller States, which felt that the Presidency of the European Council would be dominated by the larger Member States.

The Convention proceedings were influenced by the external discourse on this issue. The membership of the Convention altered in late autumn 2002, with the 'invasion of the foreign ministers',[15] the French and German foreign ministers

---

[14] G Grevi, 'The Europe We Need: An Integrated Presidency for a United Europe' (European Policy Centre, December 2002) 5.

[15] P Norman, *The Accidental Constitution, The Making of Europe's Constitutional Treaty* (Euro-Comment, 2nd edn, 2005) 129.

joined the Convention, followed by those from some other countries. Change inside the Convention was matched by political developments outside its portals. The larger Member States, Spain, the UK, and France, made it clear that they subscribed to the 'separate hats' view. The idea of a longer-term strengthened Presidency of the European Council was central to the 'ABC' view, expressed by Aznar, Blair, and Chirac.[16] In January 2003 Germany was brought on board. This was made clear in a Franco-German paper, in which Germany accepted the long-term Presidency of the European Council, the *quid pro quo* being that France accepted that the Commission President should be elected.[17]

The Franco-German paper, combined with the 'ABC' view, shaped developments inside the Convention in early 2003. It provoked a fierce reaction from the smaller States, which saw the idea of long-term Presidency of the European Council as encroaching on the power of the Commission President, and as leading to acrimony and stalemate between the two Presidents.[18] While the revolt of the smaller States appeared to have dealt the Franco-German proposals a serious blow, it was nonetheless the case that the 'joint proposals were to be the template for all future discussions on the institutional settlement'.[19]

Giscard d'Estaing may well have inclined to the views of the larger Member States. The Franco-German paper, combined with the opinions of the UK and Spain, nonetheless had a marked impact on his thinking. He was not about to produce a Draft Constitution with key provisions about the institutional disposition of power that were opposed by the larger Member States. The announcement of the provisions on the Presidency of the European Council was nonetheless dramatic. The proposals were leaked to the press on 22 April 2003, just as he was unveiling them to the Praesidium. The proposals 'provoked shock and awe in about equal measure, particularly among the integrationist Convention members from the European Parliament and some of the smaller Member States'.[20] It is safe to say that they were not welcomed by the Commission either.

The 'shock and awe' provoked by Giscard's proposals was explicable because they not only provided for an extended Presidency of the European Council, which was to be the highest authority of the Union, but also for a 'board' of seven including a Vice-President, the EU Foreign Minister, two other members of the European Council, plus the Presidents of Ecofin and the Justice and Home Affairs Council. This reconfigured European Council was to have its own bureaucracy.[21] The 'most developed' form of these proposals did not survive long within the Convention. Substantial parts hit the 'cutting room floor' and

---

[16] ibid 110–111.   [17] ibid 143–144.   [18] ibid 148–149.   [19] ibid 149.
[20] P Norman, 'From the Convention to the IGC (Institutions)' (Federal Trust, September 2003) 3; Norman (n 15) 189–192.
[21] Norman (n 15) 190.

those opposed to the 'separate hats' view congratulated themselves on curbing the Giscardian vision.

The result as expressed in the Constitutional Treaty nonetheless embodied the central feature of the 'separate hats' view. Article I-22(1) CT stipulated that the European Council shall elect a President, by qualified majority, for two and half years, renewable once. This same provision has been carried over into the Lisbon Treaty and is now contained in Article 15(5) TEU.

(b) The President(s) of the Union: power and authority

The victory for the 'separate hats' view is only part of the story. Article 15(5) tells us that there is going to be a long-term President of the European Council. It tells us nothing about the division of power between the President of the Commission and the President of the European Council. The nature of their respective powers *de jure* and *de facto* would be crucial in shaping executive power within the EU. It is therefore unsurprising that there was much contestation as to the powers of the President of the European Council. It is only through an understanding of the contending proposals that one can appreciate the provisions that were finally agreed on in the Lisbon Treaty.

(i) The far-reaching vision: the UK paper and the Giscardian vision

A vision of the powers of the President of the European Council emerged from what Grevi has termed a non-paper leaked by the UK Government in January 2003.[22] This paper envisioned the President of the European Council preparing and controlling its agenda; developing jointly with the Commission President the multi-annual strategic agenda; being head of the Council Secretariat that would become 'his administration'; chairing the General Affairs Council (GAC); supervising the work of sectoral Council formations; approving agendas for sectoral Councils; chairing trialogue meetings with the Commission and the European Parliament; attendance at Commission meetings as observer when the President of the European Council so decided; 'ownership' of major summits with great powers; coordination and supervision on aspects of crisis management and defence.[23]

A similarly expansive view of the European Council and the role of its President were apparent in the original version of the institutional proposals submitted by Giscard d'Estaing to the Convention in April 2003.[24] The European Council was characterized as the 'highest authority of the Union', to be chaired by the long-term President who would hold the post for two and half years, renewable once. The President would 'prepare, chair and drive' its work,

---

[22] G Grevi, 'Options for Government of the Union' (Federal Trust, March 2003) 6.
[23] Norman (n 15) 112.   [24] ibid 190–194.

represent the EU to the outside world, and the GAC would be chaired by the
Vice-President of the European Council. The President of the European Council
would be supported by a board, composed of the President, Vice-President, two
members of the European Council, the EU foreign Minister, and the chairs of
the ECOFIN Council and the Council on Justice and Security. This schema
thereby provided for the European Council to be highest authority within the
EU, to be run by a powerful cabinet, which would be chaired by its new
President. It is unsurprising that these proposals provoked fierce criticism,[25]
more especially because they were part of a package of institutional provisions
that diminished the role of the Commission and upset pre-established orthodoxy
on qualified majority voting in the Council. The original version of Giscard's
proposals survived for barely 24 hours, and revised drafts were produced by the
Praesidium, which significantly modified the earlier schema.

(ii) The limited vision: the Commission and the IGC

The power accorded to the European Council and its President continued to be
debated in the intergovernmental conference (IGC) convened to consider the
draft Constitutional Treaty produced by the Convention.

The Commission had, not surprisingly, been opposed to the idea of a long-
term Presidency of the European Council. When it became clear that this was
embodied in the draft Constitutional Treaty produced by the Convention, the
Commission focused its efforts in the subsequent IGC on limiting the power and
authority that would be wielded by the new President. Thus the Commission
stated that despite its reservations about the Presidency of the European Council
'the Commission does not propose to bring into question the compromise which
the Convention reached after prolonged debate'.[26] It nonetheless expended
considerable efforts in constraining the powers of the new Presidency.

It was vital, said the Commission, to maintain the balance of the President of
the European Council's role defined by the Convention.[27] It argued that any
extension of the President's duties beyond chairing meetings of the European
Council and representing the Union in relation to the Common Foreign and
Security Policy (CFSP) 'would inevitably change the institutional architecture
agreed in the Convention and create confusion as to how responsibility was
shared'.[28] The President of the European Council should not organize the work
of the Council, since a person 'who is not accountable for his/her action to any
parliamentary assembly cannot exert influence over the modus operandi of the

---

[25] ibid 194–195.
[26] A Constitution for the Union, Opinion of the Commission, pursuant to Art 48 of the Treaty
on European Union, on the Conference of Representatives of the Member States' governments
convened to revise the Treaties, COM(2003) 548 final, [14].
[27] ibid [14].   [28] ibid [14].

Council, which is supposed to be transparent and democratic'.[29] The extension of judicial review to acts of the European Council was a further element in the Commission's strategy for limiting its power.[30]

(iii) *A* via media: *the Lisbon Treaty*

The provisions concerning the distribution of power between the President of the European Council and the President of the Commission that finally emerged in the Constitutional Treaty were largely taken over into the Lisbon Treaty. They are central to the division of executive power, but are not, however, simple to divine.[31]

We can begin with the legal provisions relating to the European Council. These contain a subtle modification of established orthodoxy. Prior to the Lisbon Treaty Article 4 EU stated that the European Council shall provide the Union with the necessary impetus for its development and shall define the general political guidelines thereof. This has been modified by Article 15(1) TEU, which states that the European Council shall provide the Union with the necessary impetus for its development, and shall define its general political directions *and priorities*. It is the addition of the reference to priorities that is the formal novelty in Article 15(1) TEU. This is subject to the caveat that the European Council does not exercise legislative functions.

Article 15(6) TEU specifies the powers of the President of the European Council. It states that the President shall chair the European Council and drive forward its work; shall ensure preparation and continuity of the European Council's work with the President of the Commission, and on the basis of the work of the GAC; shall endeavour to facilitate cohesion and consensus within the European Council; and shall present a report to the European Parliament after each of its meetings; and the President shall ensure the external representation of the EU on issues concerning its CFSP, without prejudice to the responsibilities of the High Representative.

The provisions concerning the Council, and its relationship with the European Council, are also vital for an understanding of the President's powers. The original Giscardian proposals for the European Council provided, as we have seen, for a crucial overlap with the Council, since the Presidents of Ecofin and the Justice and Home Affairs Council were to be members of the European Council. This would have enabled the European Council and its President to exert a direct influence on the workings of important Council formations, more especially because the original Giscardian proposals provided for the Vice-President of the European Council to chair the GAC.

---

[29] ibid [14].   [30] ibid [14] fn 6.
[31] House of Lords, Select Committee on the European Union, The Future of Europe—The Convention's Draft Constitutional Treaty (HL 169; 2003) [153].

The Lisbon Treaty does not encapsulate the degree of power for the European Council within the Council as envisaged either by the Giscardian or UK proposals. It is for the European Council acting by qualified majority to adopt the list of Council configurations,[32] although pending this decision, the GAC, acting pursuant to transitional provisions in the Lisbon Treaty, produced a list of Council formations.[33] It is nonetheless clear from Articles 16(6) and 16(9) TEU that the Presidency of the Council configurations, other than Foreign Affairs, is to be held by Member States on the basis of the team Presidency, and a draft Decision to this effect was appended to the Lisbon Treaty.[34] This was to meet the fears of the smaller States that a long-term Presidency of the European Council would lead to domination by the larger States. The draft Decision setting out the team Presidencies has now been acted on.[35]

The essence of the scheme is that the Presidency of the Council, with the exception of the Foreign Affairs configuration, is held by pre-established groups of three Member States for a period of 18 months. The groups are composed on the basis of equal rotation among the Member States, taking into account their diversity and geographical balance within the Union. Each member of the group in turn chairs for a six-month period all configurations of the Council, with the exception of the Foreign Affairs configuration. The other members of the group assist the Chair in its responsibilities on the basis of a common programme. It is open to members of the team to decide alternative arrangements among them-selves. The scheme also makes provision for chairing of preparatory bodies.[36] A Decision has been made by the Council to implement the regime on team Presidencies,[37] and the Council has modified its Rules of Procedure to accord with the new modalities.[38]

The influence of the European Council, and hence its President, is nonetheless still apparent within the Council. It is, as we have seen, the European Council that adopts the decision establishing the Council configurations,[39] and the Presidency of those configurations, in accordance with criteria in the Treaty.[40]

---

[32] Art 236 TFEU.

[33] Council of the European Union, 16520/09, 26 November 2009. The formations are: General Affairs; Foreign Affairs; Economic and Financial Affairs; Justice and Home Affairs; Employment, Social Policy, Health and Consumer Affairs; Competitiveness (Internal Market, Industry and Research); Transport, Telecommunications and Energy; Agriculture and Fisheries; Environment; Education, Youth and Culture.

[34] Declaration 9 LT.

[35] Council of the European Union, 16534/1/09, 27 November 2009.

[36] Coreper is chaired by a representative of the Member State chairing the GAC. The Chair of the Political and Security Committee is held by a representative of the High Representative of the Union for Foreign Affairs and Security Policy. The chair of the preparatory bodies of the various Council configurations, with the exception of the Foreign Affairs configuration, is normally held by the member of the group chairing the relevant configuration.

[37] Council of the European Union, 16517/09, 30 November 2009.

[38] Council of the European Union, 16183/09, 17 November 2009.

[39] Art 236(1) TFEU.

[40] Art 16(9) TEU, Art 236(2) TFEU.

The relationship between the European Council and the GAC is especially significant. Article 16(6) TEU provides that the GAC is to ensure consistency in the work of different Council configurations. It also prepares and ensures follow-up to meetings of the European Council, in liaison with the Commission and the President of the European Council.

This is significant because of the centrality of the GAC to the functioning of the Council.[41] The obligation cast upon the GAC to prepare and ensure follow-up to meetings of the European Council provides the latter, and hence its President, with an important power. It was of course the case that even prior to the Lisbon Treaty the 'conclusions' reached by the European Council would frame detailed deliberations in the Council and in the Commission.[42] This was especially so where the European Council expressed specific policy objectives, as was increasingly common. Article 16(6) TEU is significant nonetheless. It creates a cognizable legal obligation on the GAC to ensure that the European Council's conclusions are followed up. It creates a more formal mechanism than hitherto for the European Council to influence the priorities of the EU. It may enable it to press for legislation on specific issues, where this is necessary to effectuate conclusions reached by the European Council. The formal right of legislative initiative would remain with the Commission. The obligation on the GAC to ensure that the meetings of the European Council are followed up may nonetheless require legislation on specific issues deliberated on by the European Council.

The influence of the President of the European Council is also apparent in the proximate connection between the holder of this office and the regime of team Presidencies of the Council. Thus it is not fortuitous that the background briefing to a meeting of the GAC held on 7 December 2009, which dealt with the 18-month programme of the Spanish, Belgian, and Hungarian delegations for January 2010 to June 2011, stated that the programme would require close cooperation with the new President of the European Council and the High Representative.[43] This is evident once again in the new Council Rules of Procedure, which emphasize more generally that the draft 18-month programme of the three Member States taking on the Presidency of the Council is to be prepared in close cooperation with the Commission, the President of the European Council, and with the President of the Foreign Affairs Council with regard to that configuration's activities during that period.[44]

---

[41] F Hayes-Renshaw and H Wallace, *The Council of Ministers* (Macmillan, 2nd edn, 2006) 36–42.

[42] S Bulmer and W Wessels, *The European Council* (Macmillan, 1987); P de Schoutheete and H Wallace, *The European Council* (Notre Europe, 2002); P Ludlow, *The Making of the New Europe: The European Council in Brussels and Copenhagen 2002* (EuroComment, 2004); P de Schoutheete, 'The European Council' in J Peterson and M Shackleton (eds), *The Institutions of the European Union* (Oxford University Press, 2nd edn, 2006) ch 3.

[43] Background, 2984th General Affairs Council, 7 December 2009.

[44] Council Rules of Procedure (n 38) Art 2(6).

We shall return to the inter-institutional balance of power and the way in which the Presidents of the European Council and Commission are likely to interrelate after considering the other major changes that affect the disposition of executive power in the EU.

3. The High Representative of the Union for Foreign Affairs and Security Policy

There were debates in the Convention on the Future of Europe as to the changes that should be made concerning institutional responsibility for external relations.[45] These will be considered more fully below.[46] Suffice it to say for the present that the Constitutional Treaty created the post of EU Minister for Foreign Affairs, who was to 'conduct' the Union's common foreign and security policy.[47] The idea that executive power within the Union was divided between the European Council and the Commission was personified in this post. The Minister for Foreign Affairs was appointed by the European Council by qualified majority, with the agreement of the Commission President.[48] The EU foreign minister was one of the Vice-Presidents of the Commission, and was responsible for handling external relations and for coordinating other aspects of the Union's external action.[49] The EU Foreign Minister therefore wore a 'shared hat'. The holder of the office was to take part in the work of the European Council,[50] chair the Foreign Affairs Council,[51] and was also a Vice-President of the Commission.

The nomenclature changed in the Lisbon Treaty, but the substance remains the same. The rationale for the change was that some Member States were unhappy about the 'statist' connotations of the title 'EU Minister for Foreign Affairs',[52] and hence it was altered in the Lisbon Treaty to be High Representative of the Union for Foreign Affairs and Security Policy.[53] The substance of the provisions concerning the High Representative in the Lisbon Treaty is, however, the same as that in the Constitutional Treaty. Thus the High Representative is appointed by the European Council by qualified majority, with the agreement of the Commission President.[54] The incumbent is one of the Vice-Presidents of the Commission, and is responsible for handling external relations and for coordinating other aspects of the Union's external action.[55] The holder of the office takes part in the work of the European Council,[56] chairs

---

[45] CONV 459/02, Final Report of Working Group VII on External Action, Brussels, 16 December 2002, 19–23.
[46] Ch 10.   [47] Art I-28 CT.
[48] Art I-28(1) CT.   [49] Art I-28(4) CT.
[50] Art I-21(2) CT.   [51] Art I-28(4) CT.
[52] Brussels European Council, 21–22 June 2007, Annex 1, [3].
[53] Art 18 TEU.   [54] Art 18(1) TEU.
[55] Art 18(4) TEU.   [56] Art 15(2) TEU.

the Foreign Affairs Council,[57] and is also a Vice-President of the Commission. The High Representative therefore wears 'two hats', or perhaps three if one regards the role of chairing the Foreign Affairs Council as distinctive from the functions performed within the European Council and Commission.

The idea that executive power within the Union is shared between the European Council and the Commission is clearly personified in this post. The inter-institutional implications of the positions accorded to the High Representative will be considered below.

4. The Commission

(a) The Commission President: election and legitimacy

An issue of significance for executive power in the EU concerned the method of choosing the Commission President. The Commission had hitherto generally been opposed to the idea that its President should be elected, fearing the politicization that might result. Its attitude changed, however, by the time that the Convention deliberated. An important consideration inclining the Commission towards election was that this would enhance the legitimacy of the Commission President, thereby strengthening his claim to be President of the Union as a whole, or at the very least providing grounds for resisting the grant of far-reaching powers to the President of the European Council. Norman captures related sentiments at work.[58]

For its advocates, election of the Commission President by the European Parliament would kill several birds with one stone. It would increase the democratic legitimacy of the Commission and so, it was argued, strengthen it as an institution. Election by the Parliament would enhance its own role, and could generate some positive spin-off in terms of greater voter interest in the European Parliament elections. As a properly elected office holder, the Commission President should also enjoy more clout in the European Council, where he (and it has always been 'he' so far) is the only non-elected leader. All three consequences would be good news for integrationists. It was thus unsurprising that the election of the Commission President was strongly supported by most MEPs and representatives of smaller governments and by Germany, the most federally inclined of the big Member States.

The Commission's contribution to the debate concerning the emerging institutional architecture for the EU was timely, appearing in December 2002, just before the Convention discourse on institutions was set to begin in January 2003. Its vision for the method of choosing the Commission President featured prominently in this document.[59] The Commission argued that its responsibility

---

[57] Art 18(3) TEU.   [58] Norman (n 15) 120–121.
[59] CONV 448/02, For the European Union Peace, Freedom, Solidarity—Communication from the Commission on the Institutional Architecture, 5 December 2002, [2.3]; Peace, Freedom and Solidarity, COM(2002) 728 final.

for setting out the general interests of the Union meant that it must derive its political legitimacy from the European Council and the European Parliament, and therefore recommended that both should be involved in the appointment. The Commission proposed that its President should be elected by the European Parliament, subject to approval by the European Council. The Commission urged that in order that it could retain the necessary independence in relation to national and partisan interests, the Treaty should specify the procedure whereby the European Parliament could put any candidacy for the Commission Presidency to the vote and also specify that the vote should take place under a secret ballot with a two-thirds majority of MEPs required. It also made recommendations for appointment of other members of the Commission. These should be designated by the Council, acting by qualified majority in agreement with the Commission President, subject to approval of the full College of Commissioners by the European Parliament.

The solution ultimately adopted in the Constitutional Treaty brought a sharp dose of political reality to the debate. The European Parliament was in favour of an indirectly elected Commission President. However, it was always doubtful whether the Member States would be willing to accept a regime in which they surrendered control over the Commission Presidency to the European Parliament. The Member States were, unsurprisingly, not willing to surrender this power. They were not willing for just any candidate to be considered for the post and desired greater control over appointment of the Commission President than the mere approval that was embodied in the Commission proposal considered above.

The 'solution' in the Constitutional Treaty[60] was carried over directly into the Lisbon Treaty. Thus Article 14(1) TEU duly states that the European Parliament shall elect the President of the Commission. The retention of State power, however, is apparent in Article 17(7) TEU. The European Council, acting by qualified majority, after appropriate consultation,[61] and taking account of the elections to the European Parliament, puts forward to the European Parliament the European Council's candidate for Presidency of the Commission. This candidate shall then be elected by the European Parliament by a majority of its members. If the candidate does not get the requisite majority support, then the European Council puts forward a new candidate within one month, following the same procedure. Thus while there had been some limited support for the idea that the Commission President should be directly elected, the argument being that this would help to foster a European demos, the result is that the Commission President is indirectly-indirectly elected.

---

[60] Arts I-20(1), 27(1) CT.
[61] Declaration 11 LT emphasizes consultation between the European Council and European Parliament preceding choice of the candidate for Commission President.

It will be interesting to see the consequences of the new regime. There were some who felt that indirect election would not markedly affect the *modus operandi* of the Commission. It would be very much business as usual, except the Commission would have added legitimacy from election of its President. There were others who accepted that election would significantly alter the character of the Commission. They acknowledged that election would lead to politicization, since an indirectly elected President would be likely to have a more prominent political platform or agenda than hitherto. They nonetheless regarded such a development with equanimity. They argued that the legislative and executive powers of the Commission inevitably entailed political choices. The exercise of these powers could not be politically neutral, any more than it could in domestic polities. It was then better for this to be out in the open. This would moreover have the virtue of securing a greater link between power and responsibility than had been the case previously.

There is almost certainly something to be said for both sides of this argument. The very fact that the Commission President is indirectly elected means that in reality the 'candidate' will have to secure the support of the dominant grouping within the European Parliament. Thus President Barroso was the official candidate of the European People's Party, when he secured re-election in autumn 2009.[62] This means that the prospective incumbent will increasingly have to present some form of political platform or agenda for the term of office. The President of the Commission would, moreover, under the draft of the Constitutional Treaty presented to the IGC, have exercised some real control over the choice of Commissioners, since it was for the President to choose from a list of three names presented by each Member State. He could therefore have fashioned a Commission that cohered with his political credo, and that of the dominant grouping within the European Parliament, while at the same time being mindful of the need to satisfy the different political groupings represented within the EU as a whole.[63]

There remain, however, real limits to the extent to which the voters will be able even indirectly to 'throw out' incumbents of political office they dislike. The voters' inability to do this at present is one aspect of the critique concerning the EU's democratic deficit. While the indirect election of the Commission President goes some way to alleviate this concern, it does not remove it.[64] The Commission President may be *primus inter pares*, but the other Commissioners will, under the Lisbon Treaty, be chosen by the Member States, albeit in common accord with the President-elect of the Commission.[65] They will have diverse political backgrounds/beliefs and Commission policy will have to be

---

[62] <http://www.euractiv.com/en/future-eu/barroso-elected-lisbon-majority/article-185513>.

[63] Art I-26(2) Draft CT. For some more recent indications of increasing politicization within the Commission, see <http://www.euractiv.com/en/future-eu/eu-leaders-shape-commission-coalition-government/article-188233>.

[64] pp 71–75.   [65] Art 17(7) TEU.

acceptable to the College of Commissioners as a whole. The Commission, moreover, does not have a monopoly over the direction of EU policy, with the European Council and Council both being important institutional players in this respect.

It will also be interesting to see whether the regime in the Lisbon Treaty leads to pressure on the Commission's 'gold standard', its near monopoly of legislative initiative, which is now enshrined in Article 17(2) TEU. It could be argued that the retention of this monopoly will be strengthened by the election of the Commission President, since the incumbent will have the support of those in the European Parliament who voted in his or her favour. The fact that a member of the executive is elected by the legislature does not, however, mean that the latter will accept with equanimity that the executive thus chosen has a legal monopoly over the introduction of legislation. The European Parliament might feel that it has more direct democratic credentials than those of an indirectly elected Commission President, and that it should also have the right to initiate legislation. The nature of such a right would then be a matter for further debate. It might exist in parallel to that exercised by the Commission President, such that the European Parliament could draft its own legislation, which would become law subject to approval from the Council. The European Parliament might alternatively press for a right to initiate legislation that would then be drafted by the Commission. We should not forget that the European Parliament has pressed for a right of legislative initiative in the past. The fact that it has not always done so is explicable on the ground that it wished to prioritize other issues.

(b) The Commission: size and appointment

(i) The Convention: conflicting pressures

There had been considerable debate, going back at least to the Nice Treaty 2000, concerning the overall size of the Commission. In the IGC leading to the Nice Treaty opinion was divided as to whether there should continue to be one Commissioner from each State, or whether there should be an upper limit combined with rotation.[66] The Nice Treaty embodied a compromise. The Protocol on Enlargement provided that from 1 January 2005 Article 213(1) EC should be amended to provide that the Commission should consist of one national from each State. The Council, acting unanimously, could alter the number of members of the Commission. When the Union had 27 Member States Article 213(1) would be further modified such that the number of Commissioners would be less than the number of Member States. The Council, acting on the principle of equality, would adopt a rotation system, and would decide on the number of Commissioners.

---

[66] CONFER 4813/00, Presidency Note, 1 December 2000.

The composition and size of the Commission featured prominently in the Convention deliberations. It came to the fore because of the then pending enlargement. There was, as Norman noted, a paradox in the Convention deliberations, which was rooted in different conceptions of the Commission.[67] The Commission's role as depicted in the original Treaty was a Collegiate body, the guardian of the Treaties, in which individual Commissioners were independent and represented the general Community interest, not that of their own Member States. This vision of the 'platonic, non-national, pan-European Commissioner',[68] however, was shaken by the belief in many of the then future Member States that they should have their own Commissioner to safeguard their national interests. It was also argued by those who held to the vision of the independent Commissioner that the system of one Commissioner per Member State should be retained, since it enhanced the representative nature of the Commission and Member State confidence in its deliberations.[69]

The issue concerning the composition of the Commission was further complicated by the fact that mixed messages were forthcoming from the Commission itself. Thus there was one strand of thought that saw a large Commission as a weak Commission. A body with 25 or 27 Commissioners would cross the line between a collegiate body and a deliberative assembly, such that it would be more difficult to maintain policy coherence and control. This was the view espoused by the Prodi Commission in the wake of the resignation of the Santer Commission in 1999. Commission policy nonetheless remained ambiguous in 2002–2003, with Prodi both supporting the idea of one Commissioner per Member State, while at the same time voicing suggestions for an inner cabinet of senior Commissioners.[70]

The Draft Constitution as it emerged from the Convention on the Future of Europe embodied a compromise. It provided that the Commission should consist of a College comprising the President, the Union Minister for Foreign Affairs, and 13 Commissioners selected on the basis of a rotation system between the Member States.[71] The system of rotation was to be established by a decision of the European Council, on the basis of two principles. There was a State equality principle,[72] which mandated that Member States should be treated on an equal footing as regards the sequence of, and time spent by, their national as Members of the College. There was also a demographic and geographic equality principle, which mandated that subject to the first principle, each

---

[67] Norman (n 15) 118–119.   [68] ibid 119.

[69] J Temple Lang, 'The Commission: The Key to the Constitutional Treaty for Europe' (2003) 26 Fordham ILJ 1598.

[70] CONV 448/02 (n 59) [2.3.2]; Norman (n 15) 228–229.

[71] CONV 850/03, Draft Treaty Establishing a Constitution for Europe, Brussels 18 July 2003, Art I-25(3) Draft CT.

[72] CONV 850/03, Art I-25(3)(a) Draft CT.

successive College of Commissioners should be so composed as to reflect satisfactorily the demographic and geographical range of all Member States.[73] These
provisions of the Draft Constitution reflected the view that there should be a
small Commission, with a number of Commissioners that was less than that
of the Member States. However, this was undermined by the provision that
the Commission President should appoint non-voting Commissioners from all
the other Member States.

(ii) Commission response: opposition and modification

The 'solution' embodied in the Draft Constitution was problematic. It would
have created a two-tier Commission, with voting and non-voting Commissioners. This would have been the worst of all possible worlds. It would not
have produced a coherent, smaller Commission, since the views of the non-
voting Commissioners would inevitably have had a major impact even if they did
not have the vote in the College. Moreover, it would necessarily have produced
tensions between the two groups, since non-voting Commissioners could still
head a particular Directorate-General (DG) within the Commission. A non-
voting Commissioner might therefore have developed a legislative initiative, but
have no formal vote within the College. This would have led to considerable
tensions, which would have been exacerbated if the College had rejected the
proposal or suggested modifications when the Commissioner responsible was not
able to vote.

It is therefore not surprising that the Commission expressed its opposition in
the strongest possible terms. The sharpness of the Commission response had an
added 'edge', which should be viewed against the backdrop of the increasingly
strained relationship between Giscard d'Estaing and Romano Prodi, depicted
by Norman as the 'dialogue of the deaf'.[74]

The Commission certainly did not hold back, describing the relevant provisions as 'complicated, muddled and inoperable'.[75] It argued that 'if the members
without voting rights manage a portfolio, one cannot see how they could
effectively exercise their responsibilities without being able to participate in the
collective decision'.[76] If they 'don't have a portfolio, one wonders what their role
within the College would be'.[77] The Commission also pointed to significant
issues that were unclear as to the status of non-voting Commissioners.

---

[73] CONV 850/03, Art I-25(3)(b) Draft CT.   [74] Norman (n 15) 229.
[75] COM(2003) 548 final (n 26) [2]; J Rideau, 'Conflits et compromise constitutionnels sur la
composition de la Commission et la vote a la majorité qualifiée au Conseil' in C Kaddous and
A Auer (eds), *Les Principes Fondamentaux de la Constitution Européenne* (Helbing & Lichtman,
Bruylant, LGDF, 2006) 165–179; A Mattera, 'Les zones d'ombre du projet de Constitution dans
l'architecture institutionnelle de l'Union: la composition de la Commission' (2003) Revue du droit
de l'Union européenne 5.
[76] ibid 2.   [77] ibid 2.

The general approach in Part III of the Draft Constitution was that Commissioners given the vote, and those who were not, were otherwise subject to the same responsibilities.[78] This still left open, as the Commission rightly noted, a plethora of issues on which the Draft Constitution was unclear.[79] Thus it was not apparent whether non-voting Commissioners could attend meetings of the College and take part in its discussions. Nor was it clear whether they could take decisions on behalf of the Commission. This latter issue was particularly important, given that only about 3 per cent of approximately 10,000 Commission decisions per annum are made by the College of Commissioners through the 'oral procedure' at its weekly meetings. The great majority of such decisions, approximately 60 per cent, are made either by 'empowerment', whereby a Member of the Commission is empowered to take management decisions on its behalf; or 'delegation', whereby decisions are taken by a Director-General to whom power has been delegated by the Commission.[80]

The Commission's proposed solution was shaped by the politics of the Convention. The constitutional provisions reflected opposition within the Convention to the idea of a small, slimmed-down Commission. This was recognized by the Commission, which was nonetheless strongly opposed to the divide between voting and non-voting Commissioners. The Commission's alternative solution was premised on each Member State having a Commissioner, with the same rights and obligations.[81] Some restructuring of the College would be necessary, however, within an enlarged EU. The way forward was to build on current practice, whereby informal groups of Commissioners deal with related subject matter. The Commission proposed that this should be formalized by structuring the College into a number of groups of Commissioners. The College of Commissioners, which would contain all members of the Commission, would consider only the most important issues.[82] The Commission drafted amendments, which encapsulated its preferred solution.[83] There was much to be said for the Commission's proposal, given that a slimmed-down Commission of 15 Commissioners did not seem acceptable. The proposal was certainly preferable to that in the Draft Constitution.

(iii) Constitutional Treaty and Lisbon Treaty: size of the Commission

The Italian Presidency of the IGC addressed a questionnaire to the Member States, asking whether the two-tier regime of Commissioners proposed by the Convention should be retained.[84] The Irish Presidency of the IGC brokered a

---

[78] CONV 850/03 (n 71) Arts III-250–257 Draft CT.
[79] COM(2003) 548 final (n 26) [3] n3.   [80] ibid Annex 1.
[81] ibid [3].   [82] ibid [4].
[83] ibid Annexes 2 and 3.
[84] Conference of the Representatives of the Governments of the Member States, Preparation of the IGC Ministerial Meeting on 14 October 2003: Questionnaires CIG 6/03, Brussels 7 October 2003.

compromise, which was embodied in the Constitutional Treaty[85] and taken over with some modification into the Lisbon Treaty.

Thus the Commission will, until 31 October 2014, consist of one national from each Member State, including the President and the High Representative for Foreign Affairs.[86] After that date the Commission is to consist of members, including the President and the High Representative for Foreign Affairs, which correspond to two-thirds of the number of Member States,[87] unless the European Council, acting unanimously, decides to alter this number. Member States must be treated on a strictly equal footing as regards determination of the sequence of, and the time spent by, their nationals as members of the Commission, with the consequence that the difference between the total number of terms of office held by nationals of any given pair of Member States may never be more than one. Subject to the preceding point, each successive Commission must be composed so as to reflect satisfactorily the demographic and geographical range of all the Member States.[88] This system is to be established by the European Council.[89]

The basic position in the Lisbon Treaty is therefore that there will be a slimmed down Commission in the medium term, and all members thereof will have voting rights. This is an improvement on the Convention draft, and does not preclude formalization of the present arrangements for groups of Commissioners dealing with related matters.

It is, however, open to the European Council to modify the system that is intended to govern post-1 November 2014, by unanimously voting to alter the number of Commissioners.[90] The European Council could, for example, vote to retain one Commissioner per Member State post-2014, and it has indeed made such a commitment as part of the deal struck with Ireland prior to its second referendum.[91] Thus assuming that the requisite unanimity is forthcoming in the European Council we shall see a continuation of the status quo, with one Commissioner per Member State. This would then mark the 'end' of a long debate that has come full circle, with the new regime being the same as the old. It would not, however, preclude the European Council at some later date from voting unanimously for the slimmed down Commission that is the default position established by Article 17(5) TEU.

---

[85] Art I-26 CT.   [86] Art 17(4) TEU.
[87] Declaration 10 specifies that when the Commission no longer includes nationals of all Member States, the Commission should pay particular attention to the need to ensure full transparency in relations with all Member States, and to ensure that political, social, and economic realities in all Member States are fully taken into account.
[88] Art 17(5) TEU, Art 244 TFEU.   [89] Art 17(7) TEU.
[90] Art 17(5) TEU.   [91] Brussels European Council, 10 July 2009, [I.2].

(iv) Constitutional Treaty and Lisbon Treaty: appointment of the Commission

The IGC also made significant changes to the appointment of the Commissioners. The Convention proposed that the President-elect of the Commission would choose Commissioners from a list of three names put forward by each Member State, and that these would be approved by the European Parliament.[92] Thus the President of the Commission would be in the driving seat as to the choice of the other Commissioners, subject to approval of the entire package by the European Parliament.

Developments since then, however, have 'ratcheted up' Member State input and control over choice of Commissioners. The initial revisions to the Convention Draft were made by the IGC in December 2003, and have been included in the Lisbon Treaty. Member States make suggestions for Commissioners, but it is now the Council, by common accord with the President-elect, that adopts the list of those who are to be Commissioners in accordance with the two principles set out above. The body of Commissioners is then subject to a vote of approval by the European Parliament. However the formal appointment of the Commission is made by the European Council, acting by qualified majority, albeit on the basis of the approval given by the European Parliament.[93]

The difference between the regime in the Draft Constitutional Treaty and that in the Lisbon Treaty is significant, both substantively and symbolically. Member States' influence over the choice of Commissioners has increased, since it is the Council in accord with the President-elect of the Commission that draws up the list of Commissioners. The default position is that individual Member States will therefore continue to choose their own Commissioners. Member State influence is apparent once again symbolically in the fact that the final appointment of the Commission resides with the European Council.

5. Agencies

(a) Agencies: pre-Lisbon

The discussion of EU executive power would be incomplete without mention of EU agencies. Modern democratic polities face a dilemma. The range of issues over which government now has responsibility has increased significantly. It may be decided that that the optimum strategy is not to deal with all such matters 'in house', but rather to create an agency outside of the normal departmental structure. This might be felt to be better for a number of reasons.[94] It facilitates

---

[92] Art I-26(2) Draft CT.   [93] Art 17(5) TEU.

[94] D Hague, W Mackenzie and A Barker (eds), *Public Policy and Private Interests: The Institutions of Compromise* (MacMillan, 1975) 362; Report on Non-Departmental Public Bodies, Cmnd 7797

the use of experts who are not part of the normal bureaucratic structure. It frees up the parent department so as to enable it to concentrate on strategic policy. It insulates the resolution of technical regulatory issues from the vagaries of day-to-day political change and hence increases the credibility of the choices thus made.[95] It would be a mistake to think of agencies as a modern creation. They have existed in, for example, the UK for over two centuries.[96]

It is nonetheless the case that there has been a considerable increase in the use of agencies over the last two decades. This has been linked with the regulatory State hypothesis advanced by Majone.[97] On this view the principal State function in the modern era is the correction of market failure through rule making. He argues that in the positive State the main institutions were Parliament, government departments, and State-owned industry, with the primary political actors being political parties and civil servants. In the regulatory State by way of contrast the main institutions are said to be parliamentary committees and regulatory agencies, with the primary actors being regulators, experts, and courts. Indirect political accountability replaces more traditional direct forms of holding government to account. Thus 'regulatory politics combines a rule-bound legalistic policy style, a pluralist political culture and indirect political accountability'.[98] The regulatory State thesis was undoubtedly fuelled by the changing patterns of government in many European countries over the last two decades, with privatization of previously nationalized industry and the creation of regulatory bodies to oversee the new market structures.[99] Further research on countries in Europe has found much to substantiate the claims about the 'regulatory State', with many instances of privatization, liberalization, and delegation to regulatory agencies and a shift away from State ownership. The research also revealed, however, that several features of the regulatory State were absent or only partially

(1980), [10]–[16]; R Baldwin and C McCrudden, *Regulation and Public Law* (Weidenfeld & Nicolson, 1987) ch 1; M Thatcher and A Stone Sweet, 'Theory and Practice of Delegation to Non-Majoritarian Institutions' (2002) 25 West European Politics 1.

[95] G Majone, 'Temporal Consistency and Policy Credibility: Why Democracies Need Non-Majoritarian Institutions' Working Paper RSC No 96/57, Florence EUI; F Gilardi, 'Policy Credibility and Delegation to Independent Regulatory Agencies: A Comparative Empirical Analysis' (2002) 9 JEPP 873.

[96] D Roberts, *Victorian Origins of the British Welfare State* (Yale University Press, 1960); Sir N Chester, *The English Administrative System 1780–1870* (Clarendon Press, 1981); H Parris, *Constitutional Bureaucracy, The Development of British Central Administration in the Eighteenth Century* (Allen & Unwin, 1969).

[97] G Majone, 'The Rise of the Regulatory State in Europe' (1994) 17 West European Politics 77; G Majone, *Regulating Europe* (Routledge, 1996); G Majone, 'From the Positive to the Regulatory State: Causes and Consequences of Changes in the Mode of Governance' (1997) 17 Jnl of Public Policy 139.

[98] M Thatcher, 'Analysing Regulatory Reform in Europe' (2002) 9 JEPP 859, 867.

[99] J Vickers and G Yarrow, *Privatization, An Economic Analysis* (MIT Press, 1988).

present and that there was some real diversity across countries and across different policy areas.[100]

The fact that the EU should be beset by similar problems should not come as a surprise. We saw in the previous chapter that the need for the Council to delegate power to the Commission was recognized in the original Rome Treaty. Not all matters could be dealt with through the standard process for the making of Community legislation, particularly when they concerned, for example, the detailed regulation of agriculture, where fast reaction to the exigencies of the market was of the essence. The Council, however, became unwilling to hand over a blank cheque to the Commission. It wished to have some control over the detail of the delegated norms, over and above any control that it could exert through the enabling regulation. This signalled the birth of the management and regulatory committees, an institutionalized mechanism for allowing national, normally technocratic interests, to have input into these norms. It was these committees that formed the core of what has become known as Comitology.

More recently the institutional structure of the Community has been further developed through the creation of agencies.[101] The initial two were established in 1975 and many others have been created since then. They deal with areas as diverse as air safety, medicines, border control, food safety, maritime safety, environment, trade marks, and fundamental rights,[102] and are also used in the Second[103] and Third Pillar.[104] It is unsurprising that a number of the factors that led to the choice of agencies in Nation States have also been of relevance in the

---

[100] Thatcher (n 98) 867–869; V Schmidt, 'Europeanization and the Mechanics of Economic Policy Adjustment' (2002) 9 JEPP 894.

[101] G Greco, 'Le agenzie comunitarie: aspetti procedimentali e giurisdizionali della tutela degli interessati' (1997) Riv It Dir Pub Com 27; C Franchini, 'Le relazioni tra le agenzie europee e le autorità amministrative nazionali?' (1997) Riv It Dir Pub Com 15; A Kreher, 'Agencies in the European Community—A Step towards Administrative Integration in Europe' (1997) 4 JEPP 225; M Shapiro, 'The Problems of Independent Agencies in the United States and the European Union' (1997) 4 JEPP 276; R Dehousse, 'Regulation by Networks in the European Community: The Role of European Agencies' (1997) 4 JEPP 246; E Chiti, 'The Emergence of a Community Administration: The Case of European Agencies' (2000) 37 CMLRev 309; G Majone, 'Delegation of Regulatory Powers in a Mixed Polity' (2002) 8 ELJ 319; D Keleman, 'The Politics of "Eurocratic" Structure and the New European Agencies' (2002) 25 West European Politics 93; E Chiti, 'Decentralisation and Integration into the Community Administrations: A New Perspective on European Agencies' (2004) 10 ELJ 402; D Geradin and N Petit, 'The Development of Agencies at EU and National Levels: Conceptual Analysis and Proposals for Reform' Jean Monnet Working Paper 01/04, NYU School of Law; T Groß, 'Die Kooperation zwischen europäischen Agenturen und nationalen Behörden' (2005) EuR 54; P Craig, *EU Administrative Law* (Oxford University Press, 2006) ch 5; Curtin (n 2) ch 6; E Chiti, 'Les agences, l'administration indirecte et la coadministration' in J Bernard-Auby and J Dutheil de la Rochere (eds), *Droit Administratif Européen* (Bruylant, 2007) 267–282; T Zwart, 'La poursuite du père Meroni pourquoi les agences pourraient jouer un rôle plus en vue dans l'Union européenne' in J Dutheil de la Rochere (ed), *L'execution du droit de l'Union, entre mécanismes communautaires et droits nationaux* (Bruylant, 2009) 159–173.

[102] <http://europa.eu/agencies/community_agencies/index_en.htm>.

[103] <http://europa.eu/agencies/security_agencies/index_en.htm>.

[104] <http://europa.eu/agencies/pol_agencies/index_en.htm>.

EU. Thus the Commission in its Communication on Agencies stated that they 'would make the executive more effective at European level in highly specialized technical areas requiring advanced expertise and continuity, credibility and visibility of public action'.[105] It continued in the following vein, claiming that 'the main advantage of using the agencies is that their decisions are based on purely technical considerations of very high quality and are not influenced by political or contingent considerations'.[106] The Commission also emphasized the value of agencies in enabling the Commission to focus on its core function of policy formation, with the agencies implementing this policy in specific technical areas.[107]

(b) Agencies: post-Lisbon

The inter-institutional ramifications of the Lisbon Treaty in relation to agencies will be considered below.[108] The present discussion focuses directly on the changes made in positive law in the Lisbon Treaty as they impact on agencies.

The EC Treaty contained scant reference to agencies, notwithstanding their growing significance within the EU institutional architecture. The general strategy in the Lisbon Treaty has been to revise the relevant provisions so as to make express reference to agencies. Thus the Treaty rules relating to judicial review concerning direct review for legality, review for inaction, and the plea of illegality have been modified so as to make express reference to agencies,[109] and analogous changes have been made to the regime for preliminary rulings, allowing references concerning the validity or interpretation of acts of the institutions, bodies, offices, or agencies of the Union.[110] Similar changes have been made to the Treaty provisions concerning transparency,[111] data protection,[112] the Ombudsman,[113] and the Court of Auditors.[114]

These changes are to be welcomed, and will be examined in more detail in the chapter concerning the EU courts.[115] It should nonetheless be recognized that the Lisbon Treaty did not touch the real issues of executive power and inter-institutional relations as they pertain to agencies. These are central to the workings of executive power in the post-Lisbon world and will be examined in the course of the subsequent analysis.

6. The Post-Lisbon World: The Disposition of Executive Power

The Treaty deliberations concerning executive power were, as we have seen, contentious and complex. Shared executive power won the day. The rest, as they

---

[105] The Operating Framework for the European Regulatory Agencies, COM(2002) 718 final, 5.
[106] ibid 5.   [107] ibid 2.
[108] pp 113–115.   [109] Arts 263, 265, 277 TFEU.
[110] Art 267 TFEU.   [111] Art 15 TFEU.   [112] Art 16 TFEU.
[113] Art 228 TFEU.   [114] Art 287 TFEU.   [115] Ch 4.

say, is history. It is nonetheless important to stand back and consider this picture of executive power in the EU.

(a) The argument against shared executive power

The principal argument against divided executive power was based on the simple proposition that two Presidents of the Union is one President too many. There should as a matter of principle be one locus of executive power within the Union, by parity of reasoning with domestic polities, and this should be the President of the Commission, who is responsible to the European Parliament.[116] The EU should therefore embrace a more parliamentary-type system, in which there is a single locus of executive power, the holder of which is responsible to the electorate, albeit indirectly through election by the European Parliament. The voters will then be able to express their preferences by changing the composition of the European Parliament, which will impact on the person indirectly elected as the President of the Commission.

The divide in executive power was also deprecated on grounds of clarity and transparency. An aim of the Laeken Declaration was to render EU decision making clearer and simpler. This has not been achieved in relation to executive power. An informed citizen, reading the Lisbon Treaty assiduously, would still find it difficult to understand the distribution of executive power. The lack of clarity as to the respective powers of the two Presidents will, it is argued, lead to confusion of responsibility.

The new Presidency of the European Council has also been opposed on the ground that it would have an adverse impact on the relationship between large and small States, and there is evidence of opposition to this institutional change by some smaller States in the Convention.[117]

(b) The argument for shared executive power

The argument for shared executive power is premised on the nature of the EU. Inter-institutional balance of power, rather than the separation of powers, has always characterized the EU. The major institutions represent different interests, such that it is consonant with principle for executive power to be shared by a body representing State interests, and a body representing the Community interest, each of which is legitimated in different ways. Viewed from this perspective the Lisbon Treaty is a continuation rather than a departure from

---

[116] Devuyst (n 1) 318–320; J Temple Lang, 'The Main Issues after the Convention on the Constitutional Treaty for Europe' (2004) 27 Fordham ILJ 544; Temple Lang (n 69); J Leinen, 'A President of Europe is Not Utopian, it's Practical Politics' Europe's World (Summer 2007), <http://www.europeswOrld.org/EWSettmgs/Article/tabid/78/Default.aspx?Id=14db4079-leb1–4110–9fo3-ed343139403d>.
[117] Norman (n 15) 194–195.

the status quo, since shared executive power was the order of the day both *de jure* and *de facto* under the EC Treaty, even if the nature of the sharing may have altered to some degree under the Lisbon Treaty.

The contention that shared executive power will lead to confusion is based in part on the assumption that it would be a novel development. This does not accord with reality. Executive power in the EU has not hitherto resided in a single institution.[118] It was exercised in part by the Commission, which had a plethora of executive-type functions, including administration of legislative programmes, planning the legislative agenda, negotiation of Treaties with third parties, and framing the budget. The Council[119] and the European Council also wielded executive power prior to the Lisbon Treaty. The European Council was especially important in this respect.[120] The previous Treaties said relatively little about its powers. The reality was that nothing of major importance happened without its approval. It had a say in the legislative agenda, in setting the Union's priorities, and in deciding on the pace and direction of change within the Union. The division of executive power between the Commission and European Council may not be neat, but it has been the reality, especially since the Single European Act 1986 (SEA). Moreover the two institutions have for the last decade worked well symbiotically in developing the Union's agenda.

The attempt to impose a single executive power could have been counterproductive. Thus there might have been real tensions if there had been only one President of the Union, the Commission President, more especially if the incumbent were to have chaired the European Council. The Commission President might be subject to conflicts of interest, resulting from the desire to press the Commission view, while at the same time retaining the confidence of the Member States within the European Council and articulating their views.

It should also be recognized that the consequences said to follow from a single locus of executive power would not have been feasible without radical change in the EU institutional structure. The voters would not have been able to remove those whom they disliked and thereby change policy, because even if the Commission President could be indirectly removed in this manner, that would still leave State representatives in the Council and the European Council, who would continue to have major input into agenda setting.[121]

The critique of shared executive power based on clarity has force. It was always going to be difficult to deliver on this aspiration from the Laeken Declaration in relation to executive power, more especially once it was decided that there would be two Presidents for the EU. The reality is, however, that even if we had opted for the single Presidency located in the Commission, combined with the six-monthly rotation of Presidencies of the European Council, executive power

---

[118] Curtin (n 2); Curtin (n 5).   [119] Hayes-Renshaw and Wallace (n 41) 324–326.
[120] (N 42).   [121] pp 71–74.

would continue to have been divided between the Commission and European Council as it had hitherto. It should moreover be acknowledged that clarity as to executive power in Nation States is also imperfect. A national constitution may 'locate' executive power within a certain institution. This does not mean, however, that the citizen will be clear as to who exercises particular aspects of executive power. The assumption that executive power in Nation States is 'unitary' is often belied by legal and political reality. A more realistic picture would recognize that such power is exercised not only by ministers that form the 'government' plus the 'formal bureaucracy', but also by a plethora of other agencies and firms to which power has been contracted out.

It is moreover not self-evident that smaller States would suffer under the new regime. The suggestion that the new Presidency would somehow inevitably be occupied by a candidate from the larger States has been belied by the first appointment to the post, Herman van Rompuy, the Belgian Prime Minister. There is no reason to believe that smaller States within the European Council will fare less well under the new Presidency as compared to the status quo ante. The approach within the European Council has generally been based on building consensus,[122] and it is not apparent why the concerns of smaller Member States in this process should be accorded lesser status as compared to the status quo ante where the Presidency was held in six-monthly rotations by different Member States. It is true that under the Lisbon regime the smaller States lose the opportunity to chair the European Council for six months, but so too do the larger States. The six-monthly rotation may have had symbolic value for the smaller States, but we should surely keep this in perspective, given that in a Union of 27 States it would only come round every 13 years, and given also that it imposed significant financial and administrative burdens.

The argument for shared executive power also rests on the 'lessons of history'. A constant theme in the EU's history is that institutions have developed, often outside the strict letter of the Treaties, as a response to concerns relating to the institutional balance of power. The European Council began life in this way, as did the Comitology committees. If executive power had been concentrated within a single Presidency of the Commission, and this did not prove acceptable to the Member States, then it could well have led to institutional developments outside the strict letter of the Treaty. Better therefore to recognize and structure shared executive power within the Lisbon Treaty, than have it develop outside this remit.

7. The Post-Lisbon World: The Reality of Shared Executive Power

The Lisbon Treaty embodies a regime in which executive power is shared between the European Council, the Council and the Commission, with agencies

---

[122] Art 15(4) TEU.

also fulfilling executive functions within their assigned areas. This is, as we have seen, a continuation rather than a departure from the status quo, since the legal and political reality under the EC Treaty was that executive power was shared between these players. This does not mean, however, that the precise mode of sharing is the same post-Lisbon as it was hitherto. Nor does it tell us how the component parts of the executive will interrelate in practice in the post-Lisbon world. The 'answers' to these issues will unfold over time. The Treaty provisions will frame the nature of this interrelationship, but they will not be determinative in and of themselves.

(a) Commission, Council, and European Council: priorities and agenda setting

The legal provisions that relate to setting the priorities for the EU and the planning of the overall agenda exemplify the regime of shared executive power in the Lisbon Treaty. These provisions were considered in detail above,[123] but can be briefly summarized here.

(i) Legal frame

The European Council is charged by Article 15(1) TEU with providing the EU with the necessary impetus for its development and defining the EU's general political directions and priorities. This modifies the previous Treaty formulation by mandating that the European Council should define the EU's priorities, as well as its general political direction. This language is mandatory, and the additional task of defining the EU's priorities is not expressly qualified by the adjective 'general'. European Council influence will in addition be apparent through the GAC, since the GAC not only ensures consistency in the work of different Council configurations, but also prepares and ensures follow-up to meetings of the European Council, in liaison with the Commission and the President of the European Council.[124] It is clear, moreover, that the 18-month Council programme devised by the team Presidency will be undertaken in close cooperation with the President of the European Council, the High Representative, and the President of the Commission.[125] The Commission for its part is obliged to initiate the EU's annual and multi-annual programming with a view to achieving inter-institutional agreements.[126] Thus while the Commission is accorded a general right to initiate particular pieces of Union legislation, it also has the duty to initiate the Union's more general programming strategy.

---

[123] pp 85–88.   [124] Art 16(6) TEU.
[125] Background, 2984th General Affairs Council, 7 December 2009; Council Rules of Procedure (n 38) Art 2(6).
[126] Art 17(1) TEU.

(ii) *Political frame*

The legal provisions affirm the regime of shared executive power and are delicately balanced. They frame but do not determine the inter-institutional balance of executive power, which will be decided by political forces. It is likely that the President of the European Council will exert greater influence over priorities and the legislative agenda than before, because the office will be held for up to five years. The incumbent can develop a vision for the EU that was more difficult with the six-monthly rotation system, notwithstanding the reforms made by the Seville European Council, more especially because he will not be preoccupied with running a Nation State at the same time.[127] Successive Presidents of the European Council may also wish to leave a 'legacy' on the EU, in the form of an agenda that they will press for during their term of office. Institutional support will be of importance. The European Council has not hitherto had an institutional support mechanism to rival that of the Commission, but this has not prevented it from exercising real input into the Union's development. The Lisbon Treaty provides that the European Council is to be 'assisted' by the General Secretariat of the Council of Ministers.[128] It would be surprising if this did not blossom into institutional support suited to the needs of the 'new' European Council.

Having said this, it is clear that the Commission, and its President, will continue to be important in setting the EU's overall agenda. It is the Commission that is to initiate the annual and multi-annual programming with the aim of securing inter-institutional agreement, and the Commission President cooperates with the President of the European Council in ensuring the preparation and continuity of the work of the European Council. The Commission President can moreover rely on the force of the Commission bureaucracy.

It is interesting to reflect on the likelihood of conflict or cooperation between the European Council and Commission, more especially in the light of the fears expressed in the Convention proceedings that a regime of two Presidencies would lead to acrimony and stalemate. It is possible that there will be conflict between the European Council and the Commission, redolent of the inter-institutional tensions between the Council and Commission in the late 1960s to 1970s,[129] with the result that coherence would suffer, and any agreed initiatives would be partial and fragmentary. There will doubtless be issues on which the two Presidents disagree, and we should keep a watchful eye on any attempt by the President of the European Council to circumvent or bypass the Commission.

---

[127] This was emphasized by the President of the European Council in a speech to the European Parliament, Brussels, 24 February 2010, PCE 32/10, available at <http://www.european-council.europa.eu/the-president/press-releases-(new).aspx?lang=en>.

[128] Art 235(4) TFEU.

[129] Hayes-Renshaw and Wallace (n 41) ch 7.

There are nonetheless incentives for the Presidents to cooperate and develop a coherent agenda.[130]

First, inter-institutional tension leading to failure to develop a coherent agenda would be detrimental to the EU, a consequence that would be in the interest of neither President. They would both be held responsible irrespective of whether the 'objective reality' was that one was more to blame than the other.

Second, if shared executive power fails the consequences for the two Presidents will be uncertain. They might hope that any future allocation of executive power would be more unequivocally in their favour, but they could not be certain. The only certainty would be that the future disposition of executive power would be uncertain. It might incline towards a single locus of executive responsibility, but the beneficiary would not be readily predictable. It might be the President of the Commission, but it might be the President of the European Council, along the lines of the Giscardian vision presented to the Convention. This uncertainty will be a factor inclining the relevant players to cooperation rather than conflict and intransigence.

Third, the respective 'constituencies' of the President of the European Council and the President of the Commission is likely to be a further factor engendering cooperation. The fear of conflict is based in part on the assumption that each will lead a united team, which will have strongly opposed views. The reality is more complex.

The President of the European Council will undoubtedly occupy a powerful position, and 'enhance a sense of shared direction'.[131] It should nonetheless be recognized that the interests of the President's immediate constituency, viz the Member States, will not be homogenous. We know that the smaller States fear domination by their larger neighbours, and feel that they might be better 'protected' by the Commission. Nor should it be pre-supposed that the larger Member States necessarily have an identity of interest on the substantive direction of EU policy. The priorities that emerge from the European Council are therefore likely to be the result of compromise between the Member States. The European Council may be intergovernmental in institutional terms. It would, however, be a mistake to think that this will necessarily translate into intergovernmentalism and States' rights in relation to the substantive direction of EU policy.

The President of the Commission's 'constituency' under the Lisbon Treaty is equally interesting. The incumbent will have considerable power. However, the President may also face contending pressures from his or her constituency. The indirectly elected President will have to take account of the interests of those in the European Parliament that voted him into office on the promise or

---

[130] This was stressed by the President of the European Council in a speech to the European Parliament (n 127).
[131] ibid 2.

expectation of certain policy initiatives. The Commission President, however, will be wary of alienating those in the European Parliament of a different political persuasion, and wary of offending State interests if the President hopes for a second term. There may also be constraining influences from the other Commissioners. It would be surprising if they did not reflect some real diversity of opinion on the EU's priorities. This diversity will play out in the multi-annual agenda. It will be for the Commission President to balance the legitimating force that this can bring to the EU's agenda, with the need to fulfil the expectations of the European Parliament party or coalition that put him into power.

Fourth, the *modus operandi* of the European Council and Commission in the past is indicative of likely cooperation in the future. They have worked symbiotically and to good effect on many issues, especially since the passage of the SEA. The Commission has frequently fed policy initiatives that it wishes to advance to the European Council, and gained its imprimatur. The Commission's shift in thinking about the strategy for the single market in the 1990s is but one example of this.[132] Winning the European Council's approval for the general direction of policy in a particular area facilitates the Commission's task when fashioning more specific legislation to put that policy into effect. It is to be hoped that this cooperation will not change under the new order, notwithstanding the increased power of the President of the European Council. The interrelationship between Commission and European Council in setting priorities and the multi-annual agenda may indeed lead to greater coherence than hitherto. The European Council's contribution to the overall policy agenda has been real, but somewhat fragmentary and unpredictable, because of the six-month limit on the Presidency. The five-year Presidency of the European Council is intended to allow greater planning and coherence than hitherto.

The final factor in engendering a climate of cooperation rather than conflict is law. The legal provisions of the Lisbon Treaty embody shared executive power. This is not just in the very instantiation of the extended Presidency of the European Council alongside the President of the Commission, but also in their respective powers concerning the setting of priorities and the multi-annual agenda. These powers are delicately balanced in the manner adumbrated above. The European Council has express power to define priorities, while the Commission retains the duty to initiate the multi-annual agenda with a view to securing inter-institutional agreement. Neither side can therefore use the law to argue that it should have exclusive executive power, but both can resort to legal argument to delimit the sphere of executive power possessed by the other.

The discussion thus far has largely concentrated on the inter-institutional relationship between the Commission and the European Council in relation to setting the agenda and the priorities in the post-Lisbon world. However, we should not forget the Council in this respect. We have already seen that

---

[132] P Craig, 'The Evolution of the Single Market' in C Barnard and J Scott (eds), *The Law of the Single European Market, Unpacking the Premises* (Hart, 2002) ch 1.

initiatives have been taken to try to ensure a 'fit' between the Council programme, and that of the Commission and European Council.[133] This aspect of
the inter-institutional triangle with regard to agenda setting and priorities may
yet prove to be the most interesting and unpredictable. The Commission and the
President of the European Council are both there for the medium term. The
Member State is part of a trio of States with responsibility for 18 months, but
holds the Presidency of the Council for six months. It will therefore, as in the
past, seek to prioritize and achieve certain goals within that period, as exemplified
by the Spanish Presidency in the first half of 2010.[134]

The Spanish foreign minister stated in December 2009 that Spain would play
a supporting role to the new President of the European Council and the High
Representative.[135] There can nonetheless be strains with the President of the
European Council and/or the Commission as to the issues that should be
accorded priority during this short six-month time-frame. There can also be
tensions as to who 'represents' the EU, as revealed by the 'disagreement' between
Spain and the President of the European Council as to who should meet
President Obama and where this should take place.[136]

(b) Commission, Council, and European Council: development of policy choices

The discussion thus far has focused on the way in which shared executive power
might operate in relation to the setting of the EU's priorities and the planning of
the agenda. It is equally important to consider how shared power will play out in
relation to the development of policy choices through the Council.

(i) Legal frame

The Council formations and the role of the President of the European Council
therein were considered in the course of the earlier discussion, and in the previous
chapter.[137] It is nonetheless important to draw this together briefly here, more
especially because it was of such importance in the Convention deliberations.

We have already seen that the Giscardian plan, and the UK proposals from
January 2003, accorded the President considerable control over the Council.[138]
These proposals were not incorporated in the draft Constitutional Treaty, which
opted for the system of team Presidencies of the Council.[139] The role of the
President of the European Council within the Council nonetheless continued to

---

[133] See (nn 43–44).
[134] <http://www.eu2010.es/en/index.html?idioma=en>.
[135] <http://www.euractiv.com/en/priorities/spain-vows-take-backstage-role-eu-president/article-188494>.
[136] Independent 3 February 2010.   [137] pp 39–42, pp 86–88.
[138] pp 83–84.   [139] Article I-23 Draft CT.

be central to the IGC deliberations from October to December 2003. Thus the Commission's comments on the draft Constitutional Treaty sought to confine the President's duties to chairing the European Council, and representing the Union in the CFSP,[140] while excluding the President from organizing the work of the Council.[141] The European Parliament expressed similar concerns.[142] By way of contrast some Member States in the IGC argued that the President of the European Council should be President of the GAC.[143]

Neither side won a complete victory. The Presidency of the GAC is held for six months by each member of the team Presidency, not the President of the European Council.[144] The role of the President of the European Council within the GAC, however, was strengthened by the IGC. The draft Constitutional Treaty provided that the GAC should prepare, and ensure follow up to, meetings of the European Council in liaison with the Commission. The President of the European Council was not accorded a formal role in this respect.[145] This was changed in the final version of the Constitutional Treaty,[146] which was taken over into the Lisbon Treaty,[147] such that the President of the European Council is now given the same status as the Commission in preparing and ensuring follow-up meetings of the European Council.

(ii) Political frame

It is important to stress at the outset that the Council has wielded important executive power, more particularly since the 1990s. Its influence has been especially marked in relation to foreign and security policy, and in relation to justice and home affairs.[148] The Council also has responsibility in terms of policy delivery. The relationship between the Commission, Council, and European Council in this respect will doubtless evolve. Thus the Commission will continue to have input into Council configurations. It regularly attended GAC meetings in the past and will do so in the future. The relationship between the European Council and the Council has always been important.[149] The connection will now be framed by the provisions of the Lisbon Treaty.

---

[140] COM(2003) 548 final (n 26) [14].

[141] Ibid [14].

[142] European Parliament, Report on the Draft Treaty establishing a Constitution for Europe and the European Parliament's Opinion on the Convening of the Intergovernmental Conference, A5–0299/2003/Final, [20].

[143] Conference of the Representatives of the Governments of the Member States, Reply from the UK to the Questionnaire on the Legislative Function, the Formations of the Council and the Presidency of the Council of Ministers, CIG 34/03, DELEG 25, Brussels 15 October 2003.

[144] Art 16(9) TEU, Art 236 TFEU; Art I-24 CT.

[145] Article I-23(1) Draft CT.   [146] Art I-24(2) CT.   [147] Art 16(6) TEU.

[148] Hayes-Renshaw and Wallace (n 41) 324–326; Annual Report from the Council to the EP on the Main Aspects and Basic Choices of the CFSP (European Communities, 2009); <http://consilium.europa.eu/showPage.aspx?id=248&lang=EN>.

[149] Hayes-Renshaw and Wallace (n 41) ch 6.

The GAC, in liaison with the President of the European Council and the Commission, must ensure follow-up to meetings of the European Council. This will often require work by the other sectoral Councils. The President of the European Council, when liaising with the GAC, may therefore be able to exert influence over the detailed legislative and non-legislative initiatives required to carry European Council policy into action. A significant number of legislative initiatives have their origin in suggestions from the Council.[150] The President of the European Council, reinforced by the obligation on the GAC to ensure follow up to meetings of the European Council, will be in a position to press other Council formations to take the necessary steps to carry through the detail of European Council policy. It should, by way of contrast, also be acknowledged that the President of the European Council will have to work with the successive teams that have the Council Presidency for 18 months.

The impact of the President of the European Council and the Commission on the other aspect of the GAC's role, which is to ensure consistency in the work of the other Council configurations,[151] remains to be seen. They do not have a formal role in this aspect of the GAC's work,[152] but this divide may not be sustainable. Consistency of work by Council configurations may be necessary for the efficacious follow-up to European Council meetings, and the follow-up to those meetings may have implications for all Council formations. The influence of the President of the European Council, and the Commission President, over both aspects of the GAC's work may be further enhanced by institutional factors relating to the GAC itself. Concerns have been voiced that the GAC has not in the past performed the consistency task adequately. Its members were commonly national foreign ministers, who were too busy to give proper attention to ensuring consistency in the work of Council formations. If this tendency were to persist in the new constitutional order it would increase the likelihood that the President of the European Council and the Commission President would exercise greater influence to fill this 'relative vacuum'.

(c) Commission, Council, and European Council: the High Representative

(i) *Legal frame*

The High Representative of the Union for Foreign Affairs and Security Policy is the embodiment of shared executive power,[153] appointed by the European Council with agreement of the Commission President. The incumbent, as we have seen, takes part in the work of the European Council, chairs the Foreign Affairs Council and is also a Vice-President of the Commission, with responsibility for external relations.

---

[150] Art 241 TFEU.   [151] Art 16(6) TEU; Council Rules of Procedure (n 38) Art 2(3).
[152] Art 16(6) TEU.   [153] Art 18 TEU.

(ii) Political frame

It is interesting to consider how this regime of shared executive power will operate. The High Representative 'conducts' the EU's foreign and security policy.[154] Primary authority for policy choice in this area continues to reside with the European Council and the Council. It is the European Council that identifies the strategic interests and determines the objectives of the CFSP through strategic guidelines.[155] It is the Council that adopts the decisions to implement these guidelines,[156] with the High Representative as chair of the Foreign Affairs Council having specific responsibilities in this respect.[157] The primacy of the European Council is even more marked in relation to defence.[158] It would seem therefore that executive authority within the EU in relation to CFSP continues to rest primarily with institutions of an intergovernmental nature, the European Council and the Council, and that this is so notwithstanding the creation of the High Representative who operates within the European Council, the Council, and the Commission.

This conclusion, while basically sound, should nonetheless be qualified. The pre-Lisbon regime for CFSP concentrated executive power in the European Council and the Council. Notwithstanding this, the Commission exercised some influence over CFSP matters. This was in part because the line between foreign and security policy *stricto sensu*, which came within the remit of the Council and European Council, and other aspects of external relations dealt with by the Commission, could be a fine one.[159] It was in part because Javier Solana, the High Representative for the CFSP and Secretary-General of the Council from 1999 to 2009, was institutionally 'inclusive' rather than 'exclusive' in his overall approach.[160]

The interesting issue is how the post of High Representative in the Lisbon Treaty will change matters for the future. This remains to be seen. The role played by the High Representative within the CFSP and external relations will be considered in detail below, and reference should be made to that discussion.[161] It has been argued that the triple hats worn by the High Representative could lead to institutional schizophrenia, with the incumbent being subject to conflicting loyalties.[162] There are also legal grounds for concluding that the institutional loyalty owed by the High Representative to the Commission is limited, and constrained by her responsibilities in the Foreign Affairs Council and the European Council.[163]

---

[154] Art 18(2) TEU.   [155] Arts 22–26 TEU.   [156] Arts 26(2), 28 TEU.
[157] Art 27 TEU.   [158] Arts 42–44 TEU.
[159] <http://ec.europa.eu/dgs/external_relations/index_en.htm>.
[160] <http://www.consilium.europa.eu/app/Solana/default.aspx?lang=EN&id=246>.
[161] pp 384–387, pp 426–429.
[162] Devuyst (n 1) 294–295. There have been tensions concerning the new European External Action Service, <http://www.euractiv.com/en/foreign-affairs/parliament-raises-pressure-eu-diplomatic-service-news-467697>, <http://www.euractiv.com/en/future-eu/stop-turf-wars-over-eeas-top-diplomats-plead-news-485733>.
[163] Art 18(4) TEU; A Dashwood and A Johnston, 'The Institutions of the Enlarged EU Under the Regime of the Constitutional Treaty' (2004) 41 CMLRev 1481,1504.

    Moreover, we should not too readily assume that the Commission will be
weakened by the creation of the new post. The High Representative is Vice-
President within the Commission, with responsibility for external relations. The
lessons and ideas generated by this 'front-line' work will inevitably impact on the
proposals contributed by the High Representative to the more strategic development of common foreign policy, as decided on by the European Council, and
fleshed out by the Foreign Affairs Council. This is of course a 'two-way street'.
The influence will operate the other way, such that the overall strategic focus of
the European Council will impact on the way the High Representative discharges
her responsibilities in external relations within the Commission.

    This can be accepted. It does not, however, remove the force of the point
being made here. The Commission's external relations portfolio covers a wide
range of important initiatives, as the website will confirm.[164] The fact that the
High Representative will be responsible for these matters,[165] and that she will
have a central place within the Council and the European Council may therefore
enhance the Commission's influence. This is more especially so given that
Baroness Ashton, the first appointee as High Representative under the Lisbon
Treaty, is familiar with the Commission, having previously served as Trade
Commissioner.

    It should also be noted by way of conclusion that Working Group VII on
External Relations in the Convention on the Future of Europe favoured unification of external responsibilities in one person. Its 'first order preference' was for
the incumbent of the unified post to operate purely within the Commission, but
it recognized that this was not feasible and hence proposed a version of the shared
hat view, which was similar to, but not identical with, that embodied in the final
version of the Constitutional Treaty.[166]

(d) EU institutions: financial resources and the budget

The direction of EU policy is not wholly dependent on money. The EU is rightly
regarded as a regulatory State, and many initiatives do not require expenditure
from EU funds. It is nonetheless the case that money matters in the EU, and
hence control over the EU's budget is important. The disposition of power in the
Lisbon Treaty is interesting and accords power to all institutional players, albeit
in varying degrees.

(i) Legal frame

A bare outline of the complex provisions can be provided here. In relation to
resources, the Lisbon Treaty largely preserves the status quo ante. The Council of

---

[164] <http://ec.europa.eu/dgs/external_relations/index_en.htm>.
[165] Art 18(4) TEU.
[166] Final Report of Working Group VII (n 45) 19–23, discussed below, pp 384–387.

Ministers establishes the system of Union resources, which must be approved by the Member States in accordance with their constitutional requirements. The Council of Ministers acts unanimously after consulting the European Parliament.[167]

In relation to the budget, it is necessary to distinguish between the multi-annual financial framework and the annual budget. The multi-annual financial framework, which is to be established for a period of at least five years, is designed to ensure that EU expenditure develops in an orderly manner and within the limits of its resources.[168] It determines the amounts of the annual ceilings for commitment and payment appropriations. This framework is laid down by the Council acting unanimously after obtaining the consent of the European Parliament.[169] The annual budget must comply with the multi-annual financial framework.[170]

(ii) Political frame

The decision-making regime under the EC Treaty was complex, but in effect gave the European Parliament the final say over non-compulsory expenditure, with the Council having the final word over compulsory expenditure.[171] This dichotomy led to repeated battles and skirmishes over the divide between compulsory and non-compulsory expenditure.

The Lisbon Treaty marks a significant change in this respect. It makes clear that the European Parliament jointly with the Council exercises legislative and budgetary functions.[172] The European Parliament's powers have been increased because the distinction between 'compulsory' and 'non-compulsory' expenditure has been abolished. Executive power in relation to budgetary matters is therefore shared. Thus, while the Council is in the driving seat in relation to the multi-annual framework, the annual budget is, by way of contrast, made jointly by the Council and European Parliament on a proposal from the Commission, using a variant of the ordinary legislative procedure.[173]

(e) Council and Commission: agencies

(i) Legal frame

The changes made by the Lisbon Treaty in relation to agencies have been charted above. These are to be welcomed insofar as they bring agencies formally within the reach of judicial review, the principles concerning transparency, data protection and the like. The Lisbon Treaty did not, however, address the real issues of inter-institutional contestation that beset agencies. It is to these that we now turn.

---

[167] Art 311 TFEU.   [168] Art 312 TFEU.
[169] Art 312(2) TFEU, although there is provision whereby the European Council can modify this to qualified majority.
[170] Art 314 TFEU.   [171] Art 272 EC.   [172] Arts 14(1), 16(1) TEU.
[173] Art 314 TFEU.

(ii) Political frame

EU agencies have a range of powers, but they do not have formal rule-making authority that is common among national regulatory agencies. The principal legal constraint is the *Meroni* principle,[174] which stipulated that it was not possible to delegate power involving a wide margin of discretion, since it thereby transferred responsibility by replacing the choices of the delegator for those of the body to whom power was delegated. The Commission provided the political rationale for limiting agency powers. It has been supportive of agencies, but nonetheless wished to adhere to the legal constraints for reasons that transcend the dictates of formal law.

This is in order to preserve 'the unity and integrity of the executive function' and to ensure 'that it continues to be vested in the chief of the Commission if the latter is to have the required responsibility vis-à-vis Europe's citizens, the Member States and the other institutions'.[175] The participation of agencies should therefore be 'organized in a way which is consistent and in balance with the unity and integrity of the executive function and the Commission's ensuing responsibilities'.[176] The Commission has therefore been reluctant to create real regulatory agencies exercising discretionary power through adjudication and rule making, since if such power could be delegated then the Commission's sense of the unity of the executive function vested in it would be undermined. The emphasis placed on the unity and integrity of the executive function located in the President of the Commission was not fortuitous given that the 2002 Communication was issued during the deliberations of the Convention on the Future of Europe, where the location of executive power was one of the most divisive issues.

The Commission's concern as to the unity of the executive function played out not only in relation to the powers accorded to agencies, but also in relation to agency decision-making structure. The composition of agency boards has been crucial in this respect.[177] The Commission voiced concern in its 2002 Communication about the balance between its representation on agency boards and that of the Member States.[178] It drafted an Inter-institutional Agreement on agencies in 2005,[179] which enshrined its preferred position on the composition of agency boards, but failed to secure the Agreement's passage and it was withdrawn in 2009.[180] It is nonetheless clear that the Commission adheres to the philosophy in the 2005 draft Agreement,[181] and that it remains concerned about agency decision-making structure, stating that 'the degree of accountability of the

---

[174] Case 9/56 *Meroni & Co, Industrie Metallurgiche SpA v High Authority* [1958] ECR 133, 152.
[175] COM(2002) 718 (n 105) 1.   [176] ibid 1, 9.   [177] Craig (n 101).
[178] COM(2002) 718 (n 105) 9.
[179] Draft Interinstitutional Agreement on the Operating Framework for the European Regulatory Agencies, COM(2005) 59 final.
[180] [2009] OJ C71/17.
[181] European Agencies—The Way Forward, COM(2008) 135 final, 9.

Commission cannot exceed the degree of influence of the Commission on the agency's activities'.[182]

Institutional development will commonly throw into sharp relief the balance of power within a particular polity. The EU is no different in this respect. The Commission acknowledges the utility of agencies, but continues to be concerned about their impact on what the Commission perceives to be the unity and integrity of its executive function. Agencies in this respect constitute a site in which the locus of executive power remains contested.

8. The Post-Lisbon World: Accountability and Shared Executive Power

It is important to consider the emerging regime in terms of accountability. This inquiry could well occupy a book[183] in itself. What follows, therefore, does not purport to be an exhaustive analysis. The object is rather to identify some of the central issues concerning accountability.

(a) Legal accountability: closing the gaps

The Constitutional Treaty left the general structure of the ECJ's jurisdiction unchanged, but it did close a number of legal gaps by rendering agencies and other bodies subject to judicial review. This was taken over into Lisbon Treaty, thereby giving formal Treaty imprimatur to purposive judicial decisions to bring such agencies within the purview of legal accountability.[184]

The draft Constitutional Treaty that emerged from the Convention, however, did not render the European Council subject to judicial review.[185] This was anomalous given its powers. This matter was addressed by the IGC. The relevant Article was amended so as to render the European Council subject to review in relation to acts that are intended to produce legal effects vis-à-vis third parties,[186] with a similar amendment concerning failure to act.[187] The relevant provisions have been adopted in the Lisbon Treaty.[188] It is clear, moreover, that binding acts of the European Council could also be challenged indirectly through national courts via the preliminary ruling procedure. The European Council is

---

[182] ibid 8.

[183] C Harlow, *Accountability in the European Union* (Oxford University Press, 2002); Curtin (n 2).

[184] Case T-411/06 *Sogelma—Società generale lavori manutenzioni appalti Srl v European Agency for Reconstruction (AER)* [2008] ECR II-2771.

[185] Art III-270(1) Draft CT.

[186] IGC 2003-Naples Ministerial Conclave: Presidency Proposal, CIG 52/1/03, PRESID 10, Brussels 25 November 2003, Annex 7; Art III-367(1) CT.

[187] Art III-369 CT.   [188] Arts 263, 265 TFEU.

an institution of the EU,[189] and hence is susceptible to this procedure in relation to the validity or interpretation of its acts.[190]

It should also be recognized that inter-institutional disputes concerning the disposition of executive power could end up before the ECJ. It has been argued above that there are cogent reasons to expect the European Council and the Commission to cooperate rather than conflict. If cooperation breaks down, however, then recourse to the ECJ will always be a possibility. The ECJ would have jurisdiction to hear such actions under Article 263 TFEU.

(b) Political accountability: securing political responsibility

It can be accepted that political accountability within a regime of shared executive power will be more complex than in those regimes where such power is concentrated within the 'unitary executive'. A regime of shared executive power will not have a single line of executive accountability. The force of this distinction, however, must be qualified in at least two ways.

First, the reality is that even in political systems where all executive authority can be formally traced to a single locus, most commonly the government in parliamentary systems, there will nonetheless be considerable problems in securing accountability given that executive power is now exercised in various ways by a plethora of bodies within the modern State. Thus a common feature in many political systems is for executive power to have been dispersed across a range of agencies and other bodies outside the core executive, and for some aspects of executive power to have been contracted out to private bodies. This leads to constant challenges to decide how best to secure accountability within this more complex administrative State. The challenges in this regard are especially marked for those bodies accorded executive power where part of the very rationale for their creation is that they should have some decision-making autonomy in relation to the core executive.[191]

Second, Parliamentary political systems in which executive power is located within a 'single' executive may well foster electoral accountability: the electorate can throw out the party whose policies they dislike. It should also be recognized that systems with strong, unitary executive power can often lead to problems of political accountability between elections. These problems have been especially prevalent in the UK, which has in the past been described as 'elective autocracy', whereby a government elected with a reasonable majority has very considerable power and the legislature's influence is limited.

(i) Accountability and appointment

The Lisbon Treaty regime for appointment of the Commission President and Commissioners was considered above. While the European Parliament elects the

---

[189] Art 13 TEU.   [190] Art 267 TFEU.
[191] P Craig, *Administrative Law* (Sweet & Maxwell, 6th edn, 2008) ch 4.

Commission President, the European Council retains control over the candidate put forward to the European Parliament.[192] Power over the appointment of the Commissioners resides with the Council and President-elect of the Commission, subject to the caveat that the entire Commission must be approved by the European Parliament, with the formal appointment being made by the European Council.[193] The European Parliament will continue with its 'senate-like' confirmation hearings of proposed Commissioners, in which aspiring holders of such posts are subjected to fairly intense scrutiny to determine their expertise and likely approach to the area over which they are to have responsibility.[194]

This method of choosing the Commission might well be criticized. There are, doubtless, other possible ways in which it could be done and as we have seen State control over such appointments was 'ratcheted up' in the final version of the Constitutional Treaty and Lisbon Treaty. The reality is that the method of appointment of the Commission President and other Commissioners was regarded as warranting input from State interests in the Council and European Council, as well as from the European Parliament. We should not forget, moreover, that such choices in Nation States will commonly involve input from more than one source, as exemplified by appointment procedures for agency heads, which frequently accord a role to the traditional core executive and to the legislature.

The appointment procedure for the Presidency of the European Council places the power firmly in the hands of that body. Thus the Lisbon Treaty provides that the European Council shall elect its President, by a qualified majority, for a term of two and a half years, renewable once. In the event of an impediment or serious misconduct, the European Council can end the President's term of office by the same procedure.[195] A similar regime applies to appointment of the High Representative, subject to the qualification that the President of the Commission is also involved, given that the High Representative is a Vice-President within the Commission.[196]

The choice of the President of the European Council was always going to be intensely political in the broad sense of that term, as attested to by the politicking that preceded appointment of the Belgian Prime Minister, Herman van Rompuy, to the post.[197] Commentary on the appointment was largely critical, based in part on the procedure, with the decision being concluded over dinner by the Heads of State, and in part on substance, in the sense that the chosen candidate was relatively unknown. Indeed critics over the EU did not know whether to cavil at the appointment of a person regarded as relatively lightweight on the international scene, or to criticize the EU for the fact that it might have

---

[192] Arts 14(1), 17(7) TEU.   [193] Art 17(7) TEU.
[194] <http://www.euractiv.com/en/priorities/new-european-commission>.
[195] Art 15(5) TEU.   [196] Art 18(1) TEU.
[197] <http://consilium.europa.eu/showPage.aspx?id=1823&lang=EN>.

appointed someone such as Tony Blair, who would have been more 'Presidential', thereby fostering fears of a super State.

It would nonetheless be premature to draw conclusions concerning the role of the Presidency of the European Council under its first incumbent. Herman van Rompuy proved himself to be a skilled politician as Prime Minister of Belgium, helping to diffuse an impending crisis between the principal groups within that country. Quiet diplomacy and negotiation skills will be valuable in the new job, and may well achieve much, both internally and externally, given the need for the President to forge consensus with the Heads of State and to liaise with the Commission, Council, and European Parliament.

(ii) Accountability, setting the political agenda and priorities

The general impact of the Lisbon Treaty on democracy in the EU was considered in the previous chapter and reference should be made to that discussion.[198] It can be accepted at the outset that it will not be possible for the voters to express their dislike and put another party into office with a different agenda. The fact that executive power over agenda setting is shared between the Commission, Council, and European Council prevents such direct transmission of voter preferences.

It would nonetheless be mistaken to believe that such preferences will have no effect. The Commission President is elected by the European Parliament and the European Council must take account of the election results in deciding which person to put forward to the European Parliament as Commission President. Thus, if the electorate dislike the direction of EU policy they may, subject to the caveats discussed in the previous chapter,[199] be able to express this through a change in the European Parliament, which will have some impact on the European Council's decision as to the candidate for Commission President.

It is important to be realistic, moreover, about how far voter preferences could lead to a change of policy even if the Lisbon Treaty had opted for a single President of the EU, this being the President of the Commission, indirectly elected by the European Parliament. This would have accorded the voters greater electoral influence over the policy agenda. There would, however, still have been constraints flowing from the Council and European Council. The President of the Commission, acting as the sole President of the EU, would still have to take account of Member State preferences in the Council and European Council, as well as voter preferences expressed by MEPs.

The reality under the Lisbon Treaty is that the multi-annual agenda will be the result of a discourse between the major institutional players. This discourse will incorporate voter preferences partly through the Commission President, and partly through consultation with the European Parliament on the multi-annual agenda. The discourse will also include State interests as mediated through the

---

[198] pp 71–75.   [199] pp 72–75.

European Council and the Council. This process may be 'messier' than that in States with a single executive power. It does, however, avoid the kind of executive dominance over the political agenda adverted to above. The dialogue fostered by shared executive power can be healthy in making actors re-think their own pre-conceived positions concerning the direction of EU development. The dangers of this leading to conflict between Commission and European Council are, as we have seen, more likely to be outweighed by factors that engender cooperation.

(iii) Accountability, legislation and individual policy choice

The annual and multi-annual agenda will be developed through legislative acts, which are legitimated through the ordinary legislative procedure initiated by the Commission. The Council and European Parliament function as co-legislators in the passage of such legislative acts. The ordinary legislative procedure,[200] which is the successor to co-decision, encourages and facilitates a discursive process between Commission, Council, and European Parliament and hence fosters a deliberative dialogue.[201]

The new-style delegated regulations will also feature prominently. There have in the past been difficulties in relation to the Comitology regime that has accompanied the passage of such secondary regulations, which are reflective of the difficulty of rendering secondary rule making both workable and legitimate. The political impact of the Lisbon provisions on this area has been considered above,[202] and the legal impact will be addressed below.[203]

(iv) Accountability, implementation and administration

The Commission clearly has primary responsibility for policy implementation.[204] It is, however, subject to a plethora of differing constraints. A Commissioner can be compulsorily retired for failure to comply with the duties of the office.[205] In addition, the President of the Commission can request the resignation of a Commissioner.[206]

The European Parliament has retained its 'nuclear-strike' power in relation to censure of the Commission. Thus the Lisbon Treaty stipulates that the Commission is responsible to the European Parliament and that if it votes in favour of a censure motion the members of the Commission must resign and the High Representative of the Union for Foreign Affairs and Security Policy must resign from the duties that she carries out in the Commission.[207] The European Parliament has also retained its more fine-tuned controls over Commission administrative activity, including a Committee of Inquiry,[208] citizen

---

[200] Art 294 TFEU.
[201] Subject to the concerns in this respect expressed above, pp 38–39.
[202] pp 48–66, pp 75–77.   [203] Ch 7.
[204] Art 17(1) TEU.   [205] Arts 245, 247 TFEU.   [206] Art 17(6) TEU.
[207] Art 17(8) TEU, Art 234 TFEU.   [208] Art 226 TFEU.

petition,[209] and oral or written questions.[210] There is an Ombudsman to investigate cases of maladministration.[211]

Commission expenditure and policy is also subject to oversight by the Court of Auditors.[212] The Commission is, in addition, subject to the important rules contained in the Financial Regulation 2002,[213] which covers matters such as fiscal and policy responsibility, audit, delegation, contracting-out and the like.[214] These controls emerged in response to the problems that led to the resignation of the Santer Commission. The controls in the Financial Regulation are stringent and have been further tightened by amendment to the 2002 Regulation.[215]

9. Conclusion

There was greater disagreement about the institutional provisions in the Convention on the Future of Europe than any other issue, the subsequent IGC devoted the majority of its time to them and they were taken over largely unchanged into the Lisbon Treaty. This is unsurprising. The detailed provisions on executive power embody a view as to the nature of the EU polity, and the balance therein as between intergovernmental and supranational forces.

There is little doubt that some have been disappointed by the outcome. Those who hoped for a single locus of executive responsibility, the Commission President, legitimated through election by the European Parliament, with continuation of the six-monthly Presidencies of the European Council, will not be content with the outcome. There are undoubtedly arguments for this vision of the EU polity.

It has not, however, been incorporated within the Lisbon Treaty, which contains a regime of shared executive power. It has been argued that this vision is sustainable in principle and preferable in pragmatic terms. Moreover, while there may inevitably be differences of view on a particular issue between the two Presidents, there are several factors inclining them towards cooperation rather than conflict. We should, moreover, avoid hasty conclusions based on a few months of the new regime. The relationship between the two Presidents will take time to settle and will evolve over time. It may well be that the more problematic part of the institutional triangle is the relationship between both Presidents and the Member State that chairs Council formations for a six-month period. The

---

[209] Art 227 TFEU.   [210] Art 230 TFEU.   [211] Art 228 TFEU.

[212] Art 287 TFEU.

[213] Council Regulation (EC, Euratom) 1605/2002 of 25 June 2002 on the Financial Regulation applicable to the general budget of the European Communities [2002] OJ L248/1.

[214] P Craig, 'The Constitutionalisation of Community Administration' (2003) 28 ELRev 840.

[215] Council Regulation (EC, Euratom) 1995/2006 of 13 December 2006 amending Regulation (EC, Euratom) 1605/2002 on the Financial Regulation applicable to the general budget of the European Communities [2006] OJ L390/1.

latter will have goals that it wishes to secure within its six-month tenure as the lead member of the team system introduced by the Lisbon Treaty. The EU is mindful of the need to ensure coherence between these goals and the more general EU objectives developed by the Presidents of the European Council and the Commission.[216] It remains to be seen whether this can be achieved.

[216] (Nn 43–44).

4

Courts, Continuity, and Change

The Community courts were integral to the development of the EC Treaty, and they will continue to play a major part within the new legal order post the Lisbon Treaty. The role of the European Court of Justice (ECJ) and General Court is considered throughout the different chapters of this book. It is nonetheless important to analyse the impact of the Lisbon Treaty more generally on the EU judiciary, which is the purpose of this chapter.

The discussion begins by examining the Lisbon Treaty amendments that affect the nomenclature of the Union courts and the rules relating to judicial appointment. This is followed by analysis of the provisions concerning the courts' jurisdiction, and the extent to which these have been altered by the Lisbon Treaty. The focus then shifts to the overall judicial architecture of the EU courts. This was given scant attention in the deliberations that led to the Constitutional Treaty, which largely replicated the schema in the Nice Treaty, and the same remains true for the Lisbon Treaty. The reasons why this issue never made it onto the reform agenda will be explained, and the possibilities for more coherent and rational division of power between the ECJ and the General Court will be explored. The penultimate section will address the implications of the Lisbon Treaty for central components of judicial doctrine, direct effect, and supremacy. The chapter will conclude by considering what can be learned from national courts during the ratification process, with particular attention focused on the German Federal Constitutional Court.

1. Lisbon Treaty, Courts, and Appointment

The impact of the Lisbon Treaty on the formal judicial architecture of the EU is limited for the reasons that will be considered in the section that follows. It is important nonetheless to begin by understanding the formal changes made by the Lisbon Treaty.

The schema in the Lisbon Treaty, largely replicates that in the Constitutional Treaty.[1] Article 19(1) TEU provides that:

---

[1] Art I-29 CT.

The Court of Justice of the European Union shall include the Court of Justice, the General Court and specialised courts. It shall ensure that in the interpretation and application of the Treaties the law is observed.

Member States shall provide remedies sufficient to ensure effective legal protection in the fields covered by Union law.

This nomenclature is inelegant. The appellation Court of Justice of the European Union 'includes' the Court of Justice, the General Court, which is the new name for the Court of First Instance (CFI), and specialized courts, which is the appellation now used for judicial panels. The procedure for the creation of specialized courts has been modified, such that that they can be established through the ordinary legislative procedure, with a requirement of qualified majority in the Council,[2] whereas hitherto the European Parliament had a mere right to be consulted and there was a requirement of unanimity in the Council.[3] The Statute of the Court of Justice is attached as a Protocol to the Treaty.[4]

The regime for appointments replicates many of the features of the pre-existing system. Thus the ECJ consists of one judge per Member State, while the General Court has at least one judge for each Member State.[5] The ECJ continues to be assisted by Advocates General.[6] The judges and Advocates General of the ECJ must be chosen from persons whose independence is beyond doubt, who possess the qualifications required for appointment to the highest judicial offices in their respective countries, or who are jurisconsults of recognized competence.[7] The judges of the General Court must also be chosen from persons whose independence is beyond doubt, who possess the ability required for appointment to high judicial office.[8] Appointments to the ECJ and General Court are made by common accord of the governments of the Member States for six years, and judges and Advocates General can be re-appointed.[9]

The Lisbon Treaty does, however, contain a novel element in relation to judicial appointments to the ECJ and General Court. These are now made after consultation with a panel that provides an opinion on candidates' suitability to perform their duties.[10] The panel is composed of seven persons chosen from among former members of the Court of Justice and the General Court, members of national supreme courts, and lawyers of recognized competence, one of whom is proposed by the European Parliament. The Council is to adopt a decision establishing the panel's operating rules and a decision appointing its members. It acts on the initiative of the President of the Court of Justice.

The ECJ is assisted by eight Advocates General, but it can request that this number be increased. The Council may, acting unanimously, accede to this

---

[2] Art 257 TFEU.   [3] Art 225a EC.
[4] Art 281 TFEU; Protocol (No 3) on the Statute of the Court of Justice of the European Union.
[5] Art 19(2) TEU.   [6] Art 19(2) TEU.
[7] Art 19(2) TEU, Art 253 TFEU.   [8] Art 19(2), Art 254 TFEU.
[9] Art 19(2) TEU.   [10] Art 255 TFEU.

request.[11] A Declaration appended to the Lisbon Treaty[12] provides that if the ECJ requests that the number of Advocates General be increased by three, making 11 in total, the Council will, acting unanimously, agree on such an increase. If this occurs Poland will, alongside Germany, France, Italy, Spain, and the United Kingdom, have a permanent Advocate General and no longer take part in the rotation system, while the existing rotation system will involve the rotation of five Advocates General instead of three.

2. Lisbon Treaty, Courts, and Jurisdiction

(a) Continuity: general heads of jurisdiction

The role of the Union courts in the different areas covered by the remit of this book will be considered within the respective chapters. The present focus concerns the general impact of the Lisbon Treaty on the courts' jurisdiction. Article 19(3) TEU provides scant guidance in this respect, merely stating that:

The Court of Justice of the European Union shall, in accordance with the Treaties:

(a) rule on actions brought by a Member State, an institution or a natural or legal person;
(b) give preliminary rulings, at the request of courts or tribunals of the Member States, on the interpretation of Union law or the validity of acts adopted by the institutions;
(c) rule in other cases provided for in the Treaties.

It is the TFEU that provides the real substance on this issue, and the principal heads of jurisdiction replicate the schema which existed hitherto: enforcement actions, Articles 258 to 260 TFEU; review of legality, Article 263 TFEU; review of inaction, Article 265 TFEU; preliminary rulings, Article 267 TFEU; exception of illegality, Article 277 TFEU; and damages actions, Articles 268 and 340 TFEU.

There are, however, aspects of the drafting that lead to unnecessary confusion. The principal heads of jurisdiction in the Lisbon Treaty replicate those in the EC Treaty. The provisions of the EC Treaty indicated in a straightforward manner which court had jurisdiction over different types of case. The difficulty in the Lisbon Treaty stems from the fact that on a number of occasions the wording used is that the 'Court of Justice of the European Union' adjudicates on a particular head of jurisdiction. The word 'include' covers, as we have seen above, the ECJ, General Court, and specialized courts.[13] It gives the impression at first glance that a case could be heard by the ECJ, General Court, or even a specialized court, even though this is not, in reality, so in certain instances.

---

[11] Art 252 TFEU.
[12] Declaration 38 on Art 252 of the Treaty on the Functioning of the European Union regarding the number of Advocates-General in the Court of Justice.
[13] Art 19(1) TEU.

This confusion can be exemplified by the provisions relating to enforcement actions. Such actions by the Commission can be brought before the 'Court of Justice of the European Union',[14] and the same is true for actions brought by one Member State against another.[15] This would seem to imply that the General Court has jurisdiction over such matters, by way of contrast to the analogous provision from the EC Treaty, which accorded jurisdiction to the ECJ and not the CFI.[16] This would however be inconsistent with the list of the General Court's jurisdiction,[17] which does not include enforcement actions.[18] This list can be extended to other types of action by the Statute of the Court of Justice of the EU,[19] but the Statute has not thus far extended the General Court's jurisdiction to enforcement actions,[20] nor does the General Court's website indicate any such jurisdictional competence.[21]

It might be argued that the phrase 'Court of Justice of the European Union' in this and other instances was used to provide Treaty foundation if the authority of the General Court were to be extended to new types of case. This does not, however, withstand examination. The Lisbon Treaty already provides such foundation in Article 256(1) TFEU, which lists the existing heads of the General Court's jurisdiction and then states that these can be extended by amendment of the Statute of the Court. There is therefore no need for Treaty legitimation for any extension of the General Court's jurisdiction to new areas, since this already exists, and the Lisbon Treaty in this respect simply echoes the same provision of the EC Treaty.[22]

(b) Change: particular heads of jurisdiction

The Lisbon Treaty has, however, wrought certain changes in the powers of the Union courts. There have been certain modifications to particular heads of jurisdiction.

Thus the preliminary ruling procedure is formally extended to acts of EU bodies, offices, or agencies.[23] The procedure also covers the European Council, which is listed as a Union institution.[24] The Lisbon Treaty accorded Treaty status to the urgent preliminary ruling procedure introduced in March 2008, by stipulating that the ECJ shall act with the minimum of delay if a question referred for a preliminary ruling is raised in a case pending before any court or tribunal of a Member State with regard to a person in custody.[25]

---

[14] Art 258 TFEU.   [15] Art 259 TFEU.
[16] Art 226 EC.   [17] Art 256(1) TFEU.
[18] The list specifies Arts 263, 265, 268, 270, 272 TFEU, and the General Court can also be accorded power over preliminary rulings in specific areas, Art 256(3) TFEU.
[19] Art 256(1) TFEU.   [20] Protocol (No 3) (n 4).
[21] <http://curia.europa.eu/jcms/jcms/Jo2_7033/>.   [22] Art 225(1) EC.
[23] Art 267 TFEU.   [24] Art 13 TEU.   [25] Art 267 TFEU.

There have also been changes to direct actions. Bodies, offices, and agencies[26] are subject to legality review for acts that have legal effects in relation to third parties, as is the European Council.[27] The Committee of the Regions is added to the Court of Auditors and the European Central Bank as bodies that can seek judicial review to defend their prerogatives.[28] The standing criteria for actions brought by individuals have been broadened such that the requirement of individual concern no longer applies in relation to regulatory acts that directly affect an individual and do not entail implementing measures.[29] The acts setting up bodies, offices, and agencies of the Union can lay down specific conditions and arrangements concerning actions brought by individuals against acts of these bodies, etc intended to produce legal effects in relation to them.[30] Bodies, offices, and agencies are in addition brought within the remit of liability for inaction, as is the European Council.[31]

Enforcement actions by the Commission against Member States are not applicable in relation to measures concerning police cooperation and judicial cooperation in criminal matters adopted before the entry into force of the Treaty of Lisbon. The ECJ has the powers that it had under what was Title VI of the EU Treaty in force prior to the Lisbon Treaty.[32] This circumscription of the Court's power is stipulated by the Protocol on Transitional Provisions,[33] but it is limited to a five-year period, after which the normal rules concerning enforcement actions will apply.[34]

The Lisbon Treaty has expedited the power to impose pecuniary penalties on Member States pursuant to enforcement actions. Under the EC Treaty if the Commission considered that a Member State had not taken the necessary measures to comply with the ECJ's judgment then, after giving the Member State the opportunity to submit written observations, the Commission had to issue a reasoned opinion specifying the points on which the Member State had not complied with the judgment, and it had to specify time limits within which the Member State had to take the requisite measures.[35] The new rules no longer require the Commission to issue a reasoned opinion, nor to specify a time within which the Member State must take the requisite measures.[36] The new regime is that where the Commission considers that the Member State has not taken the necessary measures to comply with the judgment of the Court, the only requirement on the Commission before taking the case to the ECJ is that it affords the Member State the opportunity to submit its observations.[37]

---

[26] There can be difficulties, however, in deciding precisely which bodies come within this phrase, especially in the complex world of the AFSJ, V Mitsilegas, *EU Criminal Law* (Hart, 2009) 227.
[27] Art 263(1) TFEU.   [28] Art 263(3) TFEU.   [29] Art 263(4) TFEU.
[30] Art 263(5) TFEU.   [31] Art 265(1) TFEU.   [32] Art 35 EU.
[33] Protocol (No 36) On Transitional Provisions, Art 10(1).
[34] ibid Art 10(3). There are special rules for the UK, ch 9.
[35] Art 228 EC.
[36] The requirement on the Commission to issue a reasoned opinion and to specify a time for compliance still applies in relation to the initial finding of a breach under Art 258 TFEU.
[37] Art 260(2) TFEU.

The Lisbon Treaty has moreover added a new provision dealing specifically with Member State failure to notify measures transposing a directive under a legislative procedure. In such cases the Commission may, when it deems appropriate, specify the amount of the lump sum or penalty payment to be paid by the Member State concerned which it considers appropriate in the circumstances. If the Court finds that there is an infringement it can impose a lump sum or penalty payment on the Member State concerned not exceeding the amount specified by the Commission.[38]

The ECJ is accorded a new jurisdiction to decide on the legality of an act adopted by the European Council or by the Council pursuant to Article 7 TEU. This provision is concerned with a finding that there is a clear risk of serious breach by a Member State of the values as listed in Article 2 TEU, such as democracy, rule of law, and human rights. The action before the ECJ can only be brought at the request of the Member State concerned by such a determination and in respect solely of the procedural stipulations contained in Article 7 TEU. The request must be made within one month from the date of such determination, and the ECJ must rule within one month from the date of the request.

(c) Change: particular heads of jurisdiction and privileged applicants

The reforms made by the Lisbon Treaty whereby acts of the European Council and EU bodies, offices, and agencies can be reviewed are welcome, but they may have inadvertently created a consequential problem: these institutions and bodies can be defendants, but are not listed among either the privileged or quasi-privileged applicants who are entitled to seek judicial review. There is thus an asymmetry built into Article 263 TFEU, which does not apply to any of the other EU institutions. It is interesting to note by way of contrast that the European Council is accorded the right to bring an action for failure to act under Article 265 TFEU. It can be both applicant and defendant in such actions, which makes the position under Article 263 TFEU look all the more odd.

It might be argued by way of response that the asymmetry in Article 263 TFEU is imagined rather than real, because there will be no instance in which the European Council would wish to bring an action against any other EU institution. This will not bear examination.

We have seen that the balance of legal power between, for example, the European Council and the Commission is nuanced.[39] While recourse to court would be likely to be a last resort it cannot be discounted, and we know full well from past experience that inter-institutional disputes have frequently ended up before the judiciary. The European Council also has an array of legal powers in different areas of the Treaties and there could well be inter-institutional disputes concerning their interpretation and application. Thus, to take but one

---

[38] Art 260(3) TFEU.   [39] Ch 3.

example, it is the European Council that is to define the strategic guidelines for legislative and operational planning in the Area of Freedom, Security and Justice.[40] There might well be instances in which it would wish to have recourse to legality review under Article 263 TFEU if it felt either that another EU institution was trespassing on its prerogatives in this area, or if it believed that legislative acts were not in accord with the strategic guidelines that it had defined.

It is not inconceivable, moreover, that the European Council might wish to resort to court in relation to demarcation disputes between Common Foreign and Security Policy (CFSP) powers and those under the remaining body of the Treaties, over which the ECJ has jurisdiction.[41] It is true that most concrete decisions in this area are taken by the Council, but it is equally true that they are taken pursuant to general guidelines and strategies adopted by the European Council.[42] Insofar as a dispute might call into question such European Council strategies it might justifiably wish to be party to such a suit.

This might of course be 'déjà vu all over again'. The ECJ in the past interpreted the predecessor to Article 263 TFEU so as to enable the European Parliament to defend its prerogatives,[43] justifying this on first principle on the grounds that it was necessary to safeguard the institutional balance under the Treaty. The European Council does not partake in the legislative process, but it does have other powers, including a role in the setting of the EU's priorities. It would then be open to the ECJ to draw on this precedent and afford the European Council claimant status, at the very least as a quasi-privileged applicant.

The position of bodies, offices, and agencies of the Union requires separate consideration. They too suffer from the infirmity of being defendants without having any separate recognition as applicants. It might once again be argued that they would have no occasion to bring an action to review the legality of acts adopted by other EU institutions. This conclusion is premature. There could, for example, be instances in which an EU agency might wish to argue that Union legislation or a delegated act had wrongfully impinged on its terrain, as laid down in its own empowering legislation. These bodies, offices, or agencies might seek to bring an action as a non-privileged applicant. Most agencies have legal personality and could therefore count as legal persons for the purposes of Article 263(4) TFEU. They would, however, then have to satisfy the criteria in that Article, including the test for standing.

---

[40] Art 68 TFEU.
[41] Art 40 TEU, Art 275 TFEU.
[42] Art 26 TEU.
[43] Case C–70/88 *European Parliament v Council* [1990] ECR I–2041.

(d) Change: particular heads of jurisdiction and standing for individual applicants

The restrictive criteria for standing for non-privileged applicants in actions to review the legality of Community acts have long been a cause for concern.[44] The ECJ, however, refused to interpret Article 230(4) EC more leniently in the manner powerfully contended for by Advocate General Jacobs, and placed the onus for reform on to the political agenda.[45]

The Convention on the Future of Europe established an ad hoc working group to consider certain issues relating to the Community Courts,[46] including the possible modification of Article 230 EC. The Discussion Circle was divided on the matter:[47] some felt that the current position was satisfactory taking account of indirect challenge, and therefore it was not necessary to change Article 230(4) EC; others argued that the interpretation of Article 230(4) was too restrictive and should be broadened. The Chairman, Antonio Vitorino, proposed a compromise, which was incorporated in the Constitutional Treaty, and taken over in Article 263(4) TFEU.

Any natural or legal person may, under the conditions laid down in the first and second paragraphs, institute proceedings against an act addressed to that person or which is of direct and individual concern to them, and against a regulatory act which is of direct concern to them and does not entail implementing measures.

The novelty of the provision is that individual concern does not have to be shown for regulatory acts that are of direct concern to a person and do not entail

---

[44] A Barav, 'Direct and Individual Concern: An Almost Insurmountable Barrier to the Admissibility of Individual Appeal to the EEC Court' (1974) 11 CMLRev 191; C Harding, 'The Private Interest in Challenging Community Action' (1980) 5 ELRev 354; H Rasmussen, 'Why is Article 173 Interpreted against Private Plaintiffs?' (1980) 5 ELRev 112; R Greaves, '*Locus Standi* under Art 173 EEC when Seeking Annulment of a Regulation' (1986) 11 ELRev 119; J Weiler, 'Pride and Prejudice—*Parliament* v. *Council*' (1989) 14 ELRev 334; K Bradley, 'Sense and Sensibility: *Parliament* v. *Council* Continued' (1991) 16 ELRev 245; A Arnull, 'Challenging EC Anti-Dumping Regulations: The Problem of Admissibility' [1992] ECLR 73; C Harlow, 'Towards a Theory of Access for the European Court of Justice' (1992) 12 YBEL 213; P Craig, 'Legality, Standing and Substantive Review in Community Law' (1994) 14 OJLS 507; A Arnull, 'Private Applicants and the Action for Annulment under Art 173 of the EC Treaty' (1995) 32 CMLRev 7; M Hedemann-Robinson, 'Article 173 EC, General Community Measures and *Locus Standi* for Private Persons: Still a cause for Individual Concern?' (1996) 2 EPL 127; N Neuwahl, 'Article 173 Paragraph 4 EC: Past, Present and Possible Future' (1996) 21 ELRev 17; J Cooke, '*Locus Standi* of Private Parties under Art 173(4)' (1997) Irish Jnl of European Law 4; A Ward, *Judicial Review and the Rights of Private Parties in EU Law* (Oxford University Press, 2nd edn, 2007) chs 6–7; A Arnull, 'Private Applicants and the Action for Annulment since *Codorniu*' (2001) 38 CMLRev 7; P Craig, 'Standing, Rights and the Structure of Legal Argument' (2003) 9 EPL 493; P Craig, *EU Administrative Law* (Oxford University Press, 2006) ch 10; P Craig and G de Búrca, *EU Law, Text, Cases and Materials* (Oxford University Press, 4th edn, 2007) ch 14.

[45] Case C-50/00 P *Union de Pequenos Agricultores v Council* [2002] ECR I-6677.

[46] CONV 543/03, Discussion Circle on the Court of Justice, Brussels 7 February 2003.

[47] Discussion Circle on the Court of Justice, CIRCLE I, Working Document 08, Brussels 11 March 2003.

implementing measures. Liberalization of this kind is to be welcomed, and goes some way to meet the difficulties exemplified by the existing case law. It should be recognized, however, that this reform does not address the more general difficulties with indirect challenge, which were set out by Advocate General Jacobs in the *UPA* case.[48] Moreover, there are difficulties with this new provision, and whether this particular cup is 'half empty rather than half full' or vice-versa will depend upon how these problems are judicially resolved.

(i) The meaning of 'regulatory act'

The liberalization in Article 263(4) TFEU applies only to 'regulatory acts' and hence the meaning of this term is central in assessing the impact of the reforms.

The same term was used in the analogous provision in the Constitutional Treaty,[49] and its meaning was uncertain. Article I-33(1) CT distinguished between European laws, European framework laws, European regulations, European decisions, recommendations, and opinions. European laws and European framework laws were regarded as legislative acts corresponding to old-style regulations and directives respectively. A European regulation was said to be a non-legislative act of general application for the implementation of legislative acts and could in effect be a secondary European law or a secondary European framework law. It seemed, therefore, that the liberalization in Article III-365(4) CT would only have operated in relation to regulatory acts, secondary norms, and not in relation to EU laws, framework laws, decisions, or implementing acts. Thus on this reading if there was a European law that did not require implementing measures, it would still have been necessary for the individual to show direct and individual concern.

The only way to avoid this conclusion would have been to read the phrase 'regulatory act' to mean something broader than the term European Regulation within Article I-33(1) CT. This might have been possible, but it would have been difficult both textually and historically. The formulation proposed by Commissioner Vitorino to the Discussion Circle left open the type of act to which the new liberalization should apply: the draft had suggested that it might apply either to regulatory acts or to an act of general application. The Constitutional Treaty embodied the former, not the latter. The significance of this choice should now be apparent. If the latter criterion had been adopted it could have been applicable to primary European laws, and not just secondary norms.

The same uncertainty pervades the Lisbon Treaty, although it assumes a somewhat different form because of change in the language used to describe legal acts. The Lisbon Treaty retains a hierarchy of norms, which will be considered in a later chapter.[50] Legislative acts are those enacted by a legislative

---

[48] Case C-50/00 P (n 45).   [49] Art III-365(4) CT.   [50] Ch 7.

procedure, and can take the form of a regulation, decision, or directive.[51] A legislative act can delegate power to the Commission to adopt a non-legislative act, which may once again take the form of a regulation, decision, or directive, although it will normally be a regulation.[52] These are termed delegated acts.[53] There is also a separate category of implementing acts,[54] but it should be noted that such acts, notwithstanding their names, may, but need not, involve implementing measures at national level.

The term 'regulatory act' does not fit easily with the Lisbon classification of legal acts. It could be construed broadly to cover any legally binding act, whether legislative, delegated, or implementing, provided that it does not entail implementing measures. It could be interpreted more narrowly to cover any legislative, delegated, or implementing act, provided that it takes the form of a regulation or decision that does not entail implementing measures. It could cover only delegated and implementing acts in the form of regulations or decisions, which do not entail implementing measures, or only delegated acts subject to the same condition.

The interpretation adopted by the ECJ will therefore markedly affect the impact of Article 263(4) TFEU. The construction that best fits the framers' intent would be the last, which is the narrowest. It would nonetheless be regrettable if it were given this narrow remit. It would do little to ease the pre-existing problems of standing for non-privileged applicants. It would not apply to legislative acts that are of direct concern and do not entail implementing measures. This constraint on the ambit of the reformed provision would be all the more marked given the formalistic nature of the definition of legislative act in the Lisbon Treaty, which covers any act passed by a legislative procedure. It is therefore perfectly possible for there to be a 'legislative act' that applies to a very narrow group of applicants, which is *de facto* a closed group, where no one could challenge the measure because they would not come within the scope of the reformed standing provision, they would hence have to show individual concern and would be unable to do so under existing case law.

(ii) Substance and form

The preceding discussion leads naturally to a further potential difficulty with Article 263(4) TFEU. It contains nothing equivalent to the provision in Article 230(4) EC which stated that an act in the form of a regulation might in reality be a decision that was of direct and individual concern to the applicant. Article 263(4) TFEU therefore contains no invitation to look behind the form of the measure to its substance.

---

[51] Art 289 TFEU.   [52] Art 290 TFEU.
[53] Art 290(3) TFEU.   [54] Art 291 TFEU.

It would still be possible in principle for the courts to undertake this task *within* a particular category of legal act. Thus an applicant might contend that a delegated act in the form of a regulation was in substance a decision that was of direct and individual concern, or that it was of direct concern and there was no need to show individual concern because it should be regarded as a regulatory act and did not entail implementing measures.

It will perforce be more difficult for an individual to contend that the courts should look to the substance of a measure *across* the categories of legal act. This is because the very nature of the test for a legislative act is formalistic in nature: enactment by a legislative procedure.[55] There are requirements, moreover, that must be satisfied for the passage of delegated acts.[56] The consequence of reclassifying a legislative act as a delegated act, or vice-versa, would therefore inevitably be to condemn it as invalid, since it would not have been enacted by the proper procedure.

(e) Change: scope of jurisdiction

The discussion thus far has been concerned with modifications to particular heads of the courts' jurisdiction. The scope of the courts' power has, however, been affected by other changes made by the Lisbon Treaty.

The most important change in this respect concerns the Pillar structure introduced by the Maastricht Treaty. Subject to the caveat entered below, this no longer applies, with the consequence that the jurisdiction of the Court of Justice of the European Union extends to all EU law, unless the Treaties stipulate to the contrary. The injunction that the Court of Justice of the European Union shall ensure that in the interpretation and application of the Treaties the law is observed,[57] is therefore of general application, save whether it is limited by specific Treaty provisions.

This will be of most significance in relation to the Area of Freedom, Security and Justice (AFSJ),[58] discussed below.[59] The courts' jurisdiction over the Third Pillar had been limited,[60] notwithstanding teleological interpretation which stretched the limits to afford the maximum possible judicial oversight. Thus in relation to police and judicial cooperation in criminal matters, the ECJ will have jurisdiction to give preliminary rulings and this will no longer be subject to a declaration by each Member State recognizing that jurisdiction and specifying the national courts that may request a preliminary ruling. Thus, subject to transitional provisions,[61] police and criminal justice will become part of the general law, and any court or tribunal can request a preliminary ruling from the Court of Justice.

---

[55] Art 289 TFEU.   [56] Art 290 TFEU.   [57] Art 19(1) TEU.
[58] Arts 67–89 TFEU.   [59] Ch 9.   [60] Art 35 EU.
[61] Protocol (No 36) On Transitional Provisions, Art 10.

The courts' jurisdiction in relation to the other aspect of the AFSJ, dealing with visas, asylum, immigration, and other policies related to free movement of persons,[62] had also been constrained, since only national courts of last resort could send preliminary rulings to the ECJ.[63] Any national court or tribunal can now seek a preliminary ruling from the ECJ.

While the Pillar structure has formally disappeared under the Lisbon Treaty, the reality is that the Union courts continue to have only very limited competence in relation to CFSP. The general rule is that the Union courts have no jurisdiction over these areas,[64] subject to two exceptions. The Court has jurisdiction to police the delimitation of the Union's competences and the CFSP.[65] It also has jurisdiction over annulment actions brought against decisions providing for restrictive measures against natural or legal persons adopted by the Council in cases concerned with, for example, combating terrorism.[66]

Another major innovation that affects the scope of the courts' jurisdiction is the Charter of Fundamental Rights, which is rendered legally binding and has the same legal value as the Treaties themselves.[67] The legal and political implications of this change are considered in a subsequent chapter.[68]

The scope of the courts' jurisdiction has in addition been affected in relation to subsidiarity. This principle was always amenable to judicial review, with the action being brought by the Member State complaining that the principle had not been respected by the Community institutions when enacting legislation. This is still possible, but the Lisbon Treaty now also makes provision for the Member State to notify such an annulment action in accordance with their legal order, on behalf of a national Parliament or one of its chambers.[69] Similarly, the Committee of the Regions can invoke subsidiarity, provided the acts are those on which it is required to be consulted.

3. Lisbon Treaty, Judicial Architecture and the Status Quo

(a) Judicial architecture: Convention deliberations

The discussion thus far has focused on changes made by the Lisbon Treaty as they pertain to judicial appointment and jurisdiction. The general judicial architecture of the EU, including relations between the ECJ and General Court, and those between the ECJ and national courts, were, however, left unchanged by the Lisbon Treaty. This was so notwithstanding significant discussion concerning such issues at the end of the millennium when the Nice Treaty was being considered. It is a truism within political science that inaction constitutes a decision every bit as much as positive action. It might be argued that

---

[62] Title IV EC.   [63] Art 68(1) EC.   [64] Art 275 TFEU.
[65] Art 40 TEU.   [66] Art 275 TFEU.   [67] Art 6 TEU.   [68] Ch 6.
[69] Protocol (No 2) On the Application of the Principles of Subsidiarity and Proportionality, Art 8.

the issues concerning judicial architecture that preoccupied earlier official and academic discourse were somehow resolved or rendered otiose in the interim. This hypothesis, however, does not bear serious scrutiny, as we shall see. We should therefore press further to understand why judicial architecture received scant if any consideration in discussions of Treaty reform that spanned almost a decade.

The answer to this inquiry requires us to step back to the deliberations in the Convention in the Future of Europe, since the provisions on courts in the Lisbon Treaty replicate those in the Constitutional Treaty. The Constitutional Treaty made significant changes in a number of areas, but not the Community judicial architecture. The Convention on the Future of Europe gave little time to the role of the Community courts, even though it would have been the obvious locus for a thorough debate on the judicial system of a kind lacking hitherto. This is so independently of the substantive conclusions that might have been reached from such a discourse. The debate never happened, there was no discourse, and the Constitutional Treaty simply took over, with minor modifications, the regime embodied in the Nice Treaty.

The reason for this lies in the more general *modus operandi* of the Convention. Working Groups were, as we have seen,[70] established to consider many of the main issues prior to discussion in the plenary sessions. It was felt, however, that institutional reform could only be dealt with in the plenary, because issues such as the role of the European Council, and the composition of the Commission, were important and controversial. These deliberations did not begin until January 2003. They were divisive with strongly held divergent views being proffered. It also became apparent that the Convention was subject to a tight deadline for the production of a Draft Constitutional Treaty and that the IGC was unwilling to extend this. The net effect was that the spring of 2003 was principally taken up with fights about the main institutional issues, plus the drafting of provisions on topics that had been dealt with by Working Groups on which consensus had been reached.

There had, at this point, been no discussion about the Community courts, and the Praesidium hurriedly convened a 'Discussion Circle' to consider judicial matters.[71] The group was, however, subject to severe time constraints. Its first meeting took place on 17 February 2003[72] and it finished its work on 17 March 2003.[73] This fortuitous temporal symmetry was not reflected in the roundedness of substantive deliberation. This was constrained by the terms of reference set by the plenary session. The temporal exigencies were readily

---

[70] Ch 1.   [71] CONV 543/03 (n 46).
[72] CONV 551/03, Meeting Concerning the Circle of Discussion of the Court of Justice, Brussels 12 February 2003.
[73] CONV 636/03, Final Report of the Discussion Circle on the Court of Justice, Brussels 25 March 2003.

apparent from this document, which stated that the 'composition of this circle should be more restricted than that of the working groups and its members should ideally be able to contribute expertise in a specific area in order to ensure efficiency and swift results'.[74]

The empowering document then listed topics that should be considered by the Discussion Circle, these being the procedure for appointing Judges and Advocates General; the possibility of shifting from unanimity to qualified majority to facilitate the application of Articles 225a, 229a, and 245 EC; whether the names of the ECJ and CFI should be altered; possible alteration to the standing rules for individual applicants, and inclusion of agencies among those susceptible to judicial review; and revision of the system of penalties for non-compliance with an ECJ judgment in an enforcement action. The empowering document left open the possibility that other topics would be examined by the Discussion Circle, but any such discussion was circumscribed by the fact that the Circle would meet only three or four times and present its report by the beginning of March 2003.[75] The Discussion Circle duly met four times during this period. It held discussions with the President of the Court of Justice,[76] the President of the Court of First Instance[77] and representatives of the Council of the Bars and Law Societies of the European Union, who addressed the issues listed above, and certain other matters.

There was therefore no general overview of the Community judicial architecture, and no discussion as to how this might be modified in the light of the more general precepts of Treaty reform. It can be accepted that the issues considered the Discussion Circle were of some importance, and the results of these deliberations were included in the Constitutional Treaty and thereafter the Lisbon Treaty. This does not alter the fact that the Convention was a major missed opportunity. It should have been the locus for a wide-ranging discussion about the Community judicial system, including the allocation of power between the ECJ and CFI, and the relationship between Community courts and national courts.

These are the key issues that shape the Community judicial architecture, as is readily apparent from the fact that it was precisely such matters that were addressed by the earlier official reports,[78] and in much of the academic

---

[74] CONV 543/03 (n 46) 2.   [75] ibid 3.

[76] CONV 572/03, Oral Presentation by M Gil Rodriguez Iglesias, President of the ECJ, to the Discussion Circle on the Court of Justice, Brussels 10 March 2003.

[77] CONV 575/03, Oral Presentation by M Bo Vesterdorf to the Discussion Circle on the Court of Justice, Brussels 10 March 2003.

[78] The Future of the Judicial System of the European Union (Proposals and Reflections) (May 1999), available at <http://europa.eu.int/cj/en/instit/txtdocfr/autrestxts/ave.pdf> (hereafter referred to as the Courts' Paper); Report by the Working Party on the Future of the European Communities' Court System (January 2000) (hereafter referred to as the Due Report).

commentary.[79] The deliberations in the Convention would therefore have been the natural place for consideration of issues raised, but not hitherto resolved, in these reports, and of other related matters that were not examined by these studies. It did not happen. The heads of jurisdiction remained much the same as before, subject to the changes noted above, as did the general division of jurisdiction between the Union courts.

It is therefore fitting to provide some more detailed consideration of the EU's judicial architecture, and the challenges to be faced in the years after the Lisbon Treaty. There will doubtless be differences of view as to these issues, but this does not thereby obviate the significance of the discourse.

(b) Judicial Architecture: ECJ, General Court, and direct actions

(i) Nomenclature, reality, and principle

The nomenclature of the CFI was always somewhat problematic, since it was never a first instance court for all actions. This disjunction between appellation and reality has been heightened further by the Lisbon Treaty, since the circumscription of the General Court's[80] jurisdictional competence sits uneasily with its new title. The jurisdiction of the CFI grew in an ad hoc manner. Heads of jurisdiction were given to it primarily to relieve the ECJ's workload, hence the assignment of staff cases and competition cases to the CFI. The transfer of all direct actions brought by non-privileged applicants was fuelled by similar concerns. The jurisdiction of the General Court remains central to the overall judicial architecture of the EU.

It is important at the outset to be clear as to the principles that should guide the division of jurisdiction between the ECJ and the General Court. This inquiry depends, explicitly or implicitly, on certain assumptions about the principal

[79] A Arnull, 'Judicial Architecture or Judicial Folly? The Challenge Facing the European Union' (1999) 24 ELRev 516; H Rasmussen, 'Remedying the Crumbling EC Judicial System' (2000) 37 CMLRev 1071; P Craig, 'The Jurisdiction of the Community Courts Reconsidered' in G de Búrca and J Weiler (eds), *The European Court of Justice* (Oxford University Press, 2001) ch 6; J Weiler, 'Epilogue: The Judicial Après Nice', ibid, 215; R Caranta, 'Diritto comunitario e tutela giuridica di fronte al giudice amministrativo italiano' (2001) Rivista Trimestrale di Diritto Pubblico 81; A Dashwood and A Johnston (eds), *The Future of the Judicial System of the European Union* (Hart, 2001); N Forwood, 'The Judicial Architecture of the European Union—the Challenges of Change' in M Hoskins and W Robinson (eds), *A True European, Essays for Judge David Edward* (Hart, 2003) 81; B Vesterdorf, 'The Community Court System Ten Years from Now and Beyond: Problems and Possibilities' (2003) 28 ELRev 203; C Timmermans, 'The European Union's Judicial System' (2004) 41 CMLRev 393; I Pernice, J Kokott and C Saunders (eds), *The Future of the European Judicial System in Comparative Perspective* (Nomos, 2006); H Rasmussen, 'Present and Future European Judicial Problems after Enlargement and the Post-2005 Ideological Revolt' (2007) 44 CMLRev 1661; N Forwood, 'The Court of First Instance, its Development, and Future Role in the Legal Architecture of the European Union' in A Arnull, P Eeckhout and T Tridimas (eds), *Continuity and Change in EU Law, Essays in Honour of Sir Francis Jacobs* (Oxford University Press, 2008) ch 3.

[80] Art 19 TEU.

objectives of a reformed regime. The earlier official reports posited three fundamental requirements that should be taken into account when thinking about the future of the judicial system:[81] the need to secure the unity of Community law by means of a supreme court; the need to ensure that the judicial system is transparent, comprehensible, and accessible to the public; and the need to dispense justice without unacceptable delay.

Two further considerations should be added to this list. The division of judicial power between the ECJ and General Court should be as coherent and symmetrical as possible; and the system should be structured to ensure that the most important points of law are decided by the ECJ, and that it is, so far as possible, not troubled by less important cases. These considerations have been acknowledged by the judges themselves. Thus Vesterdorf argued convincingly that 'in the long term, the ECJ should focus only on deciding the main constitutional issues and on safeguarding the consistency of EU law where necessary',[82] and the same theme was echoed by Forwood, who advocated a sensible system of allocation of judicial tasks 'that would reserve to the highest Community court and give it time to reflect on only those cases that truly merit the attention of a "supreme" court'.[83]

These criteria can provide the foundation for a rational system of Union judicial architecture. A significant step in this direction would be for the jurisdiction of the General Court to reflect its nomenclature and become a real general court of first instance for all direct actions, with limited rights of appeal to the ECJ.

(ii) Jurisdiction, principle, and attainment

The possibility that the General Court might have initial jurisdiction over all types of direct action has come closer to being attained, although it is not yet a reality.

The possibility that the CFI might become a court of first instance for all direct actions was considered by both reports that preceded the Nice Treaty. The Courts' paper was hesitant, however, about the possible transfer of further competence to the CFI to hear direct actions. It stated that there were no grounds at that time for proposing the transfer of any heads of jurisdiction over and above those whose transfer had already been proposed by the ECJ, while leaving open the possibility that 'it may become necessary, if the volume of cases continues to grow, to review the basis on which jurisdiction is allocated between the two Community courts and to transfer further heads of jurisdiction to the Court of First Instance'.[84]

---

[81] The Future of the Judicial System (n 78) 18; Report by the Working Party (n 78) 10.
[82] B Vesterdorf, 'A Constitutional Court for the EU' in Pernice, Kokott and Saunders (n 79) 87.
[83] Forwood 'The Court of First Instance' (n 79) 36.
[84] The Future of the Judicial System (n 78) 21.

The Due Report was more forthcoming in this respect.[85] Its starting point was that the CFI should, as a matter of principle, be the first judicial forum for direct actions, including review for legality and compensation. The CFI's jurisdiction would include actions brought by a Member State or Community institution. This principle was then qualified in the Report such that direct actions involving matters of urgency and importance would be assigned to the ECJ.[86] Only those cases where a rapid judgment was essential to avoid serious problems in the proper functioning of the Community institutions would fall into this category.[87]

The changes made by the Nice Treaty moved matters in the direction suggested by the Due Report. The position hitherto had been that the CFI would be accorded jurisdiction over certain classes of case as a result of a determination made by the Council, albeit at the request of the ECJ, subject to the Treaty limitation at the time that the CFI could not hear preliminary rulings. The Nice Treaty modified Article 225(1) EC by formally assigning certain categories of case to the CFI, and this format has been carried over to the Lisbon Treaty, Article 256(1) TFEU of which provides, as we have seen, that the General Court has jurisdiction in relation to Articles 263, 265, 268, 270, and 272 TFEU, with the exception of those assigned to a specialized court set up under Article 257 TFEU and those reserved in the Statute for the Court of Justice. The Statute can provide for the General Court to have jurisdiction for other classes of action.

The General Court's jurisdiction over direct actions has also been extended as a result of changes to the Statute of the Court, since the narrower the class of case reserved by the Statute for the ECJ the broader the jurisdictional remit of the General Court. Article 51 of the Statute of the Court had hitherto reserved jurisdiction to the ECJ in all actions brought by Member States, the Community institutions, and the European Central Bank (ECB). This Article was amended in 2004 so as to give the CFI increased jurisdiction over direct actions,[88] and this formulation has been preserved in the version of the Statute appended to the Lisbon Treaty.[89]

Thus Article 51 of the Statute continues to reserve jurisdiction for the ECJ in relation to direct actions for review of legality and failure to act brought by a Union institution against certain other Union institutions.[90] Jurisdiction also remains with the ECJ where a Member State seeks to challenge the legality of an act or failure to act by the European Parliament or Council, or where these

---

[85] Report by the Working Party (n 78) 23–29.
[86] ibid 24–25.   [87] ibid 25.
[88] Council Decision 2004/407/EC, Euratom of 26 April 2004, Amending Arts 51 and 54 of the Protocol of the Statute of the Court of Justice [2004] OJ L132/5.
[89] Protocol (No 3) On the Statute of the Court of Justice of the European Union, available at <http://curia.europa.eu/jcms/jcms/Jo2_7031/>.
[90] Council, European Parliament, Commission and ECB.

institutions act jointly, subject to limited exceptions.[91] The General Court, however, is accorded jurisdiction in actions brought by Member States against the Commission, subject to a limited exception.[92]

The thrust of the Due Report's proposal is to be welcomed, as are the steps in that direction taken by the Nice Treaty and Lisbon Treaty. There is a strong case for rationalizing the present regime and making it more coherent by transforming the General Court into a real first instance court in all direct actions. This would be a rational working through of Declaration 12 attached to the Nice Treaty, which stipulated that the ECJ and the Commission should, as soon as possible, present proposals for the division of jurisdiction between the ECJ and the CFI, particularly in the area of direct actions.

We should move away from the idea that the General Court is a court solely for technical or factually complex cases. We should not accept that the jurisdiction of the General Court is destined forever to remain eclectic and ad hoc. The changes made to Article 51 of the Statute, which have increased the General Court's jurisdiction over direct actions, are welcome, but serve by their very patchwork nature to complicate the jurisdictional divide between the ECJ and the General Court.

It is, moreover, difficult to sustain a principled argument as to why the General Court should be accorded jurisdiction in these areas and not others. The General Court is already the first instance court for direct actions involving non-privileged applicants, who seek to challenge the validity of Union norms, and for the great majority of actions brought by a Member State against the Commission. Its jurisdiction should be extended to enable it to hear all direct actions under Articles 263 and 265 TFEU, even where the case is brought by a privileged applicant such as the Council, Commission, European Parliament, or a Member State.

It would also be desirable if the General Court could operate as a first instance court in enforcement actions brought under Article 258 TFEU.[93] The wording of this provision is, as we have seen,[94] ambiguous, but the General Court does not at present have jurisdiction over such actions. The Member States may be particularly resistant to a change which would mean that they could be sued before the General Court for non-compliance with Union obligations, rather than before the ECJ itself. This should not dissuade us from making the General Court a court of first instance in all direct actions under Articles 263 and 265 TFEU, with the possibility of appeal to the ECJ. General Court decisions made

---

[91] An action by a Member State can be heard by the General Court where it relates to a Council decision under sub-para three of Art 108(2) TFEU concerning State aids; where it concerns Council acts adopted pursuant to a regulation to protect trade pursuant to Art 207 TFEU; and most significantly in relation to acts of the Council where the Council exercises implementing powers in accord with the second para of Art 291 TFEU.

[92] Except in the area covered by Art 331 TFEU dealing with enhanced cooperation.

[93] Forwood (n 79) 87.   [94] p 125.

pursuant to Article 256(1) TFEU are in any event subject to appeal to the ECJ on a point of law, under the conditions laid down by the Statute.

The vision of the General Court as first instance court in direct actions does moreover fit well with other developments in the general regime of Union adjudication. To an increasing extent cases which come before the Union courts will already have been the subject of some form of adjudication. This has always been the case in the context of competition and State aids where the Commission gives a formal, legally binding decision, which can be challenged before the General Court. The development of a specialist agency in the context of trade marks is a further move in the same direction. Staff cases are now dealt with through the Civil Service Tribunal,[95] subject to appeal to the General Court, and further review by the ECJ where there is a serious risk of the unity or consistency of Community law being affected, and consideration is being given to the creation of a panel to deal with patents.

If we put together these ideas then a rational division of jurisdiction begins to emerge. The General Court should become the court of first instance in direct actions irrespective of the nature of the applicant. If this requires more judges in the General Court this can be done within the limits of Article 19(2) TEU, which specifies that the General Court should have at least one judge per Member State, leaving open the possibility of more. The General Court works in Chambers and this can be used to accommodate the need for subject-matter specialization. Article 256(1) TFEU limits appeal to the ECJ to points of law, and the details of such appeals are specified further by Articles 56 to 62 of the Statute.

(c) Judicial architecture: ECJ, General Court, and preliminary rulings

The discussion thus far has concentrated on the role of the General Court in direct actions. This still leaves open the issue of preliminary rulings. Possible reform of the preliminary ruling procedure raises important issues concerning the nature of the relationship between the national courts and the Union courts. It also has implications for the relationship between the ECJ and the General Court.

Prior to the Nice Treaty all requests for a preliminary ruling were heard by the ECJ, because the Treaty precluded the CFI from hearing such actions. The ECJ's workload problem, however, arose in part from the increasing burden of preliminary rulings. The reports prior to the Nice Treaty therefore considered whether this problem could be alleviated by allowing the CFI to give preliminary rulings. This possibility was canvassed positively, albeit cautiously, in the Courts' paper.[96] The Due Report, however, was opposed to this change, except in a

---

[95] Council Decision 2004/752/EC, Euratom of 2 November 2004 establishing the European Union Civil Service Tribunal [2004] OJ L333/7; Protocol (No 3) (n 89) Annex 1.
[96] The Future of the Judicial System (n 78) 27.

limited number of special areas. Such rulings should, said the Report, be given by the ECJ because this was the most important task for the development of Community law. The Due Report was influenced in reaching this conclusion by the fact that preliminary rulings take the form of a reference of a question from a national court to the ECJ, while the substance of the case remains for resolution by the national court. It was felt that the consequence must be a 'one-stop-shop', in the sense that the questions referred by the national court should go to only one Community court, because of the time delays thereby involved, and thus there would be difficulties in providing for an appeal to the ECJ from the CFI's rulings.[97]

The Nice Treaty, however, accorded the CFI power for the first time to hear preliminary rulings. Article 225(3) EC provided that the CFI had jurisdiction to determine preliminary rulings in areas specified by the Statute of the Court of Justice. Where the CFI believed that the case required a decision of principle which was likely to affect the unity or consistency of Community law, it could refer the case to the ECJ. Preliminary rulings given by the CFI could, exceptionally, be subject to review by the ECJ, under the conditions laid down in the Statute, where there was a serious risk to the unity or consistency of Community law being affected.

This system has been retained in the Lisbon Treaty, Article 256(3) TFEU of which replicates Article 225(3) EC. The circumstances in which there is a serious risk to the unity or consistency of EU law are spelt out in more detail in the Statute of the Court.[98] There is much to be said for the idea that the General Court should be able to give preliminary rulings.[99] It is therefore unfortunate that the power to create categories of such cases that can be heard by the CFI, now the General Court, has not been acted on for the past decade.

(i) Preliminary rulings, the general court, and indirect challenge to community norms

A category of preliminary ruling involved indirect challenges to the validity of Community norms through Article 234 EC, where the non-privileged applicants

---

[97] Report by the Working Party (n 78) 22. However, compare the discussion in the Courts' paper, which explicitly considered the possibility of two adjudications on preliminary rulings in the context of its discussion of decentralized judicial bodies, The Future of the Judicial System (n 78) 28–29.

[98] Protocol (No 3) (n 4) Art 62.

[99] J Azizi, 'Opportunities and Limits for the Transfer of Preliminary Reference Proceedings to the Court of First Instance' in Pernice, Kokott and Saunders (n 79) 241–256; J Azizi, 'Die Institutionenreform in der EU aus der Sicht der Gerichtsbarkeit' in W Hummer (ed), *Paradigmen-wechsel im Europarecht zur Jahrtausendwende* (Wien, 2004) 181–229; S Prechal, 'Who should do what?' in *La Cour de Justice des Communautés européennes, 1952–2002: Bilan et Perspectives* (Bruylant, 2004) 63–85; U Everling, 'The Future of the European Judiciary within the enlarged European Union' in *Mélanges en hommage à Michel Waelbroeck* (Bruylant, 1999) 333–354; P Dyrberg, 'What should the Court of Justice be doing?' (2001) 26 ELRev 291.

could not satisfy the standing criteria under Article 230 EC. The perverse institutional consequence of the restrictive standing rules limiting access under Article 230 EC was therefore to compel such applicants to use Article 234 EC, thereby further overburdening the ECJ. The reform to the standing rules in Article 263(4) TFEU may render such cases less likely in the future, but how far this is so depends upon the interpretation given to the new provision, and the uncertainties surrounding this were considered earlier.[100]

This does not alter the fact that the substance of such cases is concerned with just the kind of issues that would be heard by the General Court in a direct action under Article 263 TFEU. The subject matter of such cases relates to the validity or interpretation of a Union act. It cannot therefore be argued that the General Court is ill-equipped to hear such actions if they emerge indirectly via national courts as requests for preliminary rulings. Moreover, many of these cases involve no general point of importance for Union law. The paradigm is normally a technical issue concerning the meaning of an article in a Union regulation, directive, or decision, which requires judicial resolution, but not the scarce resources of the ECJ.

Lenaerts has argued that this analogy should be treated with caution, because the direct action is subject to appeal on points of law, whereas if such matters were to be heard by the General Court as preliminary rulings then its judgment would in principle be definitive, subject to exceptional review by the ECJ.[101] However, this does not alter the fact that the subject matter of such indirect challenges to the validity of Union norms would be heard as a direct action by the General Court if the standing rules were more liberally interpreted.

Given that this is so, it is difficult to see why the subject matter of such actions should be regarded as ill-suited to the General Court if they arose as indirect actions. The legal arguments that might be addressed against a Union regulation, whether framed in terms of proportionality, legitimate expectations, fundamental rights, etc, will not alter depending on whether the challenge is direct or indirect. Insofar as there is concern that there would be less recourse to the ECJ from the General Court in such indirect actions than there is from direct actions, this would be a general problem and not one restricted to this category of case. We shall return to this issue below.

(ii) Preliminary rulings, the general court, and indirect challenge to Member State action

The paradigm case of preliminary ruling, however, is a challenge to Member State action, but we should not be wedded to the idea that these must necessarily

---

[100] pp 130–132.
[101] K Lenaerts, 'The Unity of European Law and the Overload of the ECJ—The System of Preliminary Rulings Revisited' in Pernice, Kokott and Saunders (n 79) 235.

be heard by the ECJ. The Treaty framers' clearly did not believe that all such cases should be the exclusive preserve of the ECJ, since this runs counter to the very reforms made by the Nice Treaty, which empowered what is now the General Court to hear such cases within specific areas to be delineated by the Statute. It is, moreover, mistaken to think that all such cases are significant either for the development of Union law, or for the Member State. Many such cases involve technical issues as to whether, for example, a Member State provision is compatible with EU rules on VAT and the like.

There is no reason why preliminary rulings should not go initially to the General Court, with the possibility of further recourse to the ECJ in accord with Article 256(3) TFEU. This provides two mechanisms for getting a case from the General Court to the ECJ: either the General Court refers it on to the ECJ because the General Court considers that the case raises an issue of principle likely to affect the unity or consistency of EU law, or the General Court's decision can be subject to review by the ECJ where there is a serious risk that the unity or consistency of EU law will be affected. The General Court could, subject to this caveat, be the first instance court for preliminary rulings as well as direct actions.

This conclusion can be reinforced by considering the plausibility of the strategy in the Nice Treaty, now embodied in the Lisbon Treaty, that the General Court has jurisdiction to give preliminary rulings only in specific areas. There is some evidence that members of the ECJ are not eager to empower the General Court,[102] and there has been no progress thus far in delineating these 'areas'. This is not fortuitous. A moment's reflection will reveal the difficulty in applying this precept. The phrase 'specific areas' indicates that the criterion is to be subject matter: the General Court would be afforded competence to give preliminary rulings in relation to energy or agriculture, transport or customs.

However, this is problematic. Cases do not always fit neatly into such pigeon-holes, and hence there would inevitably be boundary problems leading to uncertainty for national courts and costly procedural litigation. The strategy is flawed more importantly because there is no correlation between subject matter area and the importance of the point of Union law raised by the case, a point acknowledged by members of the Union courts.[103] We know full well from existing jurisprudence that preliminary rulings in, for example, agricultural and customs cases generated some of the most important points of Community law principle, even where the sums at stake were small. We know equally well that there were many cases in these areas that entailed no issue of Community law principle at all, often being concerned with the relative minutiae of statutory

---

[102] Vesterdorf (n 82).
[103] Lenaerts (n 101) 233; Azizi (n 99) 249–251; F Jacobs, 'Recent and Ongoing Measures to Improve the Efficiency of the European Court of Justice' (2004) 29 ELRev 823, 826.

interpretation. There is therefore no ready method of choosing 'specific areas' in which the General Court should be competent to give preliminary rulings.

The only way to avoid this conclusion would be to limit the General Court's competence to very specialist areas, such as judicial cooperation in civil matters, which give rise to specific issues of private international law,[104] or in relation to matters such as customs classification.[105] However, this would have relatively little impact on the overall work problem of the ECJ. Nor would it furnish any reason as to why the General Court should be precluded from acting as the first instance court for preliminary rulings in other areas. Forwood took the view that the mere fact that an area is important or central to the Community legal order should not necessarily preclude a transfer to what was then the CFI, although he argued that the relative maturity of the case law should be taken into account.[106] It seems clear that judges on the General Court and ECJ take differing views as to which areas might be suited for the exercise of preliminary ruling jurisdiction by the General Court.[107]

The principled and pragmatic solution would be to accord the General Court with a general competence to hear preliminary rulings, with the possibility of further recourse to the ECJ where necessary.[108] Article 256(3) TFEU already embodies sound criteria in this respect: the General Court can refer the matter on to the ECJ where the case requires a decision of principle likely to affect the unity and consistency of Union law, and the ECJ can review the decisions made by the General Court where there is a serious risk of the unity or consistency of Union law being affected.

Lenaerts argues that this would be undesirable because it would introduce an unwarranted distinction between direct actions and preliminary rulings. In relation to the former, the General Court would be a true first instance court, with onward appeal on points of law to the ECJ. In relation to the latter, the General Court's preliminary ruling would be *prima facie* definitive, subject to invocation of exceptional review by the ECJ in accord with Article 256(3) TFEU.[109] There is force in this argument. There are, however, two responses.

First, the criteria contained in Article 256(3) TFEU reflect the considered view of those who framed the Nice Treaty and the Lisbon Treaty that preliminary rulings by the General Court should only be subject to limited oversight by the ECJ, and not general appeal on point of law. Moreover, it should not be too readily assumed that the criteria in Article 256(3) allow for less control by the

---

[104] Report by the Working Party (n 78).
[105] Lenaerts (n 101) 234; Azizi (n 99) 251.
[106] Forwood (n 79) 86.
[107] Compare Lenaerts (n 101) 234–236; Forwood, 'The Court of First Instance' (n 79) 45–46; Azizi (n 99) 251–252.
[108] See also, Rasmussen (n 79) 1098–1103; Weiler (n 79) 222–223; Prechal (n 99) 66. For a contrary view, Lenaerts (n 101) 235–236.
[109] Lenaerts (n 101) 235–236.

ECJ than for direct actions where there is an appeal on point of law. The control is different, but the criteria in Article 256(3) allow the ECJ to be proactive in taking a case, whereas the regime for appeal on law is premised on one of the parties seeking to exercise such appellate rights, and they only do so in approximately 25 per cent of cases.[110] The existing criteria in Article 256(3) TFEU in any event allow for two routes whereby a preliminary ruling can go from the General Court to the ECJ: exceptional review by the ECJ; and the General Court deciding that the case warrants the attention of the ECJ. Both could be liberally interpreted in areas where the unity or consistency of EU law was placed in jeopardy. Indeed Vesterdorf argued strongly that the criteria in Article 256(3) provide ample safeguards to secure the unity and consistency of EU law.[111]

Second, if this interpretation of the criteria in Article 256(3) TFEU was felt to be insufficient then the criteria could be modified. It might be argued that more control by the ECJ over the General Court would be warranted if the latter were to be become the court of first instance for preliminary rulings. Parity in this respect between direct actions and preliminary rulings heard by the General Court could be ensured by allowing appeal on points of law from the latter actions as well as the former. Alternatively such appeals on point of law could be added to the existing criteria in Article 256(3). It might be contended that such changes would undermine the benefits of the primary reform, since the ECJ would still be regularly beset by such appeals and hence its workload would not be reduced. This is not self-evidently so: only approximately 25 per cent of General Court decisions are appealed to the ECJ and only approximately 20 per cent of such appeals are successful.[112] Moreover, the very fact that the case has already been subject to detailed scrutiny by the General Court will normally facilitate consideration of any appeal on point of law by the ECJ, since the arguments will already have been subject to such analysis.[113] It would also be possible to render any appeal on point of law subject to permission from either the General Court or the ECJ, a feature common in a number of domestic legal systems.

4. Lisbon Treaty, Courts, and Judicial Doctrine

It is important to consider the impact of the Lisbon Treaty on foundational judicial doctrine, in particular direct effect and supremacy.

---

[110] V Skouris, 'Self-Conception, Challenges and Perspectives of the EU Courts' in Pernice, Kokott and Saunders (n 79) 26; Forwood, 'The Court of First Instance' (n 79) 43.

[111] Vesterdorf (n 82) 88–89.

[112] Skouris (n 110) 26; Forwood, 'The Court of First Instance' (n 79) 43–44.

[113] Forwood, 'The Court of First Instance' (n 79) 43.

(a) Direct effect

The doctrine of direct effect was created by the ECJ and developed thereafter by the Community courts. The Lisbon Treaty does not signal any change in the doctrine itself, but it does have significant implications for its scope of application.

The most significant change in this respect is the result of de-pillarization. Article 34 EU had provided for a distinct set of legal norms that were used in the context of the Third Pillar, dealing with Police and Judicial Cooperation in Criminal Matters. Framework Decisions and Decisions were the most important legal norms used in this area, and Article 34(2) EU stated that they should not have direct effect. The ECJ had interpreted this stricture narrowly, and held that it did not preclude indirect effect.[114]

The Lisbon Treaty has brought what was the Third Pillar into the main body of EU law, and it falls within Title V of Part Three of the TFEU. Article 34 EU has been repealed and the general regime of legal acts specified in the Lisbon Treaty applies to measures adopted in the Area of Freedom, Security and Justice. The Lisbon Treaty specifies the nature of the legislative procedure that is applicable for measures adopted in the AFSJ; on some occasions this is the ordinary legislative procedure, on others a special legislative procedure is specified.

The net result of these changes is that it will henceforth be possible to argue that a Treaty article, or a legislative, delegated, or implementing act dealing with the AFSJ adopted after entry into force of the Lisbon Treaty, gives rise to direct effect, provided that it meets the judicially created criteria for direct effect. This change is likely to generate significant litigation as to whether those criteria have been met, given the plethora of measures adopted by the EU concerning the AFSJ.[115]

There are, however, transitional provisions that limit the legal impact of the Lisbon Treaty on measures concerning Police and Judicial Cooperation in Criminal Matters adopted before its entry into force.[116] The transitional provisions operate for five years, and their impact will be considered in a subsequent chapter.[117]

(b) Supremacy

The primacy of EU law over national law had not hitherto been enshrined in the Treaties. The supremacy doctrine was developed by the ECJ, and, as is well

---

[114] Case C-105/03 *Criminal Proceedings against Maria Pupino* [2005] ECR I-5283.

[115] Protocol (No 21) On the Position of the United Kingdom and Ireland in respect of the Area of Freedom, Security and Justice, makes special provision for the UK and Ireland. It is considered below, ch 9.

[116] Protocol (No 36) On Transitional Provisions, Arts 9–10.   [117] Ch 9.

known, met with a mixed reception from national courts.[118] The Constitutional Treaty did bite this particular constitutional bullet. Article I-6 CT provided that:

The Constitution and law adopted by the institutions of the Union in exercising competences conferred on it shall have primacy over the law of the Member States.

This provision was dropped from the Lisbon Treaty at the behest of the European Council in 2007, the rationale being that this would, with other changes, thereby diminish its 'constitutional character'.[119] It was replaced in the Lisbon Treaty by a Declaration concerning primacy.[120]

The Conference recalls that, in accordance with well settled case law of the Court of Justice of the European Union, the Treaties and the law adopted by the Union on the basis of the Treaties have primacy over the law of Member States, under the conditions laid down by the said case law.

The Conference has also decided to attach as an Annex to this Final Act the Opinion of the Council Legal Service on the primacy of EC law as set out in 11197/07 (JUR 260).

The opinion of the Council Legal Service appended to the Declaration was brief, reiterating the basic *communautaire* view on the topic.

It results from the case-law of the Court of Justice that primacy of EC law is a cornerstone principle of Community law. According to the Court, this principle is inherent to the specific nature of the European Community. At the time of the first judgment of this established case law (Costa/ENEL, 15 July 1964, Case 6/64 (1) there was no mention of primacy in the treaty. It is still the case today. The fact that the principle of primacy will not be included in the future treaty shall not in any way change the existence of the principle and the existing case-law of the Court of Justice.

The wisdom of dropping the primacy clause from the Lisbon Treaty, and the status of primacy under the Lisbon Treaty require separate consideration.

(i) Supremacy and the Constitutional Treaty

There are doubtless differences of view as to whether dropping the primacy clause from the Lisbon Treaty was a wise move. Its removal from the Lisbon Treaty might cause some national courts to doubt the continuing validity of the supremacy principle, though this is unlikely. Any such dangers are however outweighed by the problems with Article I-6 CT.[121]

---

[118] P Craig and G de Búrca, *EU Law, Text, Cases and Materials* (Oxford University Press, 4th edn, 2007) ch 10.

[119] Brussels European Council, 21–22 June 2007, Annex 1, para 4.

[120] Declaration 17 Concerning Primacy.

[121] P Craig, 'The Constitutional Treaty and Sovereignty' in C Kaddous and A Auer (eds), *Les Principes Fondamentaux de la Constitution Européene/The Fundamental Principles of the European Constitution* (Dossier de Droit Europeen No 15, Helbing & Lictenhahn/Bruylan/LGDJ, 2006) 117–134.

The most significant, but by no means the only problem was that the wording
of Article I-6 CT was crucially ambiguous. The phrase 'shall have primacy over
the law of the Member States' could have been interpreted to mean, following
the jurisprudence of the ECJ,[122] that supremacy operated over all national law,
including provisions in a national constitution. It could alternatively have been
read so as to accord primacy to EU law over national law, but not the national
constitution itself.

This ambiguity was reinforced by the wording of the Article viewed in its
entirety: the early part of Article I-6 CT, which referred to the EU, distinguished
between the Constitution and law adopted by the institutions. It would have
been perfectly possible to have drafted Article I-6 'symmetrically' so as to read
that 'the Constitution and law adopted by the institutions of the Union in
exercising competences conferred on it shall have primacy over the *constitution*
and law of the Member States', thereby removing the ambiguity.

The fact that such a formulation was not chosen by the Convention on the
Future of Europe was almost certainly because it would have been very controversial. It would have been more difficult to secure agreement on the Constitutional Treaty in the Convention and the subsequent IGC.

It would in addition have created serious problems in some national Constitutional Courts, which might either have decided that according primacy of EU
law over the national constitution was simply not constitutionally possible, or
that it would require a constitutional amendment. The issue might have come
before some national Constitutional Courts prior to ratification of the EU
Constitution. It would in any event have surely arisen after the Constitutional
Treaty entered into force. The ECJ would in all probability have interpreted
Article I-6 CT in accordance with its existing jurisprudence, such that any norm
of EU law, even the lowliest implementing act, took priority over any norm of
national law, including the national constitution. This conclusion would almost
certainly have been unacceptable to many national Constitutional Courts, which
would have held either that it was not constitutionally possible for their respective Member States to accede to a Treaty on these terms, or that it could only have
been done through explicit constitutional amendment. The result would have
been a constitutional crisis.

It might be argued by way of response that primacy of EU law over all national
law has been the 'law' as far as the ECJ is concerned ever since the early 1970s.
This may well be true, but the legal reality is that it has not been generally
accepted by national courts. This 'disjunction' was almost certainly acknowledged by Community and national courts. Neither side, however, was spoiling
for the ultimate fight on the issue, which is why 'constitutional tolerance'
prevented constitutional crisis.

---

[122] Case 11/70 *Internationale Handelsgesellschaft mbH v Einfuhr- und Vorratstelle für Getreide
und Futtermittel* [1970] ECR 1125, [3].

This was possible in part precisely because there was no hard-edged Treaty provision embodying the ECJ's view. If Article I-6 CT had been brought into the picture this would have changed. Inclusion of this provision would have 'invited' legal interpretation, which would perforce have come before the ECJ. The resultant decision would have constituted a formal ruling on a provision of constitutional principle embodied in Part I of the Constitutional Treaty. It would have inevitably raised the 'stakes' as between national Constitutional Courts and the ECJ, and could well have precipitated a crisis of the kind mentioned above. It is therefore sometimes better not to write things down in hard-edged Treaty provisions.

(ii) Supremacy and the Lisbon Treaty

This still leaves open the status of the supremacy principle under the Lisbon Treaty. This will, subject to what is said below, very likely continue much as it had under the EC Treaty. The ECJ will continue to espouse its version of primacy, using the Declaration appended to the Lisbon Treaty to reinforce this.

It should be noted, however, that the Declaration suffers from the very same infirmity that pervaded Article I-6 CT. It too is framed in terms of the EU law having 'primacy over the law of the Member States', which once again is ambiguous as to whether it covers all national law, including the constitution, or whether the latter is excluded. It could be argued that the broader construction should be given, because the Declaration states that such primacy is to operate 'under the conditions laid down by the said case law'. This refers to the ECJ's jurisprudence, under which all EU law has primacy over all national law, including national constitutions.

It is nonetheless very unlikely that national Constitutional Courts will be persuaded to forget their previous concerns, and accept that EU law prevails over national constitutions, based on a Declaration appended to the Treaties. The 'disjunction' of view between EU and national judiciaries noted above will therefore be likely to continue under the new legal order. It is unlikely that either side will be eager to pick a fight on this issue, although changes of judicial personnel can lead to altered perspectives in this respect.

There is nothing to suggest, moreover, that the Lisbon Treaty has 'resolved' the *Kompetenz-Kompetenz* issue, as to who is to decide on the ultimate boundary of Union competences.[123] Nor is there anything in the Lisbon Treaty that

---

[123] N MacCormick, *Questioning Sovereignty* (Oxford University Press, 1999); C Schmid, 'From Pont d'Avignon to Ponte Vecchio: The Resolution of Constitutional Conflicts between the EU and the Member States through Principles of Public International Law' (1998) 18 YBEL 415; M Kumm, 'Who is the Final Arbiter of Constitutionality in Europe?: Three Conceptions of the Relationship between the German Federal Constitutional Court and the European Court of Justice' (1999) 36 CMLRev 351; N Walker, 'The Idea of Constitutional Pluralism' (2002) 65 MLR 317; N Walker, 'Late Sovereignty in the European Union' in N Walker (ed), *Sovereignty in Transition*

strengthens the ECJ's claim to be the ultimate decider in such instances. There is no doubt that the ECJ would have authority to pronounce on a disputed issue as to whether the EU has competence to act or not, pursuant to its general jurisdiction to interpret EU law in Article 19 TEU. This does not mean, however, that its judgment would be conclusive in this respect. Moreover, the wording of Article 5(2) TEU, which is framed in terms of the Union acting within the limits of the competences conferred on it by the Member States, and competences not conferred on the EU remaining with the Member States, does nothing to bolster the claims of the EU to decide on the ultimate boundaries of competence.

The problem of *Kompetenz-Kompetenz* might well be more significant under the Lisbon Treaty than hitherto. Boundary problems can arise either as a result of judicial or legislative action. An individual might argue before a national court that action is beyond the EU's competence because the ECJ accorded an interpretation to a Treaty article that it could not properly bear. An individual might in a similar vein contend that the EU legislature enacted acts beyond those that could be based on the particular Treaty article. The very fact that Union competences have been divided into categories renders this type of challenge more likely than before, because the boundary lines between these heads of competence, as seen below, can be difficult to discern.[124]

The Lisbon Treaty, however, will reinforce the primacy of EU law in an important respect. There was debate under the pre-existing regime as to whether the primacy of Community law applied in relation to the Second and Third Pillars,[125] although the matter was never ultimately tested in the courts. The de-pillarization that is integral to the Lisbon Treaty means that the ECJ will surely resolve this conceptual issue in favour of the primacy of EU law covering matters that were hitherto part of the Third Pillar and are now shifted to the TFEU. It should be noted, however, that the potential for clashes between Union acts and national constitutional precepts is especially prevalent in this area. This could in turn lead to cases that test the boundaries of the primacy doctrine when the conflict with EU law involves national constitutional provisions.

The Union courts do not have jurisdiction over the CFSP, except to ensure that acts passed under the CFSP do not trespass on issues that are the preserve of the general Treaties and vice-versa, and to review the legality of restrictive measures taken by the Council that affect natural or legal persons.[126] There is

---

(Hart, 2003) ch 1; M Maduro, 'Contrapunctual Law: Europe's Constitutional Pluralism in Action' in Walker ibid ch 21; A von Bogdandy, 'Pluralism, Direct Effect, and the Ultimate Say: On the Relationship between International and Domestic Constitutional Law' (2008) 6 I-CON 397.

[124] Ch 5.

[125] K Lenaerts and T Corthaut, 'Of Birds and Hedges: The Role of Primacy in Invoking Norms of EU Law' (2006) 31 ELRev 287; A Hinarejos, *Judicial Control in the European Union: Reforming Jurisdiction in the Intergovernmental Pillars* (Oxford University Press, 2009).

[126] Art 275 TFEU.

no reason, however, why decisions on these matters should not have primacy over any inconsistent national law. This issue is explored in more detail in the discussion of the CFSP below.[127]

5. Lisbon Treaty, Ratification, and National Courts

The evolution of EU legal doctrine has always been a two-dimensional process, more especially in relation to key concepts such as supremacy. The ECJ elaborated its far-reaching vision, which embodied the idea that all EU law was supreme over all national law, including national constitutional precepts. However, most national constitutional courts placed various limits on the acceptance of EU supremacy, and were in addition unwilling to cede the ultimate *Kompetenz-Kompetenz* to the ECJ in the determination of the scope of Community power.[128] The 'legal discourse' between the ECJ and national courts continued over time, with neither side anxious to test its abstract claims in concrete contestation. This may well continue to be the pattern for the future, and we have already seen that the Lisbon Treaty reduced the probability of conflict by removing the supremacy clause that had been contained in the Constitutional Treaty.

The potential for conflict is nonetheless still there, as revealed by the decision of the German Federal Constitutional Court, *Bundesverfassungsgericht*, in its decision on the Lisbon Treaty.[129] The decision is long and complex, and hence its full implications cannot be examined here.[130] The analysis will concentrate on the issues that are most pertinent to the topics considered in this chapter. The Court held that, subject to the caveats discussed below, it was open to Germany to ratify the Lisbon Treaty, but that the national implementation law was defective in certain respects and hence had to be revised. The Court's decision was truly a blend of the old and the new.[131]

The very fact that the Court chose to reiterate and reinforce a vision of the relationship between the EU and its Member States that it had articulated

---

[127] pp 432–434.
[128] Craig and de Búrca (n 44) ch 10; M Claes, *The National Courts' Mandate in the European Constitution* (Hart, 2006).
[129] Lisbon Case, BVerfG, 2 BvE 2/08, from 30 June 2009, available at <http://www.bverfg.de/entscheidungen/es20090630_2bve000208.html>. English translation available at <http://www.bundesverfassungsgericht.de/entscheidungen/es20090630_2bve000208en.html>.
[130] F Schorkopf, 'The European Union as an Association of Sovereign States: Karlsruhe's Ruling on the Treaty of Lisbon' (2009) 10 German LJ 1219; D Halberstam and C Möllers, 'The German Constitutional Court says "Ja zu Deutschland!"' (2009) 10 German LJ 1241; D Thym, 'In the Name of Sovereign Statehood: A Critical Introduction to the *Lisbon* Judgment of the German Constitutional Court' (2009) 46 CMLRev 1795; F Mayer, '"Rashomon in Karlsruhe" The German Constitutional Court's Lisbon Decision and the Changing Landscape of European Constitutionalism', forthcoming (2010) I-CON.
[131] Halberstam and Möllers (n 130).

hitherto was itself significant. The *Bundesverfassungsgericht* premised its reasoning on the foundations it had laid in the earlier *Maastricht* ruling:[132] the empowerment to exercise supranational competences came from the Member States, who remained 'Masters of the Treaties', the corollary being that the international agreement through which such power was exercised was a 'derived fundamental order'.[133] The German Basic Law did not allow German statal bodies to transfer sovereign powers such that their exercise could independently establish other competences for the EU, and hence it prohibited transfer of competence to decide on its own competence, *Kompetenz-Kompetenz*.[134] The *Bundesverfassungsgericht* was equally wary of broad Treaty provisions that lent themselves to expansive interpretation, whether by the EU legislature or the ECJ. The *Bundesverfassungsgericht* echoed warnings from its earlier judgments that it might not apply such measures within Germany.[135]

Under the constitution, however, the trust in the constructive force of the mechanism of integration cannot be unlimited. If in the process of European integration primary law is amended, or interpreted in an extending sense, by institutions, a tension that is constitutionally important will occur towards the principle of conferral and towards the individual Member State's constitutional responsibility for integration. If legislative or administrative competences are only transferred in an undetermined manner or with the intention of their being further developed dynamically, or if the institutions are allowed to newly establish competences, to round them off in an extending manner or to factually extend them, they risk transgressing the predetermined integration programme and acting beyond the powers which they have been granted. They move on a path at the end of which there is the power of disposition of their foundation laid down in the Treaties, i.e. the competence of freely disposing of their competences. There is the risk of a transgression of the mandatory principle of conferral and of the conceptual responsibility for integration which is due to the Member States if institutions of the European Union may unrestrictedly, i.e. without any outside control—such control being very moderate and regarding itself as an exceptional one—decide about how the law under the Treaties is interpreted.

The Federal Constitutional Court made clear that it would ensure adherence to these principles.[136] It held that Declaration 17 attached to the Lisbon Treaty did not confer an absolute primacy to EU law, which would be constitutionally objectionable from the German perspective, but merely confirmed 'the legal situation as it has been interpreted by the Federal Constitutional Court'.[137] The Court would exercise *ultra vires* review, where EU institutions transgressed the boundaries of their competences, which included non-compliance with subsidiarity. It also asserted the power to exercise 'identity review', to examine whether the 'inviolable core content of the constitutional identity' of the Basic Law in

---

[132] *Brunner v European Union Treaty* [1994] 1 CMLR 57.
[133] Lisbon Case (n 129) [231].   [134] ibid [233].   [135] ibid [238].
[136] ibid [235], [241].   [137] ibid [331].

Article 23.1 read together with Article 79.3, was respected.[138] The Court, moreover, raised the possibility of the creation by the legislature of an additional type of proceedings that was especially tailored to *ultra vires* review and identity review to 'safeguard the obligation of German bodies not to apply in Germany, in individual cases, legal instruments of the European Union that transgress competences or that violate constitutional identity'.[139]

The reach and impact of 'identity review' are noteworthy in this respect. Integral to the Court's judgment is a thesis concerning functions that must to some considerable extent remain with the Nation State, although how far is not clear. Thus the Court states that European unification may not be realized in such a way 'that the Member States do not retain sufficient space for the political formation of the economic, cultural and social circumstances of life'.[140] It articulated five areas that were deemed 'especially sensitive for the ability of a constitutional state to democratically shape itself':[141] criminal law; the use of force internally and externally; fundamental fiscal decisions on public revenue and public expenditure, with the latter being particularly motivated, *inter alia*, by social-policy considerations; decisions on the shaping of circumstances of life in a social State; and decisions which are of particular importance culturally, as regards, for example, family law, education, and religion.

The Federal Constitutional Court justified its willingness to call EU law into question and refuse to apply it in part by adverting to the *Kadi*[142] case in which the ECJ had refused to apply UN resolutions because of conflict with fundamental principles of Community law. The ECJ had therefore 'in a borderline case, placed the assertion of its own identity as a legal community above the commitment that it otherwise respects'.[143] It was said the Federal Constitutional Court 'no contradiction to the objective of openness towards European law, i.e. to the participation of the Federal Republic of Germany in the realization of a united Europe ... if exceptionally, and under special and narrow conditions, the Federal Constitutional Court declares European Union law inapplicable in Germany'.[144]

There is much in this complex judgment that is controversial and has been the subject of critical comment.[145] Space precludes consideration of other aspects of the judgment that relate to the democratic credentials of the European Parliament,[146] and the strengthening of the role accorded to the German legislature in relation to EU measures enacted under Article 352 TFEU and where the passerelle clauses are invoked.[147]

---

[138] ibid [240]. See also [226], [228], [332].
[139] ibid [241].   [140] ibid [249].
[141] ibid [252]. See also [264].
[142] Cases 402 and 415/05 P *Yassin Abdullah Kadi and Al Barakaat International Foundation v Council and Commission* [2008] ECR I-6351.
[143] Lisbon Case (n 129) [340].   [144] ibid [340].
[145] Halberstam and Möllers; Thym (n 130).
[146] Lisbon Case (n 129) [280]–[284].
[147] ibid [315]–[325].

The judgment is, however, a powerful reminder of the tensions that can exist between the 'world view' of the ECJ and of some national courts. This is so notwithstanding the fact that other national courts may not share all the legal sentiments of their German colleagues. It remains to be seen whether the German court exercises its powers in the post-Lisbon world, or whether, as in the case of the earlier *Maastricht* judgment, it seeks to avoid conflict by raising the legal hurdles for pursuit of such claims. This may depend, *inter alia*, on the composition of the Federal Constitutional Court, which changes over time. We should not, however, imagine that the Lisbon Treaty has resolved the perennial issues concerning the relationship between the legal orders within the EU.

6. Conclusion

The Lisbon Treaty continues the same general regime that applied hitherto in relation to the courts, albeit with some modification in relation to nomenclature, appointment, and jurisdiction. The amendments are largely positive. It is nonetheless regrettable that the modified schema has introduced confusion in certain respects, concerning the language used to describe which court has jurisdiction over certain types of case. It is also unfortunate that the laudable aim of bringing the European Council and bodies, offices, and agencies formally within the remit of judicial review has in turn generated a new problem, this being the asymmetry that flows from the fact that they are accorded no role as claimants. The jury moreover remains out for the present on the impact of the reformed rules on standing for non-privileged applicants, since so much turns on the interpretation given to the term 'regulatory act'.

The failure to consider the overall architecture of the Union courts is to be regretted. This is so irrespective of one's view as to the desirable outcome. The Constitutional Treaty was a major exercise in Treaty reform, and most of the provisions were taken over into the Lisbon Treaty. It was an exercise that spanned nearly a decade, from the close of the deliberations of the Nice Treaty. It would have been the ideal opportunity for more considered reflection on the disposition of power between the Union courts. There is unlikely to be such an opportunity for some considerable time, given the Treaty reform 'fatigue' that prevails after the efforts required to secure agreement on the Lisbon Treaty.

The implications of the Lisbon Treaty for direct effect and supremacy were considered above. While the basic framework of these central judicial doctrines has not altered, the very fact that they will in the future be applicable to areas hitherto excluded, in particular the topics covered by what was the Third Pillar, is likely to pose fresh challenges for the Union courts, and for national courts that are charged with applying such precepts within the Member States.

5

Competence, Categories, and Control

It has never been easy to specify with exactitude the division of competence between the EU and Member States.[1] Concerns about the scope of EU power had been voiced for some time, and it was therefore unsurprising that it was an issue identified for further inquiry after the Nice Treaty 2000. The Constitutional Treaty addressed this issue and many of the provisions have been taken over into the Lisbon Treaty.

The discussion begins by considering the nature of the competence problem, and the objectives that the framers of the Laeken Declaration sought to attain via Treaty reform. This will be followed by analysis of the principal heads of EU competence set out in the Lisbon Treaty. They will be considered against the criteria of clarity and containment, which bear the meanings described below. It will be argued that while 'definitional categorization' of the kind undertaken in the Lisbon Treaty has value, there are nonetheless limits as to what can be achieved by this method of delimiting competence. The discussion of the Lisbon Treaty will therefore be set against other existing techniques, legal and political, that are designed to ensure that the EU remains within the remit of its powers.

---

[1] V Constantinesco, *Compétences et pouvoirs dans les Communautés européennes: contribution à l'étude de la nature juridique des communautés* (Librairie générale de droit et de jurisprudence, 1974); A Dashwood, 'The Limits of European Community Powers' (1996) 21 ELRev 113; *The Division of Competences in the European Union*, Directorate-General for Research, Working Paper, Political Series W 26 (1997); I Pernice, 'Kompetenzabgrenzung im europäischen Verfassungsverbund' (2000) JZ 866; F Mayer, 'Die drei Dimensionen der europäischen Kompetenzdebatte' (2001) 61 ZaöRV 577; G de Búrca, 'Setting Limits to EU Competences?' Francisco Lucas Pires Working paper 2001/02; U di Fabio, 'Some Remarks on the Allocation of Competences between the European Union and its Member States' (2002) 39 CMLRev 1289; A von Bogdandy and J Bast, 'The European Union's Vertical Order of Competences: The Current Law and Proposals for its Reform' (2002) 39 CMLRev 227; V Michel, 'Le Défi de la Repartition des Compétences' (2003) 38 CDE 17; D Hanf and T Baumé, 'Vers une Clarification de la Répartition des Compétences entre l'Union et ses Etats Membres?' (2003) 38 CDE 135; P Craig, 'Competence: Clarity, Conferral, Containment and Consideration' (2004) 29 ELRev 323; S Weatherill, 'Better Competence Monitoring' (2005) 30 ELRev 23; F Mayer, 'Competences—Reloaded? The Vertical Division of Powers in the EU and the New European Constitution' (2005) 3 I-CON 493; V Vadapalas, 'La répartition des compétences entre l'Union européenne et les Etats membres' in C Kaddous and A Auer (eds), *Les principes fondamentaux de la Constitution européenne* (Helbing & Lichtenhahn, Bruylant, LGDJ, 2006) 135–145; R Schutze, *From Dual to Cooperative Federalism, The Changing Structure of European Law* (Oxford University Press, 2009).

1. The Nature of the 'Competence Problem'

The issue of competence is central to the relationship between the EU and the Member States. It was one of the key issues singled out for further investigation after the Nice Treaty in 2000.[2]

It is important at the outset to understand the nature of the 'competence problem'. The EU has always had attributed competence. It could only operate within the powers granted to it by the Member States, as made clear by the first paragraph of Article 5 EC and Article 7(1) EC. A predominant concern was that Article 5 provided scant protection for State rights, and little safeguard against an ever-increasing shift of power from the States to the EU, notwithstanding the strictures about subsidiarity and proportionality contained in the second paragraph of Article 5 EC. This was the rationale for the inclusion of competence as an issue to be addressed after the Nice Treaty.

This view of the 'competence problem', however, is based on implicit assumptions as to how the EU acquires competence. The inarticulate premise is that the shift in power upward towards the EU is the result primarily of some unwarranted arrogation of power by the EU to the detriment of States' rights, which Article 5 EC has been powerless to prevent. This is an over-simplistic view of how and why the EU has acquired its current range of power. The matter is more complex and more interesting.

The reality is that EU competence has resulted from the symbiotic interaction of four variables: Member State choice as to the scope of EU competence, as expressed in Treaty revisions; Member State, and since the Single European Act 1986 (SEA), European Parliament acceptance of legislation that has fleshed out the Treaty articles; the jurisprudence of the Community courts; and decisions taken by the institutions as to how to interpret, deploy, and prioritize the power accorded to the EU.[3]

Thus, the judicial contribution to the expansion of competence has been but one factor in the distribution of power between Member States and the EU. Political choice by the Member States to grant the EU competence in areas such as the environment, culture, health, consumer protection, employment, and vocational training expressed through Treaty revision after extensive discussion in successive intergovernmental conferences (IGCs) has been equally important; so, too, has political choice embodied in Community legislation, accepted by the Member States in the Council, and in many instances after the SEA also by the

---

[2] Treaty of Nice, Declaration 23 [2001] OJ C80/1.
[3] P Craig, 'Competence and Member State Autonomy: Causality, Consequence and Legitimacy' in B de Witte and H Micklitz (eds), *The European Court of Justice and the Autonomy of Member States* (Intersentia, 2010) ch 1.

European Parliament. The action of Community institutions in deciding how to use the power formally accorded to them is also of real significance.

This does not mean that there is no competence problem in the EU. It does mean that we should avoid mistaken and simplistic premises that the problem is all reducible to some unwarranted arrogation of power by some reified entity called the EU. We should also be wary of analogies with other systems where judicial interpretation of open-textured constitutional provisions concerning the divide between federal and State power has been the sole or principal factor in delimiting competence.

2. The Aims of the Laeken Declaration

It is axiomatic that any view concerning the provisions on competences in the Lisbon Treaty will necessarily be affected by perceptions as to the aims that those provisions were designed to serve. We cannot judge the success or failure of the enterprise without some understanding as to the objectives.

The Laeken Declaration[4] specified in greater detail the nature of the inquiry into competence that had been left open after the Nice Treaty 2000. There were four more particular issues addressed under the heading of 'a better of division and definition of competence in the European Union'. These were the need to make the division of competence clearer and more transparent; the need to ensure that the Union had the powers required to perform the tasks conferred on it by the Member States, thereby ensuring that the European dynamic did not come to a halt; the need to ensure that there was not a 'creeping expansion' of EU competence or its encroachment upon areas left exclusively to the Member States; and the desirability of considering whether there should be some reorganization of competence between the EU and the Member States.

There were then four principal forces driving the reform process: clarity, conferral, containment, and consideration. The desire for *clarity* reflected the sense that the Treaty provisions on competences were unclear, jumbled, and unprincipled. The idea of *conferral* captured not only the idea that the EU should act within the limits of the powers attributed to it, but also carried the more positive connotation that the EU should be accorded the powers necessary to fulfil the tasks assigned to it by the enabling Treaties. The desire for *containment* reflected the concern, voiced by the German *Länder* as well as some Member States, that the EU had too much power, and that it should be substantively limited.[5] This argument must nonetheless be kept in perspective, since a significant factor in the distribution of competence has been the conscious decision of

---

[4] European Council, 14–15 December 2001, 21–22.
[5] Mayer, 'Competences' (n 1) 504–505.

the Member States to grant new spheres of competence to the EU. This is where the fourth factor came into play, *consideration* of whether the EU should continue to have the powers that it had been given in the past, a re-thinking of the areas in which the EU should be able to act.

The reality is that there was little systematic re-thinking of the areas in which the EU should be able to act. The Convention on the Future of Europe did not conduct any root and branch re-consideration of all heads of EU competence.[6] Nor would this realistically have been possible within the time available. The strategy was, in general terms, to take the existing heads of competence as given. The emphasis was on clarity, conferral, and containment. When consideration was given to the areas in which the EU should be able to act, and the degree of its competence within those areas, the general tendency was to reinforce EU power, not to 'repatriate' it to the Member States. This is exemplified by the Treaty provisions on economic policy, and by those on foreign policy and defence.

3. Categories and Consequences

The provisions on competence in the Lisbon Treaty repeat with some minor modifications those in the Constitutional Treaty, although the organization of the relevant provisions was a good deal clearer in the latter. The general approach is to delineate different categories of competence for different subject matter areas and to specify the legal consequences for the EU and Member States of this categorization.

The provisions are contained in the Treaty on European Union (TEU) and in the Treaty on the Functioning of the European Union (TFEU). Thus Article 4 TEU states that competences not conferred on the Union remain with the Member States. Article 5 TEU stipulates that the limits of Union competences are governed by the principle of conferral, under which the Union shall act only within the limits of competence conferred by the Member States, and repeats once again that competences not conferred on the Union remain with the Member States. The Lisbon Treaty thereby reaffirms the central principle that the EU operates on the basis of attributed competence. The use of Union competences is governed by the principles of subsidiarity and proportionality, which are dealt with in the remainder of Article 5 TEU. The revised TEU therefore tells us little about the existence of competence and is unnecessarily repetitious in the little that it does say.

It is to the TFEU, Articles 2 to 6, that we must look to find the substantive provisions concerned with competence. These Articles replicate with minor

---

[6] Economic governance was one of the limited substantive areas where the Convention did take stock of the limits of existing EU powers, and the desirability of reinforcing them so as to enable the EU to be able to perform its tasks properly within this area, CONV 357/02, Brussels 21 October 2002.

modification those found in the Constitutional Treaty. There are categories of competence that apply to specified subject matter areas, and concrete legal consequences flow from such categorization. The categories therefore matter, since the categorization has consequences, in terms of the possession and retention of power to legislate and make legally binding acts.

The principal categories are where the EU's competence is exclusive, where it is shared with the Member States, where the EU is limited to supporting/coordinating action, with special categories for EU action in the sphere of economic and employment policy, and Common Foreign and Security Policy (CFSP). The divide between these categories was the subject of intense debate within the Convention on the Future of Europe. The 'walls' between the categories shifted significantly.

4. Exclusive Competence

(a) Basic principles: meaning and scope

Article 2(1) TFEU establishes the category of exclusive competence, which carries the consequence that only the Union can legislate and adopt legally binding acts, the Member States being able to do so only if so empowered by the Union or for the implementation of Union acts.

The subject matter areas that fall within exclusive competence are set out in Article 3(1) TFEU: customs union; the establishing of the competition rules necessary for the functioning of the internal market; monetary policy for the Member States whose currency is the euro; the conservation of marine biological resources under the common fisheries policy; and the common commercial policy. Article 3(2) TFEU states that the Union shall also have exclusive competence for the conclusion of an international agreement when its conclusion is provided for in a legislative act of the Union, or is necessary to enable the Union to exercise its internal competence, or insofar as its conclusion may affect common rules or alter their scope.

(b) Area exclusivity: demarcation and delimitation

Article 3(1) TFEU lists a limited number of areas that are regarded as always falling within the EU's exclusive competence. These areas are in that sense to be regarded as *a priori* within the EU's exclusive competence, without the need for further inquiry. The areas thus listed are limited and relatively discrete. We have seen that a pressing concern in the Laeken Declaration and the Convention on the Future of Europe was to contain EU power. The domain of *a priori* exclusive competence fares pretty well when judged by this criterion, given that the areas that come within this category are relatively discrete and the overall list is small.

This is important because the consequences of inclusion within this category are severe: the Member States have no autonomous legislative competence and they cannot adopt any legally binding act. They can neither legislate, nor make any legally binding non-legislative act. A broad concept of exclusive competence would therefore have had the opposite effect of containment, since it would have enhanced the power of the centre at the expense of the Member States.

The importance of this point can be seen from earlier formulations of this category. The original text produced by the Convention included the four freedoms within the sphere of exclusive competence, but they were then re-assigned to the category of shared competence. The formal reason given for this change was the creation of a specific provision dealing directly with the four freedoms,[7] which was said to make their legal and political importance more visible than hitherto, and to underline the fact that they are directly applicable. While it might be felt to be desirable for political reasons to emphasize the centrality of the four freedoms, the argument based on direct applicability was odd to say the least, given that many other Treaty provisions have this quality. The real reason for the excision of the four freedoms from exclusive competence was rather different. If they had remained within this category, Member States would have had no legislative capacity in these areas, nor could they have adopted any legally binding non-legislative act. Taken literally, this would have meant that a Member State would have been precluded from enacting legislation that, for example, liberalized trade in postal services, unless it had been empowered by the Union or the Member State action was implementing Union acts. Thus, Member State action which was 'ahead' of EU action would have been precluded even though it might have been in accord with the overall aims of the EU, and even though it might well have been the catalyst for EU action in such areas.

The very creation of categories of competence nonetheless inevitably means that there will be problems of demarcating borderlines between the different categories. Such problems can arise in demarcating the line between exclusive and shared competence.

There are, for example, some ambiguities about the relationship between the competition rules, which are a species of exclusive competence, and the internal market, which is shared competence. It is clear that the basic competition rules in Articles 101 and 102 TFEU dealing with cartels and abuse of a dominant position fall within the domain of exclusive competence. The EU's exclusive competence relates only to the 'establishment' of these rules, and not their 'application'. This is in recognition of the new reality in competition law, whereby national courts have full competence to apply the entirety of Articles 101 and 102 TFEU.[8] The key issue is whether, subject to that caveat, the EU's

---

[7] Art I-4 CT.

[8] Council Regulation 1/2003 on the implementation of the rules on competition laid down in Arts 81 and 82 of the Treaty [2003] OJ L1/1.

exclusive competence applies not just to Articles 101 and 102 TFEU, but also to instances where the competition rules have an impact outside of this 'immediate area', such as Article 106 TFEU, which deals with the extent to which public undertakings are subject to the ordinary norms of Articles 101 and 102.

It is unclear whether this aspect of the competition rules also falls within the domain of exclusive competence, or whether it is to be dealt with through shared competence, which covers, *inter alia*, the internal market. The wording of Article 3(1) TFEU is important in this respect. It provides that the EU has exclusive competence in the 'establishing of the competition rules necessary for the functioning of the internal market'. This indicates that the exclusive competence attaches not only to the establishment of the basic competition rules in Articles 101 and 102 TFEU, but also to Article 106 TFEU, given that this concerns the relationship between public undertakings and the competition rules in the overall functioning of the internal market.

This conclusion is reinforced by the structure and content of this Part of the TFEU. Part III, Title VII, deals with competition, with the basic rules about cartels and abuse of a dominant position contained in Articles 101 and 102 TFEU, while the rules on public undertakings are found in Article 106 TFEU. This is one of the Titles dealing with 'Union Policies and Internal Actions'. It is therefore rational to conclude that the wording of Article 3(1) TFEU, which accords the EU exclusive competence in the 'establishing of the competition rules necessary for the functioning of the internal market' covers all competition rules relating to undertakings in the internal market, including as they apply within the context of Article 106 TFEU.

There may also be difficult borderline problems between provisions relating to the customs union, and other aspects of the internal market, since the customs union falls within exclusive competence, while the internal market is shared competence. There can be difficulties, however, in deciding whether a case is concerned with the customs union, tariffs, quotas and the like, or whether it is really 'about' discriminatory taxation.[9] There may also be 'categorization difficulties' in relation to the divide between tariffs/quotas and other quantitative measures that might limit imports.[10] The fact that the customs union falls within the domain of exclusive competence, while the other issues come within shared competence, renders such divisions more significant.

(c) Conditional exclusivity: demarcation and delimitation

The EU is also accorded exclusive competence to conclude an international agreement, provided that the conditions in Article 3(2) are met. The scope of

---

[9] P Craig and G de Búrca, *EU Law, Text, Cases and Materials* (Oxford University Press, 4th edn, 2007) ch 18.
[10] ibid chs 18–19.

the EU's exclusive competence in relation to such external matters is problematic. Article 3(2) TFEU provides that:

The Union shall also have exclusive competence for the conclusion of an international agreement when its conclusion is provided for in a legislative act of the Union or is necessary to enable the Union to exercise its internal competence, or insofar as its conclusion may affect common rules or alter their scope.

The case law on the scope of the EU's external competence, and the extent to which it is exclusive or parallel with that of the Member States, is complex.[11] Article 3(2) TFEU stipulates three instances in which the EU has exclusive external competence: where the conclusion of such an agreement is provided for in a legislative act of the Union; where it is necessary to enable the Union to exercise its competence internally; or where it affects an internal Union act.

The interpretation of this provision is by no means easy,[12] and the reason is not hard to divine. The very complexity of the case law in this area necessarily means that embodying the principles in a Treaty Article was always going to be difficult. It was almost inevitable that the translation of complex jurisprudence into a Treaty Article would lead to some change, since the limits of Treaty drafting render it difficult to capture all the nuances from that jurisprudence. This is especially manifest in the way in which Article 3(2) read together with Article 216 TFEU in effect elides the EU's power to act via an international agreement with the exclusivity of that power, an issue which pre-occupied much of the case law in this area.

The content of Article 3(2) TFEU is in contrast to the more cautious recommendations of Working Group VII on External Action. The Working Group consciously disaggregated the existence of EU competence to conclude an international agreement and the impact that this would have on the delimitation of competence between the EU and the Member States, and thus distinguished between the existence of external competence and exclusivity.[13]

---

[11] T Tridimas and P Eeckhout, 'The External Competence of the Community and the Case-Law of the Court of Justice: Principle versus Pragmatism' (1994) 14 YBEL 143; M Cremona, 'External Relations and External Competence: the Emergence of an Integrated Policy' in P Craig and G de Búrca (eds), *The Evolution of EU Law* (Oxford University Press, 1999) ch 4; A Dashwood and C Hillion (eds), *The General Law of EC External Relations* (Sweet & Maxwell, 2000); P Eeckhout, *External Relations of the European Union: Legal and Constitutional Foundations* (Oxford University Press, 2004); M Cremona, 'The Draft Constitutional Treaty: External Relations and External Action' (2003) 40 CMLRev 1347; P Koutrakos, *EU International Relations Law* (Hart, 2006); Craig and de Búrca (n 9) 95–100, and ch 6; P Koutrakos, 'Legal Basis and Delimitation of Competence in EU External Relations' in M Cremona and B de Witte (eds), *EU Foreign Relations Law, Constitutional Fundamentals* (Hart, 2008) ch 6; M Cremona, 'Defining Competence in EU External Relations: Lessons from the Treaty Reform Process' in A Dashwood and M Maresceau (eds), *Law and Practice of EU External Relations, Salient Features of a Changing Landscape* (Cambridge University Press, 2008) ch 2.
[12] Cremona, 'Draft Constitutional Treaty' (n 11); Craig (n 1).
[13] CONV 459/02, Final Report of Working Group VII on External Action, Brussels 16 December 2002, 4, 16.

(i) External competence and exclusivity: pre-Lisbon

We need therefore to take a brief step back to the pre-Lisbon case law to understand the significance of Article 3(2) TFEU. The European Court of Justice (ECJ) had for some considerable time recognized Community competence to conclude an international agreement where this was necessary to effectuate its internal competence, even where there was no express external competence.[14] The issue of whether this implied external power was exclusive, however, was treated as distinct from the existence of such power. Implied external competence could be exclusive or shared.[15] While it was clear that the EC's implied external competence could be shared with the Member States, the ECJ also held that this implied external power could be exclusive. However, the precise circumstances where this would be so were not entirely clear,[16] although the formulations used by the ECJ as to when exclusivity could arise were far-reaching.

Thus in *ERTA* the ECJ held that when the Community acted to implement a common policy pursuant to the Treaty, the Member States no longer had the right to take external action where this would affect the rules thus established or distort their scope.[17] This position was modified in *Kramer*.[18] The ECJ held that the EC could possess implied external powers even though it had not taken internal measures to implement the relevant policy, but that until the EC duly exercised its internal power the Member States retained competence to act, provided that their action was compatible with Community objectives. The scope of exclusivity was thrown into doubt in the *Inland Waterways* case,[19] where the ECJ held that the EC could have exclusive external competence, even though it had not exercised its internal powers, if Member State action could place in jeopardy the Community objective sought to be attained.

The ECJ, however, pulled back from the very broad reading of exclusivity contained in the *Inland Waterways* case in *Opinion 1/94 on the WTO Agreement*.[20] It held that exclusive external competence was in general dependent on

---

[14] (N 11); Case 22/70 *Commission v Council* [1971] ECR 263; Cases 3, 4, and 6/76 *Kramer* [1976] ECR 1279; Opinion 1/76 *On the Draft Agreement Establishing a Laying-up Fund for Inland Waterway Vessels* [1977] ECR 741; Opinion 2/91 *Re the ILO Convention 170 on Chemicals at Work* [1993] ECR I-1061; Opinion 2/94 *Accession of the Community to the European Human Rights Convention* [1996] ECR I-1759.

[15] Opinion 1/03 *Competence of the Community to conclude the new Lugano Convention on jurisdiction and the recognition and enforcement of judgments in civil and commercial matters* [2006] ECR I-1145, [114]–[117].

[16] Cremona, 'External Relations' (n 11); A Dashwood and J Heliskoski, 'The Classic Authorities Revisited' in Dashwood and Hillion (n 11) 3.

[17] Case 22/70 *Commission v Council* (n 14).

[18] Cases 3, 4, and 6/76 *Kramer* (n 14).

[19] Opinion 1/76 *Inland Waterways* (n 14).

[20] Opinion 1/94 *Competence of the Community to Conclude International Agreements Concerning Services and the Protection of Intellectual Property, WTO* [1994] ECR I-5267.

actual exercise of internal powers and not their mere existence.[21] The *Inland Waterways* case was distinguished on the ground that the EC's internal objective could not be attained without the making of an international agreement and internal EC rules could not realistically be made prior to the conclusion of such an agreement.[22] This rationale was held not to apply to the subject matter of the *WTO* case.[23] This reasoning has been followed in later decisions.[24]

Subsequent jurisprudence nonetheless revealed that the ECJ would construe broadly the idea of the EC having exercised its powers internally, and that the ECJ was also prepared to give a wide interpretation to the circumstances in which this gave rise to exclusive external competence for the EC. This was apparent from the 'open skies' litigation, involving Commission actions against a number of Member States.[25] The Commission brought actions under what was Article 226 EC, alleging that Member States had infringed the Treaty by concluding bilateral 'open skies' agreements with the USA, on the ground that the EC had exclusive external competence in this area. It argued, *inter alia*, that the EC had exclusive external competence in line with the *ERTA* ruling, because it had exercised its internal competence to some degree within the relevant area. The ECJ accepted this argument. The Council had adopted a package of legislation based on Article 80(2) EC. The ECJ held that the *ERTA* ruling could apply to internal power exercised in this manner and therefore the EC had an implied external competence. It followed that when the EC made common rules pursuant to this power, the Member States no longer had the right, acting individually or collectively, to undertake obligations towards non-Member States, which affected those rules or distorted their scope.

The importance of the judgment lies in its confirmation of the broad reading given to the phrase 'affected those rules or distorted their scope', since it was this that transformed external competence into exclusive external competence. The ECJ, in accordance with prior case law, held that this would be so where the international agreement fell within the scope of the common rules, or within an area that was already largely covered by such rules, and this was so in the latter case even if there was no contradiction between the international commitments and the internal rules. EC legislative provisions relating to the treatment of non-Member State nationals, or expressly conferring power to negotiate with non-Member States, gave the EC exclusive external competence. This was so even in the absence

---

[21] ibid [88]–[89].   [22] ibid [85]–[86].   [23] ibid [86], [99], [100], [105].
[24] See, eg, Opinion 2/92 *Competence of the Community or one of its Institutions to Participate in the Third Revised Decision of the OECD on National Treatment* [1995] ECR I-521.
[25] Case C-466/98 *Commission v United Kingdom* [2002] ECR I-9427; Case C-467/98 *Commission v Denmark* [2002] ECR I-9519; Case C-468/98 *Commission v Sweden* [2002] ECR I-9575; Case C-469/98 *Commission v Finland* [2002] ECR I-9627; Case C-471/98 *Commission v Belgium* [2002] ECR I-9681; Case C-472/98 *Commission v Luxembourg* [2002] ECR I-9741; Case C-475/98 *Commission v Austria* [2002] ECR I-9797.

of express provision authorizing the EC to negotiate with non-Member States in areas where the EC had achieved complete harmonization, since if Member States were able to conclude international agreements individually it would affect the common rules thus made. Distortion in the flow of services in the internal market that might arise as a result of the bilateral agreement did not, by way of contrast, affect the common rules adopted in the area.

The same general message emerged from the *Lugano* Opinion:[26] implied external competence could be exclusive or shared, but where the EC had exercised its powers internally, then the ECJ would be inclined to conclude that this gave rise to exclusive external competence, whenever such exclusive competence was needed to 'preserve the effectiveness of Community law and the proper functioning of the systems established by its rules'.[27]

(ii) External competence and exclusivity: post-Lisbon

It is important, before considering the meaning of Article 3(2) TFEU, to be mindful of Article 216 TFEU. Article 216 is concerned with whether the EU has competence to conclude an international agreement. Article 3(2) deals with the related, but distinct, issue as to whether that competence is exclusive or not. Article 216 TFEU reads as follows.

1. The Union may conclude an agreement with one or more third countries or international organisations where the Treaties so provide or where the conclusion of an agreement is necessary in order to achieve, within the framework of the Union's policies, one of the objectives referred to in the Treaties, or is provided for in a legally binding Union act or is likely to affect common rules or alter their scope.

2. Agreements concluded by the Union are binding upon the institutions of the Union and on its Member States

The catalyst for Article 216 TFEU was the report of the Working Group on External Action. Prior to the Lisbon Treaty the EC Treaty accorded express power to make international agreements in certain limited instances,[28] and this was supplemented by the ECJ's jurisprudence delineating the circumstances in which there could be an implied external competence to make an international agreement. The Working Group recommended that there should be a Treaty provision that reflected this case law.[29] This was embodied in the Constitutional Treaty,[30] and taken over into the Lisbon Treaty as Article 216 TFEU. The breadth of Article 216 is readily apparent, and the reality is that it will be rare, if ever, for the EU to lack power to conclude an international agreement. The scope of this Article and its relationship with Article 3(2) TFEU are considered in a

---

[26] Opinion 1/03 *Lugano* (n 15) [114]–[115].   [27] ibid [131].
[28] Arts 111, 133, 174(4), 181, 310 EC.
[29] Final Report of Working Group VII (n 13) [18].   [30] Art III-323 CT.

later chapter, to which reference should be made.[31] The present focus is Article 3 (2) TFEU and examination of the three situations in which the EU has exclusive external competence.

The first is where the conclusion of an international agreement is provided for by a legislative act of the Union. The wording is significant. Article 3(2) TFEU does not state that the Union shall have exclusive external competence where a Union legislative act says that this shall be so. Nor does it state that the EU shall have such exclusive external competence only in the areas in which it has an exclusive internal competence. It states that where the conclusion of an international agreement is provided for in a legislative act, the Union will have exclusive external competence in this regard. The consequence is that express external empowerment to conclude an international agreement is taken to mean exclusive external competence, with the corollary that Member States are pre-empted from concluding any such agreement independently, from legislating or adopting any legally binding act. The same reasoning would seem to apply *a fortiori* where a Treaty article, as opposed to a legislative act, accords the Union power to conclude an international agreement, unless there is some indication in the Treaty article to the contrary,[32] but there is no mention of this in Article 3(2) TFEU.

The same elision of external power and exclusive external power is evident in the second of the situations listed in Article 3(2) TFEU. There is, as we have seen, well-known ECJ jurisprudence that accords the EU competence to conclude an international agreement where this is necessary to effectuate its internal competence, even where there is no express external competence.[33] The effect of Article 3(2) TFEU is nonetheless that the EU has exclusive external competence to conclude an international agreement where it is necessary to enable the Union to exercise its competence internally, and this is so irrespective of the type of internal competence possessed by the EU. Taken literally this means that exclusive external competence to conclude an international agreement resides with the Union if this is necessary for the exercise of internal competence, where the internal competence is shared, and where the EU can only take supporting or coordinating action. This conclusion could be limited by fastening on the word 'necessary' and arguing that the conclusion of the international agreement did not fulfil this pre-condition. The conclusion might also be limited by arguing that any EU external competence to make an international agreement must be bounded by the nature of its internal competence in the relevant area. This would mean that the EU could not make such an agreement if the content thereof were to take the EU beyond, for example, supporting or coordinating action in an area where its internal competence was thus limited. Even if this qualification were to be accepted, the effect of Article 3(2) TFEU would still be that the EU would have exclusive external competence to conclude an international agreement that was necessary to enable the EU to exercise an internal competence, even where

---

[31] Ch 10.   [32] See, eg, Art 209(2) TFEU.   [33] (N 14).

the internal competence only allowed supporting action, provided that the international agreement did not contain provisions that went beyond this type of action.

The third of the situations mentioned in Article 3(2) TFEU is that the EU shall have exclusive competence insofar as the conclusion of an international agreement 'may affect common rules or alter their scope'. This is in accord with the ECJ's case law considered above. The reality is, as we have seen, that this phrase has been interpreted broadly by the ECJ, such that in most instances where the EU has exercised its power internally it will be held to have an exclusive external competence.

Cremona has argued convincingly that Article 3(2) 'conflates the two separate questions of the existence of implied external competence and the exclusivity of that competence',[34] and that the combination of this Article when read with Article 216 TFEU is that implied shared competence could disappear. This does indeed seem to be the outcome from the Treaty provisions, subject to the caveats mentioned above, and it is, as Cremona states, one that is hard to defend in policy terms.[35]

There may well be a more general lesson here. The translation of highly complex case law into the form of a Treaty article is always difficult. The almost inevitable tendency is to shed certain of the nuances from that jurisprudence in order to be able to put something down on paper in manageable form.

5. Shared Competence

(a) Basic principles: meaning and scope

Article 2(2) TFEU defines shared competence. The wording is important and Article 2(2) states that:

When the Treaties confer on the Union a competence shared with the Member States in a specific area, the Union and the Member States may legislate and adopt legally binding acts in that area. The Member States shall exercise their competence to the extent that the Union has not exercised its competence. The Member States shall again exercise their competence to the extent that the Union has decided to cease exercising its competence.

The categories of shared competence are delineated in Article 4 TFEU. It is clear from Article 4(1) TFEU that shared competence is the general residual category, since it provides that the Union shall share competence with the Member States where the Treaties confer on it a competence which does not relate to the

---

[34] Cremona 'Defining Competence' (n 11) 61.
[35] ibid 62. See also, A Dashwood, 'Mixity in the Era of the Treaty of Lisbon' in C Hillion and P Koutrakos (eds), *Mixed Agreements Revisited, The EU and its Member States in the World* (Hart, 2010) ch 18.

categories referred to in Articles 3 and 6 TFEU, which deal respectively with exclusive competence, and that where the Union is restricted to taking action to support, coordinate, or supplement the action of the Member States. This follows also from Article 4(2), which states that shared competence applies in the principal areas listed, implying thereby that the list is not necessarily exhaustive.

Article 4(2) TFEU specifies the more particular areas that are subject to shared competence. They are: the internal market; social policy, for the aspects defined in the TFEU; economic, social, and territorial cohesion; agriculture and fisheries, excluding the conservation of marine biological resources; the environment; consumer protection; transport; trans-European networks; energy; the area of freedom, security, and justice; and common safety concerns in public health matters, for the aspects defined in the TFEU.

Article 4(3) then stipulates that in the areas of research, technological development, and space, the Union shall have competence to carry out activities, in particular to define and implement programmes, but that the exercise of that competence shall not result in Member States being prevented from exercising theirs.

In a similar vein, Article 4(4) states that in the areas of development cooperation and humanitarian aid, the Union shall have competence to carry out activities and conduct a common policy, but that the exercise of that competence shall not result in Member States being prevented from exercising theirs.

The idea that shared competence is the default position must nonetheless be read subject to the special category of competence dealing with economic and employment policy, Article 5 TFEU, and that dealing with foreign and security policy, Article 2(4) TFEU, Title V TEU. The rationale for these separate categories will be considered below. It is true that in some general sense the regime that operates in these areas can loosely be regarded as one of shared power. It is clear, however, that the very existence of these categories is indicative that they are not to be regarded as ordinary examples of shared power. It is clear, moreover, that the legal consequences of inclusion within the general category of shared competence, set out in Article 2(2) TFEU, do not capture the reality of the divide between EU and Member State power in economic and employment policy, and the CFSP, as is apparent from the detailed provisions on these areas in the Lisbon Treaty.

In the Convention on the Future of Europe, Working Group V on Complementary Competencies was rather vague about the nature of the divide between exclusive and shared competence, and concluded that the respective areas should be defined in accordance with the ECJ's jurisprudence.[36] This ambivalent approach to the divide between exclusive and shared power would not have enhanced clarity. Nor would recourse to the case law have been conclusive,

---

[36] CONV 375/1/02, Final Report of Working Group V on Complementary Competencies, Brussels 4 November 2002, 6–7.

since it does not embody clear principles in this regard, as exemplified by the fact that the jurisprudence failed to provide a definitive answer to the meaning of exclusive competence for the purposes of applying subsidiarity. The general approach in the Constitutional Treaty and the Lisbon Treaty is therefore to be preferred.

(b) Shared competence: demarcation and delimitation

We saw in the discussion of exclusive competence the boundary problems that might arise between that category and shared competence. We shall see below that there can be analogous problems concerning the divide between shared competence and the category of supporting, coordinating, or complementary action.

The difficulties can be exemplified in relation to social policy. Article 4(2)(b) TFEU provides that social policy comes within the area of shared competence 'for the aspects defined in this Treaty'. Article 151 TFEU sets out the general objectives of EU social policy, which include promotion of employment, improved living and working conditions, proper social protection, dialogue between management and labour, the development of human resources with a view to lasting high employment, and the combating of exclusion. The Article mentions harmonization, but in guarded tones: the promotion of employment and improved living and working conditions is to 'make possible their harmonization while the improvement is being made'. However, other more specific Treaty articles on social policy expressly preclude harmonization.[37] The remaining Treaty provisions on social policy are specified in Articles 152 to 161 TFEU and the reality is that they do not provide explicit guidance as to which areas fall within shared competence, and which do not. Insofar as the Lisbon Treaty provisions on competence were intended to be conducive to greater clarity as to categories of competence the result in this area is unsatisfactory. The nature of the competence can only be divined through close reading of the individual Treaty provisions and interpreting them in the light of the previous jurisprudence.

When approached in this manner it would seem that Article 156 TFEU, which encourages the Commission to foster cooperation and coordination between the Member States in broad areas of social policy, does not come within shared competence, but is covered rather by the special category of competence dealing with economic, employment, and social policy,[38] or perhaps by that dealing with supporting, coordinating, and supplementing Member State action.[39] By way of contrast Article 157 TFEU, which deals with gender discrimination and equal pay, would seem to come within shared competence, with the consequences that flow for the balance between EU and Member State power.

---

[37] Art 153(2)(a) TFEU.   [38] Art 5 TFEU.
[39] Art 6 TFEU. However social policy is not included in the list in Art 6.

Article 153 TFEU falls betwixt and between. It is framed in terms of EU action to complement and coordinate the activities of the Member States in a wide variety of fields,[40] in order to attain the objectives of EU social policy in Article 151 TFEU. It would therefore seem to fall more naturally within the scope of competence to support, coordinate, and supplement Member State action considered below, although it does not come within the relevant list in Article 6 TFEU. The language of Article 153 TFEU couched in terms of complementing and coordinating Member State action does not fit naturally with shared competence. However, the EU is empowered to enact directives imposing 'minimum requirements for gradual implementation' in relation to many of these areas,[41] and it is not clear whether in this respect social policy is deemed to be within shared competence.[42]

The Treaty provisions on shared competence reveal moreover a further, somewhat different dimension to the demarcation problem. Shared competence is, as we have seen, the default position in the Lisbon Treaty. The area of research, technological development, and space, and that of development co-operation and humanitarian aid are not among those expressly listed as falling within shared competence in Article 4(2). They are, however, clearly regarded as falling within shared competence, subject to the special treatment accorded to them under Articles 4(3) and 4(4) TFEU. Moreover, they are not listed as areas coming within the category of supporting, coordinating, and supplementing Member State action.

There is nothing untoward in this, given that the list in Article 4(2) is non-exhaustive. These areas nonetheless reveal in more general terms the difficulties of deciding whether to assign a particular area to that of shared competence, or to place it within the category of supporting, coordinating, and supplementing Member State action, considered below. This is because inspection of the detailed provisions relating to the area of research, technological development, and space, and that of development cooperation and humanitarian aid, reveals that many of the provisions are indeed couched explicitly or implicitly in the language of supporting and complementary action.[43] These would seem to make them a more natural fit with the category of supporting, coordinating, and supplementing Member State action.

---

[40] Improvement in particular of the working environment to protect workers' health and safety; working conditions; social security and social protection of workers; protection of workers where their employment contract is terminated; the information and consultation of workers; representation and collective defence of the interests of workers and employers, including co-determination; conditions of employment for third-country nationals legally residing in Union territory; the integration of persons excluded from the labour market, without prejudice to Art 166 TFEU; equality between men and women with regard to labour market opportunities and treatment at work; the combating of social exclusion; the modernization of social protection systems.

[41] Art 153(2)(b) TFEU.

[42] Art 153(2)(a) TFEU expressly precludes harmonization.

[43] Arts 179(2), 180, 181, 208, 210, 214(1), 214(6) TFEU.

It is unclear why this option was not chosen. It is certainly true that the EU is allowed to make legally binding decisions in these areas, and the implication of the wording of Articles 4(3) and 4(4) TFEU seems to be that it is the legal capacity to define and implement such programmes, or conduct a policy, that is felt to bring the areas within the sphere of shared competence. However, this does not fit with the Treaty language, since legally binding acts are not prohibited within the category of supporting etc action, which only bars harmonization measures.[44] Whatsoever was the reason as to why these areas were regarded as falling within shared competence, it demonstrates the absence of fit between this categorization and the reality of the provisions that govern these topics.

(c) Shared competence: EU action and pre-emption

Shared competence was always central to the EU and remains so in the reformed Treaty provisions. We should nonetheless be mindful of the legal implications of the new provisions on the divide between EU and Member State competence. Article 2(2) TFEU stipulates that the Member State can only exercise competence to the extent that the Union has not exercised or has decided to cease to exercise its competence within any such area.

Taken literally this looks like automatic pre-emption of Member State action where the Union has exercised its competence. The consequence is that the amount of shared power held by the Member State in these areas will diminish over time. Power sharing would on this view be a one-way bet, subject to the possibility that the EU decided not to exercise its competence within a specific area. If containment is a concern, then there is little here to give comfort to supporters of States' rights. This conclusion as to the import of Article 2(2) TFEU must, however, be qualified in four ways.

First, Member States will only lose their competence within the regime of shared power to the extent that the Union has exercised *its* competence. Precisely what the EU's competence actually is within these areas can, as will be seen below, only be divined by considering the detailed provisions that divide power in areas as diverse as social policy, energy, the internal market, and consumer protection. The upshot is that the real limits on Union competence must be found in the detailed provisions which delineate what the EU can do in the diverse areas where power is shared. It is these provisions, the judicial interpretation thereof, and the way that the EU decides to legislate within these areas, which will determine the practical divide between Member State and EU competence. This is in reality what we have always had to do in order to determine the boundaries between State and EU power.

---

[44] Art 2(5) TFEU.

Second, the pre-emption will only occur *to the extent* that the EU has exercised its competence in the relevant area. There are different ways in which the EU can intervene in a particular area.[45] The EU may choose to make uniform regulations, it may harmonize national laws, it may engage in minimum harmonization, or it may impose requirements of mutual recognition. Thus, for example, where the EU chooses minimum harmonization, Member States will have room for action in the relevant area. The Member States were nonetheless sufficiently concerned as to the possible pre-emptive impact of Article 2(2) TFEU to press for the inclusion of the Protocol on Shared Competence,[46] which seeks to reinforce the point made above. It provides in effect that where the Union has taken action in an area governed by shared competence, 'the scope of this exercise of competence only covers those elements governed by the Union act in question and therefore does not cover the whole area'.[47] It should nonetheless be recognized that notwithstanding the Protocol it would be possible for Union acts to cover the entire area subject to shared power, provided that the EU was able to do so under the relevant Treaty provisions.

Third, Article 2(2) TFEU expressly provides for the possibility that the EU will cease to exercise competence in an area subject to shared competence, the consequence being that competence then reverts to the Member States. A Declaration attached to Treaty[48] specifies different ways in which this might occur. The EU might decide to repeal a legislative act, because of subsidiarity and proportionality. The Council could, in accordance with Article 241 TFEU, request the Commission to submit proposals for repealing a legislative act. There could moreover be a Treaty amendment to increase or to reduce the competences conferred on the EU.

The final qualification concerns Article 4(3) and Article 4(4) TFEU. The essence of both Treaty provisions is to make clear that the Member States can continue to exercise power even if the EU has exercised its competence within these areas. Thus even if the EU has defined and implemented programmes relating to research, technological development, and space, this does not preclude Member States from exercising their competence in such areas. The same reasoning is applied in the context of development cooperation and humanitarian aid.

---

[45] S Weatherill, 'Beyond Preemption? Shared Competence and Constitutional Change in the European Community' in D O' Keefe and P Twomey (eds), *Legal Issues of the Maastricht Treaty* (Chancery Law Publishing, 1994) ch 2; M Dougan, 'Minimum Harmonization and the Internal Market' (2000) 37 CMLRev 853; M Dougan, 'Vive la Différence? Exploring the Legal Framework for Reflexive Harmonisation within the Single Market' (2002) 1 Annual of German and European Law 13; CONV 375/1/02, Final Report of Working Group V (n 36) 12–13.

[46] Protocol (No 25).   [47] See also, Declaration 18.   [48] Declaration 18.

(d) Shared competence: variation and specification

Shared competence may, subject to what was said above, constitute the default position in relation to the division of competence within the Lisbon Treaty, but that does not mean that the precise modality of the sharing will be the same in all the areas to which shared competence applies. The legal as well as the political reality is that shared competence is simply an umbrella term, with the consequence that there is significant variation as to the division of competence in different areas of EU law. It follows that the precise configuration of power sharing in areas such as the internal market, consumer protection, energy, social policy, the environment, and the like can only be determined by considering the detailed rules that govern these areas, which are found in the relevant provisions of the TFEU.

The sharing of power in relation to, for example, the four freedoms is very different from the complex world of power sharing that operates within the area of freedom, security, and justice. There are indeed significant variations of power sharing that operate within the overall area of freedom, security, and justice.[49] There is nothing in the provisions on 'Categories and Areas of Union Competence' that will help the interested onlooker to work this out, nor is there any magic formula that applies to all areas of shared power that determines the precise delineation of power in any specific area.

This is not a criticism as such. It is rather the consequence of the fact that the EU has been attributed competence in different areas through successive Treaty amendments, coupled with the fact that the precise degree of power it has been accorded differs as between these areas. This is recognized by Article 2(6) TFEU, which states that 'the scope of and arrangements for exercising the Union's competences shall be determined by the provisions of the Treaties relating to each area'.

6. Supporting, Coordinating, or Supplementary Action

(a) Basic principles: meaning and scope

The third general category of competence allows the EU to take action to support, coordinate or supplement the actions of the Member States, without thereby superseding their competence in these areas, and without entailing harmonization of Member State laws', Article 2(5) TFEU. While the EU cannot harmonize the law in these areas, it can pass legally binding acts on the basis of the provisions specific to them, and the Member States will be constrained to the extent stipulated by such acts. The meaning of supporting etc action, and hence

---

[49] Ch 9.

the precise extent of EU power, varies somewhat in the different areas listed, but it is clear that the EU has a significant degree of power in these areas, albeit falling short of harmonization.[50]

The areas that fall within such competence are set out in Article 6 TFEU: protection and improvement of human health; industry; culture; tourism; education, vocational training, youth and sport; civil protection; and administrative cooperation. A bare reading of Article 6 TFEU gives the impression that the list is finite. This impression is reinforced by the wording of the Article, since the listed areas are not regarded as examples, but as the totality of this category. This impression is however belied when reading the TFEU as a whole. It then becomes clear that there are other important areas in which the EU is limited, prima facie at least, to supporting etc action, notably in respect to some aspects of social policy,[51] and certain facets of employment policy.[52]

We shall consider below why the EU chose to deal with these policies within a different head of EU competence, rather than include them within Article 6 TFEU. Suffice it to say for the present that the underlying rationale was an unwillingness to be tied in these areas to the legal consequences, in terms of the limits of EU action, specified in Article 2(5) TFEU.

(b) Supporting, coordinating, or supplementing: demarcation and delimitation

The creation of categories of competence inevitably means that there will be boundary problems as between them, as is apparent from the discussion thus far. Such problems may be especially prevalent between this category and that of shared competence.

This was acknowledged in the Praesidium's comment in the Convention, where it accepted that, for example, regulation of the media might come under the internal market, which is shared competence, or it might be regarded as falling within culture, where only supporting etc action is allowed.[53] We have seen, moreover, the difficulties of deciding which aspects of social policy fall within shared competence, and which come within this category.[54]

(c) Supporting, coordinating, or supplementing: scope and variation

It is important to press further to understand the scope of EU power for areas that fall within this category. The meaning of EU action supporting, coordinating,

---

[50] See, eg, Art 167 TFEU, culture; Art 168 TFEU, public health; Art 173 TFEU, industry.
[51] Art 153 TFEU.   [52] Art 147 TFEU.
[53] CONV 724/03, Brussels 26 May 2003, 82.   [54] pp 169–171.

or supplementing action by the Member States varies somewhat in the different areas listed, but the general approach is as follows.

Each substantive area begins with a provision setting out the objectives of Union action. Thus in relation to public health Article 168 TFEU lists, *inter alia*, the improvement of public health, prevention of illness, and the obviation of dangers to health. The EU is to complement national action on these topics. Member States have an obligation to coordinate their policies on such matters, in liaison with the Commission.[55] The Commission can coordinate action on such matters by, *inter alia*, exchanges of best practice, periodic monitoring, and evaluation.[56] The EU can also pass laws to establish 'incentive measures' designed to protect human health, and combat cross-border health scourges, subject to the mantra that this shall not entail harmonization.[57] Thus while harmonization is ruled out, the EU still has significant room for intervention through 'persuasive soft law', in the form of guidelines on best practice, monitoring and the like, and through 'legal incentive measures'.[58]

The same combination of soft law and legal incentive measures falling short of harmonization can be found in the other areas within this category.[59] The relative scope of EU power within these areas should not, however, be underestimated. The standard approach under the Lisbon Treaty is for the EU to be empowered to take measures to attain the objectives listed concerning that area. The language of the empowerment varies. It is sometimes framed in terms of taking 'incentive measures',[60] on other occasions the language is in terms of 'necessary measures',[61] in yet other instances the terminology is 'specific measures'.[62]

The salient point for present purposes is that whatsoever the precise terminology, these measures constitute legally binding acts, normally passed in accordance with the ordinary legislative procedure. The boundary of this EU legislative competence is that such legal acts must be designed to achieve the objectives listed for EU involvement in the area. These objectives are, however, normally set at a relatively high level of generality, with the consequence that the EU is legally empowered to take binding measures provided that they fall within the remit of these broadly defined objectives and do not constitute harmonization of national laws. This is evident in relation to all areas that fall within this category of competence, and can be exemplified in relation to civil protection and industry.

---

[55] Art 168(2) TFEU.   [56] Art 168(2) TFEU.   [57] Art 168(5) TFEU.

[58] There are also aspects of public health that come within the shared power, where the scope for EU intervention is greater, Art 4(2)(k), Art 168(4) TFEU.

[59] Art 165(4), Art 166(4) TFEU, education and vocational training; Art 167 TFEU, culture; Arts 173(2)–(3) TFEU, industry; Art 195 TFEU, tourism; Art 196 TFEU civil protection.

[60] Art 165(4), Art 166(4) TFEU, education and vocational training; Art 167(5) TFEU, culture; Art 168(5) TFEU, public health.

[61] Art 196(2) TFEU, civil protection.

[62] Art 195(2) TFEU, tourism; Art 173(3) TFEU, industry.

Thus in the context of civil protection Article 196 TFEU provides that the EU shall encourage cooperation among Member States to improve the effectiveness of systems for preventing and protecting against natural or man-made disasters. EU action shall aim to support and complement Member States' action at national, regional, and local level in risk prevention, in preparing their civil-protection personnel, and in responding to natural or man-made disasters within the Union; promote swift, effective operational cooperation within the Union between national civil-protection services; and promote consistency in international civil-protection work. The EU can use the ordinary legislative procedure to establish the measures necessary to achieve these objectives, subject to the caveat that they do not constitute harmonization of national laws.[63]

The provisions relating to industry follow the same conceptual pattern. Article 173(1) TFEU provides that the Union and the Member States shall ensure that the conditions necessary for the competitiveness of the Union's industry exist. Their action must be aimed at speeding up the adjustment of industry to structural changes; encouraging an environment favourable to initiative and to the development of undertakings throughout the Union, particularly small and medium-sized undertakings; encouraging an environment favourable to cooperation between undertakings; and fostering better exploitation of the industrial potential of policies of innovation, research, and technological development. The EU is then empowered to take legally binding acts to achieve these objectives in support of action taken in the Member States, subject once again to the caveat that they must not harmonize national laws.

The scope of EU legislative activity within these areas will of course be bounded by what is acceptable to the Member States in the Council and the European Parliament. It will doubtless be influenced by the very fact that the EU action is designed to support, coordinate, or supplement the action of the Member States. This can be acknowledged, but does not alter the force of the point being made here. The legal reality is that the scope of EU competence within these areas is broader than might initially have been thought, and leaves ample room for the passage of legally binding acts across a broad terrain. This is more especially so given that the meaning of harmonization, and hence the scope of the caveat to EU competence, is unclear, as will be seen below.

(d) Tensions: legal acts and Member State competence

There are limits to what the EU can do in the areas listed in Article 6 TFEU. That is, after all, the very purpose of the category. The EU nonetheless has more competence in these areas than might be thought, and there is a tension in the framing of the Treaty provisions. This tension has been present since the relevant

---

[63] Art 196(2) TFEU.

provisions were devised in the Convention deliberations[64] and it remains in the Lisbon Treaty.

Article 2(5) TFEU provides that EU action designed to support, coordinate, or supplement Member State action does not supersede Member State competence. It also states that legally binding acts of the Union adopted on the basis of the provisions specific to these areas cannot entail harmonization of Member State laws. Thus while the EU cannot harmonize the law in these areas, it can pass legally binding acts on the basis of the provisions specific to these areas.

Where, however, the EU does enact such legal acts they will bind the Member States and the competence of the Member States will be constrained to the extent stipulated by the legally binding act. Thus while Member State competence is not per se superseded merely because the EU has enacted legally binding acts, it will perforce be constrained to the degree entailed by the EU legal act. The degree of this constraint will depend on the nature of the EU legal act passed. It is, however, clear that the EU is not prevented from enacting legally binding acts, which includes legislative acts, within the listed areas, provided that they do not entail harmonization and provided that there is foundation for the passage of such laws in the detailed provisions of the TFEU.

(e) Tensions: legal acts and harmonization

This naturally leads to consideration of a related issue, which is the very meaning of harmonization. This will be of increased importance post-Lisbon, since it defines the outer limits of what can be undertaken by the EU in areas that fall within this overall category.

It can be acknowledged that the proscription on adoption of harmonization measures for areas that fall within this category means that legally binding acts cannot be adopted pursuant to Article 114 TFEU. This is the successor provision to Article 95 EC, and will continue to be the principal Treaty Article through which harmonization measures designed to attain the objectives of the internal market will be enacted. A legally binding act made in an area where the EU only has competence to support, coordinate, or supplement Member State action could not therefore be made pursuant to Article 114, since this would by its very nature be an admission that the objective was to harmonize national law, which is the very thing prohibited by Article 2(5) TFEU.

This, however, only takes us so far. The EU may enact a legally binding act in one of the areas covered by this category of competence, which is based on the relevant Treaty article authorizing the making of such acts. It may then be argued that the enacted measure is tantamount to harmonization of national laws or regulations, even though it does not bear this imprint on the face of the measure. The scope of the EU's power to make legally binding acts was considered above,

---

[64] Art I-12(5) CT.

and its breadth means that disputes as to whether a particular legal act is in effect harmonization may well arise.

It would then be for the ECJ to decide whether in substance the contested measure constituted harmonization and was therefore caught by the limit in Article 2(5) TFEU. This could well give rise to difficult cases for the ECJ, since harmonization measures have assumed various forms. The EC hitherto enacted maximum and minimum harmonization measures, and it was not always clear from the face of the measure which form of harmonization was in issue.[65] In such instances it was for the ECJ to interpret the measure and decide whether it established both a floor and a ceiling, or only the former. Article 2(5) TFEU precludes all forms of harmonization measure for areas covered by this category of competence, and hence it should preclude minimum and maximum harmonization or any other variant thereof. The line between a legitimate legally binding act that advances the objectives of the areas covered by this category of competence, and illegitimate harmonization of national laws, may nonetheless be a fine one in a particular case.

It should not be assumed, moreover, that the consequences for the Member States of enactment of legally binding acts in these areas will necessarily be less far-reaching than harmonization. The assumption behind Article 2(5) TFEU is that harmonization of national laws is by its very nature more intrusive for Member States than other EU legal norms. This then is the rationale for precluding its use within the category of supporting, coordinating, or supplementing action.

This rationale may hold true, but it may not. It depends on the nature of the particular harmonization measure and the non-harmonization legally binding act. The assumption in Article 2(5) that legally binding acts in this category do not supersede Member State competence, by way of contrast to harmonization, is equally difficult to sustain. Thus harmonization may not always supersede the entirety of Member State competence. More important for these purposes is that acts enacted in this category of competence will by virtue of being legally binding constrain what Member States can do with a competence that continues to reside with them.

7. Economic, Employment, and Social Policy

(a) Basic principles: meaning and scope

There is symmetry to the categories of competence discussed thus far. A division between exclusive, shared, and supporting competence can be understood, notwithstanding the difficulties mentioned above. The creation of a particular

---

[65] (N 45).

head of competence to deal with economic and employment policy, however, does little to enhance the symmetry of the new scheme. The Lisbon Treaty, following the Constitutional Treaty, has a separate category of competence for these matters, Article 2(3) TFEU states that 'the Member States shall coordinate their economic and employment policies within arrangements as determined by this Treaty, which the Union shall have competence to provide'. The detailed rules are then set out in Article 5 TFEU.

1. The Member States shall coordinate their economic policies within the Union. To this end, the Council shall adopt measures, in particular broad guidelines for these policies.
   Specific provisions shall apply to those Member States whose currency is the euro.

2. The Union shall take measures to ensure coordination of the employment policies of the Member States, in particular by defining guidelines for these policies.

3. The Union may take initiatives to ensure coordination of Member States' social policies.

It should be noted at the outset that the 'fit' between Article 2(3) and Article 5 TFEU is not perfect, insofar as the former refers to economic and employment policy, while the latter also covers social policy. There is moreover a difference in language, in that the EU is enjoined in mandatory language to coordinate economic and employment policy, whereas it is accorded discretion in relation to social policy.

The existence of this category was controversial in the Convention on the Future of Europe, with some members calling for these areas to come within shared competence, while others argued for the inclusion of employment and social policy, as well as economic policy, within this separate category.[66] The Praesidium felt that the category should remain distinct because the specific nature of coordination of economic and employment policy merited separate treatment.[67] This Delphic utterance provides little by way of reasoned justification.

The real explanation for the separate category was political. There would have been significant opposition to the inclusion of these areas within the head of shared competence. The very depiction of economic policy as an area of shared competence, with the consequence of pre-emption of State action when the EU had exercised power within this area, would have been potentially explosive in some quarters at least. It is equally clear that there were those who felt that the category of supporting, coordinating, and supplementary action was too weak. This was the explanation for the creation of a separate category, and its placement

---

[66] The same tensions were evident in CONV 357/02 (n 6) Final Report of Working Group VI on Economic Governance, Brussels 21 October 2002, 2.
[67] CONV 724/03 (n 53) 68.

after shared power, but before the category of supporting, coordinating, and supplementary action.

(b) Social policy: demarcation and delimitation

The boundary problems that we have seen in the preceding discussion are evident here too, particularly in relation to social policy. The difficulties in this area are especially marked, since certain aspects of social policy fall within shared competence, although it is not clear which;[68] other aspects appear to fall within the category of supporting, coordinating, and supplementary action, even though they are not within the relevant list;[69] and there is in addition separate provision for social policy in the category being considered here.

The reach of Article 5(3) TFEU and its relationship with the more detailed Treaty provisions on social policy is not clear. The most natural 'linkage' would seem to be Article 156 TFEU, which empowers the Commission to encourage cooperation between Member States and facilitate coordination of their action in all fields of social policy,[70] albeit through soft law measures. Assuming this to be so, the wording of the respective provisions does not fit, since Article 5(3) is framed in discretionary terms, 'the Union may take initiatives', while Article 156 TFEU is drafted in mandatory language, to the effect that the 'Commission shall' encourage the relevant cooperation and coordination.

(c) Economic, employment, and social policy: category and consequence

The Treaty schema for competence in Article 2 TFEU is in general premised on the ascription of legal consequences for EU and Member State power as the result of coming within a particular category. Thus, as we have seen, Member States cannot take legally binding action for matters that fall within the EU's exclusive competence, unless empowered by the EU or for the implementation of EU acts. In the sphere of shared competence the EU and Member States can both make legally binding acts, subject to the caveat that the Member States cannot do so where the EU has exercised its competence. Legal consequences are also spelt out for the category of supporting, coordinating, and supplementary action.

Article 5 TFEU is an exception in this respect, since Article 2(3) TFEU does not spell out the legal consequences of inclusion within this category. It simply provides that the 'Member States shall co-ordinate their economic and employment policies

---

[68] pp 169–171.   [69] pp 169–171.

[70] The particular areas listed are: employment; labour law and working conditions; basic and advanced vocational training; social security; prevention of occupational accidents and diseases; occupational hygiene; the right of association and collective bargaining between employers and workers.

within the arrangements as determined by this Treaty, which the Union shall have competence to provide'. The legal consequences of inclusion within this category can therefore only be divined by considering the language of Article 5 TFEU, which is couched largely in terms of coordination, and by considering the detailed provisions that apply to these areas.

(d) Economic policy: power and limits

We have seen that the rationale for creating this category was the political fear of placing such matters in the category of shared competence, balanced by an unwillingness to limit EU power by placing these areas in the category of supporting, coordinating, and supplementing Member State action. We have seen also that the legal consequences of this category for the division of power between the EU and the Member States are unclear, and can only be divined by placing close attention to the more specific provisions of the TFEU. These propositions can be exemplified by considering economic policy.[71]

The detailed provisions concerning economic policy are to be found in Chapter 1 of Title VIII of Part 3 of the Lisbon Treaty. It is clear that the EU has a range of powers that would not easily be accommodated in the category of competence concerning supporting, co-ordinating, or supplementing action. The EU's powers over economic policy allow it to take dispositive and peremptory action in certain circumstances. The powers can be regarded as relating to the 'coordination' of economic policy for the purposes of Article 2(3) TFEU, but it should be recognized that this is a broad reading of that language.

Thus Article 121(6) TFEU empowers the EU to enact regulations laying down detailed rules for the multilateral surveillance procedure, which is central to the strategy concerning broad guidelines of the economic policies of the Member States. Article 122(1) TFEU allows the Council to adopt a decision laying down measures appropriate to an economic situation, in particular if severe difficulties arise in the supply of certain products. Article 123 TFEU prohibits overdraft facilities by Union or State bodies with the ECB or national central banks, and Article 124 TFEU bans privileged access by Union or State bodies to financial institutions. The complex rules designed to control excessive budgetary deficits by Member States are ultimately backed up by the power to make binding decisions, which can lead to the imposition of fines and other disadvantageous consequences, Article 126(7)–(11) TFEU. It is clear moreover that the possession of these powers by the EU was felt to be even more important in the light of enlargement.

---

[71] See Ch 8 for more detailed discussion.

8. Common Foreign and Security Policy and Defence

The three-pillar structure that characterized the previous EU Treaty has not been preserved in the Lisbon Treaty. There are nonetheless distinct rules that apply in the context of foreign and security policy, and this warrants a separate head of competence for this area. It is set out in Article 2(4) TFEU.

The Union shall have competence, in accordance with the provisions of the Treaty on European Union, to define and implement a common foreign and security policy, including the progressive framing of a common defence policy.

The rules concerning the common foreign and security policy (CFSP) are set out in Title V TEU. Decision making in this area continues to be more intergovernmental and less supranational by way of comparison with other areas of Union competence.[72] The European Council and the Council dominate decision making, and the legal instruments applicable to CFSP are distinct from those generally applicable for the attainment of Union objectives. There will be detailed consideration of these provisions in a later chapter.[73]

Suffice it to say for the present that Article 2(4) does not specify which type of competence applies in the context of the CFSP. In truth none of the categories is a good fit. It is clearly not within exclusive competence, since it is not listed in Article 3 TFEU, and in any event the substance of the CFSP simply does not accord with the idea of exclusive EU competence. Nor is it mentioned in the list of those areas that are subject to supporting, coordinating, or supplementing Member State action in Article 6 TFEU. This would seem to imply that it falls within the default category of shared competence in Article 4 TFEU, even though not mentioned in the non-exhaustive list. The reality is, however, that the world of the CFSP may not readily fit within the frame of shared administration, insofar as this connotes strict pre-emption of Member State action when the EU exercised its power in the area, nor does this idea cohere with Declarations appended to the Lisbon Treaty.[74] If the CFSP is regarded as within shared administration, the point made earlier concerning the need for close examination of the respective powers of the EU and Member States, in order to be clear about the nature of the power sharing, is of especial significance.

9. The 'Flexibility' Clause

Article 308 EC has long been viewed with suspicion by those calling for a clearer delimitation of Community competences and in particular by the German

---

[72] Cremona (n 11).   [73] Ch 10.
[74] Declarations 13 and 14 on the common foreign and security policy.

Länder. Various calls for reform were made before and during IGCs. This issue was placed on the post-Nice and Laeken agenda for reform of the EU. The Laeken Declaration expressly asked whether Article 308 EC ought to be reviewed, in light of the twin challenges of preventing the 'creeping expansion of competences' from encroaching on national and regional powers, and yet allowing the EU to 'continue to be able to react to fresh challenges and developments and...to explore new policy areas'.[75] The Working Group on Complementary Competences recognized the concerns about the use of Article 308. The Group nonetheless recommended the retention of the Article in order that it could provide for flexibility in limited instances.[76] The flexibility clause is now enshrined in Article 352 TFEU.

1. If action by the Union should prove necessary, within the framework of the policies defined in the Treaties, to attain one of the objectives set out in the Treaties, and the Treaties have not provided the necessary powers, the Council, acting unanimously on a proposal from the Commission and after obtaining the consent of the European Parliament, shall adopt the appropriate measures. Where the measures in question are adopted by the Council in accordance with a special legislative procedure, it shall also act unanimously on a proposal from the Commission and after obtaining the consent of the European Parliament.

2. Using the procedure for monitoring the subsidiarity principle referred to in Article 5 (3) of the Treaty on European Union, the Commission shall draw national Parliaments' attention to proposals based on this Article.

3. Measures based on this Article shall not entail harmonisation of Member States' laws or regulations in cases where the Treaties exclude such harmonisation.

4. This Article cannot serve as a basis for attaining objectives pertaining to the common foreign and security policy and any acts adopted pursuant to this Article shall respect the limits set out in Article 40, second paragraph, of the Treaty on European Union.

Article 352(1) TFEU is framed broadly in terms of the 'policies defined in the Treaties', with the exception of the CFSP. It can therefore serve as the basis for competence in almost all areas of EU law. The unanimity requirement means, however, that it will be more difficult to use this power in an enlarged EU, and Article 352 TFEU also requires the consent of the European Parliament, as opposed to mere consultation, as was previously the case under Article 308 EC. The need for recourse to this power will also diminish, given that the Lisbon Treaty has created a legal basis for action in the areas where Article 308 EC had previously been used.[77] The German Federal Constitutional Court was nonetheless concerned about the scope of Article 352 and stipulated that the

---

[75] Laeken Declaration (n 4) 22.
[76] Final Report of Working Group V (n 36) 14–18.
[77] See, eg, Energy, Art 194(2) TFEU; Civil Protection, Art 195(2) TFEU; Economic Aid to Third Countries, Art 209(1), 212(2) TFEU.

exercise of any such competence constitutionally required ratification by the German legislature.[78]

The conditions in Article 352(2)–(4) are novel. The import of Article 352(2) is not entirely clear. Weatherill has argued that uniquely within the Lisbon Treaty it provides national parliaments with the opportunity to contest the existence of competence when legislative action is based on the flexibility clause, as opposed to other contexts where national parliaments can simply challenge on grounds of subsidiarity.[79] This may be so. It does not, however, sit comfortably with the wording of Article 352(2), which is framed in terms of subsidiarity and is not suggestive of national parliamentary power to challenge the existence of competence. The more natural interpretation is that because the flexibility clause entails an exceptional use of EU legislative power, the quid pro quo is that the Commission has an additional obligation, viz to draw this to the attention of national parliaments, in order that they might contest it on the grounds of subsidiarity.

10. Subsidiarity, Proportionality, and the Role of National Parliaments

The Lisbon Treaty distinguishes between the existence of competence and the use of such competence, which is determined by subsidiarity and proportionality.[80] The relevant principles are now embodied in Article 5(3)–(4) TEU.[81]

3. Under the principle of subsidiarity, in areas which do not fall within its exclusive competence, the Union shall act only if and insofar as the objectives of the proposed action cannot be sufficiently achieved by the Member States, either at central level or at regional and local level, but can rather, by reason of the scale or effects of the proposed action, be better achieved at Union level.

   The institutions of the Union shall apply the principle of subsidiarity as laid down in the Protocol on the application of the principles of subsidiarity and proportionality. National Parliaments ensure compliance with the principle of subsidiarity in accordance with the procedure set out in that Protocol.

4. Under the principle of proportionality, the content and form of Union action shall not exceed what is necessary to achieve the objectives of the Treaties.

---

[78] Lisbon Case, BVerfG, 2 BvE 2/08, from 30 June 2009, [326]–[328], available at <http://www.bverfg.de/entscheidungen/es20090630_2bve000208.html>. English translation available at <http://www.bundesverfassungsgericht.de/entscheidungen/es20090630_2bve000208en.html>.
[79] Weatherill (n 1).
[80] Art 5(1) TEU.
[81] J-V Louis, 'National Parliaments and the Principle of Subsidiarity—Legal Options and Practical Limits' in I Pernice and E Tanchev (eds), *Ceci n'est pas une Constitution—Constitutionalization without a Constitution?* (Nomos, 2009) 131–154; G Bermann, 'National Parliaments and Subsidiarity: An Outsider's View' ibid 155–161; J Peters, 'National Parliaments and Subsidiarity: Think Twice' (2005) European Constitutional L Rev 68.

The institutions of the Union shall apply the principle of proportionality as laid down in the Protocol on the application of the principles of subsidiarity and proportionality.

The Protocol on the Application of the Principles of Subsidiarity and Proportionality should be read in tandem with the Protocol on the Role of National Parliaments in the EU.[82] It should be noted at the outset that the Subsidiarity Protocol only applies to draft legislative acts,[83] and does not cover delegated or implementing acts. It is certainly possible that a detailed delegated act might be felt to infringe subsidiarity, but the Protocol provides no mechanism for checks by national Parliaments on such measures.

The Subsidiarity Protocol imposes an obligation on the Commission to consult widely before proposing legislative acts.[84] The Commission must provide a detailed statement concerning proposed legislation so that compliance with subsidiarity and proportionality can be appraised. The statement must contain some assessment of the financial impact of the proposals, and there should be qualitative and, wherever possible, quantitative indicators to substantiate the conclusion that the objective can be better attained at Union level.[85] The Commission must submit an annual report on the application of subsidiarity to the European Council, the European Parliament, the Council, and to national parliaments.[86] The ECJ has jurisdiction to consider infringement of subsidiarity under Article 263 TFEU, brought by the Member State, or 'notified by them in accordance with their legal order on behalf of their national Parliament or a chamber of it'.[87]

The most important innovation in the Protocol on Subsidiarity is the enhanced role accorded to national parliaments. The Commission must send all legislative proposals to the national parliaments at the same time as to the Union institutions.[88] A national parliament or Chamber thereof, may, within eight weeks, send the Presidents of the Commission, European Parliament, and Council a reasoned opinion as to why it considers that the proposal does not comply with subsidiarity.[89] The European Parliament, Council, and Commission must take this opinion into account.[90] Where non-compliance with subsidiarity is expressed by national parliaments that represent one-third of all the votes allocated to such parliaments, the Commission must review its proposal.[91]

---

[82] Protocol (No 1). See above, p 46.
[83] Protocol (No 2) On the Application of the Principles of Subsidiarity and Proportionality, Art 3.
[84] ibid Art 2.
[85] ibid Art 5.
[86] ibid Art 9.
[87] ibid Art 8.
[88] ibid Art 4. The national Parliaments must also be provided with legislative resolutions of the EP, and common positions adopted by the Council.
[89] ibid Art 6.   [90] ibid Art 7(1).
[91] ibid Art 7(2). This threshold is lowered to one-quarter in cases of acts concerning the area of freedom, justice, and security that are based on Art 76 TFEU.

The Commission, after such review, may decide to maintain, amend, or withdraw the proposal, giving reasons for the decision.[92] Where a measure is made in accordance with the ordinary legislative procedure, and at least a simple majority of votes given to national parliaments signal non-compliance with subsidiarity, then the proposal must once again be reviewed, and, although the Commission can decide not to amend it, the Commission must provide a reasoned opinion on the matter and this can, in effect, be overridden by the European Parliament or the Council.[93]

It should, however, be noted that while the Protocol imposes obligations on the Commission to ensure compliance with the principles of subsidiarity and proportionality, national parliaments are afforded a role only in relation to the former and not the latter. The reasoned opinion submitted by the national parliament must relate to subsidiarity. This is regrettable, as Weatherill rightly notes,[94] since it is difficult to disaggregate the two principles, and insofar as one can do so there is little reason why national parliaments should not be able to proffer a reasoned opinion on proportionality as well as subsidiarity.

It remains to be seen how subsidiarity operates in practice. It is clear that there will continue to be many areas in which the comparative efficiency calculus in Article 5(3) TFEU favours Union action, more especially in an enlarged Union. It is equally clear that subsidiarity has had an impact on the existence and form of EU action. If Union action is required, the Commission will often proceed through directives rather than regulations, and there has been a greater use of guidelines and codes of conduct.

Time will tell how far the new provisions in the Protocol according greater power to national parliaments affect the incidence and nature of EU legislation. Much will depend on the willingness of national parliaments to devote the requisite time and energy to the matter. The national parliament has to submit a reasoned opinion as to why it believes that the measure infringes subsidiarity. It will have to present reasoned argument as to why the Commission's comparative efficiency calculus is defective. This may not be easy. It will be even more difficult for the requisite number of national parliaments to present reasoned opinions in relation to the same Union measure so as to compel the Commission to review the proposal. The Commission is nonetheless likely to take seriously any such reasoned opinion, particularly if it emanates from the parliament of a larger Member State.

There is the possibility of recourse to the ECJ for infringement of subsidiarity under Article 263 TFEU, brought by the Member State, or notified by the State on behalf of the national parliament. It remains to be seen whether this is used and if so how it works. There may well be instances where the Member State has agreed in the Council to the EU measure which the national parliament then regards as infringing subsidiarity. This is the rationale for the provision allowing

---

[92] ibid Art 7(2).   [93] ibid Art 7(3).   [94] Weatherill (n 1).

the Member State to notify the action on behalf of its parliament. This still leaves open interesting questions as to how such a case will be argued. If the Member State has voted for the legislative act in the Council it will be odd for it then to contend before the Court that the measure violates subsidiarity.[95] If the legal action is to be a reality the Member State will not simply have to notify the action on behalf of its Parliament, but also allow the Parliament through its chosen legal advocate to advance its arguments about the fact that the measure does not comply with subsidiarity, even if the Member State does not agree with those arguments.

11. Conclusion

(a) Clarity: aim and realization

We saw at the inception of this chapter that a principal aim of the Treaty reform was to attain greater clarity as to the division of competence between the EU and Member States. It is therefore important by way of conclusion to assess how far this aim has been realized.

The basic tripartite division introduced by the Constitutional Treaty and taken over into the Lisbon Treaty has gone some way towards greater clarity. The categories of exclusive competence, shared competence, and competence to support, coordinate, or supplement Member State action are helpful in this respect. So too is the fact that the Lisbon Treaty specifies the legal consequences of assignment of a subject matter area to a particular category.

The preceding discussion has, however, also revealed the limits of what can be achieved through categorization. This is not a critique of the Lisbon Treaty as such. It is rather testimony to the inherent limitations of categorization in clearly demarcating the boundaries of competence between the EU and Member States. The difficulty of dividing power between different levels of government is an endemic problem within any non-unitary polity.[96] The principal difficulties in relation to clarity are nonetheless as follows.

First, any regime of categorization will perforce generate problems of demarcating the boundaries of each category. This is inevitable, as evidenced by the preceding analysis. The scale of the problem will be affected by the complexity of the legal provisions that apply in any particular area, and the extent to which the Treaty does or does not specify with greater exactitude which of those provisions fall into which category of competence. This is exemplified most acutely in relation to social policy.

---

[95] I am grateful for this point to a participant in a Conference on the Lisbon Treaty held in Brussels.

[96] E Young, 'Protecting Member State Autonomy in the European Union: Some Cautionary Tales from American Federalism' (2002) 77 NYULRev 1612.

Second, shared competence is the default position both formally and substantively in the Lisbon Treaty. This is to be expected given the nature of the EU and the range of areas over which it has some degree of authority. The broad range of areas that fall within shared competence nonetheless has inevitable consequences in terms of the clarity of the divide between EU and Member State competence. It means that the informed observer can only determine the reality of this divide by looking at the detailed Treaty provisions that govern the relevant area, and the nature of the divide will differ, often significantly, as between different areas that fall within the remit of shared competence. It also means that the informed observer who wishes to understand what the Member State is allowed to do in any such area will have to be acutely aware of whether and how the EU has exercised its power, since the Member States lose their competence to the extent that the EU has exercised its competence. This necessarily requires close attention to the legal norms made by the EU within any such area. The devil is always in the detail.

Third, analogous problems are apparent in relation to the category of competence whereby the EU supports, coordinates, or supplements Member State action. The Lisbon Treaty places boundaries on EU competence in these areas, through the proscription on harmonization. We have seen, however, that the specific provisions in the TFEU governing the areas that fall within this head of competence allow persuasive soft law and binding hard law to achieve the objectives spelt out for each area. The formal message from the Lisbon Treaty is that such measures, including the hard law, do not supersede Member State competence. The choice of this verb was either finely judged or fortuitous. The legal reality in any event is that such legally binding acts made by the EU will constrain Member State competence, and, as we have seen, the scope for such legal norms is broader than one might have expected. The informed observer who wishes to understand the division between EU competence and that of the Member States will therefore once again have to be cognizant of the specific Treaty provisions that govern each of these areas, and of any EU legislation made pursuant thereto.

(b) Containment: aim and realization

The Laeken Declaration and subsequent discussion of Treaty reform was also premised on the need to contain EU power. There were concerns voiced about 'competence creep', more especially in relation to two of the most 'general' Treaty provisions, Articles 95 and 308 EC. These concerns were echoed by academic literature discussing 'competence creep'.[97] It is therefore important

---

[97] M Pollack, 'Creeping Competence: The Expanding Agenda of the European Community' (1994) 14 Journal of Public Policy 95; S Weatherill, 'Competence Creep and Competence Control' (2004) 23 YEL.

to consider how far the Lisbon reforms have addressed this issue. The answer is that they have done so to some extent, but problems still remain.

The Lisbon Treaty will render 'competence creep' based on Article 352 TFEU, the successor to 308 EC, less likely in the future for the reasons given above. Article 352 TFEU requires unanimity in the Council, which will not be easy to achieve in a Union of 27 Member States. It now demands consent from the European Parliament, and national parliaments are specifically alerted to use of this provision. Equally important is the fact that the EU has been given specific legislative competence in the areas where Article 308 EC had been used in the past, and hence recourse to this provision will be obviated for the future.

The Lisbon Treaty will, by way of contrast, do little if anything to alleviate problems of 'competence creep' in the terrain covered by Article 114 TFEU, the successor to Article 95 EC. The reason is not hard to divine. Article 114 TFEU replicates Article 95 EC. Concerns about over-extensive use of this legislative competence arose because it was felt that the EU was too readily assuming power to harmonize national laws based on mere national divergence, with scant attention being given to the impact, if any, of that divergence on the functioning of the internal market.[98] The ECJ's ruling in the *Tobacco Advertising* case[99] appeared to signal some tightening up in this respect, by stating that mere divergence in national laws was insufficient to warrant EU regulatory competence under Article 95 EC, it being necessary to show some more discrete impact on the functioning of the internal market. Subsequent case law[100] has, however, revealed at the very least some softening of the ECJ's position on this issue.[101] It is now more willing to find that regulatory competence exists because divergent national laws constitute an impediment to the functioning of the internal market and EU harmonization contributes to the elimination of obstacles to the free movement of goods or to the freedom to provide services, or to the removal of distortions of competition.

There are, however, other techniques for dealing with this problem. The new subsidiarity provisions will provide one mechanism for checks concerning use of Article 114 TFEU. It is unlikely, however, that subsidiarity could ever serve as the principal control device in this respect. The EU did not, however, cease to function during the period when Treaty reform featured prominently on the

---

[98] Weatherill (n 1); Weatherill (n 97).

[99] Case C-376/98 *Germany v European Parliament and Council.*

[100] Case C-377/98 *Netherlands v Parliament and Council* [2001] ECR I-7079; Case C-491/01 *The Queen v Secretary of State for Health, ex p British American Tobacco (Investments) Ltd and Imperial Tobacco Ltd* [2002] ECR I-11453; Case C-210/03 *R v Secretary of State for Health, ex p Swedish Match* [2004] ECR I-11893; Case C-380/03 *Germany v European Parliament and Council* [2006] ECR I-11573.

[101] D Wyatt, 'Community Competence to Regulate the Internal Market' in M Dougan and S Currie (eds), *50 Years of the European Treaties, Looking Back and Thinking Forward* (Hart, 2009) ch 5.

agenda. To the contrary, the first decade of the new millennium saw the passage of major legislative initiatives across a variety of fields.[102]

The development of Impact Assessment is especially important in this context. It began in earnest in the new millennium,[103] and has developed significantly since then.[104] Impact assessment is a set of steps to be followed when policy proposals are prepared, alerting political decision makers to the advantages and disadvantages of policy options by assessing their potential impacts. The results of this process are summarized and presented in an Impact Assessment Report.[105] The lead department within the Commission in the relevant area will be responsible for the Impact Assessment, and there is an Impact Assessment Board which controls the quality of such Impact Assessments, and provides support and advice. The Impact Assessment work is seen as a key element in the development of Commission proposals, which is taken into account by the College of Commissioners when making decisions. The Impact Assessment Report does not, however, replace decision making and the adoption of a policy proposal remains a political decision made by the College.

A typical Impact Assessment will address a range of issues including: the nature and scale of the problem, how is it evolving, and who is most affected by it; the views of the stakeholders concerned; should the Union be involved; if so, what objectives should it set to address the problem; the main policy options for reaching these objectives; the likely economic, social, and environmental impacts of those options; a comparison of the main options in terms of effectiveness, efficiency, and coherence in solving the problems; and the organization of future monitoring.

Impact Assessment developed as part of the Better Regulation strategy. The Impact Assessment Reports are regarded as an important component of this strategy. They help the EU to design better laws; facilitate better-informed decision making throughout the legislative process; take into account input from external stakeholders; foster coherence of Commission policies and consistency with Treaty objectives such as the respect for Fundamental Rights; improve the quality of policy proposals by revealing the costs and benefits of different policy options; and help to ensure that the principles of subsidiarity and proportionality are respected.[106]

The Commission initiatives subject to Impact Assessment are decided each year by the Secretariat General, Impact Assessment Board, and the departments concerned. They are in general used for the most important Commission initiatives and those with most far-reaching impact. This includes a broad range

---

[102] Craig (n 3).
[103] Impact Assessment, COM(2002) 276 final; Impact Assessment—Next Steps, SEC(2004) 1377; Better Regulation and Enhanced Impact Assessment, SEC(2007) 926.
[104] Impact Assessment Guidelines, SEC(2009) 92.
[105] ibid 1.1.   [106] ibid 1.2.

of initiatives:[107] all legislative proposals in the Commission's Legislative and Work Programme (CLWP); all non-CLWP legislative proposals with clearly identifiable economic, social, and environmental impacts; non-legislative initiatives, such as White Papers, action plans, and expenditure programmes, which define future policies; and certain Comitology implementing measures that are likely to have significant impacts.

The Impact Assessment strategy is not some panacea that will magically dispel concerns as to 'competence creep' or 'competence anxiety'. It is nonetheless central to addressing these concerns. The Impact Assessment Report considers the very issues that are pertinent to our inquiry. This includes the justification for EU action in terms of, for example, the need for harmonization because of the impact of diverse national laws on the functioning of the internal market. It also includes the subsidiarity calculus, which is an explicit step in the overall Impact Assessment process,[108] with a specific section devoted to verification of the EU's right of action and justification thereof in terms of subsidiarity.[109] It is acknowledged in the documentation that assessment of subsidiarity can evolve over time, such that EU action may be scaled back if it is no longer justified, or it may be expanded if circumstances so require. In the latter instance there should be the 'clearest possible justification'[110] in terms of subsidiarity and proportionality.[111]

The Impact Assessment strategy therefore constitutes a framework within which to address concerns as to competence anxiety. The strategy is not perfect, but it has been improved since its inception and assessments, both official[112] and academic,[113] have generally been positive. The strategy looks set to stay, providing the justificatory foundation for EU action and verification of the subsidiarity calculus. If the data in a particular Impact Assessment Report are felt to be wanting in these respects, then we should press for further improvement and not be satisfied with exiguous or laconic argument. The very fact that there is a framework within which these issues are now considered is, however, a positive step, which facilitates scrutiny as to the nature of the justificatory arguments and their adequacy.

This should in turn facilitate judicial review. The ECJ should be willing to consider the adequacy of the reasoning for EU legislative action, and to look behind the formal legislative preamble to the arguments that underpin it derived from the Impact Assessment. The ECJ should be properly mindful of the

---

[107] ibid 1.4.   [108] ibid 2.1, 2.3.
[109] ibid 5.2.   [110] ibid 5.2.   [111] ibid 7.2.
[112] Evaluation of the Commission's Impact Assessment System, Final Report–Executive Summary (April 2007, Secretariat General of the Commission); Impact Assessment Board Report for 2008, SEC(2009) 55.
[113] European Policy Forum, *Reducing the Regulatory Burden: The Arrival of Meaningful Regulatory Impact Analysis* (City Research Series No 2, 2004); C Radaelli and F de Francesco, *Regulatory Quality in Europe, Concepts, Measures and Policy Processes* (Manchester University Press, 2007); C Cecot, R Hahn, A Renda, L Schrefler, 'An Evaluation of the Quality of Impact Assessment in the European Union with Lessons for the US and the EU' (2008) 2 Regulation & Governance 405.

Commission's expertise as evinced in the Impact Assessment. It should also be
fully cognizant of the precepts in the Treaty, which in the case of Article 114
TFEU condition EU intervention on proof that approximation of laws is
necessary for the functioning of the internal market. If the justificatory reasoning
to this effect in the Impact Assessment is wanting then the ECJ should invalidate
the relevant instrument, and thereby signal to the political institutions that the
precepts in the Treaty are to be taken seriously. This is equally the case in relation
to subsidiarity. If the verification or justification for EU action contained in the
Impact Assessment appear merely formal, scant, or exiguous then the ECJ should
not hesitate to so conclude,[114] thereby indicating that the enhanced role
accorded to subsidiarity in the Lisbon Treaty will be taken seriously.

[114] The Community courts have generally not engaged in intensive review of subsidiarity, Case
C-84/94 *United Kingdom v Council* [1996] ECR I-5755; Case C-233/94 *Germany v European
Parliament and Council* [1997] ECR I-2405; Case C-377/98 *Netherlands* (n 100); Cases
C-154–155/04 *The Queen, on the application of Alliance for Natural Health and Nutri-Link Ltd v
Secretary of State for Health* [2005] ECR I-6451, [99]–[108]; Case C-491/01 *British American
Tobacco* (n 100) [177]–[185]; Case C-103/01 *Commission v Germany* [2003] ECR I-5369 [46]–[47].

6

Rights, Legality, and Legitimacy

The Lisbon Treaty rendered the Charter of Fundamental Rights legally binding, thereby resolving an issue that had been left open since the Charter was initially drafted almost a decade earlier. The Lisbon Treaty in addition imposed an obligation on the EU to join the European Convention on Human Rights (ECHR), thereby resolving another issue that had been on the agenda for even longer. The legal and political consequences of these developments will be significant for the EU polity, and will be analysed in this chapter.

The discussion begins with a brief account of the evolution of fundamental rights in the EC, followed by the genesis and drafting of the Charter. The status accorded to the Charter in the Lisbon Treaty is examined, as is the EU's obligation to accede to the ECHR. The focus then turns to the Charter itself. It would clearly be beyond the scope of this chapter to analyse every provision of the Charter, since that would require a book dedicated to human rights. The approach is therefore to provide a brief overview of the overall content of the Charter, with attention thereafter being on important issues that arise from Title VII, which contains general provisions concerning the interpretation and application of the Charter. The discussion concludes by examining some of the broader implications of the Charter for the profile and legitimacy of judicial review within the EU.

1. Charter of Fundamental Rights

(a) Fundamental rights: origins and development

The evolution of the fundamental rights' jurisprudence is well known.[1] The original Treaties contained no express provisions concerning the protection of

---

[1] M Dauses, 'The Protection of Fundamental Rights in the Community Legal Order' (1985) 10 ELRev 398; A Cassese, A Clapham, and J Weiler (eds), *European Union: The Human Rights Challenge* (Nomos, 1991); A Clapham, 'A Human Rights Policy for the European Community' (1990) 10 YEL 309; K Lenaerts, 'Fundamental Rights to be Included in a Community Catalogue' (1991) 16 ELRev 367; J Weiler, 'Thou Shalt not Oppress a Stranger: On the Judicial Protection of the Human Rights of Non-Community Nationals—a Critique' (1992) 3 EJIL 65; J Coppel and A O'Neill, 'The European Court of Justice: Taking Rights Seriously?' (1992) 12 Legal Studies 227;

human rights. This may have been a reaction to the failure of the ambitious attempts to create a European Political Community (EPC) in the mid-1950s, which convinced advocates of closer integration to scale down their plans. The 1957 EEC Treaty focused on economic integration and contained no mention of human rights. The absence of human rights may also have been because the framers did not realize that the EEC Treaty, with its economic focus, could encroach on traditionally protected fundamental human rights. This was belied by subsequent events. It quickly became apparent that Community action could affect social and political, as well as economic, issues. The expansion of Community competences attendant upon successive Treaty amendments re-inforced this.

It was the European Court of Justice (ECJ) that developed what amounted to an unwritten charter of rights.[2] The ECJ's early approach was unreceptive to rights-based claims.[3] It was however *Internationale Handelsgesselschaft* which secured fundamental rights within the Community legal order.[4] The applicant, a German import–export company, argued that a Community Regulation, which required forfeiture of a deposit if goods were not exported within a specified time, was contrary to principles of German constitutional law. The ECJ's response was a mixture of stick and carrot. It forcefully denied that the validity of a Community measure could be judged against principles of national constitutional law. It then held that respect for fundamental rights formed an integral part of the general principles of Community law protected by the ECJ. The ECJ would decide whether the deposit system infringed these fundamental rights. In subsequent case law the ECJ emphasized that it would draw inspiration from the constitutional traditions of the Member States, international human rights Treaties,[5] and the ECHR.[6] The early case law was concerned with the

G de Búrca, 'Fundamental Human Rights and the Reach of EC Law' (1993) 13 OJLS 283; P Twomey, 'The European Union: Three Pillars without a Human Rights Foundation' in D O'Keeffe and P Twomey (eds), *Legal Issues of the Maastricht Treaty* (Wiley, 1994) 121; J Weiler and N Lockhart, ' "Taking Rights Seriously" Seriously: The European Court and its Fundamental Rights Jurisprudence' (1995) 32 CMLRev 51, 579; S O'Leary, 'The Relationship between Community Citizenship and the Protection of Fundamental Rights in Community Law' (1995) 32 CMLRev 519; N Neuwahl and A Rosas (eds), *The European Union and Human Rights* (Kluwer, 1995); P Alston, with M Bustelo and J Heenan (eds), *The EU and Human Rights* (Oxford University Press, 1999).

[2] B de Witte, 'The Past and Future Role of the European Court of Justice in the Protection of Human Rights' in Alston (n 1) ch 27.

[3] Case 1/58 *Stork v High Authority* [1959] ECR 17; Cases 36, 37, 38, and 40/59 *Geitling v High Authority* [1960] ECR 423; Case 40/64 *Sgarlata and others v Commission* [1965] ECR 215.

[4] Case 11/70 *Internationale Handelsgesellschaft v Einfuhr- und Vorratstelle für Getreide und Futtermittel* [1970] ECR 1125.

[5] Case 149/77 *Defrenne v Sabena* [1978] ECR 1365.

[6] See, eg, Case 4/73 *Nold v Commission* [1974] ECR 491; Case 44/79 *Hauer v Land Rheinland-Pfalz* [1979] ECR 3727; Case C-235/99 *The Queen v Secretary of State for the Home Department, ex p Kondova* [2001] ECR I-6427; Case C-25/02 *Rinke v Arztekammer Hamburg* [2003] ECR I-8349; Cases C-465/00, 138 and 139/01 *Rechsnungshof v Osterreichischer Rundfunk and others* [2003] ECR I-4989.

compatibility of Community norms with fundamental rights. The ECJ later confirmed that these rights could be binding on the Member States when they acted within the sphere of Community law.[7] The ECJ did not, however, allow fundamental rights to be pleaded against a Member State where there was no real connection with EC law.[8]

It would nonetheless be a mistake to think that the ECJ made the sole contribution to the evolution of human rights within the Community. The Treaty itself contained certain provisions that would find a place in any modern Bill of Rights. Non-discrimination on the grounds of nationality was secured by Article 12 EC, and also in the Treaty provisions on free movement. Gender equality was protected by Article 141 EC.[9] The ECJ's approach to fundamental rights was cloaked with legitimacy in a declaration of the three major Community institutions on 5 April 1977.[10] They emphasized the importance of fundamental rights, as derived from the constitutions of the Member States and the ECHR, and stated that they would respect them in the exercise of their powers. This was followed by several other non-binding political initiatives. These included a Joint Declaration of the three institutions in 1986; various Declarations and Resolutions on Racism and Xenophobia by the European Council;[11] a Declaration of Fundamental Rights and Freedoms by the European Parliament in 1989;[12] a Community Charter of Fundamental Social Rights, signed by 11 of the then 12 Member States in 1989;[13] as well as references in the preamble to the Single European Act 1986 (SEA) to the ECHR, the European Social Charter, and to 'equality and social justice'.

Treaty amendments contributed to the profile of fundamental rights within the legal order. The Amsterdam Treaty was especially important in this respect. Article 6(1) EU was strengthened so as to provide that the Union was founded on the principles of liberty, democracy, and respect for human rights and fundamental freedoms. Article 6(2) EU stipulated that the Union should respect fundamental rights as guaranteed by the ECHR and as they result from the

---

[7] Case 222/84 *Johnston v Chief Constable of the Royal Ulster Constabulary* [1986] ECR 1651; Case 5/88 *Wachauf v Germany* [1989] ECR 2609; Cases C-74/95 and 129/95, *Criminal Proceedings against X* [1996] ECR I-6609; Case C-260/89 *Elliniki Radiophonia Tileorassi AE v Dimotiki Etairia Pliroforissis and Sotirios Kouvelas* [1991] ECR I-2925, [43]; Case C-368/95 *Vereinigte Familiapress Zeitungsverlags- und vertriebs GmbH v Heinrich Bauer Verlag* [1997] ECR I-368, [24]; Case C-60/00, *Carpenter v Secretary of State for the Home Department* [2002] ECR I-6279, [40]–[41]; Cases C-482 and 493/01 *Orfanopoulos v Land Baden-Wurttemberg* [2004] ECR I-5257, [97]–[98].

[8] Case C-144/95 *Maurin* [1996] ECR I-2909; Case C-299/95 *Kremzow v Austria* [1997] ECR I-2629; Case C-309/96 *Annibaldi v Sindaco del Commune di Guidonia and Presidente Regione Lazio* [1997] ECR I-7493.

[9] C Barnard, 'Gender Equality in the EU: A Balance Sheet' in Alston (n 1) ch 8.

[10] [1977] OJ C103/1; K Bradley, 'Reflections on the Human Rights Role of the European Parliament' in Alston (n 1) ch 26.

[11] See eg [1986] OJ C158/1, Bull EC 5–1990, 1.2.247, Bull EC 6–1991, I.45, and Bull EC 12–1991, I.19.

[12] [1989] OJ C120/51.   [13] COM(89) 471 Final.

constitutional traditions of the Member States as general principles of law. It was made justiciable by Article 46(d) EU. Article 7 EU enabled the Council to suspend certain Member State rights, where it committed serious and persistent breach of the principles set out in Article 6(1) EU. The Amsterdam Treaty also added an important new head of legislative competence, Article 13 EC, to combat discrimination based on sex, racial or ethnic origin, religion or belief, disability, age, or sexual orientation.[14]

(b) Charter: genesis and drafting

Prior to the Charter the protection of rights was nonetheless fragmented and piecemeal, thereby making it more difficult for the citizenry to understand the legal status quo.[15] Moreover, the very fact that the scope of Community power had increased considerably made the promulgation of some form of Community bill of rights more pressing. It is a basic tenet of liberal democratic regimes that a *quid pro quo* for governmental power is the existence of rights-based constraints on the exercise of that power. This fundamental idea is just as applicable to the EU as to traditional Nation States. Thus even if the ECJ had not been 'pressed' into recognizing fundamental rights by the threat of revolt from the German and Italian courts, it would, in all likelihood, have realized the necessity for such limits on governmental power of its own accord, more especially because it was at that time developing administrative law controls on Community action.

While the ECJ laid the groundwork for rights-based protection, the decision to draft a Charter meant that consideration could be given to the range of rights which should be recognized, and enabled a spectrum of views to be taken into account when doing so, thereby enhancing the legitimacy of the resulting document.[16]

The immediate catalyst for the Charter of Fundamental Rights came from the European Council. In June 1999 the Cologne European Council[17] decided that there should be a Charter of Fundamental Rights to consolidate the fundamental rights applicable at Union Level and to make their overriding importance more visible to EU citizens.[18] The Charter was to contain fundamental rights and

---

[14] L Flynn, 'The Implications of Article 13—After Amsterdam Will Some Forms of Discrimination be More Equal than Others?' (1999) 36 CMLRev 1127; G de Búrca, 'The Role of Equality in European Community Law' in S O'Leary and A Dashwood, (eds), *The Principle of Equal Treatment in EC Law* (Sweet & Maxwell, 1997) 13–34.

[15] A Vitorino, *The Charter of Fundamental Rights as a Foundation for the Area of Freedom, Justice and Security* (Centre for European Legal Studies, Exeter Paper in European Law, No 4, 2001) 12–14.

[16] See, however, J Weiler, 'Editorial: Does the European Union Truly Need a Charter of Rights?' (2000) 6 ELJ 95.

[17] 3–4 June 1999.

[18] J Dutheil de la Rochere, *La Charte des droits fondamentaux de l'Union europeene* (2001); G de Búrca, 'The Drafting of the European Charter of Fundamental Rights' (2001) 26 ELRev 126; M Maduro, 'The Double Constitutional Life of the Charter of Fundamental Rights of the

freedoms, as well as the basic procedural rights guaranteed by the ECHR. It was to embrace the rights derived from the constitutional traditions common to the Member States that had been recognized as general principles of Community law. It was also made clear that the Charter should include economic and social rights.

The institutional structure for the discussions about the Charter was laid down in the Tampere European Council in October 1999.[19] It was decided to establish a body called the Convention. It consisted of representatives of the Member States, a member of the Commission, members of the European Parliament, and representatives from national Parliaments. The first meeting took place in December 1999. The Convention was instructed to conclude its work in time for the Nice European Council in December 2000. The discussion in the Convention was therefore conducted in parallel with the Intergovernmental Conference (IGC) concerning the institutional consequences of enlargement that led to the Nice Treaty.

The draft Charter was submitted by the Chairman of the Convention, Roman Herzog, to President Chirac, who held the Presidency of the European Council, on 5 October 2000.[20] It was considered at an informal meeting of the European Council at Biarritz on 14 October 2000.[21] The Charter was accepted, and this was reinforced at the Nice European Council. The Charter was drafted so as to be capable of being legally binding. The precise legal status of the Charter was, however, left undecided in Nice. It is important, at this juncture, to stress two things about the genesis of the Charter.

In substantive terms, the catalyst was the Heads of State meeting in the European Council. Some of the press coverage painted the Charter as but yet another example of expansionism by some reified entity called the EU, with the Commission playing a Machiavellian role in the process. This is wrong. The Commission was in favour of the initiative, but it was launched by the Member States. It was the Member States meeting in the European Council that set the broad terms for the Charter, more particularly the fact that it should include social and economic, as well as traditional civil rights, although it should also be acknowledged that this broad remit had been recommended by an independent group of experts in February 1999. Indeed, given that the development of fundamental rights had hitherto been in the hands of the Community courts there is force in Maduro's observation that the drafting of the Charter

European Union' in T Hervey and J Kenner (eds), *Economic and Social Rights under the EU Charter of Fundamental Rights: A Legal Perspective* (Hart, 2003) 272–276; G de Búrca and J Beatrix Aschenbrenner, 'European Constitutionalism and the Charter' in S Peers and A Ward (eds), *The EU Charter of Fundamental Rights, Politics, Law and Policy* (Hart, 2004) ch 1; J Schonlau, *Drafting the EU Charter, Rights, Legitimacy and Process* (Palgrave, 2005).

[19] 15–16 October 1999.
[20] Charte 4960/00, Convent 55, 26 October 2000.
[21] Charte 4955/00, Convent 51, 17 October 2000.

represented 'the political process taking back into its own hands the definition of the system and catalogue of fundamental rights in the EU'.[22]

In procedural terms, the deliberations of the Convention were transparent, with discussion papers readily available on the website. There were public meetings in which individuals, non-governmental organizations (NGOs) and the like were invited to submit their views. It is moreover worth noting how much was achieved within such a short time. The Convention had to submit a document to the Nice European Council in December 2000. This meant that it had but one year in which to forge a far-reaching document that would be acceptable to the 15 Member States. In reality the period in which it had to complete its work was even shorter than this. The members of the Convention recognized that the Charter would have to be ready by autumn 2000, in order that it could be presented to the Heads of State prior to the Nice European Council. The framing of the Charter has therefore much to commend it as an exercise in efficient and inclusive governance. This is so even though the process was not perfect with regard to, for example, the inclusion of civil society or the power wielded by the Praesidium and Secretariat.[23]

We should nonetheless be mindful of a duality in the Charter project, which is captured well by Maduro.[24]

[T]he Charter of Fundamental Rights of the European Union represents a constitutional paradox. It reflects an emerging trend to agree on the use of the language of constitutionalism in European integration without agreeing on the conception of constitutionalism underlying such language. For some, the Charter is the foundation upon which to build a true constitutional project for the European Union. It will promote the construction of a European political identity and mobilize European citizens around it. For others, the Charter is simply a constitutional guarantee that the European Union will not threaten the values of the Member States. It is a constitutional limit to the process of European integration. The Charter reflects this tension between its conception as a constitutional instrument for polity building and its conception as a simple consolidation of the previous fundamental rights *acquis* aimed at guaranteeing regime legitimacy. These two conceptions confronted each other in the drafting of the Charter and are reflected in many of its provisions.

(c) EU: human rights policy

The Charter will be the primary focus for the remainder of this chapter. It should nonetheless be emphasized that the Charter does not constitute the entirety of EU human rights policy. Indeed the most far-reaching concern voiced prior to the Charter was the need for the Community to develop a more general, coherent

---

[22] Maduro (n 18) 276.
[23] de Búrca (n 18); de Búrca and Aschenbrenner (n 18); O de Schutter, 'Europe in Search of its Civil Society' (2002) 8 ELJ 198.
[24] Maduro (n 18) 269.

human rights policy,[25] particularly when contrasted with the EU's external policy in this regard,[26] and to think beyond the judicial focus.

An EU Network of Independent Experts on Fundamental Rights was created in 2002,[27] and a Fundamental Rights Agency in 2007.[28] Space, however, precludes examination of the general human rights policy for the EU,[29] since it raises a plethora of more particular concerns relating to diverse areas where the EU operates and proper discussion of these matters would require a book in itself. Suffice it to say for the present that the debate about a human rights policy for the EU raises three general issues that cut across particular subject matter areas: competence, content, and desirability.

2. Lisbon Treaty

(a) Charter: status and place

The Nice Treaty did not, as we have seen, resolve the legal status of the Charter. This issue was addressed in the Convention on the Future of Europe. The status of the Charter of Fundamental Rights, and its position in the constitutional architecture of the Constitutional Treaty, was clear. The Charter was 'recognized' in Article I-9 CT and the entire text became Part II of the Constitutional Treaty, which also mandated that the EU should accede to the ECHR.[30]

The European Council of June 2007 signalled a re-thinking of the way in which the Charter would be dealt with,[31] and its conclusions laid the foundations for the relevant provisions in the Lisbon Treaty. The status of the Charter is dealt with in Article 6(1) TEU.

[25] P Alston and J Weiler, 'An "Ever Closer Union" in Need of a Human Rights Policy: The European Union and Human Rights' in Alston (n 1) ch 1. See also, A von Bogdandy, 'The European Union as a Human Rights Organization: Human Rights and the Core of the European Union' (2000) 37 CMLRev 1307; G de Búrca, 'Convergence and Divergence in European Public Law' in P Beaumont, C Lyons and N Walker (eds), *Convergence and Divergence in European Public Law* (Hart, 2002) ch 8; N Nic Shuibhne, 'The European Union and Fundamental Rights: Well in Spirit but Considerably Rumpled in Body?' ibid ch 10.

[26] B Simma, J Beatrix Aschenbrenner and C Schulze, 'Human Rights Considerations in Development Co-operation' in Alston (n 1) ch 18; A Williams, 'Enlargement of the Union and Human Rights Conditionality: A Policy of Distinction?' (2000) 25 ELRev 601; L Bartels, *Human Rights Conditionality in the EU's International Agreements* (Oxford University Press, 2005).

[27] <http://www.europa.eu.int/comm/justice_home/cfr_cdf/index_en.htm>.

[28] <http://europa.eu/agencies/community_agencies/fra/index_en.htm>; The Fundamental Rights Agency, Public Consultation Document, COM(2004) 693 final; Commission Proposal for a Council Regulation establishing a European Union Agency for Fundamental Rights, COM (2005) 280 final; Council Regulation (EC) No 168/2007 of 15 February 2007 establishing a European Union Agency for Fundamental Rights [2007] OJ L53/1.

[29] <http://europa.eu/pol/rights/index_en.htm>; <http://ec.europa.eu/justice_home/fsj/rights/fsj_rights_intro_en.htm>; <http://ec.europa.eu/justice_home/web/policy/rights/web_rights_en.htm>.

[30] Art I-9(2) CT.

[31] Brussels European Council, 21–22 June 2007, Annex 1, 17, 27.

The Union recognises the rights, freedoms and principles set out in the Charter of
Fundamental Rights of the European Union of 7 December 2000, as adapted at
Strasbourg, on 12 December 2007, which shall have the same legal value as the Treaties.

The provisions of the Charter shall not extend in any way the competences of the
Union as defined in the Treaties.

The rights, freedoms and principles in the Charter shall be interpreted in accordance
with the general provisions in Title VII of the Charter governing its interpretation and
application and with due regard to the explanations referred to in the Charter, that set out
the sources of those provisions.

The Charter itself is not therefore incorporated in the Lisbon Treaty, but it is
accorded the same legal value as the Treaties. The Lisbon Treaty is premised on
the version of the Charter as amended by the IGC in 2004,[32] and this version has
been reissued in the Official Journal.[33]

Notwithstanding the clear wording of Article 6(1) TEU and of the Charter
itself,[34] the Member States nonetheless re-emphasized once again in a Declaration attached to the Lisbon Treaty[35] that the Charter does not extend the field
of application of Union law beyond the powers of the Union or establish any new
power or task for the Union, or modify powers and tasks as defined by the
Treaties. The UK and Poland negotiated a Protocol designed to limit the
application of the Charter in certain respects[36] and its impact will be considered
below.[37]

The approach adopted by the Lisbon Treaty to the Charter is 'messier' than
that in the Constitutional Treaty. The clear constitutional architecture of Article
I-9 CT, combined with inclusion of the Charter as Part II of the Constitutional
Treaty, was not replicated in the Lisbon Treaty. Insofar as the objective was to
prevent the Lisbon Treaty from becoming too cumbersome by inclusion of the
Charter within the main fabric of the Treaty, this is belied by the fact that it is
accorded the same legal value as the Treaties, and hence any political or legal
adviser will necessarily have it to hand when considering the legality of EU law,
or national law that 'implements' EU law. It is likely that the changes in this
respect were motivated by the political need at EU level to show that the Lisbon
Treaty differed in certain ways from the Constitutional Treaty, even if in legal
reality the force of the Charter under the Lisbon Treaty will be the same as it
would have been under the Constitutional Treaty.

[32] ibid n 21.
[33] Charter of Fundamental Rights of the European Union, [2007] OJ C303/1; Explanations
Relating to the Charter of Fundamental Rights, [2007] OJ C303/17. The Charter has been reissued
with the Lisbon Treaty, [2010] OJ C83/2.
[34] Art 51(2) Charter of Fundamental Rights.
[35] Declaration 1 concerning the Charter of Fundamental Rights of the European Union.
[36] Protocol (No 30) on the Application of the Charter of Fundamental Rights of the European
Union to Poland and to the United Kingdom.
[37] 237–240.

(b) ECHR: status and place

(i) ECHR: obligation to accede

The relationship between the EU and the ECHR has been much debated, but prior to the Lisbon Treaty the formal legal position was that the EU did not have authority to join the ECHR.[38] This ruling had been controversial, but the issue has now been addressed by the Lisbon Treaty. Article 6(2) TEU stipulates that the Union shall accede to the ECHR, and that such accession shall not affect the Union's competences as defined in the Treaty on European Union (TEU) and the Treaty on the Functioning of the European Union (TFEU). The EU is therefore not merely empowered to accede to the ECHR, but has a duty to do so, although it is a duty without a specific 'time line'. Many commentators advocated the step,[39] as did Working Group II of the Convention on the Future of Europe.[40] While Article 6(2) TEU does not specify a time, the Stockholm Programme is framed in terms of rapid accession by the EU to the ECHR.[41]

A Protocol attached to the Lisbon Treaty[42] states that the agreement relating to accession to the ECHR must make provision for preserving the specific characteristics of the Union and Union law. This is in particular with regard to the arrangements for the Union's possible participation in the control bodies of the ECHR, and the mechanisms necessary to ensure that proceedings by non-Member States and individual applications are correctly addressed to Member States and/or the Union as appropriate.[43] The Protocol repeats the injunction that accession to the ECHR does not affect EU competences or the powers of its institutions,[44] and seeks to preserve derogations made by Member States pursuant to Article 15 ECHR and reservations made by Member States in relation to their membership of the ECHR.[45]

The injunction that accession to the ECHR should be arranged in such a way as to preserve the specific features of Union law is repeated in a Declaration appended to the Lisbon Treaty, which also emphasizes the existence of

---

[38] Opinion 2/94 *On Accession by the Community to the ECHR* [1996] ECR I-1759.

[39] Vitorino (n 15); Assembly of the Council of Europe (n 175); House of Lords' Select Committee on European Union, Eighth Report, *EU Charter of Fundamental Rights* (2000; HL 67); S Fredman, C McCrudden and M Freedland, 'The EU Charter of Fundamental Rights' [2000] PL 178, 180; K Lenaerts and E de Smijter, 'The Charter and the Role of the European Courts' (2001) 8 MJ 90, 99–101; A Arnull, 'From Charter to Constitution and Beyond: Fundamental Rights in the New European Union' [2003] PL 774, 785–787.

[40] CONV 354/02, Final Report of Working Group II, 22 October 2002, 11.

[41] The Stockholm Programme—An Open and Secure Europe Serving and Protecting the Citizen, Council 16484/1/09, Brussels, 25 November 2009, [2.1]; Delivering an area of freedom, security and justice for Europe's citizens, Action Plan Implementing the Stockholm Programme, COM(2010) 171.

[42] Protocol (No 8) Relating to Article 6(2) of the Treaty on European Union on the Accession of the Union to the European Convention on the Protection of Human Rights and Fundamental Freedoms.

[43] Protocol (No 8) Art 1.   [44] Protocol (No 8) Art 2.   [45] ibid.

regular dialogue between the ECJ and the European Court of Human Rights, stating that such dialogue could be reinforced when the Union accedes to that Convention.[46]

The conceptual status accorded to ECHR rights is dealt with in Article 6(3) TEU, which provides that the fundamental rights, as guaranteed by the ECHR, and as they result from the constitutional traditions common to the Member States, constitute general principles of EU law. This approach follows that in the Constitutional Treaty.[47] It has been argued in the past that the very fact that the ECJ conceived of fundamental rights in terms of general principles meant that they were accorded less force than if they had been conceptualized as rights, as they are within Member States.[48] This critique was, however, largely misconceived. It elided the conceptual basis through which the ECJ read fundamental rights into the Community legal order, with the interpretation of those rights within that order. The window through which fundamental rights were brought into EC law was as general principles of law. This was in accord with Article 6(1) EU and Article 230 EC, the latter laying down the grounds for judicial review, which include breach of the Treaty or any rule of law relating to its application. Fundamental rights were regarded as one such rule of law, as were principles such as proportionality, legitimate expectations and the like. However, once they were read into the Treaty the fundamental rights were interpreted in the same general manner as in domestic legal orders, and this was so notwithstanding the fact that there could be disagreement as to the interpretation of a right in a particular case.

The precise terms on which the EU accedes to the ECHR remain to be seen. Decisions will have to be made as to whether, for example, to build in a preliminary reference relationship between the Luxembourg and Strasbourg courts.[49] Accession will not, however, as is sometimes claimed, obviate the need for the EU to have its own Charter. This is so for both substantive and jurisdictional reasons.

In substantive terms, a political entity with the power of the EU should, as a matter of principle, be subject to rights-based constraints on the exercise of that power. The absence of such constraints was the source of the initial revolt by the German and Italian courts, which served as the catalyst for the introduction of the ECJ's fundamental rights jurisprudence. The Charter has enhanced the political legitimacy of the EU by furnishing its citizens with a comprehensive, transparent document that includes a broad range of rights. The Charter was premised on the political choice made by the Heads of State in the European Council that it should cover social and economic, as well as more traditional civil and political rights. The ECHR covers only some of the rights included in the

---

[46] Declaration 2 on Art 6(2) of the Treaty on European Union.

[47] Art I-9(3) CT.

[48] L Besselink, 'Entrapped by the Maximum Standard: On Fundamental Rights, Pluralism and Subsidiarity in the European Union' (1998) 35 CMLRev 629, 633–638.

[49] Arnull (n 39) 788–789.

Charter, and for that reason accession would not obviate the need for the EU's own document enshrining the rights that it believes are worthy of protection. Moreover, the Charter protection accorded to certain civil rights differs from that in the ECHR, as exemplified by the broader remit of the Charter protection for equality.

In jurisdictional terms, accession to the ECHR would not render moot the choices open to citizens as to how they protect their human rights. This point would hold true even if the EU's Charter had been an exact copy of the ECHR. This is because of the differing impact of the EU and ECHR Treaties in at least some States, as exemplified by the UK. The supremacy doctrine is a central principle of EU law. The UK courts have held that even primary legislation that is inconsistent with EU law can be declared inapplicable to the instant case. Such legislation will be 'disapplied' by the national court.[50] The status of the ECHR is different. Under the Human Rights Act 1998, where primary legislation is incompatible with Convention rights, the court can issue a declaration of incompatibility.[51] This declaration does not, however, affect the validity of the legislation. It serves to send the legislation back to the political forum, with the expectation that Parliament will remove the offending provision. There is therefore an incentive for those minded to challenge primary legislation to do so through EU rights where that is possible.

(ii) ECHR: relationship between EU and ECHR prior to accession

The relationship between the EU and the ECHR prior to accession will continue to be governed by existing case law.

From the perspective of the ECJ, the ECHR has always been regarded as an important source of inspiration for its decisions on fundamental rights,[52] and there is even prior to accession an obligation that Charter rights that correspond to rights under the ECHR should be given the same scope and meaning.[53]

From the perspective of the European Court of Human Rights the leading decision on the relationship between fundamental rights protection afforded by the EU and the ECHR was the *Bosphorus* case.[54] The Strasbourg Court held that it was legitimate for contracting parties to the ECHR to transfer power to an

---

[50] *R v Secretary of State for Transport, ex p Factortame Ltd (No 2)* [1991] 1 AC 603; *R v Secretary of State for Employment, ex p Equal Opportunities Commission* [1995] 1 AC 1.

[51] Human Rights Act 1998, ss 2–4.

[52] Case C-94/00 *Roquette Freres SA v Directeur General de la Concurrence, de la Consommation et de la Repression des Fraudes and Commission* [2002] ECR I-9011, [29]; Cases C-238, 244, 245, 247, 250–252, and 254/99 P *Limburgse Vinyl Maatschappij (LVM) and Others v Commission* [2002] ECR I-8375, [273]–[275].

[53] Art 52(3) Charter.

[54] *Bosphorus Hava Yollari Turizm Ve Ticaret Anonim Sirketi v Ireland*, ECHR (2005) No 45036/98; I Canor, '*Primus Inter Pares:* Who is the Ultimate Guardian of Fundamental Rights in Europe?' (2000) 25 ELRev 3; C Costello, 'The *Bosphorus* Ruling of the European Court of Human Rights: Fundamental Rights and Blurred Boundaries in Europe' [2006] Human Rights Law Rev 1.

international organization such as the EU, even if the organization was not itself a contracting party under the ECHR. The State contracting party, however, remained responsible for all acts and omissions of its organs, irrespective of whether they were the result of domestic law or the need to comply with an international obligation flowing from membership of an international organization. If this were not so then the State's obligations under the ECHR could be evaded when power was transferred to an international organization.

State action taken in compliance with such international obligations could nonetheless be justified as long as the relevant international organization was considered to protect fundamental rights 'as regards both the substantive guarantees offered and the mechanisms controlling their observance, in a manner which can be considered at least equivalent to that for which the Convention provides'.[55] The Strasbourg Court made it clear that 'equivalent' meant comparable, not identical, and that the finding of equivalence might alter if there was a relevant change in fundamental rights' protection by the international organization.[56] Where equivalent protection was provided by the international organization, there was a presumption that a State had not departed from the ECHR when it did no more than implement legal obligations flowing from its membership of that international organization. This presumption could be rebutted if it could be shown in the circumstances of a particular case that the protection of Convention rights was manifestly deficient.[57] The Strasbourg Court found that the protection afforded to fundamental rights by the EU was equivalent in the preceding sense and that the protection afforded in the instant case was not manifestly deficient so that the presumption was not rebutted.[58]

The Strasbourg Court, however, also emphasized that a 'State would be fully responsible under the Convention for all acts falling outside its strict international legal obligations',[59] that numerous Convention cases had confirmed this, and that such cases concerned review by the Strasbourg Court 'of the exercise of State discretion for which EC law provided'.[60] Detailed discussion of this exception, interpretation of which is problematic, can be found elsewhere.[61] The fact that the EU now has a legal obligation to accede to the ECHR renders it less likely that such potential problems will become a reality.

3. Charter Content

There was, as might be imagined, considerable debate as to issues concerning the content of the Charter. It will, however, be easier to understand these against the

---

[55] *Bosphorus Hava Yollari* (n 54) [155].   [56] ibid [155].
[57] ibid [156].   [58] ibid [165]–[166].   [59] ibid [157].
[60] ibid [157].
[61] P Craig, *EU Administrative Law* (Oxford University Press, 2006) ch 14.

backdrop of the finished document.[62] A bare outline of the structure of the Charter will be given here,[63] with more detailed discussion of selected issues below.[64]

Title I of the Charter is labelled Dignity, and contains five articles. Article 1 states that human dignity is inviolable and that it must be respected and protected. Article 2 protects the right to life and outlaws the death penalty. The right to the integrity of the person is enshrined in Article 3. This covers physical and mental integrity, Article 3(1). It also deals with medical practices, forbidding, *inter alia*, reproductive cloning of human beings and eugenics. Torture and inhuman and degrading treatment or punishment is prohibited in Article 4. Article 5 prohibits slavery, forced labour, and trafficking in human beings.

Title II of the Charter covers Freedoms, and contains 14 articles. The right to liberty and security of the person is guaranteed in Article 6; respect for private and family life in Article 7; protection of personal data, Article 8; the right to marry and found a family, Article 9; freedom of thought, conscience, and religion, Article 10; freedom of expression and information, Article 11; freedom of assembly and association, Article 12; freedom of the arts and sciences, Article 13; the right to education, Article 14; freedom to choose an occupation and the right to engage in work, Article 15; freedom to conduct a business, Article 16; the right to property, Article 17; the right to asylum, Article 18; and protection in the event of removal, expulsion, or extradition, Article 19.

Title III deals with Equality, and has seven articles. Equality before the law is covered by Article 20. Article 21(1) prohibits discrimination based on a variety of grounds such as sex, race, colour, and sexual orientation, while Article 21(2) prohibits discrimination on the grounds of nationality. Respect for cultural, religious, and linguistic diversity is dealt with in Article 22; gender equality in Article 23; children's rights, Article 24; the rights of the elderly, Article 25; and the integration of those with disabilities, Article 26.

Title IV is concerned with Solidarity and contains 12 articles. Article 27 covers workers' right to information and consultation; Article 28, the right of collective

---

[62] Charter of Fundamental Rights (n 33).
[63] A Heringa and L Verhey, 'The EU Charter: Text and Structure' (2001) 8 MJ 11; C McCrudden, 'The Future of the EU Charter of Fundamental Rights' (Harvard Jean Monnet Working Paper No 10/01); Lord Goldsmith, 'A Charter of Rights, Freedoms and Principles' (2001) 38 CMLRev 1201; P Craig, 'The Community, Rights and the Charter' (2002) 14 ERPL 195.
[64] E Eriksen, J Fossum and A Menéndez (eds), *The Chartering of Europe* (Arena Report No 8/2001); K Feus (ed), *An EU Charter of Fundamental Rights: Text and Commentaries* (Federal Trust, 2000); Hervey and Kenner (n 18); Peers and Ward (n 18); I Pernice and R Kanitz, 'Fundamental Rights and Multilevel Constitutionalism in Europe', WHI Paper 2004, available at <http://www.whi-berlin.de/documents/whi-paper0704.pdf>; I Pernice, 'The Treaty of Lisbon and Fundamental Rights' in S Griller and J Ziller (eds), *The Lisbon Treaty, EU Constitutionalism without a Constitutional Treaty?* (Springer, 2008) 235–256; J Dutheil de la Rochere, 'The Protection of Fundamental Rights in the EU: Community of Values with Opt-out?' in I Pernice and E Tanchev (eds), *Ceci n'est pas une Constitution—Constitutionalisation without a Constitution?* (Nomos, 2009) 119–129.

bargaining; Article 29, right of access to placement services; Article 30, protection against unjustified dismissal; and Article 31, fair and just working conditions. Article 32 prohibits child labour and deals with protection of young people at work. Article 33 is concerned with the protection of family life and the reconciliation of work with the family. Article 34 deals with social security; Article 35 with health care; Article 36 with access to services of general economic interest; Article 37 with environmental protection; and Article 38 with consumer protection.

Title V is entitled Citizens' Rights, and has eight articles. The right of Union citizens to vote and stand for election to the European Parliament is covered by Article 39, and the corresponding right to stand for municipal elections in Article 40. The right to good administration is enshrined in Article 41; access to documents in Article 42; the right to refer maladministration to the Ombudsman, Article 43; the right to petition the European Parliament, Article 44; freedom of movement and residence, Article 45; and diplomatic protection, Article 46.

Title VI deals with Justice. There are four articles. The right to an effective remedy and fair trial is provided in Article 47, and the presumption of innocence in Article 48. The proscription of retrospective criminal penalties is dealt with in Article 49, and the right not to be punished twice for the same offence is found in Article 50.

Title VII contains General Provisions which pertain to the Charter as a whole. Article 51(1) defines the scope of application of the Charter, while Article 51(2) is designed to prevent new EU competences flowing from the Charter. The scope of the guaranteed rights is covered by Article 52. Article 53 addresses the 'level of protection' for rights, and is concerned with the relation between the Charter, national law, international law, and international agreements. The final provision of the Charter, Article 54, contains a prohibition on abuse of rights.

This chapter will not seek to consider the detailed interpretation of all rights contained in the Charter. That would require a book about human rights law. The principal focus will be on the General Provisions in Title VII, since these Articles raise important issues concerning the scope and reach of the Charter.

4. Reach of the Charter

(a) Union institutions: verticality and horizontality

(i) Textual argument: literal and radical interpretation

Charter rights seem only to have a vertical impact. The governing provision is Article 51(1) of the Charter, which stipulates that:

The provisions of this Charter are addressed to the institutions, bodies, offices and agencies of the Union with due regard for the principle of subsidiarity and to the Member States only when they are implementing Union law. They shall therefore respect the rights, observe the principles and promote the application thereof in accordance with their respective powers and respecting the limits of the powers of the Union as conferred on it in the Treaties.

Treaty articles can, by way of contrast, have direct effect, which can be horizontal and hence bind private parties, as well as vertical, binding the State. The same is true for regulations and decisions. Directives by way of contrast can lead to vertical but not horizontal direct effect, although doctrines such as indirect effect and the like can produce similar results.[65]

The importance of this difference can be exemplified in the context of equality. Article 23 of the Charter stipulates that equality between men and women must be ensured in all areas, including employment, work, and pay. In accordance with Article 51(1) of the Charter it will have a vertical impact and bind the Union institutions and the Member States when they are implementing Union law. It will not bind private parties such as employers. The most proximate Treaty provision is Article 157 TFEU, which has both vertical and horizontal direct effect, with the consequence that it can be relied on against the State and private parties.[66]

While the Charter appears to have only a vertical dimension we should pause to consider a more radical reading of Article 51(1). The second sentence thereof provides that Charter rights are addressed to, *inter alia*, Union institutions, which must respect the rights, observe the principles, and promote the application thereof. The paradigm is Union legislation or executive action that infringes a right, with a subsequent annulment action brought by the aggrieved individual. This is the classic vertical application of constitutional rights to protect private autonomy.

It should be noted, however, that the Union courts are Union institutions[67] and are bound to 'respect the rights, observe the principles and promote the application thereof in accordance with their respective powers and respecting the limits of the powers of the Union as conferred on it in the Treaties'. There is nothing that expressly limits this obligation to cases brought against public authorities, whether at Union or national level. It might therefore be argued that this obligation is equally applicable where an individual seeks to rely on a Charter right against another private individual, provided that the subject matter falls within EU law. If this were the case then the Charter would have horizontal direct effect or something close thereto.

---

[65] P Craig and G de Búrca, *EU Law, Text, Cases and Materials* (Oxford University Press, 4th edn, 2007) ch 8.
[66] There are differences in the wording between Art 157 TFEU and Art 23 of the Charter, but they do not alter the point being made in the text.
[67] Art 13 TEU.

This reading might, however, seem too radical. It could be argued that if this were the intent then the Article could have been drafted explicitly to make this clear. There is nothing in the explanatory memorandum to give the impression of horizontal direct effect.[68] This analysis might nonetheless be accepted in a somewhat weaker form, as the justification for indirect horizontal effect, in the manner discussed below.

(ii) Normative argument: choice and tension

Any legal system that protects fundamental rights has to decide how far those protections are to apply. The view that protection of rights should only apply vertically is premised, as Hunt has argued, on a 'rigid distinction between the public and private sphere and presupposes that the purpose of fundamental rights protection is to preserve the integrity of the private sphere against coercive intrusion by the state'.[69] Legal relations between individuals are, by way of contrast, seen as part of private autonomy, with the consequence that the choices individuals make about how to live their lives and deal with each other should not be dictated by the State.

The view that rights-based protections should apply even as between private parties is premised ultimately on the hypothesis that all legal relations are constituted by the State, in the sense that the law itself is constructed and supported by the State.[70] Viewed from this perspective, choices are constantly being made and expressed through legal rules as to the limits on private freedom of action. Legal rules frequently impose limits on private choice whether in the sphere of contract, tort, property, or restitution.

When the matter is viewed in this light the formal divide between the public and private sphere begins to crumble. The issue becomes which types of restraint on private action are felt to be normatively warranted. It becomes more difficult to argue that rights-based protections should have no application in the private sphere, more especially since power which is nominally private may be just as potent as power which is formally public. Even if constitutional rights are applied horizontally this does not mean that there would be no difference in the way in which they would be interpreted in public and private contexts.

The Charter embodies a choice in this respect and the choice seems to be to accord the rights only a vertical dimension, subject to the possible more radical reading considered above. This is readily explicable in 'political' terms. There is

---

[68] Charte 4473/00, Convent 49, 11 October 2000, 46; CONV 828/03, Updated Explanations Relating to the Text of the Charter of Fundamental Rights, 9 July 2003, 45–46; Explanations Relating to the Charter (n 33) 16.

[69] M Hunt, 'The "Horizontal Effect" of the Human Rights Act' [1998] PL 423, 424.

[70] A Clapham, *Human Rights in the Private Sphere* (Oxford University Press, 1993); P Alston (ed), *Non-State Actors and Human Rights* (Oxford University Press, 2005).

little doubt that agreement on the Charter would have been considerably more difficult if its scope of application had been horizontal as well as vertical. This is especially so given the broad range of rights included in the Charter. The 'solution' embodied in Article 51(1) does, however, give rise to tensions if it is read as being restricted to the vertical dimension.

There is an uneasy tension in normative terms between the solely vertical scope of the Charter rights, when compared to the vertical and horizontal scope of some Treaty articles. The very fact that the comparable Treaty article is thought suited to a horizontal as well as a vertical application sits uneasily with the proposition that the analogous Charter right is limited to a vertical impact. It could be argued by way of response that the distinction is justified since a Treaty article will only have horizontal direct effect if it satisfies the requirements of that doctrine: it must be intended to confer rights on individuals and must be sufficiently clear, precise, and unconditional. There are, however, many Charter rights that would satisfy these criteria, and they could in any event be made a condition for horizontal application of Charter rights.

There is furthermore a strain between those Charter rights that do have some readily identifiable provision in other parts of the Treaty, and those that do not. Where there is some comparable provision with horizontal direct effect the individual can rely on it in an action against another private party. This is perforce not possible where there is no readily identifiable provision in the Treaty that deals with the same subject matter as the Charter right.

There is moreover an uneasy practical tension between the vertical scope of the Charter and the wording of some of the rights contained therein. Thus Article 24 (2) of the Charter provides that 'in all actions relating to children, whether taken by public authorities or private institutions, the child's best interests must be a primary consideration'. The Article imposes a substantive obligation, *inter alia*, on private institutions, even though the general field of application of the Charter is limited to Union institutions and Member States when implementing Union law. This tension might be reconciled by allowing an action to compel a public body to ensure that the private institution complies with the obligation contained in this Article. The issue might be addressed more generally by considering ways in which Charter rights might have an impact on private parties, notwithstanding the limits imposed by Article 51(1). It is to this issue that we now turn.

(iii) Indirect horizontal effect: textual and normative dimensions

It is clear that a legal system might decline to afford 'direct horizontal effect' to rights contained in a constitutional document, but be willing nonetheless to give them some limited 'indirect horizontal effect'. Canadian, German, and UK jurisprudence indicate that the values and principles enshrined in the protection

Article 51 that 'it follows unambiguously from the case law of the Court of Justice that the requirement to respect fundamental rights defined in a Union context is only binding on the Member States when they act *in the scope of Union law*.'[81] This formulation was retained in the version of the explanatory memorandum endorsed when the Charter was re-issued in 2007 at the time of the signature of the Lisbon Treaty.[82] The memorandum cited established case law for this proposition, including jurisprudence on the application of fundamental rights when Member States attempted to 'derogate' from EU law.[83] The message from these explanatory memoranda is therefore that Member States are bound by fundamental rights when they act in the scope of Union law, and that the phrase 'implementing Union law' is intended to capture the various senses in which Member States could be said to be acting in the scope of Union law. If the narrow view had really been intended then the Member States had ample opportunity over the last decade to cast the explanatory memorandum in those terms, but did not do so. To the contrary, the formulation in the later versions of the memorandum reinforces the broader reading of Article 51(1).

Third, the broader interpretation is preferable in normative terms. The narrow view would lead to formalistic distinctions between situations where Member States would be bound by the Charter, and those where they would not, which make little sense in terms of principle. It is difficult to think of sound normative argumentation for the consequences that would follow from the narrow view. The normative arguments for Member State action of the *ERT* kind to be subject to fundamental rights review are equally strong, if not stronger, than those that pertain in relation to other types of Member State action. Thus in the *ERT* type of case the Member State has *prima facie* broken one of the four fundamental freedoms that lie at the heart of EU substantive law. There is therefore good reason to condition its ability to rely on such exceptions by requiring compliance with fundamental rights.

Fourth, if the narrow view were to be taken the Member States would in all likelihood continue to be bound by the ECJ's prior jurisprudence, including the *ERT* case, independently of the Charter. It is certainly possible in principle for the Treaty to overrule prior case law. This might be argued by those who subscribe to the narrow view, so that insofar as implementation bears the narrow meaning for which they contend, this must then mean that prior case law entailing a broader application of fundamental rights against Member States has been implicitly overruled. There are, however, considerable difficulties with this argument: there is nothing in the Lisbon Treaty that expressly overrules this case law; the Charter is repeatedly said to be declaratory of existing law; and the

---

[81] CONV 828/03, Updated Explanations (n 68) 45, emphasis added.
[82] Explanations Relating to the Charter (n 33) 16.
[83] Case 5/88 *Wachauf* (n 7); Case C-260/89 *ERT* (n 7); Case C-309/96 *Annibaldi* (n 8); Case C-292/97 *Kjell Karlsson* [2000] ECR I-2737.

very authorities that are said to be overruled are expressly cited in the Explanatory Memorandum. If the narrow view of implementation were to be taken it should then still be possible to rely on the rights-based protections contained in prior case law against Member State action independently of the Charter. The effect of the narrow view would then be a complex world, whereby Member States were caught by the Charter in some instances, and in others by the Court's prior case law. We should not subscribe to such a conclusion unless forced to do so, and there is no such imperative.

(ii) Implementation: scope and application

The following should be regarded as merely examples of the general precept that Member States are bound by Charter rights when acting in the scope of EU law.

The Charter will be applicable when the Member States act as agents for the EU in the context of shared administration,[84] and when they seek to take advantage of a defence to what would otherwise be the applicable EU norm.[85] The Charter should apply to Member States when their action falls within the bounds of a Treaty article, regulation, or decision. Thus if a Member State acting in the area of free movement of goods has national provisions that arguably infringe, for example, the right to protection for personal data, then this Charter right should be capable of being raised by the affected individual. The claimant would have to show a sufficient connection between the Charter right allegedly infringed and the particular area of EU law in order to justify the conclusion that the Member State action fell within the scope of Union law.[86]

The Charter should also be applicable when a Member State implements a directive. Member States have an obligation to implement directives, and thus if the choice of form and methods are felt to violate a Charter right then this should be capable of being raised in the national or Union courts. It is, as de Witte rightly states,[87] difficult to argue that the choice of form and methods of implementation should include the choice of whether to violate a fundamental right, and natural by way of contrast to argue that respect for fundamental rights should be regarded as an implicit part of the result to be achieved under the directive. There is direct support for this view in the ECJ's jurisprudence.[88]

(iii) Implementation: verticality and horizontality

The preceding discussion about verticality and horizontality is relevant in relation to Member States as well as Union institutions. It is clear in principle that the obligation on Member States in Article 51(1) applies to central authorities,

---

[84] Case 5/88 *Wachauf* (n 7).   [85] Case C-260/89 *ERT* (n 7).
[86] Case C-299/95 *Kremzow* (n 8); Case C-309/96 *Annibaldi* (n 8).
[87] de Witte (n 2) 873.
[88] Case C-442/00, *Caballero v Fondo de Garantia Salarial (Fogasa)* [2002] ECR I-11915, [29]–[32]; Cases C-465/00, 138 and 139/01 *Rechnungshof* (n 6).

regional and local bodies, and the explanatory memorandum is cast in these terms.[89] The obligation must also be incumbent on national courts, which would have the duty to 'respect the rights, observe the principles and promote the application thereof in accordance with their respective powers'. An individual could argue in an action against a national public body that it had breached a Charter right in the way that it had implemented a directive.

Whether a Charter right could be invoked in an action against another individual before a national court in circumstances where EU law was applicable raises the same issue about horizontality considered above. The 'radical reading' of Article 51(1) would countenance this, but the objections to this reading would be equally pertinent here. The argument in favour of some measure of indirect horizontal effect would, however, be equally applicable.

5. Competence and the Charter

There was concern during the negotiations that led to the Charter that it might broaden the scope of EU competence or power. The concern was addressed by Article 51(2), which originally stipulated that the Charter does not establish any new power or task for the Community or Union, or modify powers and tasks defined by the Treaties. This was reaffirmed by Working Group II at the Convention on the Future of Europe, which proposed to make this clearer through an amendment to Article 51(2).[90] Article 51(2) now provides that:

The Charter does not extend the field of application of Union law beyond the powers of the Union or establish any new power or task for the Union, or modify powers and tasks as defined in the Treaties.

The 'fit' between Article 51(2) and the substantive provisions of the Charter may be questioned.[91] Much turns on the precise meaning accorded to the key words 'power or task'. These words could be interpreted to mean a new head of legislative competence. If viewed in this way Article 51(2) prohibits construction of the Charter such as to afford new or modified legislative competence to the Union.[92] The application of this precept may, however, be problematic given the uncertainties concerning competence under the Lisbon Treaty.[93] It is important to note, however, that the denial of new heads of legislative competence would not preclude, for example, claims to new social entitlements from the EU 'on the

---

[89] Explanations Relating to the Charter (n 33) 16.
[90] CONV 354/02, Final Report of Working Group II, 22 October 2002, 5.
[91] Maduro (n 18) 277.
[92] Explanations Relating to the Charter (n 33) 16; Charte 4423/00, Convent 46, 31 July 2000, 35; Charte 4473/00, Convent 49, 11 October 2000, 46–47.
[93] Ch 5.

basis of fundamental social rights so long as those claims can be satisfied through the exercise of an existing competence'.[94]

It is clear, moreover, that the Charter will add to the matters that can be taken into account when determining the legality of Union action. It can be accepted that the fact that the Charter, for example, protects religious freedom in Article 10 will not of itself accord the EU any new legislative competence in this area, although it may exercise any such competence as it has under existing provisions. The recognition of freedom of religion in Article 10 will nonetheless be relevant in assessing the legality of Union legislation even where it does not seek to regulate religion as such, but may be felt to impinge directly or indirectly on the protected right. This is equally true of all Charter rights. The point is especially significant in relation to those rights that were wholly or partly based on international conventions and the like, rather than primarily on existing Treaty provisions.[95] Thus Article 24, concerned with the protection of children, was said to be based on the New York Convention on the Rights of the Child 1989, which had been ratified by the Member States. It seems that the provision within the Article that children may express their views freely could affect the legality of Union or State action. It is doubtful, however, whether there would be a ground for such reasoning under existing EU law. The same point can be made about other Charter provisions, such as the proscription of eugenics and cloning contained in Article 3.[96] These rights could affect the interpretation and validity of Union acts that are alleged to infringe them.

The Charter might also have a validating rather than potentially invalidating impact on the legality of Union action. Thus while Article 51(2) might make it difficult for the EU to adopt legislation specifically requiring the social partners or CEN (European Committee for Standardization) and CENELEC (European Committee for Electrotechnical Standardization) to observe fundamental rights, it would not necessarily preclude attaching human rights considerations based on the Charter to action founded on other competences. It would, as Bernard states, be possible for the Council in deciding whether to adopt a Union act to implement an agreement between the social partners under Article 155 TFEU 'to consider whether the agreement complies with the Charter', and when mandating CEN or CENELEC to adopt standards to implement directives 'it would be appropriate to include human rights clauses in the contract, where relevant'.[97]

---

[94] Maduro (n 18) 286 and 289.

[95] See, eg, Arts 1, 3, 8, 18, 12(1), 21(1), 24, 49.

[96] Explanations Relating to the Charter (n 33) 2; Charte 4473/00, 5, where the source of this provision is said to be the Convention on Human Rights and Biomedicine adopted by the Council of Europe. However in January 2001 only 10 Member States had signed the Convention and only three had ratified it.

[97] N Bernard, 'A "New Governance" Approach to Economic, Social and Cultural Rights in the EU' in Hervey and Kenner (n 18) 260.

It is clear, moreover, that the line between prohibition and positive action can be a fine one. The ECHR jurisprudence contains several instances where a basic prohibition is held to generate a duty of positive action on the part of the relevant State authorities.[98] The relevant right might not generate legislative competence, but it might well require some positive action by Union and/or Member State authorities to safeguard the right in question. There is some recognition of a positive duty to act on the EU institutions to protect fundamental rights, but this was in the context of a Community scheme that gave a discretionary power to act, the ECJ taking the view that this power should be triggered where fundamental rights were at stake.[99]

6. Rights, Principles, and the Charter

(a) Rights and principles: rationale for the divide

The classic form of rights-based action is for an individual to rely on a provision in the Charter in order to challenge the legality of a legislative, executive, or administrative norm, and to do so via judicial review either directly or indirectly. This will be the paradigm for many cases where reliance is placed on the Charter. Certain Charter provisions, however, have been held to embody principles rather than rights, and this may have consequences for judicial review.

The catalyst for discussion of the rights-principles dichotomy was the broad range of rights, political, social, and economic, enshrined in the Charter, in accordance with the remit given to the Convention established to draft the Charter by the European Council in Cologne and Tampere. There was, not surprisingly, much discussion within the Convention about the structure of the Charter as a whole,[100] and the particular place of social and economic rights therein.[101]

The issue was addressed directly by Commissioner Vitorino, the Commission representative to the Convention that drafted the Charter.[102] He distinguished between rights enforceable in the courts and principles that could be relied on against official authorities, and said that this was the basis for a consensus in the Convention, particularly as regards social rights. The Commissioner argued that rights could be pleaded directly in the courts. Principles, by way of contrast, were mandatory in relation to the authorities which had to comply with them when exercising their powers, and could be used as a basis for censuring their acts.

---

[98] See (ns 109, 110, 111).

[99] Case C-68/95 *T. Port GmbH & Co KG v Bundesanstalt fur Landwirtschaft und Ernahrung* [1996] ECR I-6065, [37]–[41].

[100] See, eg, Charte 4428/00, Contrib 282, 20 July 2000; Charte 4423/00, Convent 46, 31 July 2000; Charte 4470/00, Convent 47, 14 September 2000.

[101] See, eg, Charte 4383/00, Convent 41, 3 July 2000; Charte 4401, Contrib 258, 4 July 2000.

[102] Vitorino (n 15) 25–26.

Private individuals would not, however, be able to bring a legal action to enforce them.

Vitorino admitted that the Charter did not, at that time, state explicitly what was to be regarded as a right and a principle. He concluded, however, that there is 'a right where the holder is clearly designated and that there is a principle where the Union is referred to as having to respect or recognize a specific value such as a healthy environment or protection of consumers'.[103] Future practice and case law would, he said, refine this dichotomy.

This issue was addressed, albeit indirectly, by the Convention in two explanatory memorandums.[104] Thus health care and access to services of general economic interest were, for example, said to be principles and not rights. This issue was considered again in Working Group II of the Convention on the Future of Europe, which considered the issue of rights. It recommended a modification to the effect that provisions of the Charter that contained principles might be implemented by legislative and executive acts taken by the EU institutions, and by acts of the Member States when implementing EU law. They were, however, to be judicially cognizable only in the interpretation of such acts when ruling on their legality.[105]

The suggestions of Commissioner Vitorino and the Working Group were taken up in the final version of the Constitutional Treaty and in the Lisbon Treaty. Article 52(5) of the Charter now provides that:

The provisions of this Charter which contain principles may be implemented by legislative and executive acts taken by institutions, bodies, offices and agencies of the Union, and by acts of Member States when they are implementing Union law, in the exercise of their respective powers. They shall be judicially cognisable only in the interpretation of such acts and in the ruling on their legality.

(b) Rights and principles: nature of the divide

This necessarily raises the issue as to which Charter articles will be regarded as rights, and which as principles. Commissioner Vitorino and the Working Group believed that it would be for the ECJ to decide on this. This must be correct in terms of principle, although the Explanatory Memorandum has provided some guidance in this respect.[106] It specifies as principles the 'rights' of the elderly, Article 25; integration of those with disabilities, Article 26; and environmental protection, Article 37. The Memorandum also acknowledges that in some instances an Article of the Charter may contain elements of a right and of a

---

[103] ibid 26.
[104] Charte 4423/00, Convent 46, 31 July 2000, 24; Charte 4473/00, Convent 49, 11 October 2000, 31–32.
[105] CONV 354/02, Final Report of Working Group II, 22 October 2002, 8.
[106] Explanations Relating to the Charter (n 33) 19.

principle, giving as examples gender equality, Article 23; family and professional life, Article 33; and social security and social assistance, Article 34. It will then be for the ECJ to delineate the divide between rights and principles, taking into account this guidance. We should, however, resist falling into two common errors when thinking about this divide.

It is tempting to think that there is an equation between rights and the civil and political Charter provisions, and principles and the social/economic provisions of the Charter. This would be mistaken. The matter is more complex.[107] Many of the Charter provisions dealing with social matters can properly be thought of as rights, capable of individual legal enforcement. The following are merely examples. The injunction in Article 29 that everyone has the right to a free placement service provides one such example. There is no reason why an individual should not be able to bring a legal rights-based claim against a State that sought to charge for such services. The same is true for the right to working conditions which respect the health, safety, and dignity of the worker, Article 31. This is amenable to an individual rights-based legal claim by a particular worker that, for example, the conditions of his employment by the Union were unsafe. The injunction against unfair dismissal in Article 30 provides a further example. This provision, like a number of others, stipulates that this protection operates in accordance with 'Union law and national law and practices'. This does not, however, preclude interpretation of the relevant Article as an enforceable right. Thus if a Member State agency was implementing Union law and dismissed a worker in breach of relevant Union legal norms and national law, it would violate the Article. There is no reason why this should not be cognizable by a court as a legal right.

It is equally tempting to think in terms of an equation between rights and prohibition, and principles and positive action. This, too, would be mistaken. It is true that the classic response to an individual rights claim is to prohibit the State or Union from intruding on the protected sphere of private autonomy defined by the right. It is equally true that there are principles that require positive action, by the legislative or executive branch of government, such that failure to take the requisite action is a cause for censure, but not the basis for a legal action. It is nonetheless clear that a right can be infringed by inaction as well as action,[108] and that protection of a right can require positive action by the State or other public body. The ECHR jurisprudence provides ample examples of the derivation of positive obligations from Convention rights.[109] The positive

---

[107] P Alston, 'The Contribution of the EU Fundamental Rights Agency to the Realization of Economic and Social Rights' in P Alston and O de Schutter (eds), *Monitoring Fundamental Rights in the EU, The Contribution of the Fundamental Rights Agency* (Hart, 2005) 161–165.

[108] Human Rights Act 1998, s 6(6).

[109] A Mowbray, *The Development of Positive Obligations under the European Convention on Human Rights by the European Court of Human Rights* (Hart, 2004); S Fredman, *Human Rights Transformed: Positive Rights and Positive Duties* (Oxford University Press, 2008).

obligation imposed on the State may be designed to ensure the effective exercise of the right.[110] It may require the State to act so as to prevent a third party from interfering with the right.[111] The Strasbourg case law has been mainly concerned with positive obligations in the context of civil or political rights, since that is the principal remit of the ECHR. The same arguments could readily be made in relation to the civil rights in the Charter, and there is no reason why positive obligations could not attach to Charter social rights. The argument would have to be considered on its merits in relation to the particular social right in question, but there is no reason in principle why it should not be accepted. If, for example, an employer were to dismiss employees for seeking to conclude a collective agreement, the State could, pursuant to Article 28, have a positive obligation to secure this right against the actions of the private party,[112] provided that the relevant action fell within the scope of Union law.

(c) Rights and principles: consequences of the divide

We should tread carefully when considering the legal consequences of the distinction between rights and principles.

Charter provisions that are deemed to be rights will be judicially enforceable by individuals. This can arise in two kinds of case. There may on the one hand be instances where the individual claims that the EU has provided insufficient protection for the right, and this may be so even in the absence of Union action. This is borne out by the Explanatory Memorandum, which states by implication that rights may give rise to claims for positive action by the Union or Member States when implementing Union law.[113] The majority of cases will, on the other hand, be those where the Union has taken action and the individual argues that it is inconsistent with a Charter right, and hence should be annulled, or that it should be interpreted in a particular way because of a Charter right.

Charter provisions characterized as principles differ in two respects in terms of legal consequences. An individual cannot claim that the Union must take positive action in the absence of Union legislation or executive action. This follows directly from the wording of Article 52(5), which provides that Charter principles may be fulfilled through legislative or executive action and are judicially cognizable only when Union courts interpret such acts and rule on their legality.[114] The other legal difference that flows from characterization as a

---

[110] *Airey v Ireland* (1979–80) 2 EHRR 305; *Markcx v Belgium* (1979–80) 2 EHRR 330.

[111] *X and Y v Netherlands* (1986) 8 EHRR 235; *Lopez Ostra v Spain* (1995) 20 EHRR 513; *Plattform 'Arzte fur das Leben' v Austria* (1991) 13 EHRR 204; *Young, James and Webster v United Kingdom* (1982) 4 EHRR 38.

[112] The converse argument succeeded before the Strasbourg Court in *Young, James and Webster* (n 111) where the Court accepted that the State could be required, under Art 11, to take action to prevent an employer from dismissing employees who did not wish to join a union.

[113] Explanations Relating to the Charter (n 33) 19.

[114] Explanations Relating to the Charter (n 33) 19; CONV 828/03, Updated Explanations (n 81) 51.

principle rather than a right is that where the Union has taken legislative or executive action to implement the Charter principle there may be more room for argument as to whether such action respects the principle of, for example, integration of those with disabilities.

It should be noted, however, that there is an ambiguity latent in Article 52(5). A narrow interpretation would dictate that the courts can only take cognizance of such principles when interpreting or ruling on the legality of acts that directly seek to implement such principles. If this view were to be adopted such cognizance could only be taken when a Union or Member State act could be said to implement directly the Charter principle on, for example, the integration of those with disabilities. This reading does not, however, fit with the Explanatory Memorandum, which exemplifies the judicial role in relation to Charter principles by analogy to existing jurisprudence on the precautionary principle and principles used in agricultural law.[115] These principles, however, do not only apply when the challenged act is designed directly to implement those principles.

Thus the precautionary principle was used to contest the legality of, for example, a Community act withdrawing the authorization of a particular product;[116] to challenge the legality of the regime for genetically modified foods;[117] and to assess the legality of Member State action concerning marketing requirements for vitamins.[118] The challenged acts in these cases were not designed directly to implement the relevant principle, but it was nonetheless used to test the legality of the measure. This is surely the better view, which would mean that Charter provisions regarded as principles could be taken cognizance of when interpreting or ruling on the legality of Union acts, irrespective of whether the Union act was directly implementing the relevant principle or not.

If this is so then the legal consequences of the divide between rights and principles may be less clear cut and dramatic than might initially be thought. In both instances the paradigm claim will be one where an individual seeks to challenge Union norms, whether of a legislative or executive nature. Where such a norm violates a Charter right, this will constitute the individual's cause of action in the judicial review claim. Where a Charter provision is characterized as a principle the individual will still be able to argue that the legislative or executive norm should be interpreted in the way best designed to enhance the relevant principle, even where there was little in the way of ambiguity in the challenged measure.

---

[115] Explanations Relating to the Charter (n 33) 19.

[116] Cases T-74, 76, 83–85, 132, 137, and 141/00 *Artegodan GmbH v Commission* [2002] ECR II-4945.

[117] Case C-236/01 *Monsanto Agricultura Italia SpA v Presidenza del Consiglio dei Ministri* [2003] ECR I-8105. See also, Case C-6/99 *Association Greenpeace France v Ministère de l'Agriculture et de la Pêche* [2000] ECR I-1651, [40]–[44].

[118] Case C-95/01 *Criminal Proceedings against John Greenham and Leonard Abel* [2004] ECR I-21333.

It should be noted, moreover, that Article 52(5) of the Charter countenances taking cognizance of Charter principles when ruling on the legality of Union acts or Member State acts when implementing Union law. A claimant who felt that the challenged action gave insufficient protection to the Charter principle could then contest its legality on that ground, or on the basis of, for example, proportionality. This is supported by the Explanatory Memorandum, which exemplifies the judicial approach to Charter principles by reference to existing case law on the precautionary principle and certain principles in agricultural law.[119] This jurisprudence enables the Union courts to assess conformity with, for example, the precautionary principle either in a direct action for judicial review, or indirectly via a preliminary reference, with the consequence that if the Union or Member State action fails to comply with the relevant principle it is annulled.[120]

7. Limitations and the Charter

(a) Limitation of rights: prior jurisprudence

The precise test for limitation of rights hitherto applied by the Community courts was not absolutely clear.[121] Suffice it to say for the present that the general test applied by the ECJ was that such a limitation was allowed provided that it corresponded to objectives of general interest pursued by the Community and did not constitute, with regard to the aim pursued, a disproportionate and unreasonable interference that undermined the very substance of the right.[122] Having said this, the ECJ had in some other cases employed a test closer to that used by the ECHR.[123]

A high profile example of the ECJ's approach to the limitation of rights was *Schmidberger*.[124] The Austrian Government gave implicit permission for a demonstration by an environmental group on the Brenner motorway, the effect of which was to close it for 30 hours. Schmidberger ran a transport firm and argued that the closure of the motorway was in breach of EU law on free movement of goods. The issue for the ECJ was the relation between Article

---

[119] Explanations Relating to the Charter (n 33) 19.
[120] Case T-13/99 *Pfizer Animal Health SA v Council* [2002] ECR II-3305; Cases T-74, 76, 83–85, 132, 137, and 141/00 *Artegodan* (n 116); P Craig, *EU Administrative Law* (Oxford University Press, 2006) ch 19.
[121] Craig (n 61) ch 16.
[122] Case 5/88 *Wachauf* (n 7) [18]; Case C-292/97 *Karlsson* (n 83) [45].
[123] S Peers, 'Taking Rights Away? Limitations and Derogations' in Peers and Ward (n 18) 142–149.
[124] Case C-112/00 *Schmidberger Internationale Transporte und Planzuge v Austria* [2003] ECR I-5659.

28 EC on free movement, and freedom of expression and assembly as protected by Articles 10 and 11 ECHR and the Austrian Constitution.

The ECJ reaffirmed that Article 28 EC required the State to refrain from imposing obstacles to free movement of goods, and also to take all necessary action to ensure that free movement was not impeded by the acts of private parties.[125] The failure by the Austrian Government to ban the demonstration was therefore *prima facie* a breach of Article 28 EC, unless it could be objectively justified.[126] The justification proffered by the Government was respect for the right to freedom of expression and assembly guaranteed by the ECHR and the Austrian Constitution.

The ECJ accepted this justification. It held that Member States and the Community were both required to respect fundamental rights, and that therefore those rights could justify a restriction of other Community obligations, even a fundamental freedom such as free movement of goods.[127] The ECJ noted, however, that Articles 10 and 11 ECHR protecting freedom of expression and assembly were not absolute. They could be limited, provided that the restrictions corresponded to objectives of general interest and did not constitute disproportionate and unacceptable interference that impaired the very substance of the right.[128] It was therefore necessary to decide whether the restrictions placed on Community trade were proportionate in the light of the relevant fundamental rights. The ECJ held that they were: the disruption of Community trade was for a limited time on a limited route; it was in pursuit of a genuine environmental aim; it was not designed to keep foreign goods out of a particular State; efforts had been made to limit the disruption caused by the demonstration; and a ban on the demonstration would have been an unacceptable limit on the right to peaceful demonstration.[129]

(b) Limitation of rights: Article 52(1)

The criterion in the Charter is set out in Article 52(1), which specifies the conditions in which a Charter right can be limited.

Any limitation on the exercise of the rights and freedoms recognized by this Charter must be provided for by law and respect the essence of those rights and freedoms. Subject to the principle of proportionality, limitations may be made only if they are necessary and genuinely meet objectives of general interest recognized by the Union or the need to protect the rights and freedoms of others.

The Explanatory Memorandum confirms that this wording is based on the case law of the ECJ. It also states that the reference to general interests recognized by the Union covers both the objectives mentioned in Article 3 TEU and other

---

[125] ibid [59], reaffirming Case C-265/95 *Commission v France* [1997] ECR I-6959.
[126] ibid [64].   [127] ibid [74].   [128] ibid [80].   [129] ibid [83]–[94].

interests protected by specific provisions of the Treaties such as Article 4(1) TEU and Articles 35(3), 36 and 346 TFEU.[130]

The formulation in Article 52(1) combines criteria some of which, such as proportionality, are similar to those used by the Strasbourg court, others of which owe their origin to German law, such as the requirement that the essence of the right should be protected.[131] These criteria were present in the ECJ's case law.[132] There are nonetheless important issues concerning the interpretation of this Article.

(i) General limitation v specific limitation

The Charter enshrines a general limitation clause, whereas the ECHR's limitations are attached to certain rights, others of which are not capable of derogation. Peers has correctly pointed out, however, that the Article does not actually state that any Charter right can be limited, but rather that if such rights are limited the conditions laid down in the Article apply.[133] It would therefore be open to the ECJ to conclude that certain Charter rights are not open to limitation or derogation at all. The ECJ recognized in *Schmidberger*[134] that the ECHR rights to life and freedom from torture were non-derogable. The ECJ stopped short of expressly stating that EU law would preclude derogation from such rights, but this is a reasonable inference.

The Charter formulation makes no reference to the needs of a democratic society, although given that the EU is founded on respect for democracy, human rights, and the rule of law,[135] it is therefore, as Peers argues, 'hard to see how limitations on human rights can be justified without taking account of the element of democracy'.[136]

(ii) Criteria for limitation: I

An additional difference between the Charter test and that found in the ECHR is that the former allows limitations 'only if they are necessary and genuinely meet objectives of general interest recognized by the Union or the need to protect the rights and freedoms of others', as compared with the more discrete justifications found in Articles 8 to 11 ECHR. The breadth of the possible justifications allowed by the Charter test is exemplified by the Explanatory Memorandum, which construed reference to 'general interest' to cover objectives mentioned in Article 3 TEU and other interests protected by specific provisions of the Treaties such as Article 4(1) TEU and Articles 35(3), 36, and 346 TFEU.[137]

---

[130] Explanations Relating to the Charter (n 33) 16. [131] de Witte (n 2) 880.
[132] Case 5/88 *Wachauf* (n 7) [18]; Case C-292/97 *Karlsson* (n 83) [45].
[133] Peers (n 123) 163. [134] Case C-112/00 *Schmidberger* (n 124) [80].
[135] Art 2 TEU. [136] Peers (n 123) 168.
[137] Explanations Relating to the Charter (n 33) 16.

However, the relationship between Article 52(1) and Article 52(3) insofar as limitation of rights is concerned is important in this context. Article 52(3) provides that the 'meaning and scope' of Charter rights that correspond to ECHR rights should be the same. This should include the rules on limitations and this is supported by the Explanatory Memorandum.[138] Thus for rights falling in this category Union legislation limiting such rights must comply with the ECHR rules on limitations. The EU, however, is permitted by Article 52(3) to provide more extensive protection. It would therefore be possible for the limitation conditions laid down in Article 52(1) to apply in addition to those of the ECHR for Charter rights that correspond to ECHR rights, assuming that the Charter limitation was read as granting more extensive protection than application of the ECHR rules on limitations in the instant case.[139]

(iii) Criteria for limitation: II

The Charter stipulates that any limitation on the exercise of a right or freedom must be provided for by law and respect the essence of those rights and freedoms. The meaning accorded to the phrase 'respect the essence of those rights and freedoms' is particularly important. This formulation is derived from German law.[140] It captures the important idea that a restriction should not be deemed lawful if it undermines the essence of the guaranteed right.

It was part of the test for limitation of rights hitherto applied by the ECJ. However, its application by the Community courts was often subtly different from their German counterparts. The ECJ would commonly conclude that the restriction was lawful, *provided* that it did not infringe the essence of that right.[141] Whether intended or not, the wording of the ECJ's formulation was that restrictions would be lawful provided that they did not constitute a disproportionate and intolerable interference that impaired the substance of the right. This gave the relevant phrase a different role from that accorded to it by the German courts.

The interpretation of this phrase within the context of the Charter is therefore especially important. It should be interpreted in accordance with its German origins and the structure of Article 52(1) facilitates this. The Article makes it clear that any limitation must respect the essence of the right, and that even if it does it will still only be lawful if proportionate, necessary, and in the general interest.

---

[138] Explanations Relating to the Charter (n 33) 17.

[139] K Lenaerts and E de Smijter, 'A "Bill of Rights" for the European Union' (2001) 28 CMLRev 273, 292–293.

[140] de Witte (n 2) 880.

[141] Case C-491/01 *R v Secretary of State for Health, ex p British American Tobacco (Investments) Ltd and Imperial Tobacco Ltd* [2002] ECR I-11453; Cases C-20 and 64/00 *Booker Aquacultur Ltd and Hydro Seafood GSP Ltd v Scottish Ministers* [2003] ECR I-7411; Cases C-184 and 223/02 *Spain and Finland v European Parliament and Council* [2004] ECR I-7789.

(iv) Criteria for limitation: III

A further interpretative issue that arises concerning Article 52(1) is whether the margin of appreciation is applicable in this context. The rationale for its use in the ECHR is that it enables the Strasbourg court to take cognizance of the different views on morality and the like prevalent in the diverse countries that are signatories to the Convention.

This argument would be inapplicable in relation to rights-based review of Union institutions undertaken by the ECJ. It would, however, be open to the ECJ to develop an autonomous concept of deference to Union institutions when assessing rights-based arguments, as exemplified by the approach of the UK courts under the Human Rights Act 1998.[142] While this would be possible, such deference is not a common feature in constitutional adjudication by the courts of most Member States, and would therefore be unlikely to be adopted by the ECJ when reviewing acts of the Union institutions for compatibility with Charter rights.

It should nonetheless be acknowledged that the ECJ has often reached the same result, albeit by different means. It commonly found that, for example, property rights and rights to pursue a trade were not absolute. It then considered whether the restrictions imposed by the measure corresponded to objectives of general interest pursued by the Community and whether they constituted a disproportionate and intolerable interference, which impaired the very substance of the rights guaranteed.[143] This approach thereby enabled the ECJ to give weight to the views of the Community institutions by treating Community legislation encapsulating those views as pursuing objectives of Community interest, and through adjudication on the proportionality criterion.

This leaves the possible application of a margin of appreciation when the Charter is applied to the Member States. It has been argued that a margin of appreciation is not warranted here, principally on the ground that there are already a number of ways in which national diversity can be taken into account.[144] There is some force in this argument, but the contrary view is preferable. The rationale for according Member States some margin of appreciation is applicable when Member States are, for example, derogating from EU law. It enables the strength of national preferences on issues as diverse as abortion[145] or pluralism of the press to be given due weight.[146] This is

---

[142] P Craig, *Administrative Law* (Sweet & Maxwell, 6th edn, 2008) ch 18.

[143] Case 265/87 *Schräder HS Kraftfutter GmbH & Co KG v Hauptzollamt Gronau* [1989] ECR 2237, [15]; Case C-280/93 *Germany v Council* [1994] ECR I-4973, [78]; Case C-200/96 *Musik Metronome GmbH v Music Point Hokamp GmbH* [1998] ECR I-1953, [21]; Case C-293/97 *R v Secretary of State for the Environment and Ministry of Agriculture, Fisheries and Food, ex p Standley* [1999] ECR I-2603, [54].

[144] Peers (n 123) 168.

[145] Case C-159/90 *SPUC v Grogan* [1991] ECR I-4685.

[146] Case C-368/95 *Vereinigte Familiapress Zeitungsverlags-und Vertreibs GmbH v Heinrich Bauer Verlag* [1997] ECR I-368.

particularly so given that cases on derogations may entail a balance between a fundamental right, such as freedom of the press or assembly, and a Community freedom, such as free movement of goods.[147] The ECJ has been willing to accord Member States a margin of appreciation in assessing derogations from the four freedoms,[148] and there is no reason why it should cease to do so under the Charter.

This argument is reinforced by Article 52(3): Charter rights that correspond to those in the ECHR must be given the same meaning and scope. The margin of appreciation has an impact on the meaning accorded to a particular right. It would be odd, moreover, for the margin of appreciation to apply in relation to some Charter rights, those that correspond to the rights in the ECHR, but not to other rights contained in the Charter.

8. Treaty and Charter

Interpretation of rights-based provisions is often complex because of contestability as to the meaning of the particular rights and as to their application in concrete circumstances. These difficulties are exacerbated in the EU because the Charter subsists alongside the TEU and TFEU, many of the provisions of which touch on the same subject matter as rights contained in the Charter.[149] This issue was addressed by Article 52(2) of the Charter, which states that 'rights recognized by this Charter for which provision is made in the Treaties shall be exercised under the conditions and within the limits defined by those Treaties'.

The Explanatory Memorandum states that Article 52(2) refers to rights which were expressly guaranteed in the EC Treaty and have been recognized in the Charter, and which are now found in the TEU or TFEU, notably the rights derived from Union citizenship. The Memorandum emphasizes that Charter rights remain subject to the conditions and limits applicable to the Union law on which they are based, and for which provision is made in the Treaties, and that the Charter does not alter the system of rights conferred by the EC Treaty and taken over by the Treaties.[150]

---

[147] In Case C-112/00, *Schmidberger* (n 124) [82], [89], the ECJ spoke of the wide margin of discretion of the Austrian Government in balancing freedom of assembly and freedom of trade, albeit the ECJ then undertook a reasonably searching proportionality analysis of its own; the margin of appreciation was expressly referred to in Case C-274/99 P *Connolly v Commission* [2001] ECR I-1611, although it was not applied to the facts.

[148] Case C-124/97 *Laara, Cotswold Microsystems Ltd and Oy Transatlantic Software Ltd v Finland* [1999] ECR I-6067; Case C-36/02 *Omega Spielhallen- und Automatenaufstellungs-GmbH v Oberburgermeiste der Bundesstadt Bonn* [2004] ECR I-9609.

[149] G de Búrca, 'Fundamental Rights and Citizenship' in B de Witte (ed), *Ten Reflections on the Constitutional Treaty for Europe* (Robert Schumann Centre for Advanced Studies, 2003) 29–44.

[150] Explanations Relating to the Charter (n 33) 16.

The Memorandum attached to Article 52(2), however, gives no list of Charter rights that are based on existing Treaties. The matter is addressed in relation to explanations of particular Charter rights, but inconsistently. Thus comments on some Charter articles state expressly that they are based on a Treaty provision and that Article 52(2) applies;[151] the comments on other Charter rights state that they are based wholly or partly on a Treaty provision, but make no reference to Article 52(2).[152] Three types of problems will therefore arise in deciding on the reach of Article 52(2).

(a) Application: Charter rights and Treaty rights

The initial difficulty will be to decide in relation to which Charter rights there are Treaty provisions. This will not be easy, more especially given that, as noted above, the Explanatory Memorandum specifies that certain rights are based on a Treaty article, without making any link to Article 52(2). The difficulties can be exemplified in relation to discrimination, which were considered by Lenaerts and de Smijter.[153]

The Charter deals with this in Article 21(1), which prohibits discrimination on grounds such as sex, race, colour, ethnic or social origin, genetic features, language, religion or belief, political or other opinion, membership of a national minority, property, birth, disability, age, or sexual orientation. This is broader than Article 19 TFEU in a number of ways. The list in Article 21(1) is more extensive and it prohibits discrimination on the listed grounds, whereas Article 19 TFEU merely empowers Union action to tackle discrimination.

The framers of the Explanatory Memorandum were cognizant of tensions between Article 21(1) of the Charter and Article 19 TFEU, but the resolution of these difficulties was neither clear nor convincing. The Explanatory Memorandum states that Article 21(1) 'draws on' Article 19 TFEU, as well as Article 14 ECHR.[154] It states that there is no 'contradiction or incompatibility' between Article 21(1) and Article 19 TFEU, because the latter confers power to adopt legislative acts, including harmonization, to combat the listed forms of discrimination, and such legislation may cover action of Member State authorities and relations between private individuals in any area within the limits of the Union's powers. This is contrasted with Article 21(1), on the grounds 'that it does not create any power to enact anti-discrimination laws in these areas of Member State or private action, nor does it lay down a sweeping ban of discrimination in such wide-ranging areas',[155] and only covers discrimination by Union institutions and

---

[151] Arts 15(3), 39, 40, 41(4), 42, 43, 44, 45(1), and 46; Peers (n 123) 155.
[152] Arts 11(2), 18, 21(2), 22, 23, 32, 34(1), 35, 37, and 38; Peers (n 123) 155–156.
[153] Lenaerts and Smijter (n 139) 283–289.
[154] Explanations Relating to the Charter (n 33) 8, as well as Art 11 of the Convention of Human Rights and Biomedicine as regards genetic heritage.
[155] Explanations Relating to the Charter (n 33) 8.

by Member States when they are implementing Union law. The Memorandum concludes by stating that Article 21(1) does not therefore alter the extent of powers granted under Article 19 TFEU.

The reality is, however, that the list in Article 21(1) of the Charter is broader, not narrower, than that in Article 19 TFEU, and that the Charter prohibits such discrimination. It is true that the Charter does not authorize legislative acts and is in this respect narrower than Article 19 TFEU, but this does not alter the preceding point as to the respects in which Article 21(1) is broader than Article 19 TFEU.

The solution proposed by Lenaerts and Smijter was complex, but they argued in essence that the grounds listed in Article 21(1) which are not in Article 19 TFEU are not based on the latter, and therefore Article 52(2) is inapplicable.[156] They contended that this was probably also true for the listed grounds common to both provisions where the Council had not yet taken any measures. When the Council had exercised its power under Article 19 TFEU they argued that the Union act would serve as a basis for construing the scope of the corresponding right recognized by Article 21(1).

(b) Application: Charter rights and Union legislation

There is a further difficulty concerning the relationship between Charter rights and Union regulations, directives etc. Article 52(2) specifies that Charter rights for which provision is made in the Treaties must be exercised under the conditions and limits defined by those Treaties. It is common, however, for a Treaty provision to be set in general terms and for the more specific conditions for its exercise to be laid down in legislation. The issue is therefore whether Article 52(2) is applicable in these instances, such that conditions and limits contained in a regulation or directive would then impose constraints on the interpretation of an analogous Charter right. This in turn depends on whether the Charter right could be said to be based on the Treaty in such instances. The issue is further sharpened by the fact that certain Charter rights are said in the Explanatory Memorandum to be based wholly or partly on Union legislation.[157]

It is clear as a matter of principle that the legislation must be *intra vires* the Treaty article on which it is based. If conditions are imposed on the Treaty article which are inconsistent with it then the legality of the legislation could be contested on that ground. It might be argued in the light of this that in the converse case, where the regulation or directive is not open to challenge on this ground, any conditions to the right could be said to be defined by the Treaties and hence the Charter right would have to be interpreted subject to those limits.

This is a possible view. It is, however, unconvincing and would be regrettable. In addressing this issue we should not lose sight of the fact that the fundamental

---

[156] Lenaerts and Smijter (n 139) 284–285.   [157] Arts 5(3), 11(2), 23, 31(1)–(2), and 32.

rights doctrine as developed by the ECJ was used to challenge the legality of Community regulations, directives and the like. This was premised on a normative hierarchy in which fundamental rights were superior to Community legislation and hence operated as a ground of judicial review. Thus under the fundamental rights' regime that preceded the Charter the meaning given to those rights was not bounded by conditions laid down in Community legislation. On the contrary, the legality of Community legislation and any conditions laid down therein was tested for conformity with fundamental rights as developed by the Community courts. This is exemplified by the jurisprudence on the right to be heard, where it was held that provisions concerning hearings contained in a regulation could be complemented by recourse to the fundamental right itself.[158] The fundamental principle of the rights of the defence could not be excluded or restricted by any legislative provision, and respect for the right to be heard should be ensured both where there was no specific legislation and where legislation existed, but did not take sufficient account of the right.[159]

It would therefore be a retrograde step to interpret the Charter as in effect reversing this normative hierarchy, such that conditions laid down by Union legislation defined the boundaries of Charter rights, more particularly given that the Charter has the same value as the Treaties,[160] and therefore in normative terms sits above Union legislation. It follows that it should be open to the ECJ to read any conditions or limits to a Treaty article laid down in legislation made pursuant thereto in the light of the Charter right when assessing the legality of those conditions.[161] This is more especially so where the Treaty article is opentextured, and does not in terms specify particular limits or conditions for its exercise. The interpretation of the Charter right should not be subject to Article 52(2) and should not be formally bounded by the conditions laid down in the Union legislation. The extension of Article 52(2) to the latter would diminish the sense of Charter rights as constitutional rights and risk ossifying their interpretation by the conditions attached to legislation.

It can also be maintained, however, consistently with the preceding argument, that where the Union legislature has given considered thought to the more particular meaning to be accorded to a right laid down in a Treaty article and expressed this through legislation, the ECJ should treat this with respect and should not lightly find this to be inconsistent with the Charter right.

---

[158] Case C-49/88 *Al-Jubail Fertilizer v Council* [1991] ECR I-3187, [15]. See also, Cases T-33-34/98 *Petrotub and Republica SA v Council* [1999] ECR II-3837; Case C-458/98 P *Industrie des Poudres Spheriques v Council and Commission* [2000] ECR I-8147, [99].

[159] Case T-260/94 *Air Inter SA v Commission* [1997] ECR II-997, [60].

[160] Art 6(1) TEU.

[161] Moreover, it is the case that the requirements of the general limitation clause in Article 52(1) of the Charter would be applicable in such a situation. Thus it would be necessary, for example, to show that such limitations respected the essence of the relevant right.

(c) Application: Charter rights and the Courts' jurisprudence

A further difficulty with the application of Article 52(2) is whether it applies to the courts' jurisprudence. We need to tread carefully here.

There will be many instances where the meaning and hence the conditions and limits of a particular Treaty article will only become apparent in the light of case law from the Union courts. Thus the meaning of State aid, competition, agreement, and many other prominent terms in Treaty provisions that serve to define their scope or the conditions in which they apply will only become apparent through judicial interpretation. In such instances it is natural to think of Article 52(2) applying, subject of course to the Charter right being based on the relevant Treaty article. Where this is met then the definition of the conditions and limits for application of the relevant Treaty article should include the courts' jurisprudence defining them.

There are, however, other instances where the right or principle is in reality created by the courts and where it is based on an open-textured or generally worded Treaty article. Consider in this respect the possible relation between Article 52(2) and Article 41 of the Charter, concerned with the right to good administration. Article 41(1) imposes an obligation on Union institutions to be impartial in the handling of the affairs of every person, and to deal with them in a reasonable time. Article 41(2) then provides that the right in Article 41(1) shall be taken to *include* the 'right of every person to be heard, before any individual measure which would affect him or her adversely is taken'. It also includes the right of access to the person's file, subject to exceptions for confidentiality, and the obligation to give reasons. Article 41(3) covers damages actions against the Union, and the right to communicate to the Union institutions in a person's own language is guaranteed in Article 41(4). The Explanatory Memorandum[162] makes it clear that the rights contained within Articles 41(1) and most of Article 41(2)[163] are derived from the courts' case law. The Memorandum also states that the rights contained in Articles 41(3)–(4) are, in accordance with Article 52(2), to be applied under the conditions and within the limits defined by the Treaties.[164]

This leaves open the issue of principle as to whether Article 52(2) can or should apply to such Charter rights based on the courts' jurisprudence. The wording of the Article, framed in terms of rights 'for which provision is made' in the Treaties, is ambiguous in this respect. This could be read to include rights derived from case law that is conceptually based on Articles 19 TEU and

---

[162] Explanations Relating to the Charter (n 33) 12; Charte 4423/00, Convent 46, 31 July 2000, 27; Charte 4473/00, Convent 49, 11 October 2000, 36–37.
[163] The obligation to give reasons, the third indent of Art 41(2), is based on Art 253 EC.
[164] Explanations Relating to the Charter (n 33) 12; Charte 4473/00, Convent 49, 11 October 2000, 37; CONV 828/03, Updated Explanations (n 81) 37.

263 TFEU.[165] The wording of Article 52(2) states, however, that Charter rights based on the Treaties must be exercised 'under the conditions and within the limits defined by those Treaties'. The Treaties do not define the conditions and limits to rights fashioned by the ECJ, except in the attenuated sense that all of the ECJ's jurisprudence will constitute an interpretation of some Treaty provision. However, where the Union courts read extensive principles into vaguely framed Treaty articles it is strained to say that the Treaty article itself established the conditions and limits to the exercise of that right.

When addressing this issue we should not lose sight of the underlying point of principle. Thus even if one subscribes to the thesis that in formal terms the courts' jurisprudence is premised on some Treaty article, the salient issue here is whether conditions and limits placed on principles or rights derived by the judiciary from broadly framed Treaty articles should necessarily constrain the interpretation of the analogous Charter right. It is one thing to say that Charter rights must respect the conditions and limits defined by the Member States when they ratified the Treaty. It is another thing altogether to say that where Charter rights owe their origin to the courts' jurisprudence, the interpretation of the Charter right must forever be constrained by the limits and conditions of that jurisprudence.

It should also be acknowledged that even if it was felt that Charter rights based on the courts' jurisprudence should be constrained by the limits and conditions in that case law, this would not impede a creative court minded to develop the law in the relevant area. Such a court could if it so wished simply develop its traditional case law under the Treaties so as to make it conform to the interpretation that it would like to give to the relevant Charter right.

The actual coverage of Article 41 raises further questions about the relationship between it and Article 52(2). Article 41(1) is the *lex generalis*, and Article 41(2) the *lex specialis*, which sets out three specific rights which are said to be *included* in Article 41(1). It seems, therefore, that the rights listed in Article 41(2), which all relate to the hearing by the initial decision-maker, are not exhaustive. There is nothing explicitly within Article 41 that is directed towards judicial review, either the rules on standing, or the grounds thereof. It might be contended that this is because the Article as a whole is directed towards obligations imposed on the initial decision-maker. This will not withstand examination, since Article 41(3), concerning damages actions against the Community, directly addresses the individuals' remedial rights when an error in the original decision has been made. It is axiomatic that judicial review, leading to

---

[165] Art 19 TEU (ex Art 220 EC) is the foundational provision in relation to the ECJ and provides that the Court of Justice shall ensure that in the interpretation and application of this Treaty the law is observed. Art 263 TFEU (ex Art 230 EC) sets out the grounds for judicial review, which include breach of the Treaty or any rule of law relating to its application, and it was this that served as the window for the ECJ to read into the EC Treaty many of the principles of good administration.

annulment, and damages actions, leading to compensation, are both methods of recourse when an error in the initial decision has occurred.

It will, therefore, be interesting to see whether there are attempts made to base claims concerning judicial review on Article 41(1).[166] An individual might argue that the restrictive rules on standing to seek judicial review violated the right to have one's affairs handled fairly by the institutions of the Union. It would of course be open to the ECJ to respond either by raising Article 52(2), or by interpreting Article 41(1) so as not to require more extensive standing requirements than currently exist. It would also be open to the ECJ if so minded to use Article 41(1) as the *raison d'être* for broadening the existing restrictive rules.

(d) Principle: to replicate or not to replicate

It might be felt in the light of the above that it would have been more sensible to avoid replication in the Charter of provisions found elsewhere in the Treaties. There is force in this argument.[167] The avoidance of replication, however, would have required the identification of rights found in the Charter that already exist in the Treaties and the removal thereof. This would not have been easy, as the preceding discussion revealed. It would moreover be very odd for a Charter of Fundamental Rights not to include, for example, important provisions concerning equality on the ground that the existing Treaties covered the issue. This point is reinforced by the possibility that over time the Charter rights may come to have a higher status *de facto* than other Treaty provisions.

9. ECHR and Charter

(a) Approach: Charter rights that correspond to ECHR rights

The relation between the Charter and the ECHR was an issue that occupied much time in the drafting process.[168] The result is encapsulated in Article 52(3), which provides that Charter rights that correspond to rights guaranteed by the ECHR shall have the same scope and meaning as those in the ECHR. This is subject to the caveat that Union law can provide more extensive protection.[169]

Article 52(3) requires the identification of those rights which 'correspond' to those guaranteed by the ECHR. The task is facilitated by guidance from the drafting process, and was addressed by the Explanatory Memorandum. It

---

[166] See below, at pp 241–242.

[167] Arnull (n 75) 778–779.

[168] See, eg., SN 3340/00, 29 June 2000; Charte 4423/00, Convent 46, 31 July 2000; Charte 4961/00, Contrib 356, 13 November 2000; P Lemmens, 'The Relationship between the Charter of Fundamental Rights of the EU and the ECHR: Substantive Aspects' (2001) 8 MJ 49.

[169] This was reconfirmed by CONV 354/02, Final Report of Working Group II, 22 October 2002, 7.

concluded that the right to life, the prohibition of torture, the prohibition on slavery and forced labour, the right to liberty and security, respect for private and family life, freedom of thought, conscience, and religion, freedom of expression and information, freedom of assembly and association, right to property, protection in the event of removal, expulsion, or extradition, and the presumption of innocence and right of defence, had the same meaning and scope as the corresponding Articles of the ECHR.[170]

There are, however, Charter articles where the relationship with ECHR rights is more complex,[171] albeit for different reasons. Some Charter rights, such as Article 5 dealing with slavery and forced labour, are based on an ECHR right in part, but go beyond it, by expressly prohibiting trafficking in human beings. Other rights, such as Article 8 dealing with personal data, are based on more than one source, in this instance a Treaty article plus directive, as well as an ECHR right. Yet other Charter rights modify the analogous ECHR right. This is exemplified by Article 9, which countenances the possibility of marriage by those of the same sex, where this is permitted by the relevant national law. There are also instances where the Charter article is based on more than one source, and modifies the relevant ECHR right. This is so for the right to education, and for the important right to equality. This complexity is recognized by the Explanatory Memorandum, which lists Charter articles where the meaning is the 'same' as the corresponding ECHR right, but the scope is wider.[172]

(b) Consequence: same meaning and scope

The other major injunction in Article 52(3) is that the meaning and scope of Charter rights that correspond to ECHR rights should be the same as those laid down in the ECHR.

It should be noted that earlier versions of the Charter were crucially different in this respect, requiring only that the meaning and scope of such Charter rights were 'similar' to the corresponding ECHR right.[173] This would have given rise to significant problems of interpretation. While the present formulation does not refer expressly to the case law of the Strasbourg court, this must be implicit in the injunction that the meaning and scope of Charter rights corresponding to rights contained in the ECHR should be the same.

It should be recognized, however, that the present formula, requiring the interpretation of corresponding rights to be the same, may still be problematic.

---

[170] Explanations Relating to the Charter (n 33) 17–18; Charte 4473/00, Convent 49, 11 October 2000, 49.

[171] Explanations Relating to the Charter (n 33) 18.

[172] ibid 18. The list contains Arts 9, 12(1), 14(1), 14(3), 47(2)–(3), 50, and the case law on aliens.

[173] Charte 4423/00, Convent 46, 31 July 2000, 36.

This will especially be so in areas where the ECHR jurisprudence on the point is unclear, or where the point is a novel one, as emphasized by comments from the Council of Europe observers' on the drafting of the Charter.[174] They expressed concern that the Charter would generate a large increase in the number of preliminary references, and that this would raise the risk that ECJ decisions would be at variance with those of the Strasbourg Court. This in turn would lead to courts of Member States being under mutually inconsistent Treaty obligations. Harmony between the Charter and the ECHR could, they said, only be secured if the EU acceded to the ECHR.[175]

10. National Constitutions and the Charter

We have already considered the extent to which Member States are bound by the Charter. There are, however, further provisions that serve to define the relationship between the Charter and fundamental rights at national level.

(a) National constitutions: interpretative obligation

Working Group II of the Convention on the Future of Europe recommended a new provision,[176] which was added to the Charter by the Constitutional Treaty. Article 52(4) of the Charter states that 'insofar as this Charter recognizes fundamental rights as they result from the constitutional traditions common to the Member States, those rights shall be interpreted in harmony with those traditions'. It imposes an interpretative obligation on courts and legislature alike. The obligation is one which the institutions would in any event be minded to comply with, at least as a starting point.

The interpretative duty is triggered when the Charter recognizes fundamental rights as they result from the constitutional traditions common to the Member States, and the duty is one of harmonious interpretation, rather than identity of result. However, as we have seen, there is a stricter duty in relation to Charter rights that correspond to those contained in the ECHR, and many of these rights will also be found in national constitutions.

There is moreover the fact that the particular conception or meaning accorded to a right can vary as between Member States. This does not present an insuperable problem because the obligation is one of harmonious interpretation rather than identity of result. There will nonetheless be cases where the construction of a Charter right might arise in a case concerning Member State

---

[174] Charte 4961/00, Contrib 356, 13 November 2000, 3.
[175] ibid 3–4. This view was echoed by the Committee on Legal Affairs and Human Rights of the Parliamentary Assembly of the Council of Europe, Charte 4499/00, Contrib 349, 4 October 2000.
[176] CONV 354/02, Final Report of Working Group II, 22 October 2002, 7–8.

implementation of EC law, where, as in *ERT*[177] or *Familiapress*,[178] another Member State's laws are directly implicated in the action. It is possible for an interpretation of the Charter right to affect adversely the constitutional right protected by one Member State, while the contrary construction would be regarded as constitutionally objectionable by the other State. In these circumstances the ECJ will necessarily have to make difficult choices.

(b) National constitutions: substantive obligation

Article 53 is entitled 'Level of Protection'. It deals with the interrelationship of the Charter and other bodies of law. The aim of this provision was said to be to maintain the level of protection 'currently afforded within their respective scope by Union law, national law and international law'.[179] Special mention was made of the ECHR because of its importance.

Nothing in this Charter shall be interpreted as restricting or adversely affecting human rights and fundamental freedoms as recognised, in their respective fields of application, by Union law and international law and by international agreements to which the Union or all the Member States are party, including the European Convention for the Protection of Human Rights and Fundamental Freedoms, and by the Member States' constitutions.

The present discussion will concentrate on the relation between the Charter and Member States' constitutions. It should be noted at the outset that there is an ambiguity as to the meaning of the phrase 'in their respective spheres of application'. It appears to mean that nothing in the Charter should be interpreted as restricting or adversely affecting human rights recognized in the respective areas to which public international law, international agreements, and Member State constitutions apply. It therefore delineates the spheres of application of human rights norms derived from these other areas.

This raised concerns that the supremacy of EU law might be jeopardized,[180] in part because of the absence of a supremacy clause in the Charter, in part because jurisprudence from German and Italian courts had not in the past been premised on the assumption that their human rights norms only applied within a limited field, being that to which Community rules did not apply. It had been premised rather on the assumption that such national constitutional protection continued to be generally applicable, but that national courts might choose not

---

[177] Case C-260/89 (n 7).
[178] Case C-368/95 (n 7).
[179] Explanations Relating to the Charter (n 33) 19; Charte 4473/00, Convent 49, 11 October 2000, 50.
[180] J Liisberg, 'Does the Charter of Fundamental Rights Threaten the Supremacy of Community Law?' (2001) 38 CMLRev 1171.

to exercise their jurisdiction if satisfied that the protection of rights within the Community legal order was sufficient.[181]

These concerns should be kept in perspective.[182] The approach of, for example, the German courts has softened in the last decade. The *Bundesverfassungsgericht* emphasized that the level of protection provided by the ECJ could differ from that of the German courts in individual cases and that it was only if the overall level of protection generally fell below a minimum acceptable level would the German courts reassert their control function.[183] It is therefore the case that from the perspective of German constitutional law there is less of a problem than hitherto about the delineation of the respective spheres of application of EU law and national law in relation to fundamental rights. It should also be noted, however, that the *Bundesverfassungsgericht*'s decision[184] on the Lisbon Treaty contained strictures concerning the inability of the EU to impinge on areas that were regarded as central to German constitutional identity.[185]

11. International Law and the Charter

We have seen that Article 53 addresses the relationship between the Charter and fundamental rights as recognized and protected by, *inter alia*, international law. Space precludes detailed elaboration of the relationship between international law and EU law in relation to fundamental rights,[186] but the nature of the difficulties can be exemplified by the *Kadi* case,[187] which highlights the pressing need for administrative law safeguards at the international level.[188]

---

[181] *Re Wunsche Handelsgesellschaft*, Dec. of 22 Oct. 1986 [1987] 3 CMLR 225; J Frowein 'Solange II' (1988) 25 CMLRev 201; W Roth, 'The Application of Community Law in West Germany: 1980–1990' (1991) 28 CMLRev 137; *SpA Granital v Amministrazione delle Finanze*, Dec 170, 8 June 1984; *SpA Fragd v Amministrazione delle Finanze*, Dec 232, 21 April 1989, (1989) 72 RDI; R Pettricione, 'Italy: Supremacy of Community Law over National Law' (1986) 11 ELRev 320; G Gaja, New Developments in a Continuing Story: The Relationship between EEC Law and Italian Law' (1990) 27 CMLRev 83; P Craig, 'National Courts and Community Law' in J Hayward and A Menon (eds), *Governing Europe* (Oxford University Press, 2003) ch 2.
[182] Maduro (n 18) 296–297.
[183] Thym (n 75) 15–16; Schwarze (n 76) 411–417; F Hoffmeister, 'Case Note' (2001) 38 CMLRev 791.
[184] Lisbon Case, BVerfG, 2 BvE 2/08, from 30 June 2009, available at <http://www.bverfg.de/entscheidungen/es20090630_2bve000208.html>. English translation available at <http://www.bundesverfassungsgericht.de/entscheidungen/es20090630_2bve000208en.html>.
[185] pp 151–154.
[186] G de Búrca, 'The European Court of Justice and the International Legal Order after *Kadi*', Jean Monnet Working Paper, No 1/09; T Tridimas and J Guitierrez-Fons, 'EU Law, International Law, and Economic Sanctions against Terrorism: The Judiciary in Distress?' (2009) 32 Fordham ILJ 660.
[187] Cases C-402 and 415/05 P *Yassin Abdullah Kadi and Al Barakaat International Foundation v Council and Commission* [2008] ECR I-6351; C Eckes, *EU Counter-Terrorist Policies and Fundamental Rights, The Case of Individual Sanctions* (Oxford University Press, 2009).
[188] B Kingsbury, N Krisch and R Stewart, 'The Emergence of Global Administrative Law' (2005) 68 LCP 15.

The applicant challenged a Community Regulation that froze the funds of those suspected of supporting Al-Qaeda. The Regulation was passed pursuant to Security Council Resolutions, which established a Sanctions Committee to designate those who should be subject to such freezing orders. This Committee obtained its information from States and regional organizations and the names placed on the list were reviewed after 12 months. The applicant's name was included on the list and his assets in the EU were frozen in accordance with the Community Regulation. He argued that he was never involved in the provision of financial support for terrorism and that his fundamental rights were infringed by the Regulation.

The ECJ held that the EC was based on the rule of law, and could not therefore avoid review of conformity of its acts with the EC Treaty. An international agreement could not affect the allocation of powers fixed by the Treaties or the autonomy of the Community legal system. It was not for the Community judiciary to review the lawfulness of a resolution of an international body, even if it was limited to examination of the compatibility of that resolution with *jus cogens*.

The Community courts should rather review the lawfulness of the implementing Community measure, including full review for compliance with EC fundamental rights. The ECJ held that the right to be heard did not, in this type of case, require communication to a person before a name was placed on the list as being subject to freezing of assets, since this would jeopardize the objectives of the regulation. The right to be heard, however, was violated because the regulation provided no opportunity for those listed to challenge their inclusion, or to test the evidentiary basis thereof, within a reasonable time after being listed. This same infirmity also constituted breach of the right to an effective legal remedy, and to the right to property.

12. UK/Poland Protocol and the Charter

(a) Protocol: content

The UK and Poland negotiated a Protocol[189] designed to limit the application of the Charter in certain respects, and the Protocol will be extended to the Czech Republic.[190] The Protocol contains a lengthy preamble, which, *inter alia*, reaffirms that Article 6 TEU requires the courts of the UK and Poland to interpret and apply the Charter in accordance with the explanations referred to

---

[189] Protocol (No 30) On the Application of the Charter of Fundamental Rights of the European Union to Poland and to the United Kingdom.
[190] Brussels European Council, 29–30 October 2009, Annex 1.

in that Article. The preamble moreover 'notes' the wish of Poland and the United Kingdom to clarify certain aspects of the application of the Charter.

The Protocol has two substantive articles. Article 1(1) states that the Charter does not extend the ability of the Union courts, or any court or tribunal of Poland or of the United Kingdom, to find that the laws, regulations, or administrative provisions, practices, or action of Poland or of the United Kingdom are inconsistent with the fundamental rights, freedoms, and principles that it reaffirms. Article 1(2) further states that for the avoidance of doubt nothing in Title IV of the Charter, which concerns solidarity rights, creates justiciable rights applicable to Poland or the United Kingdom except insofar as Poland or the United Kingdom has provided for such rights in its national law. Article 2 provides that insofar as a provision of the Charter refers to national laws and practices, it shall only apply to Poland or the United Kingdom to the extent that the rights or principles that it contains are recognized in the law or practices of Poland or of the United Kingdom.

(b) Protocol: political background

In political terms, the UK's insistence on the Protocol is problematic. The UK had, two years earlier, signed the Constitutional Treaty, which included the Charter, and did so without any such reservations of the kind found in the Protocol attached to the Lisbon Treaty. It can therefore be assumed that had the Constitutional Treaty ratification process not been stopped as a result of the negative referenda in France and the Netherlands, the UK Government would have campaigned for the Constitutional Treaty, including the Charter, notwithstanding the absence of any opt-out or reservation. The relevant terrain had not altered in the ensuing two years, and the rationale for the Protocol is in that sense unclear.

The 'official view' is that the Government engaged in some re-thinking of the possible impact of the Charter on UK business, in particular relating to the solidarity rights contained in Title IV, although insofar as this was so it is of course highly contestable whether Charter rights should be limited in this manner. However, it is difficult to avoid the conclusion that the inclusion of the Protocol was motivated as much if not more by the Government's desire to show that the Lisbon Treaty differed in certain respects from the Constitutional Treaty, and that therefore a referendum on the former was not necessary.

(c) Protocol: legal effect

We need to tread carefully when considering the legal effect of the Protocol, and to distinguish between a broad and a narrow view.

The 'broad view' of Article 1(1) of the Protocol would be that the Charter creates no legally enforceable rights that can be pleaded against the UK or Poland, either before Union or national courts. This view is not sustainable when read in the light of the Protocol as a whole. If the intent had been for the Protocol to create a complete opt-out for the UK and Poland in relation to the entire Charter, then this could have been simply done. It would only have required a single article, suitably and simply worded to achieve this result. If this had been the intent behind Article 1(1) of the Protocol, then Article 1(2) and Article 2 would have been legally redundant. There would, by definition, have been no need for anything to have been said about, for example, solidarity rights not being enforceable against the UK and Poland if Article 1(1) constituted a complete opt-out from the entirety of the Charter. It should moreover be noted that the very wording of Article 2 assumes that the Charter applies to the UK and Poland. The broad view is moreover inconsistent with the wording of the preamble to the Protocol, in which the contracting parties 'note' that the UK and Poland wish to clarify 'certain aspects of the application of the Charter', and 'reaffirm' that 'references in this Protocol to the operation of specific provisions of the Charter are strictly without prejudice to the operation of other provisions of the Charter'. These extracts from the preamble, and especially the latter, contradict a reading of the Protocol as a complete opt-out.

The 'narrow view' focuses on the precise wording of Article 1(1), which states that the Charter does not 'extend the ability' of Union or national courts to find that national laws etc are inconsistent with rights reaffirmed by the Charter. On this view Article 1(1) has less impact. The Community courts could, prior to the Charter, consider the legality of Community measures, and Member State action where it fell within the sphere of EU law, for violation of fundamental rights. The matter would often arise in the context of a preliminary ruling from a national court, which had the duty to consider the legality of, for example, Member State action for compliance with Community law, including fundamental rights. Viewed from this perspective the Charter does not 'extend the ability' of Union or national courts to find that national laws etc are inconsistent with Charter rights. Thus Article 1(1) affirms established orthodoxy, and reaffirms the injunction in Article 51(2) that the Charter does not extend the field of application of EU law. It fits, moreover, with the statement in the preamble that the UK and Poland wish to clarify certain aspects of the application of the Charter.

Article 1(2) is, by way of contrast, a substantive limit, which reduces the impact of Title IV of the Charter concerning solidarity rights.[191] So, too, more generally is the stipulation in Article 2 that insofar as a provision of the Charter

---

[191] C Barnard, 'The "Opt-Out" for the UK and Poland from the Charter of Fundamental Rights: Triumph of Rhetoric over Reality?' in Griller and Ziller (n 64) 257–283.

refers to national laws and practices, it shall only apply to Poland or the United Kingdom to the extent that the rights or principles that it contains are recognized in the law or practices of those countries. It should nonetheless be noted that the crucial wording is 'recognized in the law or practices' of the UK and Poland, and that this wording provides the ECJ with interpretative discretion as to when a Charter right might be regarded as recognized by the law or practice of that country.

It should moreover be remembered that the Protocol does not in itself affect the *acquis communautaire*, including the fundamental rights' jurisprudence that preceded the Charter. It would therefore still be open to claimants to rely on this body of established law if they could not rely directly on the Charter because of the limits imposed by the Protocol.[192]

13. Remedies and the Charter

Rights demand remedies. This is an obvious proposition, but important nonetheless. It is axiomatic, as van Gerven states, that 'fundamental rights are only truly respected when the legal order concerned makes them enforceable against those who have breached them'.[193] An individual may seek redress for a violation of fundamental rights through a national legal system, the ECHR, or EU law, and van Gerven provides a comprehensive overview of the possibilities open to the aggrieved individual.

The present discussion will focus on legal remedies under EU law, although we should be cognizant of the possibilities of also using the Open Method of Coordination.[194] The principal remedies are review of legality leading to annulment of the offending measure, and damages liability. Review of legality can be direct through Article 263 TFEU, or indirect through Article 267 TFEU.

The main obstacle for direct actions hitherto has been the narrow criterion for standing. There has always been an uneasy tension between Charter rights and the standing rules for direct actions, and this has been thrown into sharp relief by the fact that the Charter is now legally binding. The Charter accords 'individual rights', yet the application of the standing rules meant that a person who claimed that such rights were infringed by Community law was often not able to meet the requirements of 'individual concern'. There was something decidedly odd about

---

[192] See also the preceding discussion pp 212–213.
[193] W van Gerven, 'Remedies for Infringements of Fundamental Rights' (2004) 10 EPL 261.
[194] G de Búrca, 'The Constitutional Challenge of New Governance in the European Union' (2003) 28 ELRev 814; O de Schutter, 'The Implementation of Fundamental Rights through the Open Method of Coordination' in O De Schutter and S Deakin (eds), *Is the Open Coordination of Employment and Social Policies the Future of Social Europe?* (Bruylant, 2005) 279–342.

the infringement of an individual right not counting as a matter of individual concern.

The ECJ touched on this in *Bactria*,[195] where the applicant argued that it should be regarded as individually concerned by a Community regulation because it affected its property and data-protection rights. The ECJ briefly concluded that the alleged infringiene of the applicant's property right was insufficient to distinguish it individually for the purposes of standing. This conclusion was sustainable in formalistic terms, since the regulation could equally have affected the property rights of other operators in the area. This merely served to demonstrate the limits of the formalistic reasoning. The fact that a regulation might affect equally a number of traders did not alter the fact that the effect in each such case was on the claimant's individual right. Thus *Bactria* failed to resolve or indeed recognize the tension between individual rights and individual concern.

The deliberations in the Convention on the Future of Europe on standing were considered above,[196] such that the criterion in Article 263(4) TFEU was altered, so as to provide that:

Any natural or legal person may, under the conditions laid down in the first and second paragraphs, institute proceedings against an act addressed to that person or which is of direct and individual concern to them, and against a regulatory act which is of direct concern to them and does not entail implementing measures.

The novelty of the provision is that individual concern does not have to be shown for regulatory acts that are of direct concern to a person and do not entail implementing measures. Liberalization of this kind is to be welcomed, and goes some way to meet the difficulties exemplified by the existing case law. The difficulties of construction concerning Article 263(4) TFEU were, however, considered above.[197] It is not clear in the light of these difficulties that the reformed standing rules will do much to alleviate the problems faced by individuals in securing standing to challenge EU legislative acts on rights-based grounds, more especially because it seems unlikely that the reformed rules will apply to primary legislative acts. The claimant will in many instances still be forced to bring right-based challenges by recourse to indirect challenge to Union acts under Article 267 TFEU.

It remains to be seen what impact if any the Charter might have. Article 41 enshrines a right to good administration, which is said to inhere in every person. Article 41(2) sets out certain more specific rights that are included in this right. Article 47 provides that everyone whose rights and freedoms guaranteed by EU

---

[195] Case C-258/02 P *Bactria Industriehygiene-Service Verwaltungs GMbH v Commission* [2003] ECR I-15105, [48]–[51].
[196] p 129.   [197] pp 130–132.

law are violated has the right to an effective remedy before a tribunal in compliance with the conditions laid down in this Article. Standing rules are not explicitly mentioned in either article. It would be open to the Union courts, if they wished to do so, to regard these provisions as the basis for expanding the existing standing rules. They are, however, unlikely to do so given their approach to standing hitherto. This is especially so given that the Explanatory Memorandum stated in relation to Article 47 that there was no intent for this provision to make any change to the rules on standing other than those embodied in Article 263(4).[198]

It would have been possible to make special provision for rights-based actions by drawing on the *Verfassungsbeschwerde* in German law, or the *recurso de amparo* in Spanish law. They are subsidiary procedures in the sense that a direct complaint to the Constitutional Court is possible where it can be shown that the ordinary courts have failed to uphold the applicant's constitutional rights. The applicant has to show some personal, direct, and present effect from the contested measure, but this criterion has not prevented thousands of such complaints each year to the German and Spanish Constitutional Courts.[199] However, as de Witte has argued, if the criterion for standing were broadened there would be no need for such a mechanism in relation to challenge to Union acts.[200] It would by way of contrast have had a marked impact on judicial review of Member State action for violation of fundamental rights, since it would have allowed the aggrieved individual to bring an action before the Union courts without the need for a preliminary reference by a national court.[201] De Witte nonetheless concluded against the creation of a European *amparo*.

Liability in damages is the other main remedy that might be sought for violation of fundamental rights. The general principles that govern Union liability under Article 340 TFEU and Member State liability under the *Francovich* doctrine[202] will apply here. Thus, provided that the applicant can show that the provision was intended to confer rights on individuals, and can prove breach, causation, and damage, then liability will ensue. It may well be necessary to show a sufficiently serious breach where the contested measure entailed the exercise of meaningful discretion. Damages will not readily be available in relation to Charter provisions judged to be principles rather than rights, since such provisions are intended to guide legislative and executive action rather than confer rights on individuals.

---

[198] Explanations Relating to the Charter (n 33) 13; Charte 4473/00, Convent 49, 11 October 2000, 41; CONV 828/03, Updated Explanations Relating to the Text of the Charter of Fundamental Rights, 9 July 2003, 41.
[199] de Witte (n 2) 894.
[200] ibid 895.
[201] ibid 895–896.
[202] Cases C-6 and 9/90 *Francovich and Bonifaci v Italy* [1991] ECR I-5357.

14. Conclusion: Judicial Review, Legitimacy and the Charter

It is fitting to conclude this chapter by reflecting more generally on the impact of the Charter on judicial review.

(a) Charter: the profile of judicial review

The fact that the Charter is rendered binding by the Lisbon Treaty may well alter the profile of judicial review within the EU, and pose new challenges for the Union courts. They have hitherto fashioned the fundamental rights jurisprudence and been required to adjudicate on complex and contentious issues. The role of rights-based claims within judicial review may nonetheless expand considerably, forcing the Union courts to adjudicate on an increasing number of complex claims relating to both Union and national action.

An analogy with developments in the UK is interesting. The UK enacted the Human Rights Act in 1998 and it came into effect in 2000. Prior to that the UK courts had made it clear that fundamental rights were embedded in the common law and would be protected by the UK courts in judicial review actions. The advent of the Human Rights Act 1998 nonetheless transformed judicial review in the UK. There has been a significant expansion in the number of cases that raise rights-based arguments in the context of judicial review actions. The 'message' or 'lesson' from this is that enshrining fundamental rights in statutory form has a marked impact on the extent to which they will be relied on in legal actions. This is not surprising. Claimants are likely to feel on more secure foundations when relying on a statute that clearly lists rights and has received Parliament's imprimatur.

In the EU there has been a 'common law style' development of fundamental rights by the Community courts since the 1970s. The number of such cases has nonetheless remained limited. Claimants, Advocates General, the Court of First Instance (CFI), and more recently the ECJ relied on the Charter for interpretative guidance even prior to the Lisbon Treaty. The fact that the Charter is now rendered legally binding by the Lisbon Treaty will in all likelihood increase the profile of rights-based claims within judicial review actions. Claimants will be able to point to a clear set of rights, which are legally binding on EU institutions and Member States when they act within the sphere of EU law. The Union courts will then be faced by a change in the profile of judicial review actions, with an increasing number of such claims having a strong rights-based component.

The analogy between the UK and the EU cannot be pressed too far. There are obstacles to bringing actions within the EU, whether directly or indirectly, and these obstacles will serve to limit the number of actions that can be brought. This can be accepted, but even if there is no net increase in the number of judicial

7

Legal Acts, Hierarchy, and Simplification

The Constitutional Treaty included reform of legal acts and created a hierarchy of norms. The Lisbon Treaty retained a hierarchy of legal acts,[1] although the nomenclature was altered because it was felt by the European Council that the words 'law' and 'lawmaking' in the Constitutional Treaty should be excised on the ground that they carried 'federal' and 'constitutional' resonance.

The reforms relating to the classification of legal acts were intended to introduce greater simplification and to signal the appropriate degree of political oversight and control over each type of legal act. This chapter will consider whether this has been achieved. The Working Group on Simplification noted that nothing is more complex than simplification, and the significance of this insight will be apparent from the ensuing discussion. It is equally important to be aware of the political dimension of reform of legal acts. It was not simply a technical tidying up exercise. The Treaty provisions have broader implications for the inter-institutional balance of power within the EU, which must be revealed and assessed.

The analysis begins with consideration of the provisions in the Constitutional Treaty and the objectives that were sought to be achieved by reform of legal acts. This will be followed by explication of the relevant provisions in the Lisbon Treaty. There will then be detailed evaluation of the categories of legal act in the Lisbon Treaty, with consideration being given to the political and legal dimension of these provisions.

---

[1] A von Bogdandy, J Bast and F Arndt, 'Legal Instruments in European Union Law and their Reform: A Systematic Approach on an Empirical Basis' (2004) 23 YEL 91; P Craig, 'The Hierarchy of Norms' in T Tridimas and P Nebbia (eds), *European Union Law for the Twenty-First Century, Rethinking the New Legal Order* (Hart, 2004) 75–93; K Lenaerts and M Desomer, 'Towards a Hierarchy of Legal Acts in the European Union? Simplification of Legal Instruments and Procedures' (2005) 11 ELJ 744; J Liisberg, 'The EU Constitutional Treaty and its Distinction between Legislative and Non-Legislative Acts' in B Olsen and K Sorensen (eds), *Regulation in the EU* (Thomson, 2006) 133–168; P Stancanelli, 'Le système décisionnel de l'Union' in G Amato, H Bribosia and B de Witte (eds), *Genesis and Destiny of the European Constitution* (Bruylant, 2007) 485–543; B de Witte, 'Legal Instruments and Law-Making in the Lisbon Treaty' in S Griller and J Ziller (eds), *The Lisbon Treaty, EU Constitutionalism without a Constitutional Treaty* (Springer, 2008) 79–108; H Hofmann, 'Legislation, Delegation and Implementation under the Treaty of Lisbon: Typology Meets Reality' (2009) 15 ELJ 482.

1. Constitutional Treaty and the Hierarchy of Norms

It is impossible to understand the provisions concerning legal acts in the Lisbon Treaty without awareness of the analogous provisions in the Constitutional Treaty and this is so notwithstanding the fact that the Lisbon Treaty departed in certain respects from the nomenclature used in the Constitutional Treaty. It is equally important to comprehend the objectives underlying the reforms.

(a) Rationale: simplification, democratic legitimacy, and separation of powers

The provisions in the Constitutional Treaty on the hierarchy of norms followed, with some modifications, the recommendations of Working Group IX on Simplification.[2] It is instructive to note the cautionary warning of the Group, that 'nothing is more complicated than simplification'.[3] The Working Group sought to attain a number of objectives, three of which featured prominently in its Report: simplification, democratic legitimacy, and separation of powers.

Simplification, as the name of the Group suggests, was a major concern, both in relation to the types of Union instrument and the legislative procedures for enactment.[4] This was especially prominent in the Group's thinking, given the multiplicity of procedures for enactment of Community measures that existed under the EC Treaty.

This initial aim was to be secured while at the same time respecting democratic legitimacy. The Working Group proceeded on the assumption that the democratic legitimacy of the Union was based on the Member States and the people. Legislation should secure approval from both bodies, and acts that had the same nature and effect should be produced by the same procedure.[5]

The separation of powers also informed the Working Group's thinking. The hierarchy of legislation was said to be 'the consequence of a better separation of powers',[6] the aim being not to pay tribute to Montesquieu, 'but out of concern for democracy'.[7] It is clear from reading the Working Group's report that separation of powers was regarded as the basis for a clearer delineation between matters that should fall to the legislative arm of government and those that should fall within the province of the executive. It recognized that the divide could not be as clear cut in the Union as in some national polities, but it felt that some advances could be made. This was the rationale for the new breed of delegated acts, whereby the Commission would be empowered to fill in the

---

[2] CONV 424/02, Final Report of Working Group IX on Simplification, Brussels, 29 November 2002.
[3] ibid 1.   [4] ibid 1.   [5] ibid 2.   [6] ibid 2.   [7] ibid 2.

details of the legislative scheme, thereby avoiding excessive detail in the primary legislation.[8]

We shall consider in the course of this chapter whether these aims have been realized, the implications for the inter-institutional balance of power, and the less obvious institutional consequences of these reforms.

(b) Constitutional Treaty: categories and hierarchy of legal act

The Lisbon Treaty modified the nomenclature used to describe Union legal acts. It is nonetheless important to advert briefly to the taxonomy used in the Constitutional Treaty as background for understanding the schema in the Lisbon Treaty.

The provisions concerning the hierarchy of norms were set out in Title V of Part I of the Constitution, entitled 'Exercise of Union Competence'. The foundational provision was Article I-33(1) CT. It provided that in exercising the competences conferred on it by the Constitution, the Union should use as legal instruments European laws, European framework laws, European regulations, European decisions, recommendations, and opinions. Article I-38(1) CT stipulated that the choice as between these measures was to be in accordance with the principle of proportionality, and Article I-38(2) CT imposed a duty to give reasons when making these Union acts.

(i) Legislative acts

The Constitutional Treaty specified two types of legislative act, European laws and European framework laws, Article I-33(1). A European law corresponded to an EC regulation: it was binding in its entirety and directly applicable in all Member States. A European framework law corresponded to an EC directive: it was a legislative act binding as to the result to be achieved on the Member States to which it is addressed, but leaving the national authorities to choose the form and means of achieving the result.

Article I-34(1) CT specified the way in which legislation was made. The general rule was that European laws and framework laws were to be adopted on the basis of a Commission proposal jointly by the European Parliament and the Council, under the ordinary legislative procedure, the old co-decision procedure. This reflected the centrality of the idea that the European Parliament and the Council were the joint legislatures within the Union.[9] Provision was also made for specific cases where European laws and framework laws were to be adopted by the European Parliament with the participation of the Council, or by the Council with the participation of the European Parliament, in accordance with special legislative procedures.[10]

---

[8] ibid 8.   [9] Arts I-20(1) and I-23(1) CT.   [10] Art I-34(2) CT.

(ii) Non-legislative acts

Article I-33(1) CT provided for what were termed non-legislative acts. A European regulation was a non-legislative act of general application for the implementation of legislative acts and certain specific provisions of the Constitution. It could either be binding in its entirety and directly applicable in all Member States, or be binding as regards the result to be achieved on all the Member States to which it was addressed, while leaving the national authorities to choose the form and means of achieving that result. This provision therefore provided for secondary European laws and secondary European framework laws.

Article I-33(1) CT also specified a category of European decisions, which were non-legislative acts that were binding in their entirety. Where the decision specified those to whom it was addressed it was binding only on them. The other type of non-legislative act was the recommendation or the opinion, which did not have binding force.

Articles I-36 CT, entitled 'Delegated European Regulations', dealt with the way in which non-legislative acts were made. It provided, in Article I-36(1), that European laws and framework laws could delegate power to the Commission to enact delegated regulations to 'supplement or amend certain non-essential elements of the European law or framework law'. The objectives, content, scope, and duration of the delegation should be explicitly defined in the laws and framework laws. The delegation could not cover the essential elements in the area, which were reserved for the law or framework law. Article I-36(2) specified that the conditions to which the delegation was subject should be determined in the law or framework law, and that these conditions might specify that the European Parliament or the Council could decide to revoke the delegation; or that the delegated regulation could enter into force only if no objection was expressed by the European Parliament or the Council within a period set by the law or framework law.

(iii) Implementing acts

Article I-33(1) CT listed the principal types of Union act, but did not list all such measures. Implementing acts were not mentioned in the list, but were dealt with in Article I-37 CT.

The Member States had a duty to adopt all measures of national law necessary to implement legally binding Union acts.[11] The category of implementing acts was also relevant to the Commission. Where uniform conditions were required for implementing binding Union acts, those acts could confer implementing powers on the Commission, or in specific cases concerned with common foreign and security policy, on the Council.[12] European laws were to lay down in advance rules

---

[11] Art I-37(1) CT.   [12] Art I-37(2) CT.

and general principles for the mechanisms of control by Member States over implementing acts of the Union.[13] Implementing acts could take the form of European implementing regulations or European implementing decisions.[14]

2. Lisbon Treaty and the Hierarchy of Norms

(a) Lisbon Treaty: types of legal act

(i) Regulations, directives, decisions

The European Council of June 2007, which initiated the process leading to the Lisbon Treaty, decided that the terms 'law', and 'framework law' should be dropped. The rationale given was that the Lisbon Treaty was not to have a 'constitutional character',[15] although it is not readily apparent why the terminology of 'law' or 'framework law' should be assumed to have such a character.

It was decided to retain the existing terminology of regulations, directives, and decisions. A version of the hierarchy of norms is, however, preserved in the Lisbon Treaty, which distinguishes between legislative acts, non-legislative acts of general application, and implementing acts. The foundational provision is Article 288 TFEU.

To exercise the Union's competences, the institutions shall adopt regulations, directives, decisions, recommendations and opinions.

A regulation shall have general application. It shall be binding in its entirety and directly applicable in all Member States.

A directive shall be binding, as to the result to be achieved, upon each Member State to which it is addressed, but shall leave to the national authorities the choice of form and methods.

A decision shall be binding in its entirety. A decision which specifies those to whom it is addressed shall be binding only on them.

Recommendations and opinions shall have no binding force.

There are some instances where the Treaty specifies that a particular legal act should be used, as in the case of, for example, services, where Article 59 TFEU stipulates that a directive shall be used for a legislative act that seeks to liberalize a specific service. In other instances Article 296 TFEU contains the default position: where the Treaties do not specify the type of act to be adopted, the institutions shall select it on a case-by-case basis, in compliance with the applicable procedures and with the principle of proportionality.

The formulation of regulations and directives replicates that in the EC Treaty.[16] The wording used in relation to decisions is slightly different. A decision is said to be binding in its entirety, and a decision which specifies

---

[13] Art I-37(3) CT.   [14] Art I-37(4) CT.
[15] Brussels European Council, 21–22 June 2007, Annex 1, para 3.   [16] Art 249 EC.

those to whom it is addressed is binding only on them. This captures the duality in the use of decisions as legal acts prior to the Lisbon Treaty. In most instances decisions were used as binding legal acts in relation to specific addressees, as exemplified by the many such decisions made in the context of competition and State aids. Some decisions, however, were of a more generic nature, setting out the legal rules to govern an inter-institutional issue such as Comitology, or providing the legal foundation for Community programmes.[17] The English version of the wording of Article 288 is capable of covering both types of decision. The German and Dutch wording, however, signifies the generic rather than the individualized version of decision.[18] It remains to be seen, therefore, whether the individualized sense of decision will subsist. It would be very odd if it did not, since it has been a staple and important form of legal act ever since the inception of the EEC.

(ii) Atypical legal acts

The preceding point leads naturally to consideration of the status of atypical acts under the Lisbon Treaty. This was the name accorded to acts other than those listed in Article 249 EC, some of which were soft law, others of which involved legally binding acts, such as the more generic decision considered above,[19] which were used prior to the Lisbon Treaty.

Article 296(3) TFEU provides some guidance in this respect, stating that when considering draft legislative acts, the European Parliament and the Council shall refrain from adopting acts not provided for by the relevant legislative procedure in the area in question. Hofmann has argued, with justification, that this precludes the use of acts other than regulations, directives, and decisions for the adoption of legislative acts.[20] He argues, moreover, that because Article 296(3) only relates to legislative acts, therefore atypical acts could be used for the enactment of delegated and implementing acts, provided that there was nothing to preclude this in the legislative act.[21] Whether this latter proves to be the case depends on the interpretation given to Article 288, which provides that in exercising the Union's competences, the institutions shall adopt regulations, directives, decisions, recommendations, and opinions. It would certainly be possible for the European Court of Justice (ECJ) to interpret this provision as precluding recourse to atypical acts when making delegated and implementing acts.

The EU will, in any event, doubtless continue to use a variety of soft law instruments in the post-Lisbon world as it has done hitherto, and these will, as before, continue to be used alongside binding legal norms.

---

[17] von Bogdandy, Bast and Arndt (n 1) 103–106.
[18] de Witte (n 1) 95–96.
[19] S Lefevre, *Les actes communautaires atypiques* (Bruylant, 2006).
[20] Hofmann (n 1) 487 n 23.
[21] ibid 487 n 23.

(iii) Inter-institutional agreements and international agreements

The list of legal acts provided in Article 288 TFEU must moreover be supplemented by Article 295 TFEU, which provides that inter-institutional agreements can be concluded between the European Parliament, Council, and Commission and that such agreements may be binding in nature.

Article 216 TFEU is also relevant. It provides that the Union may conclude an agreement with one or more third countries or international organizations where the Treaties so provide, or where the conclusion of an agreement is necessary in order to achieve, within the framework of the Union's policies, one of the objectives referred to in the Treaties, or is provided for in a legally binding Union act, or is likely to affect common rules or alter their scope. Such agreements concluded by the Union are binding upon the institutions of the Union and on the Member States. Article 216 is considered in detail below.[22]

(iv) Open method of coordination

The Open Method of Coordination has been an important policy tool for over a decade. It will doubtless continue to be used in the future. It finds no formal place in the list of legal acts, or in the accompanying provisions. However, it is mentioned in substance in certain articles of the Lisbon Treaty.[23]

(b) Lisbon Treaty: categories and hierarchy of legal act

While the framers of the Lisbon Treaty rejected the terminology of law and framework law used in the Constitutional Treaty, the categories and hierarchy of legal act in the Lisbon Treaty nonetheless owe much to the thinking that went into the Constitutional Treaty.

(i) Legislative acts

Article 289 TFEU is the governing provision that deals with legislative acts. It provides as follows.

1. The ordinary legislative procedure shall consist in the joint adoption by the European Parliament and the Council of a regulation, directive or decision on a proposal from the Commission. This procedure is defined in Article 294.

2. In the specific cases provided for by the Treaties, the adoption of a regulation, directive or decision by the European Parliament with the participation of the Council, or by the latter with the participation of the European Parliament, shall constitute a special legislative procedure.

3. Legal acts adopted by legislative procedure shall constitute legislative acts.

---

[22] pp 398–400.
[23] See, eg, Arts 149, 153(2), 156, 168(2), 173(2), 181(2) TFEU.

4. In the specific cases provided for by the Treaties, legislative acts may be adopted on the initiative of a group of Member States or of the European Parliament, on a recommendation from the European Central Bank or at the request of the Court of Justice or the European Investment Bank.

Thus the basic premise of Article 289 TFEU is that legislative acts are legal acts adopted by a legislative procedure. The legal acts that can be legislative in this sense can be regulations, directives, or decisions: provided that they are adopted in accord with a legislative procedure they will constitute legislative acts for the purposes of the Lisbon Treaty. The default position is that this will be the ordinary legislative procedure, which is the successor to co-decision. A special legislative procedure is, however, mandated in certain instances whereby a regulation, directive, or decision is adopted by the European Parliament with the participation of the Council, or by the Council with the participation of the European Parliament. Article 289(4) TFEU also provides for legislative acts to be adopted in the circumstances mentioned therein.

(ii) Delegated acts

The continuity of thought between the Constitutional Treaty and the Lisbon Treaty is equally apparent in relation to non-legislative acts, Article 290 TFEU drawing directly on Article I-36 CT. Article 290 TFEU is framed as follows:

1. A legislative act may delegate to the Commission the power to adopt non-legislative acts of general application to supplement or amend certain non-essential elements of the legislative act.

   The objectives, content, scope and duration of the delegation of power shall be explicitly defined in the legislative acts. The essential elements of an area shall be reserved for the legislative act and accordingly shall not be the subject of a delegation of power.

2. Legislative acts shall explicitly lay down the conditions to which the delegation is subject; these conditions may be as follows:

   (a) the European Parliament or the Council may decide to revoke the delegation;
   (b) the delegated act may enter into force only if no objection has been expressed by the European Parliament or the Council within a period set by the legislative act.

   For the purposes of (a) and (b), the European Parliament shall act by a majority of its component members, and the Council by a qualified majority.

3. The adjective 'delegated' shall be inserted in the title of delegated acts.

Thus power is delegated to the Commission, subject to the conditions in Article 290 TFEU. The non-legislative acts can supplement or amend certain non-essential elements of the legislative act, but the legislative act must define the objectives, content, scope, and duration of the delegation of power. The essential elements of an area cannot be delegated. The legislative act must specify the conditions to which the delegation is subject. The conditions may allow the European Parliament or the Council to revoke the delegation, and/or enable the European Parliament or the Council to veto the delegated act within a specified period of time set by the legislative act.

It is important to appreciate that a delegated act can in principle be a regulation, directive, or decision. This follows from Article 288 TFEU read in conjunction with Article 290 TFEU. Thus Article 288 specifies the list of legal acts that can be adopted by the EU, regulations, directives, and decisions. Article 290(1) then stipulates that a legislative act can delegate to the Commission power to make a non-legislative act of general application. The non-legislative act, termed a delegated act, must perforce fall within the specified list of legal acts in Article 288.[24] It follows therefore that the delegated acts made pursuant to Article 290 are in effect secondary regulations, directives, and decisions. Regulations and decisions are in reality the legal acts that will be used most often when making delegated acts under Article 290, but there may well be situations in which a directive is felt to be the most appropriate instrument.

(iii) Implementing acts

The third category in the hierarchy of norms, implementing acts, is dealt with in Article 291 TFEU, which once again draws directly on the analogous provision of the Constitutional Treaty, Article I-37 CT. Article 291 TFEU is framed in the following terms:

1. Member States shall adopt all measures of national law necessary to implement legally binding Union acts.

2. Where uniform conditions for implementing legally binding Union acts are needed, those acts shall confer implementing powers on the Commission, or, in duly justified specific cases and in the cases provided for in Articles 24 and 26 of the Treaty on European Union, on the Council.

3. For the purposes of paragraph 2, the European Parliament and the Council, acting by means of regulations in accordance with the ordinary legislative procedure, shall lay down in advance the rules and general principles concerning mechanisms for control by Member States of the Commission's exercise of implementing powers.

4. The word 'implementing' shall be inserted in the title of implementing acts.

Thus Member States have an obligation to adopt all measures of national law necessary to implement legally binding Union acts. The Commission is empowered, as it was in the Constitutional Treaty. Thus where uniform conditions for implementing legally binding Union acts are needed, those acts shall confer implementing powers on the Commission, or, in certain cases on the Council. It is for the European Parliament and Council to lay down in advance the rules and general principles concerning mechanisms for control by Member States of the Commission's exercise of implementing powers.

[24] Subject to the discussion above, p 251.

The point made above concerning the legal form of delegated acts is in principle applicable here too. There are, as we shall see below, significant interpretive difficulties with this category of act. Implementing acts can take one of the legal forms listed in Article 288 TFEU, regulations, directives, or decisions.

3. Lisbon Treaty and Legislative Acts

The discussion thus far has explicated the regime for the hierarchy of norms in the Constitutional Treaty and the Lisbon Treaty. We now explore difficulties attendant upon the new regime, being mindful of the twin precepts identified at the outset: there is nothing more complicated than simplification, and reform will perforce have political as well as legal consequences. It is fitting to begin with analysis of legislative acts.

(a) Political dimension: democracy and enhanced legitimacy

The political consequences of the new regime are readily apparent in relation to legislative acts. They were explored in detail in an earlier chapter.[25] The general approach in the Lisbon Treaty is to be commended, and builds on the pre-existing regime. The Commission has, subject to limited exceptions, retained its gold standard, the right of legislative initiative.[26] The European Parliament and Council are said to jointly enact legislation.[27] The co-decision procedure under which such legislation is jointly enacted is now deemed to be the ordinary legislative procedure for the making of legislative acts, and the reach of this procedure has been extended to cover more areas than hitherto.[28]

This treatment of legislative power in the Lisbon Treaty is to be welcomed. The co-decision procedure allowed input from the European Parliament representing the electorate directly, and from the Council, representing State interests. It provided a framework for deliberative dialogue on the content of the legislation between the European Parliament, Council, and Commission. The extension of what is now termed the ordinary legislative procedure to cover new areas is a natural development, building on what occurred in earlier Treaty reform. It enhances the legitimacy of Union legislation and its democratic credentials by enabling the European Parliament to have input into the making of legislation in these areas.

This should, however, be read subject to the caveat discussed earlier as to the worrying development whereby trilogues are increasingly used at first reading stage and early in the second reading stage, thereby foreclosing broader consid-

---

[25] Ch 2.   [26] Art 17(2) TEU.
[27] Arts 14(1), 16(1) TEU.   [28] Arts 289, 294 TFEU.

eration of the merits of a legislative act by European Parliament committees and in plenary.[29]

(b) Legal dimension: formalism and attendant problems

(i) Formalism and legislative acts

Legislative acts are those passed pursuant to the ordinary or special legislative procedure. The ordinary legislative procedure is clear, and the details of the procedure are laid down in Article 294 TFEU, the successor provision to Article 251 EC. The nature of the special legislative procedure requires more elaboration.

Article 289(2) TFEU states, as seen above, that the special legislative procedure constitutes, 'in the specific cases provided for by the Treaties, the adoption of a regulation, directive, or decision by the European Parliament with the participation of the Council, or by the latter with the participation of the European Parliament'. It is only by looking at particular Treaty provisions that one can fully understand what this means. It becomes clear that particular Treaty articles state expressly that the special legislative procedure is to be used, and specify its meaning in the relevant area. Thus in most instances it signifies that the legal act is to be adopted by the Council unanimously, combined with a requirement of consent or consultation by the European Parliament.[30] In a few instances, notably those concerned with the organization of the European Parliament, the special legislative procedure signifies that the European Parliament adopts the legal act after approval from the Council.[31]

The new schema for legislative acts is not free from legal difficulty. It should be noted that the definition of a legislative act is purely formal. This follows from the wording of Article 289(3) TFEU: any legal act, whether in the form of a regulation, directive, or decision, which is enacted in accordance with either the ordinary or special legislative procedure, is deemed to be a legislative act for the purposes of the Lisbon Treaty. This formalism is symmetrical: any legal act enacted by the ordinary or special legislative procedure is by definition a legislative act; and if a legal act is not enacted in this manner then it does not constitute a legislative act for the purposes of the Lisbon Treaty. There are two noteworthy consequences of this formalism.

The first is that the content of the act is not relevant to its status as a legislative act. If a legislative procedure is prescribed for the enactment of a legal act then it is *ipso facto* a legislative act, notwithstanding that the content of the measure

---

[29] pp 38–39.
[30] Art 48 TEU; Arts 19, 21 22, 23, 25, 64, 77(3), 81(3), 83(2), 86(1), 87(3), 89, 113, 115, 118, 126, 127(6), 153(2), 182(4), 192, 194(3), 203, 218(6), 223(1), 262, 308, 311, 312(2), 314, 333(2), 349, 352 TFEU.
[31] Arts 223(2), 226, 228(4).

might well be regarded as administrative in nature. The converse is equally true. If the Lisbon Treaty does not prescribe a legislative procedure for the passage of a legal act then it is not a legislative act, even if judged by its content it lays down rules of general application that would in substantive terms be regarded as legislative in nature.

The second consequence of the formalistic approach is that the only legal acts that constitute legislative acts for the purposes of the Lisbon Treaty are those made in accordance with the ordinary or special legislative procedure as those are defined in Article 289(1) to (2) TFEU, including in the case of the latter the requirement that this special procedure is mandated in the specific cases provided for by the Treaties.

(ii) Formalism and fit

The difficulties that this creates can be exemplified in relation to competition policy. Article 103 TFEU provides for the passage of regulations or directives to give effect to the key principles of competition policy concerning cartels and abuse of a dominant position, which are specified in Articles 101 to 102 TFEU. Article 103 TFEU stipulates that such regulations or directives are to be laid down by the Council, on a proposal from the Commission after consulting the European Parliament.

This is not the ordinary legislative procedure, since the European Parliament has a mere right of consultation, as opposed to the co-equal status in the legislative process provided for by the ordinary legislative procedure. Nor does the procedure in Article 103 TFEU appear to constitute a special legislative procedure. It is true that Article 103 provides for the adoption of a legal act by the Council, with some form of participation by the European Parliament, in this instance, consultation. It might therefore be argued that this falls within the wording of Article 289(2) TFEU as a special legislative procedure. The obstacle to this interpretation is that Article 289(2) states that the special legislative procedure applies where there is participation by the European Parliament in acts adopted by the Council, or vice-versa, 'in the specific cases provided for by the Treaties', and the pattern throughout the Treaties is that where a special legislative procedure is intended to apply this is expressly signified in the relevant Treaty article.[32] There is no such signification in Article 103 TFEU.

Thus regulations and directives adopted pursuant to Article 103 TFEU would not seem to constitute legislative acts for the purposes of the Lisbon Treaty. The tension that this causes is immediately apparent when one reflects on the type of legal provisions that were adopted under Article 83 EC, the equivalent provision in the EC Treaty. Article 83 EC was the legal base for the adoption of Regulation

---

[32] See (nn 30–31).

1/2003,[33] which revolutionized the interrelationship between national courts, national competition authorities, and the Community institutions in the application and enforcement of EC competition law. It was clearly legislative in nature judged by any substantive criterion, but such a measure would not count as a legislative act for the purposes of Article 289 TFEU if enacted post the Lisbon Treaty.

This problem is not isolated to competition law. It is also apparent in other subject matter areas.[34] Thus, for example, Article 109 TFEU, which is the provision that empowers the making of regulations in relation to State aid, states that they shall be made by the Council on a proposal from the Commission after consulting the European Parliament.[35] Such regulations would not constitute legislative acts for the same reasons as identified in the discussion of competition: the regulations are not made in accord with the ordinary legislative procedure, nor does the Treaty state that a special legislative procedure applies when such State aid regulations are made. The analogous provision under the EC Treaty, Article 89 EC, was used relatively infrequently, but there were undoubtedly instances where it was used to enact a regulation that was legislative in nature.[36]

(iii) Formalism and consequence

The analysis thus far has revealed the difficulties flowing from the fact that the formalistic definition of legislative act does not, in some areas, cover the passage of legal acts that would clearly be regarded as legislative judged by their scope, content, and importance.

The problems are compounded when the rules relating to the passage of delegated acts are considered. These were set out above and will be considered in more detail below. The salient point for present purposes is that Article 290 TFEU states that, subject to certain conditions, a legislative act can delegate power to the Commission to make further regulations, directives, or decisions, which are termed delegated acts. These delegated acts are subject to the controls specified in Article 290 TFEU.

The difficulty should now be apparent: if the 'primary' regulation in areas such as competition or State aids does not, for the reasons given above, constitute a legislative act then the condition precedent for recourse to Article 290 TFEU for the making of delegated acts is not met. Such delegated acts could not be made in these areas, precisely because the 'primary regulation' did not constitute a

---

[33] Council Regulation (EC) No 1/2003 of 16 December 2002 on the implementation of the rules on competition laid down in Articles 81 and 82 of the Treaty [2003] OJ L1/1.
[34] See, eg, Art 95(3) TFEU.
[35] Art 109 TFEU.
[36] Council Regulation (EC) No 994/98 of 7 May 1998 on the application of Arts 92 and 93 of the Treaty establishing the European Community to certain categories of horizontal State aid [1998] OJ L142/1.

legislative act and hence could not contain provisions delegating power to the Commission.

This would lead to considerable problems and a potential 'black hole'. Regulation 1/2003, which embodied the new framework for application and enforcement of competition law, contained an express provision allowing implementing provisions to be made by the Commission.[37] The Commission duly made an implementing regulation pursuant to this power.[38] There is nothing untoward in this. To the contrary, this was the standard method of proceeding under the EC Treaty, whereby a primary regulation would enable power to be delegated to the Commission to make more detailed secondary regulations to flesh out certain provisions of the primary regulation. This is still possible under the Lisbon Treaty, subject, however, to the conditions in Article 290. This requires, as we have seen, the existence of a legislative act, which contains a provision enabling the Commission to make delegated acts. If the 'primary regulation' does not constitute a legislative act as defined by Article 289 then, subject to what is said below, this condition precedent is not met, with the consequence that power cannot be delegated to the Commission.

(iv) Formalism and adjustment

The problems considered above are not wholly insurmountable. Legal reasoning is a rich resource. Difficulties created by formalism can always be overcome if the judiciary is minded to do so. This can only be achieved, however, by qualifying the very formalism that underlies the existing schema.

The ECJ could therefore craft a legal judgment along the following lines. It could have recourse to the time-honoured technique of construing Treaty provisions whereby they are read as not containing an exclusive list. If this approach were to be taken the ECJ could conclude that Article 289 TFEU merely provided the principal examples of legislative act, and that this did not preclude the recognition of other kinds of legislative act, such as those made pursuant to Article 103 TFEU in the context of competition policy. The Court might reinforce this conclusion by adverting to the substantive nature of some legal acts concluded under Article 103, which are indubitably legislative when judged by this criterion. It could alternatively choose to regard the regulations or directives made pursuant to Article 103 as instances of a special legislative procedure, notwithstanding that the Article did not expressly signify this.

If the ECJ declined to take this step, it might nonetheless seek to address the conundrum that if a 'primary regulation' is not a legislative act then it would seem that the condition precedent to delegation of power to the Commission

---

[37] Reg 1/2003(n 33) Art 33.
[38] Commission Regulation (EC) No 773/2004 of 7 April 2004 relating to the conduct of proceedings by the Commission pursuant to Articles 81 and 82 of the EC Treaty [2004] OJ L123/18.

under Article 290 TFEU was not fulfilled. It could, once again, have recourse to familiar techniques of legal reasoning that it has deployed in the past. Thus it could acknowledge that the Council legitimately wished to delegate power to the Commission to make further regulations in the context of competition law. It could then reason that it would be inconsistent with the constitutional schema in the Lisbon Treaty if such delegated acts were not to be subject to the controls in Article 290 TFEU. This would then provide the conceptual foundation for the conclusion that even if the primary regulation was not a legislative act for the purposes of Article 289 TFEU, because it was not made by the ordinary or special legislative procedure, this did not preclude delegated empowerment to the Commission, subject to the conditions in Article 290.

4. Lisbon Treaty and Delegated Acts

(a) Political dimension: delegated acts and the balance of power

The precept adverted to at the outset of this chapter to the effect that 'simplification' of legal acts will have political and not just legal consequences is readily apparent in relation to the changes made to delegated acts. This is so irrespective of the view that one takes of these amendments. To pretend that these amendments are merely technical legal changes with no wider ramifications is just that, a pretence that ignores the political reality that has coloured this area for almost half a century. The political implications of the new provisions concerning delegated acts were considered in detail in an earlier chapter, and reference should be made to that discussion.[39]

A brief recap of the essence of this analysis will suffice for present purposes. The Council recognized from the outset of the EEC that not everything could be done by primary regulation and that it would need to delegate power to the Commission to make secondary norms. The Council was, however, unwilling to accord the Commission a blank cheque, because it realized that regulatory choices and contentious issues would often be resolved through such measures, the devil being in the detail. This was the rationale for the birth of what became known as Comitology, whereby national technocrats would sit with the Commission when it made these secondary measures, with the possibility of sending them to the Council in accord with the management and regulatory committee procedures if the national technocrats disagreed with the Commission proposal.

The workings of these mechanisms were analysed in a large body of literature. Rational choice institutionalists regard Comitology in principal-agent terms, whereby Member State principals use Comitology to impose constraints on a

[39] Ch 2.

supranational agent, the Commission. Sociological institutionalists and constructivists contend, by way of contrast, that decision making within Comitology is best viewed as a form of deliberative supranationalism.

The Commission has always chafed at what it regards as unwarranted Comitology constraints on its executive autonomy. It might be content with purely advisory committees, but it has never been happy with management and regulatory committees. Its strategy for over 20 years has been to devise some method whereby it could be freed from these limitations. This strategy explicitly underpinned its proposals when the Constitutional Treaty was being discussed, as is apparent from a series of high-profile Commission communications.[40] It advocated a regime of *ex ante* and *ex post* constraints on non-legislative acts of the kind that were incorporated in the Constitutional Treaty and are now contained in Article 290 TFEU, with the express hope that this might lead to the demise of management and regulatory committees. Article 290 TFEU makes no mention of Comitology.

Comitology was used hitherto primarily in relation to what are now termed delegated acts, and not in relation to implementing acts as they are defined in the Lisbon Treaty.[41] Notwithstanding this the Convention documentation considered the legitimacy of Comitology primarily in the context of implementing acts, as is apparent in the literature from the Working Group,[42] and other Convention documentation.[43] It is nonetheless unlikely that the Member States appreciated the possible demise of Comitology in the terrain where it has been used for 50 years. This may seem surprising, but it is less so when it is recognized that there was scant deliberation about the proposals for legal acts within the plenary sessions of the Convention on the Future of Europe, in part because of time constraints and in part because the subject matter was felt to be too technical.

The institutional deliberations concerning the workings of Article 290 TFEU post-ratification of the Lisbon Treaty have nonetheless been premised on the assumption that old-style management and regulatory committees will not operate in the post-Lisbon world. Scrutiny of delegated acts will be undertaken through advisory committees of national experts and committees of the European Parliament.[44] The details of the new arrangements are likely to be em-

---

[40] European Governance, COM(2001) 428 final, [20]–[29]; Institutional Architecture, COM (2002) 728 final, [1.2], [1.3.4]; Proposal for a Council Decision Amending Decision 1999/468/EC Laying Down the Procedures for the Exercise of Implementing Powers Conferred on the Commission, COM(2002) 719 final, 2; Final Report of Working Group IX on Simplification, CONV 424/ 02, Brussels 29 November 2002, 12.

[41] This was implicitly acknowledged by the Committee on Legal Affairs, On the Power of Legislative Delegation, A-7 0110/2010, Rapporteur J Sjazer, 12–13.

[42] Working Group IX (n 2) 9.

[43] CONV 724/03, Annex 2, 94.

[44] Implementation of Art 290 of the Treaty on the Functioning of the European Union, COM (2009) 673 final; Council 17477/09, Implementation of the Treaty of Lisbon, Art 290, Art 291, Brussels, 11 December 2009; Committee on Legal Affairs A-7 0110/2010 (n 41); European Parliament resolution of 5 May 2010 on the power of legislative delegation, (2010/2021(INI)).

bodied in an Inter-institutional Agreement or Common Understanding, but it is clear from the discussion thus far that there are still considerable differences between the Commission, Council, and European Parliament as to the precise role of such committees in the process of enacting delegated acts.[45]

It might be argued that the controls over delegated acts in Article 290 TFEU are actually tougher than those that existed hitherto. This is contestable. The efficacy of these constraints was considered in the earlier discussion.[46] Suffice it to say for the present that the *ex ante* constraint, to the effect that the legislative act must lay down the essential principles on the relevant topic, was a condition embodied in the ECJ's case law, although it was not interpreted rigorously. The *ex post* controls that can be exercised by the Council or the European Parliament are revocation of the delegation, or veto of the particular delegated act. It is true that this has increased the European Parliament's power over delegated acts, but this is not true in relation to the Council, which could under the previous regime veto a secondary norm pursuant to the Comitology procedures. The limits of this aspect of the new regime must moreover be firmly borne in mind.

First, neither the Council nor the European Parliament is accorded any formal right to propose amendments to a delegated act, but only the power to prevent its entry into force. While threat of a veto might act as a lever to secure amendment, this does not alter the fact that Article 290 gives no such formal power.

Second, and most important, the exercise of the veto power is crucially dependent on understanding the proposed measure. The Council and European Parliament cannot decide whether to object to the delegated act unless they understand it. The Member State representatives on the Council clearly have neither the time nor expertise to perform this task unaided. They fly in for meetings lasting one or two days, and are normally members of their national executive. It is wholly implausible to imagine that they would be able to form a view about a delegated act without assistance of the kind hitherto provided by Comitology committees. The European Parliament committees might develop such expertise. However, they have hitherto drawn on informational resources from Comitology committees, but, assuming that such committees cease to operate in relation to delegated acts, then the relevant European Parliament committee will have less material to help it to comprehend the relevant measure and decide whether to object to it. The retention of advisory committees of Member State representatives under the new regime will not necessarily avail the European Parliament, since it would not have any linkage to such committees of the kind that existed hitherto. This explains the emphasis placed by the European Parliament on information flows concerning delegated acts to its own committees in order that they can exercise adequate scrutiny over such acts.[47]

---

[45] For more detailed discussion, see pp 267–269.   [46] p 61–64.
[47] Committee on Legal Affairs A-7 0110/2010 (n 41) 10.

Third, the preceding difficulties will be more pronounced given that the European Parliament and Council will have to raise any such objection within a short period specified by the legislative act, which will normally be somewhere between two and three months. The Council and European Parliament will therefore have to 'get their act together' pretty quickly if either seeks to prevent the non-legislative act becoming law. The reality is therefore that the Council will only be able to make a reasoned choice concerning a delegated act within the limited time available if it re-invents the very type of oversight that the Commission hoped to dismantle through the Lisbon Treaty provisions, or, what amounts to the same thing, de facto invests advisory committees with power of the kind hitherto exercised by its more powerful siblings, management, and regulatory committees.

It might be argued that the Commission will nonetheless still engage with national representatives through advisory committees, and that it has an interest in doing so, even if management and regulatory committees disappear from the terrain of delegated acts.[48] This may be so. It is, however, not unreasonable to assume that if the Council insisted on certain controls over the last 40 plus years then those controls mattered. Institutional players do not commonly fight institutional battles that are irrelevant or unimportant for the disposition of power. Likewise, if the Commission went to considerable lengths to devise a scheme for delegated acts with the express intent that it might lead to the demise of a regime that it has resisted for many years, then the assumption once again is that this matters, and that it will not necessarily be business as usual under the new regime.

(b) Legal dimension: delegated acts and judicial control

There are, as will be seen, significant legal problems concerning the relationship between delegated acts and implementing acts. These are best understood when the problems concerning the meaning of implementing acts have been examined. The present discussion will focus on legal issues pertaining to delegated acts.

(i) Formalism and delegated acts

It is important to appreciate at the outset that the depiction of delegated acts in Article 290 TFEU as being non-legislative acts is true only in a formalistic sense. They are non-legislative in the formal sense that they are not legislative acts, because they have not been made in accordance with the ordinary or special legislative procedure, this being the condition precedent for an act to be regarded as legislative in Article 289 TFEU.

---

[48] P Ponzano, 'Executive and Delegated Acts: The Situation after the Lisbon Treaty' in Griller and Ziller (n 1) 135–143.

Many such delegated acts will nonetheless be legislative in nature. This view is reinforced by the fact that they are said to be of general application, and can supplement or amend certain non-essential elements of legislative acts.[49] It is reinforced also because there is a separate provision dealing with administrative decisions.[50] The reality is therefore that a delegated act will often be what would be regarded in some domestic legal systems as secondary or delegated legislation. This was recognized by the Working Group, which depicted these acts as a new category of legislation.[51] It was also acknowledged by the European Parliament, whose report was explicitly prefaced on the premise that delegation was a 'delicate operation', whereby the Commission was instructed to exercise a power that was 'intrinsic to the legislator's own role'.[52]

(ii) Comitology and delegated acts

We have already seen from the preceding discussion that there is no mention of Comitology constraints among the *ex ante* or *ex post* controls listed in Article 290 TFEU. We have already seen that the institutional discussions thus far have been premised on the assumption that management and regulatory committees will not operate in the post-Lisbon world. Input and scrutiny will henceforth be undertaken by advisory committees of national experts and European Parliament committees.[53]

This is also likely to be the view taken by the ECJ should the issue come before it. The absence of any mention of Comitology within Article 290, combined with its express mention in relation to implementing acts, means that the ECJ would probably conclude that there is no place for management and regulatory committees in relation to delegated acts. It could be argued, moreover, that Comitology should have no place within Article 290 TFEU, since it would thereby unbalance the controls therein in favour of the Council, thereby upsetting the formal equality between Council and European Parliament on which Article 290 is based.[54]

It is nonetheless worth briefly adverting to arguments that might be used to legitimate the continued existence of Comitology. The ECJ could conclude that Comitology can operate within and via Article 290(2)(b) TFEU. This enables the Council and European Parliament to veto a delegated act. The argument would then be that Comitology is simply an informational device used by the Council in deciding whether to exercise its veto power, and that it does not constitute an independent or separate constraint. There are indeed echoes of this

---

[49] Art 290(1) TFEU.   [50] Art 288 TFEU.
[51] Final Report of Working Group IX (n 2) 8.
[52] European Parliament resolution (n 44) Preamble C.
[53] (N 44).
[54] Lenaerts and Desomer (n 1) 755; Committee on Legal Affairs A-7 0110/2010 (n 41) 11–12.

reasoning in the ECJ's earlier jurisprudence on Comitology. Thus in *Koster*[55] the ECJ conceptualized Comitology committees as not distorting the institutional balance within the Community, because they did not take decisions themselves, but merely served to send the matter back to the Council. This argument could be reinforced, moreover, by suitably framed wording in future Union legislation. Thus the legislative act delegating power to the Commission could explicitly state that in deciding whether to exercise the veto power over particular delegated acts the Council and European Parliament will draw on opinions provided by management and regulatory committees.

The alternative legal route to validate the continued existence of Comitology committees would be for the ECJ to interpret Article 290(2) TFEU as a non-exhaustive list of conditions. The legislative act could therefore specify conditions other than those listed, including Comitology.

(iii) Courts and ex ante control of delegated acts

There are, as we have seen, controls over the enactment of delegated acts. The Union courts will adjudicate on disputes concerning these issues. The legal as well as political reality, however, is that the *ex post* controls relating to withdrawal of the delegation and veto of a delegated act reside with the Council and European Parliament. These issues may give rise to adjudication before the Union courts, but this does not alter the fact that it is the Council and European Parliament that decide whether to activate these constraints.

The principal focus of judicial control is therefore in relation to the *ex ante* limits on delegation in Article 290 TFEU: the legislative act can only delegate power to supplement or amend certain non-essential elements of the legislative act, and the objectives, content, scope, and duration of the delegation of power must be explicitly defined in the legislative act. It will be for the Union courts to police these limits on delegation, and the intensity with which they do so will be central to the new regime.

It is important prior to consideration of the Court's case law to be mindful of the issues dealt with through Commission implementing regulations, many thousands of which are issued each year. The paradigm prior to the Lisbon Treaty was that the primary legal norm governing an area, whether a regulation, directive, or decision, was supplemented by Commission implementing regulations. The latter were norms of general application, addressed to the relevant group, whatsoever it might be, which specified in greater detail an issue that had been mentioned at some level of generality in the primary legal act. The additional specification provided through the secondary legal acts was often very significant. Such acts would, *inter alia*, embody regulatory choices, allocate

---

[55] Case 25/70 *Einfuhr- und Vorrasstelle fur Getreide und Futermittel v Koster, Berodt & Co* [1970] 2 ECR 1161, [9].

risk and responsibility as between Community and Member States, and fill gaps revealed in the efficacy of the primary regulation, which was why the Council and the European Parliament sought input through Comitology committees.[56] This was recognized by the Committee of Legal Affairs, which prefaced its report on Article 290 TFEU by stating that delegated acts have important implications in many areas, the corollary being that it was of 'paramount importance' that such acts should be subject to democratic control.[57]

The ECJ deployed a non-delegation doctrine prior to the Lisbon Treaty, insisting that the primary legal norm should specify the essential elements of the regulatory schema, but this review was not particularly intensive. Thus in *European Parliament v Commission*[58] the former sought annulment of a Commission implementing regulation on the ground that it extended the ambit of organic foodstuffs to cover products containing genetically modified microorganisms and thereby undermined the objectives of the basic regulation relating to consumer expectations, conditions of fair competition, free movement of organic products, and balance between agricultural production and environmental protection. The Commission, by way of response, argued that the basic regulation did not prohibit the use of genetically modified organisms or microorganisms in organic farming, and did not preclude their addition to the list of substances authorized for use as ingredients or processing aids, with the consequence that the contested regulation should be regarded as lawful.

The ECJ affirmed that a basic regulation should contain the essential elements of the matter to be dealt with and that these should be respected in any implementing regulation. It held that the main purpose of the basic regulation was to define a framework of Community rules on production, labelling, and inspection so that organic farming could be protected. It concluded that the contested provisions in the secondary regulation did not go beyond the principles laid down by the basic regulation, primarily because the basic regulation did not preclude use of genetically modified organisms in organic food production.

It was not easy, therefore, to convince the ECJ to annul a secondary regulation on the ground that it violated the essential principles in the primary or basic

---

[56] See, eg, in relation to Structural Funds, Commission Regulation (EC) 1681/94 of 11 July 1994 concerning irregularities and the recovery of sums wrongly paid in connection with the financing of the Structural Policies and the organization of information systems in this field [1994] OJ L178/43; Commission Regulation (EC) 2064/97 of 15 October 1997 establishing detailed arrangements for the implementation of Council Regulation (EEC) 4253/88 regards the financial control by Member States of operations co-financed by the Structural Funds [1997] OJ L290/1; Commission Regulation (EC) 438/2001 of 2 March 2001 laying down detailed rules for the implementation of Council Regulation (EC) 1260/99 as regards the management and controls systems for assistance granted under the Structural Funds [2001] OJ L63/21; Commission Regulation (EC) 448/2004 of 10 March 2004 the eligibility of expenditure of operations co-financed by the Structural Funds [2004] OJ L72/66.

[57] Committee on Legal Affairs A-7 0110/2010 (n 41) Preamble E.

[58] Case C-156/93 *European Parliament v Commission* [1995] ECR I-2019, [18]–[25].

regulation governing that area.[59] Nor have claimants found it easy to convince the ECJ that the essential principles in the primary regulation were not set out with sufficient specificity so as to guide the Commission when it made the further regulation. It remains to be seen to what extent the ECJ polices the requirement in Article 290 TFEU that the objectives, content, scope, and duration of the delegation of power must be explicitly defined in the legislative act.

It will not be easy, however, for the legislative act to define with real precision the 'objectives, content, scope and duration' of the delegation. The Council and the European Parliament will often have neither the knowledge, nor the time to delineate precise parameters for the exercise of delegated regulatory choices in the legislative act. The real issues about the assignment of regulatory risks and choice will often only be apparent when the matter is examined in detail, which was one of the very reasons that the Comitology process was first created. These difficulties may influence the intensity of judicial review where a claimant argues that the legislative act was insufficiently precise about the 'objectives, content, scope and duration' of the delegation, the ECJ being unwilling to review too vigorously because mindful of the difficulties faced by the legislature in specifying these matters with greater precision.[60]

The net effect will nonetheless be that the delegation leaves some significant measure of regulatory choice to the Commission, and that the resolution of such choice is not pre-determined either by the essential elements in the legislative act, or by the objectives, content etc of the delegation laid down by the legislative act.

(iv) Courts and ex post control over delegated acts

It will also be for the ECJ to resolve legal issues concerning the *ex post* controls over delegated acts in Article 290 TFEU. Two issues are of particular significance.

First, there are matters concerning the exercise of the controls that are listed in Article 290, revocation of the delegation and veto of the delegated act. It should be emphasized that these controls can be exercised by the Council or the European Parliament. The Commission's position can be summarized as follows: delegations should normally not be subject to a temporal limit, more

---

[59] See also, Case 25/70 *Koster* (n 55); Case 23/75 *Rey Soda v Cassa Conguaglio Zucchero* [1975] ECR 1279, [10], [14]; Case 121/83 *Zuckerfabrik Franken v Hauptzollamt Wurzburg* [1984] ECR 2039; Case 46/86 *Romkes v Officier van Justitie* [1987] ECR 2685, [16]; Cases C-296 and 307/93 *France and Ireland v Commission* [1996] ECR I-795, [17]–[20]; Case C 303/94 *European Parliament v Council* [1996] ECR I-2943; Case C-417/93 *European Parliament v Council* [1995] ECR I-1185, [30].

[60] The non-delegation doctrine in the US is barely enforced by the courts, A Aman and W Mayton, *Administrative Law* (West Group, 2001) ch 1; J Rogers, M Healy, and R Krotoszynski, *Administrative Law* (Aspen Publishers, 2003) 312–345.

especially because there is in any event a power to revoke the delegation;[61] the institution wishing to revoke a delegation should 'ideally' give reasons for doing so, in order to explain its position to the other co-legislator and to enable the Commission to learn lessons for the future;[62] the period within which the European Parliament and Council can veto the measure should normally be two months, the time beginning to run from the moment when the delegated act is transmitted by the Commission;[63] and there should be provision for urgent situations where the delegated act becomes operative immediately, subject to the possibility of veto within a period of approximately six weeks.[64]

The European Parliament differed in certain significant points of detail:[65] it accepted that a delegation could be indefinite, because it could be revoked at any time, but also emphasized that a delegation could be for a limited period, subject to periodic renewal; it argued that the time limit for the veto power should be set on a case-by-case basis, with two months as a minimum; and it felt that use of the urgent procedure should be limited to very serious cases and that most such instances could be dealt with through a requirement of early non-objection by the Council and Parliament. These differences will have to be resolved through a Common Understanding or Inter-institutional Agreement.

Second, there is the more far-reaching issue as to whether the *ex post* controls listed in Article 290 TFEU are to be regarded as exhaustive or illustrative. The European Parliament's Committee on Legal Affairs argued strongly for the latter interpretation.[66]

Article 290 TFEU gives the Legislator the freedom to choose the control mechanism(s) to put in place. It mentions two such means of control purely by way of example. To conclude that these two means of control form an exhaustive list would not only be contrary to the plain wording of Article 290 TFEU but would also be contrary to the underlying philosophy whereby the Legislator is delegating a power which is intrinsic to its own role and must therefore be sure of being able to retain proper control over its use. This implies the widest possible margin of appreciation in determining how to control a delegation.

The controls listed in Article 290 should, in the Committee's view, operate in relation to every delegated act, but this should not preclude other controls being imposed. The Committee identified two further such controls.

It contended that there could be a requirement that the delegated act should only take effect if expressly approved by the Council and European Parliament, which would thereby complement the express veto power in Article 290 with a more powerful requirement that the Commission should have to secure affirmative approval of the delegated act before it could take effect. The other example proffered by the Committee was a condition whereby the Council and European

---

[61] COM(2009) 673 (n 44) [3.2].   [62] ibid [5.2].   [63] ibid [5.3.1].
[64] ibid [5.3.4].   [65] European Parliament resolution (n 44).
[66] Committee on Legal Affairs A-7 0110/2010 (n 41) 9.

Parliament could repeal a delegated act that was already in force, which would give the co-legislators a powerful control where the full implications of the delegated act might not be apparent when it was initially enacted.[67] The European Parliament followed its Committee's thinking on this issue when it formulated its resolution.[68]

It is not clear whether the Council would support such controls, although it might well do so since they would offset the loss of power through the demise of management and regulatory committees. It is safe to assume that the Commission would be opposed to control mechanisms other than those listed in Article 290.[69]

The difference of view in this respect is not merely explicable on the basis of practical considerations, although they will doubtless play a role in Commission thinking. The difference is also reflective of deeper divisions as to the very nature of delegated acts. The Commission's approach has always been that such measures are properly to be regarded as part of the executive function, which is vested in the Commission. It is readily apparent from the preceding quotation that the Committee on Legal Affairs does not share this view. It recognizes that delegation is necessary, but regards it as giving power that is intrinsic to its legislative role, the corollary being proper control over its use and a wide margin of institutional appreciation as to how this should be realized.

(v) Temporal dimension and delegated acts

There is a 'nice' legal question concerning the time at which the new regime in Article 290 TFEU takes effect. It is a matter of some practical importance, if the new schema is interpreted legally as having no place for Comitology committees that operated in this area hitherto. This raises the issue as to the status of such committees under Community legislation made prior to the Lisbon Treaty.

The 'radical view' would be that Article 290 TFEU operates from the moment that the Treaty enters into force, more especially because there is nothing in the Protocol on Transitional Provisions to suggest otherwise.[70] It might then be argued that if Article 290 is construed to preclude Comitology this should become operative immediately. This would cause significant practical and political problems.

The 'moderate view' would be that the regime in Article 290 TFEU takes effect whenever power is delegated under new Union legislation, or when Community legislation is amended in the post-Lisbon world. Thus Comitology

---

[67] ibid 10.
[68] European Parliament resolution (n 44) [2].
[69] COM(2009) 673 (n 44) contains no mention of any control device other than those mentioned in Art 290 TFEU.
[70] Protocol (No 36) On Transitional Provisions.

would continue to operate as mandated by previously enacted Community legislation, until it is amended.

The moderate view is to be preferred, and this is supported by the official documentation on Article 290.[71] The constraints on delegation in Article 290 must be viewed as a whole. The radical view would mean that Comitology constraints would be immediately inoperative, in circumstances where the relevant Community legislation delegating power to the Commission would not have been drafted so as to comply with the other conditions now required by Article 290 TFEU.

5. Lisbon Treaty and Implementing Acts

(a) Political dimension: objective and tension

(i) Pre-Lisbon

The nature of the difficulties created by the separate category of implementing act can only be appreciated by adverting to the pre-existing regime. We need, therefore, to take a step back before we can understand the significance of the new regime.

Article 202 EC was framed so as to allow delegation of power to the Commission for the 'implementation' of rules laid down by the Council, subject to the Comitology procedure. The term 'implementation' connoted in many instances delegated rule making or decision making subject to Comitology conditions: the Commission would, subject to Comitology procedures, enact secondary regulations or decisions that amended or supplemented the primary norm. 'Implementation' could also mean the execution of other norms, whether Treaty provisions, primary legislation, or delegated regulations. This latter sense of implementation was based on the premise that the norms would be taken as given, and they would be executed or applied: the existing rules in the primary law, or delegated regulation would not be substantively supplemented or amended. The Comitology procedure was created primarily for the first type of case, since the Member States sought input into the detailed secondary norms that would supplement or amend the primary legal act, but it applied also to implementation in the second sense.

It should, however, be emphasized that the line between the two senses of implementation could be a fine one, and there was significant variation as to the types of secondary norm concluded pursuant to Article 202. In reality there was a spectrum of secondary norms, with 'pure' rule making at one end, 'pure' implementation at the other, and many measures falling betwixt the two. This

---

[71] Council 17477/09 (n 44) Annex II; Committee on Legal Affairs A-7 0110/2010 (n 41) 12–13; European Parliament resolution (n 44) [18]–[19].

did not matter, however, pre-Lisbon since the same Treaty provision, Article 202 EC, applied to all such measures.

The term 'implementation' as used in Community legislation and on official websites thus covered what are now termed delegated acts, as well as the terrain covered by implementing acts. Thus the standard format in EC legislation was to empower the Commission to make 'implementing provisions', 'implementing rules', or 'determine detailed rules',[72] subject to Comitology, and the paradigmatic application was through delegated rule making or decision making that amended or supplemented the primary legal norm.[73] The same terminology was evident on official websites, where the term 'implementing provisions' carried the broad connotation used in Community legislation.[74]

(ii) Post-Lisbon

The discussion in the Convention on the Future of Europe revealed an important shift in thought in a double sense.

It was decided to create two categories of act below legislative acts. Delegated acts would be those which amended or supplemented the legislative act. Implementing acts were those which implemented or executed the legislative act without amendment or supplementation. Thus the Working Group on Simplification spoke in terms of implementing acts as 'acts implementing legislative acts, delegated acts or acts provided for in the Treaty itself'.[75] The idea was that there should be a hierarchy with legislative acts at the top, then delegated acts which would flesh out the detail or amend certain elements of a legislative act, to be followed by implementing acts that would, it seems, put into effect the

---

[72] See, eg, Regulation (EEC) No 729/70 of the Council of 21 April 1970 on the financing of the common agricultural policy [1970] OJ L94/13, Art 7(2); Council Regulation (EC) No 1260/1999 of 21 June 1999 laying down general provisions on the Structural Funds [1999] OJ L161/1, Arts 47–53; Council Reg 1/2003 (n 33) Art 33; Council Regulation (EC) No 1290/2005 of 21 June 2005 on the financing of the common agricultural policy [2005] OJ L209/1, Art 42.

[73] In the context of the Common Agricultural Policy, see eg, Commission Regulation (EC) 1663/95 of 7 July 1995, Laying Down Detailed Rules for the Application of Council Regulation (EEC) 729/70 Regarding the Clearance of Accounts of the EAGGF Guarantee Section [1995] OJ L158/6; Commission Decision 94/442/EC of 1 July 1994, Setting Up a Conciliation Procedure in the Context of the Clearance of Accounts of the EAGGF Guarantee Section [1994] OJ L182/45. In the context of the Structural Funds, see eg, (n 56). In the context of competition law, see eg, (n 38). In the context of public procurement, see eg, Commission Regulation (EC) No 1177/2009 of 30 November 2009 amending Directives 2004/17/EC, 2004/18/EC and 2009/81/EC of the European Parliament and of the Council in respect of their application thresholds for the procedures for the award of contracts [2009] OJ L314/64.

[74] See, eg, <http://ec.europa.eu/competition/antitrust/legislation/regulations.html>; <http://ec.europa.eu/information_society/policy/ecomm/implementation_enforcement/index_en.htm>; <http://ec.europa.eu/internal_market/services/services-dir/implementation_en.htm>; <http://ec.europa.eu/internal_market/publicprocurement/legislation_en.htm>.

[75] Working Group IX (n 2) 9.

legislative or delegated act, but without thereby adding to the substance of what had already been decided.[76]

It was also decided that Comitology procedures were not relevant directly to the making of what are now delegated acts, even though this was the true analogy with the status quo ante.[77] The Convention documentation considered the legitimacy of Comitology primarily in the context of implementing acts covered in what is now Article 291 TFEU, where the emphasis is on implementation in its second sense, as execution or application. This was apparent from the reasoning of the Working Group.[78] It was apparent again in the Convention comments on what is now Article 291(3) TFEU, which provision allows Member State control over implementing acts.[79] The Praesidium stated that several amendments were opposed to the *current* mechanisms for the committee procedure, and wished to delete this Article, while other comments proposed confining the control mechanisms to advisory committees alone. The Praesidium considered that this was a matter for secondary legislation and therefore did not amend the Article.

It might be felt that the framers of the Lisbon Treaty were right to disaggregate delegated acts from implementing acts. This would be premature and any conclusion should be reserved until the problems created by this differentiation are examined. Commentators have been mindful of the difficulties consequent on the new typology of acts, and more especially the dichotomy between delegated and implementing acts. It is, however, important to press further to understand the root cause of this dilemma. The difficulties created by this divide will be explicated below, and it will be seen that there is a very real tension built into the Lisbon schema.

(b) Legal dimension: dichotomy and tension

(i) *Implementing acts and the paradigm case*

There are, as will be seen below, difficulties in deciding on the type of situation where implementing acts can be used. It is nonetheless useful

---

[76] It should be noted that the term 'implementing' is used in relation to the passage of a legal act where it is clear that it does not connote an implementing act for the purposes of Art 291 TFEU. Thus the EU is empowered to enact 'implementing regulations' in the context of the Structural Funds, Arts 164, 178 TFEU, but they do not constitute implementing acts for the purposes of Art 291 TFEU, since these 'implementing regulations' are made pursuant to the ordinary legislative procedure, and hence are legislative acts for the purposes of the Lisbon Treaty. It is, moreover, reasonably clear that the term 'implementing measures', the absence of which is the trigger for the liberalized standing rules under Art 263(4) TFEU, does not bear the same meaning as 'implementing acts' in Art 291 TFEU.

[77] This is recognized in Committee on Legal Affairs A-7 0110/2010 (n 41) 7, 12–13.

[78] Working Group IX (n 2) 9.

[79] CONV 724/03, Annex 2, 94.

for the sake of clarity to begin with the paradigm case where Article 291 TFEU will apply. We should recall that this is where uniform conditions are required for implementing legally binding Union acts. Those acts then 'shall' confer implementing powers on the Commission, or, in certain cases on the Council.

The paradigmatic application of Article 291 TFEU is not the 'implementation' of the primary legislative act itself. If the primary legislative act is a regulation then it is directly applicable within the Member States' legal systems, and is binding as to means as well as ends. It does not require adoption or transformation before it acquires legal force within those systems.[80] The primary legislative regulation might specify facets of its implementation, but these would then be directly applicable in the same way as the remainder of the regulation. There is therefore no need for recourse to Article 291 in relation to implementation of the legislative act itself.[81]

The same conclusion is true, albeit for different reasons, where the primary legislative act is a directive. A directive leaves Member States with discretion as to means of implementation. That is its very raison d'être. It would therefore be contradictory to empower the Commission to impose uniform conditions for implementation of the directive itself. If this occurred it would create a new hybrid species of primary legislative act, in which the means of implementation, normally left to the discretion of the Member States, would be exercised or circumscribed by the Commission.

The paradigmatic case where Article 291 TFEU would be used is rather in relation to particular provisions of the regulation, directive, or decision. There can be instances where past experience reveals that particular provisions of a primary legislative act have been implemented differently in different Member States and that greater uniformity is required. There can also be instances where future changes in the subject matter dealt with by the legislative act require grant of implementing power to the Commission to ensure that such changes do not jeopardize uniformity.

This can be exemplified by the Directive on Insider Trading and Market Manipulation.[82] The Commission is granted power to adopt implementing measures in order to take account of technical developments on financial markets and to ensure uniform application of the Directive.[83] The implementing

---

[80] Case 34/73 *Variola v Amministrazione delle Finanze* [1973] ECR 981.

[81] A regulation might require consequential changes in other areas of national law, but where this is so the nature of those amendments are bound to differ as between the Member States, precisely because their previous laws in the area will often be very diverse. It will not be possible, therefore, to contemplate uniform changes to these other national legal provisions that could be stipulated by the Commission. The Member States would simply have the obligation, pursuant to Art 291(1) TFEU, to adopt all measures necessary to implement legally binding Union acts.

[82] Directive 2003/6/EC of the European Parliament and of the Council of 28 January 2003 on insider dealing and market manipulation [2003] OJ L96/16.

[83] ibid Art 6(10).

measures relate to matters such as: the technical modalities for appropriate public disclosure of inside information, and for delaying the public disclosure of inside information; the conditions under which issuers must draw up a list of those persons working for them and having access to inside information; the categories of persons subject to a duty of disclosure; and the type of transaction that triggers the duty to disclose.

The discussion thus far has been premised on the scenario in which there is a primary legislative act and an implementing act. It should be noted, however, that an implementing act may also be made pursuant to a delegated act. The Working Group on Simplification considered that it would be possible for implementing acts to be made pursuant to delegated acts, as well as legislative acts, and this is clearly correct in principle, given that delegated acts are legally binding.[84] There is nothing untoward in this as a matter of principle, and the instances where this might be desirable given above could be equally applicable here too.

An implementing act made pursuant to a delegated act could not, however, supplement or amend the primary legislative act. Any such measure would have to take the form of a further delegated act and be subject to the controls in Article 290. This leaves open the issue as to whether an implementing act made pursuant to a delegated act could supplement or amend the delegated act itself. The Treaty provides no foundation for suggesting that this is possible. It would moreover give unwarranted power to the Commission, which could, through the instrumentality of an implementing act, alter a delegated act without being subject to any of the controls in Article 290 TFEU.

Subject to this caveat, it would be possible for the Commission to enact a delegated regulation, for the Commission to decide that uniform implementing conditions are required, and for the Commission to then give itself the implementing power in the delegated regulation. This follows from the fact that where uniform conditions for implementation are required the legally binding Union act shall confer implementing power on the Commission. A delegated act is a legally binding Union act and could therefore mandate that implementing powers are given to the Commission. Whether this is desirable in normative terms is far more contestable. It would increase the Commission's degree of control over the legislative process taken as a whole. The only formal constraints would be for the Council or European Parliament to veto such a delegated act pursuant to Article 290 or for control to be exercised pursuant to Article 291(3).

(ii) Delegated acts, implementing acts, and principle

We have therefore identified the paradigm case where implementing acts are appropriate. It is now time to address the central difficulties that beset this aspect

---

[84] Working Group IX (n 2) 9–11.

of the Lisbon regime, which is the relationship between delegated acts and implementing acts.

Delegated acts can supplement or amend non-essential elements of a legislative act, subject to the conditions in Article 290 TFEU. There will therefore be difficult borderlines between instances of 'implementation', where recourse to Article 291 is warranted, and those where the later measures 'supplement or amend' the primary legislative act, where recourse must be had to Article 290 TFEU. Any measure that amends or supplements a legislative act must be a delegated act. Implementing acts are in that sense bounded by delegated acts. The two categories are mutually exclusive, as accepted by the Commission.[85]

This is especially significant because the conditions and controls over delegated acts are different from those over implementing acts. Delegated acts require a legislative statement as to the objective, scope, content, and duration of the delegation, the delegation can be revoked by the Council or the European Parliament and delegated acts are subject to veto by either institutional player. Implementing acts are under the control of the Commission, subject to the Comitology constraints devised pursuant to Article 291(3) TFEU.

The sphere of application of Article 291 is therefore limited by Article 290. A measure described as an 'implementing act' must be open to legal scrutiny. If this reveals that such a measure 'amends' or 'supplements' a primary legislative act then it should be annulled as *ultra vires*, since it should have been enacted as a delegated act subject to the conditions and controls in Article 290. This follows as a matter of first principle. It would otherwise be open to the Union institutions to undermine the schema in the Lisbon Treaty by depicting an act as an implementing act when it did not fulfil the criteria required by the Treaty itself.

The meaning given to 'amend' or 'supplement' in the context of delegated acts is therefore crucial for determining the divide between delegated acts and implementing acts. The extent to which this limits the sphere of application of implementing acts depends on the interpretation of these terms. The narrower the meaning given to 'amend' and 'supplement' when defining the sphere of application of delegated acts, the broader the remit of implementing acts. The broader the meaning accorded to 'amend' and 'supplement' for the purposes of Article 290 TFEU, the narrower the sphere left to implementing acts.

(iii) Delegated acts, implementing acts, and tension

The interpretation of these key terms is more complex than might initially be thought and reveals a tension at the heart of the Lisbon dichotomy between delegated and implementing acts.

The term 'amend' is the less problematic of the two, since it has a more definitive meaning, denoting a delegated act that formally changes some non-

---

[85] COM(2009) 673 (n 44) [2.2].

essential element of the legislative act. Thus if a legal act made pursuant to a legislative act amends the latter it must conform to the criteria and controls for delegated acts in Article 290 TFEU.[86]

The word 'supplement' is more nuanced and is not subject to such ready definition, as acknowledged by the Commission.[87] It clearly means something different from the term 'amend', since it would otherwise be redundant. It is therefore the meaning accorded to 'supplement' that will largely determine the respective spheres of application of Articles 290 and 291 TFEU. There is some 'precedent' for use of the word 'supplement' in a symmetrical manner with 'amend', such that the former connotes the addition of non-essential elements, while the latter captures the deletion thereof.

This use is evident in the 2006 amendment to the 1999 Comitology Decision,[88] which introduced the new regulatory procedure with scrutiny. Article 2 (2) of the 1999 Decision states that where a measure adopted under what was Article 251 EC provides for the adoption of measures of general scope designed to 'amend non-essential elements of that instrument, *inter alia*, by deleting some of those elements or by supplementing the instrument by the addition of new non-essential elements' then this must be done through the regulatory procedure with scrutiny. A similar interpretation is evident in the 2009 Commission Communication, where the Commission interprets 'supplement' to connote a measure that specifically adds new non-essential rules that change the framework of the legislative act, whereas conversely a measure intended only to give effect to the existing rules of the basic instrument should not be deemed a supplementary measure.[89]

It may well be questioned whether 'supplement' as used in this sense is really necessary, since the term 'amend' can cover addition as well as deletion. This meaning of the term 'supplement' serves, in any event, merely to push the issue one stage further back, since it invites inquiry as to when a secondary norm should be regarded as adding 'new' non-essential elements, and hence 'supplementing' the legislative act.

The answer depends in essence on the level of generality or specificity with which one views the relevant article of the legislative act in the manner explained below. Any conclusion as to whether a secondary measure 'supplements' a legislative act by adding 'new' non-essential elements will be premised, explicitly or implicitly, on some view as to the level of generality or specificity with which one approaches the inquiry.

This can be exemplified by reflecting on paradigm instances of secondary regulations made in the past pursuant to Article 202 EC. These secondary

---

[86] ibid [2.3].   [87] ibid [2.3].

[88] 2006/512/EC: Council Decision of 17 July 2006 amending Decision 1999/468/EC laying down the procedures for the exercise of implementing powers conferred on the Commission [2006] OJ L200/11.

[89] COM(2009) 673 (n 44) [2.3].

regulations in areas such as agriculture, the Structural Funds, energy, and financial services commonly fleshed out in greater detail an article of the primary regulation. They specified, for example, with greater exactitude the relative responsibilities of Commission and Member States when things went wrong under the Common Agricultural Policy (CAP); they delineated more clearly the requirements for independent certification bodies in relation to the Structural Funds; they articulated in more detail the authorization requirements for genetically modified foods; and they dealt with a plethora of issues large and small in the 'Lamfalussy world' that governs securities regulation, banking and the like.[90]

It is important to understand that all such measures necessarily involved some addition or supplementation to the primary norm. They were undeniably 'supplementary' in the sense that they brought greater exactitude to bear on the meaning of the relevant article of the primary norm, and often spelt out in considerably more detail the requisites of the regulatory regime. All such measures therefore added something to the primary norm. This will be equally true for any measure that is classified as an implementing act, since the very specification of uniform conditions of implementation will be 'adding' something to the enabling provision in the legislative or delegated act.

The Lisbon schema, however, demands differentiation between delegated and implementing acts. The key issue going forward is whether the measures adumbrated above will be regarded as 'supplementary' for the purposes of Article 290, insofar as this turns on whether the secondary measure introduces 'new' non-essential elements. The answer will, as stated above, depend on the level of generality or specificity with which the Union legislature and ECJ view the relevant articles of the legislative act. This demands the following inquiry and evaluation.

The legislature and Court may consider that the article in the legislative act has sufficiently resolved the relevant issues, the conclusion being that the secondary measure, while obviously imbuing the article of the legislative act with greater detail, does not supplement it by adding any 'new' non-essential element so as to trigger the need for recourse to Article 290. They might in other instances demand greater specificity from the relevant article in the legislative act, find that it is less definitive, the conclusion being that while it has provided sufficient guide as to essential principles, the secondary measure has nonetheless supplemented it by the addition of 'new' non-essential elements.

(iv) Delegated acts, implementing acts, and justification

The divide between the terrain of delegated and implementing acts will turn on the preceding determination. It is difficult to regard this as satisfactory. It is

---

[90] <http://ec.europa.eu/internal_market/securities/docs/lamfalussy/wisemen/final-report-wise-men_en.pdf>; <http://ec.europa.eu/internal_market/securities/monitoring/index_en.htm>; <http://ec.europa.eu/internal_market/finances/committees/index_en.htm#review>.

bound to generate inter-institutional disputes as to whether recourse should have been had to Article 290 or 291 TFEU. It calls into question the normative foundation for the differential controls that operate in relation to delegated and implementing acts. There will inevitably be instances where juxtaposition of acts will reveal scant reason as to why the 'supplementation' of the legislative act in the one instance should be regarded as a 'new' non-essential element, such that a delegated act is required, while in other instances this is not so, such that an implementing act can be used.

This problem will be exacerbated because the very determination of whether secondary norms should be classified in one way or another will perforce be influenced by practical political considerations. Thus the Lamfalussy regime is premised on secondary norms that are validated by processes more akin to those used in relation to implementing acts, with a strong role for a special Comitology-type regime.[91] The Lisbon schema does not fit with this regime, since Lamfalussy does not accord veto powers to the European Parliament in relation to what are now delegated acts. Lamfalussy is also premised on powerful Comitology constraints, and therefore would not fit Article 290 if such controls are not permitted in relation to delegated acts. There will be considerable pressure not to disturb the status quo, which means classifying Lamfalussy measures as implementing acts under the Lisbon Treaty. This is so even though some of these measures could well be regarded as entailing 'new' non-essential supplementation of the legislative act for the purposes of triggering delegated acts and Article 290.[92]

There are concerns, moreover, as to whether the European Parliament and Council should be excluded from the terrain of implementing acts. This made some sense on the premise that implementing acts truly accorded with a paradigm of pure implementation, which would properly be the preserve of the Commission and the Member States. If, however, the terms 'amend' and 'supplement' are interpreted narrowly, such that the sphere of implementing acts expands and that of delegated acts contracts, this justification loses force. The reality would then be that measures would be taken as implementing acts which involved in substance and reality supplementation of the legislative act through the articulation of detailed choices and value judgments that were not resolved in the legislative act itself. If this were to transpire then the European Parliament's success in securing

---

[91] See (n 90).

[92] The breadth of the 'implementing power' accorded to the Commission, subject to Comitology control, is significant. Thus, to take an example, Art 2(4) of Directive 2003/71/EC of the European Parliament and of the Council of 4 November 2003 on the prospectus to be published when securities are offered to the public or admitted to trading and amending Directive 2001/34/EC [2001] OJ L345/64 empowers the Commission, subject to Comitology controls, to adopt such implementing measures to ensure uniform conditions of application in relation to all the definitional issues listed in Art 2(1) of the Directive.

veto powers in relation to delegated acts would look increasingly like a Pyrrhic victory.

This is more especially so because while Comitology is expressly envisaged in relation to implementing acts[93] it is framed in terms of control by Member States. It is not even framed in terms of the Council, and says nothing of control by the European Parliament.

It might be argued that the preceding concerns are misplaced because recourse can be had to the ECJ's prior jurisprudence concerning the meaning of 'implementation' for the purposes of Article 202 EC. The Court, as we have seen, took a broad view of the term 'implementation', thereby legitimating delegation of power to the Commission, and did not readily find that delegation was unlawful for failure to specify the essential characteristics in the primary regulation.[94] It might be tempting to think that exactly the same jurisprudence can be applied to the legal order post-Lisbon. This cannot be correct.

The legal meaning of 'implementation' was developed by the ECJ when there was no distinction between delegated acts and implementing acts. The jurisprudence was premised on there being a single focal point for 'implementation', this being Article 202 EC, and there was no need to differentiate between different senses of implementation. The Lisbon Treaty distinguishes between delegated acts and implementing acts, specifying different conditions, criteria, and controls in the two instances.

The ECJ's task will therefore be harder. Its prior jurisprudence as to whether a legislative act enumerated the essential principles for the purposes of delegation will continue to be relevant, but that will not be the end of the inquiry. It will now have to decide whether the act made pursuant to a legislative act should properly be regarded as a delegated or implementing act, and the divide will turn on the meaning it ascribes to 'amend' and 'supplement' in Article 290 TFEU.

(v) Delegated acts, implementing acts, and interpretation

A new Treaty raises new interpretative problems, the resolution of which can sometimes lead to conclusions that might not easily be predicted. It is therefore fitting to conclude this part of the discussion by adverting to a possible argument that would cast the relationship between delegated and implementing acts in a new light.

The difficulties with the divide between delegated and implementing acts analysed above might tempt some to argue that Article 291 TFEU should be interpreted to permit supplementation and amendment of non-essential elements of the higher legal act, where this is necessary to achieve uniform conditions for implementation of binding legal acts. Any such argument should be rejected.

---

[93] Art 291(3) TFEU.   [94] pp 265–267.

If this had been the intent then it would surely have been written expressly into Article 291 TFEU, since it is far too important to be implied. It would moreover make nonsense of the divide between delegated and implementing acts, since if the latter could supplement or amend the higher legal act this would then invite the same control mechanisms as apply in relation to delegated acts. There would be no normative reason as to why the conditions and constraints should differ, thereby eradicating any distinction between the categories.

To argue the contrary in normative terms would require some reason as to why the types of conditions and controls over delegated acts that amend or supplement non-essential elements of a legislative act in the context of, for example, risk regulation, should not also be warranted if an act implementing risk regulation amended or supplemented the very same legislative act in the course of imposing uniform conditions of implementation. No such normative distinction is sustainable. It is the amendment or supplementation of the higher legal act that drives the normative argument for controls of the kind in Article 290. If such amendment of supplementation were to occur through an implementing act these normative arguments would be equally applicable. It is no answer in this respect to say that Comitology-type controls exist in relation to Article 291, since this simply begs the further inquiry that if implementing acts could supplement or amend a higher legal act then the *ex ante* and *ex post* constraints built into Article 290 should be applicable, either with or without Comitology.

It might further be contended that supplementation or amendment of the higher legal act can be countenanced where this is necessary to achieve the uniform conditions of implementation without thereby wholly eradicating the distinction between delegated acts and implementing acts because the former are non-legislative acts of general application, whereas the latter are not. This argument will not withstand examination.

It leaves unanswered the preceding point, that if the Treaty had intended such supplementation or amendment in relation to implementing acts it would have said so. It is moreover untenable in its own terms. The distinction between delegated acts and implementing acts cannot turn on the generalized nature of the former and the specific or individualized nature of the latter. This is to ignore the very wording of Article 291, which stipulates that implementing acts can be used where uniform conditions are required for implementation of a binding legal act. Thus by definition implementing acts can only be used where there is a generalized problem that requires the imposition of such uniformity across the EU. Such implementing acts do not therefore conform to an individualized measure as that term is commonly employed.

(vi) Implementing acts and the new Comitology regulation

Article 291(3) requires that there should be rules specified in advance as to the way in which a new Comitology regime might apply, to enable the Member

States to exercise control over implementing power exercised by the Commission pursuant to Article 291(2). The Commission has produced a draft regulation on this issue.[95] It is, at the time of writing, being considered by the European Parliament, and may therefore be amended. An outline of the Commission's proposal can nonetheless be given here.

The Commission emphasizes that control is to be exercised by the Member States, and that neither the Council nor the European Parliament are accorded a role on the committees, although they can have access to information about the proceedings.[96]

The Commission is equally keen to stress that the Treaty is framed in mandatory terms: where uniform conditions for implementation are required then these powers must be given to the Commission.[97] This is true, but misses the point made in the Draft Report of the Committee on Legal Affairs of the European Parliament.[98] It is for the legislators, the Council, and the European Parliament to identify in the basic act whether uniform conditions for implementation are truly required. The Commission may have a view on this, and submit a primary regulation framed in such terms. This does not alter the fact that it is for the Council and European Parliament to decide whether the condition for triggering Article 291(2) is met or not.

The Commission proposes that the new Comitology regime should have two procedures, the advisory procedure and the examination procedure. In both instances the Commission submits a draft of the implementing act to the committee composed of Member State representatives, chaired by the Commission. It is open to the Commission to revise the measure in the light of the committee discussion at any time before the committee has delivered its opinion. The committee gives its opinion within a time limit set by the Commission. The committee deliberations may be conducted through a written procedure, but a committee member may request that the committee should be convened. This request, however, is not binding on the Commission.

The advisory procedure is the default procedure, in the sense that it is to be used except on the occasions when the examination procedure is mandated. Under the advisory procedure, as the name would indicate, the Commission decides on the implementing measures 'taking the utmost account of the conclusions' from the committee deliberations.[99]

---

[95] Proposal for a Regulation of the European Parliament and of the Council laying down the rules and general principles concerning mechanisms for control by Member States of the Commission's exercise of implementing powers, COM(2010) 83 final.

[96] ibid 3; Draft Art 8.

[97] ibid 2.

[98] Committee on Legal Affairs, on the proposal for a regulation of the European Parliament and of the Council laying down the rules and general principles concerning mechanisms for control by Member States of the Commission's exercise of implementing powers, PE 441.207, Rapporteur, J Sjazer, 8.

[99] COM(2010) 83 (n 95) Draft Art 4.

The examination procedure[100] applies in relation to implementing measures of general scope and other such measures that relate to certain subject matter areas,[101] but even this is subject to the caveat that the advisory procedure may be used in these cases where it is considered to be appropriate. Under the examination procedure, the measure is, subject to limited exceptions, adopted by the Commission if it is in accordance with the committee's opinion, and it may also be adopted if the committee gives no opinion. If the committee does not agree with the draft measure then it is prima facie not adopted, but the Commission can submit an amended version or request the committee to consider the matter further. It can also adopt the measure in the face of a negative committee vote where non-adoption would significantly disrupt markets, or create a risk for the security or safety of humans or for the EU's financial interests.

The Commission's Draft Regulation also makes provision for implementing measures to be immediately applicable on grounds of urgency. It is for the enabling act in a particular area to stipulate that this option can be used.

The final shape of the Comitology regime under Article 291 depends on any amendments secured by the Council and European Parliament to the draft outlined above. The European Parliament's Legal Affairs Committee has already signalled its desire for some changes. Thus it has suggested that an implementing measure subject to the examination procedure should not be adopted where the committee has given no opinion. It has also proposed amendments that directly or indirectly call into question the Commission's view that implementing measures are about the Commission and the Member States, and not the Council or the European Parliament. Thus the Draft Report of the Legal Affairs Committee[102] recommends amendment whereby information about committee proceedings should not only be accessible to the European Parliament and the Council, but actively transmitted to them by the Commission. It has in similar vein argued for a provision whereby the European Parliament and the Council can indicate to the Commission that they consider a draft implementing act to exceed the implementing powers given in the basic act.

6. Lisbon Treaty and Incomplete Categorization

The discussion thus far has considered the schema of legal acts in the Lisbon Treaty and the problems presented by this novel regime. It would, however, be wrong to conclude this discussion without adverting to the incompleteness of the Lisbon categorization.

---

[100] COM(2010) 83 (n 95) Draft Art 5.
[101] ibid Draft Art 2(b): Common Agricultural Policy; environment, security and safety or protection of the health or safety of humans, animals or plants; common commercial policy.
[102] Committee on Legal Affairs, PE 441.207 (n 98).

We have seen that legislative acts, delegated acts, and implementing acts can in principle take the form of regulations, directives, or decisions, subject to the caveats noted above. We have also seen that each type of legal act has its own criteria. Legislative acts are defined formally in accordance with the procedure for their enactment. Delegated acts must be made pursuant to a legislative act, they must be of general application, and they amend or supplement non-essential elements of the legislative act. Implementing acts are premised on the need for uniform conditions of implementation. This leaves an interesting inquiry as to the status and nature of acts that do not seem to fit any of these categories.

Consider, for example, a standard administrative decision addressed to a particular person, which falls within the definition of decision in Article 288 TFEU. It will not be a legislative act, if it is not made by a legislative procedure. It will not be a delegated act, since these can only be made pursuant to a legislative act and must be of general application. It will not be an implementing act, since the paradigm administrative decision addressed to a particular person has nothing to do with uniform conditions for implementation as that term is used in Article 291.

There are then two possible consequences. We might conclude that such decisions cannot legally be made. This would, however, lead to very considerable practical difficulties and fly in the face of Article 288, which clearly contemplates a decision addressed to a particular person. The alternative is to accept that such decisions can be legally made, but to acknowledge that they may not fit into the categories of legislative, delegated, or implementing act, the corollary being that the hierarchy of legal acts composed of these three categories does not capture the totality of the ways in which legal norms are made in the post-Lisbon world.

7. Lisbon Treaty and the Common Foreign and Security Policy

The Lisbon Treaty establishes the hierarchy of legal acts analysed above. While the Lisbon Treaty has dismantled the formal Pillar system that applied hitherto, there are nonetheless distinct rules concerning the legal acts that can be used for the Common Foreign and Security Policy (CFSP). A brief overview of these measures will be given here, with more detailed treatment in a later chapter.[103]

Article 25 TEU provides that the Union shall conduct the common foreign and security policy through a number of measures. General guidelines must be defined, this being a matter for the European Council.[104] Decisions should be adopted defining actions to be undertaken by the Union, positions to be taken by the Union, and arrangements for the implementation of the preceding decisions. These decisions are taken primarily by the Council on the basis of the general

---

[103] Ch 10.   [104] Arts 26(1), 42(2) TEU.

guidelines decided by the European Council.[105] It is unclear, however, whether the term 'decision' used in this context bears the same meaning as in Article 288 TFEU,[106] although this seems doubtful given the specific contexts in which the decision is used in relation to the CFSP. The CFSP is also to be furthered through strengthening systematic cooperation between Member States in the conduct of policy. The CFSP is put into effect by the High Representative and by the Member States, using national and Union resources. Legislative acts cannot be undertaken in relation to the CFSP,[107] and the general rule is that decisions are taken unanimously, although there is provision for qualified majority voting in certain instances.[108]

8. Conclusion

The EEC has, from its very inception, used both primary and secondary norms to achieve Community goals. There have always been secondary norms, which were made pursuant to an earlier hierarchically superior 'parent' act. This could be discerned by the cognoscenti, but the distinction was not readily apparent from any difference in the formal label attached.

The Constitutional Treaty and Lisbon Treaty sought to simplify the pre-existing regime and to ascribe the types of control that were appropriate to different kinds of legal act. This was a laudable aim. It is nonetheless contestable how far it has been achieved. The division of legal acts in the Lisbon Treaty is problematic, particularly that between delegated and implementing acts. This in turn generates question as to the normative justification for the differential controls prescribed for these kinds of act.

Successive periods of the Community's existence have witnessed inter-institutional disputes as to the legal base on which measures have been enacted, as the key institutional players sought to maximize their input into the legislative process and defend their prerogatives against actual or perceived encroachment. The battle terrain has altered over time. Treaty reform has rendered old battles otiose and provided new grounds for legal hostilities. The Lisbon Treaty continued previous policy by extending the powers of the European Parliament via the ordinary legislative procedure to new areas, thereby obviating earlier inter-institutional skirmishes as to the proper legal base for the making of primary regulations, directives, and decisions. The Lisbon Treaty has at the same time laid the foundation for novel disputes.

The European Parliament fought long and hard over 30 years to secure its rightful involvement in the passage of secondary norms. It justly argued that it should not be excluded from the making of secondary norms where the primary

---

[105] Arts 26(2), 28, 29, 42(4), 43 TEU.
[106] de Witte (n 1) 90.   [107] Art 31 TEU.   [108] Art 31 TEU.

norm was enacted by co-decision. It regarded its role under the 1999 Comitology Decision as insufficient in this respect and its pressure finally secured the 2006 amendment and the regulatory procedure with scrutiny. It has now been accorded direct veto powers under Article 290 TFEU. It will, judged from past practice, fight hard to defend its prerogatives. It will not therefore look kindly on a narrow interpretation of 'amend' and 'supplement', the terms which are central to the divide between delegated and implementing acts. The European Parliament has already signalled its concerns, stating that 'in order to fully preserve the legislator's prerogatives, special attention should be given to the relative use of Articles 290 and 291 TFEU and to the practical consequences of having recourse to one article or the other'.[109] If such matters cannot be resolved through political discourse there will inevitably be resort to the ECJ, and the European Parliament will once again defend its prerogatives in the legislative process.

---

[109] European Parliament resolution (n 44) [20].

8

The Treaty, the Economic, and the Social

It would clearly be impossible within the scope of this book to examine in detail all the substantive provisions of the Lisbon Treaty. Nor is that the objective. It is nonetheless important to consider the principal changes made to the substance and architecture of what was hitherto the EC Treaty. The theme within this chapter is to approach the topic through examination of the balance between the economic and the social.[1] This has been a perennial concern within the EU,[2] and it is therefore instructive to view the Lisbon Treaty through this lens.

The discussion begins with consideration of the tension and debates about the balance between the economic and the social prior to the Lisbon Treaty, since it is necessary to appreciate the evolution of EU law in this respect. The focus then turns to consideration of the debates leading to the Constitutional Treaty, and more particularly the input of the Working Groups on Social Europe and Economic Governance. This is followed by analysis of the Lisbon Treaty itself, which is divided into three parts. It begins by examining the foundational precepts in the Lisbon Treaty, the values, objectives, and considerations that are mandated to be taken into account in developing EU policy. There will then be overviews respectively of the economic and social provisions of the Lisbon Treaty, to see how far they represent continuity with the past, and how far they contain novel elements.

---

[1] J Shaw (ed), *Social Law and Policy in an Evolving European Union* (Hart, 2000); P Rodière, *Droit social de l'Union européenne* (LGDJ, 2nd edn, 2002); J-F Flauss (ed), *Droits sociaux et droit européen: bilan et prospective de la protection normative* (Bruylant, 2003); T Hervey and J Kenner (eds), *Economic and Social Rights under the EU Charter of Fundamental Rights* (Hart, 2003); G de Búrca (ed), *EU Law and the Welfare State, In Search of Solidarity* (Oxford University Press, 2005); M Dougan and E Spaventa (eds), *Social Welfare and EU Law* (Hart, 2005); G de Búrca and B de Witte (eds), *Social Rights in Europe* (Oxford University Press, 2005); U Neergaard, R Nielsen and L Roseberry (eds), *The Services Directive: Consequences for the Welfare State and the European Social Model* (Djof Publishing, 2008); M Krajewski, U Neergaard, J van de Grondon (eds), *The Changing Legal Framework for Services of General Interest in Europe* (TMC Asser, 2009).

[2] There is a very large literature on social rights. A helpful bibliography can be found in de Búrca and de Witte (n 1) 383–408.

1. EC Treaty

(a) Output legitimacy: original intent and subsequent development

(i) The Treaty framers', peace, and economic prosperity

It is axiomatic that any form of collective action entails some loss of autonomy.[3] There are the direct costs of organizing the group, combined with the indirect costs of individual autonomy foregone, since the group's choice will often be expressed through majority voting. Collective action also has benefits. The group will often be more powerful than any individual; it will bring together expertise; it will spread the workload; it will normally have greater resources than any individual; and it can facilitate attainment of goals that could not have been otherwise achieved. Collective action will be the preferred option when the benefits outweigh the costs, which is increasingly the case in modern society.

The rationale for collective action serves to explain in part the Member State's willingness to sacrifice some autonomy by joining the EU.[4] This was initially perceived in terms of outcomes, the justification flowing from the peace and prosperity by being part of the club. Legitimacy was thus conceived of largely in terms of economic output, and increase in aggregate output was felt to justify diminution in Member State autonomy. Improved prosperity would result from the creation of the common market, with the attendant breaking down of trade barriers and free flow of factors of production.

The Member State's willingness to sacrifice autonomy by joining the EU was also influenced by the need to deal with externalities. An enduring insight from integration theory is that cross-border flows of goods create international policy externalities, which in turn create incentives for policy coordination.[5] The key issue then becomes not whether States interact, but how. They can do so by *ad hoc* international agreements. Some more permanent form of international cooperation may be preferred to reduce the transaction costs of *ad hoc* coordination. This is especially so when the number of parties becomes larger, and the issues on which they seek to coordinate become broader. Delegation of power

---

[3] J Buchanan and G Tullock, *The Calculus of Consent: Logical Foundations of Constitutional Democracy* (University of Michigan Press, 1962); M Olson, *The Logic of Collective Action: Public Goods and the Theory of Groups* (Harvard University Press, 1965).

[4] A Moravcsik, 'Preferences and Power in the European Community: A Liberal Intergovernmentalist Approach' (1993) 31 JCMS 473, 480–481.

[5] Moravcsik, 'Preferences' (n 4) 485; W Wessels, 'The Modern West-European State and the European Union: Democratic Erosion or a New Kind of Polity?' in in S Andersen and K Eliassen (eds), *The European Union: How Democratic Is It?* (Sage, 1996) ch 4; G Majone, 'The European Community Between Social Policy and Social Regulation' (1993) 31 JCMS 153 and 'The Rise of the Regulatory State in Europe' (1994) West European Politics 1; P Craig, 'Integration, Democracy and Legitimacy' in P Craig, and G de Búrca (eds), *The Evolution of EU Law* (Oxford University Press, 2nd edn, 2010) ch 1.

to supranational institutions can moreover lend credibility to Member State bargains.

This conception of legitimacy was prominent in the thinking of those who shaped the EEC. For Monnet and kindred spirits the legitimacy of the Community was to be secured through outcomes, peace, and prosperity. The ECSC was established in part to render a third European war impossible. The founders of the EEC hoped it would lead to further political integration, but were mindful of the economic benefits of a common market. Peace and prosperity were the potent benefits for the people of Europe after war and economic protectionism. These benefits were to be secured through technocratic elite-led guidance. Democracy was, by way of contrast, a secondary consideration, hence the limited powers accorded to the Assembly. When attention was directed towards the 'people' the notion of democracy was attenuated. The focus was on the way in which the success of the EEC, measured in terms of outcomes, would generate loyalty to, and acceptance of, the Community institutions. It was not directed towards the issue of whether normal democratic controls should form an important part of the Community order.

The same patterns of thought were central to the work of the neofunctionalists.[6] Legitimacy was conceived largely in terms of outcomes, more specifically increased economic prosperity, to be secured through gains made possible by technocracy. Discussion of democracy was directed towards the loyalty which people might display towards the Community, and to the 'permissive consensus' necessary to enable the technocratic elite to perform their tasks. Standard democratic controls were perceived as important only where governmental changes led to significant alteration in policy, with consequential deprivations or rewards to particular groups. It was felt, by way of contrast, that an agreed aim of wealth maximization would sublimate social cleavage, and dissolve political conflict. The attainment of this objective was to be entrusted to the experts, the technocrats.

(ii) The Rome Treaty, the economic, and the social

It was unsurprising then that the Rome Treaty encapsulated and reflected the predominance of the economic. It established a common market that went beyond a customs union by providing for free movement of factors of production in order to facilitate the optimal allocation of resources. It embodied what might be termed 'flanking policies' designed to prevent either the State or private parties impeding the creation of a level playing field, as exemplified by the prohibition

---

[6] E Haas, *The Uniting of Europe: Political, Social and Economic Forces 1950–1957* (Stanford University Press, 1958); L Lindberg, *The Political Dynamics of European Economic Integration* (Stanford University Press, 1963); L Lindberg and S Scheingold, *Europe's Would-Be Polity: Patterns of Change in the European Community* (Prentice-Hall, 1970); L Lindberg and S Scheingold, *Regional Integration* (Harvard University Press, 1970).

on State aids, and the rules on competition. The Treaty provisions on negative integration were complemented by those to enhance positive integration, most notably through harmonization of laws, the latter requiring unanimity.

The discussion leading to the Rome Treaty included debate as to whether the emergent Community should engage in social policy. The result was largely negative.

Social dumping was not perceived as a serious threat, and the Member States were reluctant to transfer power in the sensitive areas dealt with by national social policy. Moreover, competence was also restricted since it was believed that once economic integration had been achieved it would spill over to the social field. The creation of the internal market would boost Member States' economy, their people would be better off in terms of living standards, and thus there would be less need for a social Europe.

Social welfare was therefore addressed primarily as an adjunct of the creation of a common market.[7] Thus the principal legislative competence in relation to social welfare was found in the Treaty provisions concerning free movement of workers. It was felt with justification that the economic reality of free movement could only be secured if the workers had some social welfare entitlements in the host country. This was the rationale for Article 51 EEC, which empowered the Community to make regulations for the aggregation and payment of welfare benefits across the Member States. More ambitious efforts to make harmonization of social regulation a pre-condition of economic integration foundered.[8] It was possible in principle to harmonize social regulation through what was Article 100 EEC, if the requisite connection with market integration could be shown, but this was not fertile ground for such measures because of the unanimity requirement, combined with Member State resistance to Community regulation.

The Treaty Articles dealing directly with 'social policy' were limited in scope. Article 117 EEC recognized as an objective the need to improve working conditions and the standards of living for workers. Article 118 EEC accorded the Commission the duty of promoting close cooperation between Member States in the social field, in particular as regards, *inter alia*, employment, labour law and working conditions, vocational training, social security, and the right of association. The European Court of Justice (ECJ) gave a broad interpretation to Article 118,[9] but even when interpreted in this manner the Article gave only limited power to the Commission. The provision on gender equality in Article 119 EEC accorded the greatest power to the EEC, but even this was motivated by concern that was as much economic as social, this being the wish to ensure that

---

[7] G Falkner, *EU Social Policy in the 1990s. Towards a Corporatist Policy Community* (Routledge, 1998) 55–58.

[8] F Scharpf, 'The European Social Model: Coping with the Challenges of Diversity' (2002) 40 JCMS 645, 646.

[9] Cases 281, 283, 285, 287/85 *Germany v Commission* [1987] ECR 3203.

economies that paid women less than men did not thereby secure a competitive advantage when market barriers were broken down.[10]

The framers of the Rome Treaty did, however, take limited cognizance of another facet of social policy broadly conceived, insofar as they accorded special status to services provided by public utilities. They were not immune from the reach of Community policy, but were treated in a distinctive manner through Article 90 EEC. Thus, while public undertakings were under a duty not to maintain in force measures contrary to the Treaty, undertakings entrusted with the operation of services of general economic interest or having the character of a revenue-producing monopoly were subject to the Treaty rules, in particular those on competition, insofar as they did not obstruct the performance, in law or in fact, of the particular tasks assigned to them, subject to the caveat that the development of trade should not be affected to such an extent as would be contrary to the interests of the Community.

The economic was therefore dominant over the social in the initial Community ordering. Damjanovic and de Witte capture this succinctly.[11]

The original socio-economic model of the European Community as laid down in the Treaty of Rome could thus be described in a nutshell as follows. The well-being of the citizens is to be safeguarded in Europe by different mechanisms operating at different levels. The European Community contributes to it by promoting economic growth stemming from a common and competitive market, the establishment and functioning of which is the Community's primary task. The Member States, from their side, continue to provide specific welfare services within their social policy systems and their health and education systems (the 'core' of the welfare state), and also through their public utilities (the 'outer ring' of the welfare state), and all these are regarded to be within their primary responsibility. The Community only gets involved in these policy fields as far as strictly necessary for the functioning of the common market. Welfare integration at EC level was thus originally conceptualized as being related directly to the creation of a common market, as a precondition for the free movement of workers, or as a way of improving the efficiency of the provision of public services. True welfare values and social policy objectives outside the framework of the common market were practically not included in the original Treaty.

(iii) The Single European Act, tension, and contestation

The Rome Treaty was structured so as to lay down the principles governing core concepts such as free movement, with the stipulation that regulations, directives, and decisions should be enacted to make these principles a reality. The passage of these legislative initiatives became increasingly difficult during the 1970s and

---

[10] C Barnard, *EC Employment Law* (Oxford University Press, 2nd edn, 2000) 23.
[11] D Damjanovic and B de Witte, 'Welfare Integration through Law: The Overall Picture in the Light of the Lisbon Treaty', EUI Working Papers, Law, 2008/34, 5–6.

early 1980s, leading to what Middlemas termed a 'condition of immobility'.[12] The Council rejected social measures, such as directives on co-determination and worker consultation, and many others were stalled, awaiting a Council decision. There was growing concern that the Community's objectives were not being fulfilled.

The corollary was equally important. If the Community's legitimacy was to be judged in terms of outcomes, the prosperity that would accompany a single market, then falling short in this respect could threaten the entire Community project. The period from the early 1970s to the early 1980s has been characterized as the 'dark ages' for the Community.[13] Dankert, the President of the European Parliament, bemoaned the jungle of half-implemented treaties, and neglected Treaty articles, and spoke of institutions, such as the European Council, that owed their existence to a press release.[14] Wallace concluded that the Community had moved beyond other international regimes, but that it could drift towards them as 'recession at home and uncertainty abroad progressively undermine its authority'.[15]

It is therefore unsurprising that reform to facilitate completion of the internal market was the prominent feature of the Single European Act. The ideal of increased prosperity from a common market, freed from tariffs and quotas, in which goods and factors of production could move freely, was re-launched after the disappointment of the previous decade. This re-launch, however, served to increase the powers of the Community, most especially via Article 95 EC, and hence to intrude further on Member State autonomy, in order to deliver the economic gains that were promised from the club. The very need to increase the Community's powers to deliver the promised economic goals led to questions about the nature of 'market freedom', the limits on Member State autonomy that were deemed necessary to attain this goal, and the balance between the economic and the social within the EC.

Some commentators such as Streit and Mussler[16] defended the market orientation in the Rome Treaty, viewing it as a mechanism through which autonomous economic agents expressed their utility preferences across a European-wide market. The normative underpinnings of their view were explicitly Hayekian.

---

[12] K Middlemas, *Orchestrating Europe, The Informal Politics of the European Union 1973–1995* (Fontana, 1995) 90.

[13] J Caporaso and J Keeler, 'The European Union and Regional Integration Theory' in C Rhodes and S Mazey (eds), *The State of the European Union, Building a European Polity?* (Longman, 1995) 37; S George and I Bache, *Politics in the European Union* (Oxford University Press, 2001) ch 9.

[14] See, eg, P Dankert, 'The European Community—Past, Present and Future' in L Tsoukalis (ed), *The European Community, Past Present and Future* (Basil Blackwell, 1983) 8.

[15] W Wallace, 'Europe as Confederation: The Community and the Nation State' in *The European Community, Past Present and Future* (n 14) 68.

[16] M Streit and W Mussler, 'The Economic Constitution of the European Community—From Rome to Maastricht' in F Snyder (ed), *Constitutional Dimensions of European Economic Integration* (Kluwer Law International, 1996) 109–149.

They acknowledged that the original Treaty contained non-market elements, principally in the common policies for agriculture, iron and steel, and the like, but they deprecated such interventions in the market order, which they regarded as a failure. For Streit and Mussler it had been all down hill since then. The non-market elements had been strengthened through successive Treaty amendments. Community power over industrial policy, employment, economic and social cohesion all offered a 'considerable number of opportunities for the EC authorities to apply discretionary policies incompatible with the principle of undistorted competition'.[17] In their view the Treaty now 'allows for a broadly based policy of protecting the losers and of trying to pick the winners'.[18] It was, they believed, a rent seeking Community, using that phrase with all the opprobrium of the public choice school.[19]

Majone was the most prominent defender of the EC's market orientation.[20] He argued that the EC was a 'regulatory state', the principal objective being to combat market failure and produce outcomes that were Pareto-efficient. The Member States delegated regulatory competence to the EC to shield such issues from majoritarian government at national level. Majone therefore contended that precepts of majoritarian democracy were inappropriate for a Community which was principally concerned with economic integration. EC policy making by 'majoritarian' institutions would in his view inevitably produce outcomes that were not Pareto-efficient and would politicize regulatory policy. It would, moreover, lead to redistribution, since EU social policies would be used to compensate those who had lost out through market processes. For Majone, economic integration without political integration was only possible if economics and politics were kept as separate as possible, the conclusion being that attention should rather be focused on ensuring accountability and legitimacy within the non-majoritarian institutions that operated within the EC.

There were, however, many commentators who increasingly questioned the conception of market freedom that underpinned the Community. The 'completion' of the internal market threw this issue into sharp relief. Thus Heller responded to Streit and Mussler by noting the need for intervention to combat market failure, the fact that public intervention can be welfare enhancing, and that it would be 'shocking if the contemporary nation states of Europe which have spent so much political blood and effort in the development of sophisticated modes of organizing the labour, capital and transfer markets of mass industrial

---

[17] ibid 132.
[18] ibid 134.   [19] ibid 136–137.
[20] G Majone, 'The European Community between Social Policy and Social Regulation' (1993) 31 JCMS 153; *Regulating Europe* (Routledge, 1996); 'Europe's "Democracy Deficit": The Question of Standards' (1998) 4 ELJ 5; 'The Credibility Crisis of Community Regulation' (2000) 38 JCMS 273.

economies, were now to abandon that path in the embrace of the liberal constitution'.[21]

These concerns were echoed by Weiler who emphasized that completion of the single market went beyond the mere removal of technocratic obstacles to trade. It embraced, as Weiler noted,[22] 'a highly politicized choice of ethos, ideology and political culture: the culture of "the market"'. The removal of barriers to free movement was a means to maximize utility, premised on the assumption of formal equality of individuals, in which market efficiency was prized above other competing values.[23]

Scharpf voiced analogous concerns, speaking of the 'zealots of undistorted competition'[24] and the need for liberation from 'the tyranny of regulatory competition'.[25] He argued that the EU was premised on asymmetrical treatment of the economic and social spheres.[26] The Community economic order predominated, as evidenced by the Treaty itself, and the primacy accorded to the completion of the single market, with the attendant priority placed on market and competitive principles. Scharpf contended that matters need not have developed in this manner, and that it would have been possible when the Rome Treaty was framed to have made harmonization of social protection a pre-condition for market integration, given that the welfare regimes of the original six Member States were relatively rudimentary at that time and closer substantively than they had since become. If the Rome Treaty had been cast in this form then the debates at Community level about the interplay between social protection and the market mechanism would have replicated similar normative discourse at national level. Matters developed very differently. The Treaty focus was heavily on markets with the consequence that there was a decoupling of economic integration and social protection. This led to constitutional asymmetry. Whereas at national level economic and social policy had the same constitutional status, it was economic policy that predominated at Community level. The very predominance afforded to economic policy served moreover to reduce the Member States' ability to influence their own economies or to 'realize self-defined socio-political goals'.[27] Community law doctrines of direct effect and supremacy made these constraints even firmer.

---

[21] T Heller, 'Comments by Thomas Heller', *Constitutional Dimensions of European Economic Integration* (n 16) 161.

[22] J Weiler, 'The Transformation of Europe' (1991) 100 Yale LJ 2403, 2478.

[23] Ibid 2478.

[24] F Scharpf, *Governing in Europe: Effective and Democratic?* (Oxford University Press, 1999) 167.

[25] ibid 180.

[26] Scharpf (n 8) and 'Legitimate Diversity: The New Challenge of European Integration' in T Borzel and R Cichowski (eds), *The State of the European Union, Vol 6: Law, Politics and Society* (Oxford University Press, 2003) 79–104.

[27] Scharpf, 'The European Social Model' (n 26) 648.

(iv) Maastricht, Amsterdam, the economic, and the social

The preceding concerns generated further debate about the balance between the economic and social dimensions of the Community. This in turn was a factor that led to increase in the Community's power, so as to accord it some competence in areas of social policy, the objective being to alleviate such concerns, even if the 'price' of doing so was to limit Member State autonomy further than hitherto. The Member States were central to this process, since they debated and agreed such revisions in Treaty amendments. This does not alter the fact that the need to redress the perceived imbalance between the economic and social order was a factor that led to a net increase in Community power compared with the status quo ante. The fact that the Community's powers were limited in some such areas, and the fact that 'cooperative federalism' might well be the modus vivendi, is relevant but does not alter the force of the basic point being made here.

Political leaders, and Delors, came to see the necessity for an increase in European social policy in order to retain the support of workers.[28] Contestability as to the outcomes that the Community ought to be striving for was voiced concerning the balance between consumer and trade interests, more especially because of the deregulatory impact of the ECJ's jurisprudence.[29] Commentators spoke of the need for a strong regional policy to balance the effect of market integration on the weaker economies.[30]

The balance between the economic and the social had underpinned the 'SEA package' of reinforced provisions concerning the Structural Funds, in order to allay fears of the economically weaker Member States that they would suffer inordinately from market liberalization, and the addition of Article 118a EEC, which empowered the Community to adopt minimum directives to ensure the health and safety of workers.

The perceived need to re-balance the economic and social orders within the EU was evident more generally in the amendments in the Maastricht and Amsterdam Treaties, which created new heads of social competence, or modified those existing hitherto. Thus the Member States, through the Maastricht Treaty and Amsterdam Treaty, amended or accorded the Community some degree of competence in areas such as citizenship;[31] consumer policy;[32] discrimination;[33] social policy;[34] employment;[35] and public health.[36] The Community's competence within these areas varied.

---

[28] M Kleinman, *A European Welfare State? European Union Social Policy in Context* (Palgrave, 2002), 82–83, 86–87.

[29] A McGee and S Weatherill, 'The Evolution of the Single Market-Harmonisation or Liberalisation' (1990) 53 MLR 578; N Reich, 'Protection of Diffuse Interests in the EEC and the Perspective of Progressively Establishing an Internal Market' (1988) 11 Jnl Cons Policy 395.

[30] R Dehousse, 'Completing the Internal Market: Institutional Constraints and Challenges' in R Bieber, R Dehousse, J Pinder, J Weiler (eds), *1992: One European Market?* (Nomos, 1988) 336.

[31] Arts 17–21 EC.   [32] Art 153 EC.   [33] Art 13 EC.

[34] Arts 136–145 EC.   [35] Arts 125–130 EC.   [36] Art 152 EC.

The most powerful provision in this respect was Article 13 EC, which allowed the EC to make binding directives to combat discrimination on a wide variety of grounds.[37] By way of contrast, the new title on employment rested primarily on the open method of coordination, based on policy guidelines, benchmarks, and monitoring via peer group review. By way of contrast yet again, Article 16 EC, which dealt with services of general economic interest, did not in itself grant the EC any specific power with respect to such services, but recognized the place of these services among the shared values of the Union, as well as their role in promoting social and territorial cohesion. The general rule in relation to education and health was that the EC was limited to supporting and supplementing action taken by Member States,[38] albeit with greater power in relation to certain aspects of education and health policy.[39]

In relation to social policy, the return of the Labour Government in the UK saw the end of the UK's opt-out, with the consequence that the social chapter was integrated in to the Treaty. Article 137(1) EC empowered the Community to support and complement the activities of the Member States in a wide variety of fields.[40] This excluded harmonization of national laws, but included passage of directives with 'minimum requirements for gradual implementation', subject to the stricture that this should avoid imposing constraints that would hold back small and medium-sized undertakings.[41] The voting rules in the Council, however, differed depending on the particular type of measure adopted,[42] and the Community's power was excluded in relation to pay, right to strike, right of association, and the right to impose lock outs.[43] The social partners were granted a role beyond that of consultation and could choose to negotiate collective agreements that could be given *erga omnes* effect by decision of the Council.[44]

The re-balancing of the economic and the social was also manifest in the reconfiguring of the internal market. It is not fortuitous that the Community political organs consciously re-conceptualized the internal market in more holistic terms, to embrace not only the traditional economic sphere, but also a wider range of social, environmental, and consumer concerns, which were regarded as

---

[37] Council Directive 2000/78/EC of 27 November 2000, Establishing a General Framework for Equal Treatment in Employment and Occupation [2000] OJ L303/16; Council Directive 2000/43/EC of 29 June 2000, Implementing the Principle of Equal Treatment between Persons Irrespective of Racial or Ethnic Origin [2000] OJ L180/22.

[38] Arts 149(1), 152(1) EC.

[39] Arts 149(4), 152(4) EC.

[40] Improvement in particular of the working environment to protect workers' health and safety; working conditions; social security and social protection of workers; protection of workers where their employment contract is terminated; the information and consultation of workers; representation and collective defence of the interests of workers and employers, including codetermination; conditions of employment for third-country nationals legally residing in Community territory; the integration of persons excluded from the labour market, without prejudice to Art 150; equality between men and women with regard to labour market opportunities and treatment at work; the combating of social exclusion; the modernization of social protection.

[41] Art 137(2) EC.   [42] Art 137(2) EC.   [43] Art 137(5) EC.   [44] Art 139 EC.

important facets of the internal market strategy.[45] The single market project did
not magically come to an end in December 1992 and there was a continuing flow
of internal market legislation post-1992. This was matched by reports that
addressed various aspects of the Community regulatory process. A number of
these focused on completion of the internal market in an economic sense,[46] while
in others, although the concern for economic integration *per se* was still evident,
the internal market was consciously conceptualized in a broader, more holistic,
manner. This shift did not occur at any single moment. It developed across time.

Thus the Commission's introduction to the 1997 Action Plan consciously
stressed that 'the single market was not simply an economic structure', but also
included basic standards of health and safety, equal opportunities, and labour
law measures.[47] This theme was carried over in the 1997 Action Plan itself.
The strategic target of delivering a single market for the benefit of all citizens
was particularized through action directed towards, *inter alia*, the protection
of social rights, consumer rights, health and the environment, and the right
of residence.[48]

The Lisbon European Council constituted an important stage in this reconfi-
guration of the internal market agenda. The meeting focused on employment,
economic reform, and social cohesion. It set a 'new' strategic goal: the Union was
to become 'the most competitive and dynamic knowledge-based economy in the
world, capable of sustainable economic growth with more and better jobs and
greater social cohesion'.[49] Completion of the internal market was one way of
achieving this strategy.[50] The modernization of the European social model
through the building of an active welfare state was to be another. This was
crucial to ensure that 'the emergence of this new economy does not compound
the existing social problems of unemployment, social exclusion and poverty'.[51]
This objective was further particularized in terms of better education, an
active employment policy, modernizing social protection and promoting
social inclusion.[52]

---

[45] See, eg, Single Market Action Plan sets Agenda, 18 June 1997, 2; Action Plan, 9–11.
[46] Making the Most of the Internal Market, COM(93) 632 final; The Impact and Effectiveness
of the Single Market, COM(96) 520 final; Action Plan for the Single Market, SEC(97) 1 final;
Communication from the Commission to the European Parliament and the Council, Mutual
Recognition in the Context of the follow-up to the Action Plan for the Single Market, 16 June
1999; An Internal Market Strategy for Services, COM(2000) 888; Financial Services—Implementing the Framework for Financial Markets: Action Plan, COM(1999) 232; Institutional Arrangements for the Regulation and Supervision of the Financial Sector, January 2000; Financial Services
Priorities and Progress, Third Report, COM(2000) 692/2 final.
[47] Single Market Action Plan sets Agenda, 18 June 1997, 2.
[48] Action Plan for the Single Market, SEC(97) 1 final, 9–11.
[49] Lisbon European Council, 23–24 March 2000, [5].
[50] ibid [5], [16]–[21].
[51] ibid [24].
[52] ibid [25]–[34].

These commitments were reiterated at the Feira and Nice European Councils.[53] The latter meeting approved the Commission's European Social Agenda, endorsed by the European Parliament, which was characterized by the 'indissoluble link between economic performance and social progress'.[54] A high level of social protection, coupled with services of general interest vital for social cohesion, constituted the common core of values for the Community: economic growth and social cohesion were seen as mutually reinforcing.[55] The Stockholm European Council echoed the same idea, with 'full agreement that economic reform, employment and social policies were mutually reinforcing'.[56] The principal Commission reports concerning the internal market developed the ideas articulated by the European Council.[57]

It is therefore unsurprising that there was increased pressure for the EC to play a greater role in social policy thereby alleviating the constitutional imbalance between the market-making and market-correcting functions of a polity. There were, however, limits to the role accorded to the EC in the social sphere. The Member States closely circumscribed the grant of competence over such matters, fearful of too great an intrusion on terrain hitherto within their sphere. The effluxion of time had moreover constrained what could be done at the Community level. Thus Scharpf argued that it was not possible for the EU at the turn of the millennium to adopt the stance towards social policy that it had declined to take when the Rome Treaty was signed. It was not possible to treat social welfare and protection through uniform rules applicable to all, because of the very diversity in national systems of social welfare, which embodied differing normative assumptions about seminal issues such as the type and level of assistance to be provided to the unemployed, and the balance between support to be provided by the State and that to be left to private provision.[58] This diversity was then connected to choice of regulatory technique for Community intervention, the Open Method of Coordination.[59]

Political parties and unions promoting 'social Europe' are thus confronted by a dilemma: to ensure effectiveness, they need to assert the constitutional equality of social protection and economic integration functions at the European level—which could be achieved either through European social programmes or through the harmonization of national social-protection systems. At the same time, however, the present diversity of national social-protection systems and the political salience of these differences make it practically

---

[53] Feira European Council, 19–20 June 2000, [19]–[39], [44]–[49]; Nice European Council, 7–9 December 2000.

[54] Nice European Council (n 53) [15]; Annex 1, [8]–[9].

[55] ibid Annex 1, [9], [11].

[56] Stockholm European Council, [2].

[57] 2000 Review of the Internal Market Strategy, COM(2000) 257 final; Economic Reform: Report on the Functioning of Community Capital and Product Markets, COM(2000) 881 final; Services of General Interest in Europe, COM(2000) 580 final.

[58] Scharpf, 'The European Social Model' (n 26) 649–651.

[59] ibid 652.

impossible for them to agree on common European solutions. Faced by this dilemma, the Union opted for a new governing mode, the open method of coordination (OMC), in order to protect and promote social Europe.

(v) Legislature, courts, the economic, and the social: free movement

The discussion thus far has considered the balance between the economic and the social within the Community order primarily through focus on the principal Treaty revisions. This balance was also markedly affected by legislation and adjudication over this entire period. It would be impossible within the scope of this chapter to address this in detail across all areas of Community law, more especially because it was no easy task to map comprehensively the EC's social policy competence.[60] A snapshot of the forces at work that shaped the balance between the economic and the social in some areas can nonetheless be given. The reality was some blurring of the economic/social divide, which is exemplified in the areas considered below. It will be seen, however, that the 'forces' did not always pull in one direction.

The law concerning free movement of workers and social security provides an apposite starting point, since, as we have seen, this was an area where the Rome Treaty did accord some competence over social welfare. Regulations were duly enacted on free movement and social security.[61] What became readily apparent from subsequent adjudication on the primary Treaty articles and on the regulations made pursuant thereto was that the ECJ took a broad teleological view of the relevant provisions, thereby blurring the divide between the economic and social imperatives of free movement.

The basic economic object was to ensure the optimal allocation of resources within the Community, by enabling the labour factor of production to move to the area where it was most valued. There was, however, a social rationale underlying the proscription of discrimination on grounds of nationality within the four freedoms. This was at its most fundamental the idea that it should be regarded as natural and something to be encouraged that workers should be employed or firms should carry on business in Member States other than their home State, and that when they did so they could not be treated in a disadvantageous manner as compared with nationals of that State. This was integral to the very idea of a 'community'.

---

[60] M Freedland, P Craig, C Jacqueson and N Kountouris, *Public Employment Services and European Law* (Oxford University Press, 2007) ch 1.

[61] Regulation (EEC) No 1612/68 of the Council of 15 October 1968 on freedom of movement for workers within the Community [1968] OJ L 257/2; Regulation (EC) No 1408/71 of the Council of 14 June 1971 on the application of social security schemes to employed persons, to self-employed persons, and to members of their families moving within the Community [1971] OJ L 149/2.

The blend of the economic and the social was apparent in the broad interpretation accorded to workers.[62] The right to move to look for work served to
diminish the differential impact of Article 39 EC on different categories of
workers, since, other things being equal, it would normally be those in higher
paid or professional employment who would have a job offer before moving to
another Member State, by way of contrast to unskilled or semi-skilled workers
who might be more likely to secure employment after arrival in the host Member
State. The social dimension was also apparent in the right for the worker to raise
her standard of living, even if she did not reach the minimum level of subsistence
in a particular State. It also affected the ECJ's willingness to treat part-time
employment as within the remit of the Treaty, since this not only cohered with
good economic sense, given the changing nature of the job market, but also had
social resonance, since many part-time workers were women, who would therefore be especially disadvantaged if this type of work did not come within the
ambit of Treaty protection.

The admixture of the economic and the social was evident in the narrow
construction given to the public service exception.[63] The economic rationale for
the restrictive interpretation of the exception was the need to prevent the range of
employment relationships subject to Article 39 from being unduly diminished by
broad conceptions of public service applied within some Member States. However, there was also a social dimension to this case law, which embodied a view as
to when it was legitimate for the Member States to require nationality as a
condition for employment. The ECJ's rejection of the institutional test and its
adherence to a functional criterion challenged the prevalent Member State view.
The functional test required Member States to think the unthinkable: in a
Community the best qualified applicant for a job in the public service might
be a national from another Member State and that where the post did not require
the reciprocal bond of allegiance that characterized nationality the applicant
should be able to put forward her credentials for the job on an equal footing
with nationals from the State in which she sought employment.

The blend of the economic and the social was apparent once again in judicial
interpretation of the regulations on free movement. The economic rationale for
Regulation 1612/68[64] was readily apparent, since the objective of free movement
to facilitate optimal allocation of employment resources in the Community
would have had little impact if Member States had been able to discriminate
about the matters proscribed by the Regulation. There were, however, also
prominent social objectives underlying the Regulation. This was evident from
the provisions dealing with workers' families, which were framed so as to foster
the stability and cohesiveness that comes when people move as a family unit,

---

[62] Case 53/81 *Levin v Staatssecretaris van Justitie* [1982] ECR 1035; Case C–292/89 *R v
Immigration Appeal Tribunal, ex p Antonissen* [1991] ECR I–745.
[63] Case 149/79 *Commission v Belgium* [1980] ECR 3881.
[64] Reg 1612/68 (n 61).

thereby alleviating the social problems that can occur when families are divided for considerable periods of time.

There was in addition a more general social message in the Regulation, which was that once a person fulfilled the conditions for being a worker there should as a matter of principle be equality of treatment within the society where the person worked. The worker from another Member State should not be treated or regarded as 'second class' by way of contrast to nationals of that State. This has been aptly termed the supranational assimilation model.[65] It is this concept that underlies the ECJ's expansive reading of the requirement that workers should receive the same 'social and tax advantages' as nationals of the host State.[66]

While the linkage between the economic and the social is therefore apparent in the law on free movement of persons, the tension between the precepts of the internal market and national social policy is equally undeniable, nowhere more so than in the context of health care.[67] The rules on free movement, especially those concerning the provision of services, had a marked impact on national social systems, and the Court's jurisprudence compelled Member States to modify or redesign their social policy.

The ECJ's guiding principle on health care and provision of medical services was that although Community law did not detract from the ability of Member States to organize their own social security systems, they must nonetheless comply with Community law when exercising that power.[68] A national measure could not escape scrutiny under EC law merely because it was concerned with the national social security system.[69] Thus where the activity was considered as

---

[65] M Dougan and E Spaventa, ' "Wish You Weren't Here . . . " New Models of Social Solidarity in the European Union' in Dougan and Spaventa (n 1) 189.

[66] Case 32/75 *Fiorini (neé Cristini) v Société Nationale des Chemins de Fer Français* [1975] ECR 1085; Case 65/81 *Reina v Landeskreditbank Baden-Württemberg* [1982] ECR 33.

[67] V Hatzopoulos, '*Killing* National Health and Insurance Systems, but *Healing* Patients? The European Market for Health Care Services after the Judgments of the ECJ in *Vanbraekel* and *Peerbooms*' (2002) 39 CMLRev 683; T Hervey, 'Mapping the Contours of European Union Health Law and Policy' (2002) 8 EPL 69; M McKee, E Mossialos and R Baeten (eds), *The Impact of EU Law on Health Care Systems* (PIE-Peter Lang, 2002); T Hervey, 'The "Right to Health" in European Union Law' in T Hervey and J Kenner (eds), *Economic and Social Rights under the EU Charter of Fundamental Rights* (Hart, 2003) 193; T Hervey and J McHale, *Health Law and the European Union* (Cambridge University Press, 2004); G Davies, 'Health and Efficiency: Community law and National Health Systems in the light of Muller-Faure' (2004) 67 MLR 94; V Hatzopoulos, 'Health Law and Policy: The Impact of the EU' in de Búrca (n 1) ch 5; P Koutrakos, 'Healthcare as an Economic Service under EC Law' in Dougan and Spaventa (n 1) ch 5; D Wyatt, 'Community Competence to Regulate Medical Services' in Dougan and Spaventa (n 1) ch 6; S Leibfried and P Starke, 'Transforming the "Cordon Sanitaire": The Liberalization of Public Services and the Restructuring of European Welfare States' (2008) Socio-Economic Review 175.

[68] See, eg, Case C-157/99 *BSM Geraets-Smits v Stiching Zickenfonds VGZ and HTM Peerbooms v Stiching CZ Groep Zorgverzekeringen* [2001] ECR I-5473, [44]-[46]; Case C-385/99 *Müller-Fauré v Onderlinge Waarborgmaatschappij OZ and others* [2003] ECR I-4509; Case C-56/01 *Inizan* [2003] ECR I-12403; Case C-372/04 *Watts v Bedford Primary Care Trust and Secretary of State for Health* [2006] ECR I-4325.

[69] Case C-158/96 *Raymond Kohll v Union des caisses de maladie* [1998] ECR I-1931, [20]–[21].

economic and there was a restriction on the right to provide or receive services, the national measure was contrary to Community law, unless it could be objectively justified.

The application of this precept in the health care field, however, led to difficult and contentious judgments, as exemplified by the case law on the compatibility with EC law of national rules that required prior authorization before a person sought medical treatment in another Member State. The ECJ was willing to recognize objective justifications for the system of prior authorization, these being the maintenance of a balanced medical and hospital service open to all and the risk of seriously undermining the financial balance of the social security system. It did not accept, however, that the preservation of the essential characteristics of a Member State's health scheme constituted *per se* a justification for these purposes. It moreover examined ever more closely whether the justification proffered satisfied the criteria of necessity and proportionality, and it imposed increasingly stringent conditions in this respect.

What is especially interesting for present purposes is the difference of view concerning the balance between the economic and the social generated by this jurisprudence. Thus some, such as Lenaerts and Foubert, emphasized the socially activist role played by the ECJ's case law, highlighting the social benefits to patients through the application of the cross-border provision of medical services.[70] Others, such as Koutrakos, were more sceptical as to whether this case law should be conceived of in terms of a social welfare right.[71] Yet others, such as Hatzopoulos, expressed more general concern about the piecemeal application in this area of internal market principles through negative integration, arguing that it is 'casuistic and may not ensure a coherent and smooth coordination of the various systems',[72] and that that it has a differential impact on differing healthcare regimes.

(vi) Legislature, courts, the economic, and the social: public undertakings

The judicial developments in relation to free movement can be contrasted with those with respect to public undertakings, which was the other area of social policy broadly conceived that was addressed in the Rome Treaty. The story here was rather different. There is once again a blend of the economic and the social, but the terms thereof were rigorously set and policed by the ECJ. The Treaty was, in formal terms, agnostic as to whether economic activity was undertaken by the State, including those to whom it granted special or exclusive rights, or through the free interplay of market forces. The ECJ acknowledged that the grant of such

---

[70] K Lenaerts and P Foubert, 'Social Rights in the Case Law of the European Court of Justice' (2001) 28 LIEI 267, 293.

[71] Koutrakos (n 67) 126–129.

[72] Hatzopoulos, 'Health Law and Policy' (n 67) 167.

exclusive rights would not, *per se*, infringe Article 82 EC, but held that the exercise of such rights could do so if it was abusive. The ECJ frequently treated the exercise of such exclusive rights as abusive, with the consequence that it became more difficult for a State to organize its economic activities in this manner.[73] The consequence was that the grant of exclusive rights was normally held *prima facie* to infringe Article 86(1) EC.

The ECJ would then consider whether there was some objective justification for the exclusivity,[74] and in doing so it did take cognizance of social objectives underlying the exclusivity. Thus the ECJ was more receptive to use of the exception where the undertaking granted exclusivity had universal service obligations requiring it to perform some tasks that were not profitable, such that the only way that it could function was to have exclusive rights over those parts of the service that were profitable.[75] The fact that social concerns traditionally addressed by public undertakings were recognized by the ECJ was welcome. This should not, however, mask the preference for ordinary market mechanisms that underpinned the Court's case law. It was only where there was some market failure that a measure of exclusivity would be tolerated for the social reasons adumbrated above.

This same approach is manifest in legislative intervention in this area, as exemplified in the telecommunications sector by the Universal Service Directive.[76] It is clear from the Directive that the competitive market is regarded as the optimal method for the distribution of these services, but that legislative intervention via universal service obligations is required to correct market failure. Thus Article 1 states that the overall aim is to ensure the availability throughout the Community of good quality publicly available services 'through effective competition and choice and to deal with circumstances in which the needs of

[73] Case C–41/90 *Höfner and Elser v Macrotron GmbH* [1991] ECR I–1979; Case C–55/96 *Job Centre coop arl* [1997] ECR I–7119; Case C–179/90 *Merci Convenzionali Porto di Genova SpA v Siderurgica Gabrielli SpA* [1991] ECR I–5889; Case C–260/89 *Elliniki Radiophonia Tileorassi AE (ERT) v Dimotiki Etairia Pliroforissis (DEP) and Sotirios Kouvelas* [1991] ECR I–2925.

[74] L Hancher, 'Community, State and Market' in P Craig and G de Búrca (eds), *The Evolution of EU Law* (Oxford University Press, 1999) ch 20; D Edward and M Hoskins, 'Art 90: Deregulation and EC Law, Reflections Arising from the XVI FIDE Conference' (1995) 32 CMLRev 157.

[75] Case C–320/91 P *Procureur du Roi v Paul Corbeau* [1993] ECR I–2533; Case C–67/96 *Albany International BV v Stichting Bedrijfspensioenfonds Textielindustrie* [1999] ECR I–5751; Cases C–147–148/97 *Deutsche Post AG v Gesellschaft für Zahlungssyteme mbH and Citicorp Kartenservice GmbH* [2000] ECR I–825; Case C–209/98 *Entreprenorforeningens Affalds/Miljosektion (FFAD) v Kobenhavns Kommune* [2000] ECR I–3473.

[76] Directive 2002/22 of the European Parliament and the Council of 7 March 2002 on universal service and users' right relating to electronic communications networks and services (Universal Service Directive) [2002] OJ L108/51; W Sauter, 'Universal Service Obligations and the Emergence of Citizens' Rights in European Telecommunications Liberalization' in M Freedland and S Sciarra (eds), *Public Services and Citizenship in European Law—Public and Labour Law Perspectives* (Clarendon Press Oxford, 1998) ch 7; T Prosser, *The Limits of Competition Law, Markets and Public Services* (Oxford University Press, 2005).

end-users are not satisfactorily met by the market'. This same theme recurs in Article 2, which speaks of the provision of universal service within an environment of open and competitive markets, by defining a minimum set of services of specified quality to which all end-users have access, at an affordable price, in the light of specific national conditions, without distorting competition.

(vii) Legislature, courts, the economic, and the social: services of general economic interest

The themes considered in the previous section are also apparent in relation to Article 16 EC, introduced by the Treaty of Amsterdam,[77] which recognized services of general economic interest and thereby arguably strengthened the social dimension of EC law.[78] The precise import and effect of Article 16 EC was, however, debatable.[79] The Commission addressed the concept of services of general interest on a number of occasions,[80] including a White Paper in 2004.[81]

The Commission recognized that the term 'services of general interest' was not found in the Treaty itself, and that the closest Treaty formulation was in Article 16 EC, which was framed in terms of services of general economic interest. The concept of services of the general interest was broader and covered 'both market and non-market services which the public authorities class as being of general interest and subject to specific public service obligations'.[82] The concept of services of general economic interest, while not defined in the Treaty, was held to embrace 'services of general economic nature which the Member States or the Community subject to specific public service obligations by virtue of general interest criterion'.[83] This covered in particular the big network industries, such as transport, postal services, energy, and communications.

Services of general interest were regarded as 'one of the pillars of the European model of society',[84] reflecting Community values and goals based on 'a common set of elements, including: universal service, continuity, quality of service, affordability, as well as user and consumer protection'.[85] Access to such services

---

[77] Art 16 EC provided that: 'Without prejudice to Arts 73, 86 and 87, and given the place occupied by services of general economic interest in the shared values of the Union as well as their role in promoting social and territorial cohesion, the Community and the Member States, each within their respective powers and within the scope of application of this Treaty, shall take care that such services operate on the basis of principles and conditions which enable them to fulfill their missions'.

[78] A Héritier, 'Market Integration and Social Cohesion: The Politics of Public Services in European Regulation' (2001) 8 JEPP 825; Prosser (n 76) ch 7.

[79] M Ross, 'Art 16 EC and Services of General Interest: From Derogation to Obligation?' (2000) 25 ELRev 22.

[80] On Services of General Interest, COM(1996) 443; On Services of General Interest in Europe, COM(2000)580 final; Report to the Laeken European Council, Services of General Interest, COM (2001) 598 final; Green Paper on Services of General Interest, COM(2003) 270.

[81] White Paper on Services of General Interest, COM(2004) 374 final.

[82] White Paper (n 81) Annex 1.   [83] ibid.   [84] ibid [2.1].   [85] ibid [2.1].

was perceived as 'an essential component of European citizenship and necessary in order to allow them to fully enjoy their fundamental rights'.[86] The provision of such services meeting the needs of both consumers and business was, moreover, seen as part of the broader Lisbon agenda, whereby the EU was to become the most competitive and dynamic knowledge-based economy in the world capable of sustainable economic growth with more and better jobs and greater social cohesion.[87]

The Commission elaborated principles that underpinned its approach to the provision of these services. Community sector-specific regulations would only be promulgated when there was a clear Community dimension, as exemplified by the regulations made for the large network industries. Such regulatory instruments would protect 'universal service' and high levels of quality, security, and safety were also seen as crucial. It was nonetheless central to Commission thinking that the provision of high-quality services of general interest was compatible with an open and competitive market, and it argued that the latter had in many areas led to more affordable and better general interest services.

There is little doubt that the EU's approach to services of general interest changed over time, although commentators differed as to the extent of this change. Baquero Cruz argued that competition was still very much the dominant paradigm, with universal service obligations as being a relatively minor qualification.[88] Prosser, by way of contrast, took a more positive view. Speaking of services of general interest, he commented that:[89]

Initially they were seen as something of an irritant, limiting the creation of a full internal market. Now a much more positive view is taken, despite only cautious substantive proposals in the 2004 White Paper. Such services are confirmed an essential element of European citizenship and, rather than the main question being that of how their operation can be restricted and remodelled to become compatible with the single market, it is of how their operation can be improved and made both more efficient and more responsive to social values such as those underlying public service. This has provided a means by which the values of public service (although the term is disliked by the Commission) can be brought into the European law relating to services of general interest...

(viii) Legislature, courts, the economic, and the social: citizenship

The social dimension of the Community has more recently been enhanced by the jurisprudence on citizenship, which has accorded non-economic migrants a higher status than hitherto, with the consequence that they have access to certain

---

[86] ibid [2.1].

[87] Lisbon European Council, 23–24 March 2000, [5].

[88] J Baquero Cruz, 'Beyond Competition: Services of General Interest and European Community Law' in de Búrca (n 1) 207.

[89] Prosser (n 76) 172.

welfare benefits within the State in which they are residing. The ECJ brought all its teleological resources to bear in crafting this jurisprudence. It gave an expansive reading to Articles 12 and 17 EC, and a narrow reading to Article 18(1) EC, insofar as it limited the citizen's right to move freely within the EU by conditions laid down in the Treaty and in measures adopted pursuant thereto. The judicial statement that 'union citizenship is destined to be the fundamental status of nationals of the Member States, enabling those who find themselves in the same situation to enjoy the same treatment in law irrespective of their nationality, subject to such exceptions as are expressly provided for',[90] rapidly underwent a transition from *obiter dictum* to become the ECJ's guiding principle.

Thus the ECJ applied Union citizenship to situations where the citizen was lawfully resident within the Member State and hence was said to benefit from Article 17 and Article 12 EC, provided that the subject matter was within the scope of the Treaty *rationae personae* and *ratione materiae*,[91] notwithstanding that the applicant did not satisfy the conditions laid down by other Treaty Articles or Community legislation, and could not therefore rely on Article 18 EC. The ECJ also gave an expansive interpretation to the right to move and reside within Article 18 EC and interpreted the qualification to this right, that it is subject to limits and conditions laid down in the Treaty and in Community legislation, narrowly, thereby enabling applicants to benefit from Article 18 and Article 12 EC.[92] The Court in addition used the introduction of the citizenship provisions as a reason for expanding the interpretation of other Treaty Articles or Community legislation, thereby expanding the scope of equal treatment and Article 12 EC.[93] The citizenship jurisprudence generated, unsurprisingly, considerable academic commentary concerning the Court's reading of the Treaty provisions and the financial consequences for the Member States.[94]

---

[90] Case C-184/99 *Rudy Grzelczyk v Centre Public D'Aide Sociale d'Ottignes-Louvain-la-Neuve* (*CPAS*) [2001] ECR I-6193, [31].

[91] Case C-85/96 *Maria Martinez Sala v Freistaat Bayern* [1998] ECR I-2691; Case C-456/02 *Trojani v Centre Public D'Aide Sociale de Bruxelles* (*CPAS*) [2004] ECR I-7573.

[92] Case C-184/99 *Rudy Grzelczyk* (n 90); Case C-209/03 *The Queen (on the application of Bidar) v London Borough of Ealing and Secretary of State for Education* [2005] ECR I-2119.

[93] Case C-138/02 *Collins v Secretary of State for Work and Pensions* [2004] ECR I-2703; Case C-209/03 *Bidar* (n 92).

[94] S O'Leary, 'Nationality Law and Community Citizenship: A Tale of Two Uneasy Bedfellows' (1992) 12 YBEL 353; S O' Leary, 'Putting Flesh on the Bones of European Union Citizenship' (1999) 24 ELRev 68; R White, 'Free Movement, Equal Treatment and Citizenship of the Union' (2005) 54 ICLQ 885; C Barnard, 'EU Citizenship and the Principle of Solidarity' in Dougan and Spaventa (n 1) ch 8; A Pieter van der Mei, 'EU Law and Education: Promotion of Student Mobility versus Protection of Education Systems' in Dougan and Spaventa (n 1) ch 10; M Dougan, 'Fees, Grants, Loans and Dole Cheques: Who Covers the Costs of Migrant Education within the EU' (2005) 42 CMLRev 943; J Mather, 'The Court of Justice and the Union Citizen' (2005) 11 ELJ 722; K Hailbronner, 'Union Citizenship and Access to Social Benefits' (2005) 42 CMLRev 1245; M Dougan, 'The Constitutional Dimension to the case law on Union Citizenship' (2006) 31 ELRev 613.

(b) Input legitimacy: rationales for the shift

The discussion thus far has been concerned with the balance between the economic and the social within the Community order, and the way in which this evolved from the inception of the EEC. The analysis would be incomplete, however, if mention was not made of the increasing concern with input as well as output legitimacy. Debate concerning legitimacy, input, and democracy within the Community was evident even prior to the Single European Act 1986 (SEA).[95] These issues, however, came to the fore from the mid-1980s onwards. This is readily apparent in the rich vein of academic literature published during this period.[96] It is evident in the institutional submissions that led to the Treaty of Amsterdam in 1996.[97] There is a certain paradox in this shift in emphasis, given that it occurred when the European Parliament was being granted a measure of real power in the legislative process. There are, nonetheless, a range of reasons why these matters came to occupy centre stage in debates about the Community.

(i) Community power

The very fact that the Community had power over an increasing variety of subject matter fuelled the change whereby legitimacy was conceived not only in terms of output, but also in terms of input, more especially because the former was more difficult to measure in the social realm than in the economic context.

---

[95] W Wallace and J Smith, 'Democracy or Technocracy? European Integration and the Problem of Popular Consent' in J Hayward (ed), *The Crisis of Representation in Europe* (Frank Cass, 1995).

[96] See, eg., J Hayward (ed), *The Crisis of Representation in Europe* (Frank Cass, 1995); R Bellamy, V Bufacchi, and D Castiglione (eds), *Democracy and Constitutional Culture in the Union of Europe* (Lothian Foundation Press, 1995); S Andersen and K Eliassen (eds), *The European Union: How Democratic Is It?* (Sage, 1996); R Bellamy and D Castiglione (eds), *Constitutionalism in Transformation: European and Theoretical Perspectives* (Blackwell, 1996); F Snyder (ed), *Constitutional Dimensions of European Economic Integration* (Kluwer, 1996); R Dehousse (ed), *Europe: The Impossible Status Quo* (Macmillan, 1997); D Curtin, *Postnational Democracy, The European Union in Search of a Political Philosophy* (Kluwer, 1997); J Weiler, *The Constitution of Europe* (Cambridge University Press, 1999); P Craig, and G de Búrca (eds), *The Evolution of EU Law* (Oxford University Press, 1999); F Scharpf, *Governing in Europe: Effective and Democratic?* (Oxford University Press, 1999); C Hoskyns and M Newman (eds), *Democratizing the European Union* (Manchester University Press, 2000); F Mancini, *Democracy and Constitutionalism in the European Union* (Hart Publishing, 2000); K Neunreither and A Wiener (eds), *European Integration after Amsterdam, Institutional Dynamics and Prospects for Democracy* (Oxford University Press, 2000); R Prodi, *Europe As I See It* (Polity, 2000); P Schmitter, *How to Democratize the European Union... and why bother?* (Rowman and Littlefield, 2000); L Siedentop, *Democracy in Europe* (Penguin, 2001); K Nicolaidis and R Howse (eds), *The Federal Vision, Legitimacy and Levels of Governance in the United States and the European Union* (Oxford University Press, 2001); W van Gerven, *The European Union, A Polity of States and Peoples* (Hart, 2005).

[97] P Craig, 'Democracy and Rule-Making within the EC: An Empirical and Normative Assessment' (1997) 3 ELJ 105; G de Búrca 'The Quest for Legitimacy in the European Union' (1996) 59 MLR 349.

Successive Treaty revisions, beginning with the SEA, added further chapters or titles to Community competence. Areas such as the environment, consumer protection, economic and monetary union, health, culture, employment, and industrial policy were brought, albeit to varying degrees, within the scope of the Community. It was unsurprising that this should lead to increased questioning about the way in which policy was made in these areas. This was more especially so given that some of these issues, such as economic and monetary union, touched the very core of national sovereignty, and constrained national macro-economic policy. The fact that some of these policy issues were 'taken from' national regional bodies, which had only very limited input into decision making at Community level, created a 'constituency' eager to voice the democratic shortcomings of this shift of competence.

The increased use of this Community power also naturally led to greater focus on the Community decision-making process whereby such powers were exercised. Thus the very fact that the Community legislative process was used to enact the plethora of measures designed to complete the single market led to increased attention being focused on the nature of the process itself. It placed the Community's decision making under the spotlight.

(ii) Legislative process

The shift to qualified majority voting in the SEA, the decline in use of the Luxembourg Accords, and the increase in the European Parliament's legislative power, provide a second explanation. The Rome Treaty provided for qualified majority voting in many areas, but the applicability of these provisions was weakened by the *de facto* veto of the Luxembourg Accords.

The application of qualified majority voting to Article 95 EC, under which most harmonization measures were enacted, combined with the 'political decline' in the veto power, altered the dynamics of the legislative process. Decision making in the Council continued to be dominated by the search for consensus. There was nonetheless the possibility that Member States could truly be outvoted. The European Parliament's involvement, through the cooperation procedure and then co-decision, meant that the content of any measure was not solely in the hands of the Council. These changes led to reflection on the nature of the Community's legislative process, and the extent of its democratic pedigree.

The European Parliament post the SEA sought to increase its limited power and to keep the 'democracy issue' on the agenda in subsequent Treaty reforms. Prior to the SEA the European Parliament had very limited input into the legislative process. It had sought wide-ranging Treaty reform in the discussions leading to the SEA. These efforts were unsuccessful, but it was given the cooperation procedure. The European Parliament's strategy thereafter was predictable. It sought to extend this power to new areas, and to gain more extensive powers in the legislative process. The advent of the co-decision procedure in the

Maastricht Treaty, the strengthening of this procedure in the Treaty of Amsterdam, and its extension to other substantive areas in the Amsterdam and Nice Treaties, were the results of this strategy.

The concerns as to input democracy were alleviated by giving the European Parliament a greater role in the legislative process, but they were not fully met. This was because of the 'disjunction between power and electoral accountability'.[98] It is axiomatic within national systems that the voters can express their dislike of the incumbent party through periodic elections. There may be limits to electoral accountability, but the bottom line is that governments can be changed if they incur electoral displeasure. In the EU, legislative power is divided between the Council, European Parliament, and Commission, with the European Council playing a significant role in shaping the overall legislative agenda. The voters therefore had no direct way of signifying their desire for change in the legislative agenda. European elections could alter the complexion of the European Parliament, but it was only one part of the legislative process. The Commission, Council, and European Council had input into the legislative agenda, but they could not be voted out by the people.

(iii) Part of the solution, part of the problem

There was in addition a deeper reason for the increased attention accorded to legitimacy and democracy in the Community. This was the shift in perception of the Community as being part of the solution to being part of the problem. Weiler skilfully captures this point.[99]

He points out that the Community was, in its foundational period, 'perceived as part of a moral imperative in dealing with the heritage of World War II'.[100] The possibility of major war in Europe had indeed been removed, but so, too, he argues, was the moral imperative, the mantle of ideals, leaving us with politics as usual, with the twist that it was much less easy to change the political status quo.[101]

The concerns of modernity, such as the increased bureaucratization of life, the depersonalization of the market, and the centralization of power, became concerns voiced about the Community itself. The values of integration, as exemplified by the breaking down of local markets, and the insertion of universal norms into domestic cultures, were also 'part of the deep modern and post-

---

[98] A Follesdal and S Hix, 'Why there is a Democratic Deficit in the EU: A Response to Majone and Moravcsik' (2006) 44 JCMS 533.

[99] J Weiler, 'The European Court of Justice: Beyond "Beyond Doctrine" or the Legitimacy Crisis of European Constitutionalism' in A-M Slaughter, A Stone Sweet and JHH Weiler (eds), *The European Courts and National Courts, Doctrine and Jurisprudence* (Hart, 1998) 365, 368–371.

[100] ibid 368.   [101] ibid 368–369.

modern anxiety of European belongingness and part of the roots of European angst and alienation'.[102]

(iv) National democracy, EU democracy

The increased attention accorded to democracy was also related to more general concerns as to the health of democracy at national level, which were replicated within the EU. The 'new right' initiated the revolution in government of the 1980s. Privatization, contracting-out, and the preference for market-based solutions were the familiar features of this form of governance.

For some, such as Siedentop, these developments provoked concerns about the dominance of economics, and the withering of politics. The EU was seen as reflecting and exacerbating this trend. The dominance of economic outcomes, combined with French *étatisme*, was said to diminish yet further the realm of the political.[103]

2. Constitutional Treaty

The Lisbon Treaty was, as we have seen in the preceding chapters, shaped by the deliberations that led to the Constitutional Treaty. It is therefore important to understand the influences that affected the latter with respect to the social and economic dimensions of the Community. This is more especially so given that although the Convention on the Future of Europe did not engage in systematic discussion of the substantive scope of the Treaty, there were working parties on both social and economic governance, the conclusions of which markedly influenced the content of the Constitutional Treaty and of the Lisbon Treaty.

(a) Working Group on Social Europe

The Convention on the Future of Europe established a Working Group on 'Social Europe', with a mandate to address specific issues concerning the EU's social dimension.[104]

The Working Group nailed its colours to the mast, stating that social considerations were an essential part of European integration. The EU could not be a credible force for good in the wider world if 'it is indifferent to questions of social justice and poverty in European society or to how its citizens are treated at work and in retirement'.[105] The Working Group concluded as it had begun, rejecting

---

[102] ibid 371.   [103] Siedentop (n 96) 35–36, 216–217, 226.
[104] CONV 516/1/03, Final Report of Working Group XI on Social Europe, Brussels, 4 February 2003.
[105] ibid [2].

'any artificial opposition of economic and social objectives in European policy or any arbitrary hierarchical order between them'.[106]

It recommended that the values of the EU should include social justice, solidarity, and equality, in particular equality between men and women. This was accepted in the final version of the Constitutional Treaty, subject to the caveat that the reference was to justice, rather than social justice.[107] It also argued that social objectives should be treated as equivalent to those of an economic nature in the list of the EU's objectives,[108] and that the list of social objectives should be specific and numerous.[109] It is questionable whether the former was achieved in the Constitutional Treaty, an issue to which we shall return in due course, but the latter was not, the list of social objectives being less specific and numerous than advocated by the Working Group.[110] The Working Group also made recommendations that the Open Method of Coordination should be constitutionalized within Part I of the Constitutional Treaty, but this did not occur, and proffered suggestions relating to the voting rules that should apply for social policy.

It was, however, both interesting and significant that the Working Group felt unable to 'say very much' about Union competence over social policy. There were clearly deep divisions within the Group on this issue.[111] There was general consensus that social policy should remain an area of shared competence, but over and beyond that disagreement prevailed. The prevalence of divergent views normally signifies adherence to the status quo, since that represents the default position. If support for change cannot be mustered then the pre-existing rules will continue to apply. This was the case here, the Working Group recommending that in general the EU's competence was adequate in this area. Indeed, it could be argued that the phraseology used by the Working Group constituted a step back, rather than a step forward. Thus while the Group believed that some greater competence should exist in relation to services of general economic interest, its general position was that EU involvement 'should primarily concern areas of action closely linked to the functioning of the internal market, preventing distortions of competition, and/or areas with a considerable cross-border impact'.[112] This makes EU social policy hang firmly on the coat tails of

---

[106] ibid 29.
[107] Art I-2 CT.
[108] CONV 516/1/03, Final Report of Working Group XI (n 104) [12].
[109] ibid [22]. Full employment, social justice, social peace, sustainable development, economic, social, and territorial cohesion, social market economy, quality of work, lifelong learning, social inclusion, a high degree of social protection, equality between men and women, children's rights, a high level of public health, and efficient and high quality social services and services of general interest.
[110] Art I-3 CT.
[111] CONV 516/1/03, Final Report of Working Group XI (n 104) [23]–[35].
[112] ibid [35].

economic integration, and sits uneasily with the Group's earlier affirmation that the social should not be treated as second class in relation to the economic.

(b) Working Group on Economic Governance

The Convention on the Future of Europe established a Working Group on Economic Governance. It was principally concerned with EU monetary and economic policy, although the final report also touched on taxation and financial markets.[113] The report was brief. It recommended continuation of the status quo, whereby exclusive competence for monetary policy within the eurozone lies with the Community, exercised by the European Central Bank (ECB), and competence for economic policy lies with the Member States. There was some discussion concerning improvements to the accountability and transparency of the ECB, but the principal message to emerge from the Group was the need to improve coordination over economic policy, in particular in relation to implementation.

3. Lisbon Treaty: General

It is fitting to begin consideration of the Lisbon Treaty by adverting to certain general issues that shape consideration of more specific Treaty provisions.

(a) Values and objectives

The Lisbon Treaty drew heavily on the provisions of the Constitutional Treaty, and this is reflected in the provisions on values and objectives. Article 2 of the Treaty on European Union (TEU) sets out the EU's values, and follows the corresponding provision of the Constitutional Treaty.[114]

The Union is founded on the values of respect for human dignity, freedom, democracy, equality, the rule of law and respect for human rights, including the rights of persons belonging to minorities. These values are common to the Member States in a society in which pluralism, non-discrimination, tolerance, justice, solidarity and equality between women and men prevail.

Article 2 TEU did not have a direct forbear in the pre-existing Treaties. The values listed nonetheless replicate in part those found in what was Article 6 EU, which referred to the EU being founded upon liberty, democracy, rights, and the rule of law. Article 2 TEU now makes express reference to equality, rights of

---

[113] CONV 357/02, Final Report of Working Group VI on Economic Governance, Brussels, 21 October 2002.
[114] Art I-2 CT.

minorities, and the values listed in the second sentence, which include those having a more 'social' orientation.

The EU's objectives are contained in Article 3 TEU, which is close to, although not identical with, the analogous provision of the Constitutional Treaty.[115] Article 3 TEU is framed as follows:

1. The Union's aim is to promote peace, its values and the well-being of its peoples.

2. The Union shall offer its citizens an area of freedom, security and justice without internal frontiers, in which the free movement of persons is ensured in conjunction with appropriate measures with respect to external border controls, asylum, immigration and the prevention and combating of crime.

3. The Union shall establish an internal market. It shall work for the sustainable development of Europe based on balanced economic growth and price stability, a highly competitive social market economy, aiming at full employment and social progress, and a high level of protection and improvement of the quality of the environment. It shall promote scientific and technological advance.

   It shall combat social exclusion and discrimination, and shall promote social justice and protection, equality between women and men, solidarity between generations and protection of the rights of the child.

   It shall promote economic, social and territorial cohesion, and solidarity among Member States.

   It shall respect its rich cultural and linguistic diversity, and shall ensure that Europe's cultural heritage is safeguarded and enhanced.

4. The Union shall establish an economic and monetary union whose currency is the euro.

5. In its relations with the wider world, the Union shall uphold and promote its values and interests and contribute to the protection of its citizens. It shall contribute to peace, security, the sustainable development of the Earth, solidarity and mutual respect among peoples, free and fair trade, eradication of poverty and the protection of human rights, in particular the rights of the child, as well as to the strict observance and the development of international law, including respect for the principles of the United Nations Charter.

6. The Union shall pursue its objectives by appropriate means commensurate with the competences which are conferred upon it in the Treaties.

It is unsurprising that the objectives listed in Article 3 TEU bear comparison with those in Article 2 EU of the previous Treaty. There are differences, however, as to the more precise wording and placing of the objectives. Thus, for example, mention of the area of freedom, security, and justice has 'moved up' the list to become Article 3(2) TEU, thereby signifying its centrality to EU policy. There is also more of the 'social' within the new list of objectives, especially in Article 3(3)

---

[115] Art I-3 CT.

TEU, with its explicit reference to a social market economy, social progress, social exclusion, social justice, and solidarity.

The reference to social market economy is qualified by the phrase 'highly competitive', which signals compromise in the corridors of power. This does not undermine the significance of use of the term 'social market economy', however, nor does it downplay the other references to the 'social' within Article 3 TEU. How far this makes a difference remains to be seen, but it is in any event reinforced by the point made below in the discussion of mandatory considerations. It should nonetheless be acknowledged that other provisions of the Lisbon Treaty, notably those dealing with economic and monetary policy, are framed resolutely in terms of the Member States and Union acting in accordance with the principle of an 'open market economy with free competition, favouring an efficient allocation of resources'.[116]

(b) Competence and consequences

It is the Treaty on the Functioning of the European Union (TFEU) that contains the detailed provisions specifying the areas in which, and the conditions on which, the Union can act. Part One of the TFEU is entitled 'Principles', Title I of which deals with categories of Union competence, a topic dealt with in an earlier chapter, to which reference should be made.[117] The application of the competence provisions to social policy gives rise to particular problems, which were addressed in the earlier analysis.[118]

(c) Duties and mandatory considerations

The structure of the TFEU is interesting in that the Treaty framers included, immediately after the provisions on competence, a set of Treaty articles under the heading 'Provisions having General Application'. These provisions therefore constitute Title II of Part One of the TFEU, which deals with 'Principles'.

There are provisions which impose specific duties on Union institutions concerning transparency, access to documents, and protection of personal data.[119] Article 17 TFEU is new and requires, *inter alia*, the Union to respect and not prejudice the status under national law of churches and religious associations or communities in the Member States.

The thrust of most provisions within Title II is, however, somewhat different. It is to mandate that certain considerations should be taken into account when dealing with any EU policy. This technique was used in the EC Treaty, as exemplified by the obligation to aim to eliminate inequality, and promote gender

---

[116] Art 120 TFEU. See also, Art 119 TFEU.   [117] Ch 5.
[118] pp 169–170.   [119] Arts 15–16 TFEU.

equality, in all Community activities,[120] which is reiterated in Article 8 TFEU. Article 11 TFEU also repeats an injunction contained in the previous Treaty,[121] to the effect that environmental protection requirements must be integrated into the definition and implementation of the Union policies and activities, in particular with a view to promoting sustainable development. Likewise Article 12 TFEU reiterates the previous obligation[122] that consumer protection requirements must be taken into account in defining and implementing other Union policies and activities.

The TFEU extends this technique. Thus Article 9 TFEU provides that in defining and implementing its policies and activities, the Union shall take into account requirements linked to the promotion of a high level of employment, the guarantee of adequate social protection, the fight against social exclusion, and a high level of education, training, and protection of human health. Article 10 TFEU stipulates that in defining and implementing its policies and activities, the Union shall aim to combat discrimination based on sex, racial or ethnic origin, religion or belief, disability, age, or sexual orientation. Article 13 TFEU imposes an obligation to 'pay full regard' to animal welfare when formulating and implementing Union policy, subject to the caveat that respect should be shown for national 'religious rites, cultural traditions and regional heritage'. Article 14 TFEU is the re-modelled provision on services of general economic interest, and will be examined in more detail below.

(d) Duties and administrative cooperation

Article 10 EC proved to be of considerable importance in the ECJ's jurisprudence. It has been replaced in substance by Article 4(3) TEU, which provides that:

Pursuant to the principle of sincere cooperation, the Union and the Member States shall, in full mutual respect, assist each other in carrying out tasks which flow from the Treaties.

The Member States shall take any appropriate measure, general or particular, to ensure fulfilment of the obligations arising out of the Treaties or resulting from the acts of the institutions of the Union.

The Member States shall facilitate the achievement of the Union's tasks and refrain from any measure which could jeopardise the attainment of the Union's objectives.

The administrative arm of national governments had obligations flowing from Article 10 EC, and more generally from the supremacy of EU law. There is now a new provision concerning administrative cooperation, although it is framed in guarded tones, which is why it is expressly said to be without prejudice to Member States' obligations to implement Union law, to the prerogatives and duties of the Commission, and to other Treaty provisions providing for

---

[120] Art 3(2) EC.   [121] Art 6 EC.   [122] Art 153(2) EC.

administrative cooperation among the Member States and between them and the Union.[123]

Article 197 TFEU states that effective implementation of EU law by the Member States is essential for the proper functioning of the Union and hence is to be regarded 'as a matter of common interest'. The EU can support Member States to improve their administrative capacity to implement EU law, by, for example, facilitating the exchange of information and of civil servants and support for training schemes. No Member State is obliged to avail itself of such support. Legislative regulations can be enacted, however, to establish the necessary measures to achieve the objectives of Article 197, excluding harmonization of national laws.

4. Lisbon Treaty: The Economic

This chapter has been structured so as to reveal the balance between the economic and the social within the EU. It is therefore fitting to consider the impact of the Lisbon Treaty in this respect. This section will therefore consider in outline the schema concerning the principal economic provisions of the Lisbon Treaty, being mindful of the fact revealed by the earlier discussion that some of these provisions also have a social dimension.

(a) Continuity

(i) Internal market

The TFEU has in general left the EU's core economic precepts unchanged, although there have been some modifications. Part Three of the TFEU deals with 'Union Policies and Internal Actions'. It is the largest Part of the TFEU, with 24 separate Titles. It is neither surprising, nor fortuitous that the internal market takes pride of place as Title I. Article 26 TFEU is the 'lead provision'.

1. The Union shall adopt measures with the aim of establishing or ensuring the functioning of the internal market, in accordance with the relevant provisions of the Treaties.
2. The internal market shall comprise an area without internal frontiers in which the free movement of goods, persons, services and capital is ensured in accordance with the provisions of the Treaties.
3. The Council, on a proposal from the Commission, shall determine the guidelines and conditions necessary to ensure balanced progress in all the sectors concerned.

Article 26 TFEU thus replaces Article 14 EC, subject to the modification that the 'time line' in the latter provision, whereby the measures to establish the internal

---

[123] Art 197(3) TFEU.

market were meant to be completed by December 1992, has been dropped. This was the Treaty catching up with the real world, since this aspect of Article 14 bore scant relation to reality, given that measures designed to foster the internal market have been made continuously since 1992.

Article 27 TFEU duly replicates Article 15 EC, stipulating that the Commission, when drawing up proposals to achieve the objectives in Article 26, must take into account the extent of the effort that certain economies showing differences in development will have to sustain for the establishment of the internal market. The Commission can then propose appropriate provisions to take this into account, but if these constitute derogations then they must be temporary and cause the least possible disturbance to the functioning of the internal market.

(ii) Four freedoms

The provisions concerning free movement of goods are contained in Title II, which follow those in the EC Treaty. Thus Articles 28 to 32 TFEU deal with the basic principles of the customs union, replicating those in the EC Treaty.[124] This is followed by Article 33 TFEU on customs cooperation between Member States, and between them and the Commission. This has sensibly been moved up the Treaty to follow the provisions on customs law. Article 33 TFEU, however, is broader than the analogous provision in the EC Treaty, since the latter precluded application of national criminal law or national administration of justice, and these limits have been removed from Article 33 TFEU.

Articles 34 to 37 TFEU repeat the basic precepts on free movement of goods. The abundant case law on the meaning of a quantitative restriction and all measures having equivalent effect will therefore continue to be controlling in the post-Lisbon world. A fortuitous but 'endearing' result of the numbering of the Lisbon provisions is that Article 36 TFEU deals with the public policy defence, thereby bringing us back to the numbering of this provision in the Rome Treaty.

Title III TFEU is concerned with agriculture and fisheries, retaining in this respect the ordering of provisions in the EC Treaty. It is surprising that the opportunity for re-ordering provisions in the Lisbon Treaty did not lead to this topic being moved to a later point in the Treaty, which would have been more appropriate.

The core story of the four freedoms is nonetheless picked up once again in Title IV, which deals with persons, services, and capital. The basic rules on free movement of persons in Articles 45 to 48 TFEU are unchanged, subject to modification in the voting rules concerning EU regulations on social security in relation to workers. The voting rule under the EC Treaty was co-decision, subject

---

[124] Arts 23–27 EC.

to the limit that the Council acted unanimously throughout this procedure.[125] The default position under the Lisbon Treaty is that the ordinary legislative procedure applies. However, this is subject to the caveat that where a member of the Council declares that a draft legislative act would affect important aspects of its social security system, including its scope, cost, or financial structure, or would affect the financial balance of that system, it can request that the matter be referred to the European Council. The ordinary legislative procedure is then suspended. The European Council can then either refer the draft measure back to the Council, which terminates the suspension of the ordinary legislative procedure, the European Council can take no action, or request the Commission to submit a new proposal, in either eventuality the result being that the act originally proposed is deemed not to have been adopted.

The rules on freedom of establishment in Articles 49 to 55 TFEU reiterate those in the EC Treaty, subject to minor modification. Thus Article 50(2) TFEU accords with political correctness by stating the European Parliament, as well as the Council and Commission, should take account of the factors listed therein when making directives. The ordinary legislative procedure now also applies for measures passed concerning the exercise of official authority in Article 51 TFEU. Article 53 TFEU, which deals with mutual recognition of qualifications and coordination of national rules concerning the self-employed, has been 'tightened' by removing previous limits on EU action.[126]

There is similar continuity in the provisions on services in Articles 57 to 62 TFEU, subject once again to some upgrading of the decision-making procedures, such that the ordinary legislative procedure now applies.[127] There are in addition some subtle changes, which betoken more caution than hitherto. Thus the previous provision whereby Member States 'declared their readiness'[128] to liberalize services over and beyond that required by directives if their economic situation so permitted, has been replaced by less ambitious wording, which states that Member States 'shall endeavour' to do so.[129]

The basic principle on free movement of capital in Article 63 TFEU is unaltered. There are some modifications in the legislative procedures, the norm being a shift towards the ordinary legislative procedure.[130] Article 65 TFEU retains Member States' power to, *inter alia*, take all requisite measures to prevent infringements of national law and regulations, in particular in the field of taxation and the prudential supervision of financial institutions, or to lay down procedures for the declaration of capital movements for purposes of administrative or statistical information, or to take measures which are justified on grounds of public policy or public security. This provision has been a fertile source of case law, and will doubtless continue to be so post-Lisbon. The most

---

[125] Art 42 EC.   [126] The limits were in Art 47(2) EC.
[127] Arts 56, 59 TFEU.   [128] Art 53 EC.   [129] Art 60 TFEU.
[130] Art 64(2) TFEU.

notable shift is that Article 60 EC, which featured in case law on freezing of assets discussed below,[131] has now been moved and recast as Article 75 TFEU.

(iii) Harmonization

The Treaty provisions on positive integration were always central to the economic dimension of the Community, and they will continue to fulfil an important role in the post-Lisbon world. Continuity is once again the order of the day.

The ordering of the relevant provisions has, however, been reversed, such that what was Article 94 EC has become Article 115 TFEU, while Article 95 EC has been replicated in Article 114 TFEU. This shift recognizes the centrality of Article 114 TFEU to EU harmonization and the fact that it, rather than Article 115, is the legal foundation for most such measures. The scope of application of Article 114 TFEU will largely depend on the ECJ's jurisprudence, as has been the case hitherto. This has been considered in a previous chapter to which reference should be made.[132]

The Lisbon Treaty added a provision dealing expressly with intellectual property rights. Article 118 TFEU provides that in the context of the establishment and functioning of the internal market, the European Parliament and Council, acting by the ordinary legislative procedure, shall establish measures for the creation of European intellectual property rights to provide uniform protection of intellectual property rights throughout the Union and for the setting up of centralized Union-wide authorization, coordination, and supervision arrangements.

(iv) Competition and State aid

The Treaty provisions on competition and State aid have always been of real significance for attainment of the overall economic objectives of the EU, by preventing the single market from being undermined by the actions of private or State actors. If private actors could divide markets through cartels this could recreate national barriers to trade, and competition law is in addition important in order to enhance economic efficiency within the EU. If States could provide aid to their own firms unchecked by the EU this would unbalance the level playing field that is at the heart of the single market project.

The provisions of the Lisbon Treaty follow those of the EC Treaty. The core precepts of competition law in Articles 81 and 82 EC have been repeated in Articles 101 and 102 TFEU, save for change of nomenclature from 'common market' to 'internal market' in the Lisbon version. This does not signal substantive change, but merely harmonizes with the language used in Article 26 TFEU, which is framed in terms of the internal market. Article 103 TFEU empowers

---

[131] pp 347–348.   [132] pp 189–190.

the EU as before to make regulations to give effect to Articles 101 and 102 TFEU, although there are problems as to how this power fits with the more general hierarchy of acts.[133] Article 106 TFEU duly repeats the provision concerning public undertakings that had hitherto been in Article 86 EC. The previous foundational rule in relation to State aids[134] is repeated in Article 107 TFEU, and subsequent articles specify, as before, the procedure that is applicable in State aid cases.[135]

(v) Trans-European networks and industry

The Lisbon Treaty has retained the previous provisions concerning trans-European networks and industry. The former is designed to enable firms to get the most from an internal market without frontiers by the development of trans-European networks in relation to transport, energy, and telecommunications infrastructures. The aim is to secure interconnection and inter-operability between national networks, and access thereto.[136] The latter, the Title on Industry, has the object of ensuring that the conditions necessary for the competitiveness of the EU exist, such as through the speeding up of industrial adjustment to structural change.

(b) Change

(i) EMU

It is important when assessing the balance between the economic and the social within the Lisbon Treaty not to forget the complex provisions concerning economic and monetary policy.[137] There is much in the Lisbon Treaty that coheres with the previous provisions, but there are also some subtle changes designed to enhance EU power. Whether they do so in this highly-charged macro-economic arena is another matter entirely.

The general principles concerning economic and monetary policy in Article 119 TFEU follow those previously laid down in Article 4 EC. The first signs of attempts to reinforce EU power are found in Article 121(4) TFEU. This is the terrain of EU economic policy, which is structured through broad economic policy guidelines. If it appears that a Member State's economic policy does not cohere with these guidelines this can lead to a warning from the Commission, followed by recommendations by the Council, which can decide to make this public. The novelty lies in the fact that the decision whether to 'name and shame' is now expressly said to be made without taking into account the vote of the State

---

[133] pp 257–258.   [134] Art 87 EC.
[135] Arts 108–109 TFEU.   [136] Arts 170–171 TFEU.
[137] J-V Louis, 'Economic Policy under the Lisbon Treaty' in S Griller and J Ziller (eds), *The Lisbon Treaty, EU Constitutionalism without a Constitutional Treaty?* (Springer, 2008) 285.

under investigation. The European Parliament's role in this area is also increased, since regulations made concerning multilateral surveillance are now made by the ordinary legislative procedure.[138] The Commission also gains power under the excessive deficit procedure, being able to issue an opinion to the Member State and make a proposal to the Council.[139]

An interesting novelty in the dense provisions concerning economic and monetary policy is Article 136 TFEU. A word is necessary by way of explanation. There was always a proximate linkage between economic and monetary policy. If Member States run excessive deficits on their balance of payments this will be regarded negatively by the financial world. The consequence is not hard to divine. Excessive deficits may then lead to a drop in the euro, since its value in relation to other currencies will be determined in part by views as to the strength of the economy using that currency. In the case of the EU, this means all the Member States that subscribe to the euro. Hence bad economic management in one State can lead to a fall in the value of the euro, which may well have negative consequences for other States. The crisis for the euro precipitated by the Greek economy exemplifies this in the starkest manner. It is for this very reason that Member States treat their respective economic balance sheets as a matter of 'common concern'.[140] The EC Treaty had complex provisions for dealing with excessive deficits,[141] which have been replicated in the Lisbon Treaty.[142] It was unsurprisingly difficult to use such provisions, more especially when the culprit was a large Member State, the paradox being that default by such a State was even more likely to have negative repercussions on monetary policy and the euro.

Article 136 TFEU is designed to address this, or more accurately provide a legal window through which further regulations might be made that address the problem.

1. In order to ensure the proper functioning of economic and monetary union, and in accordance with the relevant provisions of the Treaties, the Council shall, in accordance with the relevant procedure from among those referred to in Articles 121 and 126, with the exception of the procedure set out in Article 126(14), adopt measures specific to those Member States whose currency is the euro:

   (a) to strengthen the coordination and surveillance of their budgetary discipline;
   (b) to set out economic policy guidelines for them, while ensuring that they are compatible with those adopted for the whole of the Union and are kept under surveillance.

2. For those measures set out in paragraph 1, only members of the Council representing Member States whose currency is the euro shall take part in the vote.

A qualified majority of the said members shall be defined in accordance with Article 238(3)(a).

---

[138] Art 121(6) TFEU.   [139] Arts 126(5)–(6) TFEU.
[140] Art 121 TFEU.   [141] 104 EC.   [142] Art 126 TFEU.

If one stands back from the difficult wording the intent becomes clear. The proper functioning of economic and monetary union requires that coordination and surveillance of budgetary discipline of those in the euro group should be strengthened. It requires also the power to set specific economic policy guidelines for particular Member States. Article 136 TFEU thus empowers the Council to adopt such measures. Whether it will do so remains to be seen. The tactic was nonetheless sound. It is unlikely that the Member States would have agreed to place measures that might be made pursuant to Article 136 in the Treaty itself. The EU has therefore at the least given itself power to make such measures for the future. The Greek economic crisis has, however, revealed that the Treaty rules concerning budgetary discipline may well need to be strengthened considerably if such problems are not to recur in the future.

(ii) Energy

The Lisbon Treaty has conformed to historical practice by adding Titles that had not existed hitherto. Thus there is now a new Title on Energy. The EU had enacted measures on energy hitherto, often based on a conjunction of Articles 47, 55, and 95 EC.[143]

Article 194 TFEU is premised on the economic and environmental dimensions of energy. It stipulates that Union policy on energy is to ensure: the functioning of the energy market; security of energy supply in the Union; promotion of energy efficiency, including renewable energy; and promotion of interconnection of energy networks. The European Parliament and Council establish the measures necessary to attain these objectives in accordance with the ordinary legislative procedure,[144] but the measures do not affect a Member State's right to determine the conditions for exploiting its energy resources, its choice between different energy sources, and the general structure of its energy supply.

(iii) Tourism

Tourism is an important industry in its own right. This is now reflected in the inclusion of a new Title in the TFEU.

Article 195 TFEU provides that the Union shall complement the action of the Member States in the tourism sector, in particular by promoting the competitiveness of Union undertakings. EU action is to be aimed at encouraging the

---

[143] Directive 2003/54/EC of the European Parliament and of the Council of 26 June 2003 concerning common rules for the internal market in electricity and repealing Directive 96/92 [2003] OJ L176/37; Directive 2003/55/EC of the European Parliament and of the Council of 26 June 2003 concerning common rules for the internal market in natural gas and repealing Directive 98/30 [2003] OJ L176/57.

[144] Different voting rules apply when the measure is primarily fiscal in nature, Art 194(3) TFEU.

creation of a favourable environment for the development of tourism undertakings, and promoting cooperation between the Member States, particularly by the exchange of good practice.

The European Parliament and the Council, acting in accordance with the ordinary legislative procedure, are empowered to establish specific measures to complement action within the Member States to achieve the Treaty objectives, subject to the exclusion of any harmonization.

5. Lisbon Treaty: The Social

(a) Continuity

There is much continuity in the social provisions of the Lisbon Treaty, although as with the case of the economic there are some modifications.

(i) *Citizenship*

The core provisions on citizenship replicate those in the EC Treaty. These provisions are now brought together in Part Two of the TFEU, which covers 'Non-Discrimination and Citizenship of the Union'.

The basic proscription on discrimination on grounds of nationality constitutes the lead article in this part of the TFEU, and is contained in Article 18 TFEU. The important power to take action to combat discrimination, which was found in Article 13 EC, is now enshrined in Article 19 TFEU, subject to the modification that measures enacted pursuant to this Article are made according to a special legislative procedure, after obtaining the consent of the European Parliament.

Article 20 TFEU is the lead provision on citizenship, and reiterates the core principle from Article 17 EC, to the effect that every national of a Member State is a citizen of the EU, that such citizenship is in addition to, and does not replace, national citizenship. Article 20 TFEU, as distinct from Article 17 EC, also elaborates the rights and duties, '*inter alia*', of EU citizens: the right to reside and move freely within the territory of the Member States; the right to stand and vote in municipal and European Parliament elections; the right to consular protection; and the right to petition the European Parliament and apply to the Ombudsman in any of the official languages. Article 20 TFEU concludes by stating that 'these rights shall be exercised in accordance with the conditions and limits defined by the Treaties and by the measures adopted thereunder', although, as we have seen, the previous embodiment of this principle did little to curb the ECJ's activist jurisprudence.[145]

---

[145] pp 304–305.

The remaining provisions elaborate in more detail on the particular citizenship rights listed in Article 20 TFEU. Thus Article 21 TFEU is the successor to Article 18 EC, and deals with the right to reside and move freely, 'subject to the limitations and conditions laid down in the Treaties and by the measures adopted to give them effect'. The EU is empowered to adopt provisions, in accordance with the ordinary legislative procedure, to facilitate exercise of this right. Article 21(3) TFEU does signal a modest change, by allowing such measures to be made in relation to social security and social protection, subject to the caveat that they must be enacted pursuant to a special legislative procedure, requiring Council unanimity and consultation with the European Parliament. Article 22 TFEU deals in detail with the right to vote and stand in municipal and European Parliament elections, hitherto covered by Article 19 EC. Article 23 TFEU is concerned with rights to consular protection, the relevant change from Article 20 EC being that the EU is now empowered to pass directives to coordinate Member State action on this issue. Article 24 TFEU reiterates Article 21 EC on citizen access to the European Parliament and the Ombudsman, and also empowers the making of regulations dealing with the new citizens' initiative.

(ii) Employment

The Lisbon Treaty reiterates the employment provisions of the EC Treaty. The imperative of EU employment policy in Article 125 EC is retained in Article 145 TFEU, and the EU operates so as to support and complement Member State action in seeking to attain high levels of employment.[146] The pre-existing position whereby Member States consider their employment policies within the framework of guidelines laid down by the EU is retained,[147] as is the EU's ability to enact incentive measures to encourage cooperation between Member States in the employment field, this being undertaken primarily through what is in effect the Open Method of Coordination.[148]

(iii) Social policy

It was seen from the earlier discussion that the Working Group on Social Europe did not recommend any real change to EU competence over social policy. It is therefore unsurprising that the provisions of the Lisbon Treaty largely repeat those from the EC Treaty. The difficulties of applying the new provisions on competence in this area have been considered above.[149]

Article 151 TFEU is the lead provision and remains unaltered from Article 136 EC. Article 152 TFEU is new. It states that the EU recognizes and promotes the role of the social partners, taking into account the diversity of national

---

[146] Art 147 TFEU.   [147] Art 148 TFEU.   [148] Art 149 TFEU.
[149] pp 169–170.

systems. It shall facilitate dialogue between the social partners, respecting their autonomy. The Tripartite Social Summit for Growth and Employment shall contribute to social dialogue.

The areas listed in Article 153(1) TFEU in which the EU can act to advance social policy is unchanged from Article 137 EC, as are the types of action than can be taken pursuant to Article 153(2) TFEU. The provision whereby a Member State can entrust management and labour with implementation of a directive enacted pursuant to Article 153 has been extended to implementation of decisions, Article 153(3) TFEU.

The limits and constraints from Article 137 EC have been retained in Article 153. Thus provisions adopted pursuant to Article 153 must not affect the right of Member States to define the fundamental principles of their social security systems and must not significantly affect the financial equilibrium thereof, and must not prevent any Member State from maintaining or introducing more stringent protective measures compatible with the Treaties.[150] Article 153 does not moreover apply to pay, the right of association, the right to strike, or the right to impose lock-outs.[151]

The social policy objectives in Article 151 TFEU can, as before, be advanced through measures taken by the Commission to coordinate Member State action in areas of social policy. The Open Method of Coordination is, as before, the principal vehicle used to this end.

The Lisbon Treaty retains the obligation to consult management and labour on proposals concerning social policy.[152] The option for management and labour to trigger the mechanism whereby they agree on social policy proposals and those agreements may be imbued with legal force through a Council decision has also been preserved.[153]

The important principle embodied hitherto in Article 141 EC, which proscribes gender discrimination, is preserved in Article 157 TFEU. The European Social Fund is continued in Articles 162 to 164 TFEU.

(iv) Education, vocational training, youth, and sport

The basic framework concerning education, vocational training, and youth remains unaltered, subject to the addition of provisions on sport.[154] The EU is limited to taking action to support and supplement that of the Member States. The provisions empowering the EU to act in these areas are nonetheless broader than might initially have been thought.[155] This is moreover an area where overlap between internal market principles and education has given rise to controversial ECJ decisions.[156]

---

[150] Art 153(4) TFEU.   [151] Art 153(5) TFEU.   [152] Art 154 TFEU.
[153] Art 155 TFEU.   [154] Arts 165–166 TFEU.   [155] pp 173–178.
[156] Case C-147/03 *Commission v Austria* [2005] ECR I-5969.

(v) Culture

The Treaty rules relating to culture repeat those of the EC Treaty, subject to the caveat that measures are enacted in this area by the ordinary legislative procedure shorn of the previous requirement of Council unanimity during this procedure.

(vi) Public health

Continuity with the previous regime is also the hallmark of the approach to public health. The basic philosophy is that EU action complements Member State action in relation to health, through, *inter alia*, techniques akin to the Open Method of Coordination.[157] The EU is, as before, accorded more dispositive power in relation to certain aspects of health care. It can enact measures to achieve high standards of health and safety in relation to body parts, including blood, and medicinal products and devices. It can also pass measures to protect health in the veterinary and phytosanitary fields.[158]

The Lisbon Treaty added a provision whereby incentive measures can be adopted in accordance with the ordinary legislative procedure to protect and improve human health. The measures can be made 'in particular' to: combat major cross-border health scourges; monitor, give early warning of, and combat serious cross-border threats to health. It also empowers measures 'which have as their direct objective the protection of public health regarding tobacco and the abuse of alcohol, excluding any harmonization of the laws and regulations of the Member States'.[159]

It should be recalled, moreover, that Member States' public health systems have in the past been markedly affected by the ECJ's internal market jurisprudence, and there is no reason why this should change in the post-Lisbon world.

(vii) Consumer protection

Article 169 TFEU is the same as Article 153 EC, subject to the caveat that the injunction that consumer protection should be taken into account in defining and implementing other EU policies, which had hitherto been Article 153(2) EC, has now been moved to Article 12 TFEU, as part of the list of policy considerations that must be taken into account when developing EU policy. Subject to this caveat consumer policy continues to be 'dual track': consumer protection measures can be enacted pursuant to Article 114 TFEU when they impact on the internal market, and in other instances measures can be taken that support or supplement Member State action.

---

[157] Art 168(1)–(2) TFEU.　　　[158] Art 168(4) TFEU.　　　[159] Art 168(5) TFEU.

(viii) Economic, social, and territorial cohesion

'Economic and Social Cohesion' has been renamed 'Economic, Social and Territorial Cohesion'. The fundamentals of the Treaty articles that provide the foundation for the Structural Funds nonetheless remain much the same.

Article 174 TFEU is the lead provision and repeats the substance of Article 158 EC, save for the fact that there is now greater specificity as to the nature of the disadvantaged regions that should benefit from EU disbursement. There has been some change in voting rules. Thus the ordinary legislative procedure now applies to regulations that define the tasks and organization of the Structural Funds.[160]

(ix) Environment

There has been some modification of the provisions concerning the environment in the Lisbon Treaty. Thus Article 191 TFEU now includes in the list of objectives specific mention of combating climate change. It is located within the heading that refers to the promotion of measures at the international level to deal with regional or worldwide environmental problems. The remaining provisions replicate those in the EC Treaty.

(b) Change

The Lisbon Treaty, subject to the modifications noted above, represents a continuation of the status quo in relation to social policy. There are, however, some areas where there has been greater change.

(i) Citizenship

The basic provisions on citizenship have been retained in the Lisbon Treaty, subject to the modifications noted above. The Lisbon Treaty does, however, contain new provisions pertinent to EU citizens. These are found in Article 10 and 11 TEU. Article 10(3) TEU provides that every citizen has the right to participate in the democratic life of the Union, and states that decisions shall be taken as openly and as closely as possible to the citizen. Article 11 TEU stipulates that:

1. The institutions shall, by appropriate means, give citizens and representative associations the opportunity to make known and publicly exchange their views in all areas of Union action.

2. The institutions shall maintain an open, transparent and regular dialogue with representative associations and civil society.

---

[160] Art 177 TFEU.

3. The European Commission shall carry out broad consultations with parties concerned in order to ensure that the Union's actions are coherent and transparent.

4. Not less than one million citizens who are nationals of a significant number of Member States may take the initiative of inviting the European Commission, within the framework of its powers, to submit any appropriate proposal on matters where citizens consider that a legal act of the Union is required for the purpose of implementing the Treaties.

   The procedures and conditions required for such a citizens' initiative shall be determined in accordance with the first paragraph of Article 24 of the Treaty on the Functioning of the European Union.

The possible impact of these provisions has been considered in an earlier chapter, and reference should be made to that discussion.[161]

(ii) Services of general economic interest

The previous discussion has already touched on Article 16 EC. It has now been replaced by Article 14 TFEU.[162]

Without prejudice to Article 4 of the Treaty on European Union or to Articles 93, 106 and 107 of this Treaty, and given the place occupied by services of general economic interest in the shared values of the Union as well as their role in promoting social and territorial cohesion, the Union and the Member States, each within their respective powers and within the scope of application of the Treaties, shall take care that such services operate on the basis of principles and conditions, particularly economic and financial conditions, which enable them to fulfil their missions. The European Parliament and the Council, acting by means of regulations in accordance with the ordinary legislative procedure, shall establish these principles and set these conditions without prejudice to the competence of Member States, in compliance with the Treaties, to provide, to commission and to fund such services.

The Lisbon Treaty also contains a Protocol on Services of General Interest, which elaborates the shared values of the EU with respect to services of general economic interest.[163] These are said by Article 1 to include: the essential role and wide discretion of national, regional, and local authorities in providing such services as closely as possible to the needs of the users; the diversity between such services and the differences in needs of users resulting from different geographical, social, or cultural situations; and a high level of quality, safety, and affordability, equal treatment and the promotion of universal access, and of user rights. Article 2 of the Protocol states that the Treaty provisions do not affect 'in any

---

[161] Ch 2.
[162] Krajewski, Neergaard, van de Grondon (n 1); A Winterstein, 'The Internal Market and Services of General Interest' in G Amato, H Bribosia and B de Witte (eds), *Genesis and Destiny of the European Constitution* (Bruylant, 2007) 645.
[163] Protocol (No 26) on Services of General Interest.

way' the competence of Member States to provide, commission, and organize non-economic services of general interest.

The strong wording of Article 2 of the Protocol means that much will turn on the divide between the economic and the non-economic in this respect. This is acknowledged by the Commission in its 2007 Communication.[164] It espoused the functional approach developed by the ECJ, whereby the nature of the service is determined by criteria related to the functioning of the particular service, such as the existence of a market, State prerogatives, or obligations of solidarity, rather than a simple institutional or funding test. The Commission also acknowledged that the scope of the 'economic' for these purposes was expanding in relation to areas such as social services.[165]

The novelty of Article 14 TFEU is that it accords the EU legislative competence. The wording of the Article imposes a duty, not just a power. The EU is mandated to enact legislative regulations to establish the principles and set the conditions on which services of general economic interest fulfil their mission. This is said to be without prejudice to Member States' competence to provide, commission, and fund such services. Notwithstanding this stricture, the exercise of the EU's legislative power will inevitably structure or constrain how the competence of the Member States is exercised.

It remains to be seen whether the EU will in fact enact such horizontal measures, applicable to all such services. The Commission's 2004 White Paper came down against a general framework directive for such services, doubting whether it would be useful, preferring instead to continue with its sectoral approach in combination with a horizontal approach to certain specific issues, such as the financing of services of general interest and the awarding of contracts.[166] The same sentiment is apparent in its 2007 Communication. There was little appetite for a general horizontal regulation, the preference being for a mix of sector-specific and issue-specific measures. This would entail the provision of legal guidance on cross-cutting issues, sector-specific initiatives, and in-depth monitoring and evaluation.[167]

(iii) Civil protection

The Lisbon Treaty introduced a new head of competence entitled 'Civil Protection'. Article 196 TFEU states that the EU shall encourage cooperation between Member States to improve the effectiveness of systems for preventing and protecting against natural or man-made disasters.

---

[164] Services of General Interest, including Social Services of General Interest: A New European Commitment, COM(2007) 725, 4–5.
[165] ibid 8.
[166] White Paper (n 81) [4.1]–[4.3].
[167] Services of General Interest (n 164) 11–13.

To this end, EU action shall aim to: support and complement Member States' action in risk prevention, in preparing civil-protection personnel and in responding to natural or man-made disasters within the Union; promote swift, effective operational cooperation within the EU between national civil protection services; and promote consistency in international civil-protection work. The EU is empowered to establish the 'measures necessary' to help achieve these objectives, excluding any harmonization of national laws.

(iv) Charter of Rights

It is fitting to conclude this section by mention of the Charter of Rights, which contains a number of social rights, broadly conceived. Its impact on the balance between the economic and the social will, however, depend not only on the interpretation of the particular rights, but also on the construction adopted of crucial horizontal provisions of the Charter.[168] The divide between rights and principles will be particularly significant in this respect; so too will be the interpretation of the injunction that the Charter does not add or modify EU powers or tasks as defined in the Treaties. These, and other pertinent issues, are considered in detail in an earlier chapter.[169]

6. Conclusion

There are two stories that might be told about the balance between the economic and the social in the Lisbon Treaty. The first would emphasize the increased attention given to the social in the values and objectives of the EU, the conclusion being that this constituted a meaningful re-balancing of the previous Treaty order. The second would focus on the subject-matter provisions of the TFEU, concluding that the devil is always in the detail and minimal change in these provisions heralded preservation of the status quo.

There is something to be said for both stories, but they are nonetheless both incomplete. The 'true balance' between the economic and the social at any stage of the Community's existence can only be divined in part by perusal of changes to the primary Treaty articles. Three other factors have always been crucial in this respect, and will remain so in the post-Lisbon world. The nature and content of EU legislation made pursuant to these powers, their interpretation by the Union courts, and the priority accorded to different aspects of Union policy by the key institutional players will continue to shape the reality of the divide between the economic and the social as it has done in the past.[170]

---

[168] Damjanovic and de Witte (n 11) 20–25.   [169] Ch 6.

[170] P Craig, 'Competence and Member State Autonomy: Causality, Consequence and Legitimacy' in B de Witte and H Micklitz (eds), *The European Court of Justice and the Autonomy of Member States* (Intersentia, 2010) ch 1.

Commentators will undoubtedly differ as to what the balance ought to be. This is readily apparent from the preceding discussion, where we saw sharply divergent views in the pre-Lisbon literature. My own view is that the economic and the social are not and cannot be kept separate. Economic regulation raises important normative issues as to the risks which society is willing to accept. The balance between the economic and the social is and always has been inherently political. These issues should not be excluded from the agenda of majoritarian politics. Nor should we be forced to accept a zero-sum relationship between majoritarian democracy and the accountability of non-majoritarian institutions within the EU.

9

Freedom, Security, and Justice

The Lisbon Treaty made significant changes to the EU's architecture by removing the Third Pillar and making provision for 'freedom, security, and justice' within the main fabric of the Treaty. There has, post-9/11, been much legislation enacted under what was the Third Pillar and Title IV EC. This volume of output is unlikely to change post-Lisbon.[1] It is therefore important to reflect on the Lisbon provisions dealing with 'freedom, security, and justice', more especially because measures enacted in this area have been controversial.

The chapter begins by examining the introduction of the Three Pillar Structure in the Maastricht Treaty and its subsequent modification in the Treaty of Amsterdam. The discussion then turns to the Lisbon Treaty, and the principles that now govern the Area of Freedom, Security, and Justice (AFSJ), followed by analysis of the general provisions applicable to this area. The remaining parts of the chapter consider the different component parts of the AFSJ, the strategy throughout being to give a brief exposition of the position pre-Lisbon, to consider the impact of the Lisbon Treaty, and the dualities and tensions that beset each part. The chapter concludes with more general reflections on the purpose of the AFSJ, viewed through the lens of the three major programmes, Tampere, Hague, and Stockholm, which have guided AFSJ policy. A warning should be given at the outset. This is difficult and complex terrain. Good people have slipped through legal and doctrinal fissures in this area, never to be heard of again.

---

[1] K Hailbronner, *Immigration and Asylum Law and Policy of the European Union* (Kluwer, 2000); E Guild and C Harlow (eds), *Implementing Amsterdam: Immigration and Asylum Rights in EC Law* (Hart, 2001); E Denza, *The Intergovernmental Pillars of the European Union* (Oxford University Press, 2002); N Walker (ed), *Europe's Area of Freedom, Security and Justice* (Oxford University Press, 2004); S Peers, *EU Justice and Home Affairs Law* (Oxford University Press, 2nd edn, 2006); A Baldaccini, E Guild and H Toner (eds), *Whose Freedom, Security and Justice?: EU Immigration and Asylum Law and Policy* (Hart, 2007); V Mitsilegas, *EU Criminal Law* (Hart, 2009); H Lindahl (ed), *A Right to Inclusion and Exclusion?: Normative Fault Lines of the EU's Area of Freedom, Security and Justice* (Hart, 2009).

1. Maastricht to Lisbon

(a) Maastricht: Three Pillars

(i) Creation

Intergovernmental cooperation to combat matters such as terrorism, cross-border crime, and external frontiers did not begin with the Maastricht Treaty. Numerous mechanisms for cooperation pre-dated the Treaty on European Union. Thus, for example, the Trevi Group was created in 1975 by the Rome European Council in order to coordinate the fight against terrorism, and its mandate was extended in 1985 to encompass serious international crimes such as drug trafficking, bank robbery, and arms trafficking. A further prominent example was the Schengen Agreement 1985, designed to remove border controls among the participating States, which was supplemented by the Schengen Implementing Convention 1990.

It was, however, the Treaty on European Union (TEU) which formalized and extended the Pillar Structure. It was signed by the Member States in Maastricht in February 1992.[2] It was however rejected by Denmark in a referendum, but after several 'concessions' were secured by the Danish Government a second referendum yielded a narrow majority in favour of ratification. A challenge to the constitutionality of ratification failed before the German Federal Supreme Court,[3] and the Treaty entered into force in November 1993.

The TEU established the 'Three-Pillar' structure for what was henceforth to be the European Union, with the Communities as the first of these pillars and the EEC Treaty being officially renamed the European Community (EC) Treaty. There were originally seven titles in the TEU: Title I included the 'common provisions', which set out the basic objectives of the TEU. Titles II, III, and IV covered the 'First Pillar' amendments to the EEC, ECSC, and Euratom Treaties respectively. Title V created the Second Pillar of the Common Foreign and Security Policy (CFSP), Title VI the Third Pillar of Justice and Home Affairs (JHA), and Title VII contained the final provisions. This basic architecture remained unchanged until the Lisbon Treaty, notwithstanding amendment and restructuring of the Second and Third Pillars, and the addition of a new Title VII to allow for closer/enhanced cooperation between Member States, with the final provisions thus becoming Title VIII.

The original formulation of the Justice and Home Affairs Pillar under Articles K.1 to K.9 TEU governed policies on matters such as such as asylum, immigration, and 'third country' nationals, which were later integrated into the EC

---

[2] R Corbett, *The Treaty of Maastricht* (Longman, 1993).
[3] See Cases 2 BvR 2134/92 and 2159/92 *Brunner v The European Union Treaty* [1994] 1 CMLR 57, discussed in Ch 4.

Treaty by the Treaty of Amsterdam. However, it also included cooperation on a range of international crime issues and various forms of judicial, customs, and police cooperation, including the establishment of a European Police Office (Europol) for exchanging information.[4]

Decision making under the Third Pillar was more intergovernmental and less supranational. The Council of Ministers was given the role of adopting joint positions and drawing up agreements on the basis of Member State or Commission initiatives, acting unanimously except on matters of procedure or when implementing joint actions or agreed conventions.[5] The Commission was to be 'fully associated' and the Parliament was to be informed, its views to be 'duly taken into consideration', and it could question or recommend matters to the Council.[6] A Coordinating Committee, which became the notorious and secretive K-4 committee, was set up to help the Council, and had a role similar to that of Coreper under the EC Treaty.

(ii) Rationale

The Three Pillar structure defined the EU's architecture from Maastricht to Lisbon. It is therefore important to reflect on the rationale for its creation.

Weiler argued that consociationalism was the key to understanding the Three Pillar structure.[7] In pluralistic societies functional stability was normally secured by cross-cutting cleavages. This could not, however, explain such stability in societies characterized by cleavages which reinforced each other, leading to divisive conceptions of the public good. Some countries had such reinforcing social cleavage, and yet were stable nonetheless. Consociational theory sought to explain this through the behaviour of a cartel of elites, which rendered the system both functional and stable. The 'elites would share a commitment to the maintenance of the system and to the improvement of its cohesion, functionality and stability'.[8] They would also deliver the agreement or acquiescence of their constituents. These elites would commonly operate outside normal political forums, and proceed by consensus politics rather than the dictates of majority rule.

Weiler used consociational theory to explain the Three Pillar structure.[9] Thus on this view the crucial factor explaining the emergence of the Second and Third Pillars was the sharply segmented nature of the politics which prevailed in these areas. For Weiler it was the very lack of substantive commonality that 'pushed the Member States to insist on this form of governance in this area'.[10]

---

[4] Art K.1 EU.   [5] Art K.3 EU.   [6] Arts K.4(2) and K.6 EU.
[7] J Weiler, U Haltern and F Mayer, 'European Democracy and its Critique' in J Hayward (ed), *The Crisis of Representation in Europe* (Frank Cass, 1995).
[8] ibid 30.   [9] ibid 29.   [10] ibid 29.

There is, however, an alternative explanation, which was also acknowledged by Weiler.[11] The Member States wished to have some degree of international cooperation in these areas, but were not ready for the application of the full supranational machinery that operated in the Community Pillar. Thus the Second and Third Pillars gave the Member States an institutionalized forum in which to discuss these matters, without subjecting themselves to supranational controls.

This view is not dependent, however, upon the existence of sharply segmented cleavages as between the Member States. The issues dealt with by the Second and Third Pillar were undoubtedly sensitive to national polities. There is, however, little reason for thinking that differences of view as between Member States were necessarily more severe than those that existed on Community Pillar issues. There is moreover little evidence that any such cleavages on Second and Third Pillar issues were reinforcing across different divides. This is central to consociationalism, since it gives society its segmented quality and dictates a consensual solution outside of the normal political forum. Neither is it self-evident that decision making in the Second and Third Pillar should be characterized as a consensual solution outside the normal political forum. An international agreement in which States maintain the monopoly of control is the normal method of resolving international differences. Supranationalism of the kind which exists within the Community Pillar is the exception, not the rule.

The better explanation for choosing intergovernmental rather than supranational machinery in the Second and Third Pillar is, rather, that the Member States believed that some form of cooperation would be beneficial for reasons of the kind articulated by international relations theorists.[12] The Member States wished for some established mechanism through which they could cooperate in the areas of Common Foreign and Security Policy and Justice and Home Affairs. Setting up *ad hoc* meetings to discuss such matters is cumbersome, time consuming, and involves heavy 'transaction costs', more especially as the number of players expands. The sensitive nature of the subject matter, touching closely as it did at the heart of traditional conceptions of sovereignty, meant, however, that Member States preferred the 'default position' of intergovernmentalism, thereby retaining maximum control in their own hands. The cost-benefit analysis of having supranationalism, with its attendant delegation of power to the Commission and the European Court of Justice (ECJ) was therefore negative, in the sense

---

[11] ibid 30.
[12] A Moravcsik, 'Preferences and Power in the European Community: A Liberal Intergovernmentalist Approach' (1993) 31 JCMS 473; A Moravcsik, *National Preference Formation and Interstate Bargaining in the European Community, 1955–86* (Harvard University Press, 1992); M Pollack, *The Engines of European Integration: Delegation, Agency and Agenda Setting in the EU* (Oxford University Press, 2003); M Pollack, 'International Relations Theory and European Integration' EUI Working Papers, RSC 2000/55.

that the benefits attendant on supranationalism in these areas were felt by the Member States to be outweighed by the costs.

(b) Amsterdam: Three Pillars modified

A major criticism of the Maastricht Treaty was that many of the policies under the JHA Pillar called for institutional provisions and legal controls that were quite different from the intergovernmental processes established. Unlike the foreign and security policy matters under the Second Pillar, the Third Pillar involved subjects such as immigration, asylum, border controls, and constraints on movement, which touched on fundamental human rights, and raised issues similar to those arising under the free movement provisions of the EC Treaty.

It was argued, therefore, that the need for openness and accountability in this policy field was much greater, requiring a full role for the European Parliament and review jurisdiction for the ECJ. Arguments for reform ranged from improving the institutional provisions under the existing JHA, to absorbing the Third Pillar entirely into the Community Pillar. What emerged in the Amsterdam Treaty lay between the two, with parts of JHA being incorporated into EC Title IV, and the remaining Third Pillar provisions being subjected to a range of institutional controls closer to those under the Community Pillar.

Thus the major structural substantive change was the incorporation into the Community Pillar of a large part of the former Third Pillar on the free movement of persons, covering visas, asylum, immigration, and judicial cooperation in civil matters,[13] which was shifted to what became Title IV, Articles 61 to 69 EC. The aim of this title and that of the amended Third Pillar, which covered Police and Judicial Cooperation in Criminal Matters (PJCC), were similarly described, both being intended to establish 'an area of freedom, security and justice'. Further, the *acquis* of the 1985 Schengen Treaty on the gradual abolition of common border checks was integrated by a Protocol to the Amsterdam Treaty into the EU framework.[14]

While the new Title IV on the free movement of persons was part of Community law, the close legal and institutional connection between these Community policies and those of the Third Pillar was still evident, thereby highlighting the increasing complexity of the EU constitutional order, and the move away from the relative clarity of the previous Community legal order.

The Area of Freedom, Security and Justice prior to the Lisbon Treaty was thus comprised of the remodelled Third Pillar and Title IV EC. The pre-Lisbon Treaty provisions dealing with the component parts of the AFSJ will be con-

[13] A new title on customs cooperation was also added in Art 135 EC.
[14] P Kuijper, 'Some Legal Problems Associated with the Communitarization of Policy on Visas, Asylum and Immigration under the Amsterdam Treaty and Incorporation of the Schengen Acquis' (2000) 37 CMLRev 345; S Peers, 'Caveat Emptor: Integrating the Schengen Acquis into the European Union Legal Order' (1999) 2 CYELS 87.

sidered in due course below, when analysing the changes made by the Lisbon Treaty.

2. Lisbon Treaty: General Principles

The Lisbon Treaty has had a marked impact on the AFSJ. This section will examine the general changes made by the Lisbon Treaty, with detailed examination of particular AFSJ provisions considered in the sections that follow.

(a) Values and objectives

Article 2 TEU sets out the EU's values, and follows the corresponding provision of the Constitutional Treaty.[15]

The Union is founded on the values of respect for human dignity, freedom, democracy, equality, the rule of law and respect for human rights, including the rights of persons belonging to minorities. These values are common to the Member States in a society in which pluralism, non-discrimination, tolerance, justice, solidarity and equality between women and men prevail.

The EU's objectives are contained in Article 3 TEU, which is close to, although not identical with, the analogous provision of the Constitutional Treaty.[16] Article 3 TEU is framed as follows.

1. The Union's aim is to promote peace, its values and the well-being of its peoples.
2. The Union shall offer its citizens an area of freedom, security and justice without internal frontiers, in which the free movement of persons is ensured in conjunction with appropriate measures with respect to external border controls, asylum, immigration and the prevention and combating of crime.
3. The Union shall establish an internal market. It shall work for the sustainable development of Europe based on balanced economic growth and price stability, a highly competitive social market economy, aiming at full employment and social progress, and a high level of protection and improvement of the quality of the environment. It shall promote scientific and technological advance.

   It shall combat social exclusion and discrimination, and shall promote social justice and protection, equality between women and men, solidarity between generations and protection of the rights of the child.

   It shall promote economic, social and territorial cohesion, and solidarity among Member States.

   It shall respect its rich cultural and linguistic diversity, and shall ensure that Europe's cultural heritage is safeguarded and enhanced.

---

[15] Art I-2 CT.   [16] Art I-3 CT.

4. The Union shall establish an economic and monetary union whose currency is the euro.

5. In its relations with the wider world, the Union shall uphold and promote its values and interests and contribute to the protection of its citizens. It shall contribute to peace, security, the sustainable development of the Earth, solidarity and mutual respect among peoples, free and fair trade, eradication of poverty and the protection of human rights, in particular the rights of the child, as well as to the strict observance and the development of international law, including respect for the principles of the United Nations Charter.

6. The Union shall pursue its objectives by appropriate means commensurate with the competences which are conferred upon it in the Treaties

The objectives listed in Article 3 TEU bear comparison with those in Article 2 EU of the previous Treaty. However, there are differences as to the more precise wording and placing of the objectives. Thus, for example, it is not fortuitous that mention of the area of freedom, security, and justice has 'moved up' the list to become Article 3(2) TEU, thereby signifying its centrality to EU policy.

(b) Treaty and architecture

The Lisbon Treaty has completed the transition that began with the Amsterdam Treaty. The Pillar system introduced by the Maastricht Treaty has been dismantled, although distinct rules still apply to the CFSP. The provisions concerning the AFSJ are no longer divided in the way in which they were prior to the Lisbon Treaty. They are grouped together in Title V of Part Three of the Treaty on the Functioning of the European Union (TFEU), which deals with 'Union Policies and Internal Actions'. Title V is located after those dealing with the internal market, free movement of goods, agriculture and fisheries, and free movement of persons, services, and capital.

It should be emphasized that the approach to the AFSJ adopted in the Lisbon Treaty follows very closely that in the Constitutional Treaty. This is true not only in relation to the detailed Treaty articles dealing with different aspects of the AFSJ, but also in relation to the more general principles and precepts that should apply to this area.[17] Thus it was Working Group X on 'Freedom, Security, and Justice'[18] from the Convention on the Future of Europe that strongly advocated de-pillarization, the incorporation of the Third Pillar into the main body of the Treaty, and the abolition of the distinctive categories of legal act that had previously applied to that area.

---

[17] Arts III-257–277 CT.
[18] CONV 426/02, Final Report of Working Group X, 'Freedom, Security and Justice', Brussels, 2 December, 2002.

(c) Competence and the AFSJ

The Lisbon Treaty established categories of competence for different subject matter areas, which were examined in an earlier chapter, to which reference should be made.[19] The AFSJ is deemed to be an area that falls within shared competence.[20] Two points should be noted about this placing, which are elaborated in detail in the earlier discussion.[21]

First, the nature of the power sharing between the EU and the Member States can only be divined by looking at the detailed provisions of the particular area. There is no reason why the nature of the divide will be the same in all areas of the AFSJ. We shall see that it is not. It is these particular Treaty provisions and the judicial interpretation thereof that will determine the division between Member State and EU competence. This is in reality what we have always had to do in order to determine the boundaries between State and EU power.

Second, Article 2(2) TFEU stipulates that in the context of shared competence the Member State can only exercise competence to the extent that the Union has not exercised, or has decided to cease to exercise, its competence within any such area. This looks like automatic pre-emption of Member State action where the Union has exercised its competence, with the consequence that the amount of shared power held by the Member State will diminish over time. There is truth in this, subject to the following qualifications.

Member States will only lose their competence within the regime of shared power to the extent that the Union has exercised 'its' competence. Precisely what the EU's competence actually is within these areas can, as noted above, only be divined by considering the detailed provisions in a particular area. The pre-emption of Member State action will moreover only occur 'to the extent' that the EU has exercised its competence in the relevant area. There are different ways in which the EU can intervene in a particular area.[22] The EU may choose to make uniform regulations, it may harmonize national laws, it may engage in minimum harmonization, or it may impose requirements of mutual recognition. The scope for any Member State action will depend on which regulatory technique is used by the EU.[23] It should in addition be noted that Article 2(2) TFEU expressly

---

[19] Ch 5.

[20] Art 4(2)(j) TFEU.

[21] pp 171–173.

[22] S Weatherill, 'Beyond Preemption? Shared Competence and Constitutional Change in the European Community' in D O' Keefe and P Twomey (eds), *Legal Issues of the Maastricht Treaty* (Chancery Law Publishing, 1994) ch 2; M Dougan, 'Minimum Harmonization and the Internal Market' (2000) 37 CMLRev 853; M Dougan, 'Vive la Difference? Exploring the Legal Framework for Reflexive Harmonisation within the Single Market' (2002) 1 Annual of German and European Law 13; CONV 375/1/02, Final Report of Working Group V on Complementary Competencies, Brussels 4 November 2002, 12–13.

[23] See also, Protocol (No 25) On Shared Competence.

provides for the possibility that the EU will cease to exercise competence in an area subject to shared competence, the consequence being that competence then reverts to the Member States. A Declaration attached to the Treaty[24] specifies different ways in which this might occur.

(d) Courts and judicial doctrine

The impact of the Lisbon Treaty on the Union courts was considered in a previous chapter.[25] The present discussion will focus on the changes that are directly relevant to the AFSJ.

(i) Scope of jurisdiction

The Lisbon Treaty has, as we have seen, brought all provisions concerning the AFSJ within the normal Treaty structure, with the consequence that the juris-diction of the Union courts extends to all EU law, unless the Treaties stipulate to the contrary. The injunction that the Court of Justice of the European Union shall ensure that in the interpretation and application of the Treaties the law is observed,[26] is therefore of general application, save where it is limited by specific Treaty provisions.

The Community courts' jurisdiction over the Third Pillar had been limited,[27] notwithstanding teleological interpretation which stretched the limits to afford the maximum possible judicial oversight. Thus jurisdiction to give preliminary rulings was dependent on a Member State making a declaration accepting such jurisdiction, and it could also specify which national courts should be able to make such a preliminary reference. There were limits on legality review. Enforcement actions by the Commission were not available, and there was no provision for damages. The Community courts' jurisdiction in relation to the other aspect of the AFSJ, dealing with visas, asylum, immigration, and other policies related to free movement of persons,[28] had also been constrained, since only national courts of last resort could send preliminary rulings to the ECJ.[29]

The Lisbon Treaty signals a major change in this respect. The normal rules on direct and indirect actions will be applicable to the AFSJ, subject to transitional provisions considered below. Thus preliminary rulings, legality review, and the other heads of jurisdiction will be applicable to the AFSJ in the same manner as other subject matter that falls within the Treaty.

---

[24] Declaration 18 in relation to the delimitation of competences.
[25] Ch 4.   [26] Art 19(1) TEU.   [27] Art 35 EU.
[28] Title IV EC.   [29] Art 68(1) EC.

(ii) Direct effect and supremacy

The doctrine of direct effect was created and developed by the ECJ. The Lisbon Treaty does not signal any change in the doctrine itself, but it does have implications for its scope of application.

Article 34 EU had provided for a distinct set of legal norms that were used in the context of the Third Pillar, dealing with Police and Judicial Cooperation in Criminal Matters. Framework Decisions and Decisions were the most important legal norms used in this area, and Article 34(2) EU stated that they did not have direct effect. The ECJ interpreted this stricture narrowly, and held that it did not preclude indirect effect.[30]

Article 34 EU has been repealed and the general regime of legal acts specified in the Lisbon Treaty applies to measures adopted in the AFSJ. It will henceforth be possible to argue that a Treaty article, or a legislative, delegated, or implementing act dealing with the AFSJ, gives rise to direct effect, provided that it satisfies the criteria for this doctrine to apply. This change is likely to generate significant litigation as to whether those criteria have been met, given the plethora of measures adopted concerning the AFSJ.

The general status of the supremacy principle under the Lisbon Treaty was considered in an earlier chapter.[31] There was debate under the pre-existing regime as to whether the supremacy of Community law over national law applied in relation to the Third Pillar,[32] although the matter was never ultimately tested in the courts. The de-pillarization that is integral to the Lisbon Treaty means that the ECJ will surely resolve this conceptual issue in favour of the primacy of EU law covering matters that were hitherto part of the Third Pillar and are now shifted to the TFEU. The potential for clashes between Union acts and national constitutional precepts is especially prevalent in this area. This could in turn lead to cases that test the boundaries of the primacy doctrine when the conflict with EU law involves national constitutional provisions.

(iii) Transitional provisions

The Lisbon Treaty does, however, contain transitional provisions that are relevant to Union courts and enforcement.[33]

Article 10(1) of the Protocol on Transitional Provisions specifies two limits to the powers of the institutions with respect to acts of the Union in the field of police cooperation and judicial cooperation in criminal matters that were

---

[30] Case C-105/03 *Criminal Proceedings against Maria Pupino* [2005] ECR I-5283.
[31] Ch 4.
[32] K Lenaerts and T Corthaut, 'Of Birds and Hedges: The Role of Primacy in Invoking Norms of EU Law' (2006) 31 ELRev 287; A Hinarejos, *Judicial Control in the European Union, Reforming Jurisdiction in the Intergovernmental Pillars* (Oxford University Press, 2009).
[33] Protocol (No 36) On Transitional Provisions, Art 10.

adopted before the entry into force of the Lisbon Treaty: the Commission's enforcement powers under Article 258 TFEU are not applicable; the powers of the Court of Justice under what was the Third Pillar remain the same, including where Member States have accepted the preliminary ruling jurisdiction under Article 35(2) EU. These limits cease to have effect five years after entry into force of the Lisbon Treaty.[34] The limits are also inapplicable if a Third Pillar act is amended[35] after the Lisbon Treaty enters into force.[36]

Article 10(4) of the Protocol is relevant to the UK. It states that at the latest six months before the expiry of the five-year transitional period, the United Kingdom may notify to the Council that it does not accept, with respect to the Third Pillar acts passed before the Lisbon Treaty, the powers of the institutions referred to in Article 10(1) as set out in the Treaties. If the UK makes such a notification then Third Pillar acts adopted prior to the Lisbon Treaty cease to apply to it from the expiry of the transitional period. This is subject to the caveat that a Third Pillar act amended after the Lisbon Treaty enters into force that is applicable to the UK remains so. Article 10(5) of the Protocol, however, leaves the door open to the UK to notify the Council of its wish to participate in acts that have ceased to apply to it pursuant to Article 10(4).

(e) UK and the AFSJ

The UK and Ireland negotiated three related opt-outs in the Treaty of Amsterdam that pertained to aspects of the AFSJ. These have been preserved and modified in the Lisbon Treaty.[37]

(i) Schengen 'acquis'

The Treaty of Amsterdam brought the Schengen Treaties, and implementing measures, the Schengen acquis, into the EU legal order, through a Protocol. The Schengen regime abolished internal border controls between the participating States, and established harmonized rules for visas, as well as rules on external border control, illegal migration, and criminal and police cooperation. The UK and Ireland were not bound by the Schengen acquis, but the Protocol allowed them to participate in part or all of it, provided that the participating States agreed unanimously that this should be so. Both States have participated in certain aspects of the Schengen regime.

---

[34] ibid Art 10(3).   [35] ibid Art 10(2).

[36] S Peers, 'European Commission: Action Plan on the Stockholm Programme', available at <http://www.statewatch.org/stockholm-programme.htm> for discussion of the acts that are likely to be amended.

[37] S Peers, 'British and Irish Opt-Outs from EU Justice and Home Affairs (JHA) Law', 3 November 2009, available at <http://www.statewatch.org/euconstitution.htm>.

The Lisbon Treaty preserved the Protocol relating to the Schengen regime, together with the option for the UK and Ireland to participate in some or all parts of the regime, subject to unanimous agreement from the participating States.[38] The Protocol has been amended, however, to give the UK and Ireland a right to opt out of measures building upon parts of the Schengen acquis.

(ii) Border controls

The Treaty of Amsterdam also contained a Protocol that preserved the UK's control over its borders. It was framed in broad terms, in order to preclude Treaty rules or international agreements concluded by the EU, from impinging on the UK's control over its borders. This Protocol has been retained in the Lisbon Treaty.[39]

(iii) AFSJ

The Treaty of Amsterdam contained a further Protocol. It provided in essence that the UK and Ireland were not bound by Title IV EC, but that they could choose whether or not to opt in to proposed measures in this area. When a legislative proposal was made, the UK and Ireland had three months to decide whether to opt in to a measure. If they did not do so, they were deemed to have opted out. The UK and Ireland could, however, opt in to legislation after it was made, subject to permission from the Commission.

The Lisbon Treaty has preserved and extended this Protocol, such that it now applies to the entirety of the AFSJ.[40] The default position is therefore that the UK and Ireland are not bound by measures adopted under the AFSJ Title. This constitutes an extension of the previous Protocol, since the Lisbon Protocol No 21 applies to all AFSJ measures, including those on crime and police cooperation. It is, as before, open to the UK and Ireland to signify that they wish to take part in the adoption of a proposed measure under this Title, and they can, as previously, choose to opt in after an AFSJ measure has been adopted.

The Lisbon Protocol No 21 extends the UK and Irish opt-out by providing in effect that it applies to amendments to measures in relation to which those States have previously opted in. There are consequential provisions dealing with the situation where the decision to opt out of an amendment to a measure by which they were previously bound would lead to that measure being inoperable as between the other Member States.

---

[38] Protocol (No 19) On the Schengen *Acquis* Integrated into the Framework of the European Union.

[39] Protocol (No 20) On the Application of Certain Aspects of Article 26 of the Treaty on the Functioning of the European Union to the United Kingdom and to Ireland.

[40] Protocol (No 21) On the Position of the United Kingdom and Ireland in respect of the Area of Freedom, Security and Justice, makes special provision for the UK and Ireland.

The Lisbon Protocol No 21 contains a further extension to the opt-out by providing that the United Kingdom and Ireland are not bound by the rules laid down on the basis of Article 16 TFEU, which relate to the processing of personal data by the Member States when carrying out activities which fall within the scope of Chapter 4 or Chapter 5 of Title V, where the United Kingdom and Ireland are not bound by the rules governing the forms of judicial cooperation in criminal matters or police cooperation which require compliance with the provisions laid down on the basis of Article 16.

3. Lisbon Treaty: General Provisions

The discussion in the subsequent sections will focus on the different aspects of the AFSJ. It is, however, important to consider the 'General Provisions' in the Lisbon Treaty as a prelude to this more detailed analysis, more especially as some are new.

(a) The 'lead' provision

Article 67 TFEU is the lead provision for this Title of the Lisbon Treaty and it represents both continuity with, and modification of, the previous Treaty articles.

1. The Union shall constitute an area of freedom, security and justice with respect for fundamental rights and the different legal systems and traditions of the Member States.
2. It shall ensure the absence of internal border controls for persons and shall frame a common policy on asylum, immigration and external border control, based on solidarity between Member States, which is fair towards third-country nationals. For the purpose of this Title, stateless persons shall be treated as third-country nationals.
3. The Union shall endeavour to ensure a high level of security through measures to prevent and combat crime, racism and xenophobia, and through measures for coordination and cooperation between police and judicial authorities and other competent authorities, as well as through the mutual recognition of judgments in criminal matters and, if necessary, through the approximation of criminal laws.
4. The Union shall facilitate access to justice, in particular through the principle of mutual recognition of judicial and extrajudicial decisions in civil matters.

Article 67 TFEU is based on Article 29 EU and Article 67 EC. There are differences, however, most notably in Article 67(1) TFEU, which now provides that the AFSJ is to be secured with respect for fundamental rights and the different national legal systems and traditions. Article 67(4) is new in terms of its express recognition within the general provision that guides this area.

It is worth mentioning at this juncture that Article 76 TFEU provides that legal acts passed in relation to crime and police cooperation, and measures enacted pursuant to Article 74 TFEU, can be made on a proposal from the Commission, or on the initiative of a quarter of the Member States.

(b) Role of European Council

Article 68 TFEU is novel and provides that the European Council shall define the strategic guidelines for legislative and operational planning within the area of freedom, security, and justice. This, however, represents the Treaty catching up with reality, since the European Council has been performing this function for a decade, through the five-year programmes, Tampere,[41] Hague,[42] and, most recently, Stockholm.[43] The Commission and the Justice and Home Affairs Council provide detailed input that fashions the guidelines agreed by the European Council.

(c) Role of the Council

The Council is central to all that happens within the AFSJ Title. It has been the source of many legislative initiatives in this area and this will doubtless continue in the future. It helps to structure the overall objectives of AFSJ policy, which are then fed into the European Council and this too will doubtless continue in the post-Lisbon world. The 'General Provisions' of the Lisbon Treaty on the AFSJ address the role of the Council in the following respect. Article 74 TFEU empowers the Council to adopt measures to ensure administrative cooperation among the relevant departments of the Member States in the areas covered by this Title, as well as between those departments and the Commission.

(d) Role of Council committees

Article 71 TFEU deals with support structures within the Council. A word by way of background is necessary here. The volume and nature of AFSJ initiatives has always necessitated specialist committee support for the Council.[44] There were essentially three layers of support beneath the Justice and Home Affairs Council. Coreper provided the highest level of support, with the lowest level coming from working groups of specialists,[45] which operated in all major areas of

---

[41] Tampere European Council, 15–16 October 1999.
[42] Brussels European Council, 4–5 November 2004.
[43] Council 16484/1/09, Brussels, 25 November 2009.
[44] F Hayes-Renshaw and H Wallace, *The Council of Ministers* (Palgrave, 2nd edn, 2006) 86–87.
[45] H Aden, 'Administrative Governance in the Fields of EU Police and Judicial Co-operation' in H Hofmann and A Turk (eds), *EU Administrative Governance* (Edward Elgar, 2006) 351.

AFSJ policy. However, there were also groups which operated between Coreper and the working parties. In relation to the Third Pillar there was the Article 36 Committee, also known as CATS (*Comité de l'Article Trente Six*). In relation to Title IV EC there was SCIFA, the Strategic Committee on Immigration Frontiers and Asylum, SCIFA + which included national heads of border control, a Committee on Civil law Matters, and a High Level Working Group on Asylum and Migration.[46]

Article 71 TFEU continues this tradition of committee support. It provides for a standing committee to be set up within the Council in order to ensure that operational cooperation on internal security is promoted and strengthened within the Union. It is, without prejudice to Coreper, to facilitate coordination of the action of Member States' competent authorities. Representatives of the Union bodies, offices, and agencies concerned may be involved in the committee proceedings, and the European Parliament and national Parliaments are to be kept informed of the proceedings.

The abbreviation chosen for this new committee is COSI, which has already prompted comment as to whether the title will match reality.[47] Its tasks and fit with existing committee structures within the Council can be discerned from a note issued by the General Secretariat of the Council in December 2009.[48]

COSI is to facilitate, promote, and strengthen coordination of operational actions between EU Member States in the field of internal security. This coordination role will concern, *inter alia*, police and customs cooperation, external border protection, and judicial cooperation in criminal matters relevant to operational cooperation in the field of internal security. COSI is also to be responsible for evaluating the general direction and efficiency of operational cooperation, so as to identify possible shortcomings and propose recommendations to address them. It can invite representatives from EUROJUST, EUROPOL, FRONTEX, and other relevant bodies to its meetings. COSI is also mandated, with the Political and Security Committee (PSC), to assist the Council in accordance with the 'Solidarity clause'.[49] COSI is not, however, to be involved in preparing legislative acts, nor in the conduct of operations. Coreper remains responsible for preparing legislative acts with the help of the different Council working groups.

Coreper will review the future of the Article 36 Committee (CATS) and the Strategic Committee on Immigration, Frontiers and Asylum (SCIFA) in the

---

[46] S Lavenex and W Wallace, 'Justice and Home Affairs, Towards a "European Public Order"' in H Wallace, W Wallace and M Pollack (eds), *Policy Making in the European Union* (Oxford University Press, 5th edn, 2005) 468.

[47] <http://www.statewatch.org/news/2010/feb/02iss-cosi.htm>.

[48] General Secretariat of the Council, 'The Lisbon Treaty's Impact on the Justice and Home Affairs (JHA) Council: More Co-Decision and New Working Structures', December 2009.

[49] Art 222 TFEU.

light of the creation of COSI. This review is to be undertaken prior to 1 January 2012. In the interim both committees will focus on strategic issues where COSI would not be able to contribute and meet as necessary. They will also be involved, when deemed appropriate, in legislative work, but Coreper retains responsibility for preparing legislative acts.

(e) Role of the European Parliament

The ordinary legislative procedure is the norm for areas that fall within the AFSJ. This is to be welcomed. We should be mindful, however, of the concerns adverted to in earlier discussion concerning the way in which the co-decision procedure has been modified in practice, such that many legislative initiatives have been resolved at first reading through trilogue meetings between representatives of the Council and European Parliament.[50] These concerns are especially prevalent in relation to the AFSJ, since the great majority of legislative measures are now subject to these trilogue arrangements, with a consequential loss of transparency and opportunity for democratic input.[51]

(f) Role of national parliaments

Article 69 TFEU stipulates that national parliaments ensure that the proposals and legislative initiatives submitted concerning crime and police cooperation comply with the principle of subsidiarity, in accordance with the arrangements laid down by the Protocol. This provision is new, and reflects the sensitivity of EU involvement in these areas. National parliaments would, however, even in the absence of Article 69, have been able to review such measures for compliance with subsidiarity, pursuant to Article 12 TEU.

(g) Role of evaluation

Article 70 TFEU is novel and reflects concern over Member State implementation of AFSJ policies, and over the efficacy of mutual recognition. It provides that without prejudice to the Treaty provisions on enforcement actions,[52] the Council may, on a proposal from the Commission, adopt measures laying down arrangements whereby Member States, in collaboration with the Commission, evaluate implementation of AFSJ policies, in particular in order to facilitate full application of mutual recognition.

---

[50] pp 38–39.
[51] T Bunyan, 'Abolish 1st and 2nd Reading Secret Deals—Bring Back Democracy "Warts and All"', available at <http://www.statewatch.org/analyses/no-84-ep-first-reading-deals.pdf>.
[52] Arts 258, 259, and 260 TFEU.

(h) Role of Member States

Articles 72 to 73 TFEU speak to the role of the Member States, albeit in different ways. Article 72 TFEU reiterates the injunction in the previous Treaty[53] that the AFSJ Title shall not affect the exercise of the responsibilities incumbent upon Member States with regard to the maintenance of law and order and the safeguarding of internal security. This proposition has political resonance and is not without substance. It does not, however, reflect reality. The AFSJ Title is an area of shared competence. This necessarily means that, at the very least, Member State responsibilities for law and order will be circumscribed by EU measures. The nature and degree of this circumscription will perforce depend on the particular measure adopted by the EU.

Article 73 TFEU provides that it shall be open to Member States to organize among themselves and under their responsibility such forms of cooperation and coordination as they deem appropriate between the competent departments of their administrations responsible for safeguarding national security.

(i) Substantive scope of EU power

The provisions considered thus far are important in different ways, but do not in general add to the substance of the EU's powers, which are determined by the more particular provisions analysed below.

Article 75 TFEU is an exception in this respect. It replaces Article 60 EC, which was hitherto in the chapter dealing with free movement of capital. Article 75 TFEU is, however, a very different provision. It is designed, *inter alia,* to address legal problems that arose in the *Kadi* litigation over freezing of assets,[54] in particular as to the legal base for EU action. These problems have been obviated because Article 75 TFEU has been reformulated with this directly in mind.

Where necessary to achieve the objectives set out in Article 67, as regards preventing and combating terrorism and related activities, the European Parliament and the Council, acting by means of regulations in accordance with the ordinary legislative procedure, shall define a framework for administrative measures with regard to capital movements and payments, such as the freezing of funds, financial assets or economic gains belonging to, or owned or held by, natural or legal persons, groups or non-State entities.

The Council, on a proposal from the Commission, shall adopt measures to implement the framework referred to in the first paragraph.

The acts referred to in this Article shall include necessary provisions on legal safeguards.

---

[53] Art 33 EU, Art 64(1) EC.

[54] Cases C-402 and 415/05 *Yassin Abdullah Kadi and Al Barakaat International Foundation v Council and Commission* [2008] ECR I-6351; C Eckes, *EU Counter-Terrorist Policies and Fundamental Rights, The Case of Individual Sanctions* (Oxford University Press, 2009).

4. Lisbon Treaty: Borders, Asylum, and Immigration

(a) Pre-Lisbon

The provisions on borders, asylum, and immigration were found in Title IV EC. The key enabling provision was Article 61 EC, which provided as follows.

In order to establish progressively an area of freedom, security and justice, the Council shall adopt:

(a) within a period of five years after the entry into force of the Treaty of Amsterdam, measures aimed at ensuring the free movement of persons in accordance with Article 14, in conjunction with directly related flanking measures with respect to external border controls, asylum and immigration, in accordance with the provisions of Article 62(2) and (3) and Article 63(1)(a) and (2)(a) and measures to prevent and combat crime in accordance with the provisions of Article 31(e) of the Treaty on European Union;

(b) other measures in the fields of asylum, immigration and safeguarding the rights of nationals of third countries, in accordance with the provisions of Article 63;

(c) measures in the field of judicial cooperation in civil matters as provided for in Article 65;

(d) appropriate measures to encourage and strengthen administrative cooperation, as provided for in Article 66;

(e) measures in the field of police and judicial cooperation in criminal matters aimed at a high level of security by preventing and combating crime within the Union in accordance with the provisions of the Treaty on European Union.

Article 64 EC was analogous to Article 33 TEU, and stated that Title IV should not affect the exercise of responsibilities incumbent on Member States with regard to the maintenance of law and order and the safeguarding of internal security. Article 64(2) EC also provided a mechanism for dealing with an emergency situation in a particular Member State, which was confronted with 'a sudden inflow of nationals of third countries'.

(i) Decision making and judicial control

The measures adopted pursuant to Articles 62 to 63 EC were made under the procedure laid down in Article 67 EC. This was a complex provision, with a number of qualifications and exceptions,[55] but in essence there was a gradual shift from decision-making based on Council unanimity, to the application of the co-decision procedure.[56]

---

[55] Peers (n 1) 22–29.
[56] Council Decision 2004/927/EC of 22 December 2004 providing for certain areas covered by Title IV of Part Three of the Treaty establishing the European Community to be governed by the procedure laid down in Art 251 of that Treaty [2004] OJ L396/45; S Peers, 'Transforming Decision-Making on EC Immigration and Asylum Law' (2005) 30 ELRev 283.

The ECJ's preliminary rulings jurisdiction over Title IV was limited to national courts from which there was no judicial remedy and, it had no jurisdiction over measures enacted pursuant to Article 62 EC concerning law and order and internal security.[57] There was power pursuant to Article 67(2) EC for the Council, acting unanimously with the consent of the European Parliament, to adapt the provisions relating to the powers of the ECJ. The Commission proposed that the preliminary ruling jurisdiction under Article 68 EC should be brought into line with the general regime under Article 234 EC,[58] but the need for this change was obviated by the Lisbon Treaty.

(ii) Borders

Article 62 EC expanded on Article 61(a) EC. The Council was required, within a period of five years after entry into force of the Amsterdam Treaty, to adopt measures to ensure, in compliance with Article 14 EC, the absence of controls on persons, whether they were Union citizens or nationals from third countries, when crossing internal borders. It was also required to adopt measures on the crossing of external borders, in order to establish standards and procedures to be followed by Member States in carrying out checks on persons at such borders, rules on visas for those intending to stay no more than three months, and measures setting out the conditions under which nationals from third countries had the freedom to travel within the territory of the Member States during a period of no more than three months.

(iii) Asylum and immigration

Article 63 EC built on Article 61(b) EC. The Council was obliged within the five-year period after the Amsterdam Treaty to adopt measures concerning four related areas. The first was asylum and the measures to be adopted, which had to be in accord with the Geneva Convention of 1951 and the Protocol of 1967 on the status of refugees, related to: criteria for deciding which State should be responsible for considering an asylum application; minimum standards on the reception of asylum seekers in Member States; minimum standards on whether third country nationals were refugees; and minimum standards on procedures in Member States for granting or withdrawing refugee status.

The second area on which the Council had to adopt measures concerned refugees and displaced persons. The third concerned immigration policy so far as it related to, on the one hand, conditions of entry and residence, and standards

---

[57] Art 68(2) EC.
[58] Adaptation of the provisions of Title IV establishing a European Community relating to the jurisdiction of the Court of Justice with a view to ensuring more effective judicial protection, COM (2006) 346.

on procedures for the issue by Member States of long term visas and residence permits, including those for family reunion, and, on the other hand, illegal immigration and illegal residence. The final area dealt with by Article 63 EC concerned measures defining the rights and conditions under which nationals of third countries who were legally resident in a Member State might reside in another Member State.

(b) Post-Lisbon

(i) Decision-making and judicial control

Significant aspects of the Treaty regime dealing with borders, immigration, and asylum were subject to co-decision and qualified majority voting in the Council, even prior to the Lisbon Treaty.[59] The Lisbon Treaty, as noted above and in earlier chapters, has increased the remit of qualified majority voting in the Council, coupled with use of the ordinary legislative procedure.[60] Unanimity in the Council, coupled with consultation with the European Parliament, is retained for passports and identity cards.[61] The legal acts in this area are, as explained above, now subject to the normal precepts of judicial control. It is also worth mentioning at this juncture that the Lisbon Treaty provides that Union acts adopted pursuant to this Chapter shall contain appropriate measures to give effect to the principle of solidarity and fair sharing of responsibility, including financial, between the Member States.[62]

(ii) Borders

Article 77 TFEU is now the principal provision dealing with border controls. It provides as follows:

1. The Union shall develop a policy with a view to:

   (a) ensuring the absence of any controls on persons, whatever their nationality, when crossing internal borders;

   (b) carrying out checks on persons and efficient monitoring of the crossing of external borders;

   (c) the gradual introduction of an integrated management system for external borders.

2. For the purposes of paragraph 1, the European Parliament and the Council, acting in accordance with the ordinary legislative procedure, shall adopt measures concerning:

---

[59] Part of the rules on short-stay visas and residence permits, Art 77 TFEU; asylum policy, Art 78 TFEU; illegal immigration, Art 79 TFEU.

[60] Part of the rules on short-stay visas and residence permits (namely, the list of third countries whose nationals must be in possession of visas when crossing the external borders and those whose nationals are exempt from that requirement as well as a uniform format for visas), Art 77 TFEU; legal immigration, Art 79 TFEU.

[61] Art 77 TFEU.   [62] Art 80 TFEU.

(a) the common policy on visas and other short-stay residence permits;
(b) the checks to which persons crossing external borders are subject;
(c) the conditions under which nationals of third countries shall have the freedom to travel within the Union for a short period;
(d) any measure necessary for the gradual establishment of an integrated management system for external borders;
(e) the absence of any controls on persons, whatever their nationality, when crossing internal borders.

3. If action by the Union should prove necessary to facilitate the exercise of the right referred to in Article 20(2)(a), and if the Treaties have not provided the necessary powers, the Council, acting in accordance with a special legislative procedure, may adopt provisions concerning passports, identity cards, residence permits or any other such document. The Council shall act unanimously after consulting the European Parliament.

4. This Article shall not affect the competence of the Member States concerning the geographical demarcation of their borders, in accordance with international law.

The catalyst for the changes made to the Treaty rules on borders was Working Group X on 'Freedom, Security, and Justice'.

The Treaty rules on visas had previously been split into four parts.[63] The Working Group recommended that this should be simplified into a single provision enabling the adoption, by qualified majority voting and co-decision, of all measures needed for the common visa policy.[64] This was accepted in the Constitutional Treaty,[65] and has been taken over in Article 77(2)(a) TFEU.

The Working Group was also the inspiration for the approach taken to border management. It recognized that in an area without internal border controls, the effective management of external borders was a matter of shared interest and responsibility. The Group therefore recommended that Article 62(2)(a) EC should be redrafted to create a general legal base for the adoption of measures needed to put in place this integrated system.[66] This recommendation formed the foundation for the approach taken in the Constitutional Treaty,[67] which has been adopted by the Lisbon Treaty. Thus Article 77(1) TFEU stipulates that border policy is premised on three considerations: absence of internal border controls; checks on external borders; and an integrated management system for external borders. It is these policies that are to be effectuated through measures enacted under Article 77(2) TFEU.

Article 77(3) TFEU contains a novel power, which is in reality analogous to Article 352 TFEU, albeit in miniature. If action is necessary to facilitate exercise of the right to move and reside freely in the EU in Article 20(2)(a) TFEU, and the Treaty has not provided the requisite power, then the Council can make provision about passports and the like. The sensitivity of this power is reflected in

---

[63] Art 62(2)(b) EC.   [64] Working Group X (n 18) 6.
[65] Art III-265(2)(a) CT.   [66] Working Group X (n 18) 6.
[67] Art III-265 CT.

the requirement of Council unanimity, plus consultation with the European
Parliament.

(iii) Asylum and displaced persons

The Lisbon Treaty has made separate provision for asylum and displaced
persons, and for immigration. These were previously dealt with in Article 63
EC. Asylum and displaced persons are now covered by Article 78 TFEU.

1. The Union shall develop a common policy on asylum, subsidiary protection and
   temporary protection with a view to offering appropriate status to any third-country
   national requiring international protection and ensuring compliance with the principle of *non-refoulement.* This policy must be in accordance with the Geneva Convention of 28 July 1951 and the Protocol of 31 January 1967 relating to the status of
   refugees, and other relevant treaties.

2. For the purposes of paragraph 1, the European Parliament and the Council, acting in
   accordance with the ordinary legislative procedure, shall adopt measures for a common European asylum system comprising:

   (a) a uniform status of asylum for nationals of third countries, valid throughout the
       Union;
   (b) a uniform status of subsidiary protection for nationals of third countries who,
       without obtaining European asylum, are in need of international protection;
   (c) a common system of temporary protection for displaced persons in the event of a
       massive inflow;
   (d) common procedures for the granting and withdrawing of uniform asylum or
       subsidiary protection status;
   (e) criteria and mechanisms for determining which Member State is responsible for
       considering an application for asylum or subsidiary protection;
   (f) standards concerning the conditions for the reception of applicants for asylum or
       subsidiary protection;
   (g) partnership and cooperation with third countries for the purpose of managing
       inflows of people applying for asylum or subsidiary or temporary protection.

3. In the event of one or more Member States being confronted by an emergency
   situation characterised by a sudden inflow of nationals of third countries, the Council,
   on a proposal from the Commission, may adopt provisional measures for the benefit
   of the Member State(s) concerned. It shall act after consulting the European Parliament.

Article 78 TFEU replicates the analogous provision of the Constitutional
Treaty,[68] which was once again influenced by the deliberations of Working
Group X in the Convention on the Future of Europe.[69] Its recommendations
were premised on the need for a common asylum procedure valid throughout the
EU. This was to be facilitated by a shift to qualified majority voting in the

---

[68] Art III-266 CT.   [69] Working Group X (n 18) 3–4.

Council and co-decision, and by amendment to Article 63(1)–(2) EC so as to create a general legal base for the measures needed for a common asylum system and a common policy on refugees and displaced persons.

Article 78 TFEU has gone a considerable way to achieving this aim. Article 63 (1)–(2) EC had mandated the EC to adopt 'measures on asylum', but these measures could for the most part only prescribe minimum standards. Article 78 TFEU by way of contrast obliges the EU to 'adopt measures for a common European asylum system'. The measures that can be adopted are not limited to the establishment of minimum standards. To the contrary, Article 78 TFEU is framed in terms of, for example, 'uniform status of asylum for nationals of third countries, valid throughout the Union', and a 'common system of temporary protection for displaced persons in the event of a massive inflow'. Similar language is evident in other provisions of Article 78(2) TFEU. Even where Article 78(2) is not framed in terms of uniformity or commonality, the measures that can be enacted are not limited to the establishment of minimum conditions. It remains to be seen how far the change in Article 78 is reflected in the nature of the measures enacted post-Lisbon.

(iv) Immigration

The Lisbon Treaty provisions on immigration, which had previously been included in Article 63(3)–(4) EC, are now covered by Article 79 TFEU.

1. The Union shall develop a common immigration policy aimed at ensuring, at all stages, the efficient management of migration flows, fair treatment of third-country nationals residing legally in Member States, and the prevention of, and enhanced measures to combat, illegal immigration and trafficking in human beings.

2. For the purposes of paragraph 1, the European Parliament and the Council, acting in accordance with the ordinary legislative procedure, shall adopt measures in the following areas:

   (a) the conditions of entry and residence, and standards on the issue by Member States of long-term visas and residence permits, including those for the purpose of family reunification;

   (b) the definition of the rights of third-country nationals residing legally in a Member State, including the conditions governing freedom of movement and of residence in other Member States;

   (c) illegal immigration and unauthorised residence, including removal and repatriation of persons residing without authorisation;

   (d) combating trafficking in persons, in particular women and children.

3. The Union may conclude agreements with third countries for the readmission to their countries of origin or provenance of third-country nationals who do not or who no longer fulfil the conditions for entry, presence or residence in the territory of one of the Member States.

4. The European Parliament and the Council, acting in accordance with the ordinary legislative procedure, may establish measures to provide incentives and support for the action of Member States with a view to promoting the integration of third-country nationals residing legally in their territories, excluding any harmonisation of the laws and regulations of the Member States.

5. This Article shall not affect the right of Member States to determine volumes of admission of third-country nationals coming from third countries to their territory in order to seek work, whether employed or self-employed.

There is much in Article 79 TFEU that repeats the previous Treaty provision. There are nonetheless differences of nuance and wording. Thus Article 79 is framed in terms of 'a common immigration policy', as opposed to 'measures on immigration policy', which was the case previously, although Commission thinking pre-Lisbon was nonetheless set in terms of a Common Immigration Policy.[70] There is increased emphasis on preventing and combating illegal immigration and human trafficking. The inclusion of Article 79(3) follows the recommendation of Working Group X, which felt that such agreements were more effective if negotiated by the EU. So too does Article 79(4), which allows for support to be given to Member States to integrate third-country nationals legally residing in their territory.[71]

(c) Dualities and tensions

The legislative and policy initiatives adopted pursuant to Title IV EC were, from the outset, beset by dualities and tensions. These will not suddenly disappear under the post-Lisbon regime, notwithstanding the changes that have been made.

(i) Duality and purpose

The tensions within the AFSJ can be exemplified in relation to asylum. The EU has sought a Common European Asylum System for over a decade.[72] It was at the forefront of the programme announced by the Tampere European Council.[73] It is clear nonetheless that the legislative 'output' has been circumscribed both by ambivalence as to the overall objectives of EU intervention and by what Member States have been willing to accept.

Costello highlights the first of these issues noting that references to 'freedom' and 'security' beg the question whose freedom and whose security is being

---

[70] <http://ec.europa.eu/justice_home/fsj/immigration/fsj_immigration_intro_en.htm#part_1>.
[71] Working Group X (n 18) 5.
[72] <http://ec.europa.eu/justice_home/fsj/asylum/fsj_asylum_intro_en.htm>.
[73] Tampere European Council, 15–16 October 1999, [13]–[17].

safeguarded.[74] The Tampere European Council intended the freedom to include those of the asylum seekers,[75] but the Treaty itself and subsequent legislative developments showed that this was to be carefully balanced against the freedom and security of EU citizens 'from the perceived threat of unmanaged migration'.[76]

The second factor, what the Member States have been willing to accept, is exemplified by the critique of the Asylum Procedures Directive.[77] The Directive was enacted because harmonization of asylum procedures was central to a common asylum system.[78] It was strongly criticized, however, on human rights grounds.[79] Costello captures the forces that led to this unsatisfactory result.[80]

Of all the post-Amsterdam measures in the asylum field, the Procedures Directive has been the most controversial. This is at least partly explained by the context wherein national governments jealously guard their leeway to manipulate asylum procedures, in order to pursue various goals... The highly qualified and differentiated procedural guarantees in the Procedures Directive are the result, and demonstrate a reluctance to commit to unequivocal procedural standards, or maintain access to asylum within the EU. Thus, the critiques of the Procedures Directive are well-founded. In particular, the variety of procedures permitted reflects an assumption that it is possible to determine the cogency of claims on the basis of generalizations or cursory examination. This runs counter to any informed context-sensitive understanding of the asylum process. In the worst cases under the Procedures Directive, such as the super-safe third country provisions, the generalized assessment entirely substitutes for any individual process. In the Directive, we see the result of a legislative process which should have established clear minimal guarantees, but instead cast a negotiated settlement in law, apparently reinvesting national administrations with discretion that they had lost in some measure due to domestic and ECHR rulings.

The Fundamental Rights Agency has in addition noted the gap between present reality and a Common European Asylum System.[81] It revealed the wide disparities between EU Member States concerning the granting of refugee status and subsidiary protection. It was of the view that creation of national

---

[74] C Costello, 'Administrative Governance and the Europeanisation of Asylum and Immigration Policy' in Hofmann and Turk (n 45) 290.

[75] Tampere European Council (n 73) [3].

[76] Costello (n 74) 290.

[77] Council Directive 2005/85/EC of 1 December 2005 on minimum standards on procedures in Member States for granting and withdrawing refugee status [2005] OJ L326/13.

[78] K Hailbronner, 'Asylum Law in the Context of a European Migration Policy' in Walker (n 1).

[79] Peers (n 1) 341.

[80] C Costello, The European Asylum Procedures Directive in Legal Context UNHCR, Research Paper 134, 2006, 34.

[81] European Union Agency for Fundamental Rights, The Stockholm Programme: A chance to put fundamental rights protection right in the centre of the European Agenda, available at <http://fra.europa.eu/fraWebsite/products/products_en.htm>;   <http://www.statewatch.org/stockholm-programme.htm>.

asylum procedures with comparable standards of fairness could not realistically be achieved without reducing substantially Member State discretion under the Asylum Procedures Directive, and strengthened safeguards to ensure access to asylum procedures. There have been numerous other related critiques directed towards aspects of the EU immigration regime.[82]

(ii) Duality and rights

The regime in Title IV EC was meant to be consonant with human rights, including those of migrants and asylum-seekers. We have, however, already seen the rights-based critique lodged at the Asylum Procedures Directive. The Fundamental Rights Agency (FRA) has more generally highlighted the tensions between realization of the EU's goals to manage migration and asylum, while securing protection for human rights.[83]

It drew attention to the mismatch between form and reality that could occur in this area. Thus while fundamental rights safeguards were enshrined in the Schengen regime, this was not always true in practice. It was necessary to improve fundamental rights' training for border guards, including learning methodologies that addressed the need to change deep-seated attitudes. The EU should moreover be mindful of rule of law considerations when immigration policies were 'extra-territorialized', as with mechanisms under consideration to process asylum applications outside the EU. Border control and surveillance measures at sea should moreover be designed to ensure respect for fundamental rights, as well as search and rescue obligations derived from international maritime law.

The FRA also urged that the curbing of irregular migration should still take cognizance of fundamental rights. It noted that in their effort to curb irregular migration, some Member States put in place practices to detect irregular immigrants which had the effect of discouraging them from enjoying basic rights applicable to any person, such as access to education and health care facilities. It voiced concern that implementation of the directive imposing sanctions on employers who employed illegal migrants might discourage employers from considering job applications submitted by migrants.

---

[82] R Cholewinski, 'The Need for Effective Individual Legal Protection in Immigration Matters' (2005) 7 European Journal of Migration and Law 237; A Baldaccini, 'The Return and Removal of Irregular Migrants under EU Law: An Analysis of the Returns Directive' (2009) 11 European Journal of Migration and Law 1; M Schain, 'The State Strikes Back: Immigration Policy in the European Union' (2009) 20 European Journal of International Law 93; J O'Dowd, 'Mutual Recognition in European Immigration Policy: Harmonised Protection or Co-ordinated Exclusion?' in F Goudappel, R Oostland and H Raulus (eds), *The Future of Asylum in the European Union: Problems, Proposals and Human Rights* (Asser Press, 2010).

[83] ibid.

5. Lisbon Treaty: Civil Law and Procedure

(a) Pre-Lisbon

The Rome Treaty provided little by way of foundation for EEC involvement with civil law and procedure,[84] although Article 220 EEC, later Article 293 EC, did allow Member States to negotiate agreements relating, *inter alia*, to recognition and enforcement of foreign judgments. The Brussels Convention 1968 and the Rome Convention 1980 were duly agreed.

It was the Maastricht Treaty which laid the real foundation for EU involvement in this area, with judicial cooperation in civil matters being included in the Third Pillar.[85] It did not, however, prove to be fertile ground for development of civil law initiatives. The need for Council unanimity, combined with use of conventions, did little to expedite the passage of measures in this area.

However, judicial cooperation in civil matters was transferred to the Community Pillar by the Treaty of Amsterdam. Article 65 EC empowered the Community to enact measures in the field of judicial cooperation in civil matters that had cross-border implications, insofar as necessary for the proper functioning of the internal market. These included: improving and simplifying the system for cross-border service of judicial and extrajudicial documents, cooperation in the taking of evidence, and the recognition and enforcement of decisions in civil and commercial cases; promoting the compatibility of national rules concerning the conflict of laws and jurisdiction; and eliminating obstacles to the good functioning of civil proceedings, if necessary by promoting the compatibility of national rules on civil procedure.

There were, unsurprisingly, differences of view as to the meaning to be given to the conditions in Article 65 EC, which required a cross-border dimension and that intervention be predicated on the proper functioning of the internal market. Nor was it surprising that the Commission inclined to a broad interpretation of these provisions, while the Council was more cautious.[86]

(b) Post-Lisbon

The Lisbon Treaty has now modified and expanded EU competence in relation to civil law and procedure. Article 81 TFEU largely follows the relevant provision of the Constitutional Treaty.[87]

---

[84] E Storskrubb, *Civil Procedure and EU Law—A Policy Area Uncovered* (Oxford University Press, 2008).

[85] Art K.1(6) EU.

[86] E Storskrubb, 'Civil Justice—A Newcomer and an Unstoppable Wave?' in P Craig and G de Búrca, *The Evolution of EU Law* (Oxford University Press, 2nd edn, 2010) ch 11.

[87] Art III-269 CT.

1. The Union shall develop judicial cooperation in civil matters having cross-border implications, based on the principle of mutual recognition of judgments and of decisions in extrajudicial cases. Such cooperation may include the adoption of measures for the approximation of the laws and regulations of the Member States.

2. For the purposes of paragraph 1, the European Parliament and the Council, acting in accordance with the ordinary legislative procedure, shall adopt measures, particularly when necessary for the proper functioning of the internal market, aimed at ensuring:

   (a) the mutual recognition and enforcement between Member States of judgments and of decisions in extrajudicial cases;
   (b) the cross-border service of judicial and extrajudicial documents;
   (c) the compatibility of the rules applicable in the Member States concerning conflict of laws and of jurisdiction;
   (d) cooperation in the taking of evidence;
   (e) effective access to justice;
   (f) the elimination of obstacles to the proper functioning of civil proceedings, if necessary by promoting the compatibility of the rules on civil procedure applicable in the Member States;
   (g) the development of alternative methods of dispute settlement;
   (h) support for the training of the judiciary and judicial staff.

3. Notwithstanding paragraph 2, measures concerning family law with cross-border implications shall be established by the Council, acting in accordance with a special legislative procedure. The Council shall act unanimously after consulting the European Parliament.

   The Council, on a proposal from the Commission, may adopt a decision determining those aspects of family law with cross-border implications which may be the subject of acts adopted by the ordinary legislative procedure. The Council shall act unanimously after consulting the European Parliament.

   The proposal referred to in the second subparagraph shall be notified to the national Parliaments. If a national Parliament makes known its opposition within six months of the date of such notification, the decision shall not be adopted. In the absence of opposition, the Council may adopt the decision.

Article 81 TFEU modifies Article 65 EC in a number of ways.[88] First, the reference to the internal market has been altered, such that it now reads that measures can be adopted 'particularly when necessary' for the proper functioning of the internal market, as opposed to the previous language, which was framed in terms of 'insofar as necessary'. This shift signals an extension of EU competence, since the formulation in Article 81 TFEU is facultative, rather than limiting in the manner hitherto.

Second, Article 81 TFEU accords pride of place to mutual recognition as the regulatory technique in this area. This is, as will be seen below, a theme that is

---

[88] G-R de Groot and J-J Kuipers 'The New Provisions on Private International Law in the Treaty of Lisbon' (2008) 15 MJ109.

repeated in relation to judicial cooperation in criminal matters. It remains to be seen how far this alters the previous legislative strategy in relation to civil law and procedure.

Third, the list of matters that the EU can address has been extended by the Lisbon Treaty. The additions are effective access to justice, development of alternative dispute resolution (ADR), and support for judicial training, although measures had been proposed concerning ADR and judicial training under the heading of measures 'eliminating obstacles to the good functioning of civil proceedings', which was part of Article 65 EC. It is the first of these additions, effective access to justice, which is therefore most significant. This is moreover underlined by Article 67 TFEU, which contains the general provisions relating to AFSJ, paragraph 4 of which states that the EU shall facilitate access to justice, in particular through mutual recognition of judgments in civil maters. The phrase 'effective access to justice' in Article 81(2)(e) TFEU is open to a plethora of meanings and it remains to be seen what strategies are developed under this rubric.

Fourth, Article 81 TFEU makes special provision for cross-border measures that deal with family law, requiring Council unanimity and consultation with the European Parliament. This decisional rule can be modified, however, in accordance with Article 81(3) TFEU.

(c) Dualities and tensions

EU involvement in civil law and procedure has evolved since the inception of the EEC. The topic has moved from the fringes to assume greater prominence over time. This is unlikely to change post-Lisbon. It is therefore especially important to stand back and appreciate some of the underlying currents and dualities that pervade this area.[89]

(i) Duality and purpose

The initial rationale for EU involvement with judicial cooperation in civil matters was to support the internal market. The formulation in the Maastricht Treaty legitimated EU competence in terms of attaining the objectives of the Union, in particular the free movement of persons. The linkage with the internal market became more evident in Article 65 EC, with its pre-conditions that measures could be made in relation to judicial cooperation where there was a cross-border impact, insofar as this was necessary for the proper functioning of the internal market.

Working Group X on 'Freedom, Security, and Justice' in the Convention on the Future of Europe decided after deliberation that these limits should be

---

[89] Storskrubb (n 84); M Tulibacka, 'Europeanization of Civil Procedures: In Search of a Coherent Approach' [2009], 46 CMLRev 1527.

retained.[90] The very fact that this issue was felt to be contestable was nonetheless a factor in softening the linkage with the internal market in the final version of the Constitutional Treaty. Article III-269 CT replaced the wording of the EC Treaty with the phrase that EU measures could be made 'particularly when necessary for the proper functioning of the internal market', and this softer version was retained in Article 81 TFEU.

A wealth of measures were enacted prior to the Lisbon Treaty concerned broadly with judicial cooperation in civil matters, and the dominant ideology thus far has been market integration and efficiency.[91] This is especially true of the raft of measures enacted concerning procedural issues, such as cross-border service of documents,[92] cross-border taking of evidence,[93] and the 'Brussels I Regulation',[94] regulating jurisdiction and cross-border recognition and enforcement of judgments for civil and commercial matters.

There is, however, another less articulated purpose underlying initiatives in this area, which is the possible creation of 'EU rules' of contract, tort, or private international law. Thus projects relating to harmonization of contract law have come within the sphere of civil justice.[95] While the EU has traditionally proceeded via sectoral directives concerned with, for example, aspects of consumer contract law, there have also been more broad-ranging studies supported by the EU. The first resulted in the Principles on European Contract Law (PECL)[96] and the second in the Draft Common Frame of Reference (DCFR).[97] These are not presently binding, and there has been much debate on the desirability of harmonization in this area.[98] This is not the place to take sides in this debate. It is rather to point out that while such initiatives may be linked to internal market objectives, they are also attractive for some within the EU because of their potential to create EU rules governing the relevant area, independently of the impact on market integration.

---

[90] Working Group X (n 18) 6.

[91] Storskrubb (n 84) 278–279.

[92] Council Regulation (EC) 1348/00 on the service in the Member States of judicial and extrajudicial documents in civil or commercial matters [2000] OJ L 160/37.

[93] Council Regulation (EC) 1206/01 on cooperation between the courts of the Member States in the taking of evidence in civil or commercial matters [2001] OJ L174/1.

[94] Council Regulation (EC) 44/01 on jurisdiction and the recognition and enforcement of judgments in civil and commercial matters [2001] OJ L12/1.

[95] <http://ec.europa.eu/justice_home/fsj/civil/fsj_civil_intro_en.htm>.

[96] O Lando and H Beale (eds), *Principles of European Contract Law, Parts I and II* (Kluwer Law International, 2000) and O Lando, E Clive, A Prüm and R Zimmermann, *Principles of European Contract Law, Part III* (Kluwer Law International, 2003).

[97] C von Bar and E Clive (eds), *Principles, Definitions and Model Rules of European Private Law, Draft Common Frame of Reference, Full Edition* (Oxford University Press, 2010).

[98] A more coherent European contract law, COM(2003) 68; European contract law and the revision of the acquis: the way forward, COM(2004) 651; H Collins, 'European Private Law and the Cultural Identity of States' (1995) 3 ERPRIVL 353; D Caruso, 'The Missing View of the Cathedral: The Private Law Paradigm of European Legal Integration' (1997) 3 ELJ 3.

(ii) Duality and regulatory technique

There are tensions, moreover, in relation to regulatory technique within this area. Civil justice is decentralized and the principle of mutual recognition has, as we have seen, assumed ever greater importance. This has led to two tensions. Storskrubb captures the first in the following terms:[99]

> The vision is that local domestic courts as the primary actors should cooperate with each other and as long as certain minimum standards are fulfilled their decisions should be mutually recognisable cross-borders. The feature of decentralisation has led to concerns of fragmentation in application due to a variety of factors including resources and knowledge with ensuing risk of discrimination between jurisdictions. In addition, the measures themselves have in parts been considered unclear and in part rely on national law with ensuing complexity.

A second concern echoes that which has been voiced in relation to EU involvement with criminal matters. This is that the minimum standards introduced by EU law when coupled with mutual recognition limit the options for the national court to decide whether the rights of the defence have been adequately protected.[100]

6. Lisbon Treaty: Criminal Law and Procedure

(a) Pre-Lisbon

It is impossible to understand the significance of the Lisbon Treaty on criminal law and procedure without some understanding of the prior legal position.

The EU's express competence over criminal matters was hitherto regulated by the EU Treaty. Article 31(1) EU provided that common action on criminal matters should 'include': facilitating and accelerating cooperation between competent ministries and judicial authorities of the Member States, including, where appropriate, cooperation through Eurojust, in relation to proceedings and the enforcement of decisions; facilitating extradition between Member States; ensuring compatibility in rules applicable in the Member States, as may be necessary to improve such cooperation; preventing conflicts of jurisdiction between Member States; and progressively adopting measures establishing minimum rules relating to the constituent elements of criminal acts and to penalties in the fields of organized crime, terrorism, and illicit drug trafficking. Article 31(2) EU stated that the Council should encourage cooperation through Eurojust in a number of

---

[99] Storskrubb (n 86). See also, Storskrubb (n 84) 261–262.
[100] Storskrubb (n 84) 166–167, 217–218; G Cuniberti, 'The Recognition of Foreign Judgments Lacking Reasons In Europe: Access to Justice, Foreign Court Avoidance, and Efficiency' (2008) 57 ICLQ 48.

specified ways. Unanimity in the Council was required for decision making in this area.[101] The Third Pillar thus provided some legislative competence over criminal matters, subject to the unanimity requirement.

It was nonetheless contested as to whether there was competence to enact measures relating to criminal procedure, since it was not explicitly mentioned in Article 31 EU. The need for EU initiatives in relation to criminal procedure was driven in large part by mutual recognition, which entailed the acceptance by Member State courts' of the judgments by national criminal courts.[102] The creation of the European Arrest Warrant led in turn to calls for procedural protection and defence rights for the person who had been transferred to the Member State issuing the warrant. There were nonetheless serious concerns as to the competence of the EU to enact such measures, and the content thereof.[103]

There was also controversy as to criminal law competence within the Community Pillar, since there was no express Treaty foundation for the exercise of such power. A legislative technique used to circumvent this problem was to enact two measures, one adopted under the Community Pillar dealing with the principal regulatory issues, the other made pursuant to the Third Pillar, which contained criminal law measures where these were felt to be necessary to support the regulatory scheme.

This approach was, however, thrown into question by ECJ decisions, which held that there was some criminal law competence within the Community Pillar.[104] The ECJ had, in its early jurisprudence, placed limits on national criminal law, insofar as it might impede the rules on free movement.[105] It had also positively encouraged use of national criminal law as a sanction for breach of Community law, where this form of sanction would be used at national level in analogous situations.[106] These decisions were significant, but fell short of ascribing any direct criminal law competence to the EC within the Community Pillar.

The Commission nonetheless felt that such competence could be justified in certain circumstances. This was accepted by the ECJ in the Environmental Crimes case, *Commission v Council.*[107] The Council enacted a Framework Decision under the Third Pillar, which required Member States to prescribe criminal penalties for certain environmental offences. The Commission argued that the measure should have been enacted under Article 175 EC, since it was concerned with the environment. It was opposed by the Council and 11 Member States.

---

[101] Art 34(2) EU.
[102] Mitsilegas (n 1) 101–109.
[103] V Mitsilegas, 'The Constitutional Implications of Mutual Recognition in Criminal Matters in the European Union' (2006) 43 CMLRev 1277.
[104] Mitsilegas (n 1) 69–70.
[105] Case 203/80 *Casati* [1980] ECR 2595, [27].
[106] Case C-68/88 *Commission v Greece* [1989] ECR 2965.
[107] Case C-76/03 *Commission v Council* [2005] ECR I-7879.

The ECJ found that the principal aim of the Framework Decision was to protect the environment, and that it should have been made under Article 175 EC. It accepted that, as a general rule, neither criminal law, nor criminal procedure fell within Community competence, but held that this did not prevent the Community legislature, when the application of effective, proportionate, and dissuasive criminal penalties by the competent national authorities was an essential measure for combating serious environmental offences, from taking measures which related to the criminal law of the Member States, which it considered necessary in order to ensure that the Community rules on environmental protection were fully effective.

The decision was greeted enthusiastically by the Commission, which regarded it as applicable to any sphere of Community action.[108] The Council and Member States were, unsurprisingly, less enamoured by the decision, and were unwilling to accept that it had such a broad reach.[109] The reaction in academic circles was critical, with commentators highlighting the expansion of Community competence on the basis of a generalized notion of effectiveness that was difficult to confine.[110]

The ECJ reaffirmed the Community's competence over criminal matters in the Ship-Source Pollution case, *Commission v Council*.[111] The Commission argued for a broad reading of the earlier judgment, such that it should be applicable to the sphere of transport, the subject matter at stake in the instant case. The Council, supported by 20 Member States, sought to distinguish and confine the ruling in the Environmental Crimes case. The ECJ gave a nuanced judgment.[112] It stated that the contested measure should have been adopted under the Community Pillar, and reiterated the ruling from the earlier decision concerning effectiveness and criminal law. The ECJ nonetheless refrained from holding that this principle was applicable to all spheres of Community policy and also held that the precise sanction should be determined through a Third Pillar measure.

(b) Post-Lisbon

The Lisbon Treaty has resolved some of the issues concerning the scope of EU competence over criminal law, although there are still difficult interpretive

---

[108] Communication on the implications of the Court's judgment of 13 September 2005, COM (2005) 583 final/2, [8].

[109] Mitsilegas (n 1) 75–79.

[110] E Herlin-Karnell, '*Commission v Council*: Some Reflections on Criminal Law in the First Pillar' (2007) 13 EPL 69.

[111] Case C-440/05 *Commission v Council* [2007] ECR I-9097.

[112] S Peers, 'The European Community's Criminal Law Competence: The Plot Thickens' (2008) 33 ELRev 399.

problems. The detailed articles of the Lisbon Treaty follow those in the Constitutional Treaty.[113] The 'thinking' on this issue had, however, been done in the Convention on the Future of Europe, and in Working Group X on 'Freedom, Security and Justice'. The detailed provisions in the Lisbon Treaty merely copied those in the Constitutional Treaty. Article 82 TFEU is now the lead provision in this area.[114]

It provides that judicial cooperation in criminal matters in the Union shall be based on the principle of mutual recognition of judgments and judicial decisions and shall include the approximation of the laws and regulations of the Member States in the areas referred to in Article 82(2) and in Article 83. The European Parliament and the Council, acting by the ordinary legislative procedure, shall adopt measures to: lay down rules and procedures for ensuring recognition throughout the Union of all forms of judgments and judicial decisions; prevent and settle conflicts of jurisdiction between Member States; support the training of the judiciary and judicial staff; and facilitate cooperation between judicial or equivalent authorities of the Member States in relation to proceedings in criminal matters and the enforcement of decisions. The legal acts in this area can be made at the initiative of the Commission or a quarter of the Member States.[115]

(i) Criminal law

The EU's competence to enact measures concerning the criminal law is now specified in Article 83 TFEU.

1. The European Parliament and the Council may, by means of directives adopted in accordance with the ordinary legislative procedure, establish minimum rules concerning the definition of criminal offences and sanctions in the areas of particularly serious crime with a cross-border dimension resulting from the nature or impact of such offences or from a special need to combat them on a common basis.

   These areas of crime are the following: terrorism, trafficking in human beings and sexual exploitation of women and children, illicit drug trafficking, illicit arms trafficking, money laundering, corruption, counterfeiting of means of payment, computer crime and organised crime.

   On the basis of developments in crime, the Council may adopt a decision identifying other areas of crime that meet the criteria specified in this paragraph. It shall act unanimously after obtaining the consent of the European Parliament.

2. If the approximation of criminal laws and regulations of the Member States proves essential to ensure the effective implementation of a Union policy in an area which has been subject to harmonisation measures, directives may establish minimum rules with

---

[113] Arts III-270–275 CT.

[114] C Ladenburger, 'Police and Criminal Law in the Treaty of Lisbon. A New Dimension for the Community Model' (2008) 4 ECLRev 20.

[115] Art 76 TFEU.

regard to the definition of criminal offences and sanctions in the area concerned. Such directives shall be adopted by the same ordinary or special legislative procedure as was followed for the adoption of the harmonisation measures in question, without prejudice to Article 76.

The scope of Articles 83(1) and (2) should be considered in turn. Article 83(1) TFEU provides that the ordinary legislative procedure should apply to the making of such directives, by way of contrast to unanimity in the Council, which was the decisional rule hitherto. It tightens the pre-existing wording in Article 31 EU, by expressly requiring that EU intervention relates to areas of particularly serious crime that have a cross-border dimension, although this might be regarded as inherent in the earlier formulation. The list of offences in Article 83(1) TFEU has, however, been broadened by way of comparison to Article 31 EU, and now embraces matters previously listed in Article 29 EU,[116] plus some other matters. Additions to this list can only be made if there is Council unanimity and consent by the European Parliament.

Article 83(2) TFEU is new and affirms the approach taken by the ECJ in the jurisprudence considered above. The Treaty provision, moreover, enshrines a broad interpretation of the previous jurisprudence. The EU is empowered to approximate criminal laws and regulations to ensure the effective implementation of a Union policy in an area that has been subject to harmonization measures. This power thus applies to any Union policy that has been harmonized, there being no condition that the relevant Union policy be regarded as referring to 'essential objectives' of the Union. It will be interesting to see the interpretation of the requirement that there has been harmonization within an area of the relevant Union policy. This could well be interpreted liberally, such that relatively minimal substantive harmonization is regarded as the sufficient foundation for the approximation of criminal laws and regulations. It will perforce be the Commission that makes the initial determination as to whether such approximation is 'essential' to ensure effective implementation of EU policy, subject to acceptance by the Council and European Parliament in the ordinary or special legislative procedure.

Member State concerns as to possible use of Article 83(1)–(2) furnish the explanation for Article 83(3) TFEU, which enshrines an 'emergency brake'. Thus where a member of the Council considers that a draft directive proposed under Article 83(1)–(2) would affect fundamental aspects of its criminal justice system, it can request that the draft directive should be referred to the European Council. This leads to suspension of the ordinary legislative procedure. If consensus is reached in the European Council within four months, the draft

---

[116] Art 29 EU did not contain any express power to make minimum rules relating to the constituent elements of offences listed therein, which were not also mentioned in Art 31 EU, although Art 31 did not expressly preclude this.

directive is then referred back to the Council, and the ordinary legislative procedure continues. If disagreement persists after four months then the draft directive fails, subject to the caveat that a minimum of nine Member States can notify the Council, European Parliament, and Commission of their wish to establish enhanced cooperation on the basis of the draft directive. If this occurs the authorization[117] to proceed with enhanced cooperation is deemed to be granted and the provisions on enhanced cooperation apply.

(ii) Criminal procedure

There were, as seen above, doubts as to EU competence over criminal procedure prior to the Lisbon Treaty. This issue has been addressed through Article 82(2) TFEU.

To the extent necessary to facilitate mutual recognition of judgments and judicial decisions and police and judicial cooperation in criminal matters having a cross-border dimension, the European Parliament and the Council may, by means of directives adopted in accordance with the ordinary legislative procedure, establish minimum rules. Such rules shall take into account the differences between the legal traditions and systems of the Member States.
 They shall concern:

(a) mutual admissibility of evidence between Member States;
(b) the rights of individuals in criminal procedure;
(c) the rights of victims of crime;
(d) any other specific aspects of criminal procedure which the Council has identified in advance by a decision; for the adoption of such a decision, the Council shall act unanimously after obtaining the consent of the European Parliament.

Adoption of the minimum rules referred to in this paragraph shall not prevent Member States from maintaining or introducing a higher level of protection for individuals.

The EU now has explicit competence over criminal procedure, and the Lisbon Treaty has in that sense settled the controversy that plagued passage of such measures hitherto. The terms of this competence are nonetheless carefully delineated.
 The condition precedent for competence over criminal procedure is that it is necessary to facilitate mutual recognition of judgments and judicial decisions and police and judicial cooperation in criminal matters having a cross-border dimension. The linkage with mutual recognition thereby reaffirms the primary rationale for earlier EU involvement with criminal procedure. The corollary is that 'criminal procedure measures—and the human rights implications

---

[117] Art 20(2) TEU, Art 329(1) TFEU.

which they may have—are thus subordinated to the efficiency logic of mutual recognition'.[118]

There are other limits built into Article 82(2). Thus the EU is only empowered to enact directives which lay down minimum rules, and there is a specific injunction to take account of differences between the legal systems and traditions of the Member States. The addition of any other aspect of criminal procedure requires Council unanimity and consent of the European Parliament.

Article 82(3) TFEU contains a further limit. The 'emergency brake' mechanism that was considered above in relation to the passage of criminal law measures is also applicable in this context. It is therefore open to a Member State to refer a draft directive to the European Council where it believes that it would affect fundamental aspects of its criminal justice system. The procedure thereafter is the same as that described above.

(iii) Crime prevention

The Lisbon Treaty has added a new provision that deals directly with crime prevention. Article 84 TFEU provides that the European Parliament and the Council, acting via the ordinary legislative procedure, can establish measures to promote and support the action of Member States in the field of crime prevention, excluding any harmonization of the laws and regulations of the Member States.

Article 84 exemplifies the incomplete categorization of competences. It confines the EU to supporting Member State action and excludes harmonization. This would naturally place it within the category of competence dealing with supporting, coordinating or supplementing Member State action, but it is not included in the relevant list.[119] The inclusion of the word 'promote' within Article 84 cannot make a difference in this respect, and if it did this would create further problems, since the corollary would be recognition of a category distinct from those elaborated in the earlier part of the Treaty. The scope of legitimate action where the EU is limited to supporting that taken by the Member States has been considered above, to which reference should be made.[120]

(iv) Criminal investigation and prosecution

The previous EU Treaty made provision for Eurojust. Article 31(2) EU was framed in terms of the Council 'encouraging cooperation' via Eurojust in a variety of ways, including, for example, the facilitation of coordination between Member States' prosecuting authorities. This sufficed, however, to enable the EU to adopt the Eurojust Decision.[121]

---

[118] Mitsilegas (n 1) 109.
[119] Art 6 TFEU.
[120] Ch 5.
[121] Council Decision 2002/187/JHA of 28 February 2002, setting up Eurojust with a view to reinforcing the fight against serious crime [2002] OJ L 63/1.

Article 85 TFEU is framed in a similar vein, although there are differences of detail. Thus Article 85(1) states that Eurojust's mission is to support and strengthen coordination and cooperation between national investigating and prosecuting authorities in relation to serious crime affecting two or more Member States, or requiring a prosecution on common bases, on the basis of operations conducted and information supplied by the Member States' authorities and by Europol.

The EU is now empowered to enact regulations via the ordinary legislative procedure to determine Eurojust's 'structure, operation, field of action and tasks', including arrangements for involving the European Parliament and national Parliaments in the evaluation of Eurojust's activities.[122] Eurojust's tasks may include the following.

(a) the initiation of criminal investigations, as well as proposing the initiation of prosecutions conducted by competent national authorities, particularly those relating to offences against the financial interests of the Union;
(b) the coordination of investigations and prosecutions referred to in point (a);
(c) the strengthening of judicial cooperation, including by resolution of conflicts of jurisdiction and by close cooperation with the European Judicial Network.

Article 85 TFEU has the potential to increase Eurojust's power. Legislative regulations can be made relating to its tasks, which now include the 'initiation of criminal investigations', which is expressly distinguished from proposing the initiation of prosecutions by national authorities. Eurojust's tasks also cover the resolution of jurisdictional conflicts, as part of the strengthening of judicial cooperation. It remains to be seen whether these provisions serve as the basis for EU regulations that re-shape, to some degree, the criminal investigatory process.

(v) Criminal prosecution and the European Public Prosecutor

There had, prior to the Lisbon Treaty, been debate and contestation as to whether there should be a European Public Prosecutor, with autonomous power to conduct prosecutions in relation to certain offences that had a marked impact on the EU's financial interests.[123] This provoked considerable opposition from Member States, who regarded the creation of such an office as a further incursion on national sovereignty in a sensitive field. The Lisbon Treaty nonetheless includes provision for a European Public Prosecutor. Article 86 TFEU is framed in the following terms.

---

[122] Art 85(2) TFEU makes clear that formal acts of judicial procedure shall be carried out by the competent national officials in relation to prosecutions, without prejudice to Art 86 TFEU.

[123] Mitsilegas (n 1) 229–232.

1. In order to combat crimes affecting the financial interests of the Union, the Council, by means of regulations adopted in accordance with a special legislative procedure, may establish a European Public Prosecutor's Office from Eurojust. The Council shall act unanimously after obtaining the consent of the European Parliament.

   . . . .

2. The European Public Prosecutor's Office shall be responsible for investigating, prosecuting and bringing to judgment, where appropriate in liaison with Europol, the perpetrators of, and accomplices in, offences against the Union's financial interests, as determined by the regulation provided for in paragraph 1. It shall exercise the functions of prosecutor in the competent courts of the Member States in relation to such offences.

Article 86 contains what is in effect an interesting 'emergency accelerator'. It provides that in the absence of Council unanimity, a group of at least nine Member States can request that the draft regulation be referred to the European Council. If this happens, the procedure in the Council is suspended. If consensus is forthcoming in the European Council within four months, the draft regulation is referred back to the Council for adoption. If disagreement persists beyond four months, it is still open to at least nine Member States to notify their wish to the European Parliament, Council, and Commission to establish enhanced cooperation. Authorization to proceed with enhanced cooperation shall be deemed to be granted and the provisions on enhanced cooperation apply.

Article 86(4) TFEU moreover enables the European Council, acting unanimously after obtaining the consent of the European Parliament and consulting the Commission, to adopt a decision amending Article 86(1) in order to extend the powers of the European Public Prosecutor's Office to include serious crime having a cross-border dimension, with relevant amendments to Article 86(2).

(vi) Crime and police cooperation

Article 30 EU dealt with police cooperation, and made provision for cooperation through Europol. The complex rules applicable to Europol and the EU have been expertly examined elsewhere.[124] The Lisbon Treaty builds on and modifies the pre-existing provisions.

Article 87 TFEU embodies the basic principle of police cooperation between Member States' authorities in relation to the prevention, detection, and investigation of crime. Measures can now be enacted pursuant to the ordinary legislative procedure concerning: the collection, storage, processing, analysis, and exchange of relevant information; support for staff training; and common investigative techniques in relation to the detection of serious forms of organized crime. It is, moreover, open to the Council, acting unanimously after consulting the European Parliament, to establish measures concerning operational cooperation

---

[124] ibid 161–187.

between national authorities. This is subject to an 'emergency accelerator' procedure of the kind described in the previous section, subject to the caveat that it does not apply to acts that constitute a development of the Schengen acquis.

Article 88 TFEU deals with Europol. Its mission is to support and strengthen action by the Member States' police authorities and other law enforcement services and their mutual cooperation in 'preventing and combating serious crime affecting two or more Member States, terrorism and forms of crime which affect a common interest covered by a Union policy'. The reference to forms of crime that affect a common interest covered by a Union policy extends Europol's mandate. Legislative regulations adopted by the ordinary legislative procedure determine Europol's structure, operation, field of action, and tasks, including procedures for scrutiny of Europol's activities by the European Parliament and national parliaments.

Europol's tasks include: collection, storage, processing, analysis, and exchange of information; and coordination, organization, and implementation of investigative and operational action carried out jointly with the Member States' competent authorities or in liaison with Eurojust. This wording lays the foundation for Europol to be granted operational capability, and this is reinforced by the requirement that any such operational action must be carried out in liaison and in agreement with the relevant national authorities, which have exclusive responsibility for application of coercive measures.[125]

(c) Dualities and tensions

The Lisbon Treaty has, following the lead of the Constitutional Treaty, made a number of changes to the provisions on judicial cooperation in criminal matters. It is important, nonetheless, to stand back from the detail and reflect on the broader issues that underlie this area. Judicial cooperation is beset by a series of interesting dualities. They relate to the purpose served by EU intervention, the Member States' realization of initiatives in this area, the regulatory techniques to be used, and the decisional rules embodied in the Treaty. These will be considered in turn.

(i) *Duality and purpose*
The purpose served by EU intervention over crime has evolved over time, but now has two discernible strands. This is apparent from Working Group X on 'Freedom, Security, and Justice', whose report shaped thinking on the EU's involvement with crime in the Treaty reform process.

---

[125] Art 88(3) TFEU.

The rationale for EU intervention in some instances was the need to combat the cross-border impact of serious crime, which could not be achieved effectively by individual Member States, more especially post-9/11.[126] The need for approximation of substantive criminal law was pressing because 'certain crimes have a transnational dimension and cannot be addressed effectively by the Member States acting alone'.[127] The cross-border impact of serious crime therefore created externalities in Member States, which demanded collective action. This logic could well be extended to collective action with non-Member States, since the cross-border impact of serious crime could also be felt in such contexts. The very existence of the EU nonetheless provided an institutional forum for collective action that could be used to fashion appropriate rules, more especially because many such crimes would also have negative effects on the EU economy.

There is also a second rationale for EU intervention in criminal law, which is more closely associated with the efficacy of internal market and other EU policies. The Working Group touched on this idea when it posited a further reason for EU intervention 'where the crime is directed against a shared European interest which is already itself the subject of a common policy of the Union...approximation of substantive criminal law should be part of the toolbox of measures for the pursuit of that policy whenever non-criminal rules do not suffice'.[128] The developed version of this idea was given expression in Article III-271(2) CT, and is now enshrined in Article 83(2) TFEU: approximation of criminal laws is warranted where this is essential to ensure effective implementation of Union policy in an area that has been harmonized.

(ii) Duality and realization

The history of EU intervention in relation to criminal matters reveals an interesting duality in the willingness of Member States to realize the Treaty objectives.

The Member States have been at the forefront of the augmentation of EU competence over crime. It was the Member States that agreed to the initial Three Pillar structure in the Maastricht Treaty which gave the EU competence over criminal issues, and to the revisions embodied in the Treaty of Amsterdam. It was the Member States that expressed willingness to bring crime within the main fabric of the Constitutional Treaty and Lisbon Treaty, and to extend the EU's powers in this sphere. It was the Member States once again that fashioned overall policy via the European Council in the Tampere[129] and Hague Programmes.[130]

---

[126] Working Group X (n 18) 1, 9.   [127] ibid 9.
[128] Working Group X (n 18) 10.
[129] Tampere European Council, 15–16 October 1999.
[130] Brussels European Council, 25–26 March 2004.

The Member States' willingness to embrace EU intervention over crime at the 'macro' level must, however, be balanced by difficulties of realization at the 'micro' level, as attested to by contestation over the content and passage of particular criminal measures. There is no logical inconsistency in this respect. This tension is reflective of the proposition that it is often easier to agree on general principles than on concrete measures to secure their realization. There was thus little difficulty in securing consensus on the desirability of tackling serious cross-border crime, as exemplified by drug trafficking and the like. Decisions as to the particular measures that should be taken to attain this objective were nonetheless often controversial, since they entailed assumptions concerning criminality and incursions into Member State autonomy on which Member States disagreed.

(iii) Duality and regulatory technique

The preceding point leads naturally to the duality that persists in this area as to regulatory technique. The EU has various regulatory tools at its disposal, but two are of particular significance: approximation of laws, and mutual recognition.

Prior to the Lisbon Treaty the formal rules gave prominence to approximation of laws. Article 34 EU provided that the objectives of the Third Pillar could be attained, *inter alia*, by framework decisions to approximate Member State laws and regulations. These measures were analogous to directives, save for the fact that they were said not to have direct effect. Subject to this caveat, the idea was that the principal regulatory vehicle should be approximation of laws via the framework decision.

The late 1990s, however, saw a shift to the principle of mutual recognition. The catalyst was concern as to the slow pace of integration post-Maastricht, coupled with Member State wariness as to EU harmonization.[131] This led to suggestions, voiced by the UK Presidency in 1998, that mutual recognition might be the way forward, with analogies drawn with the use of this concept to attain the objectives of the internal market. This suggestion was endorsed by the European Council in the Tampere programme,[132] and by the Commission.[133]

The centrality of mutual recognition is now firmly embedded in the Lisbon Treaty. Article 82 TFEU, the lead provision in this area, provides that judicial cooperation in criminal matters is to be based on mutual recognition, with approximation of laws denominated for the specific topics delineated in Articles 82(2) and 83 TFEU. This is reinforced by the fact that the new EU competence over criminal procedure in Article 82(2) TFEU is predicated on the need for minimum harmonization in order to facilitate mutual recognition of judgments.

---

[131] Mitsilegas (n 1) 116.
[132] Tampere European Council, 15–16 October 1999, [33].
[133] Mutual Recognition of Final Decisions in Criminal Matters, COM(2000) 495 final, 2.

The application of mutual recognition to the criminal sphere has not, however, been unproblematic. Commentators have questioned the analogy with use of this concept in the internal market. They have rightly pointed to the very real difference between mutual recognition of Member State regulatory provisions concerning the content of goods for the purpose of enhancing free movement, and mutual recognition of judicial decisions for the purpose of increasing the applicability of such rulings in other Member States.[134] It is, moreover, readily apparent from experience thus far that it can be difficult to secure agreement on the conditions for mutual recognition, as attested to by the legal and political difficulties surrounding the European Arrest Warrant.[135] This in turn has led to the need for harmonization of the area of the law giving rise to judgments where mutual recognition is desired, and to harmonization of procedural standards to govern the legal position when a judgment has been recognized.[136] These difficulties will not be obviated by changes in the Lisbon Treaty. They will rather assume greater prominence as the sphere of EU competence in this area expands.

(iv) Duality and decisional rules

The Treaty reform process often generates ingenious decisional rules, and the past decade is no exception in this respect. Decisional rules, as reflected in the preference for qualified majority or unanimity in the Council, are the site for hard fought battles in intergovernmental conferences (IGCs), and the Convention on the Future of Europe. This was especially so in relation to EU competence over crime, given the sensitive nature of the subject matter and the extent to which it touches core ideas of national sovereignty. The Constitutional Treaty and Lisbon Treaty reveal creativity and duality in the shaping of the decisional rules for this area.

The shift to qualified majority voting via the ordinary legislative procedure reflected the realization that in a Union of 27 Member States it would be difficult to move forward if each Member State possessed the veto that comes with unanimity. The sensitivity of the area led, however, to the invention of the 'emergency brake', which was fashioned in the Constitutional Treaty,[137] and taken over into the Lisbon Treaty. The impetus for Union action as embodied in

[134] S Peers, 'Mutual Recognition and Criminal Law in the European Union: Has the Council Got it Wrong?' (2004) 41 CMLRev 5; Mitsilegas (n 1) ch 3; Mitsilegas (n 103); M Maduro, 'So Close and Yet So Far: The Paradoxes of Mutual Recognition' (2007) 14 JEPP 814.

[135] Council Framework Decision 2002/584/JHA of 13 June 2002 on the European Arrest Warrant and the surrender procedures between Member States [2002] OJ L190/1; S Alegre and M Leaf, 'Mutual recognition in European Judicial Cooperation: A Step too Far too Soon? Case Study—The European Arrest Warrant' (2004) 10 ELJ 200; J Wouters and F Naert, 'Of Arrest Warrants, Terrorist Offences and Extradition Deals: An Appraisal of the EU's Main Criminal Law Measures against Terrorism after "11 September"' (2004) 41 CMLRev 911.

[136] Mitsilegas (n 1) 101–107.

[137] Art III-271(3) CT.

the rule of qualified majority was thus tempered by recognition of the impact of such measures on fundamental aspects of a national criminal justice system, hence the emergency brake.

The Constitutional Treaty and Lisbon Treaty nonetheless preserved Council unanimity for some particularly sensitive issues, such as the creation of a European Public Prosecutor and operational cooperation between national police authorities. This default position reflected the importance and sensitivity of such issues. The Constitutional Treaty contained no qualification to this unanimity requirement. The Lisbon Treaty, however, fashioned the 'emergency accelerator', which enables nine Member States to route a proposed measure to the European Council where unanimity has not been secured in the Council. The message is therefore that the default requirement of unanimity will be tempered by the emergency accelerator, and that if consensus is not reached via the European Council, enhanced cooperation between those in favour of the measure may still be an option.

7. Conclusion: Looking Back and Looking Forward

The discussion thus far has focused on the changes made by the Lisbon Treaty to the AFSJ. It has included the dualities and tensions that are present in the areas that comprise the AFSJ. This is in reality the tip of the iceberg. This is in part because the whole is greater than the sum of the parts, in the sense of connections between the component elements of the AFSJ. It is in part because the real world of the AFSJ has always depended on the plethora of complex initiatives, legislative and non-legislative, deployed in pursuance of the primary Treaty provisions. It would clearly be impossible within the scope of this chapter to examine such measures. Good books have been devoted to this very topic.[138] It is nonetheless important to advert to the broader connections between the areas covered by the AFSJ, by looking back and forward.

(a) Looking back: Tampere and Hague

While the whole is greater than the sum of the parts in relation to the AFSJ, the linkage between the component parts, and the very meaning of an area of freedom, justice, and security, have been contested.

The official line has been to stress linkage between the AFSJ, free movement of persons, and the inherently trans-border impact of matters such as immigration, asylum, and organized crime. Thus control over migration and external borders was rationalized by the free movement of goods and persons within the

[138] (N 1).

Community, and by the cross-border impact of serious crime, which demanded collective action and 'compensatory measures' to maintain public order.[139]

The AFSJ also provided a 'new' banner through which the legitimacy of the EU could be enhanced. The 1990s was a decade in which EU legitimacy came to be increasingly questioned. The institutional regime through which the AFSJ was delivered did not enhance input legitimacy, but it was said to foster output legitimacy. The initial establishment of the EEC had been justified in terms of outcomes, increased peace, and prosperity. It was therefore neither fortuitous, nor surprising, that the AFSJ should be justified in similar terms. This was apparent from the Tampere European Council in 1999.[140]

The European Union has already put in place for its citizens the major ingredients of a shared idea of prosperity and peace: a single market, economic and monetary union, and the capacity to take on global political and economic challenges. The challenge of the Amsterdam Treaty is now to ensure that freedom, which includes the right to move freely throughout the Union, can be enjoyed in conditions of security and justice accessible to all. It is a project which responds to the frequently expressed concerns of citizens and has a direct bearing on their daily lives.

The Tampere Programme was superseded by the Hague Programme in 2004. The salience of political events in the USA and Spain reinforced the sentiments in the previous extract.[141]

The security of the European Union and its Member States has acquired a new urgency, especially in the light of the terrorist attacks in the United States on 11 September 2001 and in Madrid on 11 March 2004.

The citizens of Europe rightly expect the European Union, while guaranteeing respect for fundamental freedoms and rights, to take a more effective, joint approach to cross-border problems such as illegal migration and trafficking in and smuggling of human beings, as well as to terrorism and organized crime.

The official message, however, did not obviate criticism as to the concrete realization of these objectives in particular policy initiatives. Thus, for example, it was argued that the 'compensatory measures rationale' could not readily explain the restrictiveness of the policies adopted in areas such as migration, asylum, and the like, and that the driving force behind AFSJ had in reality been security.[142] Nor more generally did the official message preclude inquiry as to whether the issues dealt with by the AFSJ could really be considered a coherent package. Thus Walker[143] questioned whether there was a thematic coherence in the AFSJ, in terms of a fundamental unity of subject matter and a clearly defined

---

[139] Lavenex and Wallace (n 46).
[140] Tampere European Council, 15–16 October 1999, 2.
[141] Brussels European Council, 4–5 November 2004, 4.
[142] Costello (n 74) 289.
[143] N Walker, 'In Search of the Area of Freedom, Security and Justice: A Constitutional Odyssey' in Walker (n 1) ch 1.

overall project, concluding that notwithstanding the 'compensatory measures' rationale for the controls introduced by the Maastricht Treaty, there was no distinct end game other than adherence to a highly abstract triumvirate of values. He acknowledged, however, the desire of the EU to fashion policy coherence across the Third Pillar and Title IV EC, as exemplified by the formal linkage between the two and by the rhetoric used in the Tampere European Council.

(b) Looking forward: Stockholm

A decade of Treaty reform did not stop the normal institutional wheels turning. Five years after the Hague Programme the Stockholm Programme was launched.[144] It is a lengthy document, in excess of 80 pages, and the Commission is encouraged to take forward a broad range of initiatives. The Commission has duly produced an Action Plan in 2010 to implement the Programme.[145] The European Council regards the challenge in the forthcoming years to 'ensure respect for fundamental freedoms and integrity while guaranteeing security in Europe'.[146]

It lists the political priorities for the next five years. It is encouraging that the 'promotion of citizenship and fundamental rights' is the first item on the list. This is followed by 'A Europe of law and justice', with emphasis placed on cross-border access to justice. The third priority is 'A Europe that protects', with emphasis on internal security strategy to protect the safety of European citizens and tackle organized crime, terrorism, and other threats. The fourth is 'Access to Europe in a globalized world'; and the penultimate item on the list is 'A Europe of responsibility, solidarity and partnership in migration and asylum matters', the objective being development of a forward-looking and comprehensive European migration policy, coupled with control of illegal migration. The final political priority is 'The role of Europe in a globalized world', which deals with the external dimension of EU policy in relation to the AFSJ.

The remainder of the Stockholm Programme elaborates in detail the way in which these priorities should be advanced, with use being made of both hard law and soft law. Thus, by way of example, the Programme specifies in some detail the measures and initiatives that should be used to achieve the first objective, citizenship and fundamental rights, including:[147] 'rapid accession' to the European Convention on Human Rights (ECHR); checking that legislation is compliant with the Charter and the ECHR; making use of the expertise of the

---

[144] The Stockholm Programme—An Open and Secure Europe Serving and Protecting the Citizen, Council 16484/1/09, Brussels, 25 November 2009.

[145] Delivering an area of freedom, security and justice for Europe's citizens, Action Plan Implementing the Stockholm Programme, COM(2010) 171.

[146] Stockholm Programme (n 145) [1.1].

[147] ibid [2.1].

European Union Agency for Fundamental Rights; pursuing efforts to bring about the abolition of the death penalty, torture, and other inhuman and degrading treatment; and continuing to fight against crimes of genocide, crimes against humanity, and war crimes.

To take a further example, 'A Europe of law and justice' is to be advanced through, *inter alia*:[148] mutual recognition in criminal law, with approximation of laws where necessary to foster this; minimum rules concerning the definition of criminal offences and sanctions in the areas of particularly serious crime with a cross-border dimension; the extension of mutual recognition to new areas of civil law, such as succession and the proprietary consequences of separation of couples; and harmonization of conflict-of-law rules at Union level.

The shape of the AFSJ over the next five years remains to be seen. The placing accorded to fundamental rights within the Stockholm Programme is to be welcomed, as are the frequent references to such principles throughout the remainder of the report. It is nonetheless the case that much will depend on delivery and on the balance in reality between concerns about security and borders on the one hand, and rights-based protections on the other. Thus the Stockholm Programme places much emphasis on development of an overarching 'Internal Security Strategy', which is to be overseen by COSI.[149] This strategy has already been worked out in detail.[150] The protection of fundamental rights is said to be part of the strategy, although how far such rights get 'squeezed' in the realization of the strategy remains to be seen.

The warning of the Fundamental Rights Agency, concerning the way in which the rights formally protected by the Schengen regime have been compromised in practice in external border controls, is apposite here.[151] Bunyan has opined that the Stockholm Programme will lead to 'a bit more freedom and justice and a lot more security'.[152] The European Civil Liberties Network has been especially critical of the Stockholm Programme, arguing that the AFSJ regime hitherto has allowed far-reaching surveillance mechanisms and has led to a fortress Europe with stringent border controls, in relation to which there is inadequate over-sight.[153]

Whether one agrees with this latter diagnosis or not, it is undeniable that AFSJ initiatives across the range of policies in Title V of the Lisbon Treaty will continue to occupy a considerable amount of time and energy of the EU

---

[148] ibid [3].

[149] ibid [4].

[150] Draft Internal Security Strategy for the European Union: 'Towards a European Union Security Model', Council 5842/10, Brussels, 2 February 2010.

[151] European Union Agency for Fundamental Rights (n 81).

[152] T Bunyan, 'Commission: Action Plan on the Stockholm Programme, A Bit more Freedom and Justice and a lot more Security', available at <http://www.statewatch.org/stockholm-programme.htm>.

[153] European Civil Liberties Network, Oppose the 'Stockholm Programme', available at <http://www.statewatch.org/stockholm-programme.htm>.

institutions. The change made by the Lisbon Treaty in bringing the AFSJ into the main body of the Treaty and hence subject to the normal judicial controls are to be welcomed in enhancing the rule of law. This change, coupled with the Charter of Rights becoming legally binding, could well see numerous AFSJ measures being tested for conformity with rights, more especially because many such initiatives have been criticized from a rights-based perspective.[154] The ability to contest such matters before the ECJ will at least provide some check to ensure that the balance between the priorities in the Stockholm Programme is maintained when they are transformed into concrete legal measures.

[154] S Douglas-Scott, 'The EU's Area of Freedom, Security and Justice: A Lack of Fundamental Rights, Mutual Trust and Democracy?' (2008–9) 11 CYELS forthcoming.

10

External Action, Foreign Policy, and Defence

This chapter explores the impact of the Lisbon Treaty on EU external action, including the Common, Foreign, and Security Policy (CFSP) and the Common Security and Defence Policy (CSDP). This is a complex world, with a wealth of sophisticated literature.[1]

The discussion begins by considering the approach taken to external action in the Lisbon Treaty, since this is necessary for an understanding of the more detailed provisions analysed thereafter. This section examines the Treaty architecture that informs this area of EU law, the principles that govern EU external action, the main institutional actors, and the changes made that affect the EU's legal personality.

The focus in the second part shifts to those aspects of EU external action that are dealt with by the Treaty on the Functioning of the European Union (TFEU). The strategy throughout this section is to address each principal head of EU external competence brought together in what is now Part Five TFEU, to outline

[1] I MacLeod, D Hendry, and S Hyett, *The External Relations of the European Communities* (Clarendon, 1996); M Koskenniemi, (ed), *International Law Aspects of the European Union* (Kluwer Law International, 1998); M Cremona, 'External Relations and External Competence: the Emergence of an Integrated Policy' in P Craig and G de Búrca (eds), *The Evolution of EU Law* (Oxford University Press, 1999) ch 4; A Dashwood and C Hillion (eds), *The General Law of EC External Relations* (Sweet & Maxwell, 2000); E Cannizzaro, (ed), *The European Union as an Actor in International Relations* (Kluwer, 2002); M Cremona, 'The Draft Constitutional Treaty: External Relations and External Action' (2003) 40 CMLRev 1347; S Griller, 'External Relations' in B de Witte (ed), *Ten Reflections on the Constitutional Treaty for Europe* (EUI Florence, 2003) 133; P Eeckhout, *External Relations of the European Union: Legal and Constitutional Foundations* (Oxford University Press, 2004); D Thym, 'Reforming Europe's Common Foreign and Security Policy' (2004) 10 ELJ 5; P Maddalon, 'L'action exterieure de l'Union européene' (2005) 40 RTDE 493; P Koutrakos, *EU International Relations Law* (Hart, 2006); P Craig and G de Búrca, *EU Law, Text, Cases and Materials* (Oxford University Press, 5th edn, 2007) ch 6; M Cremona (ed), *Developments in EU External Relations Law* (Oxford University Press, 2008); M Cremona and B de Witte (eds), *EU Foreign Relations Law, Constitutional Fundamentals* (Hart, 2008); A Dashwood and M Maresceau (eds), *Law and Practice of EU External Relations, Salient Features of a Changing Landscape* (Cambridge University Press, 2008); C Kaddous, 'External Action under the Lisbon Treaty' in I Pernice and E Tanchev (eds), *Ceci n'est pas une Constitution—Constitutionalisation without a Constitution?* (Nomos, 2009) 172–187; D Thym, 'Foreign Affairs' in A von Bogdandy and J Bast (eds), *Principles of European Constitutional Law* (Hart/Verlag CH Beck, revised 2nd edn, 2010) ch 9; C Hillion and P Koutrakos (eds), *Mixed Agreements Revisited, The EU and its Member States in the World* (Hart, 2010).

the pre-existing Treaty provisions and then to indicate the main changes made by the Lisbon Treaty.

This approach is replicated in the third part of the chapter, which analyses the changes made to the CFSP and the CSDP. It will be seen that while the Lisbon Treaty has formally removed the Three Pillar structure that prevailed hitherto, there are nonetheless still distinct rules that apply to the CFSP and the CSDP, which are located in the Treaty on European Union (TEU). There is an outline of the pre-existing Treaty provisions, followed by analysis of the impact of the Lisbon Treaty.

The final part of the chapter stands back from the detail and considers broader issues of consistency, coherence, and coordination that have been of concern in this area. These issues are addressed from the perspectives of purpose, institutions, and doctrine. Thus there is consideration of whether the purpose of EU external action can be regarded as consistent and coherent, whether the institutional ordering in the post-Lisbon world fosters these goals, and the degree to which the lack of consistency in legal doctrine persists under the Lisbon schema.

1. Lisbon Treaty: Architecture, Principles, and Institutions

The Lisbon Treaty has made a number of changes in relation to external action and Common Foreign and Security Policy, CFSP. This section will elaborate the new Treaty architecture and the institutional changes, with issues of substance being considered in later sections.

(a) Architecture

The external relations powers broadly conceived of the EU and EC were scattered throughout the previous Treaties. This has now changed. The Lisbon Treaty provisions are not exactly the same as those in the Constitutional Treaty, although there is much commonality between them. It was, moreover, Working Group VII on External Action,[2] combined with discussion in the Praesidium[3] in the Convention on the Future of Europe, which did much of the creative thinking that shaped the architecture in the Constitutional Treaty and the Lisbon Treaty.

Working Group VII had its share of disagreement, as will be seen below. There was, however, broad agreement that the provisions concerning external action should be grouped together under a new Title of the Treaty.[4] This was

---

[2] CONV 459/02, Final Report of Working Group VII on External Action, Brussels, 16 December 2002.
[3] CONV 161/02, EU External Action, Brussels, 3 July 2002.
[4] Final Report of Working Group VII (n 2) 2.

carried through in the Constitutional Treaty, with certain general provisions concerning foreign and security policy dealt with in Part I,[5] while the remainder, together with the Treaty articles on external action, set out in Part III.[6]

The Lisbon Treaty retained the sensible idea that there should be a separate section dealing with external action, which is now Part Five of the TFEU. It has seven Titles, which are: General Provisions on the Union's External Action; Common Commercial Policy; Cooperation with Third Countries and Humanitarian Aid; Restrictive Measures, International Agreements; The EU's Relations with International Organizations and EU Delegations; and the Solidarity Clause. This division follows that in the Constitutional Treaty.

There are, however, some differences in architecture as between the Lisbon Treaty and the Constitutional Treaty. The general principles that guide external action and the detailed provisions concerning the CFSP are dealt with in the TEU of the Lisbon Treaty, whereas the analogous provisions were largely included in Part III of the Constitutional Treaty. This reflects a difference of emphasis as between the Constitutional Treaty and the Lisbon Treaty. The rules concerning the CFSP are distinctive in both Treaties, and remain more inter-governmental than other EU policies.

The framers' of the Constitutional Treaty nonetheless chose to include the CFSP rules within the section dealing with External Action, thereby preserving the linkage with other external aspects of EU policy, while recognizing that the CFSP was subject to distinct rules. The framers' of the Lisbon Treaty preferred to keep 'greater distance' between the CFSP provisions and the remainder of those on external action, hence the choice to place them within the TEU, while preserving some architectural link with the main body of external action because the general principles that govern such action are included within, and directly precede, the detailed CFSP rules.

(b) Principles

There was a significant degree of consensus in Working Group VII on External Action that the Treaty should contain a provision specifying the underlying principles and objectives of EU external action, and it duly drafted such a provision.[7] This provided the foundation for the statement of principle that was included in the Constitutional Treaty,[8] and it is now found in the Lisbon Treaty in Article 21 TEU.

1. The Union's action on the international scene shall be guided by the principles which have inspired its own creation, development and enlargement, and which it seeks to advance in the wider world: democracy, the rule of law, the universality and

---

[5] Arts I-40–41 CT. [6] Arts III-292–329 CT.
[7] Final Report of Working Group VII (n 2) 2–3. [8] Art III-292 CT.

indivisibility of human rights and fundamental freedoms, respect for human dignity, the principles of equality and solidarity, and respect for the principles of the United Nations Charter and international law.

The Union shall seek to develop relations and build partnerships with third countries, and international, regional or global organisations which share the principles referred to in the first subparagraph. It shall promote multilateral solutions to common problems, in particular in the framework of the United Nations.

2. The Union shall define and pursue common policies and actions, and shall work for a high degree of cooperation in all fields of international relations, in order to:

   (a) safeguard its values, fundamental interests, security, independence and integrity;
   (b) consolidate and support democracy, the rule of law, human rights and the principles of international law;
   (c) preserve peace, prevent conflicts and strengthen international security, in accordance with the purposes and principles of the United Nations Charter, with the principles of the Helsinki Final Act and with the aims of the Charter of Paris, including those relating to external borders;
   (d) foster the sustainable economic, social and environmental development of developing countries, with the primary aim of eradicating poverty;
   (e) encourage the integration of all countries into the world economy, including through the progressive abolition of restrictions on international trade;
   (f) help develop international measures to preserve and improve the quality of the environment and the sustainable management of global natural resources, in order to ensure sustainable development;
   (g) assist populations, countries and regions confronting natural or man-made disasters; and
   (h) promote an international system based on stronger multilateral cooperation and good global governance.

3. The Union shall respect the principles and pursue the objectives set out in paragraphs 1 and 2 in the development and implementation of the different areas of the Union's external action covered by this Title and by Part Five of the Treaty on the Functioning of the European Union, and of the external aspects of its other policies.

The Union shall ensure consistency between the different areas of its external action and between these and its other policies. The Council and the Commission, assisted by the High Representative of the Union for Foreign Affairs and Security Policy, shall ensure that consistency and shall cooperate to that effect.

Article 205 TFEU is the sole Treaty Article under the heading 'General Provisions on the Union's External Action', which constitutes Title I of Part Five TFEU dealing with External Action, and Article 205 simply refers back to Article 21 TEU and Article 22 TEU, the latter of which will be considered below. Article 21 TEU therefore contains the general principles for this area. Moreover, it is clear from Article 21(3) TEU that these principles apply to all external action: CFSP; external action under Part V TFEU; and external aspects of other EU policies. This is further reinforced by Article 3 TEU, which lists the EU's objectives. The list includes Article 3(5), which states that:

In its relations with the wider world, the Union shall uphold and promote its values and interests and contribute to the protection of its citizens. It shall contribute to peace, security, the sustainable development of the Earth, solidarity and mutual respect among peoples, free and fair trade, eradication of poverty and the protection of human rights, in particular the rights of the child, as well as to the strict observance and the development of international law, including respect for the principles of the United Nations Charter.

The discussion of principles that are to guide EU external action would be incomplete without mention of Article 222 TFEU, which contains the new 'Solidarity Clause'. It provides in essence that the EU and its Member States shall act jointly in a spirit of solidarity if a Member State is subject to terrorist attack, or the victim of a natural or man-made disaster. The EU must mobilize all instruments at its disposal, including military resources made available by the Member States, to prevent the terrorist threat in the Member States; protect democratic institutions and the civilian population from any terrorist attack; and assist a Member State in its territory, at the request of its political authorities, in the event of a terrorist attack or a natural or man-made disaster. There is also provision for the Council to coordinate efforts by Member States to assist a Member State that is the object of a terrorist attack, or the victim of a natural or man-made disaster. Arrangements for EU implementation of the solidarity clause are made by Council decision, acting on a joint proposal by the Commission and the High Representative, with the European Parliament being kept informed. It is for the European Council regularly to assess the threats facing the EU in order to enable it and its Member States to take effective action.

(c) Institutions

The EU institutions all play a role to some degree in relation to External Action and the CFSP, although the precise role differs in different areas, as will be seen below. It is nonetheless important at this juncture to spotlight two of the institutional players that are accorded central importance by the Lisbon Treaty.

(i) European Council

Article 22 TEU is the other 'General Provision' that governs EU external action, and follows the analogous provision in the Constitutional Treaty.[9] Article 22 TEU provides that:

1. On the basis of the principles and objectives set out in Article 21, the European Council shall identify the strategic interests and objectives of the Union.

---

[9] Art III-293 CT.

Decisions of the European Council on the strategic interests and objectives of the Union shall relate to the common foreign and security policy and to other areas of the external action of the Union.

Such decisions may concern the relations of the Union with a specific country or region or may be thematic in approach. They shall define their duration, and the means to be made available by the Union and the Member States.

The European Council shall act unanimously on a recommendation from the Council, adopted by the latter under the arrangements laid down for each area. Decisions of the European Council shall be implemented in accordance with the procedures provided for in the Treaties.

2. The High Representative of the Union for Foreign Affairs and Security Policy, for the area of common foreign and security policy, and the Commission, for other areas of external action, may submit joint proposals to the Council.

It is therefore for the European Council to 'identify' the EU's strategic interests and objectives. This is to be done by decisions, which can relate to the CFSP and to other areas of EU external action. While it is the European Council that makes such decisions unanimously, Article 22 TEU reveals the role of the other institutional players. Thus the European Council decision is made on the basis of a recommendation from the Council, which is to be adopted under arrangements laid down for specific areas. It is moreover clear from Article 22(2) TEU that the Council recommendation can be based on joint proposals from the High Representative and the Commission.

The nature of the 'decision' made by the European Council is distinctive, in the sense that it does not fit within the hierarchy of norms laid down by the Lisbon Treaty. A 'decision' can be a legislative act, a delegated act, or an implementing act.[10] The use of the word 'decision' within Article 22 does not conform to any of these meanings. It is not a legislative act, since it is not made in accordance with a legislative procedure.[11] It is not a delegated act, since it is not made pursuant to a legislative act,[12] and in any event Article 22 'decisions' clearly do not match the paradigm of a delegated act. It is not, moreover, an implementing act, since these grant power to the Commission when certain conditions are met.[13]

(ii) The High Representative of the Union for Foreign Affairs and Security Policy

We have already seen in earlier discussion that the framers of the Lisbon Treaty decided to drop the nomenclature of EU Minister for Foreign Affairs from the Constitutional Treaty and replace it with the High Representative of the Union for Foreign Affairs and Security Policy. The role accorded to the High

[10] Ch 7. [11] Art 289 TFEU. [12] Art 290 TFEU.
[13] Art 291 TFEU.

Representative was nonetheless the same as that etched out for the EU Minister for Foreign Affairs.

The High Representative is appointed by the European Council by qualified majority, with the agreement of the Commission President.[14] The incumbent is one of the Vice-Presidents of the Commission, and is responsible for handling external relations and for coordinating other aspects of the Union's external action.[15] The holder of the office takes part in the work of the European Council,[16] chairs the Foreign Affairs Council,[17] and is also a Vice-President of the Commission. The High Representative therefore wears 'two hats', or perhaps three if one regards the role of chairing the Foreign Affairs Council as distinctive from the functions performed within the European Council and Commission. The way in which shared executive power in relation to foreign policy will operate was considered in the earlier discussion, and will be addressed in more detail later in this chapter.[18] The High Representative is to be assisted by the creation of the European External Action Service (EEAS),[19] the idea for which originated in the Working Group on External Action.[20] The EEAS is to be composed of staff drawn from the Commission, the General Secretariat of the Council, and staff seconded from national diplomatic services.[21]

It is instructive to probe further in order to understand the genesis of the new office of High Representative. The deliberations of Working Group VII on External Relations were premised on the need for greater coherence between foreign policy and other spheres of external action. It considered four options for the locus of institutional authority.[22] There were clearly divisions of opinion within the Working Group on this issue.

The first option was to retain the separate posts of High Representative and a Commissioner with responsibility for external action, while increasing the synergy between the two. There was support for this option, but it was not pursued by the Working Group because it was felt that closer cooperation 'would not be sufficient to ensure coherence across the board of EU external action' and that bolder institutional changes 'were needed to meet the challenge of increasing coherence'.[23]

There was considerable support for the second option, which entailed the full merger of the functions of the High Representative into the Commission. This was the most radical option, since it would have meant that there would have

---

[14] Art 18(1) TEU.   [15] Art 18(4) TEU.
[16] Art 15(2) TEU.   [17] Art 18(3) TEU.   [18] pp 110–112, pp 426–429.
[19] <http://eeas.europa.eu/background/index_en.htm>.
[20] Final Report of Working Group VII (n 2) 6–7.
[21] Art 27(3) TEU; Presidency Report to the European Council on the European External Action Service, 14930/09, Brussels, 23 October 2009.
[22] Final Report of Working Group VII (n 2) 19–23.
[23] ibid [30].

been a single centre for policy preparation in all fields of external action, including CFSP, which would have been located in the Commission, although decision making would have still remained in the hands of the European Council and the Council. The Commission, however, would have been responsible for policy initiation and implementation, and for external representation in all areas of Union external action, subject to the caveat that defence policy would have been subject to a different regime. While there was much support for this option it was not recommended, since the Working Group felt that the Member States were not ready to transform foreign policy into an area of shared, let alone exclusive, competence of the kind that operated in the field of the common commercial policy.[24]

It was this consideration that led the Working Group to advocate the third option, which was the origin of the double hat view. Both offices, High Representative and Commissioner, would be exercised by one person who would have the title 'European External Representative', this being preferred to that of 'EU Minister for Foreign Affairs', since the former did not correspond to a title held at national level. The incumbent of the new office would be appointed by the Council, meeting in the composition of Heads of State or Government acting by a qualified majority, with the approval of the Commission President and endorsement by the European Parliament. The 'European External Representative' would receive direct mandates from and be accountable to the Council for issues relating to CFSP, and also be a full member of the Commission, preferably with the rank of Vice-President.[25] The Working Group recognized that the procedures for CFSP matters and for other issues concerning Community external action should remain distinct.[26]

The Working Group did, however, advert to a fourth option, which recognized the central role played by the European Council in defining the general guidelines of the EU's foreign policy and that of the Council in relation to its implementation. This option would entail creation of the post of 'EU Minister of Foreign Affairs', who would be under the direct authority of the President of the European Council and who would combine the functions of the High Representative and the Commissioner. The holder of the new office would chair the External Action Council. The overall 'aim would be to increase coherence between policy guidelines agreed by the Council and the operational responsibilities of the Commission in the field of external action, while respecting the competences attributed to each institution'.[27]

The Working Group nonetheless concluded by recommending the third option, rather than the fourth. This was in part because when it produced its final report in December 2002 the issue of the Presidency of the European

24 ibid [31]–[32].   25 ibid [33].
26 ibid [34].   27 ibid [38].

Council was still unclear, more especially whether there would be a long-term Presidency to replace the rotation system. The framers of the Constitutional Treaty, as we have seen,[28] opted for the long-term Presidency and the institutional approach to external relations was closer to the fourth option than the third. This was carried over to the Lisbon Treaty, subject to the change in nomenclature to High Representative of the Union for Foreign Affairs and Security Policy.

(d) Legal personality

Prior to the Lisbon Treaty the EC was accorded legal personality by Article 281 EC. There was no direct equivalent provision in relation to the EU, although the reality was that international agreements were concluded by the EU pursuant to Article 24 EU.

The Working Group on Legal Personality[29] established by the Convention on the Future of Europe recommended that the EU should have a single legal personality. This would simplify matters, and would have the beneficial consequence that the EU could avail itself of means of international action, including the rights to conclude treaties, to submit claims or to act before an international court, to become a member of an international organization or party to international conventions, such as the European Convention on Human Rights (ECHR), as well as to bind the EU internationally.[30]

The Lisbon Treaty duly provides in Article 47 TEU that the 'Union shall have legal personality'. There is no reason why this change should have any impact on the competence of the EU. The Member States nonetheless felt the need to append a Declaration stating that the fact that the EU has legal personality does not in any way 'authorise the Union to legislate or to act beyond the competences conferred upon it by the Member States in the Treaties'.[31]

2. Lisbon Treaty: EU External Action

The Lisbon Treaty identifies a number of different policies that fall within the scope of external action. The analysis below follows the specific policy spheres as they are listed in the Lisbon Treaty.

---

[28] Ch 3.
[29] CONV 305/02, Final Report of Working Group III on Legal Personality, Brussels, 1 October 2002.
[30] ibid [19].
[31] Declaration 24 concerning the legal personality of the European Union.

(a) Common Commercial Policy

(i) Pre-Lisbon

The Common Commercial Policy (CCP) was, prior to the Lisbon Treaty, covered by Articles 131 to 134 EC. Article 131 EC established the objectives of CCP policy.

By establishing a customs union between themselves Member States aim to contribute, in the common interest, to the harmonious development of world trade, the progressive abolition of restrictions on international trade and the lowering of customs barriers.

   The common commercial policy shall take into account the favourable effect which the abolition of customs duties between Member States may have on the increase in the competitive strength of undertakings in those States.

Article 133(1) EC described the measures that could be adopted in the framework of the CCP.

The common commercial policy shall be based on uniform principles, particularly in regard to changes in tariff rates, the conclusion of tariff and trade agreements, the achievement of uniformity in measures of liberalisation, export policy and measures to protect trade such as those to be taken in the event of dumping or subsidies.

Decision making was divided between the Commission and the Council. It was the Commission that made proposals for implementing the CCP, which the Council then adopted by qualified majority. The European Parliament had no role in this process.[32] Agreements with States or international organizations were negotiated by the Commission after authorization had been given by the Council,[33] and the agreement was concluded by the Council in accordance with the relevant Treaty rules.[34]

   The European Court of Justice (ECJ) gave an expansive interpretation to Article 133 EC. It read it in conjunction with other Treaty provisions concerned with the customs union and concluded that it empowered the Community institutions 'thoroughly to control external trade by measures taken both independently and by agreement'.[35] The ECJ furthered this expansive interpretation by defining the scope of the CCP by analogy with the external trade policy of a State, and held, moreover, that the defence of the Community's common interest, the need to prevent distortions of competition between undertakings, and the principle of Member State loyalty to the EC and its institutions meant that competence must be exclusive.[36] There is little doubt that the linkage between the CCP and the common market influenced the ECJ's expansive

---

[32] Art 133(2), (4) EC.   [33] Art 133(2) EC.   [34] Art 300 EC.
[35] Case 8/73 *Hauptzollamt Bremerhaven v Massey-Ferguson GmbH* [1973] ECR 897, [4].
[36] Opinion 1/75 (*Understanding on a Local Cost Standard*) [1975] ECR 1355.

interpretation of competence in this area.[37] The ECJ confirmed in later cases that the CCP could legitimately be used to foster trade regulation, not just trade liberalization,[38] and that development could be accorded a role within Article 133.[39]

The limits of Article 133 EC, as it was then formulated, were revealed in Opinion 1/94.[40] The ECJ concluded that World Trade Organization (WTO) agreements on trade in goods fell within the Community's commercial policy competence. It held also that trade in services could not, in principle, be excluded from Article 133.[41] The ECJ nonetheless concluded that the definition of trade in services in the relevant WTO agreement did not fall within the CCP,[42] with the consequence that it was to be regarded as a mixed agreement which could be signed by the Member States as well as the Commission.

Subsequent Treaty amendments, however, expanded the scope of Article 133 EC. The Treaty of Amsterdam added a paragraph empowering the Council, acting unanimously after consulting the European Parliament, to extend Article 133(1)–(4) to agreements on services and intellectual property, insofar as this was not covered by the existing provisions of Article 133. The Nice Treaty made further changes to Article 133,[43] most significantly by extending it to cover the negotiation and conclusion of agreements on trade in services and commercial aspects of intellectual property, although the EC's competence was not exclusive in this respect. There was also the possibility of extending Community competence to make agreements relating more generally to intellectual property.[44]

(ii) Post-Lisbon

The provisions on the CCP are now included in Articles 206 to 207 TFEU, and follow those in the Constitutional Treaty.[45] Article 207(1) TFEU provides as follows.

The common commercial policy shall be based on uniform principles, particularly with regard to changes in tariff rates, the conclusion of tariff and trade agreements relating to trade in goods and services, and the commercial aspects of intellectual property, foreign direct investment, the achievement of uniformity in measures of liberalisation, export

---

[37] M Cremona, 'EC External Commercial Policy after Amsterdam: Authority and Interpretation within Interconnected Legal Orders' in JHH Weiler (ed), *Towards a Common Law of International Trade? The EU, the WTO and the NAFTA* (Oxford University Press, 2000).

[38] Opinion 1/78 (*International Agreement on Natural Rubber*) [1979] ECR 2871.

[39] Case 45/86 *Commission v Council* [1987] ECR 1493.

[40] Opinion 1/94 *Competence of the Community to Conclude International Agreements Concerning Services and the Protection of Intellectual Property, WTO* [1994] ECR I-5267.

[41] ibid [36]–[41].

[42] ibid [47].

[43] M Cremona, 'A Policy of Bits and Pieces? The Common Commercial Policy After Nice' (2002) 4 CYELS 61.

[44] Arts 133(5), (7).   [45] Arts III-313–314 CT.

policy and measures to protect trade such as those to be taken in the event of dumping or subsidies. The common commercial policy shall be conducted in the context of the principles and objectives of the Union's external action.

The most significant changes made by the Lisbon Treaty are as follows. First, Article 207(1) now mandates that the CCP must be conducted in the context of the principles and objectives that relate to the EU's external action. These principles were set out above, and include not only the trade liberalization objectives, now enshrined in Article 206 TFEU, but also matters such as respect for human rights, environmental protection, and sustainable development.

Second, the complexity of Article 133 EC has been simplified in important respects by the Lisbon Treaty. Article 133 EC was complicated, even judged by the standards of EC provisions. The political compromises that shaped EC power in this area were manifest in the exceptions and qualifications written into that provision. Article 207(1) TFEU provides some welcome simplification, in relative terms at least. It makes explicit reference to trade agreements relating to services and commercial aspects of intellectual property, and to foreign direct investment. All such areas fall within the EU's exclusive competence.[46] This is subject to the caveat expressed in Article 207(6) TFEU, which provides that exercise of the competences conferred by Article 207 in the field of the CCP shall not affect the delimitation of competences between the Union and the Member States, and shall not lead to harmonization of legislative or regulatory provisions of the Member States in so far as the Treaties exclude such harmonization.

Third, decision making in relation to the CCP has been modified. It is now for the European Parliament and the Council, acting by the ordinary legislative procedure, to enact regulations that define the framework for implementing the CCP.[47] The European Parliament has therefore been included in decision making in an area that it had previously been excluded from.

Fourth, the decisional rules relating to the conclusion of international agreements have been modified, so as to accord the European Parliament the right to be consulted.[48] The default rule for the conclusion of international agreements is that the Council acts by qualified majority.[49] The Council must, however, act unanimously in relation to agreements on services, the commercial aspects of intellectual property, and foreign direct investment, where such agreements include provisions for which unanimity is required for the adoption of internal rules. Unanimity in the Council is also required for the negotiation and conclusion of agreements relating to trade in cultural and audiovisual services, where they risk prejudicing the Union's cultural and linguistic diversity; and those relating to trade in social, education, and health services, where they risk seriously disturbing the national organization of such services and

[46] Art 3(1) TFEU. [47] Art 207(2) TFEU.
[48] Art 218(6)(b) TFEU. [49] Art 207(4) TFEU.

prejudicing the responsibility of Member States to deliver them.[50] Special provision is made for agreements concerning transport.[51]

Fifth, the Lisbon Treaty has repealed provisions of the EC Treaty concerning Member State harmonization of the system whereby they grant aid for exports to third countries, and Commission authorization to a Member State to take protective measures.[52]

(b) Cooperation with third countries and humanitarian aid

Title III of Part Five of the Lisbon Treaty covers three topics: development cooperation; economic, financial, and technical cooperation with third countries; and humanitarian aid.

(i) Pre-Lisbon

The EC, prior to the amendments made by the Maastricht Treaty, had no explicit legal base for development policy, technical cooperation, and humanitarian aid. The EC nonetheless undertook policy initiatives in these areas based on other EC external powers, such as those relating to commercial policy and association, and by using Article 308 EC.

In Opinion 1/78 the ECJ accepted that trade instruments could have a development dimension,[53] the result being that the association and trade provisions of the Treaty were used for agreements with developing countries. The ECJ, however, ruled that the EC did not have exclusive competence in relation to humanitarian aid,[54] or development, with the consequence that Member States could make their own commitments.[55]

The Maastricht Treaty provided explicit foundation for development policy in Articles 177 and 178 EC, and the Nice Treaty added a legal basis for 'financial and technical cooperation' with third States in Article 181(a) EC. In both areas, Community policy was required to contribute to the general objective of developing and consolidating democracy and the rule of law, and to that of respecting human rights and fundamental freedoms. The EU has engaged in wide-ranging activities in both of these areas.[56]

(ii) Post-Lisbon

Development cooperation is now governed by Article 208 TFEU, which is the successor to Article 177 EC. Article 208 TFEU provides that:

---

[50] Art 207(4) TFEU.   [51] Art 207(5) TFEU.
[52] Arts 132, 134 EC.   [53] Opinion 1/78 (n 38).
[54] Cases C-181 and 248/91 *European Parliament v Council and Commission* (*Bangladesh*) [1993] ECR I-3685, [14]–[16].
[55] Case C-316/91 *European Parliament v Council* (*EDF*) [1994] ECR I-625.
[56] <http://ec.europa.eu/development/index_en.cfm>.

1. Union policy in the field of development cooperation shall be conducted within the framework of the principles and objectives of the Union's external action. The Union's development cooperation policy and that of the Member States complement and reinforce each other.

   Union development cooperation policy shall have as its primary objective the reduction and, in the long term, the eradication of poverty. The Union shall take account of the objectives of development cooperation in the policies that it implements which are likely to affect developing countries.

2. The Union and the Member States shall comply with the commitments and take account of the objectives they have approved in the context of the United Nations and other competent international organisations.

There is little change of substance in the new provision. Article 208 TFEU is framed in terms of the reduction and eradication of poverty, by way of contrast to the campaign against poverty, which was the language of Article 177 EC, although it is doubtful whether this will signal any shift of policy. An initial glance at Article 208 TFEU gives the impression that other objectives mentioned in Article 177 EC, such as sustainable economic and social development of developing countries, and their integration into the world economy, have been dropped. This impression is mistaken. Article 208(1) TFEU requires that development policy is to be conducted within the framework of the principles and objectives that guide EU external action. Article 21 TEU, which lists these principles and objectives, makes express reference to both of the preceding factors and hence they will continue to shape development policy.[57] This is equally true in relation to democracy, the rule of law, and human rights.

Article 177(2) EC had hitherto stipulated that development policy should contribute to these foundational precepts. Article 208 TFEU contains no such provision, but the injunction that development policy should be conducted within the framework of the principles and objectives that guide EU external action leads to the same result, since the relevant list includes protection of these values.[58]

The ordinary legislative procedure continues to apply to measures related to development policy.[59] The rules relating to the making of international agreements in this area are also unchanged: the EU is empowered to make such agreements, subject to the express caveat that this does not prejudice Member States' competence to negotiate in international bodies and conclude agreements.[60]

The Lisbon Treaty provisions on development cooperation nonetheless highlight some of the difficulties with categorization of competence.[61] Development cooperation is not included in the list of areas where the EU has competence to

---

[57] Arts 21(2)(d)–(e) TEU.   [58] Art 21(2)(b) TEU.
[59] Art 209(1) TFEU.   [60] Art 209(2) TFEU.   [61] p 170.

support, coordinate, or supplement Member State action.[62] Nor is it specifically included in the non-exhaustive list of areas that are subject to shared competence.[63] It is, however, brought within the remit of shared competence, albeit with the caveat that the exercise of EU competence in relation to development cooperation and humanitarian aid does not pre-empt the Member States from exercising their competence.[64] It is nonetheless clear that certain Treaty provisions are framed in terms of the EU and Member States coordinating their action in relation to development cooperation and aid programmes.[65]

The discussion thus far has been concerned with development cooperation. The Lisbon Treaty has also made some changes in relation to the provisions dealing with economic, financial, and technical cooperation with third countries. Article 212 TFEU now makes explicitly clear that such cooperation applies to third countries, other than developing countries. The measures must, however, be consistent with the EU's development policy, and must be carried out within the framework of the principles and objectives that pertain to EU external action. The measures taken to implement this policy are now made by the ordinary legislative procedure,[66] by way of contrast with the previous position whereby they were made by the Council with consultation by the European Parliament. There is, as before, provision for the EU and the Member States, within their respective spheres of competence, to cooperate with third countries and international organizations. The EU is empowered to make international agreements in relation to such cooperation, subject to the caveat that this does not affect Member States' competence to negotiate in international bodies and to conclude international agreements.[67]

The nature of the EU's competence in this area is not without difficulty. It is not included in the list of areas coming within shared competence in Article 4(2) TEU, but Article 4(1) TEU states that if an area does not come within exclusive competence or within the category where the EU is limited to supporting, coordinating or supplementing Member State action then it is deemed to come within shared competence. Since economic, financial, and technical cooperation with third countries does not fall within either of these categories, it will by default be regarded as coming within shared competence. The problem is that this does not fit well with the wording of Article 212(1) TFEU, which is framed in terms of EU and Member State action complementing and reinforcing each other.

---

[62] Art 6 TFEU.   [63] Art 4(2) TFEU.
[64] Art 4(4) TFEU.   [65] Art 210 TFEU.
[66] Art 212(2) TFEU. This is subject to the qualification in Art 213 TFEU that if urgent financial assistance is required by a third country the decision is made by the Council on a proposal from the Commission.
[67] Art 212(3) TFEU.

This is a matter of some importance, given the consequences that flow from inclusion within the sphere of shared competence: the EU is allowed to harmonize national laws, and exercise of EU competence pre-empts Member State competence.[68] It could be argued that although this area falls within shared competence, this still leaves open the nature of the EU's competence; that this is restricted to complementing and reinforcing that of the Member States; and that this thereby precludes more far-reaching harmonization measures. There is force in this argument, although it does significantly blur the line between shared competence, and the category where the EU is limited to supporting, coordinating, or supplementing Member State action.

The third topic dealt with in Title III of Part Five TFEU is humanitarian aid. Community provision of such aid is not new,[69] and prior to the Lisbon Treaty the relevant regulations were made pursuant to Treaty powers concerned with development cooperation.[70] The aid was disbursed through ECHO, the EU's humanitarian aid department. The Lisbon Treaty now provides explicit and separate foundation for this aspect of EU external action.

Article 214 TFEU is the governing provision. Humanitarian aid provides relief for those in third countries who are victims of natural or man-made disasters. EU action is to be conducted within the framework of the principles and objectives that govern EU external action. It must also be in compliance with the principles of international law, and with principles of impartiality, neutrality, and non-discrimination. The measures defining the framework for such aid operations are made by the ordinary legislative procedure. The EU is empowered to conclude agreements with third countries and competent international organizations to help to achieve the objectives in this area, and those in Article 21 TEU, which lists the objectives and principles that guide EU external action. The EU is to ensure that its humanitarian aid operations are coordinated and consistent with those of international organizations and bodies, in particular those forming part of the United Nations system. There is provision for a European Voluntary Humanitarian Aid Corps, through which young Europeans can contribute to EU humanitarian aid operations.

The provision of humanitarian aid falls within shared competence. This is because it does not fall within the category of exclusive competence, or that where the EU is limited to taking supporting action and hence it is deemed to come within shared competence.[71] However, this is subject to the qualification provided in Article 4(4) TFEU: the EU has competence to carry out 'activities and conduct a common policy', but the exercise of that competence does not preclude the Member States from exercising their competence. Thus the

---

[68] Art 2(2) TFEU.
[69] <http://ec.europa.eu/echo/index_en.htm>.
[70] Thus Council Regulation 1257/96 of 20 June 1996 concerning humanitarian aid [1996] OJ L163/1 was made pursuant to Art 179 EC.
[71] Art 4(1) TFEU.

pre-emption rule that normally applies within the sphere of shared competence[72] does not operate in this context.

It should nonetheless be noted that, notwithstanding inclusion within shared competence, this still leaves open the precise scope of the EU's competence in this area. The EU is empowered to establish the framework within which humanitarian aid operations are to be conducted, but this should be read against the instruction that the EU's measures and those of the Member States 'shall complement and reinforce each other'.[73] This emphasis is reinforced by the provision enabling the Commission to take initiatives to promote coordination between EU and Member State actions, in order to enhance the efficiency and complementarity of their respective aid measures.[74] Thus, although humanitarian aid falls within shared competence, the limited nature of the EU's competence reveals the thin line that can separate this category of competence from that where the EU is limited to taking action to support etc the actions of the Member States.

(c) Restrictive measures

(i) Pre-Lisbon

Article 301 EC dealt with trade interruption. A common position or joint action adopted according to the then prevailing provisions of the TEU relating to the common foreign and security policy, could make provision for action by the Community to interrupt or reduce, in part or completely, economic relations with one or more third countries. It was for the Council to take the necessary urgent measures, acting by qualified majority on a proposal from the Commission.[75]

(ii) Post-Lisbon

This issue is now dealt with by Article 215 TFEU, which builds on the provision in the EC Treaty.

1. Where a decision, adopted in accordance with Chapter 2 of Title V of the Treaty on European Union, provides for the interruption or reduction, in part or completely, of economic and financial relations with one or more third countries, the Council, acting by a qualified majority on a joint proposal from the High Representative of the Union for Foreign Affairs and Security Policy and the Commission, shall adopt the necessary measures. It shall inform the European Parliament thereof.

---

[72] Art 2(2) TFEU.   [73] Art 214(1) TFEU.
[74] Art 214(6) TFEU.
[75] P Koutrakos, *Trade, Foreign Policy & Defence in EU Constitutional Law: The Legal Regulation of Sanctions, Exports of Dual-Use Goods and Armaments* (Hart, 2001) 69.

2. Where a decision adopted in accordance with Chapter 2 of Title V of the Treaty on European Union so provides, the Council may adopt restrictive measures under the procedure referred to in paragraph 1 against natural or legal persons and groups or non-State entities.

3. The acts referred to in this Article shall include necessary provisions on legal safeguards.

The institutional novelty of Article 215 TFEU is that the Council acts on a joint proposal from the High Representative and the Commission, with the European Parliament being kept informed. The substantive novelty of the new provision is that it contains express empowerment to take restrictive measures against natural and legal persons, groups, and non-State entities. The absence of such express provision prior to the Lisbon Treaty had led to uncertainty as to whether the EC could take such measures, and, if so, how this could be rationalized in accordance with the then existing Treaty articles.[76]

This problem has now been obviated by Article 215(2) TFEU, which gives the EU express power to impose restrictive measures, more especially when read with Article 75 TFEU, which empowers the EU to take measures related to asset freezing and the like in order to combat terrorism. The *quid pro quo* for this enhanced EU power is that its exercise is subject to judicial review. Thus while the normal rule is that the ECJ has no jurisdiction over CFSP issues, this is subject to exceptions, one of which is that it can review the legality of restrictive measures made under Article 215(2) TFEU.[77] The importance of due process and legal control in this area were emphasized in a Declaration appended to the Lisbon Treaty.[78]

(d) International agreements

(i) Pre-Lisbon

The EC's power to make international agreements prior to the Lisbon Treaty derived from two principal sources.

The Treaty itself accorded such power in limited instances. The original Rome Treaty gave express power to conclude international agreements in relation to the Common Commercial Policy,[79] and for agreements 'establishing an association' with the Community.[80] The EC was also empowered to maintain relations with other international organizations, in particular the Council of Europe, the

---

[76] Cases C-402 and 415/05 P *Yassin Abdullah Kadi and Al Barakaat International Foundation v Council and Commission* [2008] ECR I-6351.
[77] Art 275 TFEU.
[78] Declaration 25 on Arts 75 and 215 of the Treaty on the Functioning of the European Union.
[79] Art 133 EC.   [80] Art 310 EC.

Organization for Economic Development (OECD), and the organs and specialized agencies of the UN.[81] Later Treaty amendments added express treaty-making powers in relation to research and technological development,[82] the environment,[83] development cooperation,[84] and economic and monetary policy.[85]

The other principal source of EC treaty-making competence was the ECJ's jurisprudence. This was the terrain of the classic and complex case law developed by the ECJ concerning the scope of Community competence to make international agreements where the Treaty provided no express power, and whether, if such competence existed, it was exclusive or not. This jurisprudence, and in particular the exclusivity issue, was examined in the earlier discussion of competence, to which reference should be made.[86] The present concern is primarily with the former issue, the ECJ's case law as to whether the EC had competence to make an international agreement where the Treaty provided no express power to do so.

The case law is well known and has been carefully analysed.[87] The ECJ recognized Community competence to conclude an international agreement where this was necessary to effectuate its internal competence, even where there was no express external competence.[88] This was apparent from the seminal *ERTA* decision.[89] The ECJ held that the existence of express internal power over transport, including international transport, thus assumed that the powers of the Community extended to relationships arising from international law, and hence involved the need for agreements with the third countries concerned, more especially because regulations had been passed pursuant to the primary Treaty articles, which necessarily vested in the Community power to enter into any agreements with third countries relating to the subject matter governed by that regulation.

---

[81] Arts 302–304 EC.   [82] Art 170 EC.
[83] Art 174(4) EC.   [84] Art 181 EC.
[85] Art 111 EC.   [86] pp 161–167.

[87] T Tridimas and P Eeckhout, 'The External Competence of the Community and the Case-Law of the Court of Justice: Principle versus Pragmatism' (1994) 14 YBEL 143; A Dashwood and J Heliskoski, 'The Classic Authorities Revisited' in A Dashwood and C Hillion (eds), *The General Law of EC External Relations* (Sweet & Maxwell, 2000); P Koutrakos, 'Legal Basis and Delimitation of Competence in EU External Relations' in Cremona and de Witte (n 1) ch 6; M Cremona, 'Defining Competence in EU External Relations: Lessons from the Treaty Reform Process' in Dashwood and Maresceau (n 1) ch 2.

[88] Case 22/70 *Commission v Council* [1971] ECR 263; Cases 3, 4, and 6/76 *Kramer* [1976] ECR 1279; Opinion 1/76 *On the Draft Agreement Establishing a Laying-up Fund for Inland Waterway Vessels* [1977] ECR 741; Opinion 2/91 *Re the ILO Convention 170 on Chemicals at Work* [1993] ECR I–1061; Opinion 2/94 *Accession of the Community to the European Human Rights Convention* [1996] ECR I–1759.

[89] Case 22/70 (n 88) [25]–[28].

This principle was reiterated and extended in *Kramer*, which concerned fisheries conservation. The ECJ confirmed that legal authority to make an international agreement could be implied as well as express.[90] It went further than the earlier ruling, however, holding that the existence of implied external power flowed from express internal power, and was not necessarily dependent on the actual adoption of internal rules.

The expansive interpretation of implied external power reached its high watermark in Opinion 1/76,[91] where the ECJ held that implied external power could exist even where the internal power was only exercised when the international agreement had been concluded. The power to make an international agreement flowed 'by implication from the provisions of the Treaty creating the internal power and in so far as the participation of the Community in the international agreement is, as here, necessary for the attainment of one of the objectives of the Community'.[92]

The ECJ nonetheless recognized some limits to the implied external power to make an international agreement. Thus in Opinion 2/94 on accession of the EC to the ECHR,[93] the ECJ held that the EC did not at that time have competence to join the ECHR. It reasoned that the previous jurisprudence was dependent on some express internal competence over the relevant area, concluding that this was not so in relation to human rights, since there was no chapter or title of the Treaty that gave the EC authority over such matters. The ECJ's conclusion was also influenced by the fact that entry into this international agreement would have significant institutional implications for the EC, and modify its own system of protection.

(ii) Post-Lisbon

The legal history of the EU is replete with instances where Treaty amendments either catch up with, or decide to embrace, judicial doctrine. The Lisbon Treaty amendments concerning international agreements provide a striking exemplification of this theme. The ground was once again laid by the Working Group on External Action.[94]

The Group noted that the EC Treaty attributed explicit competences to the Community in external action, including for the conclusion of international agreements, and that the Court of Justice had recognised implicit external Community competences when the conclusion of international agreements were necessary for the implementation of internal policies or as a reflection of its internal competencies in areas where it had exercised this competence by adopting secondary legislation. The Group saw merit in making explicit

---

[90] Cases 3, 4, 6/76 *Kramer* (n 88) [19]–[20].
[91] Opinion 1/76 (n 88).   [92] ibid [4].
[93] Opinion 2/94 *on Accession by the Community to the ECHR* [1996] ECR I-1759.
[94] Final Report of Working Group VII (n 2) [18].

the jurisprudence of the Court to facilitate the action of the Union in a globalised world, in particular when dealing with the external dimension of internal policies and action. Therefore, the Group agreed that the Treaty should indicate that the Union is competent to conclude agreements dealing with issues falling under its internal competences, under the same voting procedure within the Council as the one applied for internal legislative action (normally QMV). The Group agreed that making this explicit in the Treaty should be without prejudice to the delimitation of competences between the Union and the Member States. . . . In the field of explicit external competences, the Group acknowledged that the delimitation of competences between the Community and the Member States varied from one policy area to another. One member considered that more external policy areas as well as more external aspects of internal policy areas should become exclusive competences of the Union.

This suggestion was embodied in the Constitutional Treaty,[95] and the relevant provision was included in the Lisbon Treaty as Article 216 TFEU.

1. The Union may conclude an agreement with one or more third countries or international organisations where the Treaties so provide or where the conclusion of an agreement is necessary in order to achieve, within the framework of the Union's policies, one of the objectives referred to in the Treaties, or is provided for in a legally binding Union act or is likely to affect common rules or alter their scope.

2. Agreements concluded by the Union are binding upon the institutions of the Union and on its Member States.

The reality post-Lisbon is that the EU will always have power to make an international agreement. Article 216 accords this power in four types of case: when the Treaties so provide; when an agreement is necessary within the framework of the Union's policies to achieve a Union objective; when it is provided for in a legally binding Union act; or when it is likely to affect common rules or alter their scope.

It may be possible in theory to envisage cases that do not fit into these four categories, but the reality is that one or more of these categories will legitimate the making of an international agreement in the post-Lisbon world. The breadth of the second category is worthy of note. Provided that it can be shown that the agreement was necessary, it can be made so as to achieve a Union objective within the framework of Union policy. Thus an international agreement could be made to effectuate one of the broad objectives in Article 3 TEU or Article 21 TEU within the context of any Union policy.

The link between Article 216 TFEU and Article 3(2) TFEU is significant. Article 216 is concerned with whether the EU has competence to conclude an international agreement. Article 3(2) deals with the related, but distinct, issue as to whether that competence is exclusive or not. The Working Group recognized

---

[95] Art III-323 CT.

the distinction between these issues, as is apparent from the preceding quotation, and from the summary of its conclusions.[96] Article 3(2) TFEU, however, takes a broad view of exclusive EU competence. It reads as follows.

The Union shall also have exclusive competence for the conclusion of an international agreement when its conclusion is provided for in a legislative act of the Union or is necessary to enable the Union to exercise its internal competence, or in so far as its conclusion may affect common rules or alter their scope.

Article 3(2) TFEU was analysed in a previous chapter, to which reference should be made.[97] The specific categories listed in Article 216 TFEU as to when the EU is empowered to make an international agreement do not 'map' perfectly on to the wording used in Article 3(2). There is nonetheless a significant overlap between the two. It is unlikely that the differences in wording will lead to differences in result.

Thus if an international agreement is made pursuant to Article 216 TFEU on the ground that it is necessary to achieve a Union objective within the framework of a Union policy, this will probably be interpreted as exclusive EU competence for the purposes of Article 3(2) on the ground that the agreement is necessary to enable the EU to exercise its internal competence, more especially because Article 7 TFEU and other Treaty provisions[98] mandate that such objectives should be taken into account in the development of EU policy. This conclusion is reinforced because an international agreement made pursuant to Article 216 will often be capable of fitting more than one of the categories, and hence will be cloaked with exclusivity on an alternative ground that does 'map' directly on to Article 3(2).

The discussion thus far has been concerned with the impact of the Lisbon Treaty on the power to conclude international agreements and whether those agreements give exclusive competence to the EU. The Lisbon Treaty has also modified the rules concerning the negotiation and conclusion of such agreements. These were hitherto contained in Article 300 EC and are now found in Article 218 TFEU.[99] The schema is as follows.

The basic principle is that the Council authorizes the opening of negotiations, adopts negotiating directives, authorizes the signing of agreements, and concludes them.[100] The European Parliament must be immediately and fully informed at all stages of the procedure. The default position is that the Council acts by qualified majority throughout the procedure. This is subject to the caveat

---

[96] Final Report of Working Group VII (n 2) 4.
[97] pp 161–167.
[98] Arts 7–14, 21(3) TFEU.
[99] Art 218 TFEU is without prejudice to the specific rules for CCP agreements in Art 207 TFEU. There is also separate provision detailing the making of agreements in relation to economic and monetary union, Art 219 TFEU.
[100] Art 218(2) TFEU.

that it must act unanimously when the agreement covers a field for which unanimity is required for the adoption of an EU act. It must also act unanimously for association agreements; agreements concerning economic/financial/technical cooperation with States that are candidates for accession; and for agreement on accession to the ECHR.[101]

The Council decision to authorize opening of the negotiations is made on a recommendation from the Commission, or the High Representative where the agreement relates exclusively or principally to the CFSP. The Council nominates a Union negotiator, depending on the subject matter of the envisaged agreement. It is open to the Council to address directives to the negotiator and designate a special committee that must be consulted on the negotiations. The Council may authorize the negotiator to approve modifications to the agreement on behalf of the EU.

The Council, on a proposal from the negotiator, adopts a decision authorizing signature of the agreement and, if necessary, its provisional application before entry into force. It is the Council, acting on a proposal by the negotiator, which adopts a decision concluding the agreement. Except where agreements relate exclusively to the CFSP, this decision is made by the Council after obtaining the consent of the European Parliament in the following cases: association agreements; agreement on EU accession to the ECHR; agreements establishing a specific institutional framework by organizing cooperation procedures; agreements with important budgetary implications for the Union; and agreements covering fields to which either the ordinary legislative procedure applies, or the special legislative procedure where consent by the European Parliament is required.[102] For other types of agreement, consultation with the European Parliament is required.[103]

It is, as before, open to a Member State, the European Parliament, the Council, or the Commission to obtain the ECJ's opinion as to whether an agreement envisaged is compatible with the Treaties. Where the opinion of the Court is adverse, the agreement may not enter into force unless it is amended or the Treaties are revised.

There is also a provision concerning suspension of an agreement, which appears stricter than the previous formulation.[104] The current formulation provides that the Council, on a proposal from the Commission or the High

---

[101] The decision concluding the agreement with the ECHR only enters into force after it has been approved by the Member States in accordance with their respective constitutional requirements.

[102] The European Parliament and the Council may, in an urgent situation, agree upon a time limit for consent.

[103] The European Parliament must deliver its opinion within a time limit which the Council may set depending on the urgency of the matter. In the absence of an opinion within that time limit, the Council may act.

[104] Art 300(2) EC.

Representative, shall adopt a decision suspending application of an agreement, and establish the position to be adopted on the EU's behalf in a body set up by an agreement, when that body is called upon to adopt acts having legal effects, subject to an exception for acts supplementing or amending the institutional framework of the agreement.[105] The novelty of this formulation is that it has a mandatory quality absent from the express wording of the previous Treaty provision. The Council 'shall' suspend application of the agreement in the preceding circumstances. It is not clear whether this change was intended. The provision will in any event only be applicable where the power to adopt acts having legal effect was not part of the original terms of the international agreement.

(e) Association agreements

(i) Pre-Lisbon

Association agreements are a particular type of international agreement. The power to make such agreements was, together with that applicable to the Common Commercial Policy, the only express external relations power prior to the Single European Act 1986 (SEA).[106] Article 310 EC was framed as follows:

The Community may conclude with one or more States or international organisations agreements establishing an association involving reciprocal rights and obligations, common action and special procedure.

The list of the EC's 'activities' included 'the association of the overseas countries and territories in order to increase trade and promote jointly economic and social development'.[107] The aims of such association were set out in Article 182 EC.

The Member States agree to associate with the Community the non-European countries and territories which have special relations with Denmark, France, the Netherlands, and the United Kingdom. These countries and territories (hereinafter called the 'countries and territories') are listed in Annex II to this Treaty.

The purpose of association shall be to promote the economic and social development of the countries and territories and to establish close economic relations between them and the Community as a whole.

In accordance with the principles set out in the preamble to this Treaty, association shall serve primarily to further the interests and prosperity of the inhabitants of these countries and territories in order to lead them to the economic, social and cultural development to which they aspire.

The initial rationale for external power in this area was French colonial policy.[108] Association agreements were concluded with Greece and Turkey, and with the

---

[105] Art 218(9) TFEU.   [106] Art 238 EEC.   [107] Art 3(1)(s) EC.
[108] L Bartels, 'The Trade and Development Policy of the European Union' in Cremona, *Developments in EU External Relations Law* (n 1) 129–132.

African, Caribbean, and Pacific (ACP) countries under the Yaoundé Convention in the early 1960s.[109] Association agreements with countries in central and eastern Europe were known as 'Europe Agreements' and have been the subject of litigation before the ECJ.[110] Important association agreements with ACP countries were made pursuant to the Cotonou Agreement, which provided for free trade in most goods, equality in establishment, and aid.[111] The Treaty provided some indication of the objectives of association,[112] and the initial association agreements touched on much of the subject matter of the Treaty.[113]

(ii) Post-Lisbon

The EC framework has been largely preserved under the Lisbon Treaty. Article 217 TFEU is the successor to Article 310 EC. It provides that:

The Union may conclude with one or more third countries or international organisations agreements establishing an association involving reciprocal rights and obligations, common action and special procedure.

Article 198 TFEU reiterates the aims of such association, which were previously included in Article 182 EC, and Article 199 TFEU repeats the objectives of association agreements hitherto contained in Article 183 EC. The reality is that the world of association agreements is one of considerable complexity, in terms of the detailed provisions of such agreements and other related initiatives, as a mere glimpse at the Commission website reveals.[114] The underlying policy objectives have, moreover, changed over time. Bartels captures this transformation.[115]

From 1957 to the 1990s... the main objective was to maintain the historical economic relationship between erstwhile colonizers and subjects. A more general trade policy for other developing countries, which slowly took shape during the 1970s, was reactive, and always contingent on not harming either the primary relationship, or, of course, domestic producers...

This has now changed. The gradual acceptance of the principle that trade with developing countries should be non-discriminatory, the growing ability to enforce this principle within the WTO, and a decline in internal EU support for a special relationship

---

[109] [1963] OJ L26/296; [1964] OJ L27/3685; [1964] OJ L93/1430.
[110] Case C-257/99 *Barkoci and Malik* [2001] ECR I-6557; Case C-268/99 *Jany* [2001] ECR I-8615; Case C-162/00 *Land Nordrhein-Westfalen* v *Pokrzeptowicz-Meyer* [2002] ECR I-1049.
[111] Bartels (n 108) 147–153.
[112] Arts 183–184 EC.
[113] S Peers, 'EC Frameworks of International Relations: Co-operation, Partnership and Association' in Dashwood and Hillion (n 1); K Lenaerts and E De Smijter, 'The European Community's Treaty Making Competence' (1996) 16 YBEL 1.
[114] <http://ec.europa.eu/development/index_en.cfm>.
[115] Bartels (n 108) 171.

with its ex-colonies has changed the overall objective of the EU's trade and development policy to one of equity among developing countries. This new objective is still not well reflected in the EU's existing legal instruments, which discriminate between developing countries by means of insupportably strict rules of origin, arbitrarily different levels of GSP preferences, and a fragmentary system of regional trade agreements . . . Nonetheless, a combination of internal political will and external legal scrutiny should finally see a proper transformation of an EU trade and development policy based on history to one based on principle.

(f) EU relations with international organizations, third countries, and union delegations

(i) Pre-Lisbon

The Rome Treaty, from its very inception, contained provisions stipulating that the Commission had responsibility for maintaining relations with the UN and international organizations,[116] that the Community should establish all appropriate forms of cooperation with the Council of Europe,[117] and that the Community should establish close cooperation with the Organization for European Economic Cooperation (OEEC).[118] Subject to minor amendment, the substance of these provisions was not altered prior to the Lisbon Treaty.[119]

(ii) Post-Lisbon

Continuity with the past has been preserved through Article 220 TFEU, which deals with EU relations with these bodies.

1. The Union shall establish all appropriate forms of cooperation with the organs of the United Nations and its specialised agencies, the Council of Europe, the Organisation for Security and Cooperation in Europe and the Organisation for Economic Cooperation and Development.

   The Union shall also maintain such relations as are appropriate with other international organisations.

2. The High Representative of the Union for Foreign Affairs and Security Policy and the Commission shall be instructed to implement this Article.

Article 220 TFEU has simplified matters, by expressing the EU's relationship with the UN, Council of Europe, and OECD in the same terms. It is now the High Representative and the Commission that are charged with implementing Article 220 TFEU.

---

[116] Art 229 EEC.   [117] Art 230 EEC.
[118] Art 231 EEC.   [119] Arts 302–304 EC.

Article 221 is new within the Treaty and states that EU delegations in third countries and at international organizations shall represent the Union. The delegations are under the authority of the High Representative and are instructed to act in close cooperation with Member States' diplomatic and consular missions. The delegations will form part of the new European External Action Service (EEAS).[120]

3. Lisbon Treaty: Common Foreign and Security Policy

(a) Pre-Lisbon

(i) *Architecture and objectives*

An outline of the pre-existing Treaty provisions is necessary in order to understand the significance of the changes made by the Lisbon Treaty. The Maastricht Treaty created the Three Pillar structure that characterized the EU prior to the Lisbon Treaty. The Second Pillar was contained in Title V EU and concerned the Common Foreign and Security Policy (CFSP). It was included in the EU's objectives, which were listed in Article 2 EU. The EU was instructed to assert its identity on the international scene, in particular through the implementation of a common foreign and security policy including the progressive framing of a common defence policy. The objectives of the CFSP were delineated in greater detail in Article 11 EU. They were framed in broad terms, and much activity has been undertaken in this area.[121]

— to safeguard the common values, fundamental interests, independence and integrity of the Union in conformity with the principles of the United Nations Charter,
— to strengthen the security of the Union in all ways,
— to preserve peace and strengthen international security, in accordance with the principles of the United Nations Charter, as well as the principles of the Helsinki Final Act and the objectives of the Paris Charter, including those on external borders,
— to promote international cooperation,
— to develop and consolidate democracy and the rule of law, and respect for human rights and fundamental freedoms.

It was moreover clear from Article 17 EU that the CFSP included all questions relating to the security of the Union, including the progressive framing of a common defence policy, which might lead to a common defence.

---

[120] <http://eeas.europa.eu/background/index_en.htm>.
[121] R Dover, 'The EU's Foreign, Security, and Defence Policies' in M Cini (ed), *European Union Politics* (Oxford University Press, 2007).

(ii) Instruments

The CFSP had a distinct range of instruments through which to attain these objectives.[122] These included: principles and general guidelines; common strategies in areas where the Member States had important interests in common; decisions necessary for defining and implementing the CFSP; joint actions which were used where operational action by the EU was required;[123] and common positions that defined the EU's approach to a particular matter of a geographical or thematic nature.[124] The objectives of the CFSP could also be furthered through information and consultation and international agreements.[125]

(iii) Institutions

The distinctiveness of the CFSP instruments was mirrored in the distinct decision-making structure, which was dominated by the European Council and the Council. Thus it was the European Council that defined the principles and general guidelines for the CFSP, and its common strategies.[126] The Council was charged with ensuring the overall unity, consistency, and effectiveness of EU action in this area.[127] It was the Council that made the decisions to implement the general principles laid down by the European Council.[128] It was the Council once again that recommended the common strategies to the European Council and implemented them through joint actions and common positions.[129]

The Presidency represented the EU in CFSP matters, had responsibility for implementing decisions, and spoke for the EU in international organizations and at international conferences.[130] The Presidency was assisted in this respect by the Secretary-General of the Council, who exercised the role of High Representative for the CFSP.[131] The High Representative took part in policy formulation and implementation.[132] The Treaty provided authorization to conclude an international agreement where this was necessary to achieve CFSP objectives. Such agreements were concluded by the Council on a recommendation of the Presidency.[133]

While decision making was concentrated in the European Council and the Council, the other institutions also played a role. Thus the Council could request the Commission to submit proposals relating to implementation of a joint action;[134] the Commission was to be 'fully associated' when the Presidency represented and spoke for the EU in international organizations;[135] the Commission could submit a question or a proposal to the Council relating to

---

[122] Art 12 EU.
[123] Art 14 EU; A Dashwood, 'The Law and Practice of CFSP Joint Actions' in Cremona and de Witte (n 1) ch 3.
[124] Art 15 EU.   [125] Art 24 EU.   [126] Art 13(1)–(2) EU.
[127] Art 13(4) EU.   [128] Art 13(3) EU.
[129] Art 13(4) EU.   [130] Art 18 EU.
[131] Art 18(3) EU.   [132] Art 26 EU.
[133] Art 24 EU. Art 38 EU provided that agreements referred to in Art 24 could cover matters falling under the Third Pillar.
[134] Art 14(4) EU.   [135] Art 18(4) EU.

the CFSP;[136] and there was a general provision stipulating that the Commission was to be fully associated with the work carried out in the CFSP field.[137] The Presidency had a duty to consult the European Parliament on the main aspects and basic choices of the CFSP, and to take its views into account. The European Parliament could, moreover, ask questions or put proposals to the Council concerning the CFSP.[138]

The Treaty rules also imposed duties on Member States. Article 11(2) EU imposed a general obligation on Member States to support the CFSP 'actively and unreservedly in a spirit of loyalty and mutual solidarity'. They were enjoined to work together to enhance and develop their mutual political solidarity, and to refrain from action contrary to the EU's interests, or likely to impair its effectiveness as a cohesive force in international relations. The Treaty in addition imposed more specific obligations on Member States. Thus they were committed to the positions that they adopted when joint action was taken.[139] There was a similar duty incumbent on Member States to ensure that their national policies conformed to common positions,[140] and to uphold such positions within international organizations.[141]

(iv) Voting

The voting rules that pertained in this area were complex. They reflected the sensitivity of the subject matter, balanced by the need to take action even though there was not complete agreement between the Member States. Thus the default position was that unanimity in the Council was required, subject to the qualification that abstention did not preclude adoption of decisions, although this qualification was itself subject to qualification.[142] The Council could, however, act by qualified majority in many areas including decisions adopting or implementing a joint action or common position. This too was subject to qualification, whereby a Member State could in effect prevent a vote being taken by qualified majority, in which case the matter was referred to the European Council for decision by unanimity.[143] However, there was provision for Member States to proceed via enhanced cooperation.[144]

(v) Courts

The ECJ's role in relation to the CFSP was very limited. It did not have jurisdiction over CFSP matters, save for the important power flowing from Article 47 EU, which stated that nothing in the EU Treaty should affect the EC Treaty.[145] Article 47 EU was therefore intentionally asymmetrical, in the

---

[136] Art 22(1) EU.   [137] Art 27 EU.   [138] Art 21 EU.
[139] Art 14(3) EU.   [140] Art 15 EU.   [141] Art 19 EU.
[142] Art 23(1) EU.   [143] Art 23(2) EU.   [144] Arts 27(a)–(e) EU.
[145] Art 46(f) EU.

sense that it was framed in terms of encroachment of the EU Treaty on the terrain of the EC Treaty and not vice-versa.

The overlap between the Second Pillar and EC policy proved problematic,[146] more especially because the determination of whether action fell within the former or the latter could have important consequences for the powers of the institutions, and for doctrines such as direct effect. The difficult boundary line was policed by the ECJ.[147]

It also held that the principle of loyal cooperation, in Article 10 EC, applied to the Member States when they acted within the scope of Union powers.[148] This decision was given in relation to the Third Pillar, but scholars argued that it could also apply to the CFSP, thereby arguably reinforcing the obligation of cooperation with regard to this area.[149] The nature of the CFSP legal order was clearly evolving prior to the Lisbon Treaty,[150] and some commentators contended that it was less intergovernmental than was commonly thought.[151]

(b) Post-Lisbon

The Lisbon Treaty modified certain of the provisions concerning the CFSP and also introduced new Treaty articles on the Common Security and Defence Policy (CSDP).

(i) Architecture, principles, and objectives

There is little doubt that the CFSP will continue to evolve in the post-Lisbon world. The Lisbon Treaty architecture in relation to external action broadly conceived was considered above.[152] The Three Pillar structure from the previous Treaty has now gone, although distinct rules continue to apply to the CFSP. The framers' of the Lisbon Treaty chose to keep some distance between the CFSP provisions and the remainder of those on external action, hence the decision to place the former within the TEU, while preserving some architectural link with

---

[146] R Baratta, 'Overlaps Between European Community Competence and European Union Foreign Policy Activity' in E Cannizzaro (ed), *The European Union as an Actor in International Relations* (Kluwer, 2002); Dashwood (n 123).

[147] Case C-124/95 *R v HM Treasury and Bank of England, ex p Centro-Com* [1997] ECR I-81; Case C-170/96 *Commission v Council (Airport Transit Visas)* [1998] ECR I-2763; Case C-70/94 *Fritz Werner Industrie-Ausrustungen GmbH v Federal Republic of Germany* [1995] ECR I-3189; Case C-83/94 *Criminal proceedings against Peter Leifer and Others* [1995] ECR I-3231; Cases C-402 and 415/05 P *Kadi* (n 76).

[148] Case C-105/03 *Pupino* [2005] ECR I-5285.

[149] C Hillion and R Wessel, 'Restraining External Competences of EU Member States under CFSP' in Cremona and de Witte (n 1) ch 4.

[150] R Gosalbo Bono, 'Some Reflections on the CFSP Legal Order' (2006) 43 CMLRev 337.

[151] Hillion and Wessel (n 149).   [152] pp 380–381.

the main body of external action because the general principles that govern such action are included within, and directly precede, the detailed CFSP rules.

Thus these objectives and principles, which are found in Article 21 TEU, must be taken into account within the CFSP, and this is reaffirmed by Article 23 TEU. The objectives of the CFSP are now specified in Article 24 TEU.

1. The Union's competence in matters of common foreign and security policy shall cover all areas of foreign policy and all questions relating to the Union's security, including the progressive framing of a common defence policy that might lead to a common defence.

    The common foreign and security policy is subject to specific rules and procedures. It shall be defined and implemented by the European Council and the Council acting unanimously, except where the Treaties provide otherwise. The adoption of legislative acts shall be excluded. The common foreign and security policy shall be put into effect by the High Representative of the Union for Foreign Affairs and Security Policy and by Member States, in accordance with the Treaties. The specific role of the European Parliament and of the Commission in this area is defined by the Treaties. The Court of Justice of the European Union shall not have jurisdiction with respect to these provisions, with the exception of its jurisdiction to monitor compliance with Article 40 of this Treaty and to review the legality of certain decisions as provided for by the second paragraph of Article 275 of the Treaty on the Functioning of the European Union.

2. Within the framework of the principles and objectives of its external action, the Union shall conduct, define and implement a common foreign and security policy, based on the development of mutual political solidarity among Member States, the identification of questions of general interest and the achievement of an ever-increasing degree of convergence of Member States' actions.

3. The Member States shall support the Union's external and security policy actively and unreservedly in a spirit of loyalty and mutual solidarity and shall comply with the Union's action in this area.

    The Member States shall work together to enhance and develop their mutual political solidarity. They shall refrain from any action which is contrary to the interests of the Union or likely to impair its effectiveness as a cohesive force in international relations.

    The Council and the High Representative shall ensure compliance with these principles.

The specific CFSP objectives that had been previously listed in Article 11(1) EU are now found in Article 21 TEU. Mention should also be made of Article 39 TEU, which mandates that the Council must make a decision laying down the rules relating to protection of individuals in relation to processing of personal data by Member States when carrying out CFSP and CSDP and the rules concerning the free movement of such data.

The first paragraph of Article 24(1) TEU reiterates the provision concerning the CFSP hitherto found in Article 2 EU. The remainder of Article 24(1) highlights the distinctive nature of the CFSP, emphasizing the centrality of the European Council and Council, the role played by the High Representative for Foreign Affairs and Security Policy, and the fact that the ECJ has no jurisdiction except to ensure compliance with Article 40 TEU and Article 275 TFEU, which will be discussed below.

Article 24(3) TEU repeats the obligation on Member States that had previously been found in Article 11(2) EU.[153] They are also subject to the duty contained in Article 32 TEU, which is a revised and expanded version of Article 16 EU. Article 32 TEU provides that Member States shall consult each other in the European Council and the Council on any matter of foreign and security policy of general interest in order to determine a common approach. Each Member State must, before undertaking any action on the international scene or entering into any commitment which could affect the Union's interests, consult the others within the European Council or the Council. Member States shall show mutual solidarity and ensure, through the convergence of their actions, that the EU is able to assert its interests and values on the international scene. When the European Council or the Council has defined a common approach of the Union within the meaning of the first paragraph, the High Representative shall coordinate their activities within the Council.

The Member States are subject to further obligations contained in Article 34 TFEU, which is the successor to Article 19 EU. Article 34 requires the Member States to coordinate their action in international organizations and at international conferences. They shall uphold the EU's position in such forums, this being coordinated by the High Representative. There are also obligations on Member States that are members of the UN Security Council to keep other Member States and the High Representative fully informed, and to defend the EU's positions and interests, without prejudice to their responsibilities under the UN Charter.[154]

---

[153] M Cremona, 'Defending the Community Interest: The Duties of Cooperation and Compliance' in Cremona and de Witte (n 1) ch 4. For a broad interpretation of the duty of cooperation in relation to the making of an international agreement pursuant to the EC Treaty, Case C-433/03 *Commission v Germany* [2005] ECR I-6985, [64]; Case C-266/03 *Commission v Luxembourg* [2005] ECR I-4805, [58].

[154] When the EU has defined a position on a subject which is on the UN Security Council agenda, those Member States which sit on the Security Council shall request that the High Representative be invited to present the Union's position, Art 34(2) TEU.

(ii) Instruments

The Lisbon Treaty made changes concerning the instruments used within the CFSP. Article 25 TEU is the governing provision.

The Union shall conduct the common foreign and security policy by:

(a) defining the general guidelines;
(b) adopting decisions defining:

    (i) actions to be undertaken by the Union;
    (ii) positions to be taken by the Union;
    (iii) arrangements for the implementation of the decisions referred to in points (i) and (ii);

and by

(c) strengthening systematic cooperation between Member States in the conduct of policy.

There is, notwithstanding the change in nomenclature, much continuity with the past. Article 25(a), read with Article 26(1) TEU, makes clear that the European Council, as before, defines the general guidelines for the CFSP, which can be embodied in a decision. Article 25(b)(i), decisions defining action to be undertaken by the EU, is analogous to the old-style joint action, to be used where operational action by the EU is required.[155] Article 25(b)(ii), decisions defining positions to be taken by the EU, fulfils the function previously performed by the common position.[156] There is, however, nothing directly analogous to the common strategy, which was one of the instruments in the pre-Lisbon world, although the revised Article 32 TEU fulfils a similar function. Whether the change in the nomenclature of CFSP instruments enhances clarity is contestable.[157]

(iii) Institutions

The Lisbon Treaty preserves continuity with the past by concentrating decision-making power in the European Council and the Council, with increased prominence given to the High Representative. This is reinforced by the Lisbon Treaty in Article 22 TEU, considered above,[158] which states that the European Council shall, in the light of the principles in Article 21 TEU, identify through decisions the EU's strategic interests and objectives in relation to the CFSP and other areas of external action.

The Lisbon Treaty continues, unsurprisingly, to concentrate power in the European Council and the Council. Thus it is the European Council that defines the general guidelines for the CFSP.[159] The Council frames the CFSP and takes

---

[155] Art 28 TEU.   [156] Art 29 TEU.
[157] Cremona 'The Draft Constitutional Treaty' (n 1).
[158] pp 383–384.   [159] Art 26(1) TEU.

the decisions for defining and implementing it on the basis of the European Council's guidelines.[160] It continues, together with the High Representative, to have responsibility for ensuring the unity, consistency, and effectiveness of EU action.[161] It is the Council, as before, that adopts decisions concerning operational action,[162] which commit the Member States to take the agreed action.[163] Continuity with the past is also evident in the ascription of power to the Council to adopt decisions that define the EU's approach to a particular matter of a geographical or thematic nature, with the corollary that Member States must ensure that their national policies conform to the Union positions.[164] The Council is, as previously, assisted by a Political and Security Committee, which contributes to policy formation and has special responsibilities for crisis management.[165]

The High Representative, assisted by the European External Action Service,[166] is accorded greater prominence. The incumbent has responsibility for putting into effect the CFSP;[167] chairs the Foreign Affairs Council; contributes to the formulation of the CFSP; ensures its implementation;[168] represents the EU for matters relating to the CFSP; liaises with and informs the European Parliament;[169] conducts political dialogue with third parties; and represents the EU's position at international organizations and international conferences.[170] It should be noted, however, that Article 15(6) TEU states that the President of the European Council shall ensure the external representation of the Union on issues concerning its common foreign and security policy, without prejudice to the powers of the High Representative. The tension that this might produce will be considered below.

There have been changes in the role played by other institutions within the CFSP, most notably in relation to the Commission. The previous general provision whereby the Commission was to be fully associated with CFSP work[171] has been repealed. Gone too is the provision whereby the Council could request the Commission to submit proposals relating to implementation of a joint action.[172] Article 28 TEU, which is the equivalent provision of the Lisbon Treaty, contains no such provision. There is, moreover, no obvious replacement for the previous provision whereby the Commission was to be 'fully associated' when the Presidency represented and spoke for the EU in international organizations.[173] This function is now performed by the High Representative,[174] but there is no Treaty article mandating that the Commission should be associated with such work. The power to make international agreements relating to the CFSP, which had previously stated that this was to be done with the assistance of the Commission,[175] no longer contains this stipulation.[176]

---

[160] Art 26(2) TEU.   [161] Art 26(2) TEU.   [162] Art 28(1) TEU.
[163] Art 28(2) TEU.   [164] Art 29 TEU.   [165] Art 38 TEU.
[166] Art 27(3) TEU.   [167] Art 26(3) TEU.   [168] Art 27(1) TEU.
[169] Art 36 TEU.   [170] Art 27(2) TEU.   [171] Art 27 EU.
[172] Art 14(4) EU.   [173] Art 18(4) EU.   [174] Art 27(2) TEU.
[175] Art 24(2) EU.   [176] Art 37 TEU.

It remains to be seen how far these changes signal re-balancing of power within this area. The 'benign' explanation is that the Commission's role has been reduced because its previous function is now being performed by the High Representative, who is a Vice-President of the Commission. This does not, however, withstand examination, since the High Representative does not 'represent' the Commission in relation to CFSP matters. This is readily apparent from Article 18 TEU, in which the High Representative's powers are articulated. It is clear from Article 18(2) TEU that the High Representative's functions in relation to the CFSP fall within the remit of the Council, and this reading is reinforced by other Treaty provisions.[177] This does not mean that there will necessarily be continuing tension between the two roles of the High Representative, an issue that has been considered earlier[178] and will be discussed again below.[179] It does mean that the reduced role of the Commission cannot simply be rationalized on the hypothesis that its view is now being represented by the High Representative. The diminished role of the Commission is exemplified by the fact that hitherto it could submit a question or a proposal to the Council relating to the CFSP.[180] The position now is that this can be done by the High Representative, or by the High Representative 'with the Commission's support'.[181] The wording should not mask the new reality, which is that while the High Representative can proffer such suggestions in her own right, the Commission cannot and has to do so through the High Representative.

The position of the European Parliament, by way of contrast, remains largely the same.[182] It is now the High Representative that is charged with consulting the European Parliament on the main aspects and basic choices of the CFSP and CSDP, including the evolution of these policies. The High Representative must take the European Parliament's views into account. The European Parliament can, as before, ask questions of the Council, and it can also make recommendations to the Council and High Representative.

(iv) Voting

The Working Party on External Action argued that in order to avoid CFSP inertia maximum use should be made of provisions for the use of qualified majority voting (QMV), and of provisions allowing for some form of flexibility, such as constructive abstention. It also advocated inclusion of a Treaty provision whereby the European Council could unanimously agree to extend the use of QMV in the field of CFSP.[183] The Lisbon Treaty has made provision for the latter, but subject to this the pre-existing rules remain largely the same.

---

[177] Arts 15(2), 16(6), 18(4) TEU.   [178] pp 110–112.   [179] pp 426–429.
[180] Art 22(1) EU.   [181] Art 30(1) TEU.   [182] Art 36 TEU.
[183] Final Report of Working Group VII (n 2) 7.

Article 31(1) TEU states that the default rule is that decisions by the European Council and Council are taken unanimously, and that the adoption of legislative acts is excluded. It is open to a Member State that abstains to make a declaration, the effect of which is that, while it is not obliged to apply the decision, it accepts that the decision commits the EU. If the Council members qualifying their abstention in this way represent at least one third of the Member States comprising at least one third of the EU population, the decision cannot be adopted. Article 31(2) TEU allows the Council to act by qualified majority in the following circumstances.

— when adopting a decision defining a Union action or position on the basis of a decision of the European Council relating to the Union's strategic interests and objectives, as referred to in Article 22(1),
— when adopting a decision defining a Union action or position, on a proposal which the High Representative of the Union for Foreign Affairs and Security Policy has presented following a specific request from the European Council, made on its own initiative or that of the High Representative,
— when adopting any decision implementing a decision defining a Union action or position,
— when appointing a special representative in accordance with Article 33.

The ability to proceed by qualified majority voting is subject to the caveat that it is open to a Member State to declare, for reasons of national policy, its opposition to the taking of a decision in this way, in which case a vote is not taken. The High Representative is charged with brokering a solution, but if this is not forthcoming the Council, acting by qualified majority, can request that the matter is decided by the European Council by unanimity.

Article 31(3) TEU contains a passerelle clause, whereby the European Council can unanimously adopt a decision stipulating that the Council shall act by a qualified majority in cases other than those referred to in Article 31(2).

The sensitivity of the issues dealt with under the CFSP, and the proximity of foreign policy to core concerns of national sovereignty, are readily apparent in these voting rules. The qualifications to Article 31(1) and (2) operate, albeit in different ways, as forms of emergency brake available to Member States. The sensitivity is manifest once again in Article 31(4) TEU, which states that Articles 31(2)–(3) do not apply to decisions having military or defence implications. The reality, having said this, is that votes are taken relatively rarely in the Council, with the emphasis being on reaching decisions by consensus.[184] The voting rules nonetheless constitute the formal backdrop against which consensus is negotiated.

---

[184] F Hayes-Renshaw, W van Aken, H Wallace, 'When and Why the EU Council of Ministers Votes Explicitly' (2006)44 JCMS 161.

(v) Courts

We have already seen that Article 24(1) TEU excludes the ECJ from the CFSP, and this is reaffirmed by Article 275 TFEU. Thus the ECJ has jurisdiction neither in relation to the Treaty provisions on the CFSP, nor in relation to acts adopted on the basis of those provisions,[185] subject to the qualifications mentioned below. Before considering these qualifications, it is important to be clear about the scope of the rule denying jurisdiction to the EU courts. Article 275 TFEU bars the EU courts from adjudicating on the CFSP provisions or acts adopted on the basis of those provisions. It does not thereby bar the EU courts from all issues concerning the CFSP since, in addition to the qualifications considered below, there are matters related to the CFSP in the main body of the Treaty. Thus, to take but one example, Article 218 TFEU specifies the procedure for the making of international agreements, including those made under the CFSP. If a legal issue arises concerning the meaning of Article 218 in relation to a CFSP agreement the ECJ would have jurisdiction to address it.

We can now turn to the three situations where the ECJ has jurisdiction. It can review the legality of restrictive measures against natural or legal persons adopted under the CFSP provisions.[186] It can review whether a proposed agreement is compatible with the Treaties; if the Court's decision is adverse the agreement cannot enter into force unless it is amended or the Treaty is revised.[187] It can also monitor compliance with Article 40 TEU, which provides as follows:

The implementation of the common foreign and security policy shall not affect the application of the procedures and the extent of the powers of the institutions laid down by the Treaties for the exercise of the Union competences referred to in Articles 3 to 6 of the Treaty on the Functioning of the European Union.

Similarly, the implementation of the policies listed in those Articles shall not affect the application of the procedures and the extent of the powers of the institutions laid down by the Treaties for the exercise of the Union competences under this Chapter.

Article 40 TEU is the successor provision to Article 47 EU, but there is an important difference between them. Article 47 EU was, as we have seen, asymmetrical. It was framed so as to prevent exercise of power under the EU Treaty from encroaching on the EC Treaty.[188] Article 40 TEU is, by way of contrast, symmetrical. It is expressly written so as to prevent encroachment by the CFSP on the general exercise of EU power, and vice-versa. It remains to be seen how far this changes pre-established judicial behaviour. The presumption that 'normal' EU law should predominate is deeply ingrained in the judicial psyche and will not easily be shifted, notwithstanding the change of wording in Article 40 TEU. The ECJ will nonetheless have to address such matters and apply a test

---

[185] Art 275 TFEU.   [186] Art 275 TFEU.   [187] Art 218(11) TFEU.
[188] Case C-91/05 *Commission v Council (Small arms)* [2008] ECR I-3651.

to determine whether the CFSP or ordinary EU law prevails in cases where the matter is contested.

It will doubtless draw on its previous jurisprudence to determine the appropriate legal base. The ECJ held that where the EU's power derives from overlapping Treaty provisions, recourse must be had to a double legal basis, together with the relevant procedural provisions. The choice of legal basis depends on objective factors that are susceptible to judicial review. The principal factor is the objective and content of the act.[189] Where a measure has a dual purpose, however, but one can be identified as predominant, the other being incidental, the measure must be based on a single legal basis.[190] The Court will not, moreover, insist on a double legal base where this would lead to the combination of incompatible procedures.

The application of these precepts in the post-Lisbon legal order will nonetheless be difficult, as can be exemplified by the *Small Arms* case,[191] decided prior to the Lisbon Treaty. The dispute turned on whether a measure to control the proliferation of small arms should have been made under the CFSP, or under development cooperation policy within the Community Pillar. The ECJ held that a measure having legal effects adopted under the CFSP affected the provisions of the EC Treaty within the meaning of Article 47 EU whenever it could have been made under the EC Treaty, it being unnecessary to examine whether the measure prevented or limited the exercise by the Community of its competences. If the CFSP measure, judged by its aim and content, had as its main purpose the implementation of a policy conferred by the EC Treaty on the Community, which could properly have been adopted on the basis of the EC Treaty, then the CFSP measure would thereby infringe Article 47 EU.[192]

The ECJ reiterated orthodoxy to the effect that where a measure pursued a number of objectives, without one being incidental to the other, and that various legal bases of the EC Treaty were therefore applicable, the measure would have to be founded, exceptionally, on those corresponding legal bases.[193] The Court held, however, that Article 47 EU precluded this solution where a measure that had a number of objectives fell within EC development cooperation policy and within the CFSP, and where neither was incidental to the other. It decided that the contested measure fell both within development cooperation and the CFSP, that neither was incidental to the other, and concluded that the effect of Article

---

[189] Case C-300/89 *Commission v Council* [1991] ECR I-2867; Opinion 1/78 (n 38); Case C-166/07 *Parliament v Council,* 3 September 2009.

[190] Case C-36/98 *Spain v Council* [2001] ECR I-779, [59]; Case C-211/01 *Commission v Council (Bulgaria and Hungary Agreements)* [2003] ECR I-8913, [39]; Case C-338/01 *Commission v Council (Recovery of Claims)* [2004] ECR I-4829, [55].

[191] Case C-91/05 (n 188).

[192] Case 176/03 *Commission v Council (Environmental Crimes)* [2005] ECR I-7879, [40]; Case C-440/05 *Commission v Council (Ship Source Pollution)* [2007] ECR I-9097, [54].

[193] Case C-211/01 *Commission v Council* (n 190) [40]; Case C-338/01 *Commission v Council* (n 190) [56]; Case C-94/03 *Commission v Council (Rotterdam Convention)* [2006] ECR I-1, [36].

47 EU was that the contested measure could not have been adopted under the CFSP.

The difficulty of applying Article 40 TEU in the post-Lisbon world can be appreciated by reflection on the reasoning in this case. Prior to the Lisbon Treaty, the ECJ was able to use Article 47 EU as the 'tie-break'. Thus where a measure had dual objectives that came within the CFSP and the EC Treaty, and neither was incidental to the other, the ECJ used Article 47 EU to accord priority to the EC Treaty. This reasoning, which was contestable in its own terms, will not be available post the Lisbon Treaty, since Article 40 TEU does not give priority to ordinary EU law in the manner hitherto. The ECJ will therefore either have to identify the predominant purpose of the measure, and apply a single legal base, CFSP or ordinary EU law, accordingly. The alternative is that where a measure has dual objectives, neither of which is incidental to the other, it will have to be grounded on the relevant legal bases in the CFSP and in ordinary EU law.

(vi) International agreements

Prior to the Lisbon Treaty the EU made international agreements under Article 24 EU. The Lisbon Treaty contains a terser provision covering the same terrain. Article 37 TEU simply states that the EU may conclude 'agreements with one or more States or international organizations in areas covered by this Chapter'. There are three points to note about this new provision.

First, it contains a general power to conclude agreements that relate to the CFSP and the CSDP. This power would also cover an international agreement where the objective included advancement of one of the principles governing external action laid down in Article 21 TEU. Although those principles are in a different Chapter, they are binding on CFSP and CSDP action and are in any event reaffirmed from within the CFSP/CSDP Chapter by Article 23 TEU.

Second, Article 37 TEU contains no indication as to how such agreements are to be made. This is to be found in Article 218 TFEU, which lays down the general rules for the making of international agreements, including specific provisions for CFSP agreements. This follows the recommendations of the Working Group on Legal Personality, which advocated placing the rules for the making of international agreements in a single Treaty provision.[194] Article 37 TEU has removed limitations previously contained in Article 24 EU, notably the provision whereby a Member State would not be bound by an agreement where it signalled in the Council that the agreement had to comply with its own constitutional procedure. The ECJ can, however, review CFSP agreements for compatibility with the Treaties before they are made if asked to do so by a Member State, the European Parliament, Commission, or Council.[195]

---

[194] Final Report of Working Group III (n 29) [22].
[195] Art 218(11) TFEU.

Third, there is a 'nice question' as to whether Article 3(2) TFEU, which specifies when the EU has exclusive external competence, applies to CFSP/CSDP agreements.[196] It might be argued that the jurisdictional bar would prevent the ECJ adjudicating on this issue, since it applies to CFSP provisions or acts adopted pursuant thereto, including international agreements. It could be countered, however, that the salient legal issue is interpretation of the scope of Article 3(2) TFEU, over which the ECJ clearly does have jurisdiction, and the determination as to whether in principle this is applicable to international agreements made under the CFSP. We have already seen from the preceding discussion that the ordinary Treaty provisions on the making of international agreements cover the CFSP,[197] so the application of related Treaty articles to CFSP international agreements is not an absurd inquiry.

Having said that it is doubtful whether the broad ambit of exclusivity given to international agreements by Article 3(2) TFEU fits with CFSP agreements. Thus exclusivity flowing from a legislative act specifying the conclusion of such an agreement could not apply to the CFSP, since legislative acts cannot be made in this area. The alternative idea that exclusivity exists when an international agreement could affect common rules or alter their scope does not fit readily with the CFSP regime. We should furthermore be mindful of the political dimension. Member States would not view with equanimity exclusive EU competence in relation to international agreements covering a broad swathe of CFSP matters, even less so in relation to CSDP. This conclusion is reinforced by the Declarations appended to the Lisbon Treaty concerning the CFSP, which are analysed below.[198] The Member States will nonetheless be subject to the duty in Article 24(3) TEU 'actively and unreservedly' to support the CFSP and must not 'impair its effectiveness as a cohesive force in international relations'.

(vii) CSDP

The Lisbon Treaty provisions on the CSDP follow closely those in the Constitutional Treaty,[199] and the latter were shaped by proposals from Working Group VIII on Defence.[200]

Prior to the Lisbon Treaty Article 17 EU provided the legal foundation for security and defence policy. Article 17(1) EU stated that this included 'all questions relating to the security of the Union, including the progressive framing of a common defence policy, which might lead to a common defence, should the European Council so decide'. Article 17(2) EU specified that security questions included the Petersburg tasks, in particular humanitarian and rescue tasks,

---

[196] Cremona 'The Draft Constitutional Treaty' (n 1) 1351–1352.
[197] Art 218 TFEU.   [198] pp 421–422.   [199] Arts III-309–312.
[200] CONV 461/02, Final Report of Working Group VIII on Defence, Brussels, 16 December 2002.

peacekeeping tasks, and those of combat forces in crisis management, including peacemaking.

There were, moreover, important political developments related to security and defence policy prior to the Lisbon Treaty. The Cologne European Council in June 1999 gave the political impetus for strengthening European security and defence policy. It decided to provide the EU with capacity for autonomous action, including credible military forces, in order to respond to international crises, albeit without prejudice to actions by NATO. These initiatives were carried forward at the Helsinki European Council in December 1999, with more concrete proposals concerning deployment of military forces capable of fulfilling the Petersburg tasks. The events of 9/11 and subsequent developments moreover convinced many that the nature of the threats faced by the EU had changed and that this should be reflected in a re-orientation of EU defence policy, with greater emphasis on protection of civilian population and democratic institutions, which could not adequately be addressed through purely national action.

The Working Group therefore recommended that the Petersburg tasks should be expanded to include reference to additional tasks involving military resources, such as conflict prevention, joint disarmament operations, military advice and assistance, post-conflict stabilization, and support for a third country's authorities, at their request, in combating terrorism. It made a number of recommendations designed to enhance the coherence and efficiency in carrying out crisis management operations, including an enhanced role for the High Representative and for the Political and Security Committee. Working Group VIII advocated further changes that would advance decision making, including greater use of enhanced cooperation, and the creation of a European Armaments and Strategic Research Agency that would, *inter alia*, facilitate harmonized defence procurement.

These recommendations shaped the resultant Treaty provisions. Article 42 TEU is now the lead provision. Article 42(1)–(2) TEU provides as follows:

1. The common security and defence policy shall be an integral part of the common foreign and security policy. It shall provide the Union with an operational capacity drawing on civilian and military assets. The Union may use them on missions outside the Union for peace-keeping, conflict prevention and strengthening international security in accordance with the principles of the United Nations Charter. The performance of these tasks shall be undertaken using capabilities provided by the Member States.

2. The common security and defence policy shall include the progressive framing of a common Union defence policy. This will lead to a common defence, when the European Council, acting unanimously, so decides. It shall in that case recommend to the Member States the adoption of such a decision in accordance with their respective constitutional requirements.

Article 42(2) is subject to the caveat that EU security and defence policy must not prejudice the specific character of security and defence policy of certain Member States. It must, moreover, respect Member States' obligations under NATO.

Article 43(3) TEU provides that Member States shall make civilian and military capabilities available to the EU for implementation of the CSDP, to contribute to objectives defined by the Council. If Member States establish multinational forces they can make them available to the CSDP. Member States undertake progressively to improve their military capabilities, and draw on the expertise of the European Defence Agency (EDA). The EDA has the remit proposed by the Working Group, which is spelt out in Article 45 TEU.

Article 48(4) TEU stipulates, unsurprisingly, that CSDP decisions, including those initiating a mission, are adopted by the Council acting unanimously on a proposal from the High Representative, or an initiative from a Member State. It is open to the Council to entrust execution of a task, within the EU framework, to a group of Member States to protect the EU's values and serve its interests.[201]

Article 42(6) TEU lays the foundations for structured cooperation between Member States 'whose military capabilities fulfil higher criteria and which have made more binding commitments to one another in this area with a view to the most demanding missions'. The details of such cooperation are laid down in Article 46.[202]

Article 42(7) TEU reinforces the concept of collective self-defence. It states that if a Member State is the victim of armed aggression on its territory, the other Member States have an obligation to assist it by all means in their power, in accordance with Article 51 of the UN Charter. This is without prejudice to the specific character of the security and defence policy of certain Member States. Such cooperation must be consistent with commitments under NATO, which, for those who are members, remains the foundation of their collective defence.

The Working Group's advocacy of broadening the list of tasks that can be undertaken under the CSDP bore fruit in Article 43 TEU. It is for the Council to adopt decisions relating to the tasks set out below, and the High Representative, acting under the Council's authority and in close contact with the Political and Security Committee, ensures coordination of the civilian and military aspects of such tasks. The tasks are defined in Article 43(1).

The tasks referred to in Article 42(1), in the course of which the Union may use civilian and military means, shall include joint disarmament operations, humanitarian and rescue tasks, military advice and assistance tasks, conflict prevention and peace-keeping tasks, tasks of combat forces in crisis management, including peace-making and post-conflict stabilisation. All these tasks may contribute to the fight against terrorism, including by supporting third countries in combating terrorism in their territories.

---

[201] Arts 42(5), 44 TEU.
[202] Protocol (No 10) On Permanent Structured Cooperation Established by Art 42 of the Treaty on European Union.

(viii) Declarations relating to CFSP/CSDP

It is fitting to conclude this section by adverting to the two Declarations attached to the Lisbon Treaty that affect the CFSP.

Declaration 13[203] states that the Conference underlines that the provisions in the TEU on the CFSP, including creation of the office of High Representative and establishment of the EEAS, 'do not affect the responsibilities of the Member States, as they currently exist, for the formulation and conduct of their foreign policy nor of their national representation in third countries and international organizations'. It further provides that the provisions on the CSDP 'do not prejudice the specific character of the security and defence policy of the Member States'. The Declaration stresses that the EU and its Member States remain bound by the UN Charter and, in particular, 'by the primary responsibility of the Security Council and of its Members for the maintenance of international peace and security'.

Declarations appended to Treaties are commonly the result of political pressure, and their fit with the formal Treaty provisions is often imperfect. This is especially true of Declaration 13, insofar as it states that the TEU provisions on the CFSP do not affect Member State responsibilities as they currently exist for the formulation and conduct of their foreign policy, or their national representation in international organizations. The key phrase 'as they currently exist' is ambiguous to say the least. The bottom line is that Member State responsibility for formulation and conduct of foreign policy is necessarily circumscribed in numerous ways by the CFSP provisions. These Treaty articles impose binding obligations on the Member States,[204] and they empower the EU to adopt a range of measures that may also impose duties on the Member States.[205] Declaration 13 is in this sense inconsistent with the Treaty provisions.

The Declaration might be read to guard against formal pre-emption of Member State power if the CFSP were to be treated as coming within shared competence. However, even if one takes that reading, and rejects the idea that exercise of power by the EU *ipso facto* precludes the Member State from doing so, it nonetheless remains the case that exercise of power by the EU under the CFSP imposes binding obligations on the Member States. These duties must perforce affect Member State responsibilities as they currently exist for the formulation of their foreign policy, at the least by foreclosing options that would be inconsistent with the binding obligations that flow from the CFSP measure.

Declaration 14[206] overlaps with Declaration 13 and suffers from analogous problems. Declaration 14 states that in addition to the specific rules and

---

[203] Declaration 13 concerning the common foreign and security policy.
[204] Arts 24(3), 32, 34 TEU.   [205] Arts 25, 28, 29, 31.
[206] Declaration 14 concerning the common foreign and security policy.

procedures referred to in Article 24(1) TEU, the Conference underlines that the provisions covering the CFSP, including in relation to the High Representative and the EEAS, will not affect 'the existing legal basis, responsibilities, and powers of each Member State in relation to the formulation and conduct of its foreign policy, its national diplomatic service, relations with third countries and participation in international organisations, including a Member State's membership of the Security Council of the United Nations'. It further provides that the provisions on the CFSP do not give new powers to the Commission to initiate decisions, nor do they increase the role of the European Parliament. The final paragraph of the Declaration states that the provisions governing the CSDP 'do not prejudice the specific character of the security and defence policy of the Member States'. The interpretative problems concerning Declaration 13 are equally applicable to Declaration 14, insofar as the latter states that the CFSP provisions do not affect Member State responsibility for formulation and conduct of its foreign policy.

4. Consistency, Coherence, and Coordination

It is fitting to conclude this chapter by adverting to broader issues relating to EU external action. There was, prior to the Lisbon Treaty, concern about the overall consistency, coherence, and coordination of external relations policy.[207] It is important to understand the nature of such concerns and assess how far they have been alleviated by changes made by the Lisbon Treaty. The very concept of coherence, however, has a plethora of possible meanings.[208] There are therefore various facets to this discourse, which will be distinguished in the ensuing analysis.

(a) Purpose

The most basic issue to consider is whether there is coherence as to the purpose served by EU external relations policy, including in this respect external action as covered by the TFEU, and the CFSP as dealt with by the TEU. This is by its very nature an issue on which opinion can differ, and the answer depends in part on the level of abstraction or specificity at which the question is posed.

It is nonetheless useful to begin with fundamentals. Nation States have plenary power, including over external relations and foreign policy broadly conceived.

---

[207] Europe in the World—Some Practical Proposals for Greater Coherence, Effectiveness and Visibility, COM(2006) 278 final, Annual Report from the Council to the European Parliament on the Main Aspects and Basic Choices of the CFSP (2008), available at <http://consilium.europa.eu/showPage.aspx?id=248&lang=EN>; C Hillion, '*Tous pour un, un pour tous!* Coherence in the External Relations of the European Union' in Cremona, *Developments in EU External Relations Law* (n 1) ch 1; P Gauttier, Horizontal Coherence and the External Competences of the European Union (2004) 10 ELJ 23.
[208] Hillion (n 207) 12–18.

This is necessarily subject to the obligations derived from general international law, from treaties, including the Lisbon Treaty for EU Member States, and the constraints imposed by the realities of international relations, whatsoever these might be at any particular point in time. This does not alter the point made here, which is that sovereign Nation States have plenary power over foreign relations. This leads to a related but distinct point. Whether the external policy of any particular Nation State is coherent or consistent at any point in time, or when viewed in the medium term, will vary. The political reality is that this is often not the case. Contending political forces within the state, the exigencies of events beyond State control and changes of political party can lead to tensions and shifts such that it may be difficult to ascribe the label 'consistent' or 'coherent' to foreign policy in that State. This, like the preceding point, is obvious, but is worth stating nonetheless, since the EU is often judged by criteria that States regularly fail to meet.

The EU, by way of contrast, does not have plenary power in the preceding sense. It has the powers ascribed to it by the foundational Treaties as amended over time. This then begs the further inquiry as to the underlying rationales behind the external relations powers that have been accorded to the EU. The answer, not surprisingly, is that these are eclectic. There is not one single reason that explains Member State willingness to grant such powers to the EU. Four primary rationales can be identified.

First, there is the rationale cast in terms of the external dimension of the internal market. The full realization of the internal market could require agreement with third countries and international organizations. This serves to explain in large part the powers in relation to the Common Commercial Policy. It also furnishes the explanation for the Court's willingness to imply powers to make international agreements where these were not expressly provided in the Treaty provisions, since attainment of the relevant internal market policy necessitated foreign interaction.

The second rationale is related to, but distinct from the first. There was a growing realization that all EU policies, whether directly related to the internal market or not, could have an external dimension.[209] It was this that drove the Court's expansive jurisprudence concerning implied external power. The EU was inevitably connected to the wider world. The broader the areas over which the EU exercised some form of internal authority, the greater the need for it to be able to connect with third States and international organizations. Article 216 TFEU is the ultimate embodiment of this idea within the Lisbon Treaty. What began as implied external power driven by the ECJ's jurisprudence is now transformed into a general competence to make international agreements, and the criteria in Article 216 mean that it will be rare, if ever, that the EU is unable to make such an agreement where it wishes to do so.

[209] COM(2006) 278 (n 207) 4–5.

A third rationale for external action competence is the EU's position as a powerful polity, the corollary being that it has the responsibilities embodied in the provisions concerning development cooperation, economic, financial, and technical aid to third countries and humanitarian aid.[210] The policy in this area has undoubtedly evolved over time. Trade policy with developing countries was, as we have seen, initially linked with the colonial past of the founding members of the EEC. The focus of the complex regime of association agreements, combined with development cooperation and economic etc cooperation with third countries, has nonetheless altered. It has become more centred on the provision of the kind of assistance, broadly conceived, which a powerful polity should give to its less advantaged neighbours. This economic focus is, however, also linked to broader concerns about security and stability, as powerfully exemplified by the *Small Arms* case,[211] in which it was acknowledged that the contested measure served objectives of development cooperation, as well as the CFSP.

This naturally leads to the fourth rationale, which is security as reflected in the Treaty provisions on the CFSP and CSDP. The Member States wished for some established mechanism through which they could cooperate in such areas. Security is the quintessential trans-border problem, even more so in the post-9/11 world where the nature of the threat has become more diffuse and difficult to combat.[212] Setting up *ad hoc* meetings to discuss such matters is cumbersome, time consuming, and involves heavy 'transaction costs', more especially as the number of players expands.[213] The sensitive nature of the subject matter, touching closely as it does at the heart of traditional conceptions of sovereignty, meant, however, that Member States preferred the 'default position' of inter-governmentalism, thereby retaining more control in their own hands. The cost-benefit analysis of supranationalism, with its attendant delegation of power to Commission and ECJ, was therefore negative, in the sense that the benefit of supranationalism was felt by the Member States to be outweighed by the costs.

It should also be acknowledged that there are forms of EU external action that cut across the preceding rationales, the most notable example being the European Neighbourhood Policy (ENP), the aims of which are security, peace, and prosperity.[214] The ENP, as the title would suggest, is directed towards the

[210] ibid 3–4; <http://consilium.europa.eu/showPage.aspx?id=260&lang=EN>.
[211] Case C-91/05 (n 188).
[212] <http://www.consilium.europa.eu/showPage.aspx?id=406&lang=EN>.
[213] A Moravcsik, 'Preferences and Power in the European Community: A Liberal Intergovern-mentalist Approach' (1993) 31 JCMS 473; A Moravcsik, *National Preference Formation and Interstate Bargaining in the European Community, 1955–86* (Harvard University Press, 1992); M Pollack, *The Engines of European Integration: Delegation, Agency and Agenda Setting in the EU* (Oxford University Press, 2003); M Pollack, 'International Relations Theory and European Integration' EUI Working Papers, RSC 2000/55.
[214] M Cremona and C Hillion, 'L'Union fait la force? Potential and Limitations of the European Neighbourhood Policy as an Integrated EU Foreign and Security Policy', EUI Working Paper 2006/39; M Cremona, 'The European Neighbourhood Policy: More than a Partnership?' in Cremona *Developments in EU External Relations Law* (n 1) ch 7.

EU's neighbouring countries. It emerged from the 'Wider Europe' initiative associated with the 2004 enlargement and expansion of EU borders, the objective being creation of a framework for increasing stability and security in the European neighbourhood.[215] It reached across all Three Pillars in the pre-Lisbon world. Thus it covered economic development and integration, cooperation in energy, transport, environment, health sectors, visas, and border controls, which came within the Community Pillar; regional conflict prevention and cooperation to prevent the spread of weapons of mass destruction, the preserve of the Second Pillar; and cooperation in the fight against organized crime and terrorism, the domain of the Third Pillar. The ENP operates through an admixture of hard and soft law measures. Action Plans feature prominently in the overall ENP strategy, and conditionality based on human rights and democracy is a common feature.[216]

The difficulties of ensuring coordination and coherence between these differing aspects of EU external policy, fuelled by differing rationales, will not disappear in the post-Lisbon world. The more coherent reorganization of the Treaty provisions on external action within the TFEU is nonetheless a positive step. So too is the creation of principles that guide all EU external action set down in Article 21 TEU and reiterated in Article 205 TFEU. This is reinforced by the injunction in Article 21(3) TEU that the EU shall ensure consistency between the different areas of its external action and between these and its other policies.[217] The Council and the Commission, assisted by the High Representative, are charged with ensuring this consistency and are enjoined to cooperate to that effect. The Treaty imperative in this respect is further strengthened by Article 22 TEU, which requires the European Council, drawing on the principles in Article 21 TEU, to identify the EU's strategic interests and objectives concerning both the CFSP and other areas of EU external action. The existence of such Treaty provisions does not in itself ensure the requisite consistency. Much will of course depend on their practical realization. The existence of such provisions is nonetheless surely a positive development.

It should be stressed, moreover, that developments in EU law did not stop during the decade of Treaty reform. There have been initiatives designed to enhance consistency and coherence across policy areas. Thus the Commission has, for example, fostered policy coherence in relation to development cooperation.[218] The essence of this policy is to identify 11 priority areas, other than aid,

---

[215] Wider Europe—Neighbourhood: A New Framework for Relations with our Eastern and Southern Neighbours, COM(2003) 104; European Neighbourhood Policy—Strategy Paper, COM (2004) 373.

[216] Regulation 1638/2006 of the European Parliament and of the Council of 24 October 2006 laying down general provisions establishing a European Neighbourhood and Partnership Instrument [2006] OJ L310/1.

[217] See also Art 13 TEU, Art 7 TFEU.

[218] <http://ec.europa.eu/development/policies/policy_coherence_en.cfm>; Policy Coherence for Development—Accelerating progress towards attaining the Millennium Development Goals, COM(2005) 134 final; EU Report on Policy Coherence for Development, COM(2007) 545 final; Policy Coherence for Development—Establishing the policy framework for a whole-of-the-Union approach, COM(2009) 458 final; <http://trade.ec.europa.eu/doclib/press/index.cfm?id=512>.

where attaining synergies with development policy objectives is considered particularly relevant. These areas include trade, the environment, security, agriculture, fisheries, equality and working conditions, migration, research and innovation, information society, transport, and energy. The policy initiatives designed to foster policy coherence in relation to development are ambitious. They reflect the interconnectedness that underlies the ENP strategies considered above. This is readily apparent from the connection forged by the Commission between development and security in the following passage:[219]

The EU will treat security and development as complementary agendas, with the common aim of creating a secure environment and breaking the vicious circle of poverty, war, environmental degradation and failing economic, social and political structures. It will enhance its policies in support of good and effective governance and the prevention of conflict and state fragility, including by strengthening its response to difficult partnerships/failing states. It will strengthen the control of its arms exports, particularly to ensure that EU-manufactured weaponry is not used against civilian populations or to aggravate existing tensions or conflicts in developing countries. The EU will promote cooperation in fighting corruption, organised crime and terrorism.

(b) Institutions

Some commentators on the Lisbon regime have expressed concern as to whether the institutional division of authority in relation to external action and the CFSP will foster consistency, or whether it will lead to divisiveness and tension. These concerns have centred in particular on the 'double or triple' hats worn by the High Representative. The negative view of the Lisbon institutional ordering highlights the difficulties that might ensue because of the High Representative's divided loyalties. The incumbent is a Vice-President of the Commission with overall responsibility for external action,[220] Chair of the Foreign Affairs Council, and takes part in the work of the European Council. The critics point, moreover, to tensions between Article 27(2) TEU, which states that the High Representative shall represent the EU in relation to the CFSP, and Article 15(6) TEU, which provides that, without prejudice to the role of the High Representative, the President of the European Council shall ensure the external representation of the EU on CFSP issues.

A further dimension to the critique of the Lisbon institutional arrangements is that the Commission and the 'Community method' have been weakened by the Lisbon Treaty. Thus Temple Lang has argued that the High Representative in her role as Vice-President of the Commission undermines its independence, because she has been appointed by the European Council, and is intimately

---

[219] <http://europa.eu/legislation_summaries/development/general_development_framework/r12534_en.htm>.
[220] Art 18(4) TEU.

engaged with Member State interests in her other roles, as Chair of the Foreign Affairs Council and as important participant in the European Council. He also regards the Lisbon regime as undermining the Commission and the 'Community method' because the CFSP is intergovernmental and less accountable than is decision making under ordinary EU law.[221]

There is force in some of these concerns. Much will depend on how the relationship between the key institutional players evolves. Tensions between the High Representative, Commission, and European Parliament have been evident in plans for the EEAS.[222] It is nonetheless important to be mindful of factors that should be balanced against the preceding concerns and support the institutional ordering embodied in the Lisbon Treaty. Three factors can be distinguished in this respect.

First, the critique or concern that is premised on there being more than one institutional locus for EU external relations policy, the High Representative and the President of the European Council, must be kept within perspective. It is clear from the relevant provisions of the Lisbon Treaty that the High Representative has the principal front line responsibility for the daily discharge of foreign relations,[223] and this has been borne out by practice since the inception of the Lisbon Treaty. It is the High Representative who has routinely responded to foreign policy developments across the globe, and this is so notwithstanding the fact that serious crises such as those in Haiti and Chile also prompted messages from the President of the European Council.

We should also be mindful in this regard of practice within Nation States. The reality is that in many instances it is the Foreign Minister that represents the State externally, but the Prime Minister or President will do so on other occasions. The divide is rarely etched in formal legal stone. It is moreover the case that other ministers will often engage in foreign policy as it affects their subject matter area, as attested to by the contributions of, for example, national environmental ministers to discussions on international agreements concerning climate change. The inarticulate premise that there is a single locus of institutional power for external relations within Nation States is therefore often belied by reality. It might be argued by way of response that the analogy is inapposite since in the Nation State the President or Prime Minister will retain ultimate authority over foreign policy. But this is equally true of the European Council in the EU,[224] and it is moreover incumbent on its President to drive forward its work.[225]

---

[221] J Temple Lang, 'The New Treaties—Institutional Problems Ahead', Lecture at Oxford University, 10 February 2010.

[222] <http://www.euractiv.com/en/foreign-affairs/Commission-wants-control-over-EU-diplomatic-corps-news-440904>; <http://www.euractiv.com/en/future-eu/ashton-puts-french-spider-centre-eeas-web-news-382034>; <http://www.euractiv.com/en/foreign-affairs/parliament-raises-pressure-eu-diplomatic-service-news-467697>.

[223] Arts 18, 27, 30, 32, 34, 36 TEU.

[224] Art 22 TEU.   [225] Art 15(6) TEU.

Having said this, there is undoubtedly some tension in terms of who represents the EU to the external world, as manifest in the 'absence of fit' between Articles 15(6) and 27(2) TEU. There may also be tension when the Commission wishes to argue that certain EU external action could have been undertaken under the TFEU, while the Council/European Council wishes to pursue the relevant policy through the CFSP. Under the previous Treaty, the Commission could ultimately take the case to the ECJ. This is still possible, but the High Representative now has overall responsibility for Commission action in the sphere of external relations,[226] and she may be 'torn' as to whether to support the Commission thinking in her guise as Vice-President, or to side with the Council/European Council.

Second, the concern as to the institutional ordering in the Lisbon Treaty is premised, explicitly or implicitly, on the assumption that something else would have been preferable and politically feasible. These assumptions are rarely explored. The origins of the new schema are to be found in the Working Group on External Relations.[227] It was composed of expert insiders, who understood the workings of the EU. They concluded that the divide between the High Representative and the External Relations Commissioner was detrimental to consistency and coherence of EU foreign policy. They explored options as to the institutional locus of a single figure with responsibility for EU external relations. Their preferred choice would have been to locate the incumbent within the Commission, which would have responsibility for initiation and implementation of EU foreign policy, including the CFSP. They recognized that this would, however, not be acceptable to the Member States, hence the birth of the 'double hatting' idea that was enshrined in the Constitutional Treaty and then carried over into the Lisbon Treaty. The new regime may lead to some tension. That can be acknowledged. It is nonetheless incumbent on critics to show that an alternative institutional division of power would have been preferable and politically feasible. This might be attempted in one of two ways.

The critic might contend that the previous regime wherein external relations power was divided between the High Representative and the External Relations Commissioner was preferable and that it ensured coherence and consistency of policy better than the new regime. Such an argument might be asserted, but it must be sustained. The insiders in Working Group VII felt strongly that the pre-Lisbon regime with the division of power did not best serve consistency or coherence, a view shared by the majority on Working Group III on Legal Personality.[228] The conclusion makes intuitive sense. The worlds of CFSP and external action were never hermetically sealed. On the contrary, there was always considerable 'seepage' both ways, as attested to by the security concerns underlying development policy, and the economic concerns underlying certain joint actions.

---

[226] Art 18(4) TEU.   [227] Final Report of Working Group VII (n 2).
[228] Final Report of Working Group III (n 29) [27].

The critic might alternatively accept that merging the functions of the High Representative and the External Relations Commissioner enhanced consistency, but contend that the incumbent of the new office should not have been 'double hatted', but should have been located within the Commission in relation to all external action, including the CFSP. This argument too must be sustained, not merely asserted. It would have to be shown that the 'political radar' of the insiders in Working Group VII was severely misguided. Argument would have to be advanced as to why the Working Group was mistaken in believing that the Member States would simply not accept such a solution. The reality is that the available evidence sustains the Working Group's intuition as to what would prove acceptable to the Member States. There is no evidence during the decade of reform that the Member States would have been willing to subject all foreign policy, including the CFSP, to something akin to the Community method.

Third, the preceding point leads naturally to the critique voiced above by Temple Lang that the Lisbon regime has in some way weakened the Community method. It can be accepted that the role of the Commission within the CFSP has been reduced in the post-Lisbon order. This is evident from the previous analysis.[229] This does not, however, sustain the argument advanced. The Lisbon Treaty represents continuity rather than departure from the past in relation to the general shape and place of the CFSP. While the Member States have been willing over time to merge the Third Pillar into the main body of the Treaty, a process begun with the Treaty of Amsterdam and concluded with the Lisbon Treaty, they have never been willing to make analogous changes with the CFSP. There have always been two institutional regimes governing the totality of foreign policy. The perpetuation of this duality within the Lisbon Treaty is not new, nor is it surprising. It can be acknowledged that the two hats worn by the High Representative might lead to tension between her role within the Commission in relation to external relations, and that in the Council concerning the CFSP. The rationale for this method of institutional ordering was, however, considered above.

(c) Doctrine

A third aspect of the debates concerning consistency and coherence is more distinctly legal in nature, and explores how far the domain of external relations and CFSP can be regarded as meeting these criteria in doctrinal legal terms. A word of warning should be given at the outset. This is difficult terrain. Books and articles have been written on this topic.[230] The very meaning of a 'unitary

---

[229] pp 412–413.
[230] D Curtin and I Dekker, 'The EU as a "Layered" International organization: Institutional Unity in Disguise' in P Craig and G de Búrca (eds), *The Evolution of EU Law* (Oxford University Press, 1999) ch 3; A von Bogdandy, 'The Legal Case for Unity: The European Union as a Single Organization with a Single Legal System' (1999) 36 CMLRev 88.

legal order' is fraught with difficulty.[231] It is therefore impossible within the confines of what is already a lengthy chapter to give exhaustive treatment to this subject. It is, however, possible to disaggregate some of the principal issues that are involved in this discourse, and relate them to the post-Lisbon world.

(i) Difference and justification

It is important to recognize at the outset that the legal domain applicable to external action governed by the TFEU, and the CFSP governed by the TEU is different. This is a trite proposition, but is easily lost sight of in the complex debates in this area. The legal instruments, modes of decision making, and allocation of institutional responsibility that pertain to external action and CFSP are very different. These differences cannot be imagined away.

There is a corollary to the preceding point that is less obvious. The fact that different legal regimes, including judicial power, apply to the CFSP and other forms of external action cannot per se be regarded as either inconsistent or incoherent. It is easy to reason from the factual premise that a different legal regime applies to the CFSP and other aspects of external action, to the conclusion that this generates incoherence or inconsistency. This is a non-sequitur. The terms coherence and consistency as applied in this context necessarily connote the idea that a distinction is unwarranted.

This would require normative argumentation as to why the distinctive legal regime applicable to CFSP and other forms of external action is unwarranted. There are doubtless arguments that might be made to this effect. It is equally doubtless that there are arguments that can be put to the contrary, and it is these arguments that have held sway ever since the EU exercised authority over the CFSP. The Member States have consistently wanted institutionalized collaboration within the EU in relation to CFSP, and at the same time been unwilling to subject this to the normal regime of supranational oversight. This is not an illogical position, nor is it devoid of normative and pragmatic justification, given the sensitive nature of the CFSP/CSDP and the way in which they touch so directly on core precepts of national interest and sovereignty.

It is for this reason that the preceding proposition was carefully framed to state that the existence of distinctive legal regimes for the CFSP and other forms of external action is not in itself incoherent or inconsistent. This is so notwithstanding the fact that some might prefer if matters were to be otherwise, such that everything fitted into some neat one-size-fits-all political and legal regime. Nor is the soundness of this proposition invalidated merely because, other things being equal, different legal regimes make life more complex than it would otherwise have been. This is a statement of the obvious that is applicable whenever we make

---

[231] C Hermann, 'Much Ado about Pluto? The "Unity of the European Legal Order" Revisited' in Cremona and de Witte (n 1) ch 2.

distinctions. It does not obviate the need for normative and political inquiry as to the basis for the distinction. The very existence of the distinctive rules, however, does necessitate, as we have seen,[232] a provision such as Article 40 TEU, the replacement of Article 47 EU, whereby the ECJ adjudicates on boundary disputes between the world of CFSP and the remainder of the Treaty.

(ii) Jurisdiction and principles

The fact that the legal regimes applicable to the CFSP and external action differ still leaves open the extent of this differentiation. There are various facets to this inquiry, one of the most important of which is the distinction between jurisdiction and principle. The Union courts do not, as we have seen, have jurisdiction over the CFSP, subject to the exceptions considered above.[233] This does not mean, however, that the procedural and substantive principles of EU law are inapplicable in this context. It simply means that the ECJ has no jurisdiction to adjudicate on their application.

This analytical proposition is reinforced in terms of positive law by Article 21 TEU, which lists the principles and objectives of all EU external action including the CFSP and is framed in mandatory terms. These include democracy, human rights, rule of law, equality, and solidarity. There is, moreover, no reason why the Charter of Rights should not in principle be applicable within this sphere. It is accorded the same value as the TEU and TFEU and there is nothing in Article 51 of the Charter, which defines its sphere of application, to suggest that its precepts are inapplicable when the EU is acting in the context of the CFSP.

It is certainly true that Article 24(1) TEU is framed in terms of the CFSP being subject to 'specific rules and procedures'. It thereby follows that the distinctive institutional regime laid down for the CFSP in the relevant Treaty articles cannot be contested. This does not, however, undermine the point made in the preceding paragraph. The principles in Article 21 TEU impose procedural and substantive obligations on the EU when implementing the CFSP, notwithstanding the fact that the ECJ has no general jurisdiction to review the legality of CFSP acts. This leads to a 'nice question' as to whether such issues could be raised before national courts, which will be considered below.

(iii) Primacy and the CFSP

The Lisbon Treaty dropped the primacy clause that had been part of the Constitutional Treaty, and therefore the sphere in which the supremacy of EU law over national law can apply will perforce be developed by the ECJ. The contestable terrain is now the CFSP, given that what was the Third Pillar has

---

[232] pp 415–416.   [233] Art 24(1) TEU, Art 275 TFEU.

been integrated into the main body of the TFEU. There have unsurprisingly been differences of view as to whether supremacy should apply within this sphere. It may be helpful to disaggregate different aspects of this argument.

It is necessary at the outset to address the analytical argument that supremacy of EU law cannot operate without direct effect, and that since direct effect does not apply in the confines of the CFSP, hence this precludes the application of the supremacy principle.[234] Let it be accepted for the sake of argument that direct effect does not apply in the context of the CFSP, although this is contestable, as will be seen below. This premise does not, however, lead to the conclusion drawn from it, because primacy is not logically dependent on direct effect. It is true that in many instances primacy arises in the context of an action in a national court where an individual seeks to rely on a directly effective provision of EU law against national law. This does not, however, mean that primacy of EU law is logically limited to such cases. It is clear in terms of principle and positive domestic law that there can be legal rules that do not give rise to individual rights, but which nonetheless impose obligations or empower organs of the State.[235] This is equally true of EU law. A legal norm may not have direct effect because it is not for the benefit of individuals, or it is not sufficiently certain and precise.[236] The Member State may nonetheless have failed to fulfil its obligations under such a norm, with the consequence that primacy would dictate that the inconsistent national law should fall. It is true that the relevant EU provision must be cognizable by the national court before there can be conflict with the applicable national rules.[237] This can, however, occur in a number of ways: it might be argued that the EU provision meets the requirements of direct effect; that it does not do so, but nonetheless satisfies the conditions for indirect effect; or that it comes before the national court in some other way, for example, as an action between different institutional organs of the same State.

There is then no logical bar to primacy applying even in the absence of direct effect. This does not, however, 'make the case' for the application of primacy in the context of the CFSP. This requires some more positive argument to sustain such a conclusion. Lenaerts and Corthaut have advanced such a justification in terms of consistency.[238] Writing before the Lisbon Treaty they argued that primacy could apply within the Second and Third Pillar. They drew on the reasons given for supremacy in the Community Pillar, and contended that they

---

[234] Dashwood (n 123) 55.

[235] See, eg, UK law on tort actions for breach of statutory duty, which is premised on this assumption, Markesinis and Deakin's *Tort Law* (Oxford University Press, 6th edn 2008) ch 3.

[236] Thus, to take but one example, a Member State is required under the Common Agricultural Policy (CAP) to ensure that agencies that audit CAP spending and disbursement are properly accredited. A Member State might be in breach of this duty, and primacy would dictate that it should amend the relevant national law to comply with EU law even though it did not have direct effect.

[237] Dashwood (n 123) 55.

[238] K Lenaerts and T Corthaut, 'Of Birds and Hedges: The Role of Primacy in Invoking Norms of EU Law' (2006) 31 ELRev 287, 289–291.

were equally applicable to the Second and Third Pillars: the EU, using that term in its pre-Lisbon sense, was established for an indefinite period, had its own decisional organs, had competences transferred by the Member States, which allowed it to do diverse things under the Second and Third Pillars. The corollary was, they argued, that Member State sovereignty in those areas had been limited, and a legal order had been created binding on the Member States, even though no enforcement mechanism analogous to Articles 226 to 228 EC was available. They rejected the argument that direct effect was a pre-condition for primacy, and focused on the imperative of consistency.[239]

It appears from *Costa* that the real concern is consistency: to the extent that a national measure is inconsistent with EC law, it cannot be allowed to apply over EC law. But if we take consistency seriously, there is no need for identifying whether a provision confers rights on individuals. The only thing that matters is that EC law, and by extension EU law, puts forward an identifiable result which cannot be thwarted by incompatible national measures. This result may often involve granting rights to individuals, but may also involve an obligation on a government to create the conditions under which rights are granted to individuals, as will almost always be the case with Directives...
When it comes to precedence the only question is whether a conflict can be identified. In principle, if that is the case the conflicting provision of national law has to yield. This also means, however, that the exclusion only applies to the extent of the conflict.

Commentators may disagree with this conclusion,[240] and argue that the distinctive nature of the CFSP militates against the extension of the primacy doctrine to this area. The argument advanced by Lenaerts and Corthaut is nonetheless reinforced by Article 24(3) TEU, which imposes three obligations on Member States:[241] a strong duty of cooperation, since the Member States are enjoined to support the CFSP 'actively and unreservedly in a spirit of loyalty and mutual solidarity';[242] a simple obligation of result, viz, that the Member States 'shall comply with the Union's action in this area'; and a duty to refrain from any action contrary to the interests of the EU, or likely to impair its effectiveness as a cohesive force in international relations. It is clear, moreover, that Member States are legally bound by decisions duly enacted in relation to the CFSP, unless they take advantage of provisions within Article 31 TEU through which the decision will not apply to it.

(iv) National courts and the CFSP

It might be argued by way of response that the preceding argument is purely theoretical, because the EU courts have, subject to the limits discussed earlier, no

---

[239] ibid 291.
[240] A Dashwood, 'The Relationship between the Member States and the European Union/ European Community' (2004) 41 CMLRev 355, 363, 379; A Dashwood, 'The EU Constitution: What will Really Change?' (2004–2005) 7 CYELS 33, 34.
[241] Hillion and Wessel (n 149).
[242] See (n 153).

jurisdiction over the CFSP. This response is premature. If primacy applies in relation to the CFSP that conclusion is important in itself, irrespective of whether it can be enforced by the EU courts. It is also significant in relation to the role of national courts.

The jurisdictional bar in Article 24 TEU and Article 275 TFEU pertains to the EU courts, not the national courts. There is moreover no provision that either states or denies the possibility that CFSP provisions could have direct effect. There is, as we have seen, a provision that embodies a strong duty of loyal cooperation on Member States in Article 24(3) TEU, which strengthens the argument that the reasoning in *Pupino*[243] could apply in this area. An individual may seek to challenge national action for failure to comply with a CFSP Treaty article or decision made pursuant thereto, or to challenge a CFSP decision itself. These will be considered in turn.

The individual might wish to argue that its Member State had not complied with a CFSP Treaty article, including the duty of support, or with a decision made under the CFSP. It would then be for the national court to decide whether such an action was possible. It should be noted that the national court might reach an affirmative answer either because it took the view that EU law required that such an action should be possible where the conditions for direct or indirect effect were fulfilled, or that national constitutional law dictated that such an action could proceed in such circumstances even if this was not demanded by EU law.[244]

The national court might determine that the CFSP decision on which the individual relied was sufficiently certain and specific to meet the requirements for direct effect. This conclusion might be possible if, for example, the subject matter of the challenge was a detailed operational CFSP decision, the content of which could be said to benefit individuals, more especially because such decisions commit the Member States in the positions they adopt and in the conduct of their activity.[245] The national court might alternatively conclude that the CFSP measure did not meet such criteria, but that Member State action could still be tested for conformity with it in accord with the doctrine of indirect effect. It would not be open to the national court in either of these scenarios to seek the ECJ's advice via a preliminary ruling under Article 267 TFEU, since the ECJ has no such jurisdiction over the CFSP. This would not preclude the national court itself from making the determination as to the compatibility of the national action with the CFSP measure if it was minded to do so.

The individual might, alternatively, wish to contest the legality of the CFSP measure itself via the national court. This raises the issue as to whether the *Foto-Frost*[246] principle would apply here, thereby precluding national courts from invalidating EU norms. It might be argued that the principle is confined to the

---

[243] Case C-105/03 (n 148).   [244] Dashwood (n 123) 56.   [245] Art 28(2) TEU.
[246] Case 314/85 *Foto-Frost v Hauptzollamt Lubeck-Ost* [1987] ECR 4199.

sphere of ordinary EU law, or that it extends to all EU law. The strongest argument against its extension to this area is that *Foto-Frost* is premised on the national court being able to make a preliminary reference to the ECJ, when in doubt as to the validity of an EU norm. This premise does not apply here, since there is no preliminary reference mechanism for the CFSP. If the national court is not able to render the EU provision inapplicable for the purposes of the claim before it, there is therefore no way for the individual to resist a CFSP provision that might be tainted by illegality. It necessarily follows that such a decision by a national court would qualify the uniformity of application of the CFSP provision. This is, however, a zero-sum game: either uniformity is accorded priority with the consequence that the national court cannot 'invalidate' the CFSP measure or 'render it inapplicable to the instant case'; or access to justice before the national court is given priority, with the consequence that the national court can at least render the CFSP provision inapplicable to the instant case if satisfied that it is tainted by illegality that warrants this result. The latter would seem preferable, more especially where the individual claims that the CFSP decision is, for example, contrary to Charter rights.

5. Conclusion

The principal changes made by the Lisbon Treaty in relation to the EU's powers of external action and the CFSP/CSDP have been analysed above. Treaty amendments are not, however, of equal significance. The articulation of principles that govern the entirety of EU external action is undoubtedly a positive step, so too is the more coherent reorganization of Treaty provisions concerning external action in Part Five TFEU.

The most significant change in relation to EU external action as regulated by the TFEU is arguably Article 216 TFEU, which provides Treaty foundation for power to make international agreements, which had hitherto been developed by the ECJ's case law. The reality is that for the future there will be few, if any, instances, in which the EU lacks the power to make an international agreement, since it will be rare for the EU to be unable to draw on one of the four justificatory rationales in Article 216 TFEU. It should be remembered, moreover, that in many instances this power will be treated as conferring exclusive external competence on the EU, because of Article 3(2) TFEU. This is subject to the caveat that there are instances where, as we have seen, the Treaty specifically states that conclusion of an agreement by the EU is without prejudice to the Member States' competence to negotiate and conclude an agreement in the relevant area.[247] The existence of such Treaty articles inevitably means that

---

[247] See, eg, Arts 191(4), 209(2), 212(3), 214(4) TFEU; Case C-316/91 *European Parliament v Council (EDF)* [1994] ECR I-625; Cases C-181 and 248/91 *European Parliament v Council and Commission (Bangladesh)* [1993] ECR I-3685.

there will, as hitherto,[248] be litigation in which the parties dispute whether an international agreement should have been made under a Treaty article that affirms the continued existence of Member State competence to conclude an agreement, or whether it should have been made under a different Treaty article where the EU's competence would be exclusive.

The most significant changes in relation to the CFSP/CSDP are arguably the new provisions concerning the CSDP and in more general terms the institutional changes that flow from creation of the High Representative and the extended Presidency of the European Council. The desirability of this new institutional ordering was considered above. The 'jury' is still out on the practicalities of the inter-institutional relationships that pertain to the CFSP. We should moreover be wary of hasty conclusions based on relatively scant data concerning the performance of particular incumbents to these offices, whomsoever they may be. If the history of the EU teaches us anything it is that new institutions take time to 'bed down' and that inter-institutional relationships develop over time. There is no reason for thinking that these lessons are not equally applicable to the new world of external relations.

---

[248] See, eg, the disputes as to whether certain agreements related to the environment or the Common Commercial Policy, Opinion 2/00 (*re Cartagena Protocol*) [2001] ECR I-9713; Case C-281/03 *Commission v Council* (*Energy Star Agreement*) [2002] ECR I-12049.

11

Enhanced Cooperation, Amendment, and Conclusion

The preceding chapters have considered the changes made by the Lisbon Treaty and their likely impact on the functioning of the EU. This concluding chapter addresses two issues that are distinct, enhanced cooperation and Treaty revision, but which are nonetheless connected, the linkage being tension between the desire that all should be brought on board as the EU advances or changes, and the difficulties that this can pose in an EU of 27 Member States.

The analysis begins by considering enhanced cooperation. There is a brief overview of the provisions on enhanced cooperation in the Nice Treaty, followed by discussion of the changes made by the Lisbon Treaty, the rationale for these amendments and their likely impact.

This is followed by examination of the Lisbon provisions on Treaty revision. These were, like much else in the Lisbon Treaty, borrowed from the Constitutional Treaty. They signal some shift away from the classic mode of Treaty revision, which was traditionally undertaken through an intergovernmental conference (IGC) coupled with ratification by Member States in accord with their respective constitutional requirements. These are still features of the revision process in the Lisbon Treaty, but they have, as will be seen, been modified in certain respects through the inclusion of an 'ordinary' and a 'simplified' revision procedure.

The chapter concludes by examining some of the broader implications of the new schema for enhanced cooperation and Treaty revision. The focus then shifts to more general reflection on process and content in the Lisbon Treaty. The objective is not to summarize the conclusions drawn in previous chapters, but rather to re-visit and reflect on the issues of process and content raised at the outset.[1]

1. Enhanced Cooperation Pre-Lisbon

The Treaty of Amsterdam introduced provisions enabling the Member States, under certain conditions, to establish closer cooperation, using the institutions and mechanisms of the Treaty on European Union (TEU) and the EC Treaty

---

[1] pp 29–31.

alike. These provisions were amended by the Nice Treaty. The general principles on enhanced cooperation were contained in Article 43 EU.[2]

Member States which intend to establish enhanced cooperation between themselves may make use of the institutions, procedures and mechanisms laid down by this Treaty and by the Treaty establishing the European Community provided that the proposed cooperation:

(a) is aimed at furthering the objectives of the Union and of the Community, at protecting and serving their interests and at reinforcing their process of integration;

(b) respects the said Treaties and the single institutional framework of the Union;

(c) respects the acquis communautaire and the measures adopted under the other provisions of the said Treaties;

(d) remains within the limits of the powers of the Union or of the Community and does not concern the areas which fall within the exclusive competence of the Community;

(e) does not undermine the internal market as defined in Article 14(2) of the Treaty establishing the European Community, or the economic and social cohesion established in accordance with Title XVII of that Treaty;

(f) does not constitute a barrier to or discrimination in trade between the Member States and does not distort competition between them;

(g) involves a minimum of eight Member States;

(h) respects the competences, rights and obligations of those Member States which do not participate therein;

(i) does not affect the provisions of the Protocol integrating the Schengen acquis into the framework of the European Union;

(j) is open to all the Member States, in accordance with Article 43b.

This was followed by Articles 43a and 43b EU, which provided respectively that enhanced cooperation should be used only as a last resort when it had been established that the same objectives could not otherwise be attained within a reasonable period, and that enhanced cooperation should be open to all Member States at any stage under the conditions provided in the Treaty, and that as many States as possible should be encouraged to take part. Article 44 indicated the relevant institutional provisions to be used in the adoption of decisions within a field of enhanced cooperation, and explained the decision-making procedures and obligations in relation to participating and non-participating States. Such decisions were declared not to be part of the Union *acquis*.

The most significant change brought about by the Nice Treaty was that only a minimum of eight Member States was necessary to establish enhanced cooperation, and some of the stricter conditions from the Treaty of Amsterdam were relaxed. Thus, enhanced cooperation was no longer prohibited where it could

---

[2] There were specific provisions dealing with the CFSP, Arts 27a–e EU, and with PJCC, Arts 40–40b.

affect[3] the *acquis communautaire* or the competences and rights of non-participating States. Article 43 provided, more positively, that any enhanced cooperation was required to *respect* the acquis and the competences and rights of non-participating States. The requirement that enhanced cooperation must not undermine the internal market or economic and social cohesion was, however, a newly added restrictive condition.

The general rules in Articles 43 to 45 EU were complemented by Article 11 EC, which dealt specifically with enhanced cooperation in the context of the EC. Member States which intended to establish enhanced cooperation in an area covered by the EC Treaty addressed a request to the Commission, which could then submit a proposal to the Council. The Commission was not obliged to submit a proposal, but if it did not do so it had to provide reasons. Authorization to establish enhanced cooperation was granted, in compliance with Articles 43 to 45 EU, by the Council, acting by a qualified majority on a proposal from the Commission, after consulting the European Parliament.[4] It was, however, open to a member of the Council to request that the matter be referred to the European Council. This did not *per se* block the move to enhanced cooperation, because once the matter had been raised before the European Council, the Council could then authorize such cooperation in accordance with the preceding requirements. The acts and decisions necessary for the implementation of enhanced cooperation were subject to all the relevant provisions of the EC Treaty, subject to any qualification provided in Article 11 EC and Articles 43 to 45 EU. It was *prima facie* open to any Member State to join a regime of enhanced cooperation that had already been established.[5]

2. Enhanced Cooperation Post-Lisbon

The political reality pre-Lisbon was that while there was some flexibility in the application of Treaty articles,[6] the provisions on enhanced cooperation did not provide the foundation for such initiatives. There is now a proposal to use enhanced cooperation in the field of divorce and legal separation,[7] and it remains to be seen whether greater use is made of such flexibility in the post-Lisbon world of 27 Member States. The conditions for enhanced cooperation are now contained in both the TEU and the Treaty on the Functioning of the European Union (TFEU).

---

[3] Art K.15(1)(e) EU.
[4] When enhanced cooperation related to an area covered by Art 251 EC, the assent of the European Parliament was required.
[5] Art 11a EC.
[6] F Tuytschaever, *Differentiation in European Union Law* (Hart, 1999); G de Búrca and J Scott (eds), *Constitutional Change in the EU, From Uniformity to Flexibility?* (Hart, 2000).
[7] Proposal for a Council Regulation (EU) implementing enhanced cooperation in the area of the law applicable to divorce and legal separation, COM(2010) 105 final/2.

(a) General rules

Article 20 TEU authorizes enhanced cooperation in accordance with the detailed conditions set out in the TFEU. It stipulates that such cooperation shall aim to further the objectives of the EU, protect its interests, and reinforce the integration process. There must be a minimum of nine Member States wishing to participate in order for enhanced cooperation to be used, and the cooperation must be open at any time to all Member States, in accordance with Article 328 TFEU. It is emphasized in Article 20(2) TEU that enhanced cooperation is a last resort, to be used where the Council has established that the objectives of such cooperation cannot be attained within a reasonable period by the EU as a whole. All members of the Council can participate in its deliberations, but only those members of the Council representing the Member States participating in enhanced cooperation take part in the vote, in accordance with the rules in Article 330 TFEU. The acts adopted in the framework of enhanced cooperation bind only participating Member States, and, as before, they do not constitute part of the *acquis* that has to be accepted by candidate States for accession to the EU.

The detailed rules on such cooperation are to be found in Articles 326 to 334 TFEU. It is incumbent on the Council and the Commission to ensure the consistency of activities undertaken in the context of enhanced cooperation and the consistency of such activities with the policies of the Union.[8] The conditions for such cooperation are contained in Articles 326 to 327 TFEU, read together with Article 20 TEU.

Article 326

Any enhanced cooperation shall comply with the Treaties and Union law.

Such cooperation shall not undermine the internal market or economic, social and territorial cohesion. It shall not constitute a barrier to or discrimination in trade between Member States, nor shall it distort competition between them.

Article 327

Any enhanced cooperation shall respect the competences, rights and obligations of those Member States which do not participate in it. Those Member States shall not impede its implementation by the participating Member States.

The net effect of these provisions is to relax the conditions for enhanced cooperation. The minimum number of participating Member States is now 9 out of 27, as compared with 8 out of 15, which was the rule hitherto under the Nice Treaty. A number of the conditions hitherto contained in Article 43 EU have been replicated in the Lisbon Treaty: Article 43a EU is replicated in Article 20 TEU; Article 43(e)–(f) is mirrored by Article 326 TFEU; and Article 43(h) is repeated in Article 327 TFEU. There are, however, some subtle changes in the

---

[8] Art 334 TFEU.

Lisbon provisions. Thus Article 327 now states that non-participating Member States have an obligation not to impede implementation of enhanced cooperation by participating Member States. The stipulation in Article 326 that 'any enhanced cooperation shall comply with the Treaties and Union law' replaces the previous formulation in Article 43(b)–(c) EU. The wording of Article 326 is clearly broad enough to ensure that enhanced cooperation respects the *acquis*, but the very fact that it is framed in terms of 'compliance' with the Treaties and EU law, as opposed to 'respect' for the *acquis* that was used previously, may signify a greater willingness to encourage enhanced cooperation. Enhanced cooperation can, as before, only be used in relation to the EU's non-exclusive competences,[9] but subject to this there is nothing that specifically replicates the injunction in Article 43(d) EU to the effect that such cooperation must remain within the limits of EU powers. This condition nonetheless appears to be inherent in the requirement that enhanced cooperation complies with the Treaties and Union law contained in Article 326 TFEU, which would include the Treaty rules on competence.

The detailed rules concerning creation of enhanced cooperation are found in Articles 328 and 329 TFEU. Article 328 reiterates Article 20 TEU, by providing that enhanced cooperation is open to all Member States, subject to compliance with any conditions of participation laid down by the authorizing decision. It makes clear that Member States can join such cooperation after it has been established, subject to compliance with acts already adopted within that framework, in addition to those conditions.[10] It is incumbent on the Commission and the Member States participating in enhanced cooperation to promote participation by as many Member States as possible. The Commission and, where appropriate, the EU High Representative for Foreign Affairs and Security Policy must keep the European Parliament and the Council regularly informed regarding developments in enhanced cooperation.

Article 329(1) TFEU provides that Member States that wish to establish enhanced cooperation in an area covered by the Treaties, with the exception of exclusive competence and the Common Foreign and Security Policy (CFSP), address a request to the Commission, specifying 'the scope and objectives of the enhanced cooperation proposed'. The Commission then has discretion to submit the proposal to the Council, but if it does not do so it must inform the Member States concerned of the reasons. Authorization to proceed with the enhanced cooperation is granted by the Council, on the proposal from the Commission, after obtaining the consent of the European Parliament. Somewhat different rules apply to requests for enhanced cooperation in relation to the CFSP. Article 329(2) provides that such requests from the Member States are addressed to the Council. The request is forwarded to the High Representative, who gives an

---

[9] Art 20(1) TEU.

[10] The detailed arrangements for joining an existing regime of enhanced cooperation are set out in Art 331 TFEU.

opinion as to whether the proposed enhanced cooperation is consistent with the CFSP. The request is also forwarded to the Commission, which give its opinion as to whether the enhanced cooperation proposed is consistent with other Union policies. The European Parliament also receives the request by way of information. Authorization to proceed with enhanced cooperation is granted by a decision of the Council acting unanimously.

Article 330 TFEU repeats the pre-Lisbon rules concerning Council deliberations in an area subject to enhanced cooperation: all members of the Council can participate in its deliberations, but only members of the Council representing the Member States participating in enhanced cooperation can take part in the vote. Unanimity is constituted by the votes of the representatives of the participating Member States only, and a qualified majority is defined in accordance with Article 238(3) TFEU. Expenditure resulting from implementation of enhanced cooperation, other than administrative costs entailed for the institutions, is borne by the participating Member States, unless all members of the Council, acting unanimously after consulting the European Parliament, decide otherwise.[11]

The Lisbon provisions on enhanced cooperation also contain two passerelle clauses concerning voting rules and voting procedures respectively. Article 333 (1) TFEU states that where a provision of the Treaties which may be applied in the context of enhanced cooperation stipulates that the Council shall act unanimously, the Council, acting unanimously in accordance with Article 330, may adopt a decision stipulating that it will act by a qualified majority. Article 331(2) does the same for voting procedures: where a Treaty provision that may be applied in the context of enhanced cooperation demands that the Council shall adopt acts under a special legislative procedure, the Council, acting unanimously in accordance with Article 330, may adopt a decision stipulating that it will act under the ordinary legislative procedure. The Council acts after consulting the European Parliament. These passerelle provisions cannot, however, apply to decisions having military or defence implications. A Declaration attached to the Lisbon Treaty[12] provides that Member States may indicate, when they make a request to establish enhanced cooperation, if they intend at that stage to make use of Article 333 providing for the extension of qualified majority voting or to have recourse to the ordinary legislative procedure.

(b) Particular rules

The discussion thus far has been concerned with the general schema for enhanced cooperation in the Lisbon Treaty. There is also mention of enhanced cooperation in relation to particular Treaty articles concerned with judicial cooperation in criminal matters and police cooperation. EU competence over crime was

---

[11] Art 332 TFEU.
[12] Declaration 40 on Article 329 of the Treaty on the Functioning of the European Union.

considered in a previous chapter, to which reference should be made.[13] The sensitivity of the subject matter in these areas is reflected in the decision-making rules that pertain in this area.

This can be exemplified by Article 82 TFEU, which is concerned with judicial cooperation in criminal matters. It provides for directives to establish minimum rules in order to facilitate mutual recognition of judgments. The directives can concern mutual admissibility of evidence between Member States, the rights of individuals in criminal procedure, the rights of victims of crime, and any other specific aspects of criminal procedure which the Council has identified in advance by a decision.

The default position is that the directives are enacted using the ordinary legislative procedure.[14] The sensitivity of the subject matter is attested to by the emergency brake procedure set out in Article 82(3) TFEU. Thus where a member of the Council considers that a draft directive would affect fundamental aspects of its criminal justice system, it may request that the draft directive be referred to the European Council. The ordinary legislative procedure is then suspended. If consensus is reached within four months of the suspension the European Council refers the draft directive back to the Council, which terminates the suspension of the ordinary legislative procedure. The draft directive is then considered in accordance with this procedure.

The possibility of enhanced cooperation becomes relevant where the European Council is unable to broker an agreement.[15] Article 82(3) TFEU then provides that if at least nine Member States wish to establish such cooperation on the basis of the draft directive concerned, they shall notify the European Parliament, the Council, and the Commission. In such a case, the authorization to proceed with enhanced cooperation referred to in Article 20(2) TEU and Article 329(1) TFEU shall be deemed to be granted, and the provisions on enhanced cooperation shall apply.

3. Amendment Pre-Lisbon

The difficulties of securing Treaty reform that lasted almost a decade may well lead those in power to pause before engaging in Treaty amendment, more especially with an EU composed of 27 Member States. There will, however, inevitably be further Treaty amendment, and it is therefore important to consider the mechanisms through which this can be attained. It will be seen that the Lisbon Treaty has attempted to ease the process of future reform by providing for both an ordinary and a simplified revision procedure.

---

[13] pp 361–374.   [14] Art 82(2) TFEU.
[15] This scheme, or one analogous thereto, also applies to other Treaty articles concerned with judicial cooperation in criminal matters and police cooperation, Arts 83(3), 86(1), 87(3) TFEU.

Prior to the Lisbon Treaty any amendment had to be carried out in accordance with Article 48 EU. This provided that the government of any Member State or the Commission could submit to the Council proposals for amendment of the Treaties on which the Union was founded. If the Council, after consulting the European Parliament and, where appropriate, the Commission, delivered an opinion in favour of calling a conference of representatives of the governments of the Member States, the conference was then convened by the President of the Council for the purpose of determining by common accord the amendments to be made to those Treaties. The European Central Bank was also consulted in relation to institutional changes in the monetary area. The amendments entered into force after being ratified by all the Member States in accordance with their respective constitutional requirements.

The paradigm Treaty reform process was therefore the intergovernmental conference (IGC) which preceded the formal process of Treaty revision. The IGCs varied in length, depending on the complexity of the issues that were tabled for reform. They would commonly last for at least a year, and often longer. The IGCs were the site of discussion, dialogue, and disagreement, with Member States assuming the dominant role.

The early IGCs were largely carried on behind closed doors, but matters improved considerably with the advent of the internet. Position papers and contributions were posted to a website dedicated to the IGC. This made it possible to follow the development of policy and understand the contending forces that shaped provisions included in the revised Treaty. There were, however, as we have seen,[16] pressures for a more inclusive forum for Treaty reform, which led to the creation of the Convention on the Future of Europe that produced the Constitutional Treaty. These more inclusive processes have, as will be seen below, been included in the Lisbon Treaty provisions on amendment.

4. Amendment Post-Lisbon

The Lisbon Treaty revised the provisions concerning Treaty amendment. There is now an ordinary and a simplified procedure for Treaty reform. These will be considered in turn.

(a) Ordinary revision procedure

The ordinary revision procedure is contained in Article 48 TEU. It is the replacement for Article 48 EU considered above, but there are a number of significant differences.

[16] Ch 1.

2. The Government of any Member State, the European Parliament or the Commission may submit to the Council proposals for the amendment of the Treaties. These proposals may, *inter alia*, serve either to increase or to reduce the competences conferred on the Union in the Treaties. These proposals shall be submitted to the European Council by the Council and the national Parliaments shall be notified.

3. If the European Council, after consulting the European Parliament and the Commission, adopts by a simple majority a decision in favour of examining the proposed amendments, the President of the European Council shall convene a Convention composed of representatives of the national Parliaments, of the Heads of State or Government of the Member States, of the European Parliament and of the Commission. The European Central Bank shall also be consulted in the case of institutional changes in the monetary area. The Convention shall examine the proposals for amendments and shall adopt by consensus a recommendation to a conference of representatives of the governments of the Member States as provided for in paragraph 4.

    The European Council may decide by a simple majority, after obtaining the consent of the European Parliament, not to convene a Convention should this not be justified by the extent of the proposed amendments. In the latter case, the European Council shall define the terms of reference for a conference of representatives of the governments of the Member States.

4. A conference of representatives of the governments of the Member States shall be convened by the President of the Council for the purpose of determining by common accord the amendments to be made to the Treaties.

    The amendments shall enter into force after being ratified by all the Member States in accordance with their respective constitutional requirements.

5. If, two years after the signature of a treaty amending the Treaties, four-fifths of the Member States have ratified it and one or more Member States have encountered difficulties in proceeding with ratification, the matter shall be referred to the European Council.

There are a number of noteworthy features of this procedure. First, the European Parliament can now be the catalyst for Treaty amendment proposals, as well as the Member States and the Commission. The enhanced status accorded to national parliaments is reflected in the fact that they must be notified of proposals, which can relate to the expansion or contraction of EU competence.

Second, the European Council is accorded a more formal and explicit role in the process of Treaty amendment than hitherto. It has *de facto* always been central to Treaty amendment, and in that respect the Lisbon Treaty represents legal form catching up with political reality. This is reflected in the fact that while proposals for Treaty reform are submitted initially to the Council, it acts primarily as a conduit for the passage of such proposals to the European Council, which then takes over the direction of Treaty revision.

Third, the European Council acts as gatekeeper in relation to the process of Treaty reform. It must decide by simple majority, after consulting the European Parliament and Commission, to examine the proposal for Treaty revision. If this majority is not secured the proposal is not taken further. If there is a simple majority the European Council is in effect given two options by Article 48(3) TEU. It can convene a Convention composed of representatives of national parliaments, Heads of State or government, the European Parliament and the Commission, plus the European Central Bank (ECB) for institutional changes that affect the monetary area. This Convention examines the proposals and makes recommendations to a conference of representatives of Member States as provided for by Article 48(4) TEU. This more inclusive forum for discussion of Treaty revision clearly draws on experience with the process used in relation to the Charter of Rights and the Constitutional Treaty. The European Council can alternatively decide that the proposed changes do not warrant a Convention, in which case it defines the terms of reference for the conference of the representatives of the Member States. This strategy is clearly intended for minor Treaty revision, which does not merit the full panoply of a Convention. It can only be used with the consent of the European Parliament.

Fourth, the retention of State power is apparent in Article 48(4) TEU. The deliberations of any Convention established pursuant to Article 48(3) take the form of recommendations, which then form the basis for the deliberations of the Member States who decide formally on the amendments to the Treaties. The Lisbon Treaty in this respect follows the process used in relation to the Constitutional Treaty, whereby the conclusions of the Convention on the Future of Europe took the form of recommendations that were discussed by an IGC composed of the Member States in the second half of 2003. The Treaty amendments must, as hitherto, be agreed in accordance with the constitutional requirements of the Member States.

Fifth, there is provision made in Article 48(5) TEU for dealing with problems of ratification. If after two years four-fifths of the States have ratified, but one or more States are having difficulties in securing ratification, the matter is referred to the European Council. This once again represents legal form playing catch up with political reality, since the European Council has undertaken this role in the past, even before the passage of two years after Treaty amendment.

(b) Simplified revision procedures

The simplified revision procedures are contained in Article 48(6)–(7) TEU, which is set out below.

6. The Government of any Member State, the European Parliament or the Commission may submit to the European Council proposals for revising all or part of the provisions of Part Three of the Treaty on the Functioning of the European Union relating to the internal policies and action of the Union.

   The European Council may adopt a decision amending all or part of the provisions of Part Three of the Treaty on the Functioning of the European Union. The European Council shall act by unanimity after consulting the European Parliament and the Commission, and the European Central Bank in the case of institutional changes in the monetary area. That decision shall not enter into force until it is approved by the Member States in accordance with their respective constitutional requirements.

The decision referred to in the second subparagraph shall not increase the competences conferred on the Union in the Treaties.

7. Where the Treaty on the Functioning of the European Union or Title V of this Treaty provides for the Council to act by unanimity in a given area or case, the European Council may adopt a decision authorising the Council to act by a qualified majority in that area or in that case. This subparagraph shall not apply to decisions with military implications or those in the area of defence.

Where the Treaty on the Functioning of the European Union provides for legislative acts to be adopted by the Council in accordance with a special legislative procedure, the European Council may adopt a decision allowing for the adoption of such acts in accordance with the ordinary legislative procedure.

Any initiative taken by the European Council on the basis of the first or the second subparagraph shall be notified to the national Parliaments. If a national Parliament makes known its opposition within six months of the date of such notification, the decision referred to in the first or the second subparagraph shall not be adopted. In the absence of opposition, the European Council may adopt the decision.

For the adoption of the decisions referred to in the first and second subparagraphs, the European Council shall act by unanimity after obtaining the consent of the European Parliament, which shall be given by a majority of its component members.

There are two forms of simplified revision procedure, the common theme being that recourse to a Convention and/or IGC is not required.

Article 48(6) TEU in effect provides for a simplified revision procedure to apply to Part Three TFEU. This is significant because Part Three TFEU deals with all the internal policies and action of the EU, and has 24 titles, which include, *inter alia*, the internal market; the four freedoms; economic and monetary union; the area of freedom, security, and justice; agriculture and fisheries; environment; social policy; employment policy; tax; and the approximation of laws.

The procedure is that a Member State, the European Parliament, or the Commission can submit a proposal to the European Council for the revision of Part Three TFEU. The change is made by decision of the European Council, acting unanimously, after consulting the European Parliament, the Commission, and the ECB in relation to institutional changes in the monetary area. The decision cannot, however, increase EU competence and must be approved by the Member States in accordance with their constitutional requirements.

Article 48(7) TEU is a different form of revision mechanism, where the focus is on the voting requirements that pertain to a particular area. It embodies a general *passerelle* clause, which can take two forms. The European Council can decide that areas in the TFEU or Title V TEU that presently require unanimity in the Council can be revised to enable the Council to decide by qualified majority. The other option is for the European Council to decide that where the TFEU currently requires legislative acts to be adopted by a special legislative procedure they can henceforth be made in accordance with the ordinary legislative procedure.

There are, not surprisingly, stringent requirements for the exercise of such revision powers. The European Council must decide unanimously and secure the consent of the European Parliament. It is moreover open to any national parliament to block use of the passerelle clause in a particular instance. The European Council must notify national parliaments of initiatives taken pursuant to Article 48(7) and if one such parliament declares its opposition within six months of being notified then the decision cannot be adopted. The German Federal Constitutional Court has also held that in Germany the legislature must positively approve the exercise of power pursuant to Article 48(7) TEU, the ability to oppose being insufficient in this respect.[17]

Article 48(7) TEU constitutes a general passerelle clause, but it is not the only such provision in the Lisbon Treaty. There are in fact numerous other, more specific, bridging clauses that enable shifts to be made between voting requirements or between legislative procedures.[18] Most of these more specific bridging clauses do not require notification to national parliaments, and do not enable such parliaments to block any such shift in voting requirements or voting procedures,[19] but they do require unanimity in the Council or European Council.

5. Conclusion

(a) Enhanced cooperation

There has always been a tension in the Treaty rules concerned with enhanced cooperation, and this reflects at one remove the ambivalence of the Treaty framers to such provisions, who have strained to resolve two conflicting impulses: the desire that all Member States should be brought on board as the EU moves forward, tempered by the unwillingness to allow resistance by one or more Member States to prevent advances desired by a significant group of other States.

This duality has always been reflected in the rules relating to enhanced cooperation, and the amendments made to those rules over time. It has been crucially evident in the provisions relating to the minimum number of States required in order to proceed with enhanced cooperation. This was reduced to 8 out of 15 by the Nice Treaty, but the change wrought by the Lisbon Treaty was more dramatic, with the target number being further reduced to 9 out of 27.

---

[17] Lisbon Case, BVerfG, 2 BvE 2/08, 30 June 2009, [319], available at <http://www.bverfg.de/entscheidungen/es20090630_2bve000208.html>. English translation available at <http://www.bundesverfassungsgericht.de/entscheidungen/es20090630_2bve000208en.html>.
[18] See, eg, Art 31(3) TEU, Arts 81(3), 153(2), 192(2), 312(2), 331(1)–(2) TFEU.
[19] See, however, Art 81(3) TFEU.

The duality is apparent once again in the other conditions required to proceed with enhanced cooperation. The original requirement that such cooperation should not 'affect' the *acquis* reflected the framers' wariness of the very provisions on enhanced cooperation which they had included in the Treaty of Amsterdam. If taken literally it could have prevented any attempts to use the new provisions. The shift from 'affect' in the Treaty of Amsterdam to 'respect' for the *acquis* in the Nice Treaty exhibited greater willingness to allow the provisions on enhanced cooperation to be used, should the Member States wish to do so. This line of thought has continued in the Lisbon Treaty. Specific mention of respect for the *acquis* has been excised, replaced by the more general obligation to comply with the Treaties and Union law. The conditions for using enhanced cooperation have also been relaxed in certain other respects, as seen above.

The framers' ambivalence towards enhanced cooperation is still evident, however, in the Lisbon provisions, notwithstanding the greater readiness to allow such initiatives as indicated by the relaxation in the conditions considered above. Thus the continuing desire that all should be brought on board in EU policy initiatives is captured by the injunction that enhanced cooperation should be seen as a 'last resort', to be utilized where it has been established that the objectives of such cooperation cannot be attained by the EU as a whole.[20] It is apparent once again in the detailed provisions stipulating that enhanced cooperation should always be open to Member States in addition to those who had initiated the cooperation.[21] The message from the Lisbon Treaty is very much that enhanced cooperation should be used where action by the EU as a whole has not proven possible, coupled with the hope that it will then be a catalyst and that other Member States will subscribe to such initiatives.

It remains to be seen how far such Treaty provisions are used in the post-Lisbon world of 27 Member States, acting under a Treaty that accords the EU some measure of competence over many different spheres. If an EU of 'multiple speeds' or 'concentric circles' does become a reality, there will then be significant legal and political challenges in the governance of such a polity. The idea that acts adopted in pursuance of enhanced cooperation only bind the parties thereto, and do not form part of the more general *acquis*, has always been central to the conceptualization of this area and remains so.[22] Leaving aside monetary union, this precept has yet to be seriously tested in reality. The idea that acts adopted pursuant to enhanced cooperation and the judicial interpretation thereof by the EU courts can be hermetically sealed from the remainder of EU law may well prove considerably more difficult in practice than in theory.

---

[20] Art 20(2) TEU.
[21] Art 20(1) TEU, Arts 328(1), 331 TFEU.
[22] Art 20(4) TEU.

(b) Amendment and revision

The framers of the Lisbon Treaty struggled, as we have seen,[23] to secure ratification by all Member States. Future Treaty revision may also be problematic in an EU of 27 Member States, although how problematic will perforce depend on the nature of the proposed amendments. Those who framed the Constitutional Treaty were mindful of the difficulties of securing Treaty revision in an enlarged EU, and the provisions in the Lisbon Treaty draw heavily on those in the failed Constitutional Treaty.[24] The divide between the ordinary and simplified revision procedure is taken directly from the Constitutional Treaty. Future Treaty revision will therefore be organized through the principles in the Lisbon Treaty analysed above.

The ordinary revision procedure retains the classic requirement of State consent given in accordance with the constitutional requirements of the Member States. It nonetheless embodies two different processes for discourse on possible Treaty revision. The default assumption in Article 48(3) TEU is that this takes place through a Convention, the nature of which has clearly been modelled on the process used for the Charter of Rights and the Constitutional Treaty. Thus whatever the differences of opinion may be as to the success of the format used in the Convention on the Future of Europe, it is this more inclusive model that is *prima facie* to be used for Treaty amendment made by the ordinary revision procedure. It is only where this is displaced because the nature of the proposed Treaty amendment does not warrant such a Convention that recourse is had to the more traditional IGC mode. The retention of State power is nonetheless still apparent within Article 48. This is not only because the amendments must be approved by each Member State in accordance with their constitutional requirements. It is also evident in Article 48(3)–(4) TEU, which stipulate that if a Convention is established it makes a recommendation to a Conference of Member State representatives, and the latter makes the formal Treaty amendments. The Lisbon Treaty therefore once again follows the Constitutional Treaty and embodies in formal Treaty law the practice used in 2003–4, whereby the Convention on the Future of Europe recommended the Constitutional Treaty for consideration by the Member States, which then deliberated in traditional IGC mode.

The simplified revision procedures are the real constitutional novelty in the Lisbon schema, and are designed to expedite Treaty revision. The very nature of proposed Treaty amendments may well be affected by the extent to which they can be brought within the simplified procedure. The procedure in Article 48(6) TEU that can be used for revision of Part Three TFEU concerning the EU's internal policies removes the need for a Convention or an IGC. The amendment is simply

---

[23] Ch 1.   [24] Arts IV-443, 444, 445 CT.

made by the European Council, acting unanimously, after consulting the European Parliament, Commission, and, where relevant, the ECB. State power is nonetheless retained, because the European Council's decision must be approved by the Member States in accordance with their constitutional requirements.

The other form of simplified revision is the general passerelle clause in Article 48(7) TEU. It is both broader and narrower in its remit than is Article 48(6). It is broader insofar as it applies to all the TFEU and to Title V TEU, which is concerned with the CFSP. It is narrower because Article 48(7) TEU only deals with amendments to Council voting requirements and voting procedures. Thus Article 48(7) cannot be used for other forms of Treaty revision. The ability to shift from Council unanimity to qualified majority and from a special to the ordinary legislative procedure through the general passerelle clause is nonetheless significant. Article 48(7) does not require a Convention or an IGC. It is triggered by a unanimous European Council decision, subject to the consent of the European Parliament. There is no requirement that the change should be ratified by Member States, but any national parliament can in effect veto such a decision if it makes known its opposition within six months.

(c) Process

The discussion thus far has been concerned directly with enhanced cooperation and Treaty revision. It is fitting in the conclusion to this chapter and the book to reflect more generally on the process of Treaty reform. This was discussed at the outset, to which reference should be made.[25]

We have already seen that the idea of a Convention for important Treaty revision has been embodied in the Lisbon Treaty. This is in my view sound in principle and has proven workable in practice. The experience with the Convention on the Future of Europe nonetheless prompts thoughts about the process of Treaty reform, which have particular relevance having considered in detail the substance of the reforms themselves.

The timetable for the Convention on the Future of Europe was dictated by the Member States. They established the Convention via the Laeken European Council, and they set the deadline for the delivery of the finished product, whatsoever the Convention might produce. It became clear by March 2003 at the latest that the Convention would struggle to complete its task by the summer of that year, but attempts by Giscard d'Estaing to secure an extension of time were unavailing. It might be contended that the Member States in the European Council were 'right' not to accede to this request, the argument being that the Convention would have simply deliberated longer to fill whatever further time was allotted, with no cognizable difference to the end product. This is unknowable.

[25] pp 29–31.

We inhabit the real world. We cannot engage in a controlled study, duplicate the Convention, keep all factors constant, save for the fact that 'Convention Mark II' had six months longer to perform its task and then estimate whether the resulting product would have been markedly different.

The very fact that we inhabit the real world, however, means that we know what happened as a consequence of the time constraints that were placed on the Convention's work, and the results were to some extent paradoxical when viewed from the very perspective of the Member States that refused to grant the extension. Thus the temporal exigencies constrained deliberation in plenary sessions concerning some of the major institutional issues considered by the Convention. It concentrated power in the Praesidium and its Secretariat, which exercised the all-important agenda-setting power, and which selected from the multitude of suggested amendments those that should be discussed at all. The time constraints also contributed to the inclusion in the Constitutional Treaty of provisions which the Member States would almost certainly not have accepted if they had realized their full implications, as exemplified by the excision of Comitology from the world of delegated acts. This problem was exacerbated because the temporal pressures in the first half of 2003 meant that certain reports of Working Groups received relatively scant attention in plenary, more especially where they were felt to address issues that were largely technical, or difficult to comprehend, as exemplified by the Working Group Report on the hierarchy of norms, the legal and political implications of which were not fully understood by the Member States.

It might be argued that this was unfortunate, but of no great significance for the provisions that ultimately found their way into the Lisbon Treaty. This would be mistaken. It is true that the IGC that succeeded the Convention on the Future of Europe elected to revisit certain of the issues in the Constitutional Treaty and duly made certain changes. The Member States in the 2003–2004 IGC were nonetheless mindful of re-opening Pandora's Box too far, for fear that the document crafted by the Convention could be rendered unworkable by a multiplicity of suggestions for amendment, modification, and change.

Similar impulses were apparent when the Reform Treaty, later to become the Lisbon Treaty, was planned in 2007. The German Presidency skilfully determined through bilateral negotiations those parts of the Constitutional Treaty that would have to be altered to be acceptable to the Member States. The default assumption was that the remainder of the Constitutional Treaty could form the content of the Lisbon Treaty, which is largely what happened, albeit subject to some re-ordering of the provisions. Political imperatives meant that this assumption was never fully voiced, given the rejection of the Constitutional Treaty in France and the Netherlands. It was nonetheless the reality that shaped the content of the Lisbon Treaty. The Member States in 2007, as in 2003, were not willing to re-open Pandora's Box too far and re-visit the debates on issues such as institutional power that had divided opinion in the Convention.

This story does not speak against the Convention model, nor against its inclusion as the default mode when the ordinary revision procedure is used. It does reinforce the need for care as to how this process is deployed and the importance of practical considerations concerning the Convention's modus operandi, including the length of time allowed for its deliberations. It may well be that this will be less problematic going forward, for the very reason that future Treaty reform is likely to be more limited than that witnessed in the first decade of the new millennium. Given that this is so, the length of time for deliberation, and its impact on the Convention process, will not assume such importance. This can be accepted, but does not alter the force of the point made above.

(d) Content

There will be no attempt to summarize the conclusions reached about the specific topics considered in the previous chapters. It is nonetheless fitting to reflect rather more generally on the content of the Lisbon Treaty.

We can begin by re-visiting the issue raised at the outset, concerning the wisdom or otherwise of attempts at 'comprehensive' Treaty reform of the kind that led to the Constitutional Treaty and the Lisbon Treaty. There will doubtless be differences of view on this. Some will argue that the strains placed on the EU by the reform process were unnecessary. The EU was 'never broken' and thus there was no need to 'fix it' in the manner that sapped the EU's energy for nearly a decade. There is force in this view, but it is not one to which I subscribe.

The EU had been engaged in piecemeal Treaty reform from the Single European Act 1986 (SEA) through to the Nice Treaty. It was marked by reform initiatives every four to five years, with the Maastricht Treaty and the Amsterdam Treaty being the staging posts between the SEA and the Nice Treaty. The original intent was for there to be yet another exercise of Treaty reform to deal with the four issues left unresolved by the Nice Treaty, which was scheduled to take place in 2004. We cannot, as noted above, give definitive answers to hypothetical political inquiries. We cannot know what the official and academic response to such a further round of piecemeal reform would have been. We can, however, make a calculated guess that there would at the very least have been criticism voiced from both quarters at the very partial nature of such reform initiatives, more especially when coupled with the traditional IGC process that was itself regarded as too narrow institutionally.

The reality was that the four issues left for further deliberation after the Nice Treaty were not discrete. They raised a plethora of more general issues concerning the nature of the EU, its institutional structure, power, and the relationship with the Member States. The very idea that there should be some more fundamental re-think of the Treaty that had been in existence for nearly 50 years, and that this should be undertaken via a more inclusive process than hitherto, was therefore readily explicable. It was this which, as we have seen,[26] motivated the major players in the year after the Nice Treaty to build the foundations for the Laeken Declaration and the Convention on the Future of Europe.

Hindsight is a wonderful thing. We know what happened. The fact that there were difficulties with securing ratification of the Constitutional Treaty and the Lisbon Treaty does not mean that attempts at more thoroughgoing Treaty reform were misguided. The difficulties certainly indicate that it may well have been politically unwise to append the word 'constitutional' to the 2004 Treaty. They are also indicative of serious concerns about how the EU is perceived by the citizenry of Europe. The complex causes of the negative French and Dutch referenda nonetheless had relatively little to do with the concrete innovations actually made by the Constitutional Treaty and later incorporated in the Lisbon Treaty.

If we turn our attention to the changes made by the Lisbon Treaty it is clear that their full impact will only become apparent over time. This is especially true of the revisions that affect the institutional division of power within the EU. The desire for instant assessment of 'success' or 'failure' has become more prevalent in an age where every word is subject to immediate scrutiny by a plethora of media forms. The reality is that institutional changes take time to 'bed down'. The political significance of the disposition of executive power under the Lisbon Treaty may only be properly evaluated after a few years rather than a few months. This is equally true of other Treaty reforms, such as the legally binding Charter of Rights, de-pillarization, the provisions on competence, and those on the hierarchy of norms.

This is more especially so given that so much depends on precisely how the new provisions in the Lisbon Treaty are used by the EU institutions and how they are interpreted by the EU courts. The idea that either the Constitutional Treaty or the Lisbon Treaty were regarded as attempts at 'finality', whether constitutional or otherwise, should be treated with considerable reserve. This is in part because there will inevitably be some further Treaty amendments. It is in part because the reality of EU power has always resulted from the symbiotic interaction of four variables: choice as to the scope of EU competence, as expressed in Treaty revisions, where the Member States have traditionally been the major players; legislation that has fleshed out the Treaty articles, initiated by the Commission, and voted on by the Member States in the Council and increasingly often by the European Parliament; the jurisprudence of the EU courts; and decisions taken by the institutions as to how to interpret, deploy, and prioritize the power accorded to the EU.

The EU did not grind to a halt in the decade when Treaty reform was prominent on the agenda. It pressed ahead with a plethora of important legislation

---

[26] pp 1–6.

relating to services, concerning banking,[27] financial services,[28] insurance,[29] and securities.[30] There was major legislation relating to goods, most notably through the long-awaited REACH regulation,[31] but also in areas such as pharmaceuticals,[32] and technical harmonization.[33] The Community legislature was active in other core areas, such as customs, enacting a modernized customs code,[34] taxation,[35] and regional policy.[36] Important primary legislation, accompanied by more numerous secondary Comitology regulations, was evident in most areas of Community activity. The ECJ's case law also developed markedly during this time in relation to issues such as citizenship and services.

The scope of EU power in the post-Lisbon world will continue to depend on the symbiotic interaction of the four variables. The primary Treaty has, notwithstanding its length, always been a framework that empowers further action in the areas over which the EU is assigned competence. Its provisions are perforce crucial in shaping the nature of the EU and its relationship with the Member States. The EU legislation made pursuant to such Treaty provisions will, as before, depend on the interplay of political forces within the EU and it will require agreement by the Council and the European Parliament. The legislative agenda will continue to be set so as to realize Treaty objectives. The relative priority accorded to these objectives will inevitably be shaped by Member State and institutional preferences, as coloured by external events such as 9/11 and the banking crisis. The role of the EU courts will remain central. The ECJ will be

---

[27] Legislation relating to matters such as: the reorganization of credit institutions, capital adequacy of investment firms, the taking up and pursuit of business of credit institutions, supervision of credit institutions, electronic money institutions, combating fraud in relation to payments, payment services in the internal market, <http://europa.eu/legislation_summaries/internal_market/single_market_services/financial_services_banking/index_en.htm>.

[28] Legislation relating to, *inter alia*, distance contracts for financial services, supervision, and markets in financial instruments, <http://europa.eu/legislation_summaries/internal_market/single_market_services/financial_services_general_framework/index_en.htm>.

[29] Legislation relating to, eg, supervision, solvency, accounts, <http://europa.eu/legislation_summaries/internal_market/single_market_services/financial_services_insurance/index_en.htm>.

[30] Legislation on shareholders' rights in listed companies, transparency, insider dealing, <http://europa.eu/legislation_summaries/internal_market/single_market_services/financial_services_transactions_in_securities/l24035_en.htm>.

[31] Regulation (EC) No 1907/2006 of the European Parliament and of the Council of 18 December 2006 concerning the Registration, Evaluation, Authorization and Restriction of Chemicals (REACH), establishing a European Chemicals Agency [2006] OJ L396/1.

[32] <http://europa.eu/legislation_summaries/internal_market/single_market_for_goods/pharmaceutical_and_cosmetic_products/index_en.htm>.

[33] <http://europa.eu/legislation_summaries/internal_market/single_market_for_goods/technical_harmonisation/index_en.htm>.

[34] Regulation (EC) 450/2008 of the European Parliament and of the Council of 23 April 2008 laying down the Community Customs Code (Modernised Customs Code) [2008] OJ L145/1.

[35] See, eg, Council Directive 2006/112/EC of 28 November 2006 on the common system of value added tax [2006] OJ L347/1.

[36] Council Regulation (EC) 1083/2006 of 11 July 2006 laying down general provisions on the European Regional Development Fund, the European Social Fund and the Cohesion Fund and repealing Regulation (EC) 1260/1999 [2006] OJ L210/25.

called on to make important judgments concerning provisions of the Lisbon Treaty, it will be faced with new challenges when adjudicating on the Charter of Rights and its jurisdictional authority has been increased as a result of de-pillarization.

It was a long road from Nice to Lisbon. The difficulties of securing agreement mean that the Lisbon Treaty is likely to provide the broad framework for the EU in the foreseeable future. We will therefore have ample time to see how its new provisions play out, and how they interact with the three other variables that shape the reality of the EU. It should be noted, however, that the European Parliament may well seek to exercise its new found power to call for Treaty revision, in order to modify the number of MEPs. This was approved in principle by the European Council. It remains to be seen whether the Member States have an appetite for yet another Treaty revision, albeit a modest one. They will in any event be wary of opening Pandora's Box too wide for fear of what might escape. The temptation for a Member State to open it just a bit wider in order to secure a further amendment that it feels is desirable is, however, often difficult to resist, and Germany has already hinted that reforms are required to strengthen the rules on budget deficits in the light of the Greek crisis. If such changes are made it might be felt 'safer' to incorporate them in a Treaty amendment made when the next country joins the EU. The Lisbon Treaty is nonetheless likely continue to provide the general frame for the EU for some time, more especially given the energies needed to tackle the considerable socio-economic problems at the end of the first decade of the new millennium.

12

Financial Crisis, Response, and Europe's Future

The previous chapter constituted the conclusion to this book when it was initially published. The financial crisis and the difficulties with Greece were unfolding at that time, and there was growing consensus on the need for stronger EU controls over national fiscal policy in order to make economic and monetary union (EMU) 'work'. Events have developed rapidly in the intervening period. The scale of the difficulties was not fully perceived in 2010, and this realization led to a plethora of legal and political responses that have had far-reaching consequences on all aspects of the EU, economic, social, political, and constitutional. This is the rationale for the inclusion of this new chapter in the paperback version of this book, which otherwise remains unchanged from the original version.

The chapter begins by charting the economic and constitutional assumptions that underpinned the Maastricht settlement concerning EMU, followed by a brief explanation of the crisis itself. The discussion then turns to the responses to the crisis. These were, as will be seen, complex and varied, but nonetheless two kinds of measure are discernible: those designed to assist Member States in economic difficulty, and those to increase supervision over national budgetary policy. These measures are analysed, including the legal difficulties attendant upon them. This is followed by consideration of further measures that will be enacted in the light of high-level deliberations as to what is required for a 'genuine economic and monetary union'.[1] The chapter concludes with analysis of the broader political, economic, and legal consequences of the crisis for the EU and its relationship with the Member States.

1. The Maastricht Settlement

The Maastricht Treaty was notable for introduction of the Pillar system and for the detailed rules on economic and monetary union, EMU. The latter were

---

[1] H Van Rompuy in close collaboration with J M Barroso, J-C Juncker, and M Draghi, 'Towards a Genuine Economic and Monetary Union', 5 Dec 2012.

complex and difficult to comprehend for the uninitiated, this problem being exacerbated by the cumbersome numbering regime of the Treaty provisions prior to the 'numerical cleansing' done by the Treaty of Amsterdam. The 'architecture' of the EMU provisions was nonetheless readily apparent for those who had the inclination and patience to read the relevant provisions. The EMU schema was predicated on a dichotomy between monetary and economic union, and this remained largely unchanged in the Lisbon Treaty. It is indeed arguable that the dichotomy was reinforced by the Lisbon Treaty.

(a) Monetary policy

Monetary union was all about the single currency and the Treaty articles were powerfully influenced by German ordoliberal economic thought, which demanded independence of the European Central Bank (ECB), governance by experts and the primacy of price stability. These foundational precepts were embodied in the primary Treaty articles.

The independence of the ECB[2] was enshrined in Article 108 EC, now Article 130 TFEU, which stipulates that the ECB shall not take any instruction from EU institutions, Member States, or any other body, and this is further affirmed by Article 282(3) TFEU. This independence is reflected in the ECB's decision-making structure: the President of the Council and a member of the Commission may participate in meetings of the ECB's Governing Council, but they do not have the right to vote.[3] The ECB has the power to make regulations and take decisions, and can, subject to certain conditions, impose fines or periodic penalty payments on undertakings for failure to comply with obligations contained in its regulations and decisions. It must be consulted on any EU act in its fields of competence and, subject to certain conditions, by national authorities regarding any draft legislative provision in its fields of competence.[4] The ECB has the exclusive right to authorize issue of banknotes within the EU, although the actual issue of the notes may also be undertaken by national central banks.[5]

---

[2] L Gormley and J de Haan, 'The Democratic Deficit of the European Central Bank' (1996) 21 ELRev 95; F Amtenbrink, *The Democratic Accountability of Central Banks* (Hart, 1999); C Zilioli and M Selmayr, *The Law of the European Central Bank* (Hart, 2001); R Lastra, 'European Monetary Union and Central Bank Independence', in M Andenas, L Gormley, C Hadjiemmanuil, and I Harden (eds), *European Economic and Monetary Union: The Institutional Framework* (Kluwer, 1997) Ch 15; T Daintith, 'Between Domestic Democracy and an Alien Rule of Law? Some Thoughts on the "Independence" of the Bank of England', ibid, Ch 17; L Smaghi, 'Central Bank Independence in the EU: From Theory to Practice' (2008) 14 ELJ 446; R Smits, 'The European Central Bank's Independence and its relation with the Economic Policy Makers' (2007–2008) 31 Fordham ILJ 1614; B Krauskopf and C Steven, 'The Institutional Framework of the European System of Central Banks: Legal Issues in the Practice of the first ten years of its Existence' (2009) 46 CMLRev 1143.
[3] Art 113(1) EC; Art 284(1) TFEU.
[4] Art 105(4) EC; Art 127(4) TFEU.
[5] Art 106(1) EC; Art 128(1) TFEU.

Governance by experts was stipulated in relation to the decision-making structure of the ECB. The Executive Board is composed of a President, Vice-President, and four other members, who must be recognized experts in monetary or banking matters.[6] The importance of expertise was further emphasized by the European System of Central Banks, ESCB, which is composed of the ECB and the national central banks, although it is the ECB and the national central banks whose currency is the euro that conduct the EU's monetary policy.[7] The basic tasks of the ESCB are:[8] to define and implement the EU's monetary policy; to conduct foreign-exchange operations; to hold and manage the official foreign reserves of the Member States; and to promote the smooth operation of the payment system.

The primacy of price stability was accorded pride of place in the objectives of EU monetary policy from the outset. It was originally embodied in Article 105 EC and is now to be found in Article 127 TFEU. Without prejudice to this objective, the ESCB must support the general economic policies of the EU with a view to attaining the objectives set out in Article 3 TEU. The ESCB is to act in accordance with the principle of an open market economy with free competition, and in compliance with the principles in Article 119 TFEU. The ESCB is moreover to 'contribute' to the smooth conduct of policies pursued by other competent authorities relating to the prudential supervision of credit institutions and the stability of the financial system.[9]

It was integral to the Maastricht settlement that monetary policy structured in the preceding manner was Europeanized. This was reinforced by mandatory Treaty provisions precluding instructions or interference from any outside party, whether that was a nation State or another EU institution. The importance of this principle is reflected in the symmetry of its drafting. It imposes an obligation on the ECB, national central banks, and those involved with their decision-making not to take or seek instructions from any other institution, including EU institutions, bodies, offices, or agencies, any government of a Member State, or any other body. It also imposes a duty on EU institutions, bodies etc and Member State governments to respect this principle and not to seek to influence the members of the decision-making bodies of the ECB or of the national central banks in the performance of their tasks.[10]

The very fact that monetary policy lay truly within the domain of the EU was further reinforced by the Lisbon Treaty provisions on competence. Article 3 TFEU stated clearly that monetary policy for those countries that subscribed to the euro was within the exclusive competence of the EU, with the consequence that only the EU could legislate and adopt legally binding acts, subject to the

---

[6] Art 112(2) EC; Art 283(2) TFEU.   [7] Art 282(1) TFEU.
[8] Art 105(2) EC; Art 127(2) TFEU.   [9] Art 127(5) TFEU.
[10] Art 108 EC; Art 130 TFEU.

caveat that the Member States could do so if empowered by the EU or for the implementation of Union acts.[11]

(b) Economic policy

The Maastricht settlement in relation to economic policy was markedly different. It was built on two related assumptions, preservation of national authority and preservation of national liability. The former was reflected in the fact that Member States retained fiscal authority for national budgets, subject to oversight and coordination from the EU designed to persuade Member States, with the ultimate possibility of sanctions, to balance their budgets and not run excessive deficits. The latter, preservation of national liability, was the quid pro quo for the former. It finds its most powerful expression in the no-bailout provision, Article 125(1) TFEU. This provides in essence that the EU should not be liable for, or assume the commitments of, central governments, regional, local, or other public authorities, or other public bodies, and nor should a Member State be liable for, or assume the commitments of such bodies within another Member State. This injunction was qualified to a limited extent by Article 122(2) TFEU, which allows the Council, on a proposal from the Commission, to grant financial assistance to a Member State that is in difficulty, or is seriously threatened with severe difficulty, caused by natural disasters or exceptional occurrences beyond its control. The message was nonetheless that national governments retained authority over national economic policy, subject to the Treaty rules designed to persuade them to balance their budgets, the corollary being that if they did not do so then the consequential liabilities in terms of debt and economic hardship would remain at the door of the nation State. The precise contours of this national liability, and the scope for any EU or Member State bailout of an ailing Member State, were, however, tested in litigation concerning the legality of the European Stability Mechanism discussed below.[12]

This was the 'deal' struck in Maastricht and the principal features were unaltered in the Lisbon Treaty, although the degree of oversight was actually weakened in the intervening years. The Member States recognized the proximate connection between economic and monetary policy. They understood that the economic health of individual Member State economies could have a marked impact on the valuation of the euro, hence the need for some oversight and coordination of national economic policy. They were, however, mindful of the policy decisions made in and through national budgets, including those of a redistributive nature, and were unwilling to accord the EU too much control over such determinations, whether at the individual or aggregative level.

---

[11] Art 2(1) TFEU.   [12] See below, pp 472–478.

The Maastricht bargain was reflected in the primary Treaty articles and in the Stability and Growth Pact,[13] which fleshed out the details of the schema. It contains, as is well known, two stages: the multilateral surveillance procedure, and the excessive deficit procedure.

Under the multilateral surveillance procedure, Member States must regard their economic policies as a matter of common concern, and coordinate them in the Council.[14] The Council acting on a recommendation from the Commission formulates a draft for the broad guidelines of the economic policies of the Member States and the EU, and reports this to the European Council. The guidelines are discussed by the European Council, and its conclusion forms the basis for a Council recommendation setting out the broad guidelines.[15] It is then for the Council, on the basis of reports from the Commission, to monitor economic developments in the Member States.[16] If it becomes apparent that the economic policies of the Member States are not consistent with the broad economic guidelines, or that they risk jeopardizing the proper functioning of EMU, the Commission may address a warning to the relevant Member States. The Council may make the necessary recommendations to the Member State concerned. The Council acts without taking account of the vote of the Member State concerned.

Under the excessive deficit procedure Member States have an obligation to avoid excessive deficits.[17] The Commission monitors the budgetary situation and government debt in the Member States to identify 'gross errors'.[18] The Commission examines compliance with budget discipline on the basis of two criteria. The first criterion is whether the ratio of the planned or actual government deficit to gross domestic product exceeds a reference value, this being 3 per cent, unless either the ratio has declined substantially and continuously and reached a level that comes close to the reference value, or, alternatively, the excess over the reference value is only exceptional and temporary and the ratio remains close to the reference value. The second criterion is whether the ratio of government debt to gross domestic product exceeds such a reference value, this being 60 per cent, unless the ratio is sufficiently diminishing and approaching the reference value at a satisfactory pace. These reference values are specified in the Protocol on the Excessive Deficit Procedure.[19]

The Commission reports where a Member State does not fulfil these criteria, and may do so if it believes that there is a risk of an excessive deficit in a Member State.[20] The Economic and Financial Committee gives an opinion on

---

[13] Council Regulation (EC) 1466/97 of 7 July 1997 on the strengthening of the surveillance of budgetary positions and the surveillance and coordination of economic policies [1997] OJ L209/1; Council Regulation (EC) 1467/97 of 7 July 1997 on speeding up and clarifying the implementation of the excessive deficit procedure [1997] OJ L209/6.

[14] Art 121(1) TFEU.   [15] Art 121(2) TFEU.   [16] Art 121(3) TFEU.

[17] Art 126(1) TFEU.   [18] Art 126(2) TFEU.

[19] Protocol (No 12) Art 1.   [20] Art 126(3) TFEU.

this report.[21] Where the Commission considers that there is an excessive deficit, or that it may occur, the Commission must address an opinion to the Member State concerned and inform the Council.[22] It is then for the Council, acting on a proposal from the Commission, and having taken account of any observations from the Member State, to decide whether the excessive deficit exists.[23]

Where the Council decides that an excessive deficit exists, it shall adopt, without undue delay, on a recommendation from the Commission, recommendations addressed to the Member State concerned with a view to bringing that situation to an end within a given period.[24] The general rule is that these recommendations are not made public, but where the Council establishes that the Member State has taken no effective action within the requisite period, then the Council may make the recommendations public.[25]

The Treaty then contains provisions specifying what should happen if the Member State fails to put into practice the recommendations of the Council. If this occurs the Council can decide to give notice to the Member State to take, within a specified time limit, measures for the deficit reduction which is judged necessary by the Council in order to remedy the situation, and to submit reports to the Council so that it can examine the adjustment efforts of that Member State.[26]

If the Member State fails to comply with such a decision, the Council may then decide to apply or intensify one or more of the following measures:[27] it can require the Member State to publish additional information, specified by the Council, before issuing bonds and securities; it can invite the European Investment Bank to reconsider its lending policy towards that Member State; it can require the Member State to make a non-interest-bearing deposit of an appropriate size with the Union until the excessive deficit has, in the Council's view, been corrected; and it can impose fines of an appropriate size. The Council must abrogate the preceding decisions and recommendations to the extent that the excessive deficit in the Member State has, in the Council's view, been corrected.[28]

2. The Financial Crisis

(a) Non-compliance

A necessary, albeit not sufficient, condition for the Maastricht settlement to work was that the players had to comply with the rules, more especially those concerned with economic policy, since it was in this context that the EU was heavily

---

[21] Art 126(4) TFEU.   [22] Art 126(5) TFEU.
[23] Art 126(6) TFEU.   [24] Art 126(7) TFEU.
[25] Art 126(8) TFEU.   [26] Art 126(9) TFEU.
[27] Art 126(11) TFEU. [28] Art 126(12) TFEU.

dependent on softer forms of governance couched in terms of coordination and the like. The fragility of the system was exposed by events between 2002 and 2003, in relation to deficits run by France, Germany, Portugal, and Italy. They undertook to balance their budget over the medium term, but departed from their corrective programmes.

This led to the Commission having recourse to legal action when Ecofin placed the excessive deficit procedure in abeyance for France and Germany.[29] The European Court of Justice (ECJ)[30] held that the Council's decision to place the excessive deficit procedure in abeyance was unlawful, since there was no authority for this in the Treaty. However, it rejected the other Commission claim, that the Council's failure to adopt the Commission's recommendations pursuant to what was then Article 104(8) and (9) EC, was a decision that should be annulled. It held that where the requisite majority for the Commission recommendations was not secured in the Council, there was no decision that could be reviewed under Article 230 EC.

This flouting of the system by France and Germany brought the Stability and Growth Pact (SGP) into disrepute. The Commission was placed in a dilemma. If reforms were not made, then resistance to the SGP was likely to continue. If, however, reform significantly weakened the pre-existing regime, then its future effectiveness would correspondingly diminish. Changes were made to the Stability and Growth Pact Regulations,[31] the net effect being to soften and render more discretionary the multilateral surveillance and excessive deficit procedures, thereby rendering it more unlikely that those soft or hard sanctions would be imposed.[32]

(b) System failure

The strains flowing from the events of 2002 to 2003 did not prepare the EU for the euro crisis that had its initial origins in the banking and financial crisis that began in 2008.[33]

---

[29] 2546th Meeting of the Council of the European Union (Economic and Financial Affairs), Brussels, 25 November 2003.

[30] Case C-27/04 *Commission v Council* [2004] ECR I-6649; I Maher, 'Economic Policy Co-ordination and the European Court: Excessive Deficits and ECOFIN Discretion' (2004) 29 ELRev 831.

[31] Council Regulation (EC) 1055/2005 of 27 June 2005 amending Regulation 1466/97 [2005] OJ L174/1; Council Regulation (EC) 1056/2005 of 27 June 2005 amending Regulation 1467/97 [2005] OJ L174/5; J-V Louis, 'The Review of the Stability and Growth Pact' (2006) 43 CMLRev 85.

[32] See, however, W Schelkle, 'EU Fiscal Governance: Hard Law in the Shadow of Soft Law?' (2007) 13 CJEL 705, who argues that the Stability and Growth Pact actually worked somewhat better than hitherto, notwithstanding the softening of the obligations through the 2005 amendments.

[33] <http://ec.europa.eu/economy_finance/focuson/crisis/2010-04_en.htm>; H James, H-W Micklitz, and H Schweitzer, 'The Impact of the Financial Crisis on the European Economic Constitution', EUI Law Working Paper, 2010/05.

Hindsight is a wonderful thing, and it is easy after the event to claim that it was foreseeable in advance. There is indeed some justification for such reasoning, since it was common knowledge that the two parts of the Maastricht settlement were out of sync.[34] It did not require doctoral qualifications in economics to realize that EU control over national budgetary policy was relatively weak, with consequential strain on the euro if the markets perceived budgetary problems in particular Member States. The events from 2002 to 2003 served to reinforce these concerns, in particular where big States might simply flout the existing rules.

The specific problem for the EU began in earnest with the fact that Greece's credit rating to repay its debt was downgraded.[35] This then led to problems for the euro, and to concerns about the budgetary health of some other countries that used the currency. The net impact of these developments was downward pressure on the euro, which was only alleviated when euro countries provided a support package for Greece that satisfied the financial markets. The sovereign debt crisis was overlaid by, and interacted with, the banking crisis that affected some lending institutions that were heavily committed to economic sectors, such as housing, which were hit badly by the downturn in the economic markets. The deeper causality underlying these events is contestable. Maduro identifies two 'narratives' of the current crisis.[36]

The first narrative lays the blame principally on States that either concealed the true nature of their finances when joining the euro, and/or conducted irresponsible fiscal policies. The natural consequence was flight of capital from such States, and increase in the cost of interest payments on debt that reflected the greater risk to those lending money in such circumstances. The economic interdependence generated by the euro meant that that these financial problems became generalized for all States that subscribed to the euro. The democratic manifestation of this self-same problem was, as Maduro states, that 'the interests of the latter states are not taken into account in the former state's democratic process'.[37]

The second narrative as articulated by Maduro regards the markets as the principal cause of the crisis, with unfettered capital flows after creation of the euro leading to large capital movements from northern banks to Member States in southern Europe. The banks 'benefited from the Euro to inject liquidity in other states in search of increased profits', and this 'artificially lowered interest

---

[34] J-V Louis, 'Guest Editorial: The No-Bailout Clause and Rescue Packages' (2010) 47 CMLRev 971.

[35] P de Grauwe, 'Crisis in the Eurozone and How to deal with it' CEPS Policy Brief No 204, February 2010.

[36] M Maduro, 'A New Governance for the European Union and the Euro: Democracy and Justice', European Parliament, Directorate-General for Internal Policies, Policy Department C: Citizens' Rights and Constitutional Affairs, PE 462.484, 2012, 9–10.

[37] ibid 9.

rates in those states, creating a credit bubble.'[38] The democratic dimension of this second narrative was that capital movement had 'a profound impact inside a state without being subject to its democratic control'.[39]

Commentators will continue to debate the relative significance of the two narratives. It is clear, however, that the two problems, sovereign debt and failing banks, were closely related, as noted by Cœuré.[40]

The tight link between sovereign and bank creditworthiness is clearly visible in the high degree of correlation between sovereign CDS[41] premia and bank CDS premia within the same jurisdiction . . . Causality runs both ways: banks' rising funding costs reflect the risk associated with banks' holdings of bonds issued by their own sovereign; and sovereign risk is exacerbated by the contingent liabilities coming from the perception that the government will have to intervene to rescue the domestic financial system. This creates a self-reinforcing loop between bank and sovereign risks, with doubts about the solvency of the sovereigns feeding doubts about the solvency of the banks, and vice versa. Such dynamics are much weaker in euro area countries considered by markets as financially solid. In the US—an example of a well-integrated fiscal and financial union, with a shock-absorbing capacity at the federal level, credible discipline at state level and a centralised mechanism to supervise and resolve banks—there is no correlation between bank and sovereign CDS premia. With hindsight, the 'original sins' of Economic and Monetary Union, an otherwise carefully thought-through and consistent project, were weak fiscal institutions, tolerance of economic imbalances and the lack of an integrated mechanism to supervise and resolve banks.

3. The Legal and Political Response: Assistance

There will doubtless be continued debate as to the ascription of responsibility for the crisis. The reality of the crisis was not, however, to be denied, and it generated a whole raft of legal responses.[42] These can broadly be divided into measures that were designed to provide assistance to euro-area Member States, and those where the primary objective was to strengthen oversight of national budgetary policy. They will be considered in turn.

The EU put in place a range of measures to give assistance to Member States that were in severe economic problems as a result, directly or indirectly, of the euro crisis. The most important common element as between the measures is conditionality, connoting the basic precept that funds are given on strict conditions

---

[38] ibid 9.

[39] ibid 10.

[40] B Cœuré, Member of the Executive Board of the ECB, Institut d'etudes politiques, Paris 20 September 2012, <http://www.ecb.int/press/key/date/2012/html/sp120920.en.html>.

[41] Credit Default Swaps.

[42] Louis (n 34); M Ruffert, 'The European Debt Crisis and European Union Law' (2011) 48 CMLRev 1777; R D'Sa, 'The Legal and Constitutional Nature of the New International Treaties on Economic and Monetary Union from the Perspective of EU Law' (2012) ECL xi.

concerning reforms that must be put in place by the recipient State. There is, however, considerable divergence as to the legal foundation for the measures, and this has created a number of legal difficulties, as will be seen below.

(a) European Financial Stabilisation Mechanism

The European Financial Stabilisation Mechanism (EFSM) is the most straightforward of the assistance measures. The capital was relatively limited, €60 billion, and was financed from the EU budget and from bonds. It was used to give financial assistance to Ireland and Portugal. The EFSM was enacted as a Council Regulation pursuant to Article 122(2) TFEU.[43] This is reflected in its objectives, which are defined in the same terms as Article 122(2) TFEU. Thus Article 1 of the Regulation provides that, with a view to preserving the financial stability of the EU, the Regulation establishes the conditions and procedures under which EU financial assistance may be granted to a Member State which is experiencing, or is seriously threatened with, a severe economic or financial disturbance caused by exceptional occurrences beyond its control. While some commentators questioned whether Article 122(2) TFEU provided a valid base for the EFSM, it can be interpreted so as to legitimate the assistance.[44]

The decision on financial assistance is made by the Council by qualified majority on a proposal from the Commission. The assistance takes the form of a loan or a line of credit extended to the Member State.[45] The conditionality of the financial assistance was emphasized throughout. Thus it was for the Member State seeking assistance to submit a draft financial and economic adjustment programme;[46] the decision to grant the loan contained 'general economic policy conditions...with a view to re-establishing a sound economic or financial situation in the beneficiary Member State and to restoring its capacity to finance itself on the financial markets';[47] and the decision granting the loan had to approve the adjustment programme submitted by the Member State to meet the economic conditions attached to the grant of the EU financial aid.[48]

The terms of loan or credit line were included in a Memorandum of Understanding (MoU) between the Member State and the Commission.[49] The conditionality was reinforced in practical terms by the fact that disbursement of the funds was by way of instalment. The Commission was charged with checking whether the Member State's economic policy was in accord with its adjustment programme and the conditions laid down by the Council. Funds could be withheld if the Commission was not satisfied in this respect.[50]

---

[43] Council Regulation (EU) No 407/2010 of 11 May 2010 establishing a European financial stabilisation mechanism [2010] OJ L118/1.
[44] Louis (n 34).   [45] Reg 407/2010 (n 43) Art 2(1).
[46] ibid Art 3(1).   [47] ibid Art 3(3)(b), Art 3(4)(b).
[48] ibid Art 3(3)(c), Art 3(4)(c).   [49] ibid Art 3(5).   [50] ibid Arts 4–5.

(b) European Financial Stability Facility

The European Financial Stability Facility, EFSF, was more complex legally and more important in terms of the quantum of financial assistance. The EFSF is a company established by the euro countries on 9 May 2010.[51] It was incorporated in Luxembourg under Luxembourg law. Its objective was to preserve the financial stability of Europe's monetary union by providing temporary financial assistance to euro-area Member States if needed. Its overall capacity was €780 billion. This was backed by guarantees given by the 17 euro-area Member States, divided in accordance with their share in the paid-up capital of the ECB. The EFSF Board of Directors is composed of high-level representatives of the 17 euro-area Member States. The Commission and the ECB have observers. The EFSF Board of Directors is headed by the Chairman of the EU's Economic and Financial Committee.

The EFSF was authorized to: issue bonds or other debt instruments on the market to raise the funds needed to provide loans to countries in financial difficulties; intervene in the primary debt market; intervene in the secondary debt markets; act on the basis of a precautionary programme; and finance recapitalizations of financial institutions through loans to governments, including in non-programme countries.

All financial assistance to Member States is linked to appropriate conditionality. Thus the EFSF can only act after a request is made by a euro-area Member State. A country programme must be negotiated with the Commission and the International Monetary Fund, the IMF, and this must be accepted by the euro-area finance ministers and a MoU must then be signed. Thus, for example, the conditions for the Irish programme included overhaul of the banking sector, fiscal adjustment, and measures to enhance growth.

(c) European Stability Mechanism

The principal instrument for financial assistance is now the European Stability Mechanism, ESM,[52] which entered into force on 8 October 2012, although the EFSF continued to finance ongoing programmes for Greece, Portugal, and Ireland.[53] The Euro Group summit agreed on the principle of the ESM in July 2011, but it took time for the details to be ironed out. It was finally agreed on 2 March 2012, and entered into force on 8 October 2012, having survived constitutional challenge to German ratification before the German Federal Constitutional Court.

---

[51] <http://www.efsf.europa.eu/about/index.htm>.
[52] <http://www.esm.europa.eu/>.
[53] Arts 39–40 ESM.

It is important to be clear concerning the legal basis for the ESM. Article 136 TFEU was amended through recourse to the simplified revision procedure, the result being a new paragraph 3, which stated that 'the Member States whose currency is the euro may establish a stability mechanism to be activated if indispensable to safeguard the stability of the euro-area as a whole'.[54] Article 136(3) also stipulates that the granting of any financial assistance under the ESM is strictly subject to conditionality. However, this amendment only enters into force on 1 January 2013, provided that all Member States whose currency is the euro have notified acceptance of the amendment in accordance with their respective constitutional requirements. Failing this, it will enter into force on the first day of the month following the last of the notifications. It is therefore readily apparent that Article 136(3) TFEU could not form the legal basis for the ESM, which came into force on 8 October 2012.

The ESM is thus an intergovernmental organization based on an international treaty between the euro-area Member States, and is located in Luxembourg. It shares facilities with the EFSF. The ESM has a Board of Governors composed of the Finance Ministers from the euro-area Member States, with a Commissioner and the ECB President able to participate as observers. The most important decisions of the Board of Governors require mutual consent, although qualified majority voting pertains in some areas.[55] The ESM also has a Board of Directors, to which tasks can be delegated by the Board of Governors, and the latter appoint a Managing Director responsible for the day-to-day management of the ESM. The ESM has thus been devised as a permanent rather than temporary mechanism for giving financial assistance to those in the euro-area. Its purpose is set out in Article 3.

The purpose of the ESM shall be to mobilise funding and provide stability support under strict conditionality, appropriate to the financial assistance instrument chosen, to the benefit of ESM Members which are experiencing, or are threatened by, severe financing problems, if indispensable to safeguard the financial stability of the euro area as a whole and of its Member States. For this purpose, the ESM shall be entitled to raise funds by issuing financial instruments or by entering into financial or other agreements or arrangements with ESM Members, financial institutions or other third parties.

Speed, certainty, and flexibility are central to the functioning of the ESM, as the following extract reveals.[56]

In order to effectively perform its purpose of providing stability support to euro area countries, the ESM pursues the following objectives with respect to funding: (i) the ESM must be able to react quickly to unexpected market developments and to that end it will

---

[54] European Council Decision 2011/199 of 25 March 2011 amending Art 136 TFEU with regard to a stability mechanism for Member States whose currency is the euro [2011] OJ L91/1.

[55] Arts 4–5 ESM.

[56] Frequently Asked Questions on the ESM, 9, <http://www.esm.europa.eu/pdf/FAQ%20ESM%2012112012.pdf>.

build up liquidity buffers during periods of heightened systemic risk to ensure market access even in difficult market conditions; (ii) the ESM must be capable of raising predictable amounts over an extended period of time covering various disbursement schedules, as well as unexpected amounts on relatively short notice; (iii) to achieve the aim of establishing itself as a reliable issuer in a difficult market environment, the ESM's funding portfolio will comprise liquid instruments with a simple, plain vanilla structure.

To this end, the ESM is entitled to raise funds by issuing financial instruments or by entering into financial or other agreements with ESM Members, financial institutions, or other third parties. The ESM has a total subscribed capital of €700 billion, €80 billion of which is in the form of paid-in capital provided by the euro-area Member States in five instalments of €16 billion. The ESM can also dispose of committed 'callable capital' from euro-area Member States up to €620 billion. There can be a general capital call, in order to increase lending capacity; there can be a capital call to replenish paid-in capital, if, for example, a beneficiary State has not repaid the sum due; and there can also be an emergency capital call, used, for example, to avoid default of an ESM payment obligation to its creditors. The principles governing disbursement of ESM funds are set out in Article 12.

1. If indispensable to safeguard the financial stability of the euro area as a whole and of its Member States, the ESM may provide stability support to an ESM Member subject to strict conditionality, appropriate to the financial assistance instrument chosen. Such conditionality may range from a macro-economic adjustment programme to continuous respect of pre-established eligibility conditions.

2. Without prejudice to Article 19, ESM stability support may be granted through the instruments provided for in Articles 14 to 18.

The grant of assistance under the ESM is conditional from 1 March 2013 on ratification by the applicant State of the Treaty on Stability, Governance and Coordination, known as the Fiscal Compact. The ESM may provide stability support by: giving loans to countries in financial difficulties; providing precautionary financial assistance in the form of a credit line; financing recapitalizations of financial institutions through loans to governments including in non-programme countries; and purchasing bonds of an ESM Member State in primary and secondary debt markets.[57] When granting stability support, the ESM shall aim to fully cover its financing and operating costs and include an appropriate margin.[58] The ESM is empowered to borrow on the capital markets from banks, financial institutions etc for the performance of its purpose.[59] The schema of the ESM is therefore for a State to apply for stability support, Article 13 ESM, which can then be granted through one of the mechanisms such as loans,

---

[57] Arts 14–20 ESM.
[58] Art 20(1) ESM. For all financial assistance instruments, pricing is detailed in a pricing guideline adopted by the Board of Governors, Art 20(2) ESM.
[59] Art 21(1) ESM.

recapitalization etc listed in Articles 14 to 18 of the ESM. A few words are necessary to explain these various forms of assistance.

The loans[60] are designed to assist ESM Members that have significant financing needs, but cannot access funds in the markets, either because lenders are unwilling to furnish loans, or because they will only do so at high prices that could not be sustained by the public coffers. The request for support is made to the Chair of the Board of Governors.[61] It is then for the Commission, in liaison with the ECB and wherever possible the IMF, to assess the financial needs of the applicant State and whether its public debt is sustainable. If a stability support loan is granted, the Commission, together with the ECB, negotiates a MoU with the State, which specifies the conditions attached to the financial assistance. The Managing Director of the ESM prepares the financial assistance facility agreement (FFA).[62] It is, however, the Commission that signs the MoU on behalf of the ESM, subject to approval by the Board of Governors.[63] The Board of Directors then approves the FFA and, where applicable, the disbursement of the first tranche of assistance.[64] It is the Commission once again that is accorded responsibility for ensuring that the conditions attached to the assistance are met.[65] The 'sanction' for non-compliance with the conditions is that further tranches of assistance can be withheld.

The objective of ESM precautionary financial assistance is, as the title suggests, preventive.[66] The objective is provision of lines of credit to prevent crisis situations from occurring by giving States such assistance before they face major difficulties raising funds in the capital markets. The lines of credit from the ESM are therefore designed to maintain access to market financing by bolstering the credibility of the State's economic record.

The financial crisis in the EU involved not only sovereign debt problems, but also severe difficulties in the banking sector. This is the rationale for the ESM covering recapitalization of financial institutions, the aim being 'to preserve financial stability of the euro area as a whole and of its Member States by addressing those specific cases in which the roots of a crisis situation are primarily located in the financial sector and not directly related to fiscal or structural policies'.[67] The assistance is therefore designed to 'limit the contagion of financial stress by ensuring the capacity of a beneficiary ESM Member's government to finance recapitalisation at sustainable borrowing costs and facilitate financial sector repair so that vulnerabilities are eliminated.'[68] The claimant State[69] must

---

[60] Art 16 ESM.　　　　[61] Art 13 ESM.
[62] Art 13(3) ESM.　　　[63] Art 13(4) ESM.
[64] Art 13(5) ESM.　　　[65] Art 13(7) ESM.
[66] Art 14 ESM.　　　　[67] Frequently Asked Questions (n 56) 12.
[68] ibid 12–13.
[69] The ESM is predicated on loans granted to euro-area Member States. However, at the June 2012 euro-area summit it was proposed that the ESM could recapitalize banks directly, provided that there was an effective supervisory mechanism involving the ECB.

demonstrate the lack of alternative financing options. It must therefore show that the financial institution is unable to address its problems through private sector solutions, such as new investment, and that the State cannot recapitalize the financial institution without serious consequences for its own financial stability. It must also be shown that the financial institution or institutions are of systemic relevance or pose a serious threat to the financial stability of the euro-area as a whole or of its Member States.

The ESM may in addition engage in primary market purchases of bonds or other debt securities[70] issued by ESM Members 'to allow them to maintain or restore their relationship with the dealer/investment community and therefore reduce the risk of a failed auction'.[71] Such bond purchases are subject to conditionality and can be made to complement assistance granted through loans. The ESM can also use secondary market support to aid the functioning of government debt markets of ESM Members 'in exceptional circumstances where the lack of market liquidity threatens financial stability, with a risk of pushing sovereign interest rates towards unsustainable levels and creating refinancing problems for the banking system of the ESM Member concerned'.[72]

(d) European Central Bank

The ECB has, unsurprisingly, provided advice and been consulted throughout the financial crisis. The no-bailout clause in Article 125 TFEU, and the prohibition on credit facilities to national governments in Article 123 TFEU, however, precluded the grant of direct financial assistance to States that were in financial difficulty. Notwithstanding this provision, the ECB, acting pursuant to Article 127(2) TFEU, which provides inter alia that the ECB shall define and implement the monetary policy of the EU, made a formal decision establishing a securities markets programme, which sanctioned ECB intervention in the euro-area private and public debt markets.[73] Article 1 of the Decision states that:

Under the terms of this Decision, Eurosystem central banks may purchase the following: (a) on the secondary market, eligible marketable debt instruments issued by the central governments or public entities of the Member States whose currency is the euro; and (b) on the primary and secondary markets, eligible marketable debt instruments issued by private entities incorporated in the euro area.

The ECB acted pursuant to this scheme to purchase State debt from secondary markets in excess of €200 billion. The scheme was intended to be temporary, and was terminated in September 2012.[74]

---

[70] Art 17 ESM.
[71] Frequently Asked Questions (n 56) 15.   [72] ibid 17.
[73] 2010/281/: Decision of the European Central Bank of 14 May 2010 establishing a securities markets programme [2010] OJ L124/8.
[74] <http://www.ecb.int/press/pr/date/2012/html/pr120906_1.en.html>.

However, it was replaced by Outright Monetary Transactions, OMTs, which concern transactions in secondary sovereign bond markets 'that aim at safeguarding an appropriate monetary policy transmission and the singleness of the monetary policy'.[75] The ECB has made clear that conditionality attached to an appropriate EFSF/ESM programme is a necessary condition for OMTs, and the ECB is keen to involve the IMF in the design of the country-specific conditionality and the monitoring of the programme. The programme can take the form of a full EFSF/ESM macroeconomic adjustment, or it can be a precautionary programme, provided that it includes the possibility of EFSF/ESM primary market purchases. There are no ex ante quantitative limits on the size of OMTs. The rationale for OMTs was brought out forcefully by the President of the ECB.[76]

OMTs will enable us to address severe distortions in government bond markets which originate from, in particular, unfounded fears on the part of investors of the reversibility of the euro. Hence, under appropriate conditions, we will have a fully effective backstop to avoid destructive scenarios with potentially severe challenges for price stability in the euro area.

The legality of OMTs has not gone unquestioned. The ECB President was asked as to its compatibility with Article 123 TFEU, to which the response was that it only precluded purchases on the primary and not the secondary bond market.[77] This answer might be formally compatible with the wording of Article 123, but reconciliation with the substantive aim is more difficult, since it matters little whether assistance to a State is provided directly through purchase of national debt instruments, or indirectly through such purchase on the secondary bond market.

(e) ESM, assistance, and Treaty imperatives: prohibition on bailouts

The preceding discussion has been concerned with the range of measures taken to provide assistance to Member States that encountered severe economic difficulties associated with the financial and euro crisis. These measures have not been legally unproblematic.[78] The ensuing analysis focuses on the legal problems flowing from the ESM, more especially because it is to be the permanent mechanism for granting assistance.

---

[75] ibid.

[76] M Draghi, President of the ECB, Frankfurt am Main, 6 September 2012, <http://www.ecb.int/press/pressconf/2012/html/is120906.en.html>.

[77] ibid.

[78] Louis (n 34); Ruffert (n 42); I Pernice, M Wendel, L Otto, K Bettge, M Mylnarski, and M Schwarz, *A Democratic Solution to the Crisis, Reform Steps towards a Democratically Based Economic and Financial Constitution for Europe* (Nomos, 2012); K Armstrong, 'Stability, Coordination and Governance: Was a Treaty such a Good Idea?', <http://eutopialaw.com/2012/03/08/stability-coordination-and-governance-was-a-treaty-such-a-good-idea/>; K Armstrong, 'Responding to the Economic Crisis: Public Law in a Post-Lisbon Age', <http://eutopialaw.com/2012/02/21/responding-to-the-economic-crisis-public-law-in-a-post-lisbon-age/>.

There was a legal challenge to the ESM in the *Pringle* case.[79] The claimants raised a number of arguments concerning the legality of the ESM, inter alia, that it was inconsistent with the Lisbon Treaty because it was incompatible with the no-bailout clause in Article 125 TFEU. This argument had some prima facie plausibility. The informed observer might well conclude that the ESM was doing just that, bailing out those Member States such as Greece, Ireland, and Portugal that were in serious financial difficulty. The very language of bailout was deployed repeatedly in the press and media coverage to capture the assistance provided to such Member States. It was nonetheless unlikely that the ECJ would condemn the ESM as being contrary to EU law, since this would precipitate further crisis in the eurozone. The interesting issue for seasoned court watchers was precisely how the ECJ would save the ESM from its alleged incompatibility with Article 125 TFEU.

(i) Teleology, aim, and interpretive consequence

It is common for textual argumentation as to the scope of a particular Treaty article to be shaped by background teleological premises, assumptions, or objectives. These may be apparent on the face of the judgment. They may be implicit in the Court's reasoning. The degree of work done by such argumentation will depend in part at least on how far the Court believes that it can go toward its desired conclusion through purely textual analysis, and how far it is willing to give voice to the values and assumptions that shape its textual reasoning.

There were hints of teleology in the legal contributions of Member States. Thus the German view in *Pringle* viewed Article 125 from a broader perspective, which was that the ESM was addressing a problem that was not envisaged by the Treaty framers, and hence the prohibition in Article 125 should be narrowly construed in this instance. On this view Article 125 was designed with individual cases in mind, preventing bailouts of particular States when national fiscal policy or irresponsibility led to problems confined to that State. Article 125, and the more general schema in Articles 122 to 126 TFEU, was not on this view structured so as to cope with the circumstance where the very future of the euro was at stake.

The asymmetry in the EU's power over monetary and economic union was no secret. It was evident from the outset of the Maastricht settlement. The proximate connection between the health of national fiscal policy and the health of the euro was readily apparent. Article 125 TFEU rightly embodied national fiscal liability as the price of EU limited oversight of economic policy. This was fine as a way of avoiding the moral hazard of the fiscally irresponsible Member State,

---

[79] Case C-370/12 *Pringle v Government of Ireland, Ireland and the Attorney General*, 27 November 2012.

which could be left to bear its own losses. The Treaty, however, contained no ready answer where economic difficulties of multiple States threatened to bring the whole euro-house down. Article 122(2) TFEU legitimated grant of EU financial assistance, but leaving aside interpretive difficulties concerning the scope of this Article, the EU did not possess funds on the scale needed to cope with the problem. The consequence was that assistance had to be provided by the Member States; considerations of moral hazard had to be severely compromised and could only be given expression through strict conditions attached to funding assistance.

This sentiment has been best captured in an academic context by Tuori, through his invocation of the idea of a double telos. There was the telos embodied in Article 125 itself, expressive of the view that fiscal liability remained with the particular Member State. This should nonetheless be read subject to a 'second-order telos' where the very survival of the euro was at stake.[80]

[T]he no-bailout provision clearly aims to induce Member States to responsible fiscal policy and to ward off the moral hazard which awareness of other Member States' coming to the rescue in a sovereign debt crisis could entail. This aim also justifies treating different forms of financial assistance in equal terms under this provision. But a teleological interpretation should heed not only the particular *telos* of the no-bailout clause but also the more general objective of the regulative whole Art 125(1) is part of. And this 'second-order' *telos* of the no-bailout clause undoubtedly includes the financial stability of the euro area as a whole. This argument supports the legal impeccability of Member-State assistance, in spite of the no-bailout clause and the inapplicability of the emergency provision in Art 122(2) TFEU. But it also justifies and even presupposes, at least to a certain extent, the 'strict condition-ality' of assistance. The viewpoint of moral hazard retains its relevance even when retreat from stringent bailout prohibition is considered legally possible.

This rationale for the ESM coheres with the economic reality and is reflected in key provisions of the ESM. Thus Article 3 and Article 12 ESM are both expressly predicated on assistance being necessary to safeguard the financial stability of the euro-area as a whole. So, too, is Article 136(3) TFEU, the amendment to the Lisbon Treaty that will provide a Treaty foundation for ESM-type assistance when the amendment comes into force. This reading reconciles Article 125 and Article 136(3) TFEU: the no-bailout provision is qualified so as to allow such assistance if the financial stability of the euro-area as a whole is in jeopardy.

Advocate General Kokott adverted to teleological argumentation in support of her textual analysis of the scope of Article 125. She focused on Member State sovereignty to help justify a reading of Article 125 that would uphold the legality of the ESM. It was sovereignty in the form of the capacity of Member States to protect their shared interest that was paramount.[81]

---

[80] K Tuori, 'The European Financial Crisis—Constitutional Aspects and Implications', EUI Working Papers, Law 2012/28, 24.

[81] Case C-370/12 *Pringle* (n 79) [139]–[140] AG Kokott.

If a prohibition under European Union law even on indirect assumption of liabilities were recognised, that would hinder the Member States from deploying financial resources in order to attempt to prevent the negative effects of the bankruptcy of another Member State on their own economic and financial situation. Given the mutual interdependence of the Member States' individual economic activities which is encouraged and intended under European Union law, substantial damage could be caused by the bankruptcy of one Member State to other Member States also. That damage might possibly be so extensive that an additional consequence would be to endanger the survival of monetary union, as submitted by a number of parties to the proceedings.

There is no question here of finding that such a danger to the stability of the monetary union exists or of examining how such a danger should best be combated. It must only be emphasized that a broad interpretation of Article 125 TFEU would, also in such circumstances, deprive the Member States of the power to avert the bankruptcy of another Member State and of the ability thereby to attempt to avert damage to themselves. In my opinion, such an extensive restriction on the sovereignty of the Member States to adopt measures for their own protection cannot be founded on a broad teleological interpretation of a legal provision the wording of which does not unambiguously state that restriction.

(ii) Text, underlying purpose, and interpretive consequence

It is axiomatic that courts will normally ground their preferred conclusion in text-driven reasoning, even if this textual interpretation is informed by teleological reasoning. The hallmark of a good judgment is, moreover, that the court will consider the underlying purpose of a legal provision when interpreting it. This purpose will then be used to help determine the scope of the particular provision. The ECJ in *Pringle* is to be commended for doing just this when interpreting Article 125 TFEU. The judgment also reveals the difficulties in moving from purpose to interpretive consequence.

The ECJ's textual conclusion was informed by arguments from the Advocate General, Commission, and some intervening Member States, who argued for a narrow construction of Article 125, such that it would only preclude bailouts in the form of guarantees of the debts of another State, in circumstances where no conditions were attached and there was no obligation to repay. This argumentation is reflected in the ECJ's reasoning and conclusion.

It held that Article 125 was not intended to prohibit either the EU or the Member States from granting any form of financial assistance whatever to another Member State, since the EU could grant assistance pursuant to Article 122(2) TFEU.[82] The ECJ reinforced this conclusion by arguing that the wording of Article 123 TFEU, which prohibits the ECB and national central banks from granting 'overdraft facilities or any other type of credit facility', was stricter than

---

[82] Case C-370/12 *Pringle* (n 79) [130]–[131].

that in Article 125 TFEU, which thereby lent support to the view that the no-bailout clause was not intended to prohibit any kind of financial assistance to a Member State.[83]

It was therefore necessary, according to the ECJ, to consider the objective underlying Article 125 to decide precisely what forms of financial assistance were prohibited.[84] The ECJ adverted to preparatory work on the Maastricht Treaty and correctly concluded that the aim of Article 125 TFEU was to ensure that Member States followed sound budgetary policy.[85]

> The prohibition laid down in Article 125 TFEU ensures that the Member States remain subject to the logic of the market when they enter into debt, since that ought to prompt them to maintain budgetary discipline. Compliance with such discipline contributes at Union level to the attainment of a higher objective, namely maintaining the financial stability of the monetary union.

The ECJ held that it followed from this objective that Article 125 TFEU must be held to 'prohibit the EU and Member States from granting financial assistance as a result of which the incentive of the recipient Member State to conduct a sound budgetary policy is diminished'.[86]

This reasoning is surely correct. The purpose of Article 125 was to engender sound national budgetary policy. It was to ensure that States remained subject to the logic of the market when they became indebted, and hence any assistance that would, in the words of the Court, 'diminish' the incentive of the Member State to conduct sound budgetary policy should fall within the prohibition of Article 125 TFEU.

It is the ECJ's conclusions drawn from this premise that are more contestable: provided that the State remains ultimately responsible to its creditors, and provided that conditions are attached to assistance designed to foster sound budgetary policy, then it is not prohibited by Article 125 TFEU.[87] Judged by this criterion, the ESM was said to be fine, because assistance pursuant to ESM Articles 14 to 18 did not render Member States the guarantor of the debts of the recipient State, nor did they assume the debts of that State.[88] The recipient State remained liable to repay the sums lent, which also included an appropriate margin. This was also said to be true for the assistance in the form of bond purchases on the primary and secondary markets pursuant to Articles 17 to 18 ESM, which were regarded as comparable to loans from the recipient State, which retained ultimate responsibility in terms of repayment.[89]

The ECJ therefore concluded that the ESM was compatible with Article 125 TFEU because the participating Member States were not 'liable for the commitments of a Member State which receives stability support and nor do they assume

---

[83] ibid [132].   [84] ibid [133].   [85] ibid [135].   [86] ibid [136].
[87] ibid [137], [143].   [88] ibid [138]–[139].   [89] ibid [140]–[141].

those commitments, within the meaning of Article 125 TFEU'.[90] This conclusion was reinforced by the fact that stability support pursuant to the ESM would not be given merely when a State was experiencing difficulty, but only where it was indispensable to safeguard the financial stability of the euro-area as a whole.[91]

The compatibility of the ESM with Article 125 TFEU was thereby secured through textual interpretation, albeit the text being read against the implicit imperative that a contrary conclusion would be very bad news for the eurozone. This conclusion was, as stated at the outset of this section, scarcely surprising, but it comes at a 'price', which is that Article 125 is denuded of much content. It can be argued that there is a fit between the ECJ's articulation of the purpose behind Article 125 and its interpretation of the scope of that provision. The economic reality renders the neat juncture between purpose and interpretation a good deal more tenuous.

The judgment is expressly predicated on the assumption that a Member State should remain subject to the logic of the market in relation to its debts, this will instil budgetary discipline, and that any assistance that diminishes the incentive to maintain sound budgetary policy is prohibited. This premise is used by the Court to yield the conclusion that any assistance is allowed, provided only that it is conditional and that ultimate responsibility for repayment resides with the recipient State. The fit between underlying purposes and interpretive realization is nonetheless more contestable. The very idea that conditional assistance given by the EFSF and the ESM does not diminish incentives for sound budgetary policy is difficult to accept for a number of reasons.

First, there is a common thread that runs through the various forms of stability financing in the ESM.[92] It is simple, fundamental and nonetheless easy to lose sight of when reading the detailed provisions: the assistance is provided on terms or in circumstances that would not be provided by the ordinary markets. That is the very raison d'être of the ESM. There is in that sense a tension between the purpose underlying Article 125 and its interpretive realization by the Court. Thus to take but one example, ESM intervention to buy bonds of the ailing State on the primary market may well, as the ECJ stated, be in effect a loan that has to be repaid. This, however, ignores the fact that such assistance is required because the market was either unwilling to provide the assistance, or only willing to do so at interest rates that the State could not afford. The existence of ESM stability support thus diminishes the incentive for budgetary probity by holding out the possibility of assistance in circumstances, or on terms, that the market would not do so. This is not altered by the fact that the recipient State must pay an 'appropriate margin' for the financial assistance granted,[93] since this will still be considerably less than the cost of such assistance from the ordinary market.

---

[90] ibid [146].   [91] ibid [142].
[92] Arts 14–18 ESM.   [93] Art 20 ESM.

Secondly, the preceding argument is not met merely because the assistance is given subject to strict conditionality. It is tempting to suggest that any diminution in national budgetary responsibility is offset by the strict conditions imposed, which have to be met before successive tranches of funding are released. It might be argued further that the stringency of these conditions is attested to by the very tough economic policies that recipient States have had to introduce, and the severe political backlash that this has produced. It is undoubtedly true that the conditions imposed have been stringent, and that the impact on national workers has been severe. We must nonetheless remain focused on the key issue, which is whether the ESM regime diminishes the incentive for national financial probity and hence falls within the prohibition in Article 125. The operative inquiry must therefore be the impact on that incentive flowing from a bailout subject to strict conditions, as compared to the incentive if there was no bailout, the market failed to provide the funds needed by the State, or did so only at a prohibitive cost. When the inquiry is put in these terms the answer becomes apparent. If a State knows that there is a strong chance that it will be bailed out if it is financially irresponsible, on terms that the market would not supply, this will, other things being equal, diminish its sense of budgetary responsibility as compared to the State for which no bailout is available. This is not altered by the strict conditions imposed on the former, with its impact on national economic life, because the disruptive results on such life would be even greater in the latter circumstance where no bailout is available. If the markets fail to provide the funds, or do so at a cost that is not sustainable for the State, then this would rapidly lead to inability to pay wages, debt, and the like, with dramatic results for employment and economic stability. There would, moreover, be no orderly recovery plan.

Thirdly, the recipient State may well default on repayment, or so extend the repayment period that the obligation to reimburse becomes more theoretical than real. The larger the assistance, and the smaller the economy, the less likely that repayment will be an economic reality. This is precisely why the ESM has provisions to deal with non-repayment, which are based on the assumption that other ESM members will pick up the unpaid tab.[94]

(f) ESM, assistance, and Treaty imperatives: competence and EU institutions

The problems concerning the legality of the ESM were not solely concerned with its compatibility with Article 125 TFEU. The *Pringle* case also raised broader issues concerning the competence of the EU and the capacity of the Member States to pursue objectives outside the context of the Lisbon Treaty.[95]

---

[94] Art 25 ESM.   [95] Case C-370/12 *Pringle* (n 79).

(i) ESM and categories of EU competence

The essence of this aspect of the claimant's argument in *Pringle* was simple: the ESM was in substance designed to ensure price stability and save the euro, this was monetary policy, which fell within the EU's exclusive competence;[96] the Member States therefore had no competence to adopt legally binding acts in the form of an international treaty, the ESM.[97] Thus on this view, even if the ESM was not incompatible with the no-bailout provision in Article 125 TFEU, any such assistance would have to be provided within the framework of the Lisbon Treaty. This was what the Member States intended through the amendment adding the new Article 136(3) TFEU, but this was not yet ratified when it was sought to bring the ESM into effect, hence recourse to the mechanism of an international agreement.

There was force in the claimant's contention that the ESM was in reality directed towards monetary policy, given the wording of Articles 3 and 12 ESM, which predicate assistance on the fact that it is indispensable to the financial stability of the euro area as a whole. The Member States nonetheless predictably contended that the ESM was concerned with economic policy, which is not within the EU's exclusive competence. The ECJ, equally predictably in this regard, reached the same conclusion, although the reasoning was strained. It held that the primary objective of monetary policy was price stability,[98] but that this was distinct from the stability of the euro area as a whole, which was the objective of Article 136(3) TFEU and the ESM. The ECJ justified this conclusion on the ground that even 'though the stability of the euro area may have repercussions on the stability of the currency used within that area, an economic policy measure cannot be treated as equivalent to a monetary policy measure for the sole reason that it may have indirect effects on the stability of the euro'.[99] This is, with respect, legal formalism, which may explain why the ECJ moved rapidly on in its judgment without further reasoning on the point.[100] In economic terms the stability of the euro area as a whole is surely a condition precedent to price stability within that area. To put the same point conversely, it is not clear how there could be price stability in relation to the euro, given the serious instability of the euro-area as a whole.

The claimant further contended that if the subject matter of the amended Article 136(3) TFEU was regarded as falling within economic policy, Member State competence to act should nonetheless be held to be pre-empted because the EU had occupied the relevant area. The ECJ rejected this contention.[101] It held that since Articles 2(3) and 5(1) TFEU restricted the EU's role in economic policy to the adoption of coordinating measures, the TEU and TFEU did not

---

[96] Art 3(1)(c) TFEU.   [97] Art 2(1) TFEU.
[98] Case C-370/12 *Pringle* (n 79) [54], [94].   [99] ibid [56], [96].
[100] The ECJ reiterated the same reasoning in [96].   [101] ibid [102]–[107].

therefore confer any specific power on the EU to establish a stability mechanism of the kind envisaged by Decision 2011/199 that brought about the amendment in Article 136(3) TFEU.[102] It followed, said the ECJ, from Article 4(1) and Article 5(2) TEU that competence in this regard remained with the Member States, who could therefore lawfully conclude the ESM.[103] It also followed that Article 136(3) was regarded as merely 'confirming'[104] Member State power to establish a stability mechanism, and created no new Union competence.[105]

(ii) ESM and EU institutions

The ECJ's preceding conclusion as to the legality of the Member States making an international agreement outside the confines of the Lisbon Treaty still left open the legality of the EU institutions participating in such an agreement. The Commission and ECB are, as seen above, integral to the ESM regime. It is the Commission, in liaison with the ECB, which deals with the initial request for assistance and decides whether the criteria in Article 13(1) ESM are met; it is the Commission, in liaison with the ECB and IMF, which negotiates the MoU that contains the conditionality requirements to be met by the applicant State, Article 13(3) ESM; it is the Commission that signs the MoU, Article 13(4) ESM; and it is the Commission together with the ECB and IMF that reports on compliance with the conditions, this being necessary for the release of funding, which is granted in tranches.

The issues of principle raised by such involvement are considered in more detail when analysing the Treaty on Stability, Coordination and Governance (TSCG) below. The ECJ's response to this institutional point in *Pringle* was brief and Delphic. It held that even though the ESM made use of the Commission and ECB, that fact could not affect 'the validity of Decision 2011/199, which in itself provides only for the establishment of a stability mechanism by the Member States and is silent on any possible role for the Union's institutions in that connection'.[106] The nature of this response may be explained in part because the ECJ was dealing with a question concerning whether Article 136(3) TFEU could be introduced pursuant to the simplified revision procedure. The legal reality was, as we have seen, that the ESM took effect as an international agreement because Article 136(3) had not yet come into effect. The legal reality was, however, also that the EU institutions were central to the ESM regime, and the ECJ provides scant if any guidance as to the legitimacy of such involvement.

This reticence was doubtless due in part to the legal difficulties that might be raised by such involvement. It was also doubtless due to the fact that when Article 136(3) comes into effect it will provide a more secure foundation for EU institutional involvement with the kind of assistance dealt with via the ESM.

---

[102] ibid [64].   [103] ibid [68], [109].   [104] ibid [72].
[105] ibid [73].   [106] ibid [74].

It is true that Article 136(3) does not explicitly address EU institutional involvement, but it is a good deal easier to infer EU institutional capacity to participate in such a schema when it is grounded in the primary Treaty itself.

The TSCG, by way of contrast, was created after the veto by the UK and prevented the desired ends from being undertaken within the framework of the Lisbon Treaty, and there is nothing analogous to Article 136(3) TFEU.

4. The Legal and Political Response: Supervision

The grant of assistance to Member States in serious financial difficulty is but one half of the overall strategy to cope with the euro crisis. The other half is increased supervision over national financial institutions. This has assumed various forms. Thus the regulatory apparatus for banking, securities, insurance, and occupational pensions has been thoroughly overhauled.[107] The discussion within this section will concentrate primarily on provisions designed to render economic union more effective through increased oversight over national economic policy. These reforms have been undertaken precisely because of the proximate connection between economic union and monetary union.

(a) Change pursuant to the Lisbon Treaty: the six-pack and the two-pack

The legislative framework for economic union was amended through the 'six-pack' of measures in 2011,[108] which were enacted pursuant to Articles 121, 126, and 136 TFEU.[109] The measures were designed to render economic union more

---

[107] Regulation (EU) No 1093/2010 of the European Parliament and of the Council of 24 November 2010 establishing a European Supervisory Authority (European Banking Authority) [2010] OJ L331/12; Regulation (EU) No 1095/2010 of the European Parliament and of the Council of 24 November 2010 establishing a European Supervisory Authority (European Securities and Markets Authority) [2010] OJ L331/84; Regulation (EU) No 1094/2010 of the European Parliament and of the Council of 24 November 2010 establishing a European Supervisory Authority (European Insurance and Occupational Pensions Authority) [2010] OJ L331/4.

[108] <http://ec.europa.eu/economy_finance/economic_governance/index_en.htm>,

[109] Regulation (EU) No 1175/2011 of the European Parliament and of the Council of 16 November 2011 amending Regulation (EC) No 1466/97 on the strengthening of the surveillance of budgetary positions and the surveillance and coordination of economic policies [2011] OJ L306/12; Council Regulation (EU) No 1177/2011 of 8 November 2011 amending Regulation (EC) No 1467/97 on speeding up and clarifying the implementation of the excessive deficit procedure [2011] OJ L306/33; Regulation (EU) No 1173/2011 of the European Parliament and of the Council of 16 November 2011 on the effective enforcement of budgetary surveillance in the euro area [2011] OJ L306/1; Council Directive 2011/85/EU of 8 November 2011 on requirements for budgetary frameworks of the Member States [2011] OJ L306/41; Regulation (EU) No 1176/2011 of the European Parliament and of the Council of 16 November 2011 on the prevention and correction of macroeconomic imbalances [2011] OJ L306/25; Regulation (EU) No 1174/2011 of the European Parliament and of the Council of 16 November 2011 on enforcement measures to correct macroeconomic imbalances in the euro area [2011] OJ L306/8.

effective by tightening the two parts of the schema, surveillance and excessive deficit, the details of which were contained in the Stability and Growth Pact (SGP).[110] The Commission also proposed a further two measures, which, at the time of writing, are going through the legislative process.[111]

The legislation is complex, in part because of the inherent difficulty of the subject matter, and in part because much of it amends previous measures, notably the principal regulations of the SGP. It can therefore be difficult to see the overall picture. What follows does not purport to be a detailed exegesis of these measures; that would be beyond the scope and purpose of this chapter. The objective is rather to highlight the principal changes made by the new measures, and how they affect the pre-existing schema concerning economic union. This was, as we have seen, organized around preventative measures that focused on surveillance of national budgets and corrective measures designed to deal with situations where the Member State had incurred excessive deficit.

(i) Multilateral surveillance and budgets: common timing, common format, and independent verification

There have been a number of changes designed to enhance budgetary oversight by focusing on its timing, the format of national budgetary determinations, and the need for these to be independently verified.

The introduction of the European Semester is crucial in this respect.[112] It is concerned with the timing and coordination of economic and fiscal policy planning. Prior to 2010, the EU discussed economic policy in the spring and fiscal policy in the autumn. This was modified in 2010 so as to ensure that all such policy is analysed at the same time. Thus EU-level discussion of matters such as fiscal policy, macroeconomic imbalances, financial sector issues, and growth-enhancing structural reforms now occurs during the European semester, the first half of the year. It is crucial to this schema that this takes place before governments draw up their draft budgets and present them to national parliaments for debate in the national semester, which is the second half of the year.

This will be complemented by duties imposed on Member States that use the euro.[113] The duties include a common budgetary timeline, such that the Member States must publish medium-term fiscal plans in accordance with

[110] SGP (n 13).

[111] Proposal for a Regulation of the European Parliament and of the Council on the strengthening of economic and budgetary surveillance of Member States experiencing or threatened with serious difficulties with respect to their financial stability in the euro area, COM(2011) 819; Proposal for a Regulation of the European Parliament and of the Council on common provisions for monitoring and assessing draft budgetary plans and ensuring the correction of excessive deficit of the Member States in the euro area, COM(2011) 821.

[112] Reg 1466/97 (n 13) Art 2-a, as amended by Reg 1175/2011 (n 109) Art 1(3).

[113] COM(2011) 821 (n 111).

their medium-term budgetary framework, which must be based on independent macroeconomic forecasts, no later than 15 April, with draft budget laws made public no later than 15 October and adopted by government no later than 31 December. The draft budget that has to be produced must be very detailed in order to test for compliance with the conditions in the SGP. It must be submitted to the Commission and the euro group by 15 October. If the Commission detects serious non-compliance with the precepts in the SGP, it can request an amended draft budget,[114] and can, if necessary, adopt an opinion on the draft budget by the end of November.

The objective of these temporal reforms is to ensure that the EU can comment in a timely and orderly manner on forthcoming budgetary proposals from the euro-area Member States. Fire prevention is clearly regarded as preferable to fire fighting, and knowing national budgetary plans in accord with a common time line and before they have been agreed at national level is regarded as crucial in this respect. The scars of recent years are etched in the very language used in the legislation, which resonates with the shared consequences of individual Member State decisions, and the consequential need for centralized controls. Thus the recitals relate how the sovereign debt crisis demonstrated the need for 'common financial backstops', given that euro-area Member States 'share enhanced spill-overs from their budgetary policy'.[115] These scars are evident once again in legislation that imposes extra surveillance on States in receipt of assistance under one EFSF, ESM etc, or where there are special reasons to fear for their financial stability within the euro-area.[116]

(ii) Multilateral surveillance and budgets: strengthening the substantive obligations

Further changes to the surveillance mechanism are substantive and require Member States to make significant progress towards medium-term budgetary objectives for their budgetary balances.[117] Respect for medium-term objectives must be included in national medium-term budgetary frameworks. The Council makes a determination as to the plausibility of the national medium-term objectives on the basis of a Commission assessment. Failure to comply with the medium-term objectives can lead to sanction in the form of an interest-bearing deposit of 0.2 per cent of gross domestic product (GDP) on non-compliant euro-area countries.[118] The medium-term objectives and attendant sanction regime must be read in tandem with the measures designed to prevent and correct macroeconomic and competitiveness imbalances.[119]

[114] ibid, Draft Art 5(5).
[116] COM(2011) 819 (n 111).
[118] Reg 1173/2011 (n 109) Art 4.
[115] ibid, Draft Preamble [10].
[117] Reg 1175/2011 (n 109) Art 1(5).
[119] Reg 1176/2011 (n 109).

The rationale for these measures was that Member States had in the past made economic choices that led to divergence in competitiveness and macroeconomic imbalances within the EU. This was addressed through a new surveillance mechanism, the Excessive Imbalance Procedure (EIP), the aim of which is to prevent and correct these divergences. It contains an alert system based on a scoreboard of indicators and country studies that are designed to identify the existence of an excessive imbalance. This then triggers action by the Commission and Council, which can lead to financial sanction for Member States that do not follow Council recommendations.[120]

The preceding changes have been further reinforced by minimum requirements for national budgetary frameworks.[121] The objective is to ensure that national fiscal planning is in accord with the requirements of economic union. Thus such planning must adopt a multi-annual perspective, in order thereby to facilitate attainment of that country's medium-term objectives. Numerical fiscal rules should also promote compliance with the Treaty reference values for deficit and debt. The national rules must, moreover, promote compliance with EU reference values on budget deficit and public debt.

(iii) Excessive deficit: strengthening the substantive and procedural obligations

The EU also made changes to the excessive deficit procedure, the other limb of economic union.[122] The Excessive Deficit Procedure (EDP) can be triggered by government debt or government deficit. Member States with debt in excess of 60 per cent of GDP must reduce their debt in line with a numerical benchmark. A non-interest-bearing deposit of 0.2 per cent of GDP may be requested from a euro-area country which is placed in EDP on the basis of its deficit or its debt.[123] Failure of a euro-area country to comply with recommendations for corrective action can also lead to a fine.[124] Member States found to have excessive deficits are also subject to enhanced monitoring, which can lead to duties to report to the Commission, carry out national audits, and the like.[125]

(b) Change outside the Lisbon Treaty: the Treaty on Stability, Coordination and Governance

The discussion thus far has been concerned with reinforcement of economic union by measures enacted pursuant to the Lisbon Treaty. The analysis now

---

[120] Reg 1174/2011 (n 109).
[121] Dir 2011/85 (n 109) Arts 5, 6, 9; COM(2011) 821 (n 111) Draft Art 4.
[122] Reg 1177/2011 (n 109).
[123] Reg 1173/2011 (n 109) Art 5.
[124] ibid Art 6.   [125] COM(2011) 821 (n 111) Draft Art 7.

shifts to the Treaty on Stability, Coordination and Governance,[126] hereafter the TSCG, also known as the Fiscal Compact, which was signed by 25 contracting States in March 2012.[127] This was also designed to reinforce economic union, but took the form of a Treaty made outside the confines of the Lisbon Treaty.

The euro crisis was not quelled by the measures considered above, and the bond markets continued to charge ever-increasing rates of interest to service Greek, Italian, and Spanish debt. This was the setting for the European Council meeting in December 2011, which was the latest in a series of such meetings designed to show that the EU had the euro crisis under control. The core proposal was for reform that would further strengthen EU oversight over Member State economic policy, and the new rules were to be incorporated in the Lisbon Treaty through amendment requiring unanimity. Germany was the principal paymaster for the bailout of other Member State economies. Chancellor Merkel pressed strongly for inclusion of the new measures in the Lisbon Treaty, in part to reflect their importance, in part to appease domestic political forces, and in part to render less likely legal challenge to German bailouts by the German Federal Constitutional Court. President Sarkozy also advocated amendment of the Lisbon Treaty.

Amendment to the Lisbon Treaty was, however, prevented by the UK veto. The UK Prime Minister, David Cameron, was concerned by the new powers over national economic policy that the embryonic Treaty amendments would give to Brussels. He was also driven by the desire to appease the strong eurosceptic wing of the Tory party, and the wish to gain something for the UK, in terms of protection for the City of London from EU financial regulation, as the price of UK support for the proposed changes. The other Member States were unwilling to accede to UK demands, the UK refused to back down, and the December 2011 summit ended in acrimony, with dire warnings of the UK being isolated in the EU.

The majority of Member States nonetheless pressed forward with the reforms, the result being the TSCG. Politics continued to be an important factor as the TSCG took shape. It is arguable that almost everything in the TSCG could have been enacted pursuant to the Lisbon Treaty. This was not politically feasible, however. Merkel and Sarkozy had committed themselves to change to the primary Lisbon Treaty. They could not be seen to back down in the light of the UK veto and accept change in the form EU legislation. This explains the insistence on finding some other method of enshrining the desired precepts in 'primary law', even if this had to be a treaty distinct from the Lisbon Treaty.

---

[126] P Craig, 'The Stability, Coordination and Governance Treaty: Principle, Politics and Pragmatism' (2012) 37 ELRev 231.

[127] Treaty on Stability, Coordination and Governance in the Economic and Monetary Union, 1–2 March 2012, available at <http://www.european-council.europa.eu/eurozone-governance/treaty-on-stability?lang=en>.

There is a paradox in all this, because if the precepts in the TSCG had been enshrined in EU legislation then they would have partaken of the normal attributes of EU law, including supremacy and direct effect.

The TSCG was concluded in March 2012, with 25 signatories, the Czech Republic joining the UK as the other non-signatory. The December 2011 summit laid the foundations for the strengthened fiscal compact,[128] but was light on detail. What became the TSCG went through six revisions before the text was finally agreed between the signatories. The amendments during its passage varied, but the dominant theme was a weakening of the precepts established in December 2011 and in the original version of the TSCG. The TSCG had to be ratified by the contracting parties in accordance with their constitutional requirements, and entered into force on 1 January 2013, given that 12 contracting States whose currency is the euro had ratified the TSCG by that date.[129] The contracting parties hope to incorporate the substance of the TSCG into the Lisbon Treaty within five years.[130]

Article 1 TSCG provides that the contracting parties agree, as Member States of the EU, to strengthen the economic pillar of EMU by adopting rules to foster budgetary discipline through a fiscal compact, to strengthen the coordination of their economic policies and to improve the governance of the euro area.

Article 2 TSCG deals with the relationship between the TSCG and the Lisbon Treaty. Article 2(1) provides that the TSCG is to be applied and interpreted in conformity with the EU Treaties, in particular Article 4(3) TEU, and with EU law, including procedural law when adoption of secondary legislation is required. Article 2(2) further stipulates that the TSCG applies insofar as it is compatible with the EU Treaties and EU law, and that the TSCG shall not encroach on the competence of the Union to act in the area of the economic union.

Articles 3 to 8 TSCG specify the provisions about fiscal compact. Article 3(1) TSCG contains the 'balanced budget' rule[131] and is the heart of the new Treaty. The budgets of the contracting parties must be balanced or in surplus.[132] This is deemed to be respected if the annual structural balance of the general government is at its country-specific medium-term objective as defined in the revised SGP, with a lower limit of a structural deficit of 0.5 per cent of gross domestic product at market prices.[133] The contracting parties must ensure rapid convergence towards their respective medium-term objective. The time frame for such convergence is proposed by the Commission, taking into consideration country-specific sustainability risks.

---

[128] European Council, 9 December 2011.
[129] Art 14(1) TSCG.
[130] Art 16 TSCG.
[131] The rules in Art 3 TSCG are without prejudice to obligations under European Union law.
[132] Art 3(1)(a) TSCG.
[133] Art 3(1)(b) TSCG, as qualified by Art 3(1)(d) TSCG.

The obligation to balance the national budget is the core of the TSCG. It is nonetheless arguable that almost everything in the TSCG might have been done under the existing Lisbon Treaty provisions, including those on enhanced cooperation. It is true that Article 126(1) TFEU is framed in terms of an obligation on Member States to avoid excessive deficits, which is different from an obligation to balance the budget contained in Article 3(1)(a) TSCG. The difference is, however, significantly reduced when the Lisbon Treaty provisions are read together with the changes made by the six-pack of EU legislation enacted in 2011.

Thus Article 3(1)(b) TSCG, which gives substance to the notion of a balanced budget, specifies that the balanced budget rule is deemed to be respected if the annual structural balance of the general government is at its country-specific medium-term objective as defined in the revised SGP, with a lower limit of a structural deficit of 0.5 per cent of the gross domestic product at market prices. There is much commonality between Article 3(1)(b) and Regulation 1466/97 as amended in 2011.[134] The deficit rule of 0.5 per cent in Article 3(1)(b) is not very different from that in revised Regulation 1466/97, where it is 1 per cent. The obligation to balance the budget in Article 3(1)(a) TSCG is further qualified by the fact that Article 3(1)(b) TSCG is expressed as an obligation on contracting States to ensure rapid convergence towards the medium-term objective, in accordance with a time frame proposed by the Commission.

The automatic correction mechanism is specified in Article 3(2) TSCG. It contains two related obligations. It provides, first, that the rules in Article 3(1) TSCG shall take effect in national law of the contracting parties at the latest one year after entry into force of the TSCG through provisions of binding force and permanent character, preferably constitutional, or otherwise guaranteed to be fully respected and adhered to throughout the national budgetary processes. The national correction mechanism is to be based on common principles proposed by the Commission, concerning the nature, size, and time frame of the corrective action to be undertaken, also in the case of exceptional circumstances, the role and independence of the national institutions responsible for monitoring compliance with the rules in Article 3(1). Article 8 TSCG provides for judicial enforcement of Article 3(2) through recourse to the ECJ via Article 273 TFEU. Article 3(2) provides, secondly, for an obligation on contracting States to put in place a correction mechanism of the kind referred to in Article 3(1)(e) TSCG in the event of deviation from the balanced budget criteria in Article 3(1).

The efficacy of Article 3(2) TSCG was weakened through successive amendments. The December 2011 version was framed in terms of a mandatory obligation to comply with the principles in Article 3(1) by enshrining this obligation in national binding provisions of a 'constitutional or equivalent

---

[134] Reg 1175/2011 (n 109) Art 2a.

nature'. This was reinforced by the fact that Article 8 TSCG mandated national courts to check that contracting States had put in place rules to comply with Article 3(2) TSCG. The final version of Article 3(2) is weaker and disjunctive: the rules in Article 3(1) must take effect in national law 'through provisions of binding force and permanent character, preferably constitutional, *or otherwise* guaranteed to be fully respected and adhered to throughout the national budgetary processes',[135] and the national courts' role of monitoring compliance with the rules has been removed. It should, moreover, be noted that existing EU legislation contains rules analogous to those in Article 3(2). The substance of Article 3(2) TSCG is addressed in Articles 5 to 7 of Directive 2011/85, although this does not apply to the UK because of Article 8.[136] The difference between the TSCG and the existing Treaty rules will be further reduced if and when a proposed regulation on ensuring correction of excessive deficits becomes law.[137]

It is important to be cognizant of the interrelationship of Article 3(1) and Article 3(2) TSCG, the latter of which is enforceable through the ECJ via Article 8. Article 3(2) is enforceable via Article 8, but breach of Article 3(2) is itself dependent on breach of Article 3(1). The reality is that it will often be difficult to determine with certainty whether the conditions for breach of Article 3(2) are met, and these difficulties will be especially marked within the constraints of the classic adjudicative setting. It is naïve to imagine that a contracting party accused of non-compliance with Article 3(2) leading to a legal action before the ECJ will simply accept the finding in the Commission's report made pursuant to Article 8 that it has violated Article 3(2) and hence Article 3(1).

The wording of Article 3(1) leaves ample room for disagreement in this respect. Article 3(1)(b) is framed in terms of the contracting State ensuring 'rapid convergence' towards its medium-term objective, which provides fertile ground for argument as to whether it has met this criterion, and this is so notwithstanding the fact that the Commission proposes the time frame for such convergence. This time frame must take account of 'country-specific sustainability risks', which may provide further opportunity for dispute as to whether this criterion was correctly assessed in relation to the particular contracting State. The difficulties of assessment and adjudication are exacerbated by the wording of Article 3(1)(e), which requires the correction mechanism in Article 3(2) to be triggered automatically, but only where there are 'significant observed deviations from the medium-term objective or the adjustment path towards it'. The State taken to court pursuant to Article 8 may, moreover, contend that its failure to meet its medium-term objective was due to 'exceptional

---

[135] Emphasis added.

[136] Council Directive 2011/85 (n 109).

[137] Proposal for a Regulation of the European Parliament and of the Council on common provisions for monitoring and assessing draft budgetary plans and ensuring the correction of excessive deficit of the Member States in the euro area, COM(2011) 821 final, draft Art 4.

circumstances', as defined in Article 3(1)(c) and Article 3(3)(b) and that the Commission report has not taken this adequately into account.

Article 4 TSCG stipulates that when the ratio of debt to gross domestic product exceeds the 60 per cent reference value in Article 1 of Protocol 12 of the Lisbon Treaty, the contracting party must reduce it at an average rate of one-twentieth per year as a benchmark, as provided for in Article 2 of Regulation 1467/97 as amended.[138] The existence of an excessive deficit due to breach of the debt criterion is decided by the procedure in Article 126 TFEU. Article 5 TSCG imposes an obligation on contracting States subject to an excessive deficit procedure under the Lisbon Treaty to put in place correction mechanisms. Article 7 TSCG embodies a reverse qualified majority voting rule: contracting States whose currency is the euro commit to supporting Commission proposals where it considers that a State whose currency is the euro is in breach of the deficit criterion in the framework of an excessive deficit procedure, subject to the qualification that this obligation does not apply if a qualified majority of such States oppose the proposed decision.

The framers of the TSCG were eager for there to be some legal mechanism to enforce the balanced budget obligation in Article 3 TSCG. This is provided in Article 8 TSCG, which applies in the event of breach of the corrective mechanism in Article 3(2) TSCG. Article 8(1) TSCG provides[139] for recourse to the ECJ via Article 273 TFEU, which accords the ECJ jurisdiction in any dispute between Member States that relates to the subject matter of the EU Treaties if the dispute is submitted to it under a special agreement between the parties. Article 8(2) TSCG provides for a further action before the ECJ, leading to a penalty if a contracting State has been found not to have complied with the original judgment under Article 273 TFEU. Article 8(1) TSCG is framed as follows.

The European Commission is invited to present in due time to the Contracting Parties a report on the provisions adopted by each of them in compliance with Article 3(2). If the European Commission, after having given the Contracting Party concerned the opportunity to submit its observations, concludes in its report that such Contracting Party has failed to comply with Article 3(2), the matter will be brought to the Court of Justice of the European Union by one or more Contracting Parties. Where a Contracting Party considers, independently of the Commission's report, that another Contracting Party has failed to comply with Article 3(2), it may also bring the matter to the Court of Justice. In both cases, the judgment of the Court of Justice shall be binding on the parties to the proceedings, which shall take the necessary measures to comply with the judgment within a period to be decided by the Court of Justice.

More general issues of economic coordination are dealt with in Articles 9 to 11 TSCG, and governance of the euro-area is dealt with in Article 12 TSCG, which provides for informal meetings of Heads of State of contracting parties whose currency is the euro at Euro Summit meetings, together with the Commission President.

---

[138] Reg 1177/2011 (n 109).   [139] Art 8(3) TSCG.

(c) TSCG, supervision and Treaty imperatives: change in the EU

The TSCG raises important issues of principle, including the legality and legitimacy of change in the EU. It might be argued that no such issue arises, because the TSCG did not formally amend the Lisbon Treaty and Article 2 TSCG makes clear that the TSCG is subordinate to EU law. This is true, but it does not obviate the present inquiry for the following reason.

The Lisbon Treaty provides clear rules on amendment in Article 48 TEU, with unanimity being required for change. There are in addition detailed Treaty provisions concerning enhanced cooperation in Article 20 TEU and Articles 326 to 334 TFEU, specifying the applicable rules if some but not all States wish to do certain things under the Lisbon Treaty. No attempt was made to use the rules on enhanced cooperation to attain the ends contained in the TSCG.[140] The EU Summit in December 2011 attempted to change the Lisbon Treaty, but failed because of the UK veto.

The Lisbon Treaty therefore embodies requirements before change can take place, viz the ordinary and the simplified revision procedure. These provisions enshrine the proposition that the rules of the game should not be altered unless all agree. They also contain criteria as to what should happen when all do not agree, by offering the possibility for enhanced cooperation. These amendment provisions might be different. They are not the only imaginable set of rules that could be devised for alteration of an international treaty, but it is common for such criteria to be applied, and they are the criteria in the Lisbon Treaty.

The assumption underlying the TSCG is that even though it has not been possible to attain unanimity, and even though the rules on enhanced cooperation have not been used, it is legitimate to attain the desired ends by a different route and EU institutions can be integral to such a project. This assumption must be examined, however, not merely accepted as if it were uncontroversial. We need to tread carefully here. It is perfectly possible for all Member States to agree to a Treaty amendment, which then only applies to some of them. This is in effect what occurred when, for example, the Schengen agreement was integrated into the EU Treaty. This is in accord with the principle of unanimity, since all Member States agreed to an amendment, the substance of which will henceforward only apply to some of them. This was not, however, the situation with the TSCG. There was no amendment to the Lisbon Treaty authorizing what became the TSCG for those who wished to become a party thereto.

A *necessary* condition for the legitimacy and legality of the TSCG is therefore that Member States retain inherent power under public international law to

---

[140] Art 10 TSCG provides that the contracting States 'stand ready' to use the rules on enhanced cooperation, but this does not alter the point made in the text: the contracting parties did not attempt to use the rules on enhanced cooperation in order to attain their overall objectives under the Lisbon Treaty, rather than conclude a separate Treaty.

make international agreements that are consistent with the Lisbon Treaty. This principle can be readily acknowledged,[141] although its application can be complex in the post-Lisbon world, because the extent of any such inherent Member State power will be bounded by, inter alia, the competence provisions of the Lisbon Treaty. Thus the TSCG had to be carefully structured to apply to economic and not monetary union.[142] This is because Article 3 TFEU stipulates that the EU has exclusive competence over monetary policy for Member States whose currency is the euro, with the consequences that flow from Article 2(1) TFEU: only the EU may legislate and adopt legally binding acts, the Member States being able to do so only if empowered by the EU or for the implementation of EU acts. The TSCG entails legal obligations for the signatory States, and the EU did not formally empower the making of the TSCG. The TSCG would therefore be incompatible with Articles 2 and 3 TFEU if it attempted to regulate monetary policy. The shared competence provisions of the Lisbon Treaty also constrain the capacity of Member States to conclude agreements outside its framework. This is because Article 2(2) TFEU stipulates that in areas covered by shared competence Member States can exercise their competence only to the extent that the EU has not done so. Let us nonetheless accept for the sake of argument that the principle at the beginning of this paragraph, which is a necessary condition for the legitimacy and legality of the TSCG, is met here.

The principle is not, however, a *sufficient* condition in this respect. It provides the foundation for Member States proceeding outside the Lisbon Treaties when development therein has been blocked by the veto. It provides no justification for EU institutions partaking in such a Treaty, where there has been no agreement amongst the 27 Member States that the institutions should be able to do so. The passage of the TSCG prompted parliamentary inquiries in the UK as to what exactly the effect of the UK veto had been. Now to be sure these inquiries were politically motivated and an answer would be that the veto prevented amendment of the Lisbon Treaty. There is nonetheless a serious dimension to this inquiry that is not addressed by the preceding answer. If Member States use the veto and hence prevent change to the Lisbon Treaty in accordance with the rules of the game embodied therein, it is unclear why an institution that only exists as a creation of that very Treaty should be able to decide to pursue the vetoed objectives via a different treaty.[143]

---

[141] Case C-370/12 *Pringle* (n 79); J-C Piris, *The Future of Europe, Towards a Two-Speed EU?* (Cambridge University Press, 2012) 138–139.

[142] Art 1(1) TSCG.

[143] It might be argued that the EU institutions have some 'autonomous capacity' to participate in such ventures, provided only that they are not incompatible with EU law. The foundation of this autonomous capacity is, however, unclear. It could in any event only provide justification for institutional participation in the TSCG if the following proposition is also accepted: the autonomous capacity enables the EU institution to proceed in this manner even where some Member States have vetoed amendment to the Lisbon Treaty, and there is no formal agreement by all Member States that EU institutions can be used outside its remit. There is no justification for according the concept of 'autonomous capacity', if it exists, this degree of 'normative force', and very good reasons for not doing so.

The TSCG therefore raises the following question of principle: if the Member States fail to attain unanimity for amendment, and do not seek or fail to attain their ends through enhanced cooperation, does it mean that 12, 15, 21 etc Member States can make a treaty to achieve the desired ends and the EU institutions can play a role therein, where the 27 Member States have not agreed to use of the EU institutions,[144] and where the treaty thus made deals with subject matter covered directly by the existing Lisbon Treaty?[145] This is the principle that underlies the TSCG, and can for ease be referred to as P1.

It might be argued that the TSCG is only authority for a more limited principle, let us call it P1A, which embodies what might be termed the 'Schmittian' exception.[146] On this view the TSCG stands for the following proposition: if the Member States fail to attain unanimity for amendment, and do not seek or fail to attain their ends through enhanced cooperation, the 12, 15, 21 etc Member States can make a treaty to achieve the desired ends and the EU institutions can play a role therein, even where there is no consent to this by all Member States, but only where the issue is so important that the very survival of the EU, or an important element thereof, such as the euro, is at stake. There was no express attempt to legitimate the TSCG in such terms, but that does not in itself preclude such an ex post rationalization. The argument must, however, be sustained, not merely stated. It would have to be shown that the conclusion of a treaty, which would not come into effect for approximately one year, played a vital role in the calming of bond markets that were reacting to European events on an hour-by-hour, day-by-day basis. It would have to be shown, moreover, that the TSCG had this impact, given that it added very little to what was contained in the Lisbon Treaty, plus the six-pack of accompanying regulations, made or revised in late 2011.[147]

It is important in evaluating P1 to consider the case law that the EU institutions can assist the Member States in attaining their collective goals outside the strict confines of EU law. Thus in *European Parliament v Council and Commission*, which was concerned with aid to Bangladesh, the ECJ held that the fourth indent of Article 155 EEC did not prevent the Member States from entrusting the Commission with the task of coordinating collective action undertaken by them on the basis of an act of their representatives meeting in the Council.[148]

---

[144] Craig (n 126) fn 27.

[145] It will be seen below that there are further problems, even if the powers are analogous to those in the existing Treaties.

[146] C Schmidt, *Political Theology: Four Chapters on Sovereignty* [1922] (trans G Schwab, MIT Press, 1988).

[147] The markets might react badly if the TSCG were now to be undermined, even if the TSCG had no effect thus far on contracting State behaviour because it was not yet in force. Insofar as this might occur, it does not undermine the point made in the text, but rather indicates something paradoxical about the 'logic' of markets.

[148] Cases C-181 and 248/91 *European Parliament v Council and Commission* [1993] ECR I-3685, [20].

Advocate General Jacobs framed the principle as follows: in cases where Member States decided to act individually or collectively in a field within their competence, there was nothing to prevent them from conferring on the Commission the task of ensuring coordination of such action. It was for the Commission to decide whether to accept such a mission, provided that it did so in a way compatible with its duties under the EC Treaty.[149] Similarly, in *European Parliament v Council* dealing with the Lomé Convention, the ECJ stated that no provision of the Treaty prevented Member States from using, outside its framework, procedural steps drawing on the rules applicable to Community expenditure and from associating the Community institutions with the procedure thus set up.[150]

The precise reach of these authorities is unclear, and they are distinguishable in several respects from the TSCG. Thus the preceding cases were dealing with limited use of Community institutions to act primarily as agents to coordinate the respective schemes and organize payment of money thereunder. This was done with the assent of the Member States. It would be a significant extension of the reasoning therein to apply it to the TSCG, in order to justify EU institutional involvement in a detailed regulatory regime for the signatory States, in circumstances where inclusion of such obligations in the Lisbon Treaty was precluded by use of the veto. The TSCG was not simply about using an EU institution as a conduit for payment of funds, nor was it an agreement of all Member States reached within the Council, in the manner of Bangladesh aid.

If the ECJ's reasoning is extended in this manner it means acceptance of P1 and acceptance also of the implications that P1 has for the way in which the EU, broadly conceived, develops. It would sanction EU institutional involvement in a treaty made by some Member States, covering subject matter dealt with in the Lisbon Treaty in circumstances where amendment to the Lisbon Treaty had been rejected by certain States, where there was no formal agreement of all States within the confines of the Lisbon Treaty allowing for such EU institutional involvement,[151] no attempt to pursue the desired outcome through enhanced cooperation, and hence no imperative to comply with the protective conditions for use of this cooperation built into the Lisbon Treaty. The non-EU treaty thus made could nonetheless markedly affect the way in which a subject matter area covered by the Lisbon Treaty is regulated; indeed that might be its very purpose, as is the case with the TSCG. There are in any event further issues to be considered, concerning the powers of the EU institutions under any such non-EU treaty. It is to these that we now turn.

---

[149] ibid [29], AG Jacobs.
[150] Case C- 316/91 *European Parliament v Council* [1993] ECR I-653, [41].
[151] Piris (n 141) 127.

(d) TSCG, supervision and Treaty imperatives: conferral of new functions

The TSCG raises important issues of principle concerning the functions of EU institutions operating outside the confines of the Lisbon Treaty. It is contrary to the Lisbon Treaty and to legal principle for new functions to be conferred on an EU institution by a treaty such as the TSCG. The contrary conclusion would entail the following proposition, let us call it P2: it is open to a group of Member States outside the confines of the existing Treaties to decide in agreement with an EU institution that it should be empowered or mandated to perform certain tasks not specified in the existing EU Treaties.

Article 13 TEU stipulates that each EU institution must act within the limits of the powers conferred on it by the EU Treaties and in conformity with the procedures, conditions, and objectives set out therein. This is reinforced by Article 5(2) TEU, which provides that the EU must act within the limits of its competence, and that competence not conferred on the EU remains with the Member States. It would be wrong if a treaty other than the Lisbon Treaty could confer new powers or functions on the EU institutions, even if those functions are exercised outside the Lisbon Treaty.

This conclusion is reinforced from the broader perspective of legal principle. P2 is not tenable, and that is so irrespective of whether the relevant States are willing to pay for the new function from their own budgets, and irrespective of whether the EU institution agrees with the new power/duty. It cannot suffice to validate such a conferral that it relates in some way to existing institutional powers and duties under the Lisbon Treaty. Nor can it suffice in this respect that the Lisbon Treaty is accorded formal superiority over the other agreement. There are procedural and substantive reasons why the grant of new powers or functions in this way is unacceptable.

In procedural terms, the powers and functions of EU institutions are specified in the formal Treaties after considerable deliberation, as attested to by the decade long discourse on treaty reform in which debate over institutional power was centre stage. The desirability of any addition to the functions of any EU institution is something on which all other EU institutions and all States might have a view, irrespective of whether a particular EU institution or State is party to a treaty made outside the formal confines of the Lisbon Treaty. There is no guarantee whatsoever that there will be opportunity for this deliberation when new powers are granted to an EU institution in a treaty made outside the confines of the Lisbon Treaty. It may indeed not be apparent that this has occurred until the ink is dry on the final version of the treaty, and may be not for some time thereafter.

In substantive terms, the EU institutions and States might differ as to whether they believe that an additional function is compatible with current powers and functions, and they might differ also as to whether they believe that the new function can be 'hermetically sealed' from those functions performed by the institution within the Lisbon Treaty. The very meaning of compatibility is itself under-theorized in this context. This is not the place for a general exegesis on this concept. Suffice it to say that a narrow conception of compatibility would unduly attenuate the substantive inquiry. It must also embrace the objection voiced by the EU institution or State that is not party to an agreement outside the Lisbon Treaty, which believes that conferral of a new power on an EU institution might deleteriously affect the operation of the EU itself, by embroiling that institution in issues for which it was ill-suited, with negative consequences for its role under the Lisbon Treaty, and more generally for the EU. The determination of the powers/functions of an EU institution has always been crucially dependent on calculations as to the advisability of according it such authority. This is an inherently political issue, which cannot be resolved by purely legal analysis. It would be wrong if the grant of a new function to an EU institution by a non-EU Treaty was judged by less demanding criteria.

Consider in this respect two brief examples. A treaty made outside the Lisbon Treaty is the foundation for involvement with a non-EU State. The initiative could not be undertaken within the EU because certain States objected. An EU institution is willing to take part and is given new functions. The non-signatories object because they believe that the EU institution is ill equipped to take on the new function and that in doing so its role within the EU will be deleteriously affected. Consider a further example drawn from the TSCG. Let us assume that it has accorded new or extended functions to an EU institution. Non-signatory States might plausibly feel that this is unwise, irrespective of whether it is formally compatible with the Lisbon Treaty, and could have negative consequences on the EU. The TSCG strategy is to toughen oversight over national economic policy, to ratchet up the controls over national budgets. It may, however, be felt with justification that this will increase tensions between the Commission and signatory States, and that the Commission lacks the political authority to undertake such oversight effectively. The consequence might then be national resistance to EU institutional oversight over economic policy, even within the framework of the rules that apply under the Lisbon Treaty.

The preceding discussion leaves open the issue as to whether the TSCG has conferred new functions/powers on the EU institutions. It may be contestable whether a function conferred by the TSCG constitutes a new task or function for an EU institution. This is more especially so because institutional functions can be specified either in the Lisbon Treaty or in EU legislation made pursuant thereto. This can be exemplified by considering Article 3(2) TSCG, which provides that the contracting parties must put in place at national level the correction mechanism mentioned in Article 3(1)(e) on the basis of common principles to be proposed by the European Commission. There are, however, obligations akin to those in Article 3(2) in existing EU legislation.[152]

(e) TSCG, supervision and Treaty imperatives: use of existing powers

The preceding analysis leaves open the legal difficulties in EU institutions using their existing powers under the Lisbon Treaty and EU legislation in the context of a treaty such as the TSCG. The phrase 'existing powers' can bear three different meanings.

(i) Taking cognizance in the TSCG of powers in the Lisbon Treaty or EU legislation

It could mean that the TSCG simply takes cognizance of powers in the Lisbon Treaty or legislation made thereunder. Thus, for example, Article 10 TSCG provides that the contracting States whose currency is the euro stand ready to use Article 136 TFEU, and that all contracting States should be willing to use the rules on enhanced cooperation in Article 20 TEU and Articles 326 to 334 TFEU. This is not problematic in terms of legal principle.[153] There is nothing wrong with a treaty making reference to existing provisions of the Lisbon Treaty, and indicating that the contracting parties intend to use such provisions in accordance with the relevant conditions.

(ii) Use of a specific power in the TSCG from the Lisbon Treaty or EU legislation

A second meaning of 'existing power' is that an EU institution such as the Commission uses a specific power or function that it possesses under the Lisbon Treaty or EU legislation in the context of the TSCG. This is exemplified by Article 4 TSCG, which is framed expressly in terms of the relevant provisions of the SGP and Article 126 TFEU.[154] This is legally problematic for the following reason.

The fact that a power is recognized in the Lisbon Treaty or EU legislation does not per se legitimate recognition and use of the same power in a different treaty context. The TSCG cannot in itself legitimate use of a power given under the

---

[152] Council Directive 2011/85 (n 109) Arts 5–7.

[153] There are difficulties concerning the specification in Art 10 TSCG of the conditions for enhanced cooperation, which do not cohere with those in Art 20 TEU and Arts 326–334 TFEU. This is, however, a separate issue. If the contracting States wish to make use of enhanced cooperation they have to comply with all the conditions in the Lisbon Treaty.

[154] See also, for example, Art 3(1)(b) TSCG: progress towards the medium-term objectives is to be decided 'in line' with the provisions of the revised SGP; Art 8(2) TSCG using criteria under Art 260 TFEU to determine penalties for non-compliance with an ECJ judgment under Art 273 TFEU.

Lisbon Treaty or EU legislation. The TSCG cannot pull itself up by its own legal bootstraps. If this were possible it would mean subscribing to the following proposition, let us call it P3: a treaty could be made outside the confines of the Lisbon Treaty and the framers of the former could decide that institutional powers accorded under the Lisbon Treaty or EU legislation could apply within the new treaty ordering. P3 is clearly untenable. Thus the statement in the Preamble to the TSCG that when reviewing and monitoring budgetary commitments under the TSCG, the Commission will act within the framework of its powers as provided by Articles 121, 126, 136 TFEU, cannot in itself determine the issue of whether those Articles of the TFEU are indeed capable of being used in this way in the TSCG.

Whether the same power can be used in a different institutional context must as a matter of principle depend on interpretation of the Lisbon Treaty or EU legislation. It would have to be argued that the proper interpretation of the relevant provisions of the Lisbon Treaty was such that the Treaty powers, and those in EU legislation, could also be used by the institutions pursuant to a different treaty, which was not ratified by all Member States.

It might be possible to reach this conclusion, but it is not self-evident or automatic. This is because the natural interpretation of EU legislation is that the institutional powers and duties contained therein apply in the legal context that is the EU. The Lisbon Treaty or EU legislation might of course empower an EU institution to take action outside the physical and legal confines of the EU. This does not alter the point made here, since in such circumstances the legal authority for an EU institution to act in this manner flows from the Lisbon Treaty or EU legislation. The default assumption is that EU legislation and the powers accorded to the institutions apply and are intended to apply within the legal entity that is the EU. It would therefore have to be argued that an institutional power given under, for example, the SGP could be interpreted to apply outside the legal entity that is the EU and be used in the context of the TSCG. It may be possible to sustain such a conclusion, but the justificatory exercise must be undertaken.

To reject the preceding argument would mean subscribing to P3: institutional powers granted under the Lisbon Treaty or EU legislation could be used, 'cut and pasted', to a different treaty by the authors of the non-EU treaty, which had not been ratified by all Member States. This proposition is not legally or politically tenable. Whether any particular power granted to an institution under the Lisbon Treaty or EU legislation can be used in a different treaty context must depend on interpretation of the relevant Lisbon Treaty provision or EU legislation to sustain the conclusion that it can be used in this manner. In deciding this interpretive issue there is, moreover, no reason why the signatories to a treaty such as the TSCG should have any privileged status as compared to non-signatories.

(iii) Use of a power in the TSCG that is analogous to that under the Lisbon Treaty or EU legislation

There is a third meaning of the phrase 'existing power', which must be disaggregated from the second. It captures the idea that an EU institution such as the Commission exercises a power under the TSCG that is analogous to one it possesses under the Lisbon Treaty or EU legislation. This is exemplified by Article 3(2) TSCG, which is framed in terms of the Commission devising principles concerning corrective action that may be analogous to those in EU legislation, but Article 3(2) does not directly seek to use such powers, and thus 'existing power' carries this third connotation. Article 7 TSCG is of the same genre. It imposes a reverse qualified majority voting requirement, whereby contracting States prima facie commit to abide by the Commission's decision, but can decide not to do so by qualified majority. There are circumstances where reverse qualified majority voting applies in EU legislation,[155] but Article 7 TSCG is not expressly based on such provisions, nor would this have been straightforward in legal terms. Thus, insofar as Article 7 can be regarded as use of 'existing power', it carries this third interpretation: the TSCG contains an institutional power that is analogous to that in the existing Lisbon Treaty or EU legislation.

This is also legally problematic. The fact that an EU institution has power pursuant to the Lisbon Treaty or EU legislation to do certain things cannot per se legitimate use of an analogous power pursuant to a different treaty. Thus to take an example, the fact that Articles 5 to 7 of Directive 2011/85[156] contain obligations on all Member States (except the UK) from 2013 to have numerical rules in place in their national law to promote compliance with obligations from the TFEU in the area of budgetary policy over a multiannual horizon, does not in itself legitimate use by the Commission of analogous powers pursuant to Article 3(2) TSCG.

The fact that a power under the TSCG is analogous to a power that is exercised under EU legislation is just that, a fact. It cannot in itself cloak with legal legitimacy the exercise of an analogous power under the TSCG. The legal legitimacy of such power can only be provided in the following manner, let us call this P4. It would have to be argued that an EU institution should be allowed to exercise powers in a non-EU context that are closely analogous to those that it exercises under the Lisbon Treaty or EU legislation. This argument might be sustained, but it is not self-evident. P4 is, moreover, certainly too broad to be sustainable in its present formulation, since it would on its face legitimate in a non-EU context use of any institutional power that was analogous in some way

---

[155] See, eg, Reg 1174/2011 (n 109) Art 3(3).
[156] Council Directive 2011/85/EU of 8 November 2011 on requirements for budgetary frameworks of the Member States [2011] OJ L306/41.

to an existing power under the Lisbon Treaty or EU legislation. It is not easy, however, to narrow P4 down, while retaining something that could still be regarded as a meaningful principle.

(f) TSCG, supervision and Treaty imperatives: legal enforcement

We have already seen that the framers of the TSCG were eager for its precepts to be legally enforceable. This was the rationale for Article 8 TSCG, which provides for recourse to the ECJ pursuant to Article 273 TFEU. There is no problem with this so far as inter-State actions are concerned. The rationale underlying Article 273 TFEU is that it obviates Member States using a settlement mechanism, such as arbitration, outside the EU, where a dispute might involve issues related to EU law. Access to the ECJ thereby protects the unity of EU law and its interpretation. The requirement for a special agreement dealing with a defined species of case is satisfied because recourse to the ECJ is limited to the circumstances of breach of Article 3(2) TSCG. The requirement that the dispute relates to the subject matter of the EU Treaties is also met, because there is a proximate connection between the TSCG and the Lisbon Treaty: the former deals with aspects of economic union, and Article 3 TSCG is closely related to the provisions of the SGP.

This still leaves open the legitimacy and legality of the Commission's role under Article 8 TSCG. Member States are very reluctant to sue each other. If this were the only method of getting a case before the ECJ then such adjudication would remain in practical terms a dead letter. Article 273 TFEU cannot, however, be read so as to allow the Commission to bring an action in its own name, in the manner akin to an infringement action, and such an action would, moreover, have been problematic in the light of Article 126(10) TFEU, which precludes recourse to Articles 258 and 259 TFEU in relation to Article 126(1)–(9) TFEU.

This was the rationale for the solution in Article 8 TSCG. The Commission is 'invited' to present a report on contracting parties' compliance with Article 3(2) TSCG. If the Commission concludes that a contracting party has failed to comply with Article 3(2) TSCG, the matter 'will' be brought to the ECJ by one or more of the contracting parties. The Council Legal Service defended the legality of this strategy.[157] It acknowledged that the Commission's report would play a decisive role in the subsequent litigation, but denied that this made the Commission the initiator of the legal action or a party thereto. The Council Legal Service argued, moreover, that it was the choice of the contracting party or parties as to whether to bring an action, and that this was so notwithstanding the fact that they had no discretion, in the sense that they had to do so following the

---

[157] Council of the European Union 5788/12, Brussels 26 January 2012.

Commission's negative report: 'an act of a Member State taken in a situation of "tied competence" remains an act of this Member State'.[158]

It is true that the Commission is not in a formal sense a party to the legal action. This cannot conceal the substantive reality, which is that Article 8 TSCG is seeking to do by the back door what it cannot do by the front. Article 8 TSCG gives the Commission the trigger as to whether a legal action should be brought. Commission oversight of the balancing of budgets is central to the TSCG schema and hence the requirement of an 'invitation' is purely formal, a sense which is heightened by the very fact that Article 8 TSCG is framed in terms of a collective invitation.

If the Commission produces a negative report on a contracting State, this triggers a mandatory obligation on another contracting party to bring the recalcitrant State to the ECJ. This is clear from the wording of Article 8 TSCG, which states that the contracting State 'will' bring such an action. This wording connotes a clear obligation, as accepted by the Council Legal Service.[159] This conclusion is, moreover, reinforced by the contrast between the first and second parts of Article 8(1) TSCG: if there is a negative Commission report a contracting State 'will' bring an action, whereas in the absence of Commission intervention a contracting State 'may' sue another State for non-compliance with Article 3(2) TSCG. The former clearly connotes a legal obligation, since otherwise the distinction between the first and second parts of Article 8(1) TSCG falls away. This interpretation gains added force by the Annex to the TSCG concerning the arrangements as to which State will bring the action under Article 8 TSCG.[160] The Annex provides that the applicant contracting States 'will be' the States that hold the Presidency of the Council in accord with Article 1(4) of the Council Rules of Procedure, and that the application under Article 273 TFEU 'will be' lodged by such States in the ECJ registry within three months of receipt of the Commission report that a contracting State has not complied with Article 3(2) TSCG. Thus the wording of Article 8 TSCG, read together with the Annex, leads inexorably to the conclusion that the relevant contracting States are obliged to bring an action based on a negative Commission report, and that this very report will be the basis of the action.

The Council Legal Service's argument is ultimately based on formalism: provided that the Commission is not a formal party to the action then Article 273 TFEU can be used in the manner envisaged by Article 8 TSCG. This formalism does injustice to the wording and structure of Article 8 TSCG for the reasons given above, but there is a deeper problem with such formalism. Let us imagine that a Member State attempted to structure its relations so as to avoid

---

[158] ibid 5.
[159] ibid 4, 5.
[160] Minutes of the Signing of the Treaty of Stability, Coordination and Governance in the Economic and Monetary Union, 2 March 2012, Annex.

clear obligations under EU law. Let us make the analogy tighter. The Member State seeks to avoid its obligations by using other players, even though they have a duty to act when directed by the Member State, and in accordance with its findings. The ECJ, the EU institutional legal services, and the great majority of academics would rightly conclude that we should look to the substance and not the form when considering the legality of such practices. They would properly condemn such recourse to formalism. The same principle should apply in relation to powers of the EU institutions. If Article 273 TFEU cannot accommodate enforcement actions brought by the Commission, we should not allow this injunction to be circumvented by devices that render a contracting State the 'formal plaintiff', when the imperative to bring the action and the substance of the argument to be made are determined by the Commission.

The stakes concerning the legality of the Commission's role in Article 8 TSCG are therefore higher than might be initially thought. It is the integrity and equality of legal reasoning within the EU legal order that is at stake. If the legality of Article 8 TSCG is upheld on the formalistic reasoning of the Council Legal Service, it is then incumbent on those who support such reasoning to explain why such formalism can be used to the advantage of the EU institutions when it would be rejected in relation to Member States.

5. 'Towards a Genuine Economic and Monetary Union'

The efforts made to meet the euro crisis through the admixture of assistance and supervision considered above do not, however, exhaust the EU initiatives in this area. The title of this section is taken from the Report produced by the President of the European Council in close collaboration with the Presidents of the Commission, ECB, and Eurogroup, which may for ease be referred to as the Four Presidents' Report.[161] It lays the groundwork for further policies to secure, as the title suggests, genuine economic and monetary union. It was produced at the behest of the European Council,[162] and was endorsed by it in December 2012.[163] The report is framed in terms of an integrated financial framework, an integrated budgetary framework, and an integrated economic policy framework. These proposals can be explained within the framework used in the preceding analysis, distinguishing between assistance and supervision.

(a) Assistance

The proposals concerning an integrated budgetary framework are concerned in part with supervision, as will be seen below. The new proposals on budgetary

---

[161] 'Towards a Genuine Economic and Monetary Union' (n 1).
[162] <http://www.consilium.europa.eu/uedocs/cms_data/docs/pressdata/en/ec/133004.pdf>.
[163] European Council, 13–14 December 2012.

frameworks, read together with those on an integrated economic policy framework, are, however, principally aimed at provision of assistance of a kind that will render it less likely that Member States will need to seek help from the ESM. There are in essence two elements to this proposed schema.

The first limb of the proposed reform seeks to address national economic vulnerability through 'limited, temporary, flexible and targeted financial incentives'[164] made operational through contractual arrangements between Member States and the EU, which would be mandatory for euro-area Member States and voluntary for other Member States. The contractual arrangements would be based on Commission reviews concerning the principal bottlenecks to growth and employment. They would cover a multiannual, specific reform agenda, capable of being monitored, which would be jointly agreed with the EU institutions. The focus would be on competitiveness and growth, since these are central to an effective EMU. The structural reforms would be supported through financial incentives in the form of temporary transfers to Member States with excessive structural weaknesses, which would be financed through 'specific resources'.[165] The schema would be embedded in the European Semester. Member States would be accountable to national parliaments and the Commission to the European Parliament concerning the content and implementation of their respective duties under the agreements.

The second limb of the proposed reform is to endow the EU with fiscal capacity, the Report noting that all other currency unions have this.[166] The objective is to facilitate adjustment to economic shocks.[167]

This could take the form of an insurance-type mechanism between euro area countries to buffer large country-specific economic shocks. Such a function would ensure a form of fiscal solidarity exercised over economic cycles, improving the resilience of the euro area as a whole and reducing the financial and output costs associated with macroeconomic adjustments. By contributing to macroeconomic stability, it would usefully complement the crisis management framework based on the European Stability Mechanism.

The insurance-type regime is designed to meet the negative fiscal externalities that can befall other countries in the euro-area where economic adjustment mechanisms to country-specific economic problems are imperfect. Insurance-based risk-sharing tools perform a shock absorption function, and help prevent contagion across the euro-area.[168] Contributions from, and disbursements to, national budgets fluctuate according to each country's position in the economic cycle. The Report stresses that the system should be structured in such a way that it does not lead 'to unidirectional and permanent transfers between countries',[169] but it also acknowledges the risk of moral hazard in an insurance system, in the

---

[164] 'Towards a Genuine Economic and Monetary Union' (n 1) 7.
[165] ibid 13.   [166] ibid 7.   [167] ibid 7.
[168] ibid 8.   [169] ibid 10.

sense that weaker economies might regard the safety net it provides as a disincentive to sound economic management.

This is the rationale for the emphasis placed on the inter-connection between insurance-based shock absorption and measures designed to induce stronger economic convergence, 'based on structural policies aiming at improving the adjustment capacity of national economies and avoiding the risk of moral hazard inherent to any insurance system'.[170] The technique for ensuring balance in this respect is to be the contractual arrangements between Member States and the EU described above. The bottom line is that Member States will not be eligible to participate in the insurance-based shock absorption function unless they comply with contractual arrangements aimed at instilling sound economic policy. The contractual approach to reform will continue when countries have gained access to the shock absorption function in order to avoid relapse or re-emergence of macroeconomic imbalances. Thus a Member State would only continue to be eligible for transfers under the shock absorption function if it continued to comply with the contractual arrangements.[171]

There is no such thing as a free transfer and hence resources have to be found to finance promotion of structural reform and absorption of asymmetric shocks. The Report envisages that the resources could take the form of national contributions, EU own resources, or a combination of both. It also, albeit tentatively, broached the possibility that EU fiscal capacity might entail ability to borrow, without this necessarily entailing mutualization of sovereign debt, given the negative political baggage associated with this concept.[172]

(b) Supervision

The proposals emanating from the Four Presidents' Report were not, however, exclusively concerned with assistance. Supervision was integral to the vision of a 'genuine EMU'. The supervisory element is composed in large part of measures considered above relating to an integrated budgetary framework designed to strengthen EU controls over national budgetary policy, these being the six-pack, the two-pack, and the TSCG.[173] The supervisory aspect of the schema is complemented by proposals for an integrated financial framework. Their importance and content are captured in the following extract.[174]

The current European arrangements for safeguarding financial stability remain based on national responsibilities. This is inconsistent with the highly integrated nature of the EMU and has certainly exacerbated the harmful interplay between the fragilities of sovereigns and the vulnerabilities of the banking sector. The set-up of the Single Supervisory Mechanism (SSM) will be a guarantor of strict and impartial supervisory

---

[170] ibid 8.   [171] ibid 8.   [172] ibid 9.
[173] ibid 7.   [174] ibid 4.

oversight, thus contributing to breaking the link between sovereigns and banks and diminishing the probability of future systemic banking crisis.

The core idea is for the SSM to be run by the ECB, which will have direct oversight of banks, the objective being 'to enforce prudential rules in a strict and impartial manner and perform effective oversight of cross border banking markets'.[175] Ensuring that banking supervision across the euro-area abides by high common standards is regarded as an essential pre-condition for introduction of any further support mechanisms. The ECB will have responsibility for key supervisory tasks that are central to a bank's viability. It will, inter alia, license and authorize credit institutions, assess qualifying holdings, ensure compliance with the minimum capital requirements, supervise financial conglomerates, and ensure compliance with provisions on leverage and liquidity. The establishment of the SSM is seen as the green light for the ESM to engage in recapitalization of banks directly. The SSM was approved by the European Council in December 2012, including the idea that, once in place, funds from the ESM could be used for direct recapitalization of banks.[176]

Supervision through the SSM is to be complemented by the Single Resolution Mechanism, SRM, which was also approved by the European Council.[177] This is in effect a mechanism whereby the EU will exercise supervisory responsibility and set the conditions for the resolution of financial problems that beset individual banks. The Commission has already engaged in work on this issue.[178] It was felt by the authors of the Four Presidents' Report that the existence of the SSM required responsibility for issues concerning bank resolution to be dealt with at EU level too, hence the proposals for the SRM. The idea is that the SRM would reduce resolution costs, break the bank-sovereign nexus, and ensure that the private sector bore the primary burden of bank resolution costs, thereby increasing market discipline, and minimizing cost for taxpayers of bank failures. It would be for the SSM to assess the need for resolution, while the single resolution authority set up pursuant to the SRM would carry through the resolution in a timely and efficient manner.

6. Political, Economic, and Legal Consequences

The preceding discussion has charted the complex array of measures that constitute the EU's response to the financial crisis. This has included analysis of

---

[175] Proposal for a Council Regulation conferring specific tasks on the European Central Bank concerning policies relating to the prudential supervision of credit institutions, COM(2012) 511 final, 2.
[176] European Council (n 163) [7], [10].
[177] ibid [11].
[178] <http://ec.europa.eu/internal_market/bank/crisis_management/index_en.htm#maincontent-Sec2>.

difficulties with particular measures such as the ESM and the TSCG. It is now time to stand back and consider in more general terms the political, economic, and legal consequences of these developments, albeit being mindful that these can overlap.

(a) Political consequences

(i) *Impact on the EU's defining political credo*

The consequences for the EU of the financial crisis and the measures taken to meet it are, as will be seen from the ensuing discussion, many and varied. It is nonetheless easy when considering complex economic and constitutional implications to miss what may be the most important and long-lasting impact on the 'EU brand', when viewed from the perspective of the ordinary citizen.

The EU was founded on the promise of peace and prosperity. This was the original Monnet vision, to be realized through technocratic-led expertise. The EU has largely delivered on this vision, although the technocracy-driven leadership that Monnet envisioned has been qualified. There has not been armed conflict within the EU countries, and Member States have benefited from the economic gains of the single market. Now to be sure there have been economic ups and downs during this period, but this was to be expected, more especially given that the EU is affected by trading conditions in other parts of the world. These bumps along the economic road were in general accepted with equanimity by the citizenry of the EU.

The financial crisis that led to the euro crisis has cast a very long shadow over this credo that lay at the heart of the EU. Politicians and academics might engage in complex argument about the relative degree of responsibility for the current malaise. This, however, matters little, if at all, from the perspective of ordinary citizens, more especially those living in countries affected most dramatically by the euro crisis and consequent economic measures imposed under the name of conditionality. For these people it is the EU and the euro that has failed, and this is so irrespective of political and academic discourse as to the 'real' causes of the crisis. The trust in the EU to deliver prosperity as well as peace has been severely shaken, and it will be a long time before the trust can be restored. It is this that may be the single most damaging fallout from the current crisis.

(ii) *Impact on EU inter-institutional power*

The euro crisis has also affected the EU inter-institutional division of political power. It would be tempting to conclude that it has had a predictably Schmittian effect, with power being concentrated to an ever-greater extent in the EU executive, the rationale being that only it can respond with sufficient speed to the profound problems generated by the euro crisis. This conclusion should be resisted, however, or at the least tempered, since the reality has been more complex. The European Parliament has not been excluded from the process, nor has the EU executive always demonstrated the will and speed to deal with the crisis. Thus the six-pack of measures to bolster the SGP was enacted by the ordinary legislative procedure in the post-Lisbon world, with input from the European Parliament as well as the Council. This is true also for the two-pack.

There is nonetheless evidence to sustain the Schmittian perspective. In terms of process, the lead on measures to address the euro crisis has been taken by the European Council, and by Germany and France acting partly within the European Council and partly through bilateral discussion. This is evident in the negotiations for the ESM, the TSCG, and the Four Presidents' Report.

In terms of substance, however, it may well prove to be the Commission within the EU executive whose power is most enhanced. This is readily apparent if one stands back from the principal measures to deal with the crisis. It is the Commission that has a central role in relation to the six-pack, two-pack, ESM, and TSCG, and its role will be even greater in relation to the measures enacted pursuant to the Four Presidents' Report. The provisions concerning reverse qualified majority voting in the six-pack and the TSCG are a powerful symbolic and substantive exemplification of this power, but there are numerous other articles in both sets of measures, as well as the ESM, which accord the Commission prominence.

The ratchet effect of increased EU economic oversight with the Commission in the driving seat carries dangers for the Commission itself, however. Increased power brings increased responsibility. The hard-pressed Commission will have to deliver on a whole series of fronts, which will bring it face to face with domestic political imperatives. This is more especially so in relation to the new measures foreshadowed in the Four Presidents' Report, given that these are mandatory for all euro-area Member States, irrespective of whether they are in economic difficulty or not. It is one thing to write down obligations, whether in Treaty provisions, legislation, other international Treaties, or contracts. It is quite another to enforce them.

(iii) Impact on EU unity

There was much talk at the time of the UK veto in December 2011 that it would lead to a radical division within the EU, with the UK and the Czech Republic on the fringes and excluded de facto, if not de jure, from important policy discussion. There has more generally been talk about a two-speed EU and how the response to the euro crisis might lead to this as a result of the tougher controls imposed on the euro-area Member States. It is important for the sake of clarity to disaggregate two senses of the phrase 'two-speed' EU.

The phrase is often used in a loose sense in literature and press coverage to capture the idea that closer cooperation on economic union, whether achieved within the confines of the Lisbon Treaty or without, will exert a gravitational force and produce what is in effect a two-speed EU for those subject to that regime and those who are not. This flows from the very subject matter of economic union, dealing as it does with national budgetary policy, combined with the degree of centralized oversight required to make economic union work. There is force in this argument. Whether and how far it becomes a reality depends on a range of factors, including the extent to which differential rules are imposed on the euro-area Member States, the reality being that some rules apply only to euro-area Member States, others, such as the TSCG, applying to 25 Member States. The two-speed vision is moreover predicated, explicitly or implicitly, on the assumption that the inner core will share a common vision, which is opposed to or different from that of other Member States. This does not represent current reality, at least when one gets down to detail, and this is unlikely to change in the future. A further factor yet again is the extent to which the inner core complies with the extra demands placed on them. It should not be forgotten that it was France and Germany that violated the SGP in 2003 to 2004, which ended in legal action before the EU courts.

The phrase two-speed EU has, however, also been used in a tighter, more defined sense by Piris. The central idea is that a two-speed Europe would be taken forward through an additional treaty, which would specify the nature of the obligations of the participating States, while continuing to respect the existing EU Treaties. The separate treaty would have separate institutions performing functions analogous to those of the Commission, European Parliament, Council, and ECJ. It is integral to this vision of a two-speed EU that 'all participating states should be fully committed to participate in all areas of cooperation, no areas being optional'.[179] Piris contends that there is a broad range of areas in which such cooperation could be undertaken by the avant garde group pursuant to the additional treaty: the economic component of EMU; security and defence policy; aspects of justice and home affairs; social policy; taxation; environmental protection; public health; culture and education; and certain procedural aspects of foreign policy implementation. It is the fact that the same States form the avant garde across all such areas that distinguishes Piris' conception of a two-speed EU from the current reality of a multi-speed EU. There are, however, very considerable difficulties with this conception of a two-speed EU. Thus there is, for example, no reason to believe that the inner core would share beliefs across these different subject matter areas, and there are

---

[179] Piris (n 141) 122. Emphasis in the original. Piris also considers the possibility of a two-speed EU without an additional treaty, but the idea that all avant garde States must participate across all areas is still central to his vision.

formidable difficulties associated with the creation of a parallel set of institutions created for the avant garde States.[180]

(iv) Impact on national politics

The crisis has had very significant implications for the precepts on which Member State democratic regimes operate. This flows in part from the degree of economic oversight to which euro-area Member State budgets are subject, an issue that will be considered below. The focus here is on the more direct political impact of the crisis.

This is manifest most significantly in the regime change at national level precipitated by the need to satisfy the EU and the markets that domestic economic reform will occur. The ousting of Berlusconi and his replacement by Monti in Italy is the most visible manifestation of this phenomenon. It led predictably to criticism that national political leadership was being determined by the EU, which also set the tight parameters within which this technocratic leadership would operate. The reality was rather more nuanced, since many Italians were keen to see Berlusconi go and welcomed the more professional perspective that Monti brought to the job. The Italian experience demonstrates, moreover, the 'limits', however ill-defined they might be, to this kind of intervention in the normal political process, and to the tensions that this can then produce. Thus Monti's decision to stand down in 2013 after the draft national budget was approved was based in part on the need for the country to get back to 'ordinary politics', but the very announcement precipitated a rise in the interest rate on Italian bonds, as the markets expressed their fears about a return to the bad old days of Italian national economic policy.

The impact on national politics is manifest more generally in the constraints placed on political choices available to national regimes subject to the economic crisis. It is axiomatic that those choices are always constrained by international obligations and economic exigency. There are nonetheless very real differences in degree. Conditionality is on its face a relatively innocuous word, but the consequences for countries such as Greece, Ireland, and Spain in terms of dictating the detailed direction of national politics is on a scale rarely if ever seen before in peacetime. This is not to say that the conditions imposed were unwarranted, although there is of course a vibrant debate as to the optimal economic response to the crisis. It is simply to say that whatever position one takes on that debate, the reality is that the national political agenda is set and monitored from outside.

It should also be recognized that if the measures adumbrated in the Four Presidents' Report become a reality then increased constraints on national

---

[180] P Craig, 'Two-Speed, Multi-Speed and Europe's Future: A Review of Jean-Claude Piris on the Future of Europe' (2012) 37 ELRev 800.

political choice will bite on all euro-area Member States, irrespective of whether they are in economic difficulty, and will also have some effect on non euro-area Member States. Whether this can be sustained remains to be seen. It depends in part at least on whether the EU, and in particular the Commission, has the political authority to carry through such measures. The economic logic is towards ever-tighter controls on national budgetary and economic policy. This may or may not be inexorable in economic terms, but it does not mean that it will prove to be politically acceptable to the Member States, nor does it mean that it will be capable of being delivered by the Commission.

The authors of the Four Presidents' Report were mindful of these concerns, which explain discussion of the need to secure democratic legitimacy and accountability for the proposed reforms.[181] The sentiments were echoed by the European Council when endorsing the Report.[182] There was much talk about the need to involve national parliaments and the European Parliament, and to ensure that there was 'national ownership' of the forthcoming changes. These are laudable sentiments, but it remains to be seen whether the reality is joint ownership achieved through discourse leading to consensus, or unilateral imposition of far-reaching constraints that are, at best, grudgingly accepted by Member States, at worst met with passive resistance or recalcitrance.

(b) Economic consequences

The measures enacted to meet the euro crisis have been concerned with assistance and supervision, as seen above. The general economic consequences of these measures will be considered from these perspectives in turn.

(i) Assistance: funding and moral hazard

From the perspective of assistance, the central economic issues are funding, who pays for the assistance, and moral hazard, the concern that the recipient State will take excessive risk and free ride on the greater fiscal rectitude practised by others.

The numbers involved with financial assistance/bailouts are significant indeed. They are normally in the billions, and commonly there are two or three digits in terms of magnitude. The money has to come from somewhere, and thus far this has been from the Member States, with Germany bearing the principal burden. This is likely to continue for the foreseeable future, given that financing of the ESM is predicated on State contributions. The economic impact of contributions from smaller countries should nonetheless be kept firmly in mind. Thus, for example, Finland's contribution to the ESM is €12.5 billion, which is

---

[181] 'Towards a Genuine Economic and Monetary Union' (n 1) 13–14.
[182] European Council (n 163) [14].

one-quarter of the annual government budget.[183] This regime is only viable because the ESM is structured on a divide between paid-up and callable shares, with the former amounting to €1.4 billion for Finland, a still not insignificant amount relative to its overall budget.

Eurostat has indicated that such contributions will not increase the government debt of the shareholder countries. They will rather be treated analogously to similar international financial organizations such as the IMF.[184] Therefore, unlike the loans provided by the EFSF, the loans provided by the ESM will not be re-routed through the accounts of other euro-area countries and will therefore not increase their government debt. An alternative conclusion would in any event have risked adding economic insult to injury. If shareholder contributions did increase government debt of donor countries, then they might thereby have crossed the forbidden line of the TSCG, the Fiscal Compact, and been subject to the sanctions imposed by that regime. To show financial solidarity with other Member States and then to be held liable for breach of the Fiscal Compact would have been ironic indeed.

While this accounting regime is therefore defensible, it cannot conceal the obvious reality, which is that the contributions are real money, and that sums expended for one purpose will not be available for alternative uses. This is of course recognized by all, although normally in somewhat muted tones. Thus the Four Presidents' Report noted that support to financial institutions had been substantial and that it had 'unduly weighed on public finances and reduced the ability to use fiscal policy to stave off the effects of the recession'.[185] This is a fortiori the case for assistance given to States pursuant to the ESM and its predecessors.

The very fact that the contributions are real money also explains the concern about moral hazard and the consequential emphasis placed on conditionality throughout the reforms enacted thus far. The overall assistance regime is delicately poised between the desire to intervene fast, prevent contagion, and shore up the system, with the equally firm desire to ensure that the recipient State does not free ride on the greater fiscal rectitude practised by others. This explains the emphasis placed on structural reform and conditionality, these being intended as the twin guarantors of fiscal probity, the one operating ex ante to try to prevent the State from getting into trouble in the first place, the other being applied ex post if it does get into trouble as the price of the bail out. The delicate balance between these impulses is forcefully exemplified by proposals in the Four Presidents' Report, which attempt to prevent the likelihood of contagion through

---

[183] Tuori (n 80) 40.
[184] Loans from the ESM to a euro-area country are recorded in the same way as a loan from the IMF to a Member State, as a direct loan from an international organization to the country in question.
[185] 'Towards a Genuine Economic and Monetary Union' (n 1) 5.

the insurance-based shock absorption system, funded by Member State contributions, while at the same time avoiding the risk of moral hazard of States claiming on the insurance system as a result of their fiscal irresponsibility.[186] The delicate balance is revealed once again by the insistence that fiscal risk sharing should not be seen as unidirectional or permanent transfers between countries.[187]

There are real challenges to maintaining this delicate balance going forward. They are, if anything, greater than hitherto, which is evident from a close reading of the Four Presidents' Report, laying the blueprint for a 'genuine economic and monetary union'. The challenge in terms of financial solidarity is still present, viz, how long will the Member States be willing to support their fellow travellers in the eurozone? The Report seeks to provide reassurance in this respect, but the reassurance is itself predicated on the recognition that this is not a short-term problem, but rather one that owes its origin to substantial divergence in economic structures and performance as between the Member States. This explains the emphasis placed on structural adjustment of national economies to improve them, make them more robust, and able to withstand shocks. The mandatory contractual arrangements for those in the eurozone are to be the medium through which this problem is addressed. Willingness to recognize the scale of the problem is in many ways laudable. It also serves to place in perspective the challenge that lies ahead.

The discussion thus far has focused on the issues of funding and moral hazard that are central to the regime for assistance. This is not, however, the only way in which assistance could be organized. Maduro has challenged the status quo and argued that financial solidarity in the EU should be detached from transfers between States and related rather to the wealth generated by the process of European economic integration.[188] It is integral to his view that the EU budget should be increased from 1 per cent to at least 3 per cent of EU GDP. The extra revenue would be derived from new EU taxes, such as a financial transaction tax and an EU corporation tax. Maduro argues that these taxes are justified because the economic activity was made possible by the internal market, or because the economic activity, while taking place within a State, has externalities for other Member States, or because it is an economic activity that States can no longer tax on their own.[189]

The idea is that such revenues would then provide the EU with the requisite economic firepower to address economic problems and prevent future crises, while removing the need for Member States to insure each other in the manner that underpins the ESM. The enhanced EU budget would be used for a stability fund that would provide collateral to State-issued debt when necessary, albeit subject to an adjustment programme, and it would also be used for EU policies that would address asymmetries in the EU's economic and monetary union.[190]

---

[186] ibid 8.   [187] ibid 10.   [188] Maduro (n 36).
[189] ibid 21.   [190] ibid 19–21.

Maduro contends that this is preferable to the ESM-type regime because it would have greater funds at its disposal, the adjustment programme would come fully within the scope of EU policies, thereby increasing accountability, and since funding would come from the EU budget, citizens would no longer think of themselves as bailing out ailing States since there would be no direct link to such State support. This is an interesting proposal. Space precludes detailed analysis, but the following brief comments on funding and moral hazard can be made.

In terms of funding, the proposal is premised on an increase in the EU budget from 1 per cent to at least 3 per cent EU GDP. It is extremely unlikely that this will occur, given the political difficulties of securing far more modest increases in the EU budget in 2012–13, and in previous budgetary negotiations. A proposal that would effectively triple the EU budget would seem doomed at the outset, whatever its merits might be. If this hurdle were to be overcome, that would still leave open a plethora of issues concerning the proposed taxation. Maduro's criteria for new tax revenue entail normative and practical assumptions. It would, for example, be difficult to determine whether an economic activity was made possible by the internal market and it is clearly not the case that all financial transactions occur because of the internal market. There are similar difficulties with the application of the precept that a tax is warranted because the activity, even though it takes place within a State, has externalities for other States. It is not clear who or how such matters would be determined. It would, moreover, also be difficult to ensure that such revenues would be ring-fenced within the EU budget to be used for the ends that Maduro specifies. There would always be the temptation to use such revenues for other purposes, more especially because they constitute such a sizable increase over the budgetary status quo.

In terms of moral hazard, Maduro's proposal might have some impact on public sentiment or perception, but it would not affect the substance of the issue. The public might be more accepting of financial solidarity where the link with their money is less direct, given that assistance would come from enhanced EU revenue rather than from direct State disbursement. Even if this were so, it would not alter the moral hazard dimension to the provision of assistance. This would still have to be secured through an admixture of conditionality/adjustment programmes, and measures designed to address imbalances in economic performance as between the Member States.

(ii) Supervision: oversight and direction

The whole is greater than the sum of the parts. This aphorism is particularly apposite in relation to the supervisory measures enacted to deal with the financial and euro crisis. The aggregate constraints thereby placed on Member State economic freedom are far-reaching and will increase further when the proposals from the Four Presidents' Report are realized. The very complexity and legal heterogeneity of the proposals makes it difficult to perceive the overall impact. There are in effect four kinds of supervisory oversight in the current regime, each of which places detailed regulatory duties on Member States, especially those in the eurozoneand those that have signed the Fiscal Compact, or on national financial institutions.

First, there are ex ante supervisory constraints designed to enhance EU budgetary oversight by focusing on the timing and format of national budgetary determinations, and the need for independent verification. These are ex ante in the sense that they are consciously designed so as to ensure that EU budgetary principles are embodied in national budgets prior to their approval by national parliaments. The draft national budget must be detailed. The Commission is assigned the role of 'assessor', decides whether the national budget meets the requisite criteria and can request an amended budget.

Secondly, there is the detailed regime of procedural and substantive obligations that flow from the Treaty provisions on economic union. The twin pillars of the SGP dealing with multilateral surveillance and excessive deficit have been strengthened through the six-pack and two-pack. Thus, for example, changes made in relation to multilateral surveillance impose enhanced obligations on Member States to make significant progress towards medium-term objectives for their budgetary balances, which is backed up by a sanction regime. It is reinforced through the Excessive Imbalance Procedure, minimum requirements for national budgetary frameworks, including numerical fiscal rules to promote compliance with the Treaty reference values for deficit and debt. The reforms have also ratcheted up the controls applicable to the excessive deficit procedure, which can be triggered by government debt or government deficit. The TSCG, the Fiscal Compact, adds a further layer to this set of obligations and is built on the duty to balance budgets.

Thirdly, there is a novel regulatory architecture for banks and financial institutions. Its core elements are the new regulatory agencies established to replace the previous Lamfalussy regime, the weaknesses of which were felt to have contributed to the EU's poor regulatory performance in the banking crisis. This has been augmented by the Single Supervisory Mechanism, SSM, run by the ECB, which will have direct oversight of banks, and enforce prudential rules to ensure that EU banking abides by high common standards. The SSM will itself be complemented by the Single Resolution Mechanism, SRM, through which supervisory responsibility will be exercised and conditions set in relation to individual banks that get into financial difficulty.

The fourth component consists of measures that will impact significantly on broader economic policy in Member States, the object being to reduce national economic vulnerability through temporary, targeted financial incentives. These are in one sense a form of assistance from the EU, but they also come with a 'supervisory bite' in the sense that the contractual arrangements through which they are made operational are mandatory for euro-area Member States, and carry the indirect sanction that Member States will not be eligible to participate in the insurance-based shock absorption function unless they comply with contractual arrangements aimed at instilling sound economic precepts. This aspect of 'genuine EMU' is akin to mandatory management consultancy directed at national economic policy broadly conceived, which will be 'good' for the recipient even if it does not quite like it at the time.

There is, as Fabbrini has pointed out,[191] a paradox in the EU regime. The EMU system was structured with the intent of preserving national fiscal sovereignty, which was thought to entail rejection of a more 'US-style federalist' model for governance of the euro area. However, as he points out, the reality is that the constraints on fiscal choice are greater in the EU and will become ever more so as the measures designed for a 'genuine economic and monetary union' come on line.

It is, moreover, worth repeating a point made earlier. The rules have been devised or ratcheted up on the logic that only such tighter constraints can produce a genuine economic and monetary union, although whether this is so is for economists to debate. The corollary is that the schema imposes far-reaching duties on EU institutions, especially the Commission, to deliver this overall policy. The complexity of the tests that the Commission has to apply to determine whether Member States and financial institutions are fulfilling their numerous duties is daunting, and ever more so given the political sensitivity of such exercises. Getting the legislation on to the statute book may with hindsight turn out to be the easier part of this venture. Making it work may prove a lot more difficult.

(c) Legal consequences

(i) Legality and legitimacy

The legal difficulties attendant on measures such as the ESM, TSCG, and other elements of the overall package, such as the OMTs, have been considered above to which reference should be made. The limits of law are always going to be tested in times of emergency, and that is true in the modern day for economic as well as physical threats. Indeed, the very language of the law is itself expressive, as reflected in the rhetoric of recent legislation, in which phrases speaking to the need to avoid 'contagion', and the necessity to avoid 'negative spill over' from national budgetary policy, frequently appear. We should be mindful of this 'Schmittian' dimension, but it should nonetheless not preclude reasoned analysis of the legal difficulties attendant on measures enacted to meet the crisis. On the contrary, it is when the law is under strain that we should spell out the legal

---

[191] F Fabbrini, 'The Fiscal Compact, the "Golden Rule" and the Paradox of European Federalism' (2013) 36 Boston Coll Int'l and Comp L Rev 1.

problems of political initiatives, while being cognizant of real-world pressures to avert severe economic outcomes.

(ii) Transparency and complexity

The range of measures enacted pursuant to the financial crisis will exacerbate problems of transparency and complexity that already beset this area, even for those skilled at navigating this complex terrain. Prior to the recent reforms, there were three layers of legal rules pertinent to control over national economic policy: the provisions of the Lisbon Treaty; EU legislation; and the broad economic policy guidelines. These rules were complex and created difficulties in terms of transparency, because they were spread across primary Treaty provisions, complex EU legislation, and high-level soft law.

The ESM and TSCG add a fourth layer to the existing schema through Treaties operating outside of the Lisbon Treaty. This exacerbates difficulties of complexity and transparency, more especially because, as seen above, there is in relation to the TSCG very significant overlap between obligations incumbent on States through the six-pack of EU legislation, and those in the TSCG. It may indeed be difficult for States to know in advance whether they should be structuring their documentation in terms of the six-pack plus two-pack, or in terms of the TSCG.

The further reforms posited in the Four Presidents' Report, as endorsed by the European Council, add a fifth layer, through the prominence accorded to contracts as the legal medium through which new obligations concerning economic policy should be realized. The broader implications of this move are considered in the next section.

(iii) Legislation and contract

The developments charted in this chapter reveal an interesting shift 'from legislation to contract'. To be sure, contractual language and metaphor were already present in this area, as exemplified by the relationship between Member States and the EU pursuant to the broad economic policy guidelines.[192] To be sure also, the contracts will subsist against the backdrop of Treaty provisions and EU legislation. Notwithstanding this, contract assumes enhanced prominence as the policy delivery tool of choice within the blueprint for a genuine economic and monetary union.

It is especially prominent in the Four Presidents' Report and in the subsequent endorsement by the European Council. These contracts are, as seen above, the mechanism for delivery of the integrated economic policy framework, whereby

---

[192] Art 121 TFEU.

the EU in tandem with the Member State will review structural features of the national economy in order to reduce economic vulnerabilities and increase competitiveness and growth. This will provide the basis for 'a tailor-made and detailed agreement on some specific reforms'.[193] The European Council encouraged further investigation as to the 'feasibility and modalities of mutually agreed contracts for competitiveness and growth', and as to the 'solidarity mechanisms that can enhance the efforts made by the Member States that enter into such contractual arrangements for competitiveness and growth'.[194]

The competence of the EU to engage in these contractual arrangements is not entirely self-evident. The general Treaty provisions on economic policy empower the passage of formal legal acts,[195] and even the broad competence in relation to euro-area Member States is to enact formal measures.[196] It follows that competence to use the contractual route could be grounded in general empowering legislation made pursuant to Articles 121, 126, 136 TFEU. Alternatively it might be argued that the Member States retain an inherent power to make contracts, provided that they are compatible with EU law. It might then be contended that the Commission or EU can be the other signatory, either because of an inherent power to make contracts to fulfil an EU objective, or through a broad reading of Articles 272 and 335 TFEU. It is nonetheless interesting to reflect on the rationale for and consequences of this regulatory choice.

The rationale for the shift from 'legislation to contract' is in part because of the very flexibility that inheres in the contract paradigm. It was Maine who famously coined the phrase 'from status to contract'[197] to capture the idea that in modern societies individuals could operate as autonomous agents expressing their choice through agreement, rather than being bound by obligations derived from status over which they had little control. Agreement is, however, a double-edged sword in this respect. It functions as a tool whereby contracting parties can express their autonomy, but also operates as a flexible mechanism for imposition of obligations, which can be tailored to a particular case. This is achieved with added legitimacy that comes from the fact that the overall package was 'agreed' by both parties, rather than being imposed through legislation, although how much freedom of choice exists in the making and terms of the contract may well be questioned. The choice of contract as a regulatory tool is also explicable in part because it does not require approval in the manner of legislative, delegated, or implementing acts. The deal, whatsoever it might be, can be struck between Commission and Member State without the need for formal imprimatur of other

[193] 'Towards a Genuine Economic and Monetary Union' (n 1) 12.
[194] European Council (n 163) [12].
[195] Arts 121, 126 TFEU.
[196] Art 136(1)–(2) TFEU.
[197] H Maine, *Ancient Law: Its Connection with the Early History of Society and its Relation to Modern Ideas* (J Murray, 1861).

EU decision-making institutions, although imperatives of legitimacy and accountability as discussed in the Four Presidents' Report mean that there will be some involvement of the national parliament and European Parliament in order to enhance the 'joint ownership' of the agreement.

The consequences of this shift to contract remain to be seen. It will, as stated above, at the very least increase the complexity of the overall regulatory landscape. It will, moreover, not be easy to ensure the desired legitimacy and accountability. This will be difficult in purely formal terms, as judged by the practical difficulties of involving the national parliament and the European Parliament before the deal has become de facto 'done'. It will also be difficult to achieve the desired legitimacy and accountability in substantive terms, as judged by the extent to which the contract really is a mutual bargain, rather than unilateral imposition of prescribed economic change by the Commission acting in paternalist management consultant mode.

7. Conclusion

There will be no attempt to summarize the previous analysis. The crisis has shaken the EU to the core and it would be premature to conclude, at the time of writing, that it is over yet. There is nonetheless a pathology evident in responses to the crisis that is unsurprising, but also worthy of note. The responses, whether in terms of assistance or supervision, have shifted from the ad hoc inspired by economic exigency, to attempts to configure longer-term solutions. It remains to be seen whether these are effective. What is indubitably true is that the crisis has placed the 'economic' ever more centre stage within the EU. The longer-term implications of this for the balance between the social and the economic within the EU polity, and the consequential ramifications for the balance at national level, will be significant. This will pose problems of its own for the EU as it moves onward through the second decade of the new millennium.

Index